A HISTORY OF ECONOMIC THEORY AND METHOD

THIRD EDITION

Robert B. Ekelund, Jr.
Auburn University

Robert F. Hébert
Auburn University

McGRAW-HILL PUBLISHING COMPANY

New York St. Louis San Francisco Auckland Bogotá Caracas
Hamburg Lisbon London Madrid Mexico Milan Montreal New Delhi
Oklahoma City Paris San Juan São Paulo Singapore Sydney Tokyo Toronto

To James P. Payne, Jr.,
and the late Alfred F. Chalk,
who each taught excellence by example.

This book was set in Times Roman by the College Composition Unit
in cooperation with General Graphic Services, Inc.
The editors were Scott D. Stratford, Michael Morales, and Sheila H. Gillams;
the production supervisor was Louise Karam.
The cover was designed by Karen Quigley/Joan E. O'Connor.
Cover illustration by Daniel Sacks.
R. R. Donnelley & Sons Company was printer and binder.

A HISTORY OF ECONOMIC THEORY AND METHOD

2 3 4 5 6 7 8 9 0 DOC DOC   9 4 3 2 1 0

ISBN 0-07-019416-5

See Acknowledgments on pages 657-659.
Copyrights included on this page by reference.

Economists shown in the cover illustration are (by row, from top left to right) François Quesnay
and Thorstein Veblen; Milton Friedman, Léon Walras, and Alfred Marshall; Adam Smith, John
Maynard Keynes, and John Stuart Mill; Karl Marx and Paul Samuelson.

Library of Congress Cataloging-in-Publication Data

Ekelund, Robert B. (Robert Burton), (date).
    A history of economic theory and method/Robert B. Ekelund, Jr.,
    Robert F. Hébert.—3rd ed.
        p.   cm.
    Bibliography: p.
    Includes index.
    ISBN 0-07-019416-5
    1. Economics—History.   I. Hébert, Robert F.   II. Title.
HB75.E47   1990
330'.09—dc20   89-12626

ABOUT THE AUTHORS

Robert B. Ekelund, Jr., earned bachelor's and master's degrees in economics at St. Mary's University in San Antonio, and a Ph.D. at Louisiana State University. He taught at Texas A & M University before joining the faculty at Auburn University in 1979, where he is currently Lowder Eminent Scholar in Economics. Dr. Ekelund is the author of several books on economic theory and policy, including a leading principles text, and he has been published in more than sixty papers on economics in such journals as the *American Economic Review,* the *Quarterly Journal of Economics,* the *Journal of Political Economy, Economica,* and the *Southern Economic Journal.*

Robert F. Hébert earned his Ph.D. from Louisiana State University in 1970. He has taught at Clemson University and has lectured widely in the United States and abroad. He is now Professor of Economics and the Benjamin and Roberta Russell Foundation Professor of Entrepreneurial Studies at Auburn University. Dr. Hébert is the author of a book on the historical development of the entrepreneur in economic literature, and he has been published widely in such journals as the *Quarterly Journal of Economics, Economica, Southern Economic Journal, Economic Inquiry, Journal of Public Economics,* and *History of Political Economy.* He has also contributed to a number of edited volumes in the history of economics.

CONTENTS

PART FIVE   TWENTIETH-CENTURY PARADIGMS

PREFACE

The history of economic ideas has changed little in the decade and a half since this book first appeared. But if Voltaire was right in believing that history is merely a pack of tricks that the living play on the dead, intellectual historians have played more than a few tricks over the past fifteen years. During that time historians of economic thought have been at work discovering new contributors and anticipators, reinterpreting past contributions, and evaluating new ideas that inform and expand the flux of contemporary economic literature. This activity has received encouragement over the past several decades by a modest resurgence of interest in the origins of economic science, and by the establishment of new journals and new professional organizations devoted to the study of the history of political economy.

CONTENTS

This third edition of *A History of Economic Theory and Method* presents, in an intelligible and readable format, the major theoretical and methodological ideas that have shaped and continue to shape contemporary economics. Although we have introduced numerous changes to the text in order to reflect ongoing research on the subject, we have once again tried to retain a balance between coverage of ideas, individuals, and methods, on the one hand, and institutions and policies on the other.

This book provides several advantages over previous editions and over others in the field. It offers an in-depth survey of the *complete* range of economic ideas from ancient times to the present. The coverage stops short of being encyclopedic, but it is sufficient to demonstrate the remarkable continuity of economic thought throughout the ages. The student who has mastered the contents of this book will understand how past analytic contributions, both those that successfully entered mainstream economics and those that did not, have shaped contemporary economic theory. In addition, this book integrates major methodological issues and modes of analysis with its historical survey of particular contributions. Moreover, it explores the broader implications of theory for unfolding social and economic policy.

DISTINCTIVE FEATURES

Some of the distinctive features of this book are: a detailed treatment of Scholastic economics that emphasizes its slow but nevertheless solid advances toward a unified theory of value during the Middle Ages; a broad evaluation of mercantilism that stresses both ideational and historico-institutional perspectives; an in-depth discussion of continental contributions, especially the performances of French economists in the nineteenth century; a carefully measured survey of the development of mathematical and quantitative methods in economics; and a selective survey of the varied applications of neoclassical price theory to contemporary "sociological" problems.

A book such as this forces authors to make judgments and choices. At certain junctures within the text we have chosen to embellish institutional detail (e.g., the chapter on mercantilism), while at other places we have chosen to economize on such detail in order to elaborate the richness of analysis. By and large, we have directed our effort less toward the so-called "institutional" approach, and more toward "mainstream" economics. This reflects two things: our own methodological preference and our informed judgment concerning what is more likely to be of immediate service to university students seeking historical perspective on the nature and the promise of contemporary economics.

THE THIRD EDITION

Compared to previous editions of this text, we have made several changes in the present edition that enlarge, embellish and hopefully, improve the text. In response to requests by users and reviewers, we have added two new chapters that extend the "contemporary history" portions of the book. Chapter 22 traces the development of mathematical and statistical tools as they have intruded on economic analysis; and Chapter 23 reviews, in cursory fashion, the recent expansion of neo-Marshallian ideas on the theory of consumer demand, household decision-making, and the nature of the firm. These chapters admittedly draw history much closer to the present, which makes a mature historical perspective difficult. However, they also show how economics continues to build on past ideas and techniques in its quest for present-day relevance and reality.

The core of the book as it formerly existed has also been altered in significant ways. We have introduced new material on the contributions of the ancient Greeks (Chapter 2), on the subject of usury as a form of medieval church policy (Chapter 2), and on the role of William Petty (Chapter 4) in the formation of economic thought before Adam Smith. The treatments of Mill (Chapter 8) and Wieser (Chapter 13) have been revised and enlarged somewhat. Joseph Schumpeter's ideas on the business cycle (Chapter 21) and on economic regulation (Chapter 24) have been introduced and/or expanded. The discussion of Austrian economics (Chapter 21) has been revamped to incorporate the monetary theories of Mises and Hayek. Rational expectations theory makes its appearance in Chapter 20. Finally, all of the end-of-chapter notes for further reading have been thoroughly revised and updated.

ACKNOWLEDGMENTS

The success enjoyed by previous editions of this book must be attributed to the users and interested readers who have delved into its contents. Many have been free with their advice on how the exposition could be improved. We are grateful to friendly and hostile critics alike who have shared their views with us, and we encourage a high measure of "audience participation" regarding the contents of the present edition as well.

Finally, we would like to express our gratitude to a number of colleagues and students who helped to bring this new edition to press. Professors Richard Ault, Auburn University; Richard Beil, Auburn University; Don Boudreaux, George Mason University; James Halteman, Wheaton College; Steve Hickerson, Mankato State University; Terrence McDonough, Canisius College; and Mark Thornton, Auburn University, offered advice and suggestions on various portions of the manuscript. Professors Richard Ault, John Jackson, Auburn University; and Charles Maurice, Texas A & M University were especially helpful in the formative stages of Chapters 22 and 23 as well as in later refinements. Professors David E. R. Gay, University of Arkansas; Martin Giesbrecht, Northern Kentucky University; E. O. Price III, Oklahoma State University; and Warren Samuels, Michigan State University made helpful suggestions on the entire manuscript. Linda Hadley, Manisha Perera, and James Tillery, graduate students at Auburn University, provided able technical assistance during the final dash to get the manuscript in under deadline. We are indebted to each of these individuals for their time and effort. We hope that this new edition will prove useful to students of the subject so as to repay in some small measure the time and effort so generously given by friends and critics.

Robert B. Ekelund, Jr.

Robert F. Hébert

PART ONE

INTRODUCTION AND EARLY BEGINNINGS

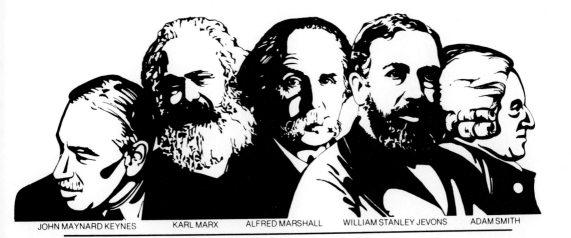

JOHN MAYNARD KEYNES   KARL MARX   ALFRED MARSHALL   WILLIAM STANLEY JEVONS   ADAM SMITH

ECONOMICS AND
ITS HISTORY

INTRODUCTION

Economic analysis has yielded a rich and extensive history since its formal inception over two hundred years ago. Just as an individual genus evolves from earlier species in the biological world, so too did economics evolve as an intellectual genus. The earlier forms of economics assumed various names and characteristics. The ancient Greeks gave us the word "economics," but confined its meaning to "household management." After the Middle Ages, economics was considered a subset of moral philosophy, but in the seventeenth century a mutant strain developed called *political arithmetic*. The eighteenth century witnessed yet another strain called *physiocracy*. Eventually, the discipline took most of its modern shape under the name *political economy* near the end of the eighteenth century. It continued to mutate in the nineteenth century, when several virulent strains of "heterodoxy" appeared. But owing to its steady acceptance and professionalization in the twentieth century, the narrower term, economics, came to represent a consensus label for a body of principles and a method of inquiry that can now be called "mainstream." This book is about the evolution and development of mainstream economic theory. As such, it is *a* history of economic analysis, but not *the* history of economic analysis.

From a holistic point of view, modern economics, like a peacock's plumage, is colorful, varied, and fanned out in several directions. Economics, in this holistic sense, embraces many heterodox viewpoints. To mention a few, it accommodates the writings of institutionalists (old and new), socialists, marxists, radicals, Austrians, post-Ricardians, and post-Keynesians. This book does not attempt to give equal time and attention to all points of view. Instead, it concentrates on the development of mainstream economic analysis as it unfolded in western culture from the time of the ancient Greeks to the present day. Our justification for this particular focus is twofold. In the first place, mainstream economics represents the consensus of what economics is all about. Secondly, a historical perspective on mainstream economics is apt to be of greater value to the contemporary student of economics. In our pedagogic approach, therefore, heterodoxy enters the historical survey either as a direct challenge to the reigning orthodoxy or as a variation on the theme of mainstream economics. Although others might treat the subject differently, the important point overall is that economics has been and is a vibrant form of intellectual discourse, not a settled body of principles.

The plain truth is that economics is anything but a settled body of thought. Even among mainstream economists, gnawing questions persist about the nature and scope of economics, as well as its value and its place among competing scientific disciplines. Because of this, not all economists approach the subject in the same way; nor do all agree on the boundaries of the subject, the role of the individual versus the group, the method of analysis to be employed, or the proper object of economic investigations. Although we emphasize continuity and consensus in the evolution of economic theory, we nevertheless advise the student to keep an open mind to alternative points of view and to look for gainful lessons in the errors of the past as well as its successes.

Historians of economics must be both historians and economists. As economists they are concerned with the theory and consequences of human decisions. As historians they are the chroniclers of these events. Modern economists who are not historians seek to emulate scientists, who are concerned primarily with the present. Yet historians are necessarily stationed at the border between past and present. They are as much concerned with the mistakes of the past as they are with its advances. Is this concern a mere waste of time, an obsession with minutiae, or does it produce constructive results? In other words, is there a positive payoff to studying the history of economic theory and method?

The subject of economics, human decision making, is forward-looking, whereas history is backward-looking. But humans can only judge where they are in terms of where they have been, and this seems to hold with the same force in the intellectual realm as it does in the world of events. History is the story of humans, and if they would understand themselves, they cannot ignore history. In this book our specific concern is the history of science, a phrase we use loosely to refer to cumulative accretions of human knowledge. The history of science is a baffling and elusive thing. One view is that it details the story of a continual progression of ideas made up of epochal contributions of new bits of knowledge added to the accumulated legacy of the past, thereby raising the edifice of scientific knowledge ever upward brick by brick. Another view is that science advances by "organic" growth—a maturation process—whereby knowledge slowly advances from the superstitious, myth-addicted infancy of early civilizations to the sophisticated state of modern science. Neither of these is a wholly accurate description of the past, nor are they likely to be faithful blueprints of the future. It often happens instead that thought progresses in a way akin to biological evolution, first by multiple subdivisions and thereafter by isolated development of various branches of knowledge, each leading to rigid orthodoxies, one-sided specializations, and collective obsessions. From this fragmentation and transmutation periodically come new syntheses that nudge us forward incrementally, until the next step of intellectual cell division occurs.

New syntheses never result from a mere adding together of two mature branches in mental evolution. Each new departure and subsequent reintegration involves the breaking down of rigid, frozen thought structures that result from past overspecialized development. Unfortunately, we do not yet know much about how or why this process comes about. What we have learned is that most geniuses responsible for the major mutations in the history of thought seem to have had certain features in common. First and foremost, the great intellectual pioneers of the past held a skeptical, almost iconoclastic, attitude toward traditional ideas. Second, they maintained (at least initially) an open-mindedness verging on naive credulity toward new concepts. Out of this combination sometimes comes the crucial capacity to see a familiar situation or problem in a new light. The creative process is a wrenching away of a concept from its traditional context or meaning.

Another precondition for basic discoveries to occur is the "ripeness" of the age, something that seems to be identifiable ex post if not ex ante. Robert Merton, among others, has explained the conditions leading up to "multiple discoveries" in knowledge—the occasions in which two or more people working independently of each other arrived at the same basic idea or approach. It is as if certain preconditions have to be fulfilled before progressive change can occur. Thomas Kuhn made much the same point in *The Structure of Scientific Revolutions,* where he argued that once an accepted way of thinking is forced to confront an increasing number of anomalies it cannot resolve, it usually gives way to a new way of thinking.

One of the things gained by a study of the history of economics, therefore, is a better understanding of the creative process. From this exposure we gain some fundamental insights into the "sociology of knowledge." Economics is a mosaic of assumptions, facts, generalizations, and techniques, and it is very difficult to understand how the current pattern of ideas emerged without any appreciation of how individual thinkers struggled with the problems of the past. Understanding the history of economics provides perspective—what Joseph Schumpeter called an appreciation for "the ways of the mind." The history of economics illustrates that the ability to analyze problems changes, not always for the better, over time. This kind of insight is seldom possible in other courses found in the traditional university curriculum.

A second thing gained from a study of the history of economics is a feel for the kind of ideas that have "staying power" in a scientific discipline. What is the appeal of an idea that lives on in economic theory long after its progenitor has gone the way of all flesh? Why do certain ideas last while others fizzle quickly and still others barely see the light of day? Although likely to be judged irrelevant in a course on contemporary economic theory, these questions are entirely appropriate in the context of the history of economic analysis.

Yet another benefit is a better understanding of contemporary economic theory through an appreciation of the shortcomings of past theories and the obstacles overcome by the principles that survive. A bonus to some students is that they find the ingestion of abstract theory more palatable when it is presented in historical context.

Undoubtedly there are many other reasons for studying the development of economics, but it is not our intention to review all of them. Not the least important is the simple fact that the subject is interesting. Many economists feel a kinship with the famous herpetologist who one day found himself confronted by a brash student demanding to know what *good* snakes are. The man who spent his entire adult life studying snakes replied quickly: "Snakes are damned interesting, *that's* what good snakes are." This defense seems no less appropriate to a study of the history of economics.

AIM, SCOPE, AND METHOD

Presenting the history of economic thought in its full cultural and intellectual diversity poses several problems. The first major problem is to identify the common strands that weave the broadloom tapestry of economics into a coherent whole. The trick is to expose the strands without unraveling the tapestry. The common strand throughout this book is the theory of value. Not every chapter emphasizes this theme to the same degree; but, whatever the emphasis, each chapter is never far removed in content from this central concern. Although value theory is generally treated as a microeconomic problem, it nevertheless provides a touchstone for macroeconomic issues as well. Thus, in the heyday of classical economic growth theory, Adam Smith, David Ricardo, and Karl Marx each paused at length to puzzle out the question of value. Furthermore, whatever definition of economics one chooses, the issue of value inevitably raises its head.

The second problem is to define the limits of economic inquiry. Because there are a number of schools of thought vying for legitimacy, choice has to be exercised by the authors of a book like this. We stated above, with justification, our choice to present this historical survey primarily in terms of mainstream economics. Certain topics in the history of economic thought, broadly defined, are not covered here in great detail. Students who wish to acquire even more breadth may profitably consult the Notes for Further Reading at the end of each chapter. In addition, we encourage each student to discuss his or her special intellectual interests, broad or narrow, with the professor responsible for teaching this course.

The third problem is to choose an appropriate "style" or approach to the subject. Just as there are many different opinions about what constitutes the proper study of economics, so there are different approaches to the history of the discipline. Some favor the "sociology of knowledge" approach, which emphasizes how ideas come about and examines the myriad social, economic, and historical forces that shape these ideas. Others regard ideas as having a life of their own. In this last view, the "soundness" of an idea is judged by whether the idea rings true once it is removed from its historical time frame. This book takes an eclectic approach somewhere between the two extreme views that (1) ideas are the *only* things that matter (regardless of time frame) and (2) *every* idea is a more or less faithful expression of the time period in which it emerged. The dilemma posed by adopting either of the above views exclusively is that the first neglects to consider the sociology of knowledge and the second makes it impossible to evaluate progress in the history of ideas.

This book is entitled *A History of Economic Theory and Method* because it attempts to impart not only a historical review of past theoretical contributions, but also something of the intellectual *gestalt* of each thinker, i.e., the *framework* of ideas handed from one thinker to the next. We believe that understanding the thought procedures followed by the great minds in economics is a valuable lesson for today's economists. Thus we employ the term "method" in an unpretentious way to convey a concern for the overall structure of thought within which theoretical contributions emerge, much as bricks and mortar, to hold the structure together. In the sense we use the term, "method" is not synonymous with "methodology." *Methodology* is the study of method. It is the systematic examination of how and why scientists came to use the methods they do and of how scientific methods differ. Methodology is therefore closely related to the sociology of knowledge. Neither methodology nor the sociology of knowledge is the main concern of this book. Rather, its concern is primarily with the questions of *what* constitutes our (mainstream) economic heritage and what are the implications that spring therefrom. The historical background is more than mere gilding on the lily, however; it radiates the ideals, pressures, and events that sparked original discovery.

Our approach is a matter of choice and is not intended to diminish the importance of these other issues. Existing studies that confront these issues, especially Mark Blaug's survey, *The Methodology of Economics, or How Economists Explain,* may be used profitably with this book. Unlike Blaug we do not attempt to present a history of methodology. Principally, this is a textbook, and its content is dictated, more or less, by the subjects with which past and present historians of thought (including ourselves) have concerned themselves. Some writers have simply been successful: for example, Adam Smith, David Ricardo, Alfred Marshall, and John Maynard Keynes. Their ideas must be included on that criterion alone. In less clear-cut instances, selective judgment must be exercised. To some our selection of individuals and topics will seem idiosyncratic. We offer no apology for this, merely an inclination to abide by the results of the marketplace.

The primary direction of this book is the development of economic abstractions per se, although social and methodological issues are frequently considered as integral parts of the intellectual landscape. We believe that economic theories do indeed have a life of their own and that a study of their development is both interesting and fruitful for the student of contemporary economics. Any book of limited scope will necessarily leave many questions unanswered. What role, if any, does the environment play in the development of economic theory? Do great empirical concerns (food shortages, income distribution, or the magnitude of unemployment and inflation) temper the nature and direction of analytical inquiry? If economic abstractions really do have a life of their own, has insularity led theorists to shut out potential areas of interest and benefit to economics? How do ideas filiate within countries and internationally? How are ideas related to the times in which they develop? How does philosophy relate to economic theory? We do not have conclusive answers to these questions, but we hope that this book will at least deepen appreciation and understanding of the issues. Nor do we attempt in the present text to confirm any single view of the development of economic analysis. Instead, we hope to expose the historical record, which must ultimately take the measure of the merits and/or shortcomings of any single view.

WHERE TO BEGIN?

Given the broad expanse of time and human experience, where does one begin a study of the history of economic analysis? The basic economic problem cannot have been far from the thoughts of humans since they took their first steps in an upright position. But intellectual historians must look to the beginning of recorded time for their raw inputs. The historian of economics, in particular, is aware that economics is a relative newcomer among the scientific disciplines. A classical situation emerged in economics in the eighteenth century. So why not start a history of economics there? Simply because every classical situation consolidates, summarizes, and synthesizes the original work of an earlier period and cannot be fully understood by itself. We therefore start with that earlier period—the cradle of western civilization, ancient Greece.

GENERAL REFERENCES

Histories of Economic Theory

Blaug, Mark. *Economic Theory in Retrospect,* 4th ed. London: Cambridge University Press, 1985.

Cannan, Edwin. *A History of the Theories of Production & Distribution in English Political Economy from 1776 to 1848,* 3d ed. London: Percival & Co., 1917.

Eatwell, J., et al. (eds.). *The New Palgrave: A Dictionary of Economics,* 4 vols. London: Macmillan, 1987.

Fellner, William. *Modern Economic Analysis.* New York: McGraw-Hill, 1960.

Gide, Charles, and Charles Rist. *A History of Economic Doctrines,* 7th ed., R. Richards (trans.). Boston: Heath, 1948.

Gray, Alexander. *The Development of Economic Doctrine.* New York: Longmans, 1933.

Heimann, Edward. *History of Economic Doctrine*. New York: Oxford University Press, 1964.

Hutchison, Terrence W. *A Review of Economic Doctrines, 1870–1929*. Oxford: Clarendon Press, 1966.

Kirzner, Israel M. *The Economic Point of View*. Kansas City: Sheed & Ward, 1970.

Lowry, S. Todd (ed.). *Pre-Classical Economic Thought*. Boston: Kluwer Academic Publishers, 1987.

Mitchell, Wesley C. *Types of Economic Theory,* vols. I and II, J. Dorfman (ed.). New York: A. M. Kelley, Publishers, 1967.

O'Brien, D. P., and J. R. Presley (eds.). *Pioneers of Modern Economics in Britain*. Totowa, N.J.: Barnes & Noble, 1981.

Pribram, Karl. *A History of Economic Reasoning*. Baltimore: Johns Hopkins University Press, 1983.

Rima, Ingrid H. *Development of Economic Analysis,* 3d ed. Homewood, Ill.: Irwin, 1978.

Rogin, Leo. *The Meaning and Validity of Economic Theory*. New York: Harper, 1956.

Roll, Eric. *A History of Economic Thought,* 4th ed. Homewood, Ill.: Irwin, 1974.

Schumpeter, Joseph A. *History of Economic Analysis,* E. B. Schumpeter (ed.). New York: Oxford University Press, 1954.

Spiegel, Henry W. *The Growth of Economic Thought,* rev. ed. Durham, N.C.: Duke University Press, 1983.

Stigler, George J. *Production and Distribution Theories: The Formative Period*. New York: Macmillan, 1941.

Readings

Abbott, Leonard (ed.). *Masterworks of Economics*. New York: McGraw-Hill, 1973.

Gherity, James A. (ed.). *Economic Thought: A Historical Anthology*. New York: Random House, 1965.

Keynes, John Maynard. *Essays in Biography*. London: Macmillan, 1933. Rev. ed., New York: The Norton Library, 1951.

Monroe, Arthur E. (ed.). *Early Economic Thought*. Cambridge, Mass.: Harvard University Press, 1924.

Patterson, S. Howard (ed.). *Readings in the History of Economic Thought*. New York: McGraw-Hill, 1932.

Rima, Ingrid H. (ed.). *Readings in the History of Economic Theory*. New York: Holt, 1970.

Schumpeter, Joseph A. *Ten Great Economists*. London: Oxford University Press, 1951.

Spengler, Joseph J., and W. R. Allen (eds.). *Essays in Economic Thought: Aristotle to Marshall*. Chicago: Rand McNally, 1960.

Spiegel, Henry W. (ed.). *The Development of Economic Thought*. New York: Wiley, 1952.

Stigler, George J. *Essays in the History of Economics*. Chicago: The University of Chicago Press, 1965.

Wilson, George W. (ed.). *Classics of Economic Theory*. Bloomington: Indiana University Press, 1964.

NOTES FOR FURTHER READING

Any serious excursion into the history of economic theory must deal with the primary sources of the major thinkers themselves. Although its bulk and advanced level render it unsuitable as a text, Schumpeter's *History of Economic Analysis* is a helpful, encyclopedic guide through the historical twists and turns of economic analysis. Another work of sweeping scope is Pribram's *History of Economic Reasoning*. More manageable, and like Schumpeter, devoted to the belief that ideas can be judged on their own merits without excessive historical trappings, is Blaug's *Economic Theory in Retrospect*, which has stood the test of time through four editions.

Collections of readings, whether of primary or secondary sources, can be helpful to the novice in the history of economics. Primary sources are contained in the collections of Abbott, Monroe, and Wilson. Gherity and Spiegel bring together both primary and secondary sources, whereas Rima and Spengler and Allen focus on secondary writings. The volumes by Keynes, Schumpeter, and Stigler contain each author's own investigations of various thinkers and contributions, and are highly recommended.

Although modern economics de-emphasizes the importance of the history of economics, several important arguments have been mounted in its defense. A representative, but nonexhaustive, list includes D. F. Gordon, "The Role of the History of Economic Thought in the Understanding of Modern Economic Theory," *American Economic Review*, vol. 55 (1965), pp. 119–127; G. J. Stigler, "Does Economics Have a Useful Past?" *History of Political Economy*, vol. 1 (Fall 1969), pp. 217–230; and F. Cesarano, "On the Role of the History of Economic Analysis," *History of Political Economy*, vol. 15 (Spring 1983), pp. 63–82. R. B. Ekelund and R. W. Ault persuasively present the case for careful study of the history of economics in "The Problem of Unnecessary Originality in Economics," *Southern Economic Journal*, vol. 53 (January 1987), pp. 650–661, where they use the historical development of peak-load pricing as a case study of the benefits to be derived from an acquaintance with earlier literature.

Many writings have appeared dealing with the factors that influence the development of economic analysis. See, especially, A. F. Chalk, "The Concept of Change and the Role of Predictability in Economics," *History of Political Economy*, vol. 2 (Spring 1970), pp. 97–117; J. J. Spengler, "Notes on the International Transmission of Ideas," *History of Political Economy*, vol. 2 (Spring 1970), pp. 133–151; and G. C. Harcourt's retrospective view, "Reflections on the Development of Economics as a Discipline," *History of Political Economy*, vol. 16 (Winter 1984), pp. 489–518. Some writers emphasize endogenous determinants, accenting their arguments with the growing "professionalism" of the science observable in the post-1870 period. See G. J. Stigler, "The Influence of Events and Policies on Economic Theory," *American Economic Review*, vol. 50 (May 1960), pp. 36–45, reprinted in Stigler's *Essays in the History of Economics;* and J. J. Spengler, "Exogenous and Endogenous Influences in the Formation of Post-1870 Economic Thought:

A Sociology of Knowledge Approach,'' in R. V. Eagley (ed.), *Events, Ideology, and Economic Theory* (Detroit: Wayne State University Press, 1968). On the subject of the rise of marginalism, philosophical determinants of various sorts—e.g., religion and utilitarianism—have been treated as major influences by Emil Kauder, ''The Retarded Acceptance of the Marginal Utility Theory,'' *Quarterly Journal of Economics,* vol. 67 (November 1953), pp. 564–575; whereas J. P. Henderson stressed the reaction of economists to Marx's labor theory of value, in his reaction to Kauder's thesis, ''The Retarded Acceptance of the Marginal Utility Theory: Comment,'' *Quarterly Journal of Economics,* vol. 69 (August 1955), pp. 465–473.

The impact of environment on economic ideas is a subject of considerable debate. Writers like Rogin (*The Meaning and Validity of Economic Theory*) attach great importance to external events in the formation of economic theories, while others argue explicitly that environment has little or nothing to do with additions to the theoretical core of economics. Frank W. Fetter, ''The Relation of the History of Economic Thought to Economic History,'' *American Economic Review,* vol. 55 (May 1965), pp. 136–142, aptly summed up the debate by noting that ''the more closely one associates economic thought with technical analysis...the greater is one likely to consider the effect of economic thought on history, and the less the effect of history on thought.'' But it remains true that a writer's argument will most likely be affected in some way by the period under consideration. All of this opens the door to the questions of ''originality'' and ''progress.'' Nobel laureate George Stigler addresses these issues in ''The Nature and Role of Originality in Scientific Progress,'' *Economica,* n.s., vol. 22 (November 1955), reprinted in Stigler's *Essays in the History of Economics*. Stigler concludes that progress in economic theory can be expected in those areas where much empirical work is being carried out.

A persuasive hypothesis regarding scientific change, related to the above issues, has been advanced by Thomas Kuhn in his *Structure of Scientific Revolutions,* 2d ed. (Chicago: The University of Chicago Press, 1970). Although Kuhn used change in the physical sciences to illustrate his thesis, his approach was quickly applied to economics by historians and by methodologists. Kuhn interprets a *paradigm* as a set of interrelated but underdeveloped principles—a body of thought that can answer questions put to it, but upon which extensions can be made freely. In this theory, new paradigms emerge when contradictions develop in the existing paradigm, which is called ''normal science.'' Old paradigms break down, in other words, when confronted with more and more questions that they cannot answer. Old paradigms are often absorbed into new ones, however, as illustrated by examples from chemistry and physics, e.g., the emergence of quantum mechanics in reaction to Newtonian physics, and absorption of the latter into the former.

Interpreting the development of economics along these lines, we might be tempted to argue that neoclassical analysis (see Chapters 12 through 16) emerged around 1870 as a result of the intellectual bankruptcy of classical economics. By this reasoning, the breakdown of the wages-fund doctrine fore-shadowed the emergence of a new paradigm. According to Keynes, in fact, the earlier paradigm gave answers to the question of how full employment is achieved and maintained that were at variance with experience. He therefore pioneered a new model. This explanation is appealing on the surface, but it glosses over certain gnawing problems. For example, how does one appropri-ately identify a paradigm in economics? What precisely is "a body of interre-lated principles"? As applied in economics the term "paradigm" has been sub-ject to rather loose interpretation. For example, Brian Loasby has advanced the intriguing interpretation that imperfect competition (see Chapter 18) arose to smite a contradiction in Alfred Marshall's theory of value. Does imperfect competition therefore constitute a competing paradigm? Perhaps, but alterna-tively, a paradigm could be identified by uniqueness of method. Thus, one could conceivably lump seemingly diverse approaches, e.g., classical, neoclas-sical, Keynesian, and others, into a single paradigm called "equilibrium eco-nomics." On this basis, contemporary concerns with macro disequilibrium (e.g., Axel Leijonhufvud, *Keynesian Economics and the Economics of Keynes,* New York: Oxford University Press, 1968) and with micro disequilibrium (e.g., Israel Kirzner, *Competition and Entrepreneurship,* Chicago: The University of Chicago Press, 1972) may be judged as a reaction to the paradigm of equilibrium economics.

Other questions naturally arise. Are there paradigms within paradigms? How are we to judge the interrelatedness of a body of thought? Much remains to be worked out if we are to apply Kuhn's interesting thesis to the history of economic thought, and indeed, much of the recent discussion has shifted away from Kuhn's provocative thesis toward other competing theses. We cannot hope to review all of this literature here, but the following citations give a fla-vor of the existing ferment: A. W. Coats, "Is There a 'Structure of Scientific Revolutions' in Economics?" *Kyklos,* vol. 22 (1969), pp. 289–296; Martin Bronfenbrenner, "The 'Structure of Revolutions' in Economic Thought," *His-tory of Political Economy,* vol. 3 (Spring 1971), pp. 136–151; L. Kunin and F. Weaver, "On the Structure of Scientific Revolutions in Economics," *History of Political Economy,* vol. 5 (Fall 1971), pp. 391–397; and D. Dillard, "Revo-lutions in Economic Theory," *Southern Economic Journal,* vol. 44 (April 1978), pp. 705–724. A paper supporting Bronfenbrenner's contention that a Hegelian dialectic process may be at work, rather than ambiguous paradigm shifts, is S. Karsten's "Dialectics and the Evolution of Economic Thought," *History of Political Economy,* vol. 5 (Fall 1973), pp. 399–419.

Developing and extending the work of Sir Karl Popper (*The Logic of Sci-entific Discovery,* New York: Basic Books, 1959), Imre Lakatos has provided an alternative methodology that many historians of economics find more to their liking than that put forward by Kuhn. See Lakatos, *The Methodology of Scientific Research Programmes. Philosophical Papers,* vol. 1 (Cambridge: Cambridge University Press, 1978); M. Blaug, "Kuhn versus Lakatos, or Par-adigms versus Research Programmes in the History of Economics," *History of Political Economy,* vol. 7 (Winter 1975), pp. 399–433; same author, *The Methodology of Economics* (see References); J. Jalladeau, "Research Program versus Paradigm in the Development of Economics," *Journal of Economic Issues,* vol. 12 (September 1978), pp. 583–608; J. V. Remenyi, "Core Demi-Core Interaction: Toward a General Theory of Disciplinary and Subdisciplinary Growth," *History of Political Economy,* vol. 11 (Spring 1979), pp. 30–63; D. W. Hands, "The Methodology of Economic Research Programmes," *Philosophy of the Social Sciences,* vol. 9 (1979), pp. 293–303; and same author, "Second Thoughts on Lakatos," *History of Political Economy,* vol. 17 (Spring 1985), pp. 1–16. Other competitors in this intellectual battle over methods are S. Latsis, "Situational Determinism in Economics," *British Journal for the Philosophy of Science,* vol. 23 (August 1972), pp. 207–245; same author (ed.), *Method and Appraisal in Economics* (Cambridge: Cambridge University Press, 1976); and P. Feyerabend, *Against Method: Outline of an Anarchistic Theory of Knowledge* (London: New Left Books, 1975). A taste of this intellectual hubris is provided by Bruce Caldwell in *Beyond Positivism: Economic Methodology in the Twentieth Century* (Boston: Allen & Unwin, 1982) and *Appraisal and Criticism in Economics: A Book of Readings* (Boston: Allen & Unwin, 1984).

REFERENCES

Blaug, Mark. *The Methodology of Economics, or How Economists Explain.* London: Cambridge University Press, 1980.

Kuhn, T. S. *The Structure of Scientific Revolutions,* 2d ed. Chicago: The University of Chicago Press, 1970.

Merton, Robert. *The Sociology of Science.* Chicago: The University of Chicago Press, 1973.

Schumpeter, J. A. *History of Economic Analysis,* E. B. Schumpeter (ed.). New York: Oxford University Press, 1954.

CHAPTER 2

ANCIENT AND MEDIEVAL ECONOMIC THOUGHT

INTRODUCTION

For most of history, economics did not have a separate identity apart from so-cial thought in general. Even as late as the eighteenth century, Adam Smith viewed economics as a subset of jurisprudence. This makes the search for first principles of economic reasoning more difficult, not because the intellectual cupboard of antiquity was bare, but because the lines of demarcation among the social sciences were blurred. Economics came into its own when it came to be identified with a self-regulating market process, and the discovery of the market as a self-regulating process was an eighteenth-century phenomenon. However, the seeds of economic analysis were sown long before, in ancient Greece, the cradle of western civilization.

CONTRIBUTIONS OF THE ANCIENT GREEKS

Our patterns of thought, the framework within which our ideas emerge and cir-culate, the forms of language in which we express ideas, and the rules which govern them, are all products of antiquity. This recognition led the philosopher Gomperz to write, "Even those who have no acquaintance with the doctrines and writings of the great masters of antiquity, and who have not even heard the names of Plato and Aristotle, are, nevertheless, under the spell of their authority."[1] The very word "economics" takes its name from Xenophon's in-structional treatise on efficient management and leadership, the *Oeconomicus*.

What the ancient Greeks contributed to economics was a rational approach to

---

[1] Theodor Gomperz, *Greek Thinkers: A History of Ancient Philosophy,* vol. 1, L. Magnus (trans.). New York: Humanities Press, 1955, p. 528.

social science in general. Their economy may be described as "premarket," not in the sense that trade was absent, but rather in the sense that products were neither uniform, nor traded on organized exchanges, nor analyzed for their own sake. Political and economic life from 500 B.C. to 300 B.C. was dominated by warfare. Greek thinkers were interested primarily in economic and organizational efficiency, and their view of the world was anthropocentric, not mechanistic. In other words, man was the center of all things. The ancient Greeks placed great stock in the self-regulating capacities of individuals charged with making rational decisions and with maximizing human happiness, but they did not discover the self-regulating marketplace, which is the essence of modern economics.

Ancient Greek culture allowed two contrasting ideas of individualism. On the one hand, an authoritarian ruler was empowered to make administrative decisions on behalf of the interests of society. This led to the development of rational calculation based on the idea of an abstractly defined individual as the basic social unit. On the other hand, each family was patriarchal and success-driven, which led to the development of the individual male citizen as a fundamental decision maker. These two contrasting forms of individualism, "macro" and "micro" as it were, contributed to the formal emphasis in Greek society on private household management (*oikonomics*) and to the development of a hedonic calculus of rational self-interest.

Because the Greeks concentrated on elements of *human* control, they developed the art of administration more than the science of economics. Their economy, after all, was basic and simple. It consisted of primary agriculture and limited palace trade. The production of goods was supervised on large, landed estates and in the halls of military chieftains. The state had few non-military expenditures; it was primarily the focal point for religious and military activities. In the course of elaborating the nature of administration, however, the Greeks developed analytic structures which have significance for economic theory. In particular, the following components of modern economics originated in Greek thought: the hedonic calculus, subjective value, diminishing marginal utility, efficiency, and resource allocation. The major writers of this period who contributed to economic analysis were Xenophon, Plato, Protagoras, and Aristotle.

Xenophon on Organization, Value, and the Division of Labor

Philip Wicksteed, a noted British economist of the nineteenth century, wrote that economics "may be taken to include the study of the general principles of administration of resources, whether of an individual, a household, a business, or a State; including the examination of the ways in which waste arises in all such administration."[2] By this criterion, Xenophon (c. 427–355 B.C.) must be

[2] P. H. Wicksteed, *The Common Sense of Political Economy.* New York: A. M. Kelley, 1966, p. 17.

judged one of the earliest economists. His writings are a paean to the science of administration.

A decorated soldier and a student of Socrates, Xenophon couched his ideas in terms of the individual decision maker, whether he be a military commander, public administrator, or head of a household. He contemplated efficient, as opposed to inefficient, courses of action. His *Oeconomicus* explores the proper organization and administration of private and public affairs, whereas his *Ways and Means* prescribes the course of economic revitalization of Athens in the middle of the fourth century B.C. Viewing the material environment as fixed, Xenophon concentrated on human capacity, directed by good leadership, as the chief variable of administration.

A good manager strives to increase the size of the economic surplus of whatever unit he supervises (e.g., family, city, state). For Xenophon, this is accomplished through skill, order, and one of the most basic of economic principles, the division of labor. The division of labor became the linchpin of economic growth in the writings of Adam Smith, as we shall see in Chapter 5, but its important economic implications were recognized in antiquity. Xenophon attributed an increase in both the quantity and the quality of goods to the principle of division of labor. Furthermore, he carried the discussion into an analysis of the relationship between population concentration and the development of specialized skills and products. This insight lies at the base of Adam Smith's famous dictum that specialization and division of labor are limited by the extent of the market.

Xenophon's leader—that exceptional individual who organizes human activity—confronts the forces of nature rather than the forces of a competitive economy. Although the leader is motivated by self-interest, acquisitive behavior as such is not considered "natural." Rather, the economic process consists of intelligent man using perception and reason to extract from nature what is necessary to fulfill human needs and to avoid discomfort. This active and rational pursuit of pleasure and avoidance of pain was formally recognized in the doctrine of *hedonism*, which was part of the larger Greek consciousness. Many centuries later, the same idea resurfaced in the subjectivist theory of value that marked the beginning of neoclassical economics (see Chapters 12 to 16).

An example of Xenophon's use of subjective value presages modern economic thought even though it is not set in an explicit market context. As regards the consumption of food, he noted in *Hiero* that "the greater the number of superfluous dishes set before a man, the sooner a feeling of repletion comes over him; and so, as regards the duration of his pleasure, too, the man who has many courses put before him is worse off than the moderate liver" (*Scripta Minora*, p. 9). Xenophon also groped toward a meaningful distinction between a purely individual subjective concept of value and a more objective general concept of wealth, or property. For example, in his discussion of estate management he observed that "the same things are wealth and not wealth, according as one understands or does not understand how to use them. A flute for example, is wealth to one who is competent to play it, but to an incompetent person it is no better than useless stones...unless he sells it..." in which case, "it becomes wealth" (*Oeconomicus*, I.10–13). Thus, in the end, "wealth is that from which a man can derive profit," but if it causes him harm, it is not wealth. "Even land is not wealth if it makes us starve instead of supporting us" (*Oeconomicus*, I.8).

The idea that it is the consequence of pleasure produced by a good, and not the good itself, lies at the center of utility theory in economics. Xenophon developed the idea of subjective utility further in the dialogue between Aristippus and Socrates, where Aristippus asks, "Do you mean that the same things are both beautiful and ugly?" And Socrates replies, "Of course—and both good and bad. For what is good for hunger is often bad for fever, and what is good for fever is bad for hunger; what is beautiful for running is often ugly for wrestling, and what is beautiful for wrestling ugly for running. For all things are good and beautiful in relation to those purposes for which they are well adapted, bad and ugly in relation to those for which they are ill adapted" (Xenophon, *Memorabilia*, III.8.6–7). This resort to subjective evaluation in the measurement of good versus bad was an important premise of Greek thought from the time of the early Sophists through Aristotle.

Plato and the Administrative Tradition

In contrast to Xenophon's concern for the practical nature of leadership and policy, Plato (c.427–327 B.C.) analyzed the entire political and economic structure of the state. Yet each writer shared a common view of the human element as the primary variable of political economy and statecraft. Plato searched for the optimum polity/economy, and he approached it by refining the moral imperative of justice. Plato's notion of an optimum state is a rigid, static, ideal situation from which he considered any change at all to be regressive.

Although his apparent concern in the *Republic* is with the nature of justice, Plato nevertheless provided a blueprint for an economy based upon several key principles. Pursuing a line of thought opened by Xenophon, Plato attributes the origin of a city to specialization and division of labor. He wrote:

> A city—or a state—is a response to human needs. No human being is self-sufficient, and all of us have many wants.... Since each person has many wants, many partners and purveyors will be required to furnish them. One person will turn to another to supply a particular want and for a different need he will seek out still another. Owing to this interchange of services, a multitude of persons will gather and dwell together in what we have come to call the city or the state.... And so one man trades with another, each assuming he benefits therefrom (*The Republic*, II.369b–c).

This passage establishes the economic foundation of every city, an insight that starts us on the road to a theory of exchange. Specialization creates mutual interdependence, and mutual interdependence establishes reciprocal exchange. But Plato did not go so far as to establish an actual *theory* of exchange. He was more interested in the ensuing pattern of distribution.

Recognizing specialization and division of labor as a source of efficiency and productivity, Plato broached the question of how goods are to be distributed. His answer was that goods are distributed through a marketplace, with money as a token of exchange. In typically Greek fashion, however, he did not consider the marketplace capable of self-regulation. Rather, it requires administrative control. The elements of control that Plato sponsored were fiat money, which must be managed to eliminate profit and usury, and custom/tradition to hold distributive shares constant according to strict mathematical principles (i.e., "rules" of justice).

Whereas Xenophon recognized that profit seekers make good managers (as long as their excesses are curbed by appropriate administrative controls), Plato saw profit and interest (i.e., profit on money) as threats to the status quo. True to the administrative tradition, he constructed an ideal state on the foundation of wise and efficient leadership. He went to great lengths to insulate his leaders from all corruption. He proposed that communism be imposed on the rulers so that they not be tempted by possessions nor diverted from the task of wise governance. He sought to make philosophers out of soldiers, to shape a ruling class of "guardians," who would combine the strength and discipline of the warrior with the wisdom and understanding of the scholar. Having pointed out the benefits of specialization and division of labor, Plato championed a kind of "class specialization" whereby an elite group of capable and high-minded rulers would be trained to direct the political economy.

Given Plato's ideal social structure, the sustenance of a ruling class is problematic without the basic production of goods by the rest of the citizenry. At this lower level of the social hierarchy, Plato tolerated money and trade as "necessary evils." Because his conception of the best society was both absolute and static, anything that threatened the status quo was likewise considered a threat to social welfare. Therefore, Plato regarded all forms of acquisitive behavior, including profit and interest, as potentially destructive. This is why money and trade must be subject to administrative control. The tendency of the Platonists was to regard exchange, in the aggregate, as a kind of "zero-sum game," whereby gains by one class came at the expense of another.

The weakness of Plato's ideal political economy is that its achievement rests on rationalism rather than on any participative social process. Plato could only envision the ideal state as being imposed by authority. The experience of western civilization in the millennia since antiquity is that where such authority exists it is more likely to impose despotism than harmony.

Protagoras and the Hedonic Calculus

Whereas Plato was an absolutist, Protagoras (c. 480–411 B.C.) was a relativist. He held that there was no objective truth, only subjective opinion. This subjectivism is exemplified in the famous maxim attributed to him, "Man is the measure of all things." In other words, although truth cannot be discovered, utility can. According to Protagoras it is up to the citizens of a state to decide what constitutes social welfare and how to achieve it. As against the absolute authority of Plato, Protagoras extolled the democratic process. He believed in common sense as against science, and in the practical social experience of mankind as opposed to the doctrines of moral and political theorists. Not surprisingly, Plato was one of his main critics.

Protagoras's subjectivism is based on the interaction between human perception and physical phenomena. Formulated at a time when vision was believed to be produced by light emanating from the eye, it suggests an active rather than a passive view of individualism. Protagoras is reputed to have said that "each of us is the measure of the things which are and the things which are not. Nevertheless there's an immense difference between one man and another in just this respect: the things which are and appear to one man are different from those which are and appear to another" (Plato, *Theaetetus,* 166d). Thus, to Protagoras, unlike Plato, the subject of *means* was more important than *ends.* Social stability was to be assured by individual participation in the choice of ends. (By analogy in economics, market stability is established by the active participation of market participants.) Like all the ancient Greeks, Protagoras was interested in the effects of leadership and administration, but the proper role of the administrator/leader was to offer advice, not to rule absolutely. Administration, in other words, would make its contribution through the informed choice of means to achieve given ends.

In his authoritative study of Greek economic thought, S. T. Lowry (*The Archaeology of Economic Ideas,* p. 159) makes certain claims on behalf of Protagoras. He asserts that Protagoras's man-measure doctrine is the parent idea of both the labor theory of value and the idea of subjective individualism. He also claims that Protagoras anticipated two of the most basic elements of modern economic theory: (1) the way the market maximizes utility through its function of allocating resources and (2) the use of hedonic measurement in the evaluation of choice. These claims are difficult to substantiate fully in view of the fact that Protagorean thought survives only in secondary sources. Nevertheless, the Sophists, of whom Protagoras was one of the earliest and greatest, definitely planted the seeds of certain ideas that were to flower in the nineteenth century.

Aristotle and Two-Party Exchange

Aristotle (c.384–322 B.C.) was interested in the analytic potential of comparing utility measurements. In his *Topics* and *Rhetoric* he presented a systematic examination of the elements of choice appropriate to public decision making. Most important for modern economic theory, Aristotle discussed value in terms of incremental comparisons. However, his systematic comparisons of value based on subjective marginal utility developed in a way completely unrelated to price theory. It is most likely that Aristotle's analysis of exchange was an attempt to determine the criteria for fairness on which the Athenian legal system was founded. In any event, equity considerations dominated economic considerations in Aristotle's analysis of exchange.

It is important to note that Aristotle set out to analyze *isolated* exchange as opposed to market exchange. The difference is especially pertinent to understanding both the procedure and conclusions of the Aristotelian model. Economists define isolated exchange as two parties exchanging goods in conjunction with their own subjective preferences, without reference to any alternative market opportunities. Market exchange, on the other hand, takes place when individual traders arrive at their decisions from their sense of continuous, pervasive trading among large numbers of participants in an organized and informed market. In market exchange, the publicly known price is the end result of an impartial working out of the interests of many buyers and sellers. In isolated exchange, by contrast, there is no going market price. Absent the interplay of large numbers of market participants, the fairness of each transaction can only be determined by a disinterested third party, such as an arbitrator or a judge. Moreover, the judgment must be rendered on a case-by-case basis. Isolated exchange was a commonplace of Aristotle's experience, and it remains fairly common today in preindustrial economies with nonuniform goods.

The Nature of the Polity   Although he was Plato's prize pupil, Aristotle did not accept his master's conception of the ideal state. Rather, he favored a mixed economy that allowed greater play for economic incentives. Unlike Plato, Aristotle defended private property for *all* classes, on the grounds that it promotes economic efficiency, engenders social peace, and encourages the development of moral character.

The Athenian polity in Aristotle's day functioned in large measure as a distributive economy. In other words, wealth and privilege were distributed by custom, tradition, and government directives. Much was distributed: honors of all sorts, free public meals, public entertainment, rations of grain, profits from the silver mines at Laurium, and payments to many citizens for jury duty and for attendance at public assemblies. In the jargon of modern social theory, these "entitlements" were the prerogative of every Greek citizen. Aristotle viewed these entitlements as protection against an unfettered democracy. The central issue of his concern, therefore, was the matter of distributive justice.

The Nature of Trade   It is against this background that Aristotle's analysis of two-party exchange must be evaluated. He viewed exchange as a bilateral process in which both parties would be better off as a result of the exchange. Exchange is induced when two parties to a potential trade each have a surplus which they are willing to give up in return for one another's goods. Thus, exchange is built upon the notion of reciprocity. From this point, the analysis proceeds on a judicial rather than a commercial footing. According to Aristotle's basic illustration of a barter trade:

Now proportionate return is secured by cross-conjunction. Let A be a builder, B a shoemaker, C a house, D a shoe. The builder, then, must get from the shoemaker the latter's work, and must himself give him in return his own. If, then, first there is proportionate equality of goods, and then reciprocal action takes place, the result we mention will be effected. If not, the bargain is not equal, and does not hold; for there is nothing to prevent the work of the one being better than that of the other; they must therefore be equated....This is why all things that are exchanged must be somehow comparable. It is for this end that money has been introduced, and it becomes in a sense an intermediate; for it measures all things, and therefore, the excess and the defect—how many shoes are equal to a house or to a given amount of food. The number of shoes exchanged for a house must therefore correspond to the ratio of builder to shoemaker. For if this be not so, there will be no exchange and no intercourse. And this proportion will not be effected unless the goods are somehow equal. All goods must therefore be measured by some one thing, as we said before. Now this unit is in truth demand, which holds all things together...; but money has become by convention a sort of representative of demand; and this is why it has the name 'money'—because it exists not by nature but by law and it is in our power to change it and make it useless. There will, then, be reciprocity when the terms have been equated so that as farmer is to shoemaker, the amount of the shoemaker's work is to that of the farmer's work for which it exchanges (*Nichomachean Ethics,* 1133ª 5–30).

This passage plus other elaborations by Aristotle became the subject of intense and repeated examination by the Scholastic writers of the Middle Ages, during which time western thought inched ever so slowly toward an understanding of supply and demand. Because of its obscure meaning and its nonmarket focus, Aristotle's analysis of two-party exchange does not move us very close to an analysis of market price. It is not clear what type of proportion Aristotle alludes to in the above passage, nor what reciprocity (or even equality) means in this context.

Later writers tried to give Aristotle's analysis geometric form. Thus, Nicole Oresme offered the diagram in Figure 2-1 in his fourteenth-century commentary on Aristotle's works. Unfortunately, this geometric "model" does not clarify the fundamental economic issues. Despite its apparent resemblance to modern supply and demand curves, the cross-diagonals of Figure 2-1 are not functional relationships in a mathematical sense. Furthermore, there is no recognition of price, although there is the suggestion of a kind of equilibrium that equates subjective utilities.[3] Moreover, the figure reveals nothing about the distribution of benefit between the two traders, nor of the justice of the exchange within the limits of voluntary choice.

Persistent confusions about the Aristotelian exchange model should not be allowed to obscure the fact it became an important foundation for the prolonged discussions of value that subsequently emerged in the Middle Ages. If

---

[3] In fact, the diagram is reminiscent of one used by W. S. Jevons, one of the founders of marginal utility analysis, in 1871 (see Chap. 14). Jevons acknowledged Aristotle's influence on his own thought.

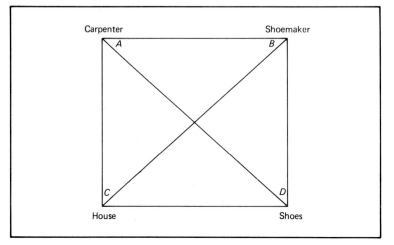

FIGURE 2-1
If the carpenter and the shoemaker trade at the intersection of the diagonals, then proportional compensation is achieved.

nothing else, Aristotle's exchange model established important preconditions for trade, and these premises became part and parcel of economic analysis. For example, Aristotle clearly established the following propositions:

1 Trade arises only when surpluses exist.
2 There must be differing subjective estimates among traders of the worth of each surplus.
3 Traders must establish a rapport that recognizes the potential mutual advantage from exchange.
4 If a dispute arises in isolated exchange regarding the specific allocation of benefits, the proper shares will have to be determined by an administrative authority, taking into account the rules of common justice and the welfare of the state.

Aristotle also made an impact on the theory of value in several other ways. For example, he approached the subject in terms of incremental comparisons. Thus, he observed that "a thing is more desirable if, when added to a lesser good, it makes the whole a greater good. Likewise, also, you should judge by means of subtraction: for the thing upon whose subtraction the remainder is a lesser good may be taken to be a greater good, whichever it be whose subtraction makes the remainder a lesser good" (*Topics,* 118^b 15). He also took account of scarcity and use value, alluding to the famous water-diamonds paradox elaborated by Adam Smith (see Chapter 5). Aristotle noted that "what is rare is a greater good than what is plentiful. Thus gold is a better thing than iron, though less useful: it is harder to get, and therefore better worth getting" (*Topics,* 1364^a 20–25). Adding that "what is often useful surpasses what is seldom useful,'' Aristotle quoted Pindar to the effect that "the best of things is water.'' His ordinal ranking of human needs in the *Politics* also presaged the theory of the great Austrian economist, Carl Menger (see Chapter 13).

Aristotle on Money and Interest

Aristotle's theory of money rationalized both the origin of money and its functions. The passage quoted above from the *Ethics* (see page 21) demonstrates his perception of money as a standard of value and a medium of exchange. Aristotle also recognized money as a store of value by observing that "if we do not need a thing now we shall have it if ever we do need it—money is as it were our surety; for it must be possible for us to get what we want by bringing the money" (*Nichomachean Ethics,* 1133^b 10). Some scholars even argue that the modern idea of money as a contractual standard of deferred payment is implicit in Aristotle's analysis of usury.

Aristotle's concern with justice and the administrative nature of the economy led him to a discussion of money as an object of acquisitive behavior, and particularly to an examination of interest as an "unnatural" return. Modern economic thought regards acquisitive behavior as a healthy manifestation of self-interest, which is demonstrated to have beneficial effects through the restraints placed upon it by competition. To the Greek mind, however, which did not grasp the self-regulating character of the marketplace, unrestrained acquisitive behavior represented a threat to social and economic stability. Aristotle believed that coined money permitted the development of "unnecessary" exchange, which was to be discouraged in the "good" state. In the context of ancient Greece, unnecessary exchange is exchange without a natural limit. Unlike the necessary exchange of households, which was restrained by the limited needs of the family and by diminishing marginal utility, unnecessary exchange (i.e., retail trade) occurs merely for the purpose of accumulating wealth for its own sake. In other words, although Aristotle recognized the use of exchange to satisfy (natural) individual and collective wants, he did not approve of the use of exchange as a device for accumulating wealth. Since such accumulation was without natural limit, its relentless pursuit runs the risk of impoverishing the many in order to profit the few.

It is this kind of thinking that underlies Aristotle's condemnation of interest as "unnatural." To Aristotle, the natural use of money is to spend it. Hoarding, or accumulation for its own sake, was unnatural, and therefore, condemned. Insofar as there can be no lending without accumulation, lending, too, was suspect. Aristotle condemned interest, which he always equated with usury, on the ground that there was no reason why a mere medium of exchange should increase in passing from hand to hand—it was not "natural" that money should reproduce itself in this way. Unfortunately, he never grappled with the question of why interest is paid in the first place. In other words, Aristotle did not develop a theory of interest, even though he had a primitive theory of money to which he linked interest.

Looking backward through the millennia, it is clear that what the Greeks contributed to western thought was a rational approach to social science. Their ideas established a continuum that stretched from the microeconomic values of the basic production/consumption unit of the household to the macroeconomic values of happiness and self-sufficiency of the collective citizenry. What they did not perceive is the marketplace as a self-regulating mechanism. Thus their framework of analysis was anthropocentric and administrative.

ROMAN AND EARLY CHRISTIAN CONTRIBUTIONS

Economic historians may debate the extent of economic activity in ancient Greece, but the record indicates that it was extensive enough to generate serious reflective thought. By the time that Rome superseded Greece as the center of western thought, important commercial interests had developed and spread throughout the empire. And by the end of the Roman Republic there were enough economic problems to employ a legion of economists and government advisers—problems of trade, finance, war, colonization, and slavery, to name a few. It is surprising, therefore, that little genuine analytical work in economics emerged during this period.

One possible answer to this enigma is that the social structure of ancient Rome was not congenial to purely intellectual interests. From the bottom up, the structure consisted of slaves, peasants, artisans, and traders, capped by a civil and military aristocracy. Although the aristocracy nurtured a considerable interest in Greek philosophy and art, it did so more as avocation than vocation, with the predictable result that little serious analytical advance in economics occurred.

The one great achievement of Roman society was the law. From a social standpoint, it was the crowning glory of one of the greatest empires in the history of the world. Roman law was divided into a civil law that applied only to relations between citizens (*jus civile*) and a kind of common law—though not in the English sense—that ruled commercial and other relations between noncitizens or between citizens and noncitizens (*jus gentium*). This last body of law became a repository of economic principles that later provided a starting point for economic analysis, especially in the Middle Ages. The Roman law of property and contract, for example, subsequently became the mainstay of legal systems in the western world. The concept of natural law, which can be traced back to Aristotle, found its way into Roman law, where it was used as a touchstone for determining the validity of human law. Finally, the modern doctrine of the corporation can be traced back to Roman law.[4] In general, Ro-

---

[4] An excellent historical treatment of the modern corporation, though brief, is contained in Robert Hessen's *In Defense of the Corporation* (Stanford: Hoover Institution Press, 1979). Curiously, Hessen does not trace the concept back as far as Roman law, stopping instead at the Middle Ages.

man law provided the framework upon which the economics of a later day was slowly but surely mounted. The focal point of subsequent discussions of market price, for example, is found in the Justinian Code:

> The prices of things function not according to the whim or utility of individuals, but according to the common estimate. A man who has a son whom he would ransom for a very large sum is not richer by that amount. Nor does he who possesses another man's son possess the sum for which he could sell him to his father; nor is that amount to be expected when he sells him. In the present circumstances he is evaluated as a man and not as somebody's son.... Time and place, however, bring about some variations in price. [Olive] oil will not be evaluated the same in Rome as in Spain, nor, since here as well prices are not constituted by momentary influences, nor by occasional scarcity, will it be evaluated the same in times of prolonged sterility as in times of abundant harvest (*Corpus Iuris Civilis,* cited in Dempsey, p. 473).

It is worth noting that from the time of the fall of Rome to the end of the eighteenth century, most of the writers on economics were by profession either businessmen or lawyers. If they were lawyers, moreover, they were either clergymen trained in canon law or jurists trained in civil law.

The rise of Christianity overlapped the decline of the Roman Empire and offered a different kind of civilizing influence. Rome's efforts at civilizing its annexations pretty much began and ended with the establishment of law and order. The only message it offered to those outside its jurisdictional limits was military surrender. Perhaps for this reason it was an inherently unstable social and political order. Christianity offered a different message, one that proved to be an inspiration and a rallying point for millions of people, but one not especially fruitful for the advance of economic analysis until a later period in its development.

Early Christian thought treated the kingdom of God as being near at hand, and so it emphasized "other worldly" treasures. Production and material welfare would be superfluous in the kingdom of God. Indeed, earthly treasures were regarded as an impediment to the attainment of this heavenly kingdom. As the passage of time made the comings of this kingdom seem more distant, wealth came to be looked upon as a gift of God, furnished to promote human welfare. Christian thought therefore came to center on the "right" use of material gifts, an idea that persisted in medieval economic thought. Thus St. Basil (c. 330–379) wrote:

> The good man...neither turns his heart to wealth when he has it, nor seeks after it if he has it not. He treats what is given him not for his selfish enjoyment, but for wise administration (*Works of St. Basil,* cited in Gray, p. 52).

This kind of thing is more of a normative admonition than a step in the direction of analysis. The same could be said of the early writings, including those of Saints John Chrysostom (c. 347–407), Jerome (c. 347–419), Ambrose (c. 339–397), and, to a lesser extent, Augustine (354–430). Augustine went further than the others in that he pointed the way to a *subjective* theory of value, where wants are individually determined. In *The City of God,* for example, he wrote:

> There is...a different value set upon each thing proportionate to its use...very frequently a horse is held more dear than a slave, or a jewel more precious than a maid servant. Since every man has the power of forming his own mind as he wishes, there is very little agreement between the choice of a man who through necessity stands in real need of an object and of one who hankers after a thing merely for pleasure (cited in Dempsey, p. 475).

By and large, however, the early Christian writers treated economic topics with indifference, if not hostility. They were primarily interested in the morality of individual behavior. The how and why of economic mechanisms seemed to be of no interest to the church's leaders or its writers.

MEDIEVAL ECONOMIC THOUGHT

The death of the last Roman emperor in 476 ushered in a long period of secular decline in the west and a concomitant rise in the fortunes of the east. For five centuries, from 700 to 1200, Islam led the world in power, organization, and extent of government; in social refinements and standards of living; in literature, scholarship, science, medicine, and philosophy. The Arab world acted as a sort of conduit to the west for Hindu wisdom and culture. It was Moslem science that preserved and developed Greek mathematics, physics, chemistry, astronomy, and medicine during this half millennium, while the west was sinking into what historians commonly call the Dark Ages. By A.D. 730 the Moslem empire reached from Spain and southern France to the borders of China and India, an empire of spectacular strength and grace. Perhaps the most significant, single innovation that the eager, inquisitive Arab scholars contributed to the west was their system of writing numbers. They displaced the clumsy Roman numerals of the previous empire with the much more utilitarian Arabic numerals of today. One of the more eccentric Arab mathematicians, Alhazen, founded the modern theory of optics around the year 1000. But for our purposes, the most important contribution of Arab culture was its reintroduction of Aristotle to the west.

After the city of Toledo, Spain, was recaptured from the Moors in 1085, European scholars flocked to that city in order to translate the ancient classics. The ancient texts were turned from Greek (which Europe had forgotten) through Arabic and Hebrew into Latin. In this last mode their philosophical gems were mined for the next four hundred years by the Schoolmen of the medieval church.

Economics in a Feudal Society

The dominant form of economic organization in the Middle Ages was feudalism. This was a system of production and distribution in which the ownership of land was neither absolute nor divorced of duties, as it had been in ancient

Rome and was to become again in modern times. Instead, the king was the repository of all legal property rights. He assigned land in large parcels to his favored chiefs and noblemen, who, could, in turn, assign the land to various subtenants. "Ownership" at the production level meant mere *right to use* (usufruct), although this right tended to become hereditary. Usufruct remained, however, subject to the performance of certain duties: military, personal, or economic.

Feudal property also became the seat of political power in the Middle Ages. Europe at this time lacked the social, economic, and political integration prerequisite to a strong central authority. Each feudal lord was consequently vested with numerous governmental functions, which he exercised in his particular territory.

Economic production under feudalism took place on the manor, or agricultural estate. Output was produced on a small scale, using relatively primitive agricultural techniques. Labor services were provided by serfs who were attached to the land rather than to the person who "owned" it. The goal of the manor was self-sufficiency; trading activities between regions and/or countries were severely limited. In sum, the economic and social framework of the manor was analogous in many respects to that of the *polis,* or Greek city-state. The principle of organization in both was status, not contract.

Two major factors that set the Middle Ages apart from Greek antiquity were its doctrinal unity, provided by the Roman Catholic Church, and the pervasiveness of the market mechanism. Medieval society somewhat grudgingly nurtured a nascent form of capitalism, as economic markets (both in products and in factors of production) became more and more entrenched in the fabric of daily life. It was against this backdrop that Scholastic economics developed.

Scholastic Economic Analysis

The power and influence of the Catholic church in the Middle Ages was due in large part to its autonomy in spiritual matters, but there was also another reason. The medieval clergy preserved the one light that shined through the Dark Ages, learning. The social hierarchy of medieval civilization was almost Platonic in its structure. One belonged to either the peasantry (who worked), the military (who fought), or the clergy (who contemplated). The last group alone emphasized the importance of knowledge, and so it was, almost by default, that the clergy became the repository and the guardians of that knowledge. Medieval economics, therefore, was the product of the clergy, particularly a group of learned writers that we now refer to as Scholastics.[5] It was they who joined together the several strands of thought that constitute medieval economics: ideas gleaned from Aristotle and the Bible, from Roman law and canon law.

---

[5] As used in this context, the term simply means "professors" or "teachers."

Scholastic economics is not held in high regard today. It is commonly perceived as a tissue of misplaced fallacies about market price, interest, and property. Although most Scholastic ideas have been expelled from the corpus of economic knowledge, this unfavorable view tends to obscure the significance of a major tradition in the painfully drawn-out evolution of modern value theory. This last phenomenon deserves a close examination.[6]

The Scholastic Method   The method of Scholasticism was as follows. The writer posed a question, then followed it with a lengthy and detailed exposition of the view that was to be either refuted or reinterpreted. Attention was always paid to the weight of authority. Eventually, an answer was given, contrary views scrutinized, and documentation brought forth. The whole process was deductive in nature, depending not so much on the rules of logic or of human experience as on faith and the weight of authority.

While this method may seem decidedly unscientific to us, it was the accepted procedure of the medieval period. There were many masters of this method, but five in particular stand out in the tradition of Aristotelian value theory. The five are Albertus Magnus (c. 1206–1280), Thomas Aquinas (c. 1225–1274), Henry of Friemar (c. 1245–1340), Jean Buridan (c. 1295–1358), and Gerald Odonis (c. 1290–1349).

As keepers of the moral code of medieval society, the main interest of the clergy was justice, not exchange. One form of justice is exchange justice (or commutative justice), which is exactly the issue broached by Aristotle in Book V, Chap. 5, of the *Nichomachean Ethics*. It was there that Aristotle developed his reciprocity model (see above), and it was from this point that Scholastic economics took its departure. The text of Aristotle's exchange analysis may have been garbled from the outset, but it seems certain that subsequent translations into Arabic, Hebrew, and Latin did little to remove any ambiguities. Perhaps it is not surprising, therefore, that the Scholastics spent four centuries trying to disentangle and clarify its meaning. In the process Scholastic analysis infused Aristotle's primitive notion of value with the idea of *equilibrium*. It also set the train of economic reasoning down two divergent tracks that were not to come together again for over half a millennium: the idea of cost-determined value on the one hand and demand-determined value on the other.

Labor and Expenses: The Analysis of Albertus Magnus   Albertus Magnus, Dominican provincial, Bishop of Regensburg, and Doctor of the church, was the first great Latin Aristotelian. His place in the history of economics is ensured by two things: his service as mentor to Thomas Aquinas, who subsequently had an enormous impact on western thought, and his commentaries on the *Nichomachean Ethics,* where he recast the ancient Greek ideas in the mold of medieval society, providing the point of departure for all subsequent

[6] The following section follows very closely the excellent study of Odd Langholm, *Price and Value in the Aristotelian Tradition*.

thought on exchange and value. What Albert did was to plant in western thought the persistent notion that value in exchange must comply with cost of production. In so doing, he set in motion a long train of thought that did not reach its fruition until the nineteenth century, notably in the work of Karl Marx (see Chapter 11).

Earlier commentators on Aristotle's exchange model did not go much past the question of the *measurement* of value. The most common references given to the measurement of value were money (*nummisma*) and need (*indigentia*). But Albert, arguing that there is a natural order and an economic order, in which things are valued differently, maintained that in the economic order goods are measured in relation to labor (*opus*). More generally, he referred to ''labor and expenses,'' mentioning both elements of cost in the same breath. Mere recognition of the role of cost in the measurement of value is not as important as the use Albert made of the insight, however. He related costs of production to the ''cross-conjunction'' in Aristotle's model, noting that if the market price does not cover costs of production, production will eventually cease. This was an important analytical leap for two reasons: it suggested that price could be treated as an *equilibrium* value, and it set up an economic variable (i.e., costs) as the *regulator* of value. Certainly Albert was a long way from presenting an integrated and systematic explanation for the determination of market price, but his was nevertheless an important advance for the thirteenth century. The fact that he brought labor into the Aristotelian framework was a lasting contribution. In subsequent chapters of this book we shall see how much mileage later economic writers got from the same notion.

Human Wants: The Analysis of Thomas Aquinas   Albert's brilliant pupil, Thomas Aquinas, did not really have any conflict with his teacher, but he quickly realized that he must improve on Albert's labor theory, and he saw the way to do this by stressing human wants (*indigentia*). Thomas harked back to St. Augustine for this point, noting that men will not always rank things according to the natural order. Augustine had toyed with subjectivism by noting that men will often value a jewel more than a servant girl (see above). But Thomas turned St. Augustine's teaching on its head. Whereas Augustine discussed the natural order and brought in economic exchange for contrast, Thomas did just the opposite, bringing economics to the fore. In one sense, though, Augustine was more astute. He did not really distinguish between need and pleasure—an approach that could have accelerated the early development of demand theory if Aquinas had taken it up. Instead, Aquinas chose to inject moral instruction into his economics, a factor that tends to discount pleasure. Consequently, Aquinas's demand theory never got beyond the simple notion of the human usefulness of goods as compared with their place in the natural order of creation.

Aquinas's formal contribution to Aristotelian value theory was a two-pronged one in which one element conditioned the other. First, he reaffirmed the *double measure* of goods (value in use versus value in exchange) that

Aristotle had established; second, he introduced need (*indigentia*) into the price formula. This last contribution is especially important because it marked the earliest root of an analytical demand theory of value. Aquinas argued that *price varies with need. Indigentia* became a regulator of value. This contribution, however, was strictly formal. Aquinas did not explain his terms; he simply made the connection between need and price. But that connection stood as an invitation to subsequent Aristotelians to work out a more complete theory of value, which they eventually did. In the Scholastic analysis that followed Aquinas, the concept of *indigentia* was gradually enlarged to include utility, effective demand, and even unmitigated desire.

It should be noted that Aquinas's mentor, Albert, did not overlook need in his discussion of value, nor did Aquinas neglect costs. Rather it is the case that each in turn helped to develop more fully one particular side of the argument. Taken together, the discussion is fairly balanced, although there was still a long way to go toward an integrated, analytical understanding of the market mechanism.

Indeed, an opinion shared by many modern historians of economics is that Aquinas's discussion mostly served to denounce market forces as antagonistic to justice. It is difficult to reconcile the medieval notion of "just price" with the modern notion of "market price," since the former is generally defended on normative grounds whereas the latter is held to be an objective result of impersonal forces. Certainly Aquinas's language was open-ended on many points, furthering the popular notion that his analysis was wrongheaded. For example, bowing to Aristotle, Aquinas wrote:

> ...if the price exceeds the quantity of the value of the article, or the article exceeds the price, the equality of justice will be destroyed. And therefore, to sell a thing dearer or to buy it cheaper than it is worth is, in itself, unjust and illicit....The just price of things, however, is not determined to a precise point but consists of a certain estimate....The price of an article is changed according to difference in location, time, or risk to which one is exposed in carrying it from one place to another or in causing it to be carried. Neither purchase nor sale according to this principle is unjust (cited in Dempsey, p. 481).

At best, "just price" was a vague and imprecise idea, unsuited to an operational theory of a purely analytical stripe. But economics, as Alfred Marshall (see Chapter 15) was later to remind us of nature, does not make sudden, gigantic leaps forward. During the Middle Ages it rather crawled, but it nevertheless headed in the right direction.

Aggregation and Scarcity: The Influence of Henry of Friemar Aquinas had developed the concept of *indigentia* in a way that essentially referred to the individual. But the modern notion of demand is an aggregate one in the sense that it comprises the wants of all those buyers who participate in the market. The next step in the Scholastic tradition was to conceive of *indigentia* as an aggregate measure, a step taken by the Augustinian friar, Henry of Friemar.

As used by the Scholastics, the concept *indigentia* is not the same as market demand in the technical sense of contemporary economics. It is not quantity demanded as a function of price; its meaning is much less precise, including elements of supply as well as of demand. The meaning most commonly attached to the concept in Scholastic literature is "amount desired in relation to what is available" (i.e., demand in the face of scarcity). As we now recognize so readily, genuine analytical progress in value theory required the separation of the two notions "demand" and "supply." Failure to separate demand and supply as elements in the value formula was the fundamental defect in the Aristotelian market model. Unfortunately, the defect was never quite remedied by the Scholastics, despite its very extensive tradition. In fact, the remedy was a lot longer in coming, having to await the full flowering of marginalism in the nineteenth century.

Progress, however slow, was nevertheless made by the Scholastics. Just as Aquinas had tilted the headlong rush of Albertine analysis toward demand factors instead of costs, so Henry tipped the Thomist formula in favor of aggregate (i.e., market) demand. Henry advanced the somewhat mixed notion that value is determined by "the *common* need of something scarce," a concept which acknowledged that as long as there is abundance in the face of strong demand, *indigentia* will not raise price.

As Odd Langholm has pointed out, a theory of exchange value can start at any one of three stages of deduction. It can start with the conditions of the market, i.e., with the abundance or scarcity of goods. Alternatively, it can start with the properties of goods that make the market conditions relevant. Finally, it can start with the needs of the people that make these properties in goods relevant, proceeding to market conditions from there. The medieval theory, which was rooted in Aristotelian soil and survived into modern economics, started at the third level. Although the Scholastics were not alone in discussing economic matters in relation to human wants, they deserve credit "for taking this concept through aggregation and scarcity into a workable argument in the price formula" (Langholm, *Price and Value,* p. 115).

Effective Demand: The Contribution of Jean Buridan   The next major step in the evolution of value theory was taken by the rector of the University of Paris, Jean Buridan. Buridan was a master logician and thoroughgoing Aristotelian whose contributions to social science and philosophy are contained in some three dozen commentaries on Aristotle's works. It was Buridan who maneuvered the Scholastic notion of *indigentia* much closer to the modern concept of *effective demand.* He described poverty as a state in which someone does not have that which he desires, so that *indigentia* could be applied to "luxuries" as well as including its more narrow Thomistic sense of "necessities." In addition, Buridan made *indigentia* into desire backed by ability to pay.

This modification, as insignificant as it may seem, provided a way out of a nettlesome problem in medieval value theory. Both Aquinas and his fellow prelate John Duns Scotus were spokesmen for a "double rule" in medieval price theory. A seller who parted with a commodity at unusually high sacrifice to himself could, with the blessing of the church fathers, compensate for his loss by charging a higher than normal price. But in the event that the sacrifice was ordinary, he could not charge a higher price merely to increase his profit. In the latter case, Aquinas argued that by profiting exorbitantly, the seller in effect sold something that was not his own (the same rationale applied to Scholastic condemnations of usury). Duns Scotus maintained that something is not precious in itself merely because of the buyer's strong preference. The gist of each argument is that it is wrong to take advantage of a buyer's intense wants.

There are several problems with this double rule. An obvious one is its basic analytical asymmetry. It is all right for a seller to do one thing if his want is high but not to do the same thing if the buyer's want is high. The other problem is how to define "unusually high want." Borrowing from both Aquinas and Henry of Friemar, Buridan advanced a line of thought that distinguished between individual "need" and aggregate "need." He tied value to aggregate need, by which he meant effective demand, and argued that the conjunction of numbers of consumers and their purchasing power works to establish a just and normal state of affairs in the marketplace. A buyer, therefore, however needy, must comply with the valuation of the market. This is the self-same line of thought that led centuries later to the laissez faire morality of Nicholas Barbon and Thomas Hobbes, the latter declaring that "the market is the best judge of value." To the extent, therefore, that the Scholastic tradition remained true to Aristotle's original meaning, we are left with the conclusion that there is no room in Aristotelian social ethics for "bleeding hearts."

What is interesting about Buridan's achievement is that it came within an Aristotelian framework that permitted the metamorphosis of a narrow medieval concept, *indigentia*—which originally took the vague connotation of need—into the indiscriminate generalization, "every desire which moves us to set store by things." It is to this notion that European price theory—as opposed to British classical value theory—owes its later success. Buridan spawned a tradition of economic inquiry that permeated not only his native France but eventually also Italy and, most especially, Austria. This tradition, with tentacles reaching all the way back to Aristotle, culminated in the nineteenth-century formulation of utility, and finally in the wedding of this last concept to the notion of the margin. This success was in no small part explained by an "emphasis on utility as a psychological experience, playing down considerations of the properties in goods which cause men to desire them, a preoccupation which is sure to take theorists away from the main point" (Langholm, *Price and Value,* p. 144).

Toward a Synthesis: Odonis and Crell   All through the Middle Ages, discussions of value theory constantly pitted a generalized concept of labor against a demand theory, so that the two were continually rubbing against each other. In these circumstances one would have expected a synthesis to be forthcoming, yet the Scholastic tradition stopped short of what we today call the "neoclassical synthesis." One man more than any other brought value theory close to the now familiar synthesis it occupies. He was a resourceful German sectarian theologist named John Crell (1590–c. 1633), whose powerful insight came from joining Buridan and another Scholastic, Gerald Odonis. The latter was a French monk of the Franciscan order, which developed its own tradition in exchange theory. Odonis had inherited a market model that went past St. Thomas and bore the stamp of Henry of Friemar. The Franciscan tradition focused on *raritas*, by which it meant scarcity in the face of need (the reverse of Henry's *indigentia*, which was need in the face of scarcity).

Odonis's approach specifically rejected a simple labor-quantity theory of value and focused on the scarcity and quality of human, productive skills. This led him to a theory of wage differentials that recognized the relative efficiencies of different skills and the relative cost of acquiring those skills. It was an important step on the path to ultimate recognition of the synthetic nature of labor and demand theories of value. Odonis's theory could explain, for example, why an architect earned more than a stonecutter, and it led to the inference that scarce labor commands a higher product price through *product* scarcity. A complete synthesis requires an additional step: the recognition that every kind of labor is always to some extent scarce, and so brings forth a scarce product. For it is in this way that labor serves as a *regulator* of value. The inference was a long time in coming; it was not made by Buridan because it required joining his own insight to that of Odonis, who had not yet written when Buridan was producing his commentaries. Fortunately for economics, Crell was born in the following century, which provided the opportunity for a resourceful thinker to put the two together.

History tells us that the problem of value was not solved completely until economists came to understand that the cost theory and the demand theory were merely components of a single principle. That single principle rested on two legs. The first leg is that labor is a regulator of value only if it is spent on something useful. The second leg is that all labor is always (to some extent) scarce. Wants and costs are, to use Alfred Marshall's felicitous analogy, but two blades of the same scissors. Yet it took a very long time to get that far in economic analysis. Ironically, in the seventeenth and eighteenth centuries a very able line of Italian and French economists had the two theories marching separately, with scarcity and utility carrying the burden of explanation. The British classical tradition somehow got off on the monotonous track of costs and failed to bring about a union, even though the idea that labor regulates product value through scarcity is very much in evidence in Senior's work (see Chapter 7). In nineteenth-century France there was a sudden flash of genius, but this was not fully reflected in economic theory until after a hiatus of nearly three decades (see Chapters 12 through 16).

The most interesting thing to surface from recent research into Scholastic economics is the remarkable continuity of the Aristotelian tradition through the years. The Scholastic economists were fully within this tradition, a fact that unfortunately serves to detract from their original contributions. But one by one, they laid the bricks and mortar on which the edifice of value theory was later erected. The chief architects of this edifice and the nature of their contributions are summarized in Figure 2-2.

The Doctrine of Usury

Insofar as interest is generally regarded as the price of money, a theory of interest may be considered merely a subset of the general theory of value. But in the Middle Ages, few topics evoked as much controversy as the conditions under which interest was to be allowed. The church, moreover, had an official position on the subject.

Although the idea that interest, or "profit," from loans is wrong can be traced back to the Old Testament (*Deuteronomy* 13:20), the Roman Catholic Church did not make the injunction against usury part of its official doctrine until the fourth century A.D. when the Council of Nicea banned the practice among clerics. During the reign of Charlemagne, the prohibition was extended

FIGURE 2-2
Aristotle, Aquinas, Albertus, Henry of Friemar, Buridan, Odonis, and Crell all helped lay the foundation for the development of value theory.

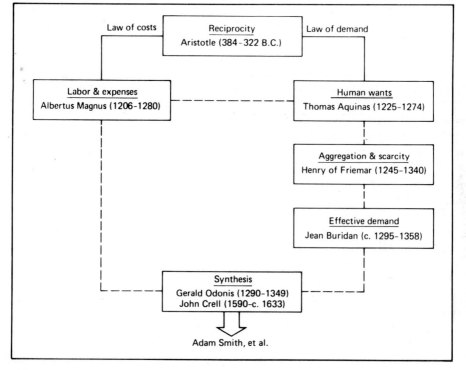

to all Christians, usury being defined as a transaction "where more is asked than is given." Subsequent practice made the ban an absolute prohibition, and for many centuries usury laws enjoyed widespread and official support. During the Middle Ages, usury and the doctrine of "just price" were the main economic topics that occupied the Scholastics.

In Latin, *usura,* from which the word "usury" derives, meant payment for the use of money in a transaction that resulted in gain (i.e., net profit) for the lender; whereas *interesse,* from which the word "interest" originates, meant "loss" and was recognized by ecclesiastic and civil law as a reimbursement for loss or expense. Interest was commonly regarded as compensation for delayed repayment or for loss of profits to the lender who could not employ his capital in some alternative use during the term of the loan. Risk was not generally considered as a justification for interest, because loans were usually secured by property worth many times the money advanced. Thus, the usury prohibition was not intended to curb the high profits of risk enterprise. For instance, the *societas* (partnership) was a recognized form of commercial organization from Roman times. Its profit objective was officially sanctioned, and gains from trade were treated as earnings for effort and risk. The *census* was a kind of early financial instrument that combined elements of a mortgage and an annuity. Under the terms of this contract, the borrower incurred "an obligation to pay an annual return from fruitful property," usually a landed estate. By its nature, a *census* was not considered usurious.

In addition, bank deposits had become a form of investment by the thirteenth century. Merchant bankers paid interest on deposits. As early as the twelfth century, bills of exchange combined foreign exchange with credit, although interest was often concealed in a high exchange rate. In other words, during the Middle Ages, the church doctrine on usury, existing alongside legitimate forms of interest-taking, helped promote a double standard that became increasingly arbitrary over time, thereby creating opportunities for exploitation by those who made the rules.[7]

Over the years, medieval economic doctrine frequently came into conflict with medieval economic practice. Up to the thirteenth century, the sweeping condemnation of usury by the church was accompanied by civil prohibitions which varied widely from country to country. Yet despite its widespread prohibition, usury was never entirely eradicated in any large part of Europe, nor for any important period of time. Professional pawnbrokers, though sometimes underground, probably always existed in medieval Europe. In fact, where they operated openly, they were licensed by the state, which received license fees.[8]

---

[7] According to Raymond De Roover ("The Scholastics, Usury and Foreign Exchange," *Business History Review,* vol. 41 (1967), p. 266), pawnbrokers and small moneylenders were the main victims of the church's campaigns against usury, "but the big bankers with international connections were left undisturbed. Far from being censured, they were called 'the peculiarly beloved sons of the Church' and prided themselves on being the Pope's exchangers."

[8] Before the Renaissance, the legal limits on personal loans from pawnshops ranged from a low of 10 percent in Italy to 300 percent in Provence. In the fourteenth century, the Lombards often

Because the church's arguments in defense of usury make little sense in the context of modern economics, the whole topic is usually considered an analytical dead end. The chief flaws of the Scholastic analysis were its neglect of the productivity of money as an economic resource, and its failure to recognize the time value of money. Some historians blame the church's doctrine for retarding the development of capitalism by suppressing the growth of credit markets. But up until recently, little research has been directed at explaining the anomalies between church doctrine and church policy on this subject.

In an attempt to break this pattern of neglect, Robert Ekelund, Robert Hébert, and Robert Tollison (see Notes for Further Reading) approached the subject by analyzing the medieval church's behavior on the basis of its "monopoly" position among religious institutions. They conclude that it was in the church's interest to selectively use the usury doctrine in order to keep its own cost of funds low, to prevent the entry of competing "firms," and to otherwise preserve its monopoly status. In the final analysis, therefore, the ultimate disappearance of the usury doctrine may have been an effect of increased doctrinal competition in the wake of the Protestant Reformation rather than of a systematic belief in the weakness of its underlying premises.

CONCLUSION

Although the period from Greek antiquity to the end of the Middle Ages constitutes roughly two thousand years, the fundamental economic structure of western civilization changed little during that time. Both Greek antiquity and European feudalism were characterized by small, insular, self-sufficient economies with little capital and low levels of production. At the level of basic production, serfdom was akin to slavery, save for the legal difference that serfs did not relinquish property rights over their own bodies. In effect, serfs were tied to the land, regardless of owner, whereas slaves belonged to a particular owner, regardless of whether or not the owner possessed land.

Throughout these two millennia, isolated exchange predominated over what we now call market exchange. Consequently, the learned treatises of the day focused primarily on the question of fairness, not on the origin of prices. This fact provided a degree of continuity stretching from Aristotle through the Scholastics. When John Crell wrote in the seventeenth century, he capped a tradition in value analysis that began with the early Scholastics four hundred years earlier. But it was a tradition within a tradition, so to speak. The Scholastic tradition, in the narrow sense, was, nevertheless, more cohesive and tight-knit, because the church in the Middle Ages enjoyed an intellectual mo-

charged 50 percent, although the most common legal pawnshop limit in effect was 43 percent. Monarchs, such as Emperor Frederick II (1211–1250), often paid interest of 30 to 40 percent to creditors, especially when collateral was not liquid. Commercial loans commonly fetched interest rates between 10 and 25 percent depending on the adequacy of commercial credits (see Sidney Homer, *A History of Interest Rates,* rev. ed. New Brunswick, N.J.: Rutgers University Press, 1977, pp. 89–103).

nopoly on learning. Its scholars all spoke the same language, Latin. They were each trained by an educational system that was the same in every country. Each figure in that tradition professed the same fundamental beliefs and acknowledged the same authority of God and church. Albert, Henry, and John Crell were Germans; Aquinas, Italian; Buridan and Odonis, French. This heterogeneity was hardly noticed, however. As Schumpeter has said of the Scholastics, "Their country was Christendom, their state the Church" (*History,* p. 75).

As Crell was writing, the Scholastic tradition was in the process of being displaced by an early modern form of inquiry. But the new economists of the eighteenth century all had classical educations, so that theirs was by no means a de novo approach to economic analysis.

NOTES FOR FURTHER READING

The ancient world is practically a never-never land to most historians of economic thought, although there is a fairly large literature on the economics of the period. A sampler of original sources, including selections from Xenophon, Aristotle, Aquinas, Oresme, and Molina, can be found in A. E. Monroe, *Early Economic Thought* (Cambridge, Mass.: Harvard University Press, 1924). For more sweeping treatments of the period, see M. L. W. Laistener, *Greek Economics* (London: Dent, 1923); Moses I. Finley, *The Ancient Economy,* 2d ed. (Berkeley: University of California Press, 1985); Marshall D. Sahlins, *Stone Age Economics* (Chicago: Aldine-Atherton, 1972); J. J. Spengler, *Origins of Economic Thought and Justice* (Carbondale, Ill.: Southern Illinois University Press, 1980); and A. M. Andreades, *History of Greek Public Finance,* rev. ed., 2 vols. (Cambridge, Mass.: Harvard University Press, 1933). The latest, and arguably the best, analysis of the Greek tradition, however, is S. Todd Lowry's *The Archaeology of Economic Ideas* (see References), from which this chapter draws freely. A useful overview of the entire period stretching from Greek to Roman to medieval economic thought is contained in Barry Gordon, *Economic Analysis before Adam Smith: Hesiod to Lessius* (New York: Harper & Row, 1975).

Much of the periodical literature on ancient economic thought centers on Aristotle, though not exclusively so. On some general topics, see A. H. M. Jones, "The Economic Basis of the Athenian Democracy," *Past & Present,* vol. 1 (February 1952), pp. 13–31; Kurt Singer, "*Oikonomia:* An Inquiry into the Beginnings of Economic Thought and Language," *Kyklos,* vol. 11 (1958), pp. 29–54; E. Simey, "Economic Theory among the Greeks and Romans," *Economic Review,* vol. 10 (October 1900), pp. 462–481; S. Todd Lowry, "The Archaeology of the Circulation Concept in Economic Theory," *Journal of the History of Ideas,* vol. 35 (July–September 1974), pp. 429–444; Gregor Sebba, "The Development of the Concepts of Mechanism and Model in Physical and Economic Thought," *American Economic Review, Papers and Proceedings,* vol. 43 (May 1953), pp. 259–271; and William Baumol's delightful excursus,

"Economics of Athenian Drama: Its Relevance for the Arts in a Small City Today," *Quarterly Journal of Economics,* vol. 85 (August 1971), pp. 365–376.

The economic ideas of other writers who fit into the ancient scheme but whose ideas have not directly impinged on this chapter are examined by J. J. Spengler, "Herodotus on the Subject Matter of Economics," *Scientific Monthly,* vol. 81 (December 1955), pp. 276–285; William F. Campbell, "Pericles and the Sophistication of Economics," *History of Political Economy,* vol. 15 (Spring 1983), pp. 112–135; and Stanley B. Smith, "The Economic Motive in Thucydides," *Harvard Studies in Classical Philology,* vol. 51 (1940), pp. 267–301.

The periodical literature on Plato's economic ideas is relatively sparse. William F. Campbell explores Plato's use of economic analogies in "The Free Market for Goods and the Free Market for Ideas in the Platonic Dialogues," *History of Political Economy,* vol. 17 (Summer 1985), pp. 187–197; C. B. Welles delves into the underpinnings of Plato's ideal society in "The Economic Background of Plato's Communism," *Journal of Economic History,* suppl., vol. 8 (1948), pp. 101–114; and Vernard Foley examines the parallels between Plato and Adam Smith in "The Division of Labor in Plato and Smith," *History of Political Economy,* vol. 6 (Summer 1974), pp. 171–191. The ideas of Protagoras have come to us mostly from the commentaries of Plato. See R. Hackforth, "Hedonism in Plato's *Protagoras,*" *Classical Quarterly,* vol. 22 (1928), pp. 39–42, for a treatment of the hedonistic elements in Greek thought.

Aristotle's discussion of exchange has drawn the most attention from historians of economic thought. Problems of equality and proportion that Aristotle was concerned with are analyzed (without, however, mention of Aristotle) by L. B. Shaynin, "Proportions of Exchange," *Economic Journal,* vol. 70 (December 1960), pp. 769–782. The search for meaning in the cryptic passage of *The Nichomachean Ethics* continues to fan a lively debate among Aristotelian scholars. The following works trace the evolution of the debate in chronological order: Van Johnson, "Aristotle's Theory of Value," *American Journal of Philology,* vol. 60 (October 1939), pp. 445–451; Josef Soudek, "Aristotle's Theory of Exchange: An Inquiry into the Origin of Economic Analysis," *Proceedings of the American Philosophical Society,* vol. 96 (1952), pp. 45–75; Karl Polyani, "Aristotle Discovers the Economy," in K. Polyani et al. (eds.), *Trade and Market in the Early Empires: Economies in History and Theory* (New York: Free Press, 1957), pp. 64–94; Whitney J. Oates, *Aristotle and the Problem of Value* (Princeton, N.J.: Princeton University Press, 1963); Barry Gordon, "Aristotle and the Development of Value Theory," *Quarterly Journal of Economics,* vol. 78 (February 1964), pp. 115–128; and S. Todd Lowry, "Aristotle's Mathematical Analysis of Exchange," *History of Political Economy,* vol. 1 (Spring 1969), pp. 44–66. William Jaffé traces Aristotle's influence on the development of neoclassical price theory in "Edgeworth's Contract Curve: Part 2. Two Figures in Its Protohistory: Aristotle and Gossen," *History of Political Economy,* vol. 6 (Fall 1974), pp. 381–404;

On the utilitarian premises of Aristotle's thought, see Kenneth D. Alpern,

"Aristotle on the Friendships of Utility and Pleasure," *Journal of the History of Philosophy,* vol. 21 (July 1983), pp. 303–315. Aristotle's distrust of market activity is based on the supposed absence of constraints on acquisitive behavior. On this topic, see S. Todd Lowry, "Aristotle's 'Natural Limit' and the Economics of Price Regulation," *Greek, Roman and Byzantine Studies,* vol. 15 (1974), pp. 57–63; T. J. Lewis, "Acquisition and Anxiety: Aristotle's Case against the Market," *Canadian Journal of Economics,* vol. 11 (February 1978), pp. 69–90; William S. Kern, "Returning to the Aristotelian Paradigm: Daly and Schumacher," *History of Political Economy,* vol. 15 (Winter 1983), pp. 501–512; and the exchange between Kern and Spencer J. Pack in the same journal, vol. 17 (Fall 1985), pp. 391–394. "Unnatural" acquisition is also the basis for Aristotle's condemnation of usury. For a competent analysis of this complex issue, see Odd Langholm, *The Aristotelian Analysis of Usury* (Bergen, Norway: Universitetsforlaget, 1984).

Related matters, both general and specific, have attracted the attention of numerous other scholars. Moses I. Finley, "Aristotle and Economic Analysis," *Past & Present,* vol. 47 (May 1970), pp. 3–25, finds "not a trace" of economic analysis in Aristotle's *Ethics* and *Politics;* whereas Barry Gordon, "Aristotle and Hesiod: The Economic Problem in Greek Thought," *Review of Social Economy,* vol. 21 (1963), pp. 147–156, is more generous in his assessment. Additional facets of Aristotle's thought are explored by J. J. Spengler, "Aristotle on Economic Imputation and Related Matters," *Southern Economic Journal,* vol. 21 (April 1955), pp. 371–389; Stephen T. Worland, "Aristotle and the Neoclassical Tradition: The Shifting Ground of Complementarity," *History of Political Economy,* vol. 16 (Spring 1984), pp. 107–134; and T. H. Deaton, R. B. Ekelund, and R. D. Tollison, "A Modern Interpretation of Aristotle on Legislative and Constitutional Rules," *Southern Economic Journal,* vol. 11 (February 1978), pp. 69–90.

The classic reference on Roman social and economic history is M. Rostovtzeff, *Social and Economic History of the Roman Empire,* 2d ed., 2 vols. (London: Oxford University Press, 1957). Very little has been done on the history of economic *analysis* of the period, with the exception of Joseph Schumpeter's encyclopedic *History of Economic Analysis* (see References). On the practical problem of price fixing in ancient economies, see H. Michell, "The Edict of Diocletian: A Study of Price Fixing in the Roman Empire," *Canadian Journal of Economics and Political Science,* vol. 13 (February 1947), pp. 1–12; and R. L. Schuettinger and E. F. Butler, *Forty Centuries of Wage and Price Controls* (Washington, D.C.: The Heritage Foundation, 1979). The pivotal role of Arabian thought as a repository of ancient Greek wisdom is explored by R. Ahmad, "The Origin of Economics and the Arabs," *Pakistani Economic Journal,* vol. 3 (August 1951), pp. 332–347.

Many historians looking for important analytical developments in economics pass over the Middle Ages in silence. Still, there are important writers who find great insights in medieval doctrine. For a trenchant survey, see J. A. Schumpeter, *History of Economic Analysis,* chap. 2; or Henry W. Spiegel, *The*

Growth of Economic Thought, chap. 3 (Englewood Cliffs, N.J.: Prentice-Hall, 1971), to which is appended an excellent bibliography on medieval economics. By far the most meticulous and convincing argument that modern value theory is a direct descendant from Aristotle, however, is Langholm's (see References). This chapter has drawn heavily on Langholm's pioneering work. Much earlier the Scholastics were defended by Bernard W. Dempsey (see References) and Raymond de Roover, "The Concept of Just Price: Theory and Economic Policy," *Journal of Economic History,* vol. 18 (December 1958), pp. 418–438; and "Scholastic Economics: Survival and Lasting Influence from the Sixteenth Century to Adam Smith," *Quarterly Journal of Economics,* vol. 69 (May 1955), pp. 161–190. The same author has traced developments in monopoly theory back to the church fathers in "Monopoly Theory Prior to Adam Smith: A Revision," *Quarterly Journal of Economics,* vol. 65 (November 1951), pp. 492–524.

Some other noteworthy contributions to the understanding of just price and to the wider significance of medieval economics are John W. Baldwin, "The Medieval Theories of Just Price," *Transactions of the American Philosophical Society,* n.s., vol. 49, part 4 (Philadelphia, 1959); E. A. J. Johnson, "Just Price in an Unjust World," *International Journal of Ethics,* vol. 48 (January 1938), pp. 165–181; Samuel Hollander, "On the Interpretation of the Just Price," *Kyklos,* vol. 18 (1965), pp. 615–634; and Stephen T. Worland. *Scholasticism and Welfare Economics* (Notre Dame, Ind.: University of Notre Dame Press, 1967). George W. Wilson extends Polyani's "status" interpretation of Aristotle's exchange model to Aquinas as well, in "The Economics of the Just Price," *History of Political Economy,* vol. 7 (Spring 1975), pp. 56–74, but his view has been challenged by Odd Langholm (see References) and by Stephen T. Worland in "*Justium Pretium:* One More Round in an Endless Series," *History of Political Economy,* vol. 9 (Winter 1977), pp. 504–521; and in Worland's review of Langholm's book in the same journal, vol. 12 (Winter 1980), pp. 638–642.

Like the idea of usury to which it is related, the idea of just price is older than Christianity. See Ephraim Kleiman, "Just Price in Talmudic Literature," *History of Political Economy,* vol. 19 (Spring 1987), pp. 23–46. The literature on usury itself is fairly extensive, but what there is sheds more economic heat than light. For historical perspective, see Carl F. Taeusch, "The Concept of 'Usury': The History of an Idea," *Journal of the History of Ideas,* vol. 3 (June 1942), pp. 291–318; and Raymond de Roover, "The Scholastics, Usury and Foreign Exchange," *Business History Review,* vol. 41 (Autumn 1967), pp. 257–271. A provocative application of public choice and monopoly theory to the church's usury policies in the Middle Ages is contained in R. B. Ekelund, R. F. Hébert, and R. D. Tollison, "An Economic Model of the Medieval Church: Usury as a Form of Rent Seeking," *Journal of Law, Economics, and Organization,* vol. 5 (Fall 1989), forthcoming.

Finally, a good perspective on the development of markets, especially in the period that marks the transition between the subject matter in this chapter and the next, can be obtained from two articles by R. H. Britnell: "English Markets and Royal Administration before 1200," *Economic History Review,* vol. 31 (May 1978), pp. 183–196; and "The Proliferation of Markets in England, 1200–1349," *Economic History Review,* vol. 34 (May 1981), pp. 209–221.

REFERENCES

Aristotle. *The Works of Aristotle,* 12 vols., W. D. Ross (ed.). Oxford: Clarendon Press, 1908–1952.

Dempsey, Bernard W. "Just Price in a Functional Economy," *American Economic Review,* vol. 25 (September 1935), pp. 471–486.

Gray, Alexander. *The Development of Economic Doctrine,* 2d ed. London: Longman, 1980.

Langholm, Odd. *Price and Value in the Aristotelian Tradition.* Bergen, Norway: Universitetsforlaget, 1979.

Lowry, S. Todd. *The Archaeology of Economic Ideas.* Durham, N.C.: Duke University Press, 1987.

Plato. *The Republic,* R. W. Sterling and W. C. Scott (trans.). New York: Norton, 1985.

———. *Theaetetus,* John McDowell (trans.). Oxford: Clarendon Press, 1973.

Schumpeter, Joseph A. *History of Economic Analysis,* E. B. Schumpeter (ed.). New York: Oxford University Press, 1954.

Xenophon. *Memorabilia and Oeconomicus,* E. C. Marchant (trans.). New York: G. P. Putnam's Sons, 1923.

———. *Scripta Minora,* E. C. Marchant (trans.). New York: G. P. Putnam's Sons, 1925.

CHAPTER 3

MERCANTILISM AND THE DAWN OF CAPITALISM

INTRODUCTION

"Mercantilism" is an ambiguous term. By the beginning of the sixteenth century, institutional changes were under way that made the next three centuries different from the preceding era of feudalism. One characteristic of these changes was the emergence of stronger, more centralized nation-states. The term mercantilism is often applied to the intellectual and institutional environment that accompanied the rise of the nation-state. By the nineteenth century, however, the intellectual and institutional environment had changed again to allow much more individual freedom and much less concentration of economic and political power. Thus mercantilism refers to an intervening period between feudalism and liberalism. It describes an economic creed that prevailed at the dawn of capitalism, before the industrial revolution.

There are two basic ways to analyze the economics of the system of thought called mercantilism. One way considers mercantilism to be a fairly cohesive, "static" set of ideas—that is, a body of thought summarized in the events of the day. We call this the *doctrinal* approach. Another approach sees mercantilism as an important *historical process*. It concentrates on the dynamics of competing interests and their role in defining economic and political institutions. We call this the *policy* approach. Both approaches view mercantilism as a system of power, but the former features a set of distinctly mercantile propositions, or "central tendencies," that characterize the thought of the age. In this approach, the propositions of mercantilism presumably withered away as mercantilism was replaced by a competing set of ideas. The doctrinal approach suggests that humans and their ideas may be arranged on a continuum with "mercantile" at one extreme and "liberal" at the other. By contrast, the policy view spotlights those self-interested forces at work in the economic system that bring about changes in power and wealth. It concentrates on the specific regulations of the mercantile period and how each affected the competing groups of interests held by the monarch, parliament, courts, and producers. It assumes that the driving force of individual behavior in the mercantilist period is the same as the driving force of twentieth-century capitalism, namely, the self-interested pursuit of gain.

Although these two approaches may be viewed as rival theories, there is no reason why they could not be treated as complementary. It is likely that the most complete comprehension of mercantilism will come through an understanding of both approaches. For purposes of discussion and learning, however, we accord separate treatment to doctrine and policy.

MERCANTILISM AS DOCTRINE: THE ECONOMICS OF NATIONALISM

The term *mercantilism* was coined by Mirabeau in 1763 to describe that loose system of economic ideas that seemed to dominate economic discourse from the beginning of the sixteenth century to almost the end of the eighteenth century. Mercantilist writers were a disparate group. Most of them were merchants, and many simply espoused their own interests. Even though it was international (mercantilism was a creed shared by England, Holland, Spain, France, Germany, Flanders, and Scandinavia), on the whole there was less consistency and continuity among mercantilists than among the Scholastics of the previous age. Lack of cohesion among mercantilist writers can be attributed in large measure to the absence of common analytical tools that could be shared and passed on to a generation of successors. Furthermore, communication among mercantilists was poor or nonexistent, in contrast to the strong network of interrelations among modern economists. Nevertheless, mercantilism was based on several unifying ideas—doctrines and policy pronouncements that appear and reappear throughout the period.

Perhaps the most concise summary of mercantilist principles was provided by Philipp Wilhelm von Hornick, an Austrian lawyer who published a nine-point mercantilist manifesto in 1684. Von Hornick's blueprint for national eminence sounds the themes of independence and treasure. His nine principal rules of national economy are:

1 That every inch of a country's soil be utilized for agriculture, mining, or manufacturing

2 That all raw materials found in a country be used in domestic manufacture, since finished goods have a higher value than raw materials

3 That a large, working population be encouraged

4 That all export of gold and silver be prohibited and all domestic money be kept in circulation

5 That all imports of foreign goods be discouraged as much as possible

6 That where certain imports are indispensible they be obtained at first hand, in exchange for other domestic goods instead of gold and silver

7 That as much as possible, imports be confined to raw materials that can be finished at home

8 That opportunities be constantly sought for selling a country's surplus manufactures to foreigners, so far as necessary, for gold and silver

9 That no importation be allowed if such goods are sufficiently and suitably supplied at home

The points in this program may not have been accepted *in toto* by all mercantilists, but they are sufficiently representative to characterize the loose system of ideas referred to at the head of this section.

In the discussion that follows, we shall be concerned primarily with a characterization of these possible tendencies rather than with specific individuals. The reader must be mindful of the fact that the characterization that follows is a *simplification* and an idealization that may not apply specifically to any mercantile nation. British, French, Dutch, and Spanish mercantilism differed in many essential respects, for instance. The disclaimer applies even more to individuals, a fact that may be easily verified by reading and comparing the writings of at least two mercantilists. (Some of the references provided at the end of this chapter may be consulted to that end.) No single individual held all the ideas that are expressed below as representing mercantile thought, and what follows is only one of a number of possible characterizations of mercantile ideas. The mercantilist period is one during which the threads of many ideas were being spun. As a consequence, mercantilism as a set of ideas remains something of a patchwork quilt.

Attention will be focused on several areas of mercantile interest: "real-world" ideas, views on international trade and finance, and examples of "dualism" in domestic policy. After an assessment of mercantile ideas, we shall turn to the historical process of mercantilism and to its role in the emergence of liberalism.

The Mercantilists and Real-World Ideas

Mercantilist writers, to a man, are typified by a concern for the real world. No longer were justice and salvation of primary concern in writings related to the economy (as in the previous period); things materialistic became the end of human activity. A few writers of the mercantile period looked back to the medieval system on some matters and other writers looked forward to laissez faire, but en masse they were concerned with a material and objective economic end. And although their overall social goal of "state power" was subjective, their opinions on the workings of the economic system were a clear reflection of real-world habits of thought.

A number of mercantilists substituted the conception of a natural law that governs social organization for the "divine-law" precepts of Aquinas and the medieval doctors. Sir William Petty (see Chapter 4) provided perhaps the best example of the attempt to draw conclusions about economic behavior from analogies with natural sciences. In his *Political Arithmetick*, Petty noted that:

> We must consider in general, that as wiser Physicians tamper not excessively with their Patients, rather observing and complying with the motions of nature, than contradicting it with vehement Administrations of their own: so in Politicks and Oeconomicks the same must be used (*Economic Writings*, I, p. 60).

Though Petty was writing late in the mercantile period, theories of social causation—that is, theories of natural tendencies ordering real-world phenomena—occur as early as the mid-sixteenth century. This aspect of certain mercantile writing is of great interest as one of the tenets of laissez faire, but for the present it is important to note that these "rationalist" ideas were not concerned with divine ends. As Eli Heckscher, a recognized authority on the period, has pointed out: "There was little mysticism in the arguments of the mercantilists...they did not appeal to sentiment, but were obviously anxious to find reasonable grounds for every position they adopted" (*Mercantilism*, II, p. 308).

International Trade

One reflection of these real-world concerns in the idealized conception of mercantilism was a seemingly incessant interest in the material gain of the state. The material resources of society (the means) were, in general, to be used to promote the enrichment and well-being of the nation-state (the end). The single most important concern of mercantile writers appeared to be that the nation's resources be used in such a manner as to make the state as powerful as possible both politically and economically. The sixteenth and seventeenth centuries were characterized by the presence of great trading nations. Power building took the form of exploration, discovery, and colonization. The major topic considered by mercantile writers was, understandably, international trade and finance. Gold, and means to acquire it, was usually at the nexus of the discussion.

The Role of Money and Trade in Mercantilism Money and its accumulation were prime concerns of the growing nation-states of the mercantile era. As already noted, a flourishing international trade followed the age of discovery and colonization, and gold bullion was the unit of international account. The acquisition of gold through trade and trade restrictions of many types were essential mercantile ideas, and money, not real goods, was commonly equated to wealth.

One of the idealized goals of trade and production was to augment wealth by increased national stockpiling of bullion. Domestic employment and industry were promoted by encouraging raw-material imports and by encouraging final-product exports. On a macro scale a surplus of exports over imports (a favorable balance of trade) was desired because the balance had to be remitted in gold. All this might sound quite reasonable if the mercantilists had been rationalizing preexisting comparative advantages within trading nations, but the disappointing truth is that many of them did not appear to understand the increased total output that might come from specialization and trade. A number of writers looked upon trade and bullion accumulation as a zero-sum game, where more for country A meant less for countries B, C, and so forth. Given these aims, protection and "beggar-thy-neighbor" were attractive policies and were thought by many mercantilists to produce the desired increase in wealth. Increases in wealth would, in turn, further the overall aim of the nation-state.

Some writers, such as Gerard de Malynes, were confirmed bullionists, opposed to any export of specie whatsoever. Such export of specie by the East India Company was the cause cèlébre of a debate on the issue in the early seventeenth century. Although he had previously taken Malynes's position, Edward Misselden (1608–1654) attacked the extreme bullionist view, which amounted to an absolute prohibition of specie export even on individual transactions. Instead, Misselden advanced the notion that governmental policies should be directed to maximizing specie earnings on the basis of an overall balance of trade.

International Trade and Finance However contradictory and misdirected their orientation toward money seems to have been, the mercantilists produced the first real awareness of the monetary and political importance of international trade and, in the process, supplied political economy with a concept of a *balance of trade* that included both visible and invisible (shipping expenses, insurance, etc.) items. In the course of attacking the bullionists, for example, Misselden developed a fairly sophisticated concept of a trade balance couched in terms of debits and credits. In *The Circle of Commerce,* published in 1623, he actually calculated a balance of trade for England (from Christmas 1621 to Christmas 1622). It was a bad year, however, for Misselden concluded disappointedly that:

> We see it to our griefe, that wee are fallen into a great Underballance of Trade with other Nations. Wee felt it before in sense; but now we know it by science: wee found it before in operation; but now wee see it in speculation: Trade alas, faile's and faint's, and we in it (*The Circle of Commerce,* p. 46).

Misselden wished to emphasize the "scientific" nature of his calculations, and it is this fact, rather than the accuracy of his data, which sets his accounting apart from the mere collection of numbers, which was earlier widespread in Egypt and Mesopotamia. Misselden arranged data for the purpose of understanding economic effects and promoting social ends.

Today the mercantile idea of "multilateral trade balance" finds expression in the balance of payments between one nation and the rest of the world. Basically, it is composed of five accounts:

1 Current account (i.e., the mercantile balance of trade)
 a Merchandise {A]
 b Invisibles (shipping services, insurance, etc.) [A]
2 Capital accounts

    a Short term [C]
    b Long term [A]
3 Unilateral transfers (gifts, military aid, etc.) [A]
4 Gold [C]
5 Errors and omissions

The balance of payments always balances because of double-entry book-keeping, and so the concepts of "deficit" and "surplus" must be derived from the arrangement and values of certain accounts. Certain accounts, those labeled A above, are regarded as *autonomous* or undertaken in response to market forces, and others, those labeled C, are regarded as *compensating*. Long-term capital positions and real-goods trade movements are, for example, regarded as motivated by fundamental economic forces, interest rate differentials, differences in relative prices of domestic and foreign goods, and the like. Such movements are regarded as autonomous. Others are compensating accounts and reflect the results of the autonomous trade and financial movements. Thus United States gold exported to France, or increased American dollar holdings by the French central bank, would be a compensation paid by the United States to France for a deficit in trade or for a net deficit in our long-term capital position with France. One might describe a deficit between the creditor country and the rest of the world as follows:

$$\begin{matrix} \text{Current} \\ \text{account} \\ \text{surplus} \end{matrix} - \left(\begin{matrix} \text{long-term} \\ \text{capital} \\ \text{deficit} \end{matrix} + \begin{matrix} \text{unilateral-} \\ \text{transfers} \\ \text{deficit} \end{matrix} \right) = \begin{matrix} \text{net} \\ \text{deficit} \end{matrix} = \begin{matrix} \text{adverse} \\ \text{movement in} \\ \text{short-term capital} \end{matrix} + \text{gold}$$

Although some of the mercantilist writers hinted at an understanding of the role of international long-term capital investment as a force in establishing a country's international position, there appears to have been no clear explication of a balance of payments in the modern sense. A cruder version was used for the analysis of trade, and on the whole, a never-ending series of restrictions related to the amount and the composition of trade were proposed in order that payments of specie in response to the autonomous trade accounts would be permanently in surplus. The Navigation Acts through which England attempted to improve her earnings on the "invisible accounts" (shipping, etc.) are good examples of such mercantile policies. These policies partly underlie one of the greatest problems of the majority of mercantilist writers—a failure to understand the quantity theory of money.

Trade and Specie Flow One of the anomalies in mercantilist literature is the pervasive belief that wealth would be maximized through specie accumulation resulting from a trade surplus. Many mercantilists misunderstood the effects of an increase in the domestic money supply (monetization), which usually followed a trade surplus. They compounded the problem by an apparent belief that a favorable balance of trade—and thus specie accumulation—could continue over long and indefinite periods. David Hume (1711–1776), the philosopher-economist contemporary of Adam Smith, finally undid this wrong. He pointed to a price-specie flow mechanism that linked the quantity of money to prices and alterations in prices to balance-of-trade surpluses and deficits. Actually Hume had predecessors in the mercantile period, and the invention of a part of the mechanism—the quantity theory of money—was anticipated by the political philosopher John Locke (1632–1704).

The idea, like most good ideas, appears simple in retrospect. Imagine a surplus in England's balance of trade. An inflow of gold occurs in England, but—assuming an extreme form of the gold standard (i.e., specie and only specie may be used as a medium of exchange)—the money stock increases in the same proportion, given, of course, the monetization of the specie. A fractional-reserve, fiat money system would magnify the increase. In all cases the price level increases, predictably as we shall see, including the prices of goods in the export sector of the economy. Foreign countries, with reduced holdings of money, experience a reduction in relative prices and, in consequence, buy less from English merchants. Simultaneously, British consumers direct purchases toward foreign goods and away from domestic wares. In time the English trade surplus becomes a deficit, gold flows out, the money stock declines, prices fall, and a surplus appears once more. The cycle continues, and the mercantile attempt to accumulate gold indefinitely is self-defeating.

The originator of this doctrine, who said of money that "'Tis none of the wheels of trade: 'Tis the oil,'' nevertheless envisioned short-term salutary effects in the acquisition of specie. Hume noted that:

> In my opinion, 'tis only in this interval or intermediate situation, betwixt the acquisition of money and rise of prices, that the increasing quantity of gold and silver is favorable to industry. When any quantity of money is imported into a nation, it is not at first disperst into many hands; but is confin'd to the coffers of a few persons, who immediately seek to employ it to the best advantage ("Of Money," p. 88).

Hume argued that in effect, money is a "veil" that hides the real workings of the economic system, and that it is of no great consequence whether a nation's stock of money is large or small, after the price level adjusts to the quantity of it.

The evidence is that most mercantilist writers, however, failed to understand the quantity theory of money. In its crudest variant this theory states that the price level, *ceteris paribus,* is a function of the quantity of money. In most early expressions, the "theory" is no more than a tautology affirming that a given increase in money (say, a doubling) produces a given increase (doubling) of the price level. A more sophisticated variant equates the money stock multiplied by velocity (the number of times money turns over per year) to the price level multiplied by the number of income-generative transactions per year. This can be written as $MV = Py$. As a theory of the price level that identifies dependent (prices) and independent (money, velocity, and transactions) variables, it is expressed as $P = MV/y$ or, more generally, $P = f(M, V, y)$. When V and y are assumed to be constant, an increase in M leads to proportionate increases in P. Although this more sophisticated version did not appear until long after Locke and Hume (but see the discussion of Richard Cantillon in Chapter 4), the mercantilists, to the detriment of their analysis, did not see even the simplest connection.

The Nation-State: Mercantilism as Domestic Policy

Most mercantilists feared too much freedom, so they relied on the state to plan and regulate economic life. The list of policies specially designed to promote the interests of the nation-state was long and varied. Among these policies were many different types of regulation of the domestic and international economy. Domestic conditions in the typical mercantile economy consisted of detailed regulations in some sectors of the economy, little or no regulation in others, taxation and subsidization of particular industries, and restricted entry in many markets. As an example of the extent to which regulations could be pushed, in 1666 French Minister Colbert issued a rule that the fabrics woven in Dijon contain no more nor less than 1,408 threads. Penalties for those weavers who strayed from this standard were severe.

Legal monopolies in the form of franchises and patents were common under mercantilism. A franchise granted exclusive trading rights to a particular merchant or league of merchants, such as the East India Company. Sometimes franchises also received massive subsidies from the king. The effect of all of this was a "mixed" economy, but with the mix far less on the side of individual freedom than was the case during the first half of the nineteenth century in England or in the United States. Some historians have suggested that the mercantilists were merely individual merchants pleading their own narrow interests. Outwardly, of course, mercantilism was an alliance of power between the monarch and the merchant-capitalist. The monarch depended on the merchant's economic activity to build up his or her treasury while the merchant depended on the authority of the monarch to protect his or her economic interests. Use of the political process to secure monopoly gains is a form of rent seeking, where "rent" refers to the profits that are attributable to the existence of monopoly. In a later section, we shall probe more deeply into this particular idea as it relates to mercantilism.

"Ambiguity" in Mercantile Policies   All mercantilists agreed on the necessity of international controls, but they were often of a different mind where domestic controls were concerned. From the very beginning we find mercantile writings that on the one hand extol international economic controls for society's enrichment but on the other hand present eloquent pleas for domestic noninterference. This dualism is somewhat of an embarrassment in the doctrinal approach. At times, individual mercantilists could sound like impassioned economic liberals (in the nineteenth-century sense).

An anonymous tract (attributed to John Hales) entitled *A Discourse on the Common Weal of This Realm of England,* written in 1549, exhibited an early and prophetic distrust of the effectiveness of legislative controls in promoting society's welfare. Analyzing various problems arising from the enclosure movement, the author argued that market forces are more efficient allocators of resources than government decree. The profit motive played a prominent role in this early analysis. Pointing up the stupidity and futility of governmental regulation of the enclosures, the author pointed out the difficulty of enacting such legislation, because vested interests will inevitably arise to challenge it; moreover, if passed, those who seek profits will find a way to subvert the law by one means or another. Market interferences are often rendered ineffectual by natural responses to prices and profits, as has been evidenced by the existence of "black markets" at every occasion (ancient and modern) of government-imposed price controls. Self-interest, which was a natural law to Hales, is the force behind economic activity. The writer in fact notes that "everie man naturally will follow that wherein he seeth most proffit." As A. F. Chalk has pointed out, "This is surely a very close approximation to Adam Smith's views concerning the self-interest motive in economic activity" ("Natural Law and the Rise of Economic Individualism in England," p. 335).

The anonymous writer of 1549 was only one of many who advanced these liberal views in the mercantile period. Pleas for free internal trade became increasingly vociferous as the mercantile system wore on, especially in the writings of John Locke, Sir Dudley North, Charles Davenant, and Bernard de Mandeville. Although these liberal beliefs relating to domestic policy are in strong contrast to mercantile views on external trade restrictions, they nevertheless represent a strand of thought that culminated in Smith's *Wealth of Nations,* which, curiously, characterized mercantilism as a system of controls. Modern research has convincingly demonstrated, however, that "what had begun as opportunistic and sporadic protests against commercial controls thus emerged, almost two centuries later, in the form of a systematized philosophy of economic individualism which proclaimed the beneficence of the laws of nature" (Chalk, "Natural Law," p. 347).

Labor and the "Utility of Poverty" The interests of the moneyed mercantile class and the aristocracy converged on the question of domestic policies toward labor and wages. The maintenance of low wages and a growing population was a clear element in mercantile literature, and it originated in a desire to maintain a skewed income distribution as well as in the mercantilists' belief in a backward-bending supply curve of labor. Fundamentally, however, the mercantile "low-wage" policy rests upon amoral grounds or upon what Edgar Furniss has called the "utility of poverty" in his classic work *The Position of the Laborer in a System of Nationalism.* The argument that labor should be kept at the margin of subsistence may be found throughout the mercantile age. In the extreme it is premised upon a belief that "suffering is therapeutic" and that, given the opportunity, a "menial" would be lazy and slothful. Because of the generally low moral condition of the lower classes, high wages would lead to all sorts of excesses, e.g., drunkenness and debauchery. In other words, if wages were beyond subsistence, the quest for physical gratification would simply lead to vice and moral ruin. Poverty (high price of subsistence and/or low wages), on the other hand, made workers industrious, which meant that they "lived better." As Arthur Young noted in his *Eastern Tour* (1771), "Everyone but an idiot knows that the lower classes must be kept poor or they will never be industrious." Unemployment, in the mercantile view, was simply the result of indolence.

The views of Bernard de Mandeville (who was a "liberal" in other contexts) were even more extreme. He argued that children of the poor and orphans should not be given an education at public expense but should be put to work at an early age. Education ruins the "deserving poor," in other words, so that "Reading, Writing and Arithmetick are very necessary to those whose Business requires such qualifications, but where People's livelihood has no dependence on these Arts, they are very pernicious to the Poor....Going to School in comparison to Working is Idleness, and the longer Boys continue in this easy sort of Life, the more unfit they'll be...for downright Labour, both as to Strength and Inclination" (*The Fable of the Bees,* p. 311).

Various proposals were put forward to limit debauchery and to make the poor industrious. In 1701, John Law proposed a tax on consumption in order to encourage frugality among the rich and industry among the poor. David Hume, who contributed to the liberal movement in other respects, supported "moderate" taxes to encourage industry, but he thought that excessive taxes destroyed incentive and engendered despair. These writers seemed to be aiming at a real wage that would support an "optimal level of frustration," one high enough to provide incentive for "luxuries" but low enough so that they could never be attained. As Furniss observed, it was of the utmost importance to mercantilist writers that

> ...the lowest ranks of the laboring classes be kept as full as possible, for upon the members of this group England relied for that economic power which was to bring her forth victorious from the struggle of nations after world supremacy. Thus the nation's destiny was conditioned upon a numerous population of unskilled laborers, driven by the very competition of numbers to a life of constant industry at minimum wages: "submission" and "contentment" were useful characteristics for such a population and these characteristics could be fostered by a destruction of social ambition amongst its members (*The Position of the Laborer,* p. 150).

Supply of Labor The belief in the utility of poverty and in the low moral condition of laborers supported the well-known mercantile theory of a backward-bending supply function for labor. The theory may be stated simply in terms of elementary graphical analysis. Given that output for domestic and international trade is a function of the input of labor and (for simplification) a constant capital, the input of labor is of crucial importance for an economy, as most mercantile writers perceived. But most mercantilists feared that after wages reached a certain point, laborers would prefer additional leisure to additional income, as shown in Figure 3-1 (the income effect would outweigh the substitution effect). Increased prosperity, as Figure 3-1 shows, if it comes in the form of an increased average wage for the whole economy—say, from W_0

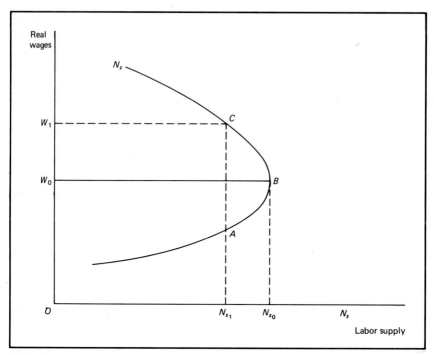

FIGURE 3-1
As wages are increased from w_0 to w_1, there is a reduction in the supply of labor from N_{s_0} to N_{s_1}.

to W_1—was to be discouraged since the quantity of labor input would decline in consequence from N_{s_0} to N_{s_1}. Output would decline, and the ability to accumulate specie through trade would be similarly reduced.

The discussion is defective, however, from a macroeconomic point of view. Unless a reallocation of real income to workers accompanied the process, the reduction in real output would ultimately cause a reduction in real wages. But these consequences were never investigated, and as it stands, the idea seems incomplete and paradoxical. It is difficult to say whether the argument rested upon an empirical judgment that the aggregate supply curve of labor (or any specific component of it) actually was backward bending or whether the argument was simply an apologetic for a certain social and economic distribution, though many statements support the former position. In any case, the idea appears and reappears in the postmercantile literature on economic thought.

Some Historical Assessments of Mercantilism

As an ideational system, mercantilism has undergone numerous assessments, beginning with the hypercritical evaluation of Adam Smith (see Chapter 5) and followed by like-minded neoclassical arguments. Not all evaluations have been so critical, however.

The Liquidity Rationale   Many writers, including members of the British and German historical schools, have stressed the rational elements in mercantilism. They see mercantile policies as appropriate for their time; that is, policies to promote a strong nation-state were justified after the chaos and disorder of the collapse of the feudal system. A further—and much more important—point is that the supply of specie was of very low elasticity at a time when the transactions requirements of commerce and trade were mushrooming. To put the matter in the frame of the quantity theory of money, velocity (or the number of times that money turns over per year) is not indefinitely expansible. A check of the identity $MV = Py$ reveals that a growing number of transactions ($+y$), given a constant money stock (M), creates pressure on velocity to rise; that is, businesses and consumers can economize just so much on cash-balance holdings (bills of exchange and other documents were invented for this purpose). Thus the mercantilist quest for specie as a means of facilitating transactions may have been a coin worth having, always granting, of course, that specie was actually monetized. However, even given that the specie game was to an extent a zero-sum game, especially in short-run situations, the mercantilist writers could be criticized for not having understood the mechanism that relates money to prices and, further, for not having oriented attention toward those factors beyond the given stock of gold that would have enhanced liquidity.

Keynesian Defense   Perhaps one of the most famous of all defenses of mercantilism was that of J.M. Keynes (see Chapter 19). In his *General Theory of Employment, Interest and Money,* Keynes praised the "practical wisdom" of the school and identified an "element of scientific truth" in the doctrine applicable to single countries, but not to the world as a whole. Keynes stated his main argument succinctly:

> At a time when the authorities had no direct control over the domestic rate of interest or the other inducements to home investment, measures to increase the favourable balance of trade were the only direct means at their disposal for increasing foreign investment; and, at the same time, the effect of a favourable balance of trade on the influx of the precious metals was their only indirect means of reducing the domestic rate of interest and so increasing the inducement to home investment (*General Theory*, p. 336).

In the now familiar Keynesian terminology, aggregate demand is raised by increases in net foreign investment plus increases in domestic investment brought about by a lowering of the rate of interest. Keynes further thought that through the "multiplier" effect the increased demand has a magnified effect on income and on aggregate employment. The critical point is that Keynes believed that the increase in the money stock, by lowering the rate of interest, caused an increase in aggregate demand and employment.

But Keynes's somewhat simplistic approach to the mercantile system belies certain gnawing problems. First, Keynes based his case upon judiciously selected passages from mercantilist literature that purportedly revealed an understanding of the relation between money and interest and the impact of increased net foreign investment upon employment. It is not altogether clear that these statements, even liberally interpreted, were not simply adventitious remarks of isolated mercantilists, as were those of some of the writers previously mentioned in this chapter.

Second, conceding "practical wisdom" to the mercantilists, one is nevertheless led to wonder about the nature of unemployment in sixteenth- and seventeenth-century Spain or England. Would unemployment in a nonintegrated and quasi-feudal, agrarian society respond to increases in the aggregate demand for goods, or would unemployment in this context be of the structural-technological type, like that of modern-day Appalachia? Certain movements of profound social significance, such as those that transformed the feudal, decentralized society into the modern state, usually take centuries to complete themselves. Frictional and structural unemployment are to be expected in these circumstances. Policies aimed at reducing unemployment in underdeveloped countries that have relied primarily upon increases in the money stock have most often succeeded in producing only inflation, for example. These reasons all weaken the Keynesian assessment of mercantilism in spite of the fact that, at first blush, the facts appear to fit his theoretical structure so nicely. In arguing that the mercantilists' policies were designed to improve general liquidity, he was on more solid ground. On other counts, the Keynesian interpretation appears overly generous.

Mercantilism as a System of Ideas: A Summary   The major theoretical defects in mercantile literature (always granting exceptions) were an inability to grasp the cyclical nature of international accounts and the linkage between domestic money stock and prices. The mercantilists failed, in short, to integrate the Locke-Hume price-specie flow mechanism (or the quantity theory of money) into their analysis, which is ironic in view of their careful collation of trade statistics and systematic record keeping.

Indeed, this penchant for assembling and keeping statistics on real-world quantities may well be the mercantilists' most important legacy to modern economics. Analytical insights in the mercantile period, such as they were, resulted from careful empiricism. Mercantilists were among the first economic writers to be more concerned with actual experience than with metaphysical speculation. They brought economic questions to prominence, and in so doing, set the stage for the advances made in the next period of economic thought.

In the meantime, economic processes within the mercantile economy (especially of England) were bringing about institutional changes that taken together provide an explanation for the historical rise and decline of mercantilism. This explanation pays little attention to what mercantilists *said*. It concentrates instead on what they did and why they did it.

MERCANTILISM AS AN ECONOMIC PROCESS

A policy, or process, view of mercantilism seeks to explain why and how mercantilism arose when it did and why it eventually gave way to a distinctly different economic system. Implied in the doctrinal approach is the notion that only nationalistic ends were appropriate to mercantilist policies. The process view examines the economic motivations of individuals or coalitions within a national economy. It focuses on the gains to economic agents of using the state to acquire profits. Such profits, in the vernacular of modern economics, are called rents (i.e., monopoly returns). Thus, mercantilism is presented here as a form of rent seeking. This process view is richer than the doctrinal view in its ability to explain historical change.

Some Basic Concepts in the Modern Theory of Regulation

A brief look at some contemporary ideas in the theory of economic regulation and politics will be helpful in examining the policy view of mercantilism.[1] The term ''rent seekers,'' for example, is simply a concept implying self-interested behavior of any or all parties to income distribution. When applied to the contemporary analysis of economic regulation, the idea is that, in *their own interests,* politicians (members of Parliament, Congress, state legislators, city councillors, etc.) will *supply* government monopoly privileges and regulations to individual business people or merchants or to any group whose self-interest leads it to *demand* regulation. This self-interested activity does not (necessarily) mean that politicians will accept direct cash payments, although we shall see that the latter were far more common in the mercantile period. The modern world is much more subtle. Since most politicians are members of law firms, patronage via company retainer fees is a feasible manner of accepting ''side payments,'' as is the promise of high-paying positions after the politician leaves office. The modern analysis seeks to explain, in terms of costs and benefits to the individuals involved, the existence or absence of monopoly privileges in some industries and activities.

The formal specification of costs and benefits need not concern us here, but a couple of examples might help in understanding how the process view works as an explanation. Consider ''industry representatives,'' or lobbyists, as potential demanders of regulation. Their demand for monopoly privileges from government (e.g., entry control and subsidies) would obviously be related to how much profit they could expect from the privileges. For example, anything increasing the uncertainty of the length of a monopoly privilege would reduce the value of the monopoly franchise to the industry. So would any costs imposed upon the regulated firm (e.g., taxes and periodic inspection) as a quid pro quo for the franchise.

---

[1] Current developments in the theories of regulation and ''public choice'' are discussed in greater detail in Chap. 24. References to this literature that are pertinent to the present discussion are provided in the Notes for Further Reading at the end of this chapter.

Now consider regulation from the supplier's side. A modern economic perspective tells us that politicians will maximize self-interest (e.g., reelection and side payments) by supplying regulation in return for money and votes. Basically, the problem of these groups or individuals is to overcome the costs of organizing an effective lobbying force. Large groups, such as retailers, are often unable to overcome the high costs of combining to establish an effective lobby, whereas small groups may be in a better position to organize lobbying activities. How much regulation politicians will seek to supply depends upon the costs and benefits of doing so together with the coalition and organization costs necessary to actually supply the regulation. Ordinarily the larger the group required to pass special-interest legislation, the higher the coalition costs.

Thus, regulation may be viewed as a "good" that is supplied and demanded like other goods. A decrease in the net benefit to those who stand to gain from regulation would, other things being equal, lead to a reduction in the amount of regulation demanded. Likewise, an increase in the costs of supplying regulation—such as when the ability to supply regulation is transferred from a single individual (a monarch or dictator) to a group of individuals (a parliament or city council)—means that we would expect the supply of regulation to be lower and the equilibrium quantity of regulation to be less. In the mercantilist era, the merchant's incentive to seek regulation was provided by the prospect of obtaining a monopoly privilege, i.e., protection by the state. In this respect, the economic logic of mercantilism is the same as that behind much present-day politico-economic activity. Some groups (e.g., artisans then, trucking firms now) possess inherent organizational advantages in lobbying for state regulatory protection from competition (e.g., the Statute of Artificers then, the Interstate Commerce Commission now) relative to other groups, such as consumers in general. Usually, then, the gains of successful interest groups are transfers of wealth from the consumers of regulated products.

The term "cartel" is also frequently used in the theory of regulation and in its application to mercantilism. A cartel—the most familiar one being the OPEC cartel—is simply a formal combination of firms acting as a single monopolist under a kind of centralized control. Prices and/or output shares are ordinarily assigned to the members of the cartel, and their behavior is in some way monitored or policed. Entry conditions are also restricted. Cartels may be privately or publicly organized. There is a strong incentive to cheat on cartel price or output agreements when there is no legal sanction to the arrangement because each firm has much to gain from reducing its price or selling outside its assigned market. Most privately organized cartels are therefore unstable; they tend to break down over time. The acquisition of regulation, therefore, is a common (and inexpensive) means for an industry to organize as a cartel, since regulation provides for the continuous enforcement of the rules. Through regulation, backed up by legal sanctions against "cheaters," the government may attempt to control such items as entry, prices, or profits.

In both the old and the new mercantilism, then, economic regulation can be seen as the outcome of a competitive process whereby interest groups seek the state's protection against competition. In the mercantilist setting, the relevant interest groups were in part groups of local administrators, merchants, and laborers in the towns, and in part monopoly interests engaged in national and international production and trade.

Internal Regulation in English Mercantilism

Economic regulation at local, national, and international levels took basically the same form in English mercantilism as in contemporary societies. Firms were licensed, and competition among suppliers was thereby restricted. It is, however, important to understand certain major differences between the conduct of institutions surrounding *local* as opposed to *national* regulation and monopoly. Local regulation of trades, prices, and wage rates in mercantilist times stemmed from the medieval guild system. Enforcement of these guild regulations in the Tudor period prior to Elizabeth I was the responsibility of the guild bureaucracy in combination with the town or shire administrative machinery. Elizabeth attempted to codify and strengthen these detailed regulations in the Statute of Artificers. This law outlined the specific enforcement duties of local justices of the peace (JP's), aldermen, and local administrators. JP's and other administrative enforcers of local regulations were paid either very little or not at all for these services, a fact that led to local alignments of economic interests. These interests ultimately rendered the local provision of monopoly rights ineffective.

At the national level, on the other hand, industrial regulation was created in three ways: (1) by statutes of Parliament, (2) by royal proclamations and letters patent, and (3) by decrees of the Privy Council of the king's "court." It should be noted that merchants and monarchs alike were alive to the possibilities of rent seeking. The meshing of private interests of monarch and monopolist was firmly enshrined in English practice as early as the fourteenth century, perhaps even earlier. The nature of this alliance was underscored in debate on the issue of monopoly in the House of Commons in 1601:

> First, Let us consider the word monopoly, what it is; *Monos* is *Unus*, and *Polis*, *Civitas:* So then the Meaning of the Word is; a Restraint of any thing Publick, in a City or Common-Wealth, to a Private Use. And the User called a Monopolitan; *quasi, cujus privatum lucrum esturbis et orbis Commune Malun.* And we may well term this Man, The Whirlpool of the Prince's Profits (Tawney and Power, *Tudor Economic Documents,* II, p. 270).

These revealing definitions of monopoly and the monopolist remind us that the motives of economic actors are usually recognizable and have not changed over the centuries. But it would be a mistake to carry the analogy too far. Although the basic nature of mercantilism then and now is the same, there are important differences in the two rent-seeking environments. The most important difference for the purposes of the discussion here concerns the supply side of the market for regulatory legislation.

National mercantilism was supplied by a monarchy, and a monarchy represents a uniquely low-cost environment for rent seeking, especially when compared with a modern democratic setting where the power to supply regulatory legislation is dispersed among various governmental powers. The consolidation of national power under the mercantile monarchies provides a logical explanation for the widespread rent seeking and economic regulation during this period of English history. In the course of our discussion, we shall see how the growth and ultimate takeover of the power to supply regulatory legislation by Parliament dramatically altered the costs and benefits to buyers and sellers of monopoly rights in such a way as to lead to the decline of mercantilist regulation. But first we must consider the pattern and fate of local regulation.

The Enforcement of Local Economic Regulation

The legal framework for the enforcement of mercantilist economic regulation at the local level was set out by the Elizabethan Statute of Artificers. This statute was an attempted codification of older rules for the regulation of industry, labor, and welfare, the important difference being that such regulations were to be *national* rather than *local* in scope. Some writers have pointed to the enormous increase in wages after the Black Death as the impetus to national regulation. The immediate economic reason was much more likely the inability of the towns to restrict cheating on local cartel arrangements. Towns attempted to buy a nationally uniform system of regulation from the king, and these local monopoly rights were to be protected against encroachment, especially by "foreigners." There were many attempts by self-interested merchants and town administrators to regulate economic activity and to prevent "interlopers" on local franchises. These sentiments are expressed in numerous Tudor documents. The city of London, especially, wished to restrict aliens and foreign technology that inhibited town profits. The solution most often proffered was to banish to the countryside aliens or those workers who did not meet "legal" qualifications for various trades.

The nationally uniform system of local monopolies was to be enforced by the JP's. As Eli Heckscher noted, "The Justices of the Peace were the agents of unified industrial legislation" (*Mercantilism*, p. 246), and several aspects of this enforcement system are of importance to our interpretation. A primary feature of the system was that the JP's were not paid. Heckscher argues that the absence of pay for the JP's led to "ineptitude" and "laziness" on their part with respect to enforcement. But it is more likely that low or no pay established a ripe setting for malfeasance and led to a self-interested pattern of enforcement—one suggesting both *sub rosa* activities and selective cartel enforcement of industries in which the JP's had interests. Evidence suggests that the regulations were enforced in such a way that the net worth of the JP's holdings in regulated enterprises increased. This could generally be accomplished either through preferential treatment—the firm in which a JP had an interest could be allowed to cheat on the cartel, while other firms could not—or through bribes made to other enforcement personnel. The Queen's Council dictated that the JP's themselves be policed by high constables, who, having less civil authority than the JP's, were often on the receiving end of bribes. By the time of James I it was open knowledge that the JP's could be easily "bought." In 1620, the following testimony was given before Parliament by a Committee of Grievances:

> There are some patents that in themselves are good and lawful, but abused by the patentees in the execution of them, who perform not the trust reposed in them from his maj.; and of such a kind is the Patent for Inns, but those that have the execution abuse it by setting up Inns in forests and bye villages, only to harbour rogues and thieves; and such as the justices of peace of the shire, who best know where Inns are fittest to be, and who best deserve to have licenses for them, have suppressed from keeping of alehouses; *for none is now refused, that will make a good composition* (Corbbett, *Parliamentary History,* vol. 1, pp. 1192–1193).

The reference to "a good composition" meant that the JP's were always ready to grant an innkeeper license, provided they received a favor or payment in return.

In every age it is difficult to find accurate records of illegal transactions because there is no incentive to report them, but in the case of mercantilism the testimony of contemporary observers seems to corroborate the view that the enforcers of internal mercantile regulations were self-interested parties. Thus, the claim that enforcers were indifferent and careless because they were not paid seems naive in retrospect. Modern economic theory leads us to *expect* malfeasance as the predictable response to low pay in occupations where an element of "trust" is dominant.[2] That is because the opportunity cost to the malfeasor of being caught (and fired) is low. From this self-interested standpoint, the behavior of the JP's during the mercantilist era was quite efficient and predictable, given the constraints imposed by the Statute of Artificers.

Local Regulation and Resource Mobility   Another difficulty in enforcement of the Elizabethan system of local regulation is that it was possible for those regulated to escape the jurisdiction of the law by moving outside the towns. Despite attempts to limit mobility, there is evidence that the rules were blatantly disregarded. Movement of artificers to the countryside was in fact blamed for the decay, impoverishment, and ruin of the cities (Tawney and Power, *Tudor Economic Documents,* I, pp. 353–365). For their part, the JP's once again "enforced" the statute in a way far different from the crown's intentions.

In effect, buyers and sellers could migrate to an unregulated sector in the suburbs and the countryside, and the existence of this unregulated sector created powerful incentives to destroy the local cartel arrangements in the towns.

---

[2] For example, see Gary Becker and G. J. Stigler, "Law Enforcement, Malfeasance, and Compensation of Enforcers," *Journal of Legal Studies,* vol. 3 (January 1974), pp. 1–18.

In this regard, however, internal regulation was different in France. According to Heckscher, "The most vital difference was that many important districts were set free from the application of the statutes in England, while in France nothing remained unregulated in principle, apart from purely accidental exceptions or subordinate points" (*Mercantilism,* p. 266). It does not appear that the English countryside was "set free" in any conscious, deliberate act of policy. Instead economic resources merely responded to the incentives produced by a pattern of enforcement of local regulation pursued by the JP's. Movement out of the towns was simply a way for some artisans and merchants to lower their costs of operation.

Migration to escape local cartel regulations did not have to involve much distance. The suburbs of towns were filled with handicraftsmen who either could not get into the town guilds or wanted to escape their control. Various efforts to bring these "cheaters" under control proved futile, because the nature of the trade carried on was akin to that of a widely dispersed flea market. Adam Smith illustrated this point nicely: "If you would have your work tolerably executed, it must be done in the suburbs where the workmen, having no exclusive privilege, have nothing but their character to depend upon, and you must then smuggle it into town as well as you can" (*Wealth of Nations,* p. 313). Cheating on the local cartels thus became the economic order of the day, and the state's lack of success in dealing with these problems is ample testimony to the inefficient nature of the Elizabethan cartel machinery.

Sometimes the crown struck back by creating institutional arrangements that increased the efficiency of enforcement. For example, Elizabeth made a practice of granting to her favorite courtiers the right to collect fines for violations of the regulatory code. Eventually these rights came to be sold to the highest bidder, the successful bidder keeping for himself whatever he could collect. Since some infringements (e.g., patents) were more lucrative to collect on than others, however, enforcement remained uneven, and a sizable unregulated sector of the economy persisted.

Ultimately, the Statute of Artificers embodied the means of its own destruction. The behavior of the unpaid JP's and the ability of firms to escape regulation were the two major factors that helped undo *local* mercantilist regulation in the long run. We now turn to a consideration of the important part played by the mercantilist judiciary in the gradual demise of *national* economic regulation.

The Mercantilist Judiciary and the Breakdown of National Monopolies

In a system of national regulations, the only way to escape legal jurisdiction is to leave the country, which is more difficult and more costly than moving from city to suburb. Thus the absence of a viable, unregulated alternative brought about more stable cartel arrangements than those described in the preceding section. The undoing of the national monopolies must therefore be explained by the changing constraints on economic activity in mercantile England.

English Common Law and the Courts The development of the judiciary in England was a long and intricate process. Basically, three common-law courts evolved in the period between the Norman invasion and the mercantile era: the Court of King's Bench, the Court of Common Pleas, and the Court of Exchequer. Matters before these courts were essentially civil in nature, and all were initially under the crown's direct control (the king even rendered decisions in the early period). During the thirteenth through the fifteenth centuries the courts grew increasingly independent of the crown, although the king retained the power to appoint and remove judges.

Up to the time of the Tudors jurisdictions between the three courts were undefined and payment of the judges depended in part on the collection of court fees. This led to a great deal of jurisdictional competition between the courts. Moreover, the functional separation of the branches of government toward the end of the fourteenth century intensified the division of interests between the King's Council, the Court of King's Bench, and Parliament. The Council became identified and allied with the executive branch of government (monarch), King's Bench with the judiciary, and Parliament as a legislative body, but with some vestiges of a judiciary (the House of Lords remains the highest appellate court in England). The separation of governmental functions brought with it a self-interested alignment between the common-law courts and Parliament. The common-law courts recognized Parliament as the body whose consent was necessary to make the laws applied by the courts. The common lawyers in parliament (of whom there were many) in turn came to believe that errors in the judiciary should be corrected in Parliament, not by the King's Council.

This alliance between the common-law courts and Parliament began centuries before the mercantile period, by which time the courts had cartelized and established firm jurisdictions and bureaucracies. Equally significant is the fact that this identity of interests between the courts and Parliament intensified by 1550, owing principally to a competing legal system in the form of the *royal* courts that were fully in place by the time of Elizabeth I.

The competing judicial system grew out of a tradition in Roman law *(curia regis)* that regarded the powers of the crown as being outside normal legal jurisdictions; therefore, outside the common-law courts. These other courts were found in branches of the Royal Council, in its subordinate court (the Court of Star Chamber) and in other parts of the executive branch of government, e.g., the Court of Chancery. As the Court of Chancery and the Court of the Star Chamber extended their jurisdictions into that of the common-law courts, they met with fierce resistance from the "cartel." One of the courts of Chancery "perished under the persistent attack of the common lawyers" (Maitland, *Selected Historical Essays,* p. 115), and the confrontation served to cement the alliance between the common-law courts and Parliament. As Parliament's power developed relative to that of the crown, it needed support for its legal actions, a support that the common-law courts were eager to provide. On the other hand, besides being composed of individuals of similar training and interest, the common-law courts were attracted to the interests of Parliament since they regarded Parliament as simply another common-law court (the House of Commons could overturn any decision made by a common-law court). Parliament, moreover, could legislate jurisdictional boundaries and other aspects of the courts, but Parliament was dependent upon the courts for the permanence and security of its law. It is against this judicial background that national mercantilist regulations must be considered.

Effects of Judicial Competition on the Durability of Monopoly Rights

The effect of competition between the king's courts and the common-law courts was to create considerable uncertainty over the durability of a monopoly right granted by governmental authority. Under competitive court systems, a monopoly right valid in one court would not necessarily be considered valid in another. Therefore the security of monopoly privilege depended on the shifting fortunes of each court system. In order to be valuable to a special interest, however, monopoly rights must be certain and durable. Consequently, after judicial competition became common practice in England, subsequent attempts by the crown to establish monopoly privileges met with less and less success.

Example 1 On grounds of national defense, Queen Elizabeth claimed regalian rights to the production of saltpeter and gunpowder in the 1580s. She granted a monopoly right to its manufacture to George and John Evlyn. The Evlyn family subsequently enjoyed lucrative benefits from rent splitting with the crown for almost fifty years, but persistent counteraction by other merchants and the common-law courts finally brought down the monopoly privilege. Subsequently the manufacture of both saltpeter and gunpowder became the object of open competition.

Example 2 Elizabeth also tried to imitate the French king's successful and lucrative salt tax, but she did not meet with the same success. Five years after a patent monopoly in salt was established, the patentees abandoned their investment, leaving huge salt pans rusting on the English coast. Private capitalists without any exclusive privileges thereafter entered the industry and profitably produced and sold salt over the next three decades, despite repeated attempts by the crown to reestablish monopoly rights (this almost literally rubbed salt in the wounds of the monarchy).

Example 3 In 1588, a paper monopoly was granted to John Spilman, who claimed to have a new process for producing white paper. Ordinarily, patents issued to protect a new invention or process were unopposed by Parliament and the common-law courts, but sometimes the patent was extended to enable its holders to "engulf" closely related products. Spilman did such a thing in 1597 when he was granted a monopoly over *all* kinds of paper manufactory.

The monopoly proved impossible to enforce, however, and within six years Spilman had to content himself with "such a share of the expanding market for papers as the efficiency of his machinery, the skill of his workmen, and the situation of his mills enabled him to command" (Nef, *Industry and Government,* p. 106). Elizabeth's luckless experiences with franchising and rent-seeking activities ended in 1603, when, given the opportunity to grant a monopoly of playing cards, she personally declared that such patents were contrary to common law. Other attempts followed, however, by her successors.

   Example 4 In the interregnum between Elizabeth and Charles I (1603–1625), the House of Commons and the common-law courts consolidated their power and succeeded in blocking the establishment of enforceable, national monopolies that interfered with their interests or the profits of merchants aligned with them. This opposition to the crown's supposed right to supply regulation reached its zenith in 1624, when the celebrated Act Concerning Monopolies legally stripped the king of all means to monopolize industry.
   In 1625, Charles I ascended to the British throne and promptly tried to reassert regalian rights to grant monopoly by letters patent or by order of the Privy Council. Together with his powerful and persuasive minister, Sir Francis Bacon, he found a loophole in the 1624 statute, and he tried to make deals with large producers in many industries, particularly in alum and soap. Between 1629 and 1640 the alum patent brought in £126,000 and the soap patent an additional £122,000. King Charles's brazen move ultimately brought him to a head-to-head confrontation with Parliament and the constitutionalists, a battle that he ultimately lost, along with his head, in 1649.
   These examples demonstrate that according to the policy, or process, analysis of mercantilism, the returns from seeking national monopolies through the state fell drastically in the sixteenth and early seventeenth centuries as the conflict between Parliament and the crown intensified. This is not to say that the conflict was motivated necessarily by monopoly policy, but rather that the conflict, however motivated, had important side effects in the rent-seeking economy of England at the time. Certainly "public interest" may have played a role in the classic decisions of the British common-law courts to transfer monopoly granting to Parliament. But the institutional facts of the centuries-old alliance between common-law courts and Parliament plus Parliament's control over jurisdictional disputes between the two court systems suggest a very powerful, self-interested economic motivation. One important question remains, however: Why was Parliament unable to effect a sustained reinstitution of mercantilist policies when it became the sole supplier of regulatory legislation?

The Decline of Mercantilism and the Rise of Parliament

The focal point of the conflict between Parliament and the crown in the struggle to supply monopoly rights was in the area of patents. Parliament's interest lay in restraint of the unlimited power of the crown to grant monopoly privileges. The struggle was not over free trade versus government grants of monopoly but rather over who would have the power to supply economic regulations.

This became abundantly clear in 1624 when the House of Commons petitioned King James I to cease and desist from granting letters patent. The controversy that provoked the petition concerned a lighthouse on the English coast known as the Wintertonness Lights. Parliament and the king came into direct conflict on the matter. Parliament had originally issued a patent to the master of Trinity House to erect and maintain the lighthouse. Under this original patent he was to charge sixpence for every 20 chaldron (1 chaldron = 32 bushels) of coals in ships passing that way. In the meantime, Sir John Meldrum successfully petitioned King James for a patent to the lighthouse. Sir John proceeded to charge a rate for coal that was nearly seven times the rate allowed the master of Trinity House. Parliament was incensed. Its petition states:

> ...the said sir John by colour of the said letters patent; for every 20 chaldron of coals, hath taken 3s. 4d. and will not suffer the ships to make their entries...before they pay the said excessive duty...to the intolerable damages and loss of your subjects, he hath taken after the rate of 35. 4d. of divers seafaring men, that sail not that way, nor in their course could take any benefit of the said lighthouse. Our humble Petition is, that your maj. will be pleased to publish the said letters patent to be void in law, and to command that they be no more put in execution (Corbbett, *Parliamentary History,* p. 1492).

In this and in numerous other cases, Parliament invoked "public welfare" as the rationale for wresting economic control from the crown. Nevertheless, it is consistent with economic incentives that its intentions were simply to acquire for itself the right to supply regulation.

Parliament ultimately bested the crown and became the sole supplier of legislation in England, but, ironically, it was unable to successfully and consistently exploit this new power to supply regulation. This inability can be attributed to the high costs of multiparty decision making. It is invariably more costly to each individual for decisions to be made by many parties than by a single party, such as the monarch. England at this time lacked an administrative bureaucracy capable of administering and enforcing economic regulation. Unable to delegate authority in this way, Parliament found it costly to legislate and even more costly to enforce economic regulations. It is a wry twist of history that after struggling long and hard with the crown for the right to operate a national system of economic regulation, Parliament discovered that the costs of sustaining the system were much larger than the pro rata benefits. On this fact, mercantilism ultimately floundered, and significant deregulation of the British economy subsequently ensued.

Some historians have made much of the "dual" nature of mercantilist thought, particularly near the end of the mercantilist era. Many later mercantilists abhorred domestic controls while they simultaneously defended protectionist measures in foreign trade. This apparent contradiction is less paradoxical if mercantilism is viewed as a form of rent-seeking activity. One particular incident, though small in itself, reveals that self-interested rent seeking was never far from the surface when mercantilist policies were shaped, despite the fact that nationalistic motives are often pressed to explain macroeconomic protectionist policies. The episode in question involves Charles I and his battle with Parliament over customs duties. King Charles claimed an ''ancient right'' to customs, but Parliament ultimately seized the exclusive power to set these duties in 1641. While Parliament was dissolved, the King reasserted his claim of absolute authority to levy taxes. However, merchant importers refused, in their own interests, to pay customs to the king, obeying instead Parliament's decree to refuse to pay any duties not authorized by itself. The King retaliated by seizing the merchants' goods, whereupon several of them resisted and were brought before the Privy Council. Merchant Richard Chambers brazenly declared that ''merchants are in no part of the world so screwed as in England. In Turkey they have more encouragement'' (Taylor, *Origin and Growth of the English Constitution*, p. 274).

TRANSITION TO LIBERALISM

Major historical turning points in the distant past are always difficult to pinpoint. Such is the case with the transition from a heavily regulated economy to one of relatively free trade. In practice, no pure laissez faire economy has ever existed, but significant structural changes in the British economy were detectible between the seventeenth and nineteenth centuries. To some extent, doctrinal and policy views of mercantilism offer different reasons for this transition.

The Doctrinal Transition: Mandeville

From a doctrinal standpoint, mercantilism broke down because it lost intellectual respectability. In the century prior to 1776, liberal criticism of mercantilism reached a high pitch. One of the most effective proponents of the new liberalism during this period was Bernard de Mandeville.

Mandeville, who has already been mentioned as a sponsor of the mercantile doctrine of the utility of poverty, was also one of the most vigorous proponents of economic liberalism. In 1705, he published an allegorical poem entitled *The Grumbling Hive; or Knaves Turn'd Honest,* in which he argued that individual vices (self-interest) produce public virtues (maximize society's welfare), one of the central themes of Smith's *Wealth of Nations*. Later the poem was reprinted and enlarged upon in *The Fable of the Bees,* published in two parts (Part I in 1714 and Part II in 1729). The book was a sensation.

Mandeville focused upon a theory of human nature that rejected a rationalist, metaphysical view of knowledge. He embraced instead an empiricist theory holding that sense impressions are all we can know of the world. Reasoning must come from facts, not from any rationalist or a priori considerations.

The importance of his espousal of an empirical view of human nature is that it is one of the fundamental tenets of the liberal revolution. Since sensations are the source of knowledge and since each individual receives different external stimuli, early empiricists argued that the optimal social organization would be one allowing a maximum of individual freedom.[3]

Mandeville thus rejected absolute criteria as the foundation for social systems or for individual behavior. Right and wrong were relative, and he noted that "Things are Good and Evil in reference to something else, and according to the Light and Position they are placed in" (*Fable*, p. 367). Although Mandeville's empiricism and moral relativism were roundly attacked during his lifetime, his position gradually gained acceptance, popularizing the view (still current) that normative problems cannot be handled by science.

Further, Mandeville's belief that man is "full of vice" (or self-interested) but promotes public benefits was a clear anticipation of liberal thought. Humans are at base selfish creatures since they "give no Pleasure to others that is not repaid to their Self-Love, and does not at last center in themselves, let them wind it and turn it as they will" (*Fable*, p. 342). But as he pointed out, "Pride and Vanity have built more Hospitals than all the Virtues together" (*Fable*, p. 261).

Although Mandeville cannot be regarded as a consistent exponent of liberalism, he nevertheless presented a clear discussion of the philosophical underpinnings of this movement. However, he did not apply his system of self-interest to actual problems of commerce, as writers such as Richard Cantillon (see Chapter 4) did. Still, he remains an important harbinger of economic liberalism.

The Institutional Transition

Regardless of which interpretation one takes of mercantilism, wealth destruction was a main feature of the system. The conventional interpretation emphasizes the misguided effort to accumulate gold and specie, whereas the process view underlines how societal wealth was dissipated through monopoly creation and rent seeking at both local and national levels. According to the doctrinal view, mercantilism declined as the "errors" of it were slowly but surely uncovered. The policy view emphasizes the unintentional consequences of rent-seeking activity—i.e., the institutional changes it spawned that gradually made rent seeking and internal regulation by the central government less feasible. Liberalism and free trade were consequently made viable alternatives under either interpretation.

Pure laissez faire never existed in England (or anywhere else) even after the dominance of Parliament's ability to supply regulation. The landed class re-

---

[3] Although he does not do so consistently, Mandeville suggests at several places in the *Fable* that man's central motivating force is pleasure. Thus some may regard him as an anticipator of utilitarian thought (see Chap. 6).

tained control of Parliament, and continued to pass legislation favorable to that class. But the deregulation of the British economy at this time was significant, and it has been so acknowledged by historians of the period, even if their characterization has been one of a willy-nilly dissolution of the old order. Whether deregulation eventually occurred because better ideas won out or because there was an increase in the cost to Parliament of supplying regulation, it should also be noted that the seventeenth and eighteenth centuries were periods of rapid technological advance and that such quick-paced innovation in a reasonably competitive environment will reduce the demand for legal cartels. This feature, too, may have played an important role in the decline of regulation in seventeenth-century England.

CONCLUSION

The analysis of mercantilism presented in this chapter has focused on the British economy. Intellectual and institutional forces interacted to produce the liberal "revolution" in England and, by export in the eighteenth century, in America as well. Even at the height of its regulatory activity, however, the British economy was a pale reflection of its European counterpart—the French economy administered by Colbert, Louis XIV's finance minister.

French mercantilism is often called "Colbertism," thus bearing the personal stamp of the man who shaped its policy. What made French mercantilism different was its very high degree of centralization and very efficient system of policing, factors that were never so great in England. The liberal reaction to French mercantilism reached its height in the writings of the Physiocrats, a group of French economists discussed in the following chapter.

NOTES FOR FURTHER READING

Until recently, the custom in economic literature has been to treat mercantilism as a set of ideas rather than as a set of institutions spawned by individual and group interest. Within this doctrinal view there have been two separate traditions, one "absolutist" in approach, the other "relativist." The absolutists tend to view the history of economics as a more or less steady progression from error to truth, whereas the relativists view past doctrines as justified within the context of their times. The absolutists emphasize the presence of grave errors in mercantilist logic, errors exposed by David Hume and the classical economists. The primary instance of such faulty reasoning was the failure of mercantilist writers to recognize the self-regulating effects that the "specie-flow mechanism" imposed on attempts to realize a perennial trade surplus. The relativists, beginning with the German historical school and their English disciples, generally defend mercantilism as historically acceptable, given its aim of national power and wealth. Representative of the German historicist view is Gustave Schmoller, *The Mercantile System and Its Historical Significance* (New York: Smith, 1931); of their English disciples, W. J. Ashley, *An*

Introduction to English Economic History and Theory, vol. 1 (New York: Putnam, 1892); and W. Cunningham, *The Growth of English Industry and Commerce,* 2 vols. (New York: A. M. Kelley, Publishers, 1968).

The clearest exponent of the absolutist view is Jacob Viner, whose two classic papers on mercantilism were originally published in 1930 as "English Theories of Foreign Trade before Adam Smith," parts 1 and 2, *Journal of Political Economy,* vol. 38 (1930), pp. 249–301, 404–457, reprinted as the first two chapters of Viner's *Studies in the Theory of International Trade* (London: G. Allen, 1937). Viner viewed the mercantilists' trade theory as "objectionable from the point of view of modern doctrine," arguing that the "simplicity and brevity of the early analysis at least resulted in fallacies of comparable simplicity, but the later writers were able to assemble a greater variety of fallacies into an elaborate system of confused and self-contradictory argument" (*Studies,* p. 109). In a trenchant criticism of the relativist position, Viner answered those who defended mercantilist policies and ideas as justified given the ends of society. According to Viner, these defenders derived from the idea that "if sufficient information were available the prevalence in any period of particular theories could be *explained* in the light of the circumstances then prevailing, the curious corollary that they can also be *justified* by appeal to these special circumstances. There are some obvious obstacles to acceptance of this point of view. It would lead to the conclusion that no age, except apparently the present one, is capable of serious doctrinal error. It overlooks the fact that one of the historical circumstances that has been undergoing an evolution has been the capacity for economic analysis. More specifically, to be invoked successfully in defense of mercantilist doctrine it needs to be supported by demonstration that the typical behavior of merchants, the nature of the gains or losses from trade, the nature of the monetary processes, and the economic significance of territorial division of labor have changed sufficiently since 1550, or 1650, or 1750 to make what was sound reasoning for these earlier periods unsound for the present-day world" (*Studies,* pp. 110–111). An interesting exploration of Viner's point is undertaken by W. R. Allen in "Modern Defenders of Mercantilist Theory," *History of Political Economy,* vol. 2 (Fall 1970), pp. 381–397.

The only work in economic literature that spans both the absolutist and relativist positions is Eli Heckscher's two-volume *Mercantilism,* published in Swedish in 1931 and translated into English (see References) and revised by the author in 1935. Fundamentally, Heckscher treats mercantilism as a coherent and interrelated system of power and economic controls in which attempts were made to maximize the well-being of the state. According to Heckscher, "The state must have one outstanding interest, an interest which is the basis for all its other activities. What distinguishes the state from all other social institutions is the fact that, by its very nature, it is a compulsory corporation or, at least in the last instance, has the final word on the exercise of force in society" (*Mercantilism,* II, p. 15). Though Heckscher's interpretations are open to dispute on specific points, his book remains the essential work on the subject.

On a simpler level, Max Beer's *Early British Economists* (London: G.

Allen, 1938) contains a less intricate discussion of mercantilism than Heckscher's or Viner's. A number of mercantilist tracts are excerpted in some of the books of readings listed under the General References at the end of Chapter 1 of this work. The original works of many of the major mercantilist writers, e.g., Gerard de Malynes, Thomas Mun, and Daniel Defoe, have been reprinted and published by A. M. Kelley.

A rich lode of secondary materials exists focusing on mercantile doctrine and on individual mercantilists. R. C. Wiles discusses the shifting aims and analysis of mercantilist writers in "The Development of Mercantilist Thought," in S. Todd Lowry (ed.), *Pre-Classical Economic Thought* (Boston: Kluwer, 1987). The dualistic or "mixed" nature of mercantilist thought is emphasized in excellent papers by A. F. Chalk (see References) and W. D. Grampp, "The Liberal Elements in English Mercantilism," *Quarterly Journal of Economics,* vol. 66 (November 1952), pp. 465–501. The process of taste acquisition and of "conditioning" in Mandeville's thought is discussed in J. J. Spengler, "Veblen and Mandeville Contrasted," *Zeitschrift des Instituts fur Weltwirtschaft,* vol. 82 (1959), pp. 35–65. Lars Magnusson, "Mercantilism and 'Reform' Mercantilism: The Rise of Economic Discourse in Sweden during the Eighteenth Century," *History of Political Economy,* vol. 19 (Fall 1987), pp. 415–434, traces the development of mercantilist doctrine and its critics in that country.

Mercantile doctrine on the question of labor, unemployment, and the relation between labor intensity and international trade are featured in three well-known papers by E. A. J. Johnson, "The Mercantilist Concept of 'Art' and 'Ingenious Labour,'" *Economic History,* vol. 2 (January 1931), pp. 234–253; "Unemployment and Consumption: The Mercantilist View," *Quarterly Journal of Economics,* vol. 46 (August 1932), pp. 698–719; and "British Mercantilist Doctrine Concerning the Exportation of Work and 'Foreign Paid Incomes,'" *Journal of Political Economy,* vol. 40 (December 1932), pp. 750–770. These papers are a very useful accompaniment to the volume by Furniss cited in the References at the end of this chapter. Also see D. Woodward, "The Background to the Statute of Artificers: The Genesis of Labor Policy, 1558–63," *Economic History Review,* vol. 33 (February 1980), pp. 32–44.

Some intellectual detective work into authorship and doctrinal influences is provided by M. Dewar, "The Memorandum 'For the Understanding of Exchange': Its Authorship and Dating," *Economic History Review,* vol. 18 (April 1965), pp. 476–487; and G. H. Evans, "The Law of Demand: The Roles of Gregory King and Charles Davanant," *Quarterly Journal of Economics,* vol. 81 (August 1967), pp. 483–492.

Political, social, and economic thought in the mercantilist era and during the transition to liberalism were also conditioned by philosophy. A reading of Thomas Hobbes's *Leviathan* (London: Dent, 1914) or Niccolo Machiavelli's *The Prince* (New York: Modern Library, 1950) exposes power as the central theme of the period. The amoral character of mercantile thought is nowhere better expressed, perhaps, than in Machiavelli's advice to the prince: "Thus it is well to seem merciful, faithful, humane, sincere, religious, and also to be so; but you must have the mind so disposed that when it is needful to be otherwise you may be able to change to the opposite qualities'' (*The Prince,* p. 65). The dualism in economic thought is explained partly by a dualism in philosophy. The impact of the ''new'' philosophies of Hume and Locke on liberalism and classical economics is admirably treated in a number of works, in particular Werner Stark, *The Ideal Foundations of Economic Thought* (New York: Oxford University Press, 1944), and Carl Becker, *The Heavenly City of Eighteenth-Century Philosophers* (New Haven, Conn.: Yale University Press, 1932).

The intellectual evolution of laissez faire may also have depended on and been supported by the development by philosophers of certain theoretical tools of economic analysis. In this regard, see Karen I. Vaughn, *John Locke: Economist and Social Scientist* (Chicago: University of Chicago Press, 1980); M. L. Myers, *The Soul of Modern Economic Man* (Chicago: University of Chicago Press, 1983); and same author, ''Philosophical Anticipations of Laissez-Faire,'' *History of Political Economy,* vol. 4 (Spring 1972), pp. 163–175.

What we have called the *process,* or *policy,* view of mercantilism is a blend of the historical conception of Heckscher and the contemporary application of self-interested behavior and property-rights theory to institutions and to institutional change. Specifically, the policy view features economic and political ''actors'' maximizing individual self-interest. This view of mercantilism was suggested as early as Adam Smith's *Wealth of Nations* (see References), but it was more forcefully stated in reviews of Heckscher's *Mercantilism.* Although a highly regarded scholar, Heckscher nevertheless incensed economic historians by his generalized treatment of economic policy and his excessive emphasis on the cohesiveness of mercantilism as doctrine and policy unaffected by actual economic events. On this point, see C. H. Heaton, ''Heckscher on Mercantilism,'' *Journal of Political Economy,* vol. 45 (June 1937), pp. 370–393.

Some historians charged that Heckscher's treatment, embedded as it was in ideas, practically ignored all reference to the political process through which the so-called unifying mercantile policies were made. D. C. Coleman, ''Eli Heckscher and the Idea of Mercantilism,'' *Scandinavian Economic History Review,* vol. 5 (1957), pp. 3–25, for example, concluded that the term mercantilism, as a label for economic policy, ''is not simply misleading but actively confusing, a red herring of historiography. It seems to give a false unity to disparate events, to conceal the closeup reality of particular times and circumstances, to blot out the vital intermixture of ideas and preconceptions, of interests and influences, political and economic, and of the personalities of men...'' (pp. 24–25). Policy, Coleman affirmed, cannot be treated in a vacuum, nor can the role and interests of parties to the political process be ignored. Thus, the application of contemporary positive economic theory dealing with economic regulation and public choice goes far in filling this important gap in Heckscher's treatment.

This policy view is described in the present chapter and expanded in R. B. Ekelund, Jr., and R. D. Tollison, "Economic Regulation in Mercantile England: Heckscher Revisited," *Economic Inquiry,* vol. 18 (October 1980), pp. 567–599; and, by the same authors, in "Mercantile Origins of the Corporation," *Bell Journal of Economics,* vol. 11 (Autumn 1980), pp. 715–720; and in B. Baysinger, R. B. Ekelund, Jr., and R. D. Tollison, "Mercantilism as a Rent-Seeking Society," in J. M. Buchanan et al. (eds.), *Towards a Theory of the Rent-Seeking Society* (College Station, Texas: Texas A & M University Press, 1980), which also includes other papers of interest on the subject.

Details of the legal and political system that was mercantilism are given in a number of references to the present chapter. The classic sources on the mercantilist judiciary, Maitland and Holdsworth, are especially recommended. A very interesting paper that illustrates the duplicity with which common-law jurists approached the subject of free trade is D. O. Wagner's "Coke and the Rise of Economic Liberalism," *Economic History Review,* vol. 6 (March 1935), pp. 30–44. The relatively new fields of public choice and regulation, from which much of the process view of mercantilism takes its foundation, are the subject of Chapter 24. However, there are several specific contemporary articles in these areas that are vital to an understanding of mercantilism as a process. See especially G. Becker and G. J. Stigler, "Law Enforcement, Malfeasance and Compensation of Enforcers," *Journal of Legal Studies,* vol. 3 (January 1974), pp. 1–18; Isaac Ehrlich and R. A. Posner, "An Economic Analysis of Legal Rule Making," *Journal of Legal Studies,* vol. 3 (January 1974), pp. 257–286; W. M. Landes and R. A. Posner, "The Independent Judiciary in an Interest-Group Perspective," *Journal of Law & Economics,* vol. 18 (December 1975), pp. 875–901; and G. J. Stigler, "The Theory of Economic Regulation," *Bell Journal of Economics and Management Science,* vol. 2 (Spring 1971), pp. 3–21.

REFERENCES

Chalk, Alfred F. "Natural Law and the Rise of Economic Individualism in England," *Journal of Political Economy,* vol. 59 (August 1951), pp. 330–347.

———. "Mandeville's Fable of the Bees: A Reappraisal," *Southern Economic Journal,* vol. 33 (July 1966), pp. 1–16.

Corbbett, W. *Parliamentary History of England,* vol. I. London: R. Bagshaw, 1966 [1806].

Furniss, Edgar S. *The Position of the Laborer in a System of Nationalism.* New York: Kelley and Millman, 1957.

Hales, John. *A Discourse of the Common Weal of This Realm of England,* E. Lammond (ed.). London: Cambridge University Press, 1929.

Heckscher, Eli. *Mercantilism,* 2 vols., Mendel Shapiro (trans.). London: G. Allen, 1934.

Holdsworth, Sir William. *A History of English Law,* vols. I–IV. London: Methuen, 1966 [1924].

Hornick, P. W. von. "Austria Over All If She Only Will," in A. E. Monroe (ed.), *Early Economic Thought*. Cambridge, Mass.: Harvard University Press, 1965.

Keynes, J. M. *General Theory of Employment, Interest and Money*. New York: Harcourt, Brace, & World, 1936.

Maitland, F. W. *Selected Historical Essays of F. W. Maitland*, Helen M. Cam (ed.). London: Cambridge University Press, 1957.

Mandeville, Bernard de. *The Fable of the Bees*, F. B. Kaye (ed.). London: Oxford University Press, 1924.

Misselden, Edward. *The Circle of Commerce*, in Philip C. Newman, Arthur T. Gayer, and Milton H. Spencer (eds.), *Source Readings in Economic Thought*. New York: Norton, 1954, pp. 43–48 [1623].

Nef, John U. *Industry and Government in France and England, 1540–1640*. New York: Russell and Russell, 1968 [1940].

Newman, Philip C., Arthur T. Gayer, and Milton H. Spencer (eds.). *Source Readings in Economic Thought*. New York: Norton, 1954.

Petty, William. *The Economic Writings of Sir William Petty*, 2 vols., C. H. Hull (ed.). New York: A. M. Kelley, 1963.

Smith, Adam. *The Wealth of Nations*. New York: Random House, 1937 [1776].

Tawney, R. H., and Eileen Power. *Tudor Economic Documents*, 3 vols. London: Longmans, 1924.

Taylor, Hannis. *The Origin and Growth of the English Constitution*, part II. Boston: Houghton Mifflin, 1898.

Viner, Jacob. *Studies in the Theory of International Trade*. London: G. Allen, 1937.

THE EMERGENCE OF A SCIENCE: PETTY, CANTILLON, AND THE PHYSIOCRATS

THE IRISH ROOTS OF POLITICAL ECONOMY

As mercantilism slowly began to unravel late in the sixteenth century, a number of enlightened writers anticipated the coming age of capitalism with its intellectual and practical focus upon the operation of free markets. Two of the most prominent figures of this transitional period were Sir William Petty (1623–1687) and Richard Cantillon (1680?–1734), both native sons of Ireland. Cantillon eventually became a citizen of France, where his ideas made an impact on an important group of economists called the Physiocrats; whereas Petty remained on British soil, moving freely back and forth between Ireland and England.

Petty and Cantillon were transitional figures: each had one foot in the mercantilist era and one in the liberal era that was to follow. Their economic writings therefore contain a mixture of liberal and mercantilist elements, particularly on the question of money, the most sensitive of mercantilist subjects. The Physiocrats, who followed Petty and Cantillon and absorbed much of their influence, represent the dawn of the liberal era. Their ideas constitute a more forceful rejection of mercantilism, if not an open embracement of laissez faire.

Sir William Petty

Petty lived in a period of emerging commercial capitalism, marked by the beginning of the agricultural revolution but as yet revealing only early signs of the incipient industrial revolution. Traveler, writer, adventurer, physician, academician, surveyor, businessman, economist—Petty was obsessed with the idea of fame and fortune. An episode from his brief medical career illustrates his flair for the sensational. While professor of anatomy at Oxford, in 1650, he revived a young woman hanged for infanticide and nursed her back to health. Soon afterward, an anonymous pamphlet appeared entitled *News from the Dead,* possibly written (at least in part) by Petty himself, extolling his miraculous medical powers that defied death and the gallows. Such bravado characterized many of Petty's efforts, including his forays into economics.

Economic Method   Petty was a positivist before that principle became the predominant research criterion of the natural sciences. As an active, charter member of the Royal Society (London), Petty once proposed, in jest, that the group's annual meeting should be held on the feast day of St. Thomas the Apostle, who believed only in what he could see or touch. Petty called his method of inquiry "political arithmetic." By this phrase he sought to express the basic idea that the introduction of quantitative methods would produce a more rigorous analysis of social phenomena. This approach represented the ascendancy of material-mechanical conceptions over the Aristotelian syllogistic-deductive approach. On such matters, Petty was influenced above all by Francis Bacon, who proposed the *inductive method,* a fusion of empiricism and rationalism. Bacon explained the new method in terms of a metaphor. Empiricists, wrote Bacon:

> ...are like the ant, they only collect and use; the reasoners resemble spiders, who make cobwebs out of their own substance. But the bee takes a middle course: it gathers its material from the flowers of the garden and of the field, but transforms and digests it by a power of its own. Not unlike this is the true business of philosophy; for it neither relies solely or chiefly on the powers of the mind, nor does it take the matter which it gathers from natural history and mechanical experiments and lay it up in the memory whole, as it finds it, but lays it up in the understanding altered and digested (*New Organon,* p. 93).

The flight from the subjectivism and logico-deductivism of the ancient Greeks and the Scholastics toward empiricism and objectivism became an important datum in the British classical tradition of political economy, as we shall see in ensuing chapters. Petty recognized the novelty of the new approach, but defended it as an improvement:

> The Method I take..., is not very usual; for instead of using only comparative and superlative words, and intellectual Arguments, I have taken the course (as a Specimen of the Political Arithmetick I have long aimed at) to express myself in Terms of Number, Weight, or Measure; to use only Arguments of Sense, and to consider only such Causes, as have visible Foundations in Nature; leaving those that depend upon the mutable Minds, Opinions, Appetites and Passions of particular Men, to the Consideration of others...(*Economic Writings,* p. 244).

Another element of Petty's methodological approach was its attempt to separate morals from science. According to Petty, science does not exist to handle moral problems—it is simply a *means* to an end. Moral problems arise only in the selection of *ends* that mankind proposes to attain by the use of science.

However, this position did not lead Petty to espouse a consistent economic philosophy. He advanced numerous proposals for state intervention even while he supported liberal propositions of nonintervention. Moreover, because his economic writings were an integral part of his political and business activities, Petty frequently and vigorously defended his own interests in the halls of power.

In the final analysis, Petty's investigations were aimed not at producing a general system of knowledge, but rather at producing solutions to practical problems. He intended only to produce general guides for policy. This was the real basis of his "political arithmetic." It was meant merely to collect the essential elements of the practical problem to be solved. It was not intended to be a perfect nor a complete description of reality. Petty recognized its limitations. Furthermore, he was aware that each economic problem confronted in the real world (whether a question of money, international trade, or whatever) must be treated as an integral part of a larger whole, not as an independent phenomenon. It is this "systemic" nature of his thought that raises Petty above his contemporaries, and it is this same feature that led Karl Marx to dub him "the founder of modern political economy."

On Money Petty recognized the three functions of money (standard of value, medium of exchange, store of value), but gave pride of place to the second function. He denied that money constitutes an *absolute* measure of value, arguing correctly that its value varies with conditions of supply and demand. He was also aware of the fiduciary operations of banks, and the "artificial" nature of money as a commodity that merely facilitates trade. Petty's analogy regarding money is what might be expected from a physician:

> Money is but the Fat of the Body-politick, whereof too much doth as often hinder its Agility, as too little makes it sick. 'Tis true, that as Fat lubricates the motion of the Muscles, feeds in want of Victuals, fills up uneven Cavities, and beautifies the Body, so doth Money in the State quicken its Action, feeds from abroad in the time of Dearth at Home; evens accounts by reason of its divisibility, and beautifies the whole, altho more especially the particular persons that have it in plenty (*Economic Writings*, p. 113).

Like the mercantilists, Petty saw a relationship between the quantity of money and the level of economic activity (production), but he did not see the relationship between the quantity of money and the level of prices, which lies at the heart of the quantity theory. He considered money to be an indirect cost of production, a cost that corresponds to the value of precious metals embodied in the stock of money. Thus, an excess of money constitutes waste, because the surplus of precious metals could have been exchanged for means of production rather than being directly employed in the production process.

Petty's chief contribution to monetary theory was his use of the velocity-of-circulation concept to determine the optimum quantity of money. This makes him an important predecessor of Locke and Cantillon. He correctly related the velocity of circulation to institutional factors, such as the length of payment periods for wages, rents, and taxes, maintaining that velocity quickens as the payment period is shortened. Petty also departed from the conventional wisdom of mercantilism by arguing that the accumulation of money was a means to an end and not an end in itself. Although favorably disposed to the influx of money from a positive trade balance, he did not consider this an absolute priority. Moreover, he considered prohibitions on the export of money to be useless. What was important, he argued, was a high level of employment and economic activity, not the accumulation of mere treasure.

On Value   Among contemporary economists, Petty is remembered for certain economic slogans more than for his solid achievements in economic analysis. Chief among the slogans popularized by Petty is his famous dictum "That Labour is the Father and active principle of Wealth, as Lands are the Mother" (*Economic Writings,* vol. 1, p. 63). Although this statement constitutes an early and profound recognition of the two "original factors of production," it contains little analytical merit. It certainly does not constitute a *theory* of value. Of much more importance was Petty's research aimed at discovering a "natural par" between land and labor. He tried to relate the values of land and labor to each other by determining how much land is required to produce "a day's food of an adult man," taking the value of such output to be equivalent to the value of a day's labor. The objective of Petty's effort was to establish a unit of measurement by which to reduce the available quantities of the two original factors, land and labor, to a homogeneous quantity of "productive power" which could then serve as the (land-labor) standard of value. Like all such efforts to find an absolute standard of value, this one, too, proved to be an analytical dead end, but it inspired Cantillon to undertake researches in the same direction.

Despite the econometric flavor of Petty's economic studies, he did not produce a satisfactory theory of prices. In particular, he failed to recognize the importance of *relative* prices, which constitutes the core of modern microeconomics. And Marx's admiration for Petty notwithstanding, the latter did not develop a labor theory of value. If anything, Petty had a land theory of value, although it is misleading to call his achievement in this area a genuine *theory* of value. What was missing was a fundamental mechanism capable of explaining exchange ratios between economic goods.

Although Petty was first and last a theorist, in retrospect his greatest achievement was providing a decisive new turn in economic method. His invention, Political Arithmetick, was an early form of econometrics, a field that has blossomed in the post-World War II era (see Chapter 22). As Joseph Schumpeter noted, Petty "was quite ready to fight for...[this methodological creed] and to start what would have been the first controversy on 'method.' But nobody attacked. A few followed. Many admired. And the vast majority very quickly forgot" (*History of Economic Analysis,* p. 211). Faced with the same issue a century later, Adam Smith chose safety over methodological novelty, declaring in the *Wealth of Nations* (Book IV, Chap. 5) that he placed little faith in Political Arithmetick. Under Smith's guidance, classical economics retained the logico-deductive method.

Richard Cantillon

In 1755, a remarkable book was published under bizarre circumstances. It was probably published in Paris, but it was done so over the imprint of a London bookseller who was no longer in business. This book, entitled *Essai sur la nature du commerce en général,* was written more than two decades earlier by Richard Cantillon, a Paris banker and London merchant of Irish extraction. The exact year of Cantillon's birth, as well as other pertinent facts about his life, remains unknown, although the circumstances of his death in 1734 were clearly sensational. He was murdered in his sleep by a discharged servant who then set the house afire in an attempt to conceal his foul deed. Economics was thereby robbed of one of its most able preclassical minds.

Cantillon's *Essai* represents the state of the art of economics before Adam Smith (see Chapter 5). It is a general treatise of penetrating insight and remarkable clarity, features that have not dimmed with the passage of time. Unlike Boisguilbert who attacked specific economic problems, Cantillon was intent on discovering basic principles. A checklist of Cantillon's original contributions to economics serves to underline his importance. He was one of the first to:

- Treat population growth as an integral part of the economic process
- Develop an economic explanation of the location of cities and sites of production
- Make a distinction between *market price* and *intrinsic value* (i.e., equilibrium price) and show how the two may converge over time
- Demonstrate that changes in velocity are equivalent to changes in the stock of money
- Trace the channels through which changes in the stock of money influence prices
- Describe the mechanism by which prices adjust in international trade
- Analyze income flows between major sectors of the economy

As impressive as this list is, it alone cannot explain Cantillon's uniqueness among eighteenth-century economists. What set him miles apart from the later mercantilists was the Newtonian cast of mind displayed on almost every page of the *Essai.* Cantillon thought of the economy as Newton thought of the cosmos—as an interconnected whole made up of rationally functioning parts. For Cantillon this meant that the economy was constantly adjusting to basic changes in population, production, tastes, etc. The animus of this adjustment process was the self-interested pursuit of profit. In Cantillon's economy, it was this last principle that took the place of Newton's "universal principle of attraction" (i.e., gravity).

Although Cantillon's masterpiece circulated rather widely in France and

England before its delayed publication in 1755, its later fate was to be ignored. Not until near the end of the nineteenth century was its full import recognized and appreciated. It was then that William Stanley Jevons, himself a prominent neoclassical economist (see Chapter 14), rediscovered Cantillon. In the first blush of this discovery, Jevons called the *Essai* "the cradle of political economy." Reflecting on Cantillon's heritage and the pioneering nature of his economic analysis, Jevons added that "the first systematic treatise on economics was probably written by a banker of Spanish name, born from an Irish family of the County Kerry, bred we know not where, carrying on business in Paris, but clearly murdered in Albermarle Street [London]" (see *Essai,* p. 360).

Although Cantillon's work betrays some concern for traditional mercantilist issues, it is far more typical of the liberal period in economics that formally began with Adam Smith decades later. Cantillon was familiar with the works of prominent English writers such as Sir William Petty and John Locke, but his immediate influence was on the French economists of the eighteenth century. His "roundabout" influence may be much wider, extending perhaps to Jevons and to the neo-Austrian economists of today (see Chapter 21). In this chapter, we emphasize three major themes of Cantillon's work: (1) his view of the market and its operation, (2) the critical role and importance of the entrepreneur in economic activity, and (3) the influence on the economy of changes in the aggregate supply of money.

The Market System Cantillon conceived of an economy as an organized system of interconnected markets that operate in such a fashion as to achieve a kind of equilibrium. The inhabitants of the economy are bound together by mutual dependence, and the institutions of the system evolve over time in response to "need and necessity." The system is kept in adjustment by the free play of self-interested entrepreneurs who conduct "all the exchange and circulation of the State" (*Essai,* p. 56). Considering the age in which Cantillon wrote, he gives the prince a remarkably low profile, a fact betraying Cantillon's conviction that a market system works best *without* interference from government. Entrepreneurs, like other market participants, are bound together in reciprocity, as they "become consumers and customers one in regard to the other." Their number is therefore regulated by the number of customers, or total demand, for their services, and their decisions are made under conditions of uncertainty about the future.

The structure of Cantillon's economic system is hierarchical. Landlords sit atop the economic and social order and are represented as financially independent, although they derive income from the inhabitants of a state, who in turn rely on the proprietors to supply natural resources in production. Private property rights are deemed essential to the successful operation of a system of markets. Entrepreneurs occupy the middle rank in Cantillon's hierarchy, but—as explained in the next section—their role is vital and pervasive. It is they who continually react to price movements in specific markets in order to bring about a tentative balance between particular supplies and particular demands.

Seeing the economy as a network of reciprocal exchanges, Cantillon provided one of the clearest early explanations of market price. His notion of *intrinsic* value (the measure of the quantity and quality of land and labor entering into production) underscores an early attempt to base price on some measure of "real" costs, at least insofar as equilibrium long-run values are concerned. When it came to short-run "market" price, however, Cantillon seemed ready to admit subjective assessments. He noted that "it often happens that many things which actually have this intrinsic value are not sold in the market at that value: that will depend on the humors and fancies of men and on their consumption" (*Essai,* p. 28). Another reason why market prices may be different from intrinsic values is that the plans of producers and their customers may be uncoordinated. Indeed, it would appear impossible always to achieve *perfect* coordination. Cantillon observed that "there is never a variation in intrinsic values, but the impossibility of proportioning the production of commodities and merchandise in a State to their consumption causes a daily variation, and perpetual ebb and flow of market prices" (*Essai,* p. 30).

The bargaining process described by Cantillon reflects the information possessed by market participants and the degree of coordination of individual plans. Cantillon described how disparate plans tend to drive prices away from costs (i.e., intrinsic value):

> If the farmers in a state sow more wheat than usual, that is to say, much more than is needed for the annual consumption, the real and intrinsic value of the wheat will correspond to the land and labor which enter into its production; but as there is an over-supply and there are more sellers of wheat than buyers, the market price of wheat will necessarily fall below the cost or intrinsic value. If on the contrary the farmers sow less wheat than is needed for consumption there will be more buyers than sellers and the market price will rise above its intrinsic value (*Essai,* pp. 28–30).

One has only to substitute the word "natural" in place of "intrinsic" to appreciate how close this analysis comes to Adam Smith's (see Chapter 5), and if Cantillon had gone no further, he would have still provided an important description of the price mechanism. But he did go further, providing a rudimentary explanation of the network of price signals that serve to connect different markets. The following passage is rich in suggestions of self-interest as a motive force, relative prices as signals to adjust resource use, and opportunity costs as a basis of economic decision making:

> For if some of the farmers sowed more grain than usual on their land they would have to graze a smaller number of sheep and would therefore have less wool and mutton to sell. Consequently there will be too much grain and too little wool for the consumption of the inhabitants. Wool will therefore be dear and this will force the inhabitants to wear their clothes longer than usual; and there will be too much grain and a surplus for the following year...the farmers...will take care the following year to have less grain and more wool, for farmers always seek to use their land for the production of those things that they think will bring the highest market price. But if the next year they have too much wool and too little grain for the demand, they will not fail to change from year to year the use of the land until they have adjusted

their production more or less to the consumption of the inhabitants. So a farmer who has adjusted more-or-less his output to the demand, will have part of his farm in grass, for hay, another part in grain, another in wool, and so on, and he will not change his plan unless he sees some considerable change in the demand (*Essai,* pp. 60–62).

In this fashion, Cantillon demonstrated how initially incompatible plans between buyers and sellers become mutually compatible over time by self-interested adjustments to changes in relative prices. The same sort of phenomenon manifests itself in the factor markets. Cantillon spoke of labor's tendency to adjust itself *naturally* to the demand for it. The emphasis on natural forces in allocating labor to different employments is clear where Cantillon speaks of the tradition of raising sons in the same line of work as their fathers. If village workers bring up a number of their sons in one trade, "the surplus adults will have to seek their living somewhere else, ordinarily in the cities: if some stay with their Fathers, since they will not find enough work, they will live in great poverty" (*Essai,* p. 22). Short-term decreases or increases in demand would engender temporarily lower or higher returns to various types of labor, but Cantillon envisioned an eventual adjustment to equilibrium. He observed correctly that after out-migration and/or in-migration, "the number left is always adjusted to the employment which suffices to give them a living; and when a permanent increase of work develops, it is profitable, and enough others come to share the work" (*Essai,* p. 24). Given a *permanent* increase in the demand for labor, Cantillon's statement of the allocative mechanism is almost as clear as that developed by neoclassical economics.

Competition and Entrepreneurship   Like Adam Smith, who was to follow, Cantillon conceived competition to be something other than what is represented in today's first-year economics texts. He did not think of competition as a list of conditions that define a specific market structure but rather as a rivalrous process between contestants who vie for the same customers. In this competitive process, Cantillon focused attention on the role and importance of the entrepreneur. He saw the economy in terms of classes of individuals, each class defined by a major economic function:

> We may conclude that, with the exception of the Prince and the Proprietors of Lands, all the Inhabitants of a State are dependent; that they may be divided into two classes, namely, Entrepreneurs and Wage-earners; and that the Entrepreneurs work for uncertain wages, so to speak, and all others for certain wages until they have them, although their functions and their rank are very disproportionate. The General who has a salary, the Courtier who has a pension, and the Domestic who has wages, are in the latter class. All the others are Entrepreneurs, whether they establish themselves with a capital to carry on their enterprise, or are Entrepreneurs of their own work without any capital, and they may be considered as living subject to uncertainty; even Beggars and Robbers are Entrepreneurs of this class (*Essai,* p. 54).

Clearly, for Cantillon there are low entrance requirements to the entrepreneurial class, and just as clearly, entrepreneurs come and go, depending on the vicissitudes of the marketplace. The essence of entrepreneurial activity is bearing risk. In the case of the merchant-entrepreneur, he buys goods at a known price in order to resell them "in large or small quantities at an uncertain price." The marketplace, therefore, is not for the fainthearted or the risk-averse. As Cantillon observed:

> These Entrepreneurs can never know the volume of Consumption in their City, nor even how long their Customers will buy of them, seeing that their Rivals will try in every way to get away their Business: all this causes so much uncertainty among all these Entrepreneurs that we see failures among them every day (*Essai*, p. 50).

Cantillon also had a "general equilibrium" notion of how a market system works. That is to say, he recognized the interconnectedness between product markets and resource markets. Entrepreneurs are "allocated" according to the same mechanism that allocates laborers or goods:

> All these Entrepreneurs become consumers and Customers of each other; the Draper, of the Wine Merchant; the latter of the Draper. They adjust their numbers in the State to their Customers or to their market. If there are too many Hatters in a City or in a street for the number of persons who buy hats there, those having the fewest customers will have to become bankrupt; if there are too few, it will be a profitable enterprise, which will encourage some new Hatters to open shop there, and it is thus that Entrepreneurs of all kinds, at their own risk, adjust their numbers in a State (*Essai*, p. 52).

One final note on Cantillon's theory of entrepreneurship—it is not something incidental to the marketplace; it is rather an integral part of the market. Cantillon sought to establish as a basic principle "that all the exchange and circulation of the State is carried on by...Entrepreneurs" (*Essai*, p. 57). Thus, for Cantillon, entrepreneurial activity is the essence of competition and vice versa.

The Effect of Money on Prices and Production   Despite the impressive treatment by Cantillon of fundamental economic principles outlined above, it is in the area of monetary theory that his genius fully blossomed. He originated the income approach to monetary theory: the analysis of the causal chain that connects changes in the money stock to changes in aggregate expenditures, income, employment, and prices (see Chapter 19 for a modern account of this theory). His analysis begins with an account of the "three rents"—the income and expenditure streams of the agricultural sector. The farmer pays a rent to the proprietor; he makes a second expenditure for labor, livestock, and manufactured goods; and he earns a residual (the third "rent") that constitutes his net income. In the next section we shall see how this rather crude notion of income flows by sector was refined by the French Physiocrat François Quesnay, in his *Tableau Économique*.

Showing an empirical bent that rivaled Petty's, Cantillon built on his three-rent concept by making estimates of the stock of money required to make the economy work smoothly. In so doing he provided the first clear explanation of monetary velocity:

> It usually happens in States where money is scarcer that there is more barter than in those where money is plentiful, and circulation is more prompt and less sluggish than in those where money is not so scarce. Thus it is always necessary in estimating the amount of money in circulation to take into account the rapidity of its circulation (*Essai,* p. 130).

Ultimately, however, it was Cantillon's analysis of the effects of changes in the stock of money that established his lasting claim to fame. Citing the "quantity theory" of John Locke, Cantillon pronounced: "Everybody agrees that the abundance of money or its increase in exchange raises the price of everything. The quantity of money brought from America to Europe for the last two centuries justifies this truth by experience...the great difficulty...[however,] consists of knowing in what way and in what proportion the increase of money raises prices" (*Essai,* p. 160).

Like Newton, whom we have already compared him to, Cantillon adorned his analytical principles with empirical research. Unfortunately this research was lost to future generations, but on its basis Cantillon was convinced that the relation between money and prices was not as simple and direct as it was usually assumed to be by early adherents of the quantity theory. He had no trouble distinguishing between relative prices and a price *level,* and he reasoned correctly that the effect of monetary changes on relative prices depends on where new money enters the economy and into whose hands it passes first. If the increased money comes into the hands of spenders, they will raise expenditures on certain goods, driving up the prices of those items. Since some goods will likely be purchased more than others, "according to the inclination of those who acquire the money," relative prices will necessarily be altered. If, instead, the increase of money comes initially into the hands of savers who thereby use it to increase the supply of loanable funds, the current rate of interest will be driven down, *ceteris paribus,* and the composition of total output will be altered in favor of investment (*Essai,* p. 214). This notion provided the germ of a distinctly Austrian theory of business cycles subsequently developed in the 1930s by Friedrich von Hayek (see Chapter 20).

It is noteworthy that Cantillon refused to separate monetary theory from value theory. He upheld a loanable-funds theory of interest, asserting that "the interest of money in a State is settled by the proportionate number of lenders and borrowers...just as the prices of things are fixed in the altercations of the market...by the proportionate number of sellers and buyers" (*Essai,* p. 198). With an eye to relative prices, Cantillon surveyed the effects of new money on interest rates and concluded once again that the demand-specific aspects are critical:

> If the abundance of money in a State comes into the hands of money-lenders it will doubtless bring down the current rate of interest by increasing the number of

money-lenders: but if it comes into the hands of those who spend it will have quite the opposite effect and will raise the rate of interest by increasing the number of entrepreneurs who will find activity by this increased spending and who will need to borrow in order to extend their enterprise to every class of customers (*Essai*, p. 214).

In effect, Cantillon saw very clearly what many writers of the next century apparently failed to see, namely, that an influx of precious metals can act in two ways. The output of the mines may be *lent*—which will tend to lower the rate of interest—or it may be *spent*—which will directly stimulate production, increase the demand for loans in anticipation of making a profit, and raise the rate that people are willing to pay for such loans.

Of all the economic writers of the mercantilist era, Cantillon came closest to founding an opposing system of economic thought. Yet even Cantillon retained some mercantilist notions concerning the balance of trade. Moreover, as a banker his point of view was rather different from that of the philosophers who were to build the new science of economics. But his performance was solid. Adam Smith cited his work by name—a rare occurrence in *The Wealth of Nations*. Cantillon's unpublished work also circulated in France and must be counted as an important factor in molding the thought of the Physiocrats.

HARBINGERS OF LIBERALISM: BOISGUILBERT AND THE PHYSIOCRATS

As the eighteenth century approached, one European country in particular, France, found itself in the grips of a long secular decline in output and national income. Historians generally agree that France's plight was due in part to the costly wars and extravagances of Louis XIV, but at least one writer attributed this wretched state of affairs directly to France's mercantilist policies.

Boisguilbert (1646–1714)

Pierre le Pesant de Boisguilbert had been a provincial magistrate in the city of Rouen for some years when he turned his attention to the problem of France's economic decline. He published five major works between 1665 and 1707, but the approach and purpose of each was essentially the same—analysis of France's secular decline. He never attempted a systematic treatment of principles; instead he tried to analyze specific economic problems. At the turn of the seventeenth century, the problem was to reverse the effects of France's mercantilist policies.

Boisguilbert's attack on mercantilism moved along three main fronts. First, as Adam Smith was to do nearly a century later, he sought to establish the true nature of national wealth as goods (and services), not as money. He termed money the mere means and method of wealth, whereas the commodities useful to life are its proper end and its aim (*Détail*, p. 198).

Gold and silver are not and never have been wealth in themselves, and are of value only in relation to, and in so far as they can procure, the things necessary for life, for which they serve merely as a gauge and an evaluation (cited in Cole, *French Mercantilism,* p. 242).

Like Petty, Boisguilbert was one of the earliest writers to recognize the importance of circulatory velocity and of money substitutes, such as bills of exchange. He argued that it is not the quantity of money alone that is important but the amount of work money does. Effective demand, not nominal money balances, is the key to national well-being. He perceived the income of a nation to be determined by flows of money expenditure, and in this sense Boisguilbert was a direct antecedent of John Maynard Keynes (see Chapter 19).

The second argument that Boisguilbert advanced against mercantilism was the primacy of agriculture. He maintained that mercantilism prejudiced resource allocation in favor of manufacturing (especially luxuries) as opposed to agriculture. Colbert's prohibition of grain exports also aggravated swings in the agricultural cycle. During times of plenty, the surplus grain could not find external markets, so its price and the income of farmers plunged. Boisguilbert argued that the consequent drop in consumption spread from the farm sector throughout the economy, thus precipitating a general crisis. He therefore denounced Colbert's prohibition on grain exports, declaring that free trade would bring stabilization of grain prices, expansion of agricultural production, and an improved distribution of income. As a supplementary measure, however (revealing lack of a total commitment to the principle of laissez faire), Boisguilbert proposed direct government action to support grain prices once they reached a "suitable" level (*Traité des grains,* p. 369).

Aside from the short-run cyclical movement of national income, Boisguilbert also concerned himself with the longer-run problem of secular decline. He estimated that between 1665 and 1695 the national income of France declined by about 50 percent (*Détail,* p. 163)—a direct consequence of the failure of aggregate demand due to an oppressive system of taxation. This opened up the third front of Boisguilbert's attack on mercantilism: the French tax system. Chief offenders in this system were the *taille,* the *aides,* and the *douanes.*

The *taille* was a property tax, divided into a levy on real property and another on personal property. The problem was not so much with the tax as with its incidence. Nobility and clergy were exempt from the tax, so that its burden pressed almost exclusively on the poorest proprietors. Administration of the *taille* was also capricious, often depending on the aggressiveness and persistence of the local "tax farmer" or on an arbitrary assessment of ability to pay. Boisguilbert reported how even in the same parish the effective tax rate could vary between 0.33 and 33 percent (*Détail,* p. 172).

Almost as damaging to consumption were the *aides* and the *douanes.* The former was originally a general sales tax, but by the end of the seventeenth century it was confined to a few products only, particularly wine. The wine tax came to be so oppressive that French workers practically ceased drinking wine (the ultimate sacrifice for a Frenchman), foreign buyers turned elsewhere, and vineyards were taken out of cultivation. In 1779, the economist Le Trosne estimated that the *aides* cost the populace of France one hundred forty millions of lost income in order to secure revenue of thirty millions for the king. The *douanes* were duties on goods moving into or out of the kingdom as well as between provinces within the kingdom. The effect of these duties was either to restrict movement of goods altogether or to raise the prices of delivered goods to a prohibitive level, at least for the poor. Taken together, these excise taxes greatly restrained trade, both domestic and foreign. Boisguilbert blamed them for the destruction of France's foreign markets in wines, hats, playing cards, tobacco pipes, and whalebone (*Détail,* p. 196).

The Physiocrats (see below) were later to react against the same oppressive tax system that confronted Boisguilbert and his contemporaries. But their intent was to substitute a natural system of finances for arbitrary reform, which is what they attributed to Boisguilbert. The link between Boisguilbert and the Physiocrats is tenuous because Boisguilbert did not anticipate either the concept of a *net product* or the exclusive productivity of agriculture. But on matters of tax reform, the Physiocrats echoed much the same concerns as Boisguilbert, who advocated an end to the regressive nature of taxes and a more equitable distribution of the tax burden. Whereas Boisguilbert sought this end so as to release the shackles on consumption, the Physiocrats had their eyes set on the salutary effects of tax reform on capital accumulation, as we shall soon see.

Physiocracy: "The Rule of Nature"

Every new science requires a philosophy, and the philosophy of capitalism that Adam Smith would soon enunciate so well was emerging, cocoonlike, by the middle of the eighteenth century. At this time a group of French writers arose to claim the name "economists." This group composed the first real "school of thought" in economics. They would later be renamed "Physiocrats," because the word "economist" took on a more generic meaning. The term "physiocracy" means "rule of nature." It is appropriate in this case because the writers in question believed in natural law and in the primacy of agriculture.

The intellectual leader of the Physiocrats was François Quesnay, court physician to Madame de Pompadour and Louis XV. Quesnay and the small group of disciples he gathered about him pushed back the theoretical frontiers of the new science and infused it with an underlying philosophy. Physiocracy appealed to rational principles: it asserted that all social facts are linked together in the bonds of inevitable laws, which would be obeyed by individuals and governments once they understood these laws. Physiocratic doctrine exerted a major influence on Adam Smith, who was an acquaintance of Quesnay.

In this chapter we shall treat the Physiocrats as a group, although like the mercantilists, they were a heterogeneous group. The publications of this group followed fairly closely on each other between 1756 and 1778. Its members included the Marquis de Mirabeau, Mercier de la Rivière, Dupont de Nemours, Le Trosne, and Nicolas Baudeau. The French minister Turgot was sympathetic to physiocratic doctrine but did not consider himself one of the inner circle.

The kind of complaints voiced by Boisguilbert at the turn of the eighteenth century were not heeded by France's then-reigning monarch, Louis XIV, nor by his next two successors to the throne. Louis XV was the last French king to exercise unrestrained royal power, and the consequences of this fact were far more injurious to France under him than under his predecessor, the "Sun King." Louis XV plunged France into unnecessary wars that depleted the state treasury. His subjects (nobility always exempted) strained under an oppressive tax system that was called on to assuage the effects of disastrous wars and an extravagant, degenerate court life presided over by the infamous Madame de Pompadour.

Land values were falling as a consequence of declining agricultural output. Two-thirds of French land was owned by clergy and nobility, each of whom was exempt from taxation. Common farmers were required to pay a large share of their produce to the landlord and were heavily taxed on the remainder. Capital accumulation at the level of production was virtually impossible. Domestic markets and personal income were further restricted by the mercantilist policy of lowering wages and other production costs in order to encourage exports. As Lewis Haney so aptly put it, "France was like a great railway or factory which has made no allowance for depreciation or depletion; her productive power was impaired and her credit shaken" (*History of Economic Thought,* p. 176). Physiocracy rose as a response to this state of affairs.

Physiocratic Economics

The Physiocrats were system builders, on a scale slightly grander than that of Cantillon but smaller than that of Adam Smith. In about 1750, Quesnay and his cohort, Vincent Gournay, asked themselves "whether the nature of things did not tend towards a science of political economy, and what the principles of this science were" (cited in Baur, "Studies," p. 100). Under Quesnay's leadership, Physiocracy devoted itself to the discovery of these principles. Its underlying philosophy was the medieval one of natural law *(jus naturae),* but Physiocracy also followed Locke in emphasizing *individual* rights and the justification of private property based on these rights. It was basically a reaction against mercantilism, but ostensibly a very odd one. For at the same time that they advocated free trade and individual self-interest, the Physiocrats continued to eulogize absolute authority. One answer to this apparent paradox is that

> the physiocrats...were a court party, though a radical one. The direct criticism of existing abuses and freedom of language were forbidden them. The only way open to reformers was to oppose to arbitrary power a higher one—the laws of nature. This, therefore, is the true origin of their *jus naturae* (Baur, "Studies," p. 106).

The point of this passage is that although much has been made of the almost metaphysical way in which the Physiocrats appealed to a "natural order" whose arrangements were perfect and whose laws were the will of God, it is more important to look retrospectively at their economic method. What they did is not very different from what economists do today. They proceeded from methodical observation of their world; they arranged and collated facts according to their causes; they tried to form an analytical system based on a theoretical model—a system that agreed with the sound state of a highly civilized country. All of this culminated, for the Physiocrats, in Quesnay's *Tableau Economique,* which was the heart and soul of Physiocratic economics.

Physiocratic Theory   The Physiocrats argued that the best way to trace out the full effects of the oppressive royal policies in France was to conceive the mutual interaction process in any one year as a *circular flow* of income and expenditure. Any policy that had the effect of enlarging the circular flow was therefore consistent with economic growth, whereas any that restricted it was inconsistent with economic growth. The same concept, considerably embellished and elaborated upon, is central to modern macro theory. Quesnay then picked out a key factor in the circular-flow process and analyzed the effects of various policies on the economy as a whole, through their effects on this key factor. (Note the familiar methodology, which economists follow still.)

The key factor that Quesnay selected—and that appears today as the most outstanding fallacy of Physiocratic doctrine—was the exclusive productivity of agriculture. In the *Tableau Économique,* which was Quesnay's own name for his visual representation of the circular flow, manufacturing and service industries are considered "sterile" in the sense that they contribute nothing to the *produit net,* or net product. The net product, in turn, was looked upon as the true source of real wealth. This reasoning involves a peculiar definition of the word "production." To the Physiocrats, production meant creating a surplus; that industry is productive that makes more than is consumed in the process. Manufacturing merely changes the form of goods. The Physiocrats did not deny that such goods become more useful in the process. But only agriculture, they reasoned, is capable of creating additional wealth. If this unique meaning is kept in mind, however strange it may seem from a modern perspective, the doctrines of the Physiocrats will be more easily understood.

The original *Tableau* was an intricate numerical table that traced in zigzag fashion the aggregate income flows between socioeconomic classes. We have opted instead for a simpler graphical representation that nevertheless captures the essence of Quesnay's model. Figure 4-1 divides the economy into three classes, or sectors: (1) a productive class made up entirely of agriculturalists (perhaps also of fishermen and miners); (2) a sterile class consisting of merchants, manufacturers, domestic servants, and professional people; and (3) a proprietary class, including not only landlords but also those who have the slightest title to sovereignty of any kind. Income flows in the diagram are depicted in clockwise motion. The net product (in money terms, net income) is

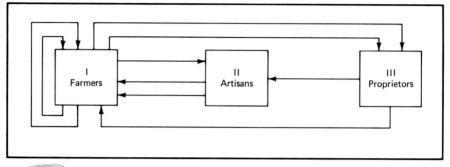

(Each line represents expenditure of one billion Francs)

FIGURE 4-1
Each expenditure made by the farm sector for upkeep, manufactured goods, rents, and taxes is returned to the farm sector by the artisans, proprietors, and the farmers themselves.

produced entirely by the first class and may be used to support its own activities or those of the other two classes.

Using Quesnay's figures and starting with a total wealth of 5 billion francs (inherited from the previous production period), 2 billion francs is assumed necessary for the upkeep of the productive class and its livestock during the year. These are represented in Figure 4-1 as payments from the farm sector to the farm sector. This portion does not circulate. In addition, the farm sector spends 1 billion francs on manufactured goods (and services), which are also necessary to sustain the farmers during the year. The remaining 2 billion francs goes to the proprietors in the form of rents and taxes. This last 2 billion represents the net product, or surplus over necessary costs (the Physiocrats did not consider rents and taxes necessary costs of production, but rather surpluses).

The circuit is completed when the proprietors spend their income (1 billion for food and 1 billion for manufactures) and those in the sterile class spend theirs (1 billion for food and 1 billion for raw materials). Thus the 3 billion francs originally spent by the agriculturalists returns to them, 1 billion coming from the proprietors and 2 billion from the artisans, and the process continues indefinitely. Note, however, that the agriculturalists are the only ones who produce a net product, i.e., more than the costs of sustaining themselves and their agricultural activities.

Physiocratic Policy This summary gives, at best, only a faint idea of the vast complexities involved in tracing the growth of revenues over time—something the Physiocrats were extremely interested in and enthusiastic about. The circular-flow model does give us important insights into their policy prescriptions, however. The Physiocrats sought policies to encourage the accumulation of capital, which was retarded by an excessive tax burden on farmers. Thus they argued for tax reform.

Quesnay had calculated the amount and productivity of capital necessary to attain a sound state of agriculture, and following Cantillon, he was convinced that the application of capital to agriculture was the only way of obtaining a taxable net product. The trick was to meet the needs of the treasury while at the same time doing away with the unreasonable means of assessment that prevented agricultural development. The solution to both problems was simply to tax the landlord. The Physiocrats viewed tax collection in prerevolutionary France as highly inefficient. The most efficient method would simply tax the group that ultimately paid the tax. Since taxes can be paid only out of the net product, they should be levied against those who receive the net product. At the same time, the tax rate set would be sufficient to meet the fiscal needs of the state.

Another source of capital accumulation for agricultural investment was land rent, insofar as landlords were responsible for improvements to the land. The mercantilist restrictions on free trade in the agricultural product, however, kept farm prices (and therefore land rents) low by restricting demand. Thus the Physiocrats argued for free trade. Removal of these restrictions, they felt, and a general "hands-off" policy by government would allow capital to flow freely into the agricultural sector and enable the size of the circular flow to grow over time, in accordance with the "laws of nature."

The tendency at this point might be to view the Physiocrats as enemies of the landed class. Nothing could be further from the truth. The Physiocrats never challenged the institution of private property or the exalted position of the landlords. Instead, they regarded proprietors as valued members of society and as necessary to the development process. After all, it was the proprietor who made the initial investment in clearing arable land and making certain improvements prior to turning the land over to the farmers for cultivation. And for this he was entitled to a share of the annual output. In Physiocratic eyes, unlike Marxian ones, the landlords were the "good guys," not social parasites.

Why, then, would the Physiocrats penalize the landlords by proposing a tax on land rents? The Physiocrats argued that any immediate disadvantage to the proprietors of the tax would be more than offset in the long run by consequential increases in agricultural investment and larger values of net product, and thus larger rents. In short, the landlords were a privileged class, but their responsibilities were considered commensurate to their exalted position in society.

In the final analysis, it is, perhaps, as important to understand *how* the Physiocrats reasoned as it is to understand what they had to say. Like many social writers to follow, they conceived of the economy as fundamentally organic. They viewed it as an extremely complex and delicate amalgam of constituent parts—linked by the mechanism of market exchange—in which any disturbance to one part eventually communicated itself to all other parts through the process of interaction and reaction. Theirs might be called the first general-equilibrium analysis (see Chapter 16), and the analogy should not be missed between this view of the economy and that of the human body commonly held by a physician, which Quesnay was. Anatomically, a disturbance to one part of the body—the stomach, for example—is sooner or later communicated to other parts, which interact and react to compensate for the initial disturbance. In the economy, a disturbance in production brings about a disturbance in demand and vice versa, because of the mutual interdependence of the two.

Criticisms of Physiocracy

Physiocratic economics ran into criticism in its own day, but by and large, as a body of systematic principles it held sway for two decades prior to the appearance of *The Wealth of Nations* in 1776. The Italian Galiani, reacting against Physiocracy, opposed both the idea of a natural order and the attempt to construct economic systems. The French philosopher Condillac correctly refuted the idea that manufactures are sterile and contributed significantly to the theory of value, an issue that only tangentially concerned the Physiocrats, who were more interested in production and distribution than the theory of exchange. But these complaints did not seriously threaten the prestige of the French economists.

Modern criticisms of Physiocracy are usually leveled on one of two fronts: (1) the pure theory of the Physiocrats did not sufficiently accord with the facts of their day, or (2) their theory was overshadowed by normative considerations. The latter criticism implies that their doctrine can be reduced to a mere rationalization of class interests. Each argument has some merit.

The first argument centers on the charge by the Physiocrats that manufacturing is sterile. But what did they really mean by that term? As explained earlier, by "productive" they did not mean the mere capability of creating utility or adding value. Those actions that were looked upon as productive by the Physiocrats certainly had this capability, but so too did most sterile occupations. "The real essence of a 'productive' occupation," says Ronald Meek, "according to the normal Physiocratic use of the term, lay in the inherent capacity to yield a disposable surplus over necessary cost; and the real essence of a 'sterile' occupation lay in its inherent incapacity to yield such a surplus" (*The Economics of Physiocracy*, p. 379).

The Physiocrats argued that manufacturing was sterile in this sense only under conditions of free competition. They were perfectly willing to admit that under monopoly conditions, a value surplus over necessary costs might result from manufacturing. Remember that under competitive conditions, long-run (equilibrium) price is just equal to average total costs of production. And in eighteenth-century France, this observation seemed in accord with the experience of the Physiocrats.

Where the Physiocrats erred badly was in maintaining that manufacturing is "naturally and inherently incapable of yielding a surplus over cost." They mistakenly concluded that because manufacturing was not yielding a value surplus over necessary costs under competitive conditions, it never *could* do so under competitive conditions (in the short run, for example). In this they were wrong, but theirs was more an error of prophecy than an error of fact. And perhaps we ask too much if we demand that economists be seers as well as scientists.

Resolution of one question brings up another, however. If competition reduces the price of manufactured products to the level of necessary costs, why does it not do the same in agriculture, thus wiping out rent? At several points in their writings the Physiocrats seemed to toy with a monopoly explanation of land rent, but in the main their answer was much less satisfactory. They regarded the net product as simply a gift of nature, or of God—a familiar argument in the early history of economic thought. But while nature might explain a surplus of physical output in agriculture, it cannot explain the existence of a *value* surplus. The latter can be explained only by a general theory of value capable of explaining the determination of product and factor prices. The Physiocrats had certain notions of value, but they failed to produce a theory of value. The task of constructing a general theory of value fell to Adam Smith, who responded admirably, as we shall soon see.

The twentieth century has produced two conflicting interpretations of Physiocracy, both of which are aimed at explaining class interests in eighteenth-century France. One view holds that the Physiocrats were merely neomedievalists, seeking to negate the tenets of mercantilism and repair the shortcomings of the old order (Beer, *An Inquiry into Physiocracy*). The other, contrary to the first, maintains that the Physiocrats were reformists seeking to serve the needs and interests of the newly established commoner-landowners (Ware, ''Physiocrats: A Study in Economic Rationalization'').

A more likely interpretation is that the Physiocrats looked in both directions—backward toward feudalism and forward toward capitalism. If this interpretation is correct, then their position in the history of economic thought is both pivotal and transitional. In Physiocratic society the exalted position of the landlord (i.e., the nobility) and the institution of private property would be retained, as under feudalism, but conditions would be right for the emergence of agricultural capitalism. The Physiocrats, in other words, were cautious reformers, unwilling to eclipse the old order entirely but eagerly awaiting the new dawn of capitalism.

In the final analysis the Physiocrats' most permanent imprint on the development of economic analysis was probably their influence on Adam Smith. At the height of their literary activity, Adam Smith made their acquaintance while conducting his own inquiry into the nature and function of capital in an agricultural society. He was thereby exposed to the systematic turn of mind that he later cultivated in himself and demonstrated in his magnum opus, *The Wealth of Nations*. For lack of this same systematic turn of mind in other writers, previous attempts at constructing a general theory of economics in England had not succeeded.

NOTES FOR FURTHER READING

Sir William Petty's writings were collected and published together for the first time in 1899 by Charles Henry Hull (see References). Hull preceded the whole with a lengthy introduction on Petty's life and writings, including the issue of

John Graunt's role in the development of statistics and his probable influence on Petty. On a more modern note, a brief but able study of Petty's economics has become available in English; see Alessandro Roncaglia, *Petty: The Origins of Political Economy* (Armonk, N.Y.: M. E. Sharpe, 1985). A. M. Endres examines Political Arithmetick in general and Petty's use of numbers in "The Functions of Numerical Data in the Writings of Graunt, Petty, and Davenant," *History of Political Economy,* vol. 17 (Summer 1985), pp. 245–264.

The details of Richard Cantillon's life have long been shrouded in mystery, but a provocative new biography by Antoin Murphy, *Richard Cantillon: Entrepreneur and Economist* (Oxford: Clarendon Press, 1986), shows painstaking research and sheds much light on this "mystery man" of economics. A major episode in Cantillon's banking career was his association with John Law's paper money scheme and his connection with the "Mississippi Bubble." For enlightening background on this period, see Earl J. Hamilton, "The Political Economy of France at the Time of John Law," *History of Political Economy,* vol. 1 (1969), pp. 123–149. Jevons hailed his rediscovery of Cantillon in "Richard Cantillon and the Nationality of Political Economy," *Contemporary Review* (January 1881), reprinted in Higgs (see References) along with a biographical essay on Cantillon by Higgs that subsumes two articles he published earlier in the *Economic Journal,* vol. 1 (June 1891), pp. 262–291, and in the *Quarterly Journal of Economics,* vol. 6 (July 1892), pp. 436–456. The Irish economist Joseph Hone, "Richard Cantillon, Economist—Biographical Note," *Economic Journal,* vol. 54 (April 1944), pp. 96–100, sought to establish 1697 as the date of Cantillon's birth, but this claim has been discredited by more recent research. The best overview of Cantillon's work and his role in the history of economics is provided by J. J. Spengler, "Richard Cantillon: First of the Moderns," *Journal of Political Economy,* vol. 62 (August, October, 1954), pp. 281–295, 406–424. Cantillon's monetary theory is discussed briefly in relation to other preclassical theorists in Joseph Ascheim and C. Y. Hsieh, *Macroeconomics: Income and Monetary Theory* (Columbus: Merrill, 1969), pp. 144–146. Other specific aspects of Cantillon's economics are treated in A. M. Huq, "Richard Cantillon and the Multiplier Analysis," *Indian Journal of Economics,* vol. 39 (April 1959), pp. 423–425; Hans Brems, "Cantillon versus Marx: The Land Theory and the Labor Theory of Value, *History of Political Economy,* vol. 10 (Winter 1978), pp. 669–678; Anthony Brewer, "Cantillon and the Land Theory of Value," *History of Political Economy,* vol. 20 (Spring 1988), pp. 1–14; and R. F. Hébert, "Richard Cantillon's Early Contributions to Spatial Economics," *Economica,* vol. 48 (February 1981), pp. 71–77. Several signs show a stirring anew of interest in Cantillon. A new French edition of Cantillon's *Essai,* based on the discovery of a manuscript copy at Rouen, has been published in Japan by Takumi Tsuda, *Richard Cantillon: Essay de la nature du commerce en général* (Tokyo: Kinokuniya Book-Store Co., 1979). Included in this volume is a detailed bibliographic essay by Tsuda. Also, Irish, British, and American economists gathered in 1980 on the coast of California to commemorate the tricentenary of Cantillon's birth (the most frequently cited, but not confirmed, year of Cantillon's birth is 1680). Papers at a three-day symposium on Cantillon's economics were presented by Michael Bordo (Carleton University), William Grampp (University of Illinois, Chicago Circle), Robert Hébert (Auburn University), Antoin Murphy (University of Dublin), David O'Mahony (University College, Cork), Vincent Tarascio (University of North Carolina), and E. G. West (Carleton University). Most of these papers, and their accompanying discussion, have been reprinted in *The Journal of Libertarian Studies,* vol. 7 (Fall 1985).

The standard reference on Boisguilbert is Hazel Roberts's *Boisguilbert, Economist of the Reign of Louis XIV* (New York: Columbia University Press, 1935), but see also J. J. Spengler, "Boisguilbert's Economic Views vis-a-vis those of Contemporary Réformateurs," *History of Political Economy,* vol. 16 (Spring 1984), pp. 69–88. C. W. Cole (see References) devotes part of his work to Boisguilbert (pp. 231–267) as, in even larger measure, does J. H. Bast, *Vauban and Boisguilbert* (Groningen: P. Noordhoff, 1935). Boisguilbert's role as an early precursor of Keynes is aptly treated by S. L. McDonald, "Boisguilbert: Neglected Precursor of Aggregate Demand Theorists," *Quarterly Journal of Economics,* vol. 68 (August 1954), pp. 401–414.

The Physiocrats helped pioneer the deductive method in economics while emerging as the first group of economic model builders. The logico-deductive background of eighteenth-century French thought is explored by Daniel Klein, "Deductive Economic Methodology in the French Enlightenment: Condillac and Destutt de Tracy," *History of Political Economy,* vol. 17 (Spring 1985), pp. 51–72; and by Martin S. Staum, "The Institute Economists: From Physiocracy to Entrepreneurial Capitalism," *History of Political Economy,* vol. 19 (Winter 1987), pp. 525–550. The standard general guide to Physiocracy for many years has been Henry Higgs, *The Physiocrats* (London: Macmillan, 1897), but it is now considered somewhat outdated. Also dated, but still accessible, is the treatment given the Physiocrats by Charles Gide and Charles Rist in their textbook *A History of Economic Doctrines from the Time of the Physiocrats to the Present Day,* R. Richards (trans.), 2d ed. (Boston: Heath, 1948). Much of the Physiocratic literature is now available in English, thanks to Meek (see References). Stephan Baur (see References) examines the role of economic thought prior to the Physiocrats, as well as the influence of the Physiocrats on Adam Smith. As noted in the text, conflicting interpretations of Physiocracy exist between Beer (see References) and Ware (see References). D. C. Carbaugh attempted a reconciliation between the two opposing views in "The Nature of Physiocratic Society: An Attempted Synthesis of the Beer-Ware Interpretations," *American Journal of Economics and Sociology,* vol. 33 (April 1972), pp. 199–207. M. Kuczynski and R. L. Meek (eds.), *Quesnay's Tableau Économique* (London: Macmillan, 1972), reveal the extraordinary story of the disappearance and reappearance of successive editions of the *Tableau.* Joseph Schumpeter's *History of Economic Analysis* (New York: Oxford University Press, 1954), part II, Chap. 4, deals with Petty and Cantillon as well as with the Physiocrats.

Some notable attempts to trace the origins of Physiocratic thought are to be found in R. S. Franklin, "The French Socioeconomic Environment in the Eighteenth Century and Its Relation to the Physiocrats," *American Journal of Economics and Sociology,* vol. 21 (July 1962), pp. 299–307; O. H. Taylor, "Economics and the Idea of 'Jus Naturale,'" *Quarterly Journal of Economics,* vol. 44 (February 1930), pp. 205–241; and L. A. Maverick, "Chinese Influences upon the Physiocrats," *Economic History,* vol. 3 (February 1938), pp. 54–67. Along the same lines, see Bert Hoselitz, "Agrarian Capitalism, the Natural Order of Things: François Quesnay," *Kyklos,* vol. 21 (1968), pp. 637–662.

Two articles that discuss the relation of Quesnay to the rest of the Physiocrats are T. P. Neill, "The Physiocrats' Concept of Economics," *Quarterly Journal of Economics,* vol. 63 (November 1949), pp. 532–553; and "Quesnay and Physiocracy," *Journal of the History of Ideas,* vol. 9, no. 2 (1948), pp. 153–173. Mary Jean Bowman, "The Consumer in the History of Economic Doctrine," *American Economic Review,* vol. 41 (May 1951), pp. 1–18, discusses, among other things, the views of the Physiocrats. Their doctrines of foreign trade in relation to mercantilist and classical ideas are investigated by A. I. Bloomfield in "The Foreign Trade Doctrines of the Physiocrats," *American Economic Review,* vol. 28 (December 1938), pp. 716–735.

An intriguing interpretation of Physiocratic tax reform is found in Luigi Einaudi, "The Physiocratic Theory of Taxation," in *Economic Essays in Honor of Gustav Cassel* (London: G. Allen, 1933). Physiocratic policy and institutions come to the fore in two articles by W. J. Samuels: "The Physiocratic Theory of Property and State," *Quarterly Journal of Economics,* vol. 75 (February 1961), pp. 96–111; and "The Physiocratic Theory of Economic Policy," *Quarterly Journal of Economics,* vol. 76 (February 1962), pp. 145–162.

The tableau as an analytical device has attracted the attention of several writers; see Almarin Phillips, "The Tableau Économique as a Simple Leontief Model," *Quarterly Journal of Economics,* vol. 69 (February 1955), pp. 137–144; I. Hishiyama, "The Tableau Économique of Quesnay," *Kyoto University Economic Review* (April 1960), pp. 1–46; T. Barna, "Quesnay's Tableau in Modern Guise," *Economic Journal,* vol. 85 (September 1975), pp. 485–496; and L. Herlitz, "The Tableau Économique and the Doctrine of Sterility," *Scandinavian Economic History Review,* vol. 9 (1961), pp. 3–55. J. J. Spengler offers some important insights as to how the Physiocratic theory of consumption may have contributed to one of the cornerstones of classical economic theory in "The Physiocrats and Say's Law of Markets," *Journal of Political Economy,* vol. 53 (September 1945), pp. 193–211; and J. Johnson treads similar ground in "The Role of Spending in Physiocratic Theory," *Quarterly Journal of Economics,* vol. 80 (November 1966), pp. 612–632. A major reinterpretation of Quesnay and his system has been undertaken by W. A. Eltis, in two parts, "François Quesnay: A Reinterpretation," *Oxford Economic Papers,* vol. 27 (July and November, 1975), pp. 167–200, 327–351. See also A. C. Muller,

"Quesnay's Theory of Growth: A Comment," *Oxford Economic Papers,* vol. 30 (March 1978), pp. 150–156; and the further comment by Eltis immediately following Muller's remarks.

In a series of papers spanning several years, Gianni Vaggi has been systematically exploring key aspects of physiocratic thought. See, for example, "The Physiocratic Theory of Prices," *Contributions to Political Economy,* vol. 2 (March 1983), pp. 1–22; "A Physiocratic Model of Relative Prices and Income Distribution," *Economic Journal,* vol. 95 (December 1985), pp. 928–947; "The Role of Profits in Physiocratic Economics," *History of Political Economy,* vol. 17 (Fall 1985), pp. 367–384; and *The Economics of François Quesnay* (London: Macmillan, 1987).

The writings of individual Physiocrats tend to be scattered and inaccessible. A notable exception concerns the most able of Quesnay's followers, Turgot. Most of Turgot's economic writings have been collected and translated by R. L. Meek, *Turgot on Progress, Economics and Sociology* (London: Cambridge University Press, 1973); and by P. D. Groenewegen, *The Economics of A. R. J. Turgot* (The Hague: Martinus Nijhoff, 1977). See also the latter's "A Reappraisal of Turgot's Theory of Value, Exchange and Price Determination," *History of Political Economy,* vol. 2 (Spring 1970), pp. 177–196; and "A Reinterpretation of Turgot's Theory of Capital and Interest," *Economic Journal,* vol. 81 (June 1971), pp. 327–340. For a summary of the economic writings of a Physiocrat who later expatriated to America, see J. J. McLain, *The Economic Writings of DuPont de Nemours* (Newark, Del.: University of Delaware Press, 1977).

Finally, for a broad sweep of French economic thought (including Cantillon) in the century prior to Adam Smith, see R. F. Hébert, "In Search of Economic Order: French Predecessors of Adam Smith," in S. Todd Lowry (ed.), *Pre-Classical Economic Thought* (Boston: Kluwer, 1987), pp. 185–210.

REFERENCES

Bacon, Francis. *The New Organon and Related Writings,* F. H. Anderson (ed.). New York: The Liberal Arts Press, 1960.

Baur, Stephan. "Studies on the Origin of the French Economists," *Quarterly Journal of Economics,* vol. 5 (1890), pp. 100–107.

Beer, Max. *An Inquiry into Physiocracy.* New York: Russell & Russell, 1966 [1939].

Boisguilbert, Pierre. *Le Détail de la France* [1695]. Reprinted in Daire.

———. *Traité de la nature, culture, commerce et interet des grains* [1707]. Reprinted in Daire.

Cantillon, Richard. *Essai sur la nature de la commerce en général,* H. Higgs (ed.). London: Macmillan, 1931 [1755].

Cole, C. W. *French Mercantilism 1683–1700.* New York: Columbia University Press, 1943.

Daire, Eugene. *Economistes financiers du 18ᵉ siècle.* Paris: Guillaumin, 1851.

Haney, L. W. *History of Economic Thought,* 4th ed. New York: Macmillan, 1949.

Meek, R. L. *The Economics of Physiocracy: Essays and Translations*. Cambridge, Mass: Harvard University Press, 1962.

Petty, William. *The Economic Writings of Sir William Petty*, 2 vols., C. H. Hull (ed.). New York: A. M. Kelley, 1963.

Schumpeter, Joseph A. *History of Economic Analysis*, E. B. Schumpeter (ed.). New York: Oxford University Press, 1954.

Ware, N. J. "Physiocrats: A Study in Economic Rationalization," *American Economic Review*, vol. 21 (December 1931), pp. 607–619.

JOHN MAYNARD KEYNES   KARL MARX   ALFRED MARSHALL   WILLIAM STANLEY JEVONS   ADAM SMITH

5

ADAM SMITH: SYSTEM BUILDER

INTRODUCTION

That new dawn of capitalism that the Physiocrats so eagerly looked forward to had not yet arrived in 1776—when many European eyes were focused on the New World and the struggles of an emerging nation—but it was certainly on its way. And it was helped along, intellectually, by the publication in that year of a book that is still read and still published (not just by and for graduate students, incidentally): Adam Smith's *Inquiry into the Nature and Causes of the Wealth of Nations*. Any book that is read and reprinted two hundred years after its initial appearance deserves attention, and in this case, the attention is not misplaced.

Adam Smith was born in Kircaldy, Scotland, in 1723, the only son of a father who had died a few months before and a mother who lived to the ripe old age of ninety. From his youth, Smith exhibited the signs of what psychiatrists might call the "professorial syndrome." His biographers describe him as an apt pupil, although given to "fits of abstraction," which later in his academic life turned to fits of reverie that frequently disturbed his colleagues (when he was observed smiling to himself at religious services, for example). In one of his early morning reveries, Smith walked 15 miles clad only in a nightgown before the church bells from a neighboring village "awakened" him. On another occasion, while walking with a friend, he is reported to have begun a lively discourse during which, not noticing his whereabouts, he fell into a tanning pit! On yet another occasion he is said to have absentmindedly dropped his bread and butter into boiling water, subsequently declaring the concoction the worst cup of tea he had ever tasted.

Although not a handsome man, Smith's other charms endeared him to his friends and students. He might be described, unkindly, as an "amalgam of protrusions.'' One cameo portrait of him reveals a protruding lower lip, a large nose, and bulging eyes. Moreover, he was troubled all his life with a nervous affliction; his head shook, and he had a speech impediment. Yet none of these flaws impaired his intellectual abilities. He described himself as ''a beau in nothing but my books.'' To be sure, he was among the leading philosophers of his day. At the University of Glasgow and later at Oxford, Smith lectured on natural theology, ethics, jurisprudence, and political economy. He was a student of Frances Hutcheson, a friend of David Hume, and an acquaintance of Quesnay. Students traveled from Russia and the Continent to attend his lectures.

In his own age, Smith's reputation as a philosopher rested largely on his very important work, *The Theory of Moral Sentiments,* first published in 1759. That work was an attempt to identify the origins of moral judgments, or moral approval and disapproval. In it Smith perceived man as a creature of self-interest who nevertheless seemed capable of making moral judgments on the basis of considerations other than selfishness. This apparent paradox is resolved, Smith charged, through the faculty of sympathy. That is, moral judgments are typically made by holding self-interest in abeyance and putting oneself in the position of a third-person, impartial observer. In this way, one reaches a sympathetic notion of morality rather than a selfish one, and morality actually transcends selfishness.

The Theory of Moral Sentiments and its problems attracted immediate interest and fame for its author. But many historians of economic thought have tended to view it as inconsistent with the importance Smith later placed on self-interest as a driving force in *The Wealth of Nations.* Informed opinion tends to view *The Wealth of Nations* as a logical extension of *The Theory of Moral Sentiments,* although that is by far not a unanimous judgment.

NATURE OF SMITH'S ECONOMIC SYSTEM

Adam Smith is today considered the father of economics because he was above all a system builder. There is evidence that he began to construct a general system of analysis two decades before the publication of *The Wealth of Nations,* and the outlines of that system were clearly visible before 1776. Smith's system combined a theory of human nature and a theory of history with a peculiar form of natural theology and some hardheaded observations of economic life. Narrowed to the economic sphere, his system featured the activities of agriculture, manufacturing, and commerce. Exchange in this system is facilitated by the use of money, and production is characterized by the division of labor. The three main features of his central analysis are the division of labor, the analysis of price and allocation, and the nature of economic growth.

Smith's accomplishments in the field of economics not only tended to render economics a serious and separate discipline of scientific inquiry but also marked the beginning of what is called the classical period in economic thought. This period extends roughly from the appearance of *The Wealth of Nations* in 1776 to the death of John Stuart Mill in 1873. Although individual differences in ideas persisted among members of the classical school, commonly held principles included belief in natural liberty (laissez faire) and the importance of economic growth as a means of bettering the condition of man's existence.[1] These two ideas, which are to be found in Physiocratic doctrine, underlie *The Wealth of Nations* as well.

Natural Law and Property Rights

In Adam Smith's day, economics was a new discipline, broadly defined as "political economy." The chief political and economic problem that Smith set out to define and resolve was the relation of the individual to the state and the proper functions of the state in relation to its members. Smith's views on these matters were grounded in his system of natural theology expounded at considerable length in *The Theory of Moral Sentiments* and carried forward, with some modifications, to *The Wealth of Nations*. That theology was none other than the Greek-Scholastic doctrine of natural law, albeit infused with Scottish common sense.

The Physiocrats, of course, had extolled a natural order based on natural law as opposed to positive law. For them, natural law reflected the mind of the creator, as inferred by human reason. Inasmuch as natural law had a higher sanction than positive law, which was the mere proclamations of a legislative assembly, positive law was thereby inferior; the less of it the better. Having come this far, they were clearly at the threshold of laissez faire as an integument of natural law. Both the Physiocrats and Adam Smith argued in essentially this vein.

Sir Alexander Gray has pointed out that "natural law is easier to talk about than to codify. But we come pretty near the core of things when we regard natural law as concerned with the personal property each individual has in himself, and as a groping effort to emphasize that there is a body of 'Rights of Man' existing anterior to, and if need be against, the State. To express it in terms nearer our subject, 'Natural Law' implied a restriction of the functions of government, in the interests of the liberty of the individual" ("Adam Smith," p. 155). All through *The Wealth of Nations* and its predecessor, *The Theory of Moral Sentiments,* Smith explained how the divine government of the universe reacts on our immediate economic and political problems. One such example is Smith's justly famous passage on the "invisible hand":

> Every individual necessarily labours to render the annual revenue of the society as great as he can. He generally, indeed, neither intends to promote the public interest, nor knows how much he is promoting it. By preferring the support of domestic to

---

[1] Although he falls within the classical period, John Stuart Mill was somewhat of an exception on both these points (see Chap. 8).

that of foreign industry, he intends only his own security; and by directing that industry in such a manner as its produce may be of the greatest value, he intends only his own gain, and he is in this, as in many other cases, led by an invisible hand to promote an end which was no part of his intention. Nor is it always the worse for the society that it was no part of it. By pursuing his own interest he frequently promotes that of the society more effectively than when he really intends to promote it. I have never known much good done by those who affected to trade for the public good. It is an affectation, indeed, not very common among merchants, and very few words need be employed in dissuading them from it (*Wealth of Nations*, p. 423).

Another passage strikes at the futility of central planning, the ineptness of the bureaucrat and the politician:

The man of system...is apt to be very wise in his own conceit; and is often so enamored with the supposed beauty of his own ideal plan of government, that he cannot suffer the smallest deviation from any part of it. He goes on to establish it completely, and in all its parts, without any regard either to the great interests, or to the strong prejudices which may oppose it. He seems to imagine that he can arrange the different members of a great society with as much ease as the hand arranges the different pieces upon a chess-board. He does not consider that the pieces upon the chess-board have no other principle of motion besides that which the hand impresses upon them; but that, in the great chess-board of human society, every single piece has a principle of motion of its own, altogether different from that which the legislature might choose to impress upon it (*Theory of Moral Sentiments*, pp. 380–381).

These passages indicate Smith's conviction that a natural harmony exists in the economic world that makes government interference in most matters both unnecessary and undesirable. The invisible hand, the doctrine of natural liberty, the wisdom of God (seen even in the folly of men) are all part of the argument. But there is a foundation underfoot stronger than mere metaphysics. There is the empirical argument on which Smith also depended that indicts government as incompetent in *fact* and underscores the brazen impertinence of the bureaucrat telling us what to do in areas where we clearly know our own interests much better than anyone else ever can. In this view there is a very clear line of influence between Adam Smith and his contemporary champion, Milton Friedman (see Chapter 20).

Human Nature

The inexpediency of control and the desirability of natural liberty become even more compelling when we consider the mechanism that drives Smith's society. Smith was neither a strict rationalist nor an idle dreamer. He was a hardheaded realist who took people as he found them and based his analysis of society on an unchanging human character. According to Smith, there were two innate features of the psychology of humans. The first is that as humans we are interested primarily in things nearest us, much less so in things at a distance (in either time or space); thus, we are all of considerable importance to ourselves:

> Every man...is first and principally recommended to his own care; and every man is certainly, in every respect fitter and abler to take care of himself than of any other person (*Theory of Moral Sentiments,* p. 359).

The second characteristic, which is actually a corollary of the first, is the overwhelming desire of every man to better his condition:

> ...the desire of bettering our condition [is] a desire which, though generally calm and dispassionate, comes with us from the womb, and never leaves us till we go to the grave. In the whole interval which separates those two moments, there is scarce perhaps a single instant in which any man is so perfectly and completely satisfied with his situation, as to be without any wish of alteration or improvement of any kind (*Wealth of Nations,* pp. 324–325).

Put in the more narrow terms of our subject, humans are *self-interested,* a characteristic not necessarily synonymous with selfishness. Smith's "economic" man in *The Wealth of Nations* is not unlike his "moral" man in *The Theory of Moral Sentiments.* Both are creatures of self-interest. In *The Theory of Moral Sentiments,* sympathy is that human faculty which holds self-interest in check, whereas in *The Wealth of Nations,* competition is the economic faculty that restrains self-interest. In fact, competition ensures that the pursuit of self-interest will improve the economic welfare of society. In Smith's day this was a liberal idea, because it implied that a society without extensive government controls would not degenerate into chaos, as might be supposed. Monopoly, on the other hand, represents unbridled self-interest and the consequent destruction of economic welfare. Although all sellers of goods and services would like to charge the highest possible prices for their wares or skills, they generally cannot, unless they have some monopoly privilege, which in Smith's day was granted by government. Competition, or the absence of monopoly, will force all sellers to lower their prices (within limits) to attract more customers, and the natural outcome of that action is lower consumer prices and improved economic welfare. To the economist, some of Smith's most memorable passages contain invectives against monopoly privileges. In one of his more lasting sayings, Smith declared: "People of the same trade seldom meet together, even for merriment and diversion, but the conversation ends in a conspiracy against the public, or in some contrivance to raise prices" (*Wealth of Nations,* p. 128). Elsewhere, he observed: "Monopoly...is a great enemy to good management, which can never be universally established but in the consequence of that free and universal competition which forces everybody to have recourse to it for the sake of self-defense" (*Wealth of Nations,* p. 147).

A Theory of History: Self-Interest and Economic Growth

In Adam Smith's view, self-interest, the development of property rights, and the division of labor were all intertwined in the historical process of economic growth. Appreciation of this fact is important for an understanding of Smith's macroeconomics in the "commercial age."

Smith's conceptual history of civilization identified four evolutionary

stages. The first two were the hunting and pastoral periods of prefeudal, nomadic cultures. These were followed by the farming stage, and finally by the
commercial era. Each stage is marked by a somewhat different structure of
property rights. A hunting culture does not recognize exclusive rights to property. All members of society stand on a relatively equal footing, both economically and socially, and there is little demand for a formal structure of civil government because the population is small and nomadic. In such a culture, the
old and the wise generally provide leadership, and subordination is self-
imposed by the rest of society in the face of experience and superior intellect.

Over time, however, self-interest brings about important sociopolitical evolution and economic growth. Civil society is to a major extent a consequence
of private property and the accumulation of wealth. Smith considered the key
role played by the shepherds in the pastoral stage of history:

> It is in the age of shepherds, in the second period of society, that the inequality of
> fortune first begins to take place, and introduces among men a degree of authority
> and subordination which could not possibly exist before. It thereby introduces some
> degree of that civil government which is indispensably necessary for its own
> preservation....Civil government, so far as it is instituted for the security of prop-
> erty, is in reality instituted for the defense of the rich against the poor, or of those
> who have some property against those who have none at all (*Wealth of Nations*, p.
> 674).

In other words, in civil society a wealth hierarchy leads to a power hierarchy
with its familiar accoutrements, hereditary transfers of power, courts, and so
forth. The poor in this structure of things grant their allegiance in return for
protection from the rich.

Eventually, nomadic cultures tend to be replaced by stationary, agricultural
communities. With this settled life comes more stable food supplies, increased
specialization, and larger population. In the Middle Ages, this kind of society
became encased in the institutional structure known as feudalism. Civil government under feudalism was greatly decentralized insofar as each of the ma-
norial barons administered justice in his local domain. In Europe, this system
lasted from the fall of the Roman Empire to about the end of the fifteenth century. Its structure is still approximated in some third world nations today.

As self-interest was responsible for the transition from nomadic to agricultural societies, so it explained for Smith the development of commercial society with its consequent growth of cities as trading centers. In the immediate
period after the fall of Rome, urban tradesmen and mechanics were given
equal tax treatment with their rural counterparts, the farmers. As particular
city dwellers became more independent, however, they succeeded in getting a
general exemption from certain "trading taxes." They therefore emerged as an
early class of "free traders," and indeed, as the first capitalists. Townspeople,
moreover, were usually allied with the monarch against a common foe, the
land barons. The king often granted concessions to the cities in return for their
allegiance against the feudal lords, and fiscal independence could be obtained

by the cities in return for a lump-sum tax paid to the king. These developments led to self-governance in the towns and the consequent establishment of a rule of law, which in turn provided a firm base for the expansion of trade, particularly in the coastal cities. Flourishing trade, in turn, made the cities even more independent of the manors. Ultimately towns became the haven of fledgling capitalists because city law protected runaway serfs provided they had evaded capture for one year. Smith underscored this tendency in the following passage:

> If in the hands of a poor cultivator, oppressed with the servitude of villeinage, some little stock should be accumulated, he would naturally conceal it with great care from his master, to whom it would otherwise have belonged, and take the first opportunity of running away to a town (*Wealth of Nations,* p. 379).

Serfdom was an institution in which peasants were tied to the land and owed a certain amount of labor to the landlord. But as peasants accumulated small surpluses, they found that they could "buy back" this obligation by paying money rents to the landlords in lieu of labor services. First the surpluses were exchanged for money at the local grain markets; then the money was used to "commute" their labor obligation. This often resulted in a situation in which the peasant became very nearly an independent, small businessman. He could rent from the lord, sell the produce to cover his rent, and keep the difference for himself. The cumulative effect of this behavior was to erode the traditional ties of the manor and to substitute the market and the search for profits as the organizing principle of production. By the middle of the fourteenth century money rents exceeded the value of labor services in many parts of Europe.

The lords seemed willing to cooperate with the new institutional arrangements, in part because of a change in their consumption patterns, which required increasing amounts of cash to buy "trinkets" and luxuries from the town merchants. Before long, the lord of the manor was a mere landlord in the modern sense; soon a "market" in land emerged, based on an individual's right to own property and supported by the law of contract. From this point it was a short step to specialization and the division of labor—the hallmarks of the industrial age.

In sum, economic growth up to the appearance of the "commercial system" was a consequence of the interaction of self-interest, property-rights modifications, and institutional change in the wider sense. With the commercial system having arrived by 1776, Smith thereupon declared economic growth to depend in a critical way on the extension of specialization and division of labor. We shall return to the central role of these twin principles after reviewing the microeconomic foundations of Smith's growth theory.

It is difficult, if not impossible, to appreciate a book without having read it, and in the case of *The Wealth of Nations* reading it through is indeed a formidable undertaking. But it is a task that every serious student of economics should attempt (at least once). For the book contains much more than Smith's celebrated attack on mercantilism (monopolies) and his justification of natural liberty (laissez faire), for which it is best known. It is, in fact, a marvelous work, even by twentieth-century standards. And it was not a late-blooming classic, as were so many other economic treatises. It was widely read and quoted during Smith's lifetime.

In many ways the least-read parts of the book are the most delightful, as when Smith digresses on the history of education in the Middle Ages or the method of selecting bishops in the ancient church. Yet despite its digressions, *The Wealth of Nations* contains important and relevant economic analysis.

A brief review of the contents of *The Wealth of Nations* reveals its extreme breadth of treatment. Book I treats of the division of labor, of the origin and use of money, and of the determination of price, wages, profits, and rent, with a lively digression thrown in on variations in the value of silver. Book II contains Smith's oft-maligned theory of capital and interest. In Book III the reader is treated to a lengthy review of the economic development of Europe from ancient times to the eighteenth century. Book IV discusses different systems of political economy, including a scathing criticism of mercantilism and barriers to free trade. Book V concludes with a lengthy treatise on taxation and fiscal policy in eighteenth-century Britain. Not surprisingly, few economists today can boast of having read the entire book from cover to cover!

The Microeconomic Foundations of The Wealth of Nations

For all its diverse coverage of numerous economic topics, the central theme of *The Wealth of Nations,* as of Physiocratic doctrine, is economic growth. Whereas the Physiocrats focused on growth of net product, Smith emphasized growth in national wealth (by which he meant, in today's terminology, national income). But more than the Physiocrats, Smith succeeded in initiating inquiry into a *theory of value,* thus overcoming a major deficiency of Physiocratic analysis. In other words, Smith's macroeconomic concern for economic growth rested, as it should have, on certain microeconomic foundations, notably the theory of value.

The Theory of Value   The chapter on value in *The Wealth of Nations* is preceded by a discussion of the advantages of division of labor and the use of money in advanced societies. The division of labor, Smith charged, arises from a propensity in human nature to exchange, for which each trader must have a surplus over his or her immediate needs with which to trade. Money enters the picture because it makes trade more convenient insofar as it is generally acceptable and portable. Value then is determined by the rules that people naturally observe in exchanging goods for money or for one another.

Smith posed the problem of value in terms of the following paradox:

> The word value...has two different meanings, and sometimes expresses the utility of some particular object, and sometimes the power of purchasing other goods which the possession of that object conveys. The one may be called "value in use";

the other, "value in exchange." The things which have the greatest value in use have frequently little or no value in exchange; and on the contrary, those which have the greatest value in exchange have frequently little or no value in use. Nothing is more useful than water: but it will purchase scarce anything; scarce anything can be had in exchange for it. A diamond, on the contrary, has scarce any value in use, but a very great quantity of other goods may frequently be had in exchange for it (*Wealth of Nations*, p. 28).

As we shall see, classical economics was incapable of solving this paradox of value, or the discrepancy between *value in use* and *value in exchange*, because as a group, the classical economists did not attempt to explain the existence and significance of marginal (i.e., incremental) valuations in the marketplace. As for Smith, he set out to explain only exchange value, or relative price, and its changes over time.

Labor as a Measure of Value Book I, Chaps. 5 to 7, of *The Wealth of Nations* contains the core of Smith's discussion of exchange value. Subsequent interpretations of Smith on this point have often been confused by the fact that in these chapters he seemed to discuss simultaneously both the *measure* of value (price) and the *cause* of value. In Chap. 5, for example, he states:

> The value of any commodity...to the person who possesses it, and who means not to use or consume it himself, but to exchange it for other commodities, is equal to the quantity of labour which it enables him to purchase or command. Labour, therefore, is the real measure of the exchangeable value of all commodities (*Wealth of Nations*, p. 30).

This idea, that what is bought with money or with goods is purchased by labor, seems to have been acquired by Smith from his friend David Hume, although the same idea was expressed by another of Smith's predecessors, Sir William Petty (see Chapter 4). There are, however, certain practical and theoretical difficulties in a labor theory of value, and Smith revealed his awareness of these problems:

> It is often difficult to ascertain the proportion between two different quantities of labour. The time spent in two different sorts of work will not always alone determine this proportion. The different degrees of hardship endured, and of ingenuity exercised, must likewise be taken into account. There may be more labour in an hour's hard work than in two hours easy business; or in an hour's application to a trade which it cost ten years labour to learn, than in a month's industry at an ordinary and obvious employment. But it is not easy to find any accurate measure either of hardship or ingenuity. In exchanging indeed the different productions of different sorts of labour for one another, some allowance is commonly made for both. It is adjusted, however, not by any accurate measure, but by the higgling and bargaining of the market, according to that sort of rough equality which, though not exact, is sufficient for carrying on the business of common life (*Wealth of Nations*, p. 31).

Prices Money is, of course, the most common measure of value, but Smith was likewise aware of the shortcomings of monetary measures, since the value of money itself changes over time. Thus he took pains in the rest of Chap. 5 to distinguish carefully between *real* and *nominal* prices. He pointed out, for example, that:

> Labour, like commodities, may be said to have a real and nominal price. Its real price may be said to consist in the quantity of the necessaries and conveniences of life which are given for it; its nominal price, in the quantity of money. The labourer is rich or poor, is ill or well rewarded, in proportion to the real, not the nominal, price of his labor (*Wealth of Nations,* p. 33).

In Chap. 6, Smith finally makes it clear that when one leaves "that early and rude state of society which precedes both the accumulation of stock and the appropriation of land," labor alone cannot adequately explain market price. Capitalist economies are marked by capital accumulation and individual property rights in land and other resources. Thus in the more advanced societies, according to Smith, market value is resolved into three component parts:

> Wages, profit, and rent are the three original sources of all revenue as well as of all exchangeable value. All other revenue [interest income, taxes, etc.] is ultimately derived from some one or other of these (*Wealth of Nations,* p. 52).

By including profit as one of the necessary components of price, Smith demonstrated an understanding of the concept of opportunity costs. He observed:

> Though in common language what is called the prime cost of any commodity does not comprehend the profit of the person who is to sell it again, yet if he sells it at a price which does not allow him the ordinary rate of profit in his neighborhood, he is evidently a loser by the trade; since by employing his stock in some other way he might have made that profit (*Wealth of Nations,* p. 55).

Notice the natural development of ideas in these two chapters of *The Wealth of Nations.* Many earlier writers had a labor-cost theory of value, and many later writers attributed the same theory to Smith. But his explanation is really something else. It is one thing to charge that the true *measure* of value, in real terms, is labor time, and another to avow that the *source* of value is the necessary costs of production for each commodity. In short, Smith felt that labor theories of value were valid only for primitive societies where labor represents the main (if not the only) factor of production.

Market Price versus Natural Price   Chapter 7 of Book I is filled with what Mark Blaug has called "the kind of 'partial equilibrium analysis' that has always been the bread and butter of economists" (*Economic Theory in Retrospect,* p. 39).

In it, Smith discusses the *natural* and *market* price of commodities. Essentially, Smith set up a dichotomy between actual (i.e., market) price and natural price. The former is determined by the interaction of supply and demand in the short run; the latter, by long-run costs of production. In his own words:

> The market price of every particular commodity is regulated by the proportion between the quantity which is actually brought to market, and the demand of those who are willing to pay the natural price of the commodity, or the whole value of the rent, labour, and profit, which must be paid in order to bring it thither. Such people may be called the effectual demanders, and their demand the effectual demand; since it may be sufficient to effectuate the bringing of the commodity to market. It is different from the absolute demand. A very poor man may be said in some sense to have a demand for a coach and six; he might like to have it; but his demand is not an effectual demand, as the commodity can never be brought to market in order to satisfy it (*Wealth of Nations*, p. 56).

Smith's discussion of actual price and natural price is not inconsistent with the more graphically precise explanation of price offered by Alfred Marshall (see Chapter 15) more than one hundred years later. Marshall's explanation is based on the now familiar concepts of supply and demand *schedules,* concepts that proved remarkably difficult for earlier writers to conceive and explain. It is not at all clear whether Smith thought of price and quantity adjustments in terms of shifting schedules of demand and supply or simply as movements along a given curve (or curves)—if, indeed, he thought of adjustments in this way at all. We use Marshall's analysis to interpret Smith simply to clarify certain theoretical points along the way.

Thus in Figure 5-1 assume some price—say, p_0—equivalent to Smith's natural price. This price is assumed invariant over time and is equal to the sum of the "natural rates of wages, rent, and profit." Smith's concept of effectual demand suggests the existence of a downward-sloping demand curve. The poor beggar who would like to have a coach and six but cannot afford it would eventually purchase one, perhaps, if the price were low enough. Others of varying degrees of wealth might find their demands becoming "effective" at lower prices. Thus in Figure 5-1 assume the existence of demand curve D_0. Smith's effectual demand (i.e., quantity demanded at the natural price) is OQ_0. Barring changes in tastes, incomes, prices of other goods, numbers of demanders and suppliers, and expectations about the future, p_0 and Q_0 would be the long-run equilibrium price and output in the industry under investigation.

Let us now juxtapose Smith's commentary and Figure 5-1:

> When the quantity of any commodity which is brought to market falls short of the effectual demand [Q_1], all those who are willing to pay the whole value of the rent, wages, and profit which must be paid in order to bring it thither, cannot be supplied with the quantity which they want [Q_0]. Rather than want it altogether, some of them will be willing to give more. A competition will immediately begin among them, and the market price will rise more or less above the natural price [to p_1, for example], according as either the greatness of the deficiency or the wealth and wanton luxury of the competitors, happen to animate more or less the eagerness of the competition. Among competitors of equal wealth and luxury the same deficiency will generally occasion more or less eager competition, according as the acquisition of the commodity happens to be of more or less importance to them. Hence the exorbitant price of the necessaries of life during the blockade of a town or in a famine (*Wealth of Nations*, p. 56).

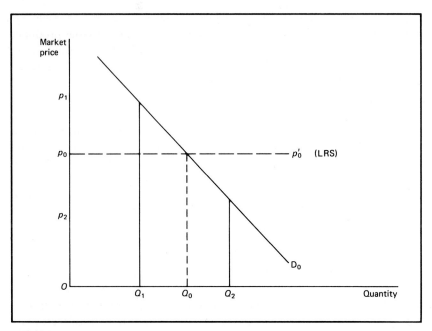

FIGURE 5-1
If Q_1 represents the quantity brought to the market, then the market price will rise above the natural price, from p_0 to p_1.

This last sentence is a clear reference to the importance of demand elasticity in the short run. On the other hand:

> When the quantity brought to market exceeds the effectual demand [Q_2], it cannot be all sold to those who are willing to pay the whole value of the rent, wages, and profit, which must be paid in order to bring it thither. Some part must be sold to those who are willing to pay less, and the low price which they give for it must reduce the price of the whole. The market price will sink more or less below the natural price [to p_2, for example], according as the greatness of the excess increases more or less the competition of the sellers, or according as it happens to be more or less important to them to get immediately rid of the commodity. The same excess in the importation of perishable, will occasion a much greater competition in that of durable commodities...(*Wealth of Nations*, p. 57).

The last sentence in this passage is likewise a clear reference to the importance of supply elasticity in the short run. Finally:

> When the quantity brought to market is just sufficient to supply the effectual demand and no more, the market price naturally comes to be either exactly, or as nearly as can be judged of, the same with the natural price [p_0]. The whole quantity on hand can be disposed of for this price, and cannot be disposed of for more. The competition of the different dealers obliges them to accept of this price, but does not oblige them to accept of less (*Wealth of Nations*, p. 57).

The foregoing analysis clearly hinges on the existence of competition, a rivalry presumed to exist among buyers as well as among sellers of the same product. It is in understanding the nature of competition and its effects, moreover, that Smith made the greatest advance over Scholastic economics and, indeed, launched economic analysis on its modern path. Smith shrewdly recognized that the economic realities of a nascent capitalism made the doctrine of just price superfluous. The "modern" world rested on the existence of atomistic competition, which implies a more or less equal diffusion of economic power. This diffusion of power provides, in turn, an automatic check to the individual *abuse* of power, which was a great concern to the Scholastics. Smith's theory of natural price filled the conditions for economic justice set forth by the church doctors, while it simultaneously rendered the normative concept of just price unnecessary in the "new world" of atomistic competition.

There is evidence that Smith was not entirely comfortable with the abstract notions of price and equilibrium. As a review of Scholastic economics (Chapter 2) clearly shows, there were two competing "theories" vying for center stage: the supply side and the demand side each made its own claim to preeminence. Since market price must cover costs of production over the long haul, value must be a function of the resources used in production. On the other hand, demand makes its own claim to being a determinant of value because people are willing to pay for something in proportion to the intensity of their desire. Smith noted that value can be influenced by utility (demand), but he did not advance this side of the analysis. His contribution to demand theory is pretty much limited to a distinction between absolute demand (aggregate desire) and effectual demand (desire + purchasing power). Effectual demand is the demand of buyers who are willing to pay the "natural price," which is the price sufficient to cover production costs. Smith evidently felt that the "cost theory" of value needed further analysis, and he seemed to want to choose labor as the common denominator underlying the supply-side elements of value. He appeared, moreover, to be groping for an absolute and universal *measure* of value, but he was not successful in this regard. Smith's attempt to resolve the two sets of claims, supply and demand, led to the description of equilibrium outlined above.

There are two points that need to be underscored regarding Smith's performance. The first is that Smith tended to view the natural price not only as an equilibrium ("the central price to which the prices of all commodities are continually gravitating") but as an *invariant* standard over the long run. In modern parlance, he saw the long-run supply curve as being horizontal. In Figure 5-1, the long-run supply curve has the same locus as the dashed line, $p_0\,p_0'$. Since this type of long-run supply curve exists only in industries characterized by constant costs of production, Smith's theory of value fits only a special case. Today economists recognize that many industries produce under conditions of increasing costs, and a few actually produce under conditions of decreasing costs.

The second point is that Smith emphasized the abstract nature of his model by showing how real markets often deviate from the ideal:

> ...though the market price of every particular commodity is in this manner continually gravitating, if one may say so, towards the natural price, yet sometimes particular accidents, sometimes natural causes, and sometimes particular regulations of police, may, in many commodities keep up the market price, for a long time together, a good deal above the natural price (*Wealth of Nations*, p. 59).

Smith's terminology is quaint by modern standards, but what he meant by "accidents" are events that conspire to hold back information from either sellers or buyers. Trade secrets or clandestine production techniques have this effect. "Natural causes" that result in prices above the "natural" level include limited acreage of certain peculiar soils. Oenophiles know, for example, that all the land fit for producing Mouton-Rothschild clarets cannot supply the effectual demand, so that the price of this wine is many times its cost of production. Adam Smith felt that little could be done about the capriciousness of nature, and that trade and manufacturing secrets could not be kept for very long. But government regulations were another story. The British economy in Smith's day contained restrictive practices that prevented the market from reaching equilibrium, thereby limiting the volume of trade, internal and external, hindering the division of labor, and retarding economic growth.

Smith was quick to point out the parallel between government grants of monopoly privileges and trade secrets:

> A monopoly granted either to an individual or to a trading company has the same effect as a secret in trade or manufacturers. The monopolists, by keeping the market constantly under-stocked, by never fully supplying the effectual demand, sell their commodities much above the natural price, and raise their emoluments, whether they consist in wages or profits, greatly above the natural rate (*Wealth of Nations*, p. 61).

In the final analysis, Smith's model of market equilibrium was based on cause and effect, but he took great pains to explain its abstract nature. Economic reality is different from theory because it entails conditions that slow or prevent smooth and certain adjustments to long-run equilibrium. On this score, Smith may be compared to the Physiocrats (see Chapter 4), who viewed the *Tableau Économique* as a rigid form of cause and effect. In their model, a given change in the primary income flows among the three socioeconomic classes of society created exact and continuing changes in national income. Despite his admiration for these "French men of system," Smith felt that the Physiocrats became unwitting captives of their own abstractions. For the Scottish realist, economic life was neither so simple nor so precise.

Perhaps as important as Smith's understanding of the principles that determine the market prices of products was his appreciation of the interdependence between product markets and factor markets. Recognition of this interdependence is basic to Smith's view of long-run price adjustments. He noted, for instance, that if at any time the quantity of a good supplied exceeded the effectual demand:

> Some of the component parts of its price must be paid below their natural rate. If it is rent, the interest of the landlords will immediately prompt them to withdraw a part of their land; and if it is wages or profit, the interest of the labourers in the one case, and of their employers in the other, will prompt them to withdraw a part of their labour or stock from their employment. The quantity brought to market will soon be no more than sufficient to supply the effectual demand. All the different parts of its price will rise to their natural rate, and the whole price to its natural price (*Wealth of Nations*, p. 57).

In other words, according to Smith, product prices cannot be in long-run equilibrium unless factor prices are also in long-run equilibrium. Almost one hundred years later, the French economist Léon Walras (see Chapter 16) developed a mathematical analysis of general economic equilibrium based on the very same principle.

An examination of the words of writers before Adam Smith heightens one's appreciation of the theoretical advance embodied in his theory of natural value. Yet there is something hauntingly tautological in all of it. The theory of natural value explains price in terms of cost of production. But costs are themselves prices. They are payments made to purchase (or hire) the various factors of production. In essence, then, the theory of natural value explains prices by prices. A complete theory of value cannot stop here but must also explain the cause and determination of the payments to each factor of production.

Factors and Their Shares   Actually, Smith did not develop a satisfactory theory of the determination of wages, rent, and profit, but he did offer numerous important insights and contributions that were later expanded by his followers. One could say, for example, that Smith offered as many as three explanations of wages, three explanations of rent, and perhaps two explanations of profit. In what follows, it is not the analytical elegance of Smith's ideas that is emphasized so much as the wide range of penetrating insights that he entertained on the subject of income distribution.

Wages   Smith begins his discussion of wages as he did his discussion of value, by harking back to "that original state of things which precedes both the appropriation of land and the accumulation of stock." In this primitive society, wages are determined by productivity, since, "In that original state of things...the whole produce of labour belongs to the labourer. He has neither landlord nor master to share with him" (*Wealth of Nations*, p. 64).

As soon as land becomes private property, the landlord demands his or her share of the annual produce, and as soon as capital accumulation occurs, the capitalist does likewise. Thus the landlord and the capitalist share in the produce of labor, and according to Smith, once this happens it becomes purposeless to trace further the possible effects of increased labor productivity upon wages. Smith's view in this respect was unfortunate, as subsequent developments in the theory of income distribution will show. Nevertheless, it set the stage for his development of the classical *wages-fund* concept, a concept that played a prominent part in the refinement of Smith's theories by Ricardo, Malthus, and many others. Smith's more refined theory of wages, such as it was, is contained in the wages-fund doctrine.

The difficulty that confronts the modern student who views, retrospectively, the wages-fund concept as an engine of analysis is that it was, simultaneously, a theory of wages *and* a theory of capital. The predominant view of wage payments throughout most of the eighteenth and nineteenth centuries can be summarized as follows. Capital accumulation makes it possible to employ labor, insofar as the accumulated capital constitutes a fund for the maintenance of a working population. This fund consists of *advances to workers* for which the owner of the fund (i.e., the capitalist) expects, and is entitled to, a return. Although the notion of the wages-fund was not original with Smith, he perhaps gave the idea its most succinct expression:

> It seldom happens that the person who tills the ground has wherewithal to maintain himself till he reaps the harvest. His maintenance is generally advanced to him from the stock of a master, the farmer who employs him, and who would have no interest to employ him, unless he was to share in the produce of his labour, or unless his stock was to be replaced to him with a profit (*Wealth of Nations*, p. 65).

In the wages-fund concept, Smith brings together the essential ingredients of the economic growth process. The existence of a wages-fund is, simultaneously, a rationale for saving (i.e., accumulation), an explanation of wages and profit, and a determinant of population growth. The doctrine maintains that workers are dependent upon capitalists to provide them with tools to work with and with food, clothing, and shelter (i.e., "wage goods of subsistence") in order to survive. The only way to increase the stock of wage goods is to induce capitalists to save, and the only way to do that is to increase profits, which, in Smith's view, constitutes the sole source of saving. In other words, savings must find an outlet in the production process—if used to hire more workers, the wages-fund grows, and so do the (average) payments to workers. Workers therefore spend more on wage goods, aggregate demand increases, and more is produced in the next period of production. In this system it is important to note that money is viewed as a medium of exchange only, not as a store of value. Hoarding appears irrational (i.e., costly), and therefore all savings are invested. That is, saving goes into the wages-fund. A particular variant of this view later came to be known as "Say's law," after the French economist and disciple of Smith, J. B. Say.

In another place, however, Smith offers a "contractual" theory of wages and yet again a "subsistence" theory. He notes, for example:

> What are the common wages of labour depends every where upon the contract usually made between those two parties, whose interests are by no means the same. The workmen desire to get as much, the masters to give as little as possible. The

former are disposed to combine in order to raise, the latter in order to lower the wages of labour (*Wealth of Nations,* p. 66).

There is clearly a lower limit to wages, Smith continues, or to the combined activity of employers, since "A man must always live by his work, and his wages must at least be sufficient to maintain him. They must even upon most occasions be somewhat more; otherwise it would be impossible for him to bring up a family, and the race of such workmen could not last beyond the first generation" (*Wealth of Nations,* pp. 67–68).

As the wages-fund grows, then, it can support a larger population, so that as average wages rise sufficiently above subsistence, workers will increase in number through propagation of the species. Population growth cannot continue unrestrained, however, since larger populations place increasing burdens on the wages-fund. Thus the long-run tendency may be toward subsistence levels of average wage rates.

Which one of these explanations represents Smith's theory of wages? Actually, all of them collapse into one; at least they are not inconsistent with one another. The size of the wages-fund explains the size of total wage payments, whereas individual or average wage rates are explained by supply-and-demand conditions. In the long run, Smith views wage rates as determined by costs of workers' maintenance and reproduction. The natural wage is a subsistence one, but "subsistence" simply means the minimum payment that workers insist on before they are willing to have children. In short, labor, too, is produced at constant costs, so that the long-run supply curve of labor is horizontal at whatever wage is consistent with Smith's notion of subsistence. In the short run, however, wage rates may be above or below the long-run equilibrium wage, since short-run supply and demand may be affected by contractual arrangements, accidents of nature, legislation, and so on.

Even in the long run, the trend in wages may be upward, since an increased demand for labor causes higher average wages and induces an increase in population, but with a sufficient time lag in the latter. In other words, in a growing economy, increases in labor supply may continually lag behind increases in labor demand.

Aside from the question of the aggregate level of wages, Smith extended the discussion of "equilibrium wage differences," by which is meant the wage premiums occasioned by certain conditions of employment. Whereas the aggregate level of wages is an important macroeconomic variable, the notion of equilibrium wage differences is an important microeconomic consideration. Cantillon was the first writer to broach the subject in a systematic way. Workers similarly trained and similarly situated in every other respect will nevertheless earn more or less according to the degree of time and expense in acquiring skills, the degree of risk and danger in employment, and the extent of trust required of employees. Cantillon opened this discussion with characteristic brevity:

The crafts which require the most time in training or most ingenuity and industry must necessarily be the best paid. A skilful cabinet-maker must receive a higher price for his work than an ordinary carpenter, and a good watchmaker more than a farrier.

The arts and crafts which are accompanied by risks and dangers like those of founders, mariners, silver miners, etc. ought to be paid in proportion to the risks. When over and above the dangers skill is needed they ought to be paid still more, e.g., pilots, divers, engineers, etc. When capacity and trustworthiness are needed the labour is paid still more highly, as in the case of jewellers, bookkeepers, cashiers and others (*Essai,* p. 21).

In the *Wealth of Nations* (Book I, Chap. 10, Part I), Smith elaborated these issues and broadened the discussion of "the inequalities of wages and profits arising from the nature of the employments themselves." A short summary of his main points follows. According to Smith:

1 *Wages vary in inverse proportion to the agreeableness of the employment.* ("The most detestable of all employments, that of public executioner, is, in proportion to the quantity of work done, better paid than any common trade whatever.")

2 *Wages vary in direct proportion to the cost of learning the business.* ("Education in the ingenious arts and in the liberal professions, is...tedious and expensive. The pecuniary recompence, therefore..., of lawyers and physicians ought to be much more liberal: and it is so accordingly.")

3 *Wages vary in inverse proportion to the constancy of employment.* ("No species of skilled labor...seems more easy to learn than that of masons and bricklayers....The high wages of those workmen, therefore, are not so much the recompence of their skill, as the compensation for the inconstancy of their employment.")

4 *Wages vary in direct proportion to the trust that must be placed in the employee.* ("The wages of goldsmiths and jewelers are every-where superior to those of many other workmen, not only of equal, but of much superior ingenuity; on account of the precious metals with which they are intrusted.")

5 *Wages vary in inverse proportion to the probability of success.* ("The counselor at law who, perhaps, at near forty years of age, begins to make something by his profession, ought to receive the retribution, not only of his own so tedious and expensive education, but of that of more than twenty others who are never likely to make any thing by it.")

Profit and Interest Of these same factors that affect wages, Smith observed that profits are affected only by the first and the last, namely "the agreeableness or disagreeableness of the business and the risk or security with which it is attended." Smith regarded profit as a return to capital rather than a return to entrepreneurship, so his theory of profits is outdated by contemporary standards. In fact, Smith offered useful insights into the profit-making process rather than a theory of how profits arise. The chief characteristic of profits, according to Smith, is their uncertainty:

> Profit is so very fluctuating that the person who carries on a particular trade cannot always tell you himself what is the average of his annual profit. It is affected, not only by every variation of price in the commodities which he deals in, but by the good or bad fortune both of his rivals and of his customers, and by a thousand other accidents to which goods when carried either by sea or land, or even when stored in a warehouse, are liable. It varies, therefore, not only from year to year, but from day to day, and almost from hour to hour. To ascertain what is the average profit of all the different trades carried on in a great kingdom, must be much more difficult; and to judge of what it may have been formerly, or in remote periods of time, with any degree of precision, must be altogether impossible (*Wealth of Nations,* p. 87).

What Smith suggested, therefore, is that in the measurement of aggregate profits, interest be viewed as a *proxy* for profit. Smith defined profit as "revenue derived from stock [i.e., capital] by the person who manages or employs it," whereas interest he defined as revenue derived from stock "by the person who does not employ it himself, but lends it to another." Smith's conception of profit emerges as the sum of two payments: (1) a return on capital advanced and (2) a compensation for bearing risk. Interest alone cannot explain all profit, although it is a good indication of profit. Thus in Smith's words:

> According...as the usual market rate of interest varies in any country, we may be assured that the ordinary profits of stock must vary with it, must sink as its sinks, and rise as it rises. The progress of interest, therefore, may lead us to form some notion of the progress of profit (*Wealth of Nations,* p. 88).

Aside from the foregoing, Smith added certain *obiter dicta* to the concepts of profit and interest. "The lowest ordinary rate of profit," he charged, "must always be something more than what is sufficient to compensate the occasional losses to which every employment of stock is exposed. It is the surplus only which is neat or clear profit." By the same token, Smith declared that: "The lowest ordinary rate of interest must...be something more than sufficient to compensate the occasional losses to which lending, even with tolerable prudence, is exposed. Were it not more, charity or friendship could be the only motives for lending" (*Wealth of Nations,* p. 96). He also made it clear what effect competition would likely have on profits:

> The increase of stock, which raises wages, tends to lower profit. When the stocks of many rich merchants are turned into the same trade, their mutual competition naturally tends to lower its profit; and when there is an increase in stock in all the different trades carried on in the same society, the competition must produce the same effect in all (*Wealth of Nations,* p. 87).

It is generally accepted that Smith viewed profit as a residual, or surplus, perhaps because this was the view taken by Smith's leading disciple in Great Britain, David Ricardo (see Chapter 7). However, the following excerpt from Smith's chapter on profit challenges this "conventional wisdom":

> In reality high profits tend much more to raise the price of work than high wages....Our merchants and master manufacturers complain much of the bad effects of high wages in raising the price, and thereby lessening the sale of their goods

both at home and abroad. They say nothing concerning the bad effects of high profits (*Wealth of Nations*, pp. 97–98).

If, indeed, profit is a residual, it seems unlikely that it could be price determining, as the above passage suggests. But we shall leave it up to the reader to determine what Smith really meant on the matter of profit. We shall, however, return to the subject of profit and capital accumulation when we examine Smith's blueprint for macroeconomic growth.

Rent   Smith's discussion of rent hinges on three factors: (1) monopoly elements, (2) the residual surplus idea, and (3) alternative costs. "The rent of land," declared Smith, "is naturally a monopoly price. It is not at all proportioned to what the landlord may have laid out upon the improvement of land, or to what he can afford to take; but to what the farmer can afford to give" (*Wealth of Nations*, p. 145).

Smith defined rent simply as "the price paid for the use of land." The sum of annual rent is usually determined by contractual arrangement between the landlord and tenant, with the landlord having the upper hand, hence the view of rent as a monopoly return. Smith wrote:

> In adjusting the terms of the lease, the landlord endeavors to leave him [the tenant] no greater share of the produce than what is sufficient to keep up the stock from which he furnishes the seed, pays the labour, and purchases and maintains the cattle and other instruments of husbandry, together with the ordinary profits of farming stock in the neighborhood. This is evidently the smallest share with which the tenant can content himself without being a loser, and the landlord seldom means to leave him any more (*Wealth of Nations*, p. 144).

Other monopoly elements involved in the determination of rent include fertility and location. Thus land fitted for a particular product may have a monopoly, such as the great wine-producing regions of the French Côte-d'Or or the Champagne districts. In this case, Smith noted that the quantity of land devoted to wine production was too small to satisfy the effectual demand, so that the market price of French wines was higher than their natural price. "The surplus of this price," argued Smith, "in this case, and in this case only, bears no regular proportion to the like surplus in corn or pasture, but may exceed it in almost any degree; and the greater part of this excess naturally goes to the rent of the landlord" (*Wealth of Nations*, p. 155).

Rent, in Adam Smith's view, is clearly a residual payment. It is the part of annual produce remaining after all other costs of production, including ordinary profit, are realized. As such, rent is price determined rather than price determining. In Smith's own words, rent "enters into the composition of the price of commodities in a different way from wages and profit. High or low wages and profit are the causes of high or low price; high or low rent is the effect of it" (*Wealth of Nations*, pp. 145–146).

Finally, Smith maintained that differential rents can be explained on the basis of alternative costs.

In Europe corn[2] is the principal produce of land which serves immediately for human food. Except in particular situations, therefore, the rent of corn land regulates in Europe that of all other cultivated land. If in any country the common and favourite vegetable food of the people should be drawn from a plant of which the most common land, with the same or nearly the same culture, produced a much greater quantity than the most fertile does of corn, the rent of the landlord... would necessarily be much greater (*Wealth of Nations,* p. 159).

In other words, the rent of land in a particular use will depend greatly on the productivity of land in its next-best alternative use.

Smith's Macroeconomics: Blueprint for Economic Growth

Although Book I of *The Wealth of Nations* is devoted primarily to the microeconomic foundations of value and distribution, it also contains the famous discussion of division of labor, which forms the starting point for Smith's theory of economic growth. This theory has to be pieced together, for all of its essentials are not to be found in any one place in *The Wealth of Nations.* The following is an overview of Smith's theory of economic growth.

Division of Labor Joseph Schumpeter has observed that for Adam Smith the division of labor "is practically the only factor in economic progress" (*History of Economic Analysis,* p. 187). While this assessment tends toward exaggeration, it is very close to the mark. Smith's discussion of the division of labor in Book I does provide an exceptionally lucid analysis of the gains from specialization and exchange—principles upon which the theory of markets rest.

In an oft-quoted passage, Smith described the gains from specialization and division of labor in a pin factory:

A workman not educated to... the trade of the pin-maker... nor acquainted with the use of the machinery employed in it... could scarce, perhaps, with his utmost industry, make one pin in a day, and certainly could not make twenty. But in the way in which this business is now carried on, not only the whole work is a peculiar trade, but it is divided into a number of branches, of which the greater part are likewise peculiar trades. One man draws out the wire, another straights it, a third cuts it, a fourth points it, a fifth grinds it at the top for receiving the head; to make the head requires two or three distinct operations; to put it on, is a peculiar business, to whiten the pins is another; it is even a trade by itself to put them into the paper; and the important business of making a pin is, in this manner, divided into about eighteen distinct operations, which, in some manufactories, are all performed by distinct hands, though in others the same man will sometimes perform two or three of them. I have seen a small manufactory of this kind where ten men only were employed, and where... each person... [averaged] four thousand eight hundred pins in a day.

---

[2] The term "corn" was at this time often used in the generic sense to mean virtually all edible grains, such as wheat, barley, oats, etc.

But if they had all wrought separately and independently, and without any of them having been educated to this peculiar business, they certainly could not each of them make twenty, perhaps not one pin in a day (*Wealth of Nations*, p. 5).

Smith concluded that there are three advantages of division of labor, each leading to greater economic wealth: (1) an increase in skill and dexterity of every worker, (2) the saving of time, and (3) the invention of machinery. The last advantage results from the narrow focus of the individual's attention on a particular object occasioned by the division of labor. As Smith puts it: "Men are much more likely to discover easier and readier methods of attaining any object, when the whole attention of their minds is directed toward that single object, than when it is dissipated among a great variety of things" (*Wealth of Nations*, p. 9).

Wealth, Income, and Productive and Unproductive Labor As noted earlier, Smith differed sharply with the mercantilists on the nature of a country's wealth. "High value of the precious metals," he observed, "can be no proof of the poverty or barbarism of any particular country....It is a proof only of the barrenness of the mines which happened at that time to supply the commercial world" (*Wealth of Nations*, p. 238). To Smith, national wealth was measured not by the value of precious metals but by "the exchangeable value of the annual produce of the land and labour of the country." Thus Smith meant by the term "national wealth" essentially the same thing economists today mean by the term "national income."

But Smith considered the essence of wealth to be the production of physical goods only, and this led in Book II to his unfortunate distinction between *productive* and *unproductive* labor. According to this distinction, productive labor is that which produces a tangible good of some market value. Unproductive labor, on the other hand, results in the production of intangibles, such as services performed by artisans or professionals. Smith characterized his own output (as a teacher) as essentially unproductive, since it did not result in tangible goods sold in the marketplace. He also so categorized the services of lawyers, physicians, and other service-oriented workers.

This distinction of Smith's has been much maligned. It is, of course, absurd to characterize the service industries as unproductive simply because they do not produce tangible goods. Yet what Smith was driving at was the distinction between those activities that increase aggregate net investment, and thus serve the end of economic growth, and those activities that serve merely the needs of households. This latter distinction is a perfectly valid one in economic theory, although the terminology Smith chose is misleading. It should be noted that Smith did not consider unproductive workers useless; he simply did not regard their activities as furthering the goal of economic growth.

The Role of Capital While division of labor (which Smith regarded as an inherent tendency in society) *starts* the growth process, it is capital accumulation that keeps it going. Key elements in the growth process are the nature, accumulation, and employment of *stock*. By "stock," Smith implied *wealth* in modern terms, a part (or all) of which is reserved for consumption and a part of which may be reserved for deriving further revenue, through investment. The larger the last share, the greater the growth potential of any nation. Capital accumulation, it will be recalled, enlarges the wages-fund, which in turn allows a larger number of workers to be engaged in productive activity, thereby increasing the size of the national output.

Workers exhaust the wages-fund over time as they draw advances from it for subsistence during the production process. At the end of the production period, however, the goods produced are sold, ordinarily at a profit, so that the stock of wage goods (capital) is replenished, and even increased, by the amount of profit earned. In this manner, through profit accumulation, the stock of capital grows over time, thus supporting more workers and greater output in the next production period.

The complete chain of economic growth as represented by Smith can be summarized in Figure 5-2, in which growth is viewed as an ongoing process as long as the chain of causation remains unbroken. Starting with division of labor, as Smith did, the line of causation proceeds in clockwise fashion. The ultimate constraint on the growth process is the increased difficulty of finding new and profitable investment outlets as the capital stock continues to grow over time.

FIGURE 5-2
Smith's theory of economic growth is an ongoing process, with division of labor starting the growth process and proceeding in a clockwise fashion in the diagram.

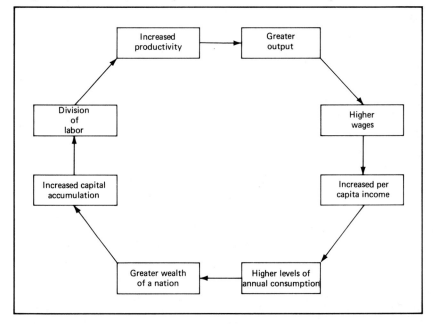

CONCLUSION

From the Middle Ages to the mid-eighteenth century, the national populations and national outputs of Europe and Great Britain increased significantly. At the time Adam Smith wrote *The Wealth of Nations,* the industrial revolution was right around the corner. These developments changed people's whole attitude toward trade and commerce. From a narrow concern with economic justice and the status quo typical of the Middle Ages, the predominant attitude changed to one of spurring economic growth and change. This evolutionary change, in turn, led to the dismantling of feudalistic and mercantilistic restraints of trade and commerce.

The reasons for this turnabout are not very obscure. In a society such as the medieval one, where economic stagnation was the hallmark, one person's gain was another's loss—hence the concern of the church fathers for economic justice and their other worldly tendency to portray want minimization as the path to happiness and economic well-being. Contrarily, when national output is expanding, one expects less preoccupation with ethics and more concentration on economic analysis to explain the underlying causes of economic growth. Quite simply, the need to curb from above the human acquisitive instinct is less important in an expanding economy where each individual can get a larger slice of the (growing) economic pie without necessarily making another worse off. By 1776, it had become possible, as well as desirable, to reduce restraints against individual profit seeking.

The idea of a self-regulating economy operating within a market system was a new one in the mid-eighteenth century. It is to be found in the writings of both the Physiocrats and Adam Smith, although Smith perhaps gave the idea its most eloquent expression. This perception of a natural order to society, existing in the absence of any form of central planning, was one of the most liberating ideas ever to emerge in the history of economic thought. It shunted economic analysis onto a new path. Adam Smith led the way by providing a framework for analyzing the economic questions of income growth, value, and distribution. For practically the next century, economists worked largely within that framework to investigate the questions raised by the quiet Scottish philosopher. No wonder he should be considered the father of economics today. He alone succeeded in weaving together his own contributions plus those of his predecessors, who were many, into a systematic, comprehensive treatise that was greater than the sum of its parts.

At the same time, Smith's book became many things to many people, a fact that accounts in no small measure for its immediate success. Business people and workers alike could find passages in *The Wealth of Nations* to support their interests. The government, of course, could not, although Smith reserved three important roles for the state: (1) to administer justice, (2) to provide for the national defense, and (3) to maintain certain enterprises in the public interest that could never be profitable if undertaken privately (i.e., the "public-goods" question). As we approach the end of the twentieth century, it seems obvious that each of these functions has weighed increasingly heavy on governments at every level.

NOTES FOR FURTHER READING

Insofar as the literature on Adam Smith is vast and varied, only a sampling can be presented here. For a glimpse of the large store of Smithiana, see Burt Franklin and F. Cordasco, *Adam Smith: A Bibliographical Checklist* (New York: Burt Franklin, 1950), and Henry W. Speigel's bibliography accompanying *The Growth of Economic Thought* (Englewood Cliffs, N.J.: Prentice-Hall, 1971). The standard works on Smith's life and thought are John Rae, *Life of Adam Smith* (New York: A. M. Kelley, Publishers, 1965 [1895]); W. R. Scott, *Adam Smith as Student and Professor* (Glasgow: Jackson, Son & Co., 1937); and C. R. Fay, *The World of Adam Smith* (Cambridge: Heffer, 1960). On the first centenary of *The Wealth of Nations,* Walter Bagehot, an economist in his own right, wrote an interesting characterization of Smith: "Adam Smith as a Person," *Fortnightly Review,* no. 115 (July 1, 1876), pp. 18–42, reprinted in Bagehot's *Biographical Studies,* R. H. Hutton (ed.) (London: Longmans, 1881). More recent evaluations of Smith and his thought include E. G. West, *Adam Smith: The Man and His Works* (New Rochelle, N.Y.: Arlington House, 1969); and Sam Hollander, *The Economics of Adam Smith* (Toronto: University of Toronto Press, 1973), a wholesale reinterpretation of Smith's significance as an economist.

A long-standing debate concerns the compatibility of intellectual arguments in Smith's *Theory of Moral Sentiments* and *The Wealth of Nations.* The preponderance of evidence seems to support the consistency thesis—there is no real conflict between the two works published almost twenty years apart. On this issue, see A. L. Macfie, "Adam Smith's *Moral Sentiments* as Foundation for His *Wealth of Nations," Oxford Economic Papers,* n.s., vol. 2 (October 1959), pp. 209–228; same author, "Adam Smith's Theory of Moral Sentiments," *Scottish Journal of Political Economy,* vol. 8 (1960), pp. 12–27; W. F. Campbell, "Adam Smith's Theory of Justice, Prudence, and Beneficence," *American Economic Review,* vol. 57 (May 1967), pp. 571–577; Ralph Anspach, "The Implications of the Theory of Moral Sentiments for Adam Smith's Economic Thought," *History of Political Economy,* vol. 4 (Spring 1972), pp. 176–206; R. L. Heilbroner, "The Socialization of the Individual in Adam Smith," *History of Political Economy,* vol. 14 (Fall 1982), pp. 427–439; J. T. Young, "The Impartial Spectator and Natural Jurisprudence: An Interpretation of Adam Smith's Theory of the Natural Price," *History of Political Economy,* vol. 18 (Fall 1986), pp. 365–382; and J. M. Evensky, "The Two Voices of Adam Smith: Moral Philosopher and Social Critic," *History of Political Economy,* vol. 19 (Fall 1987), pp. 447–468.

The sesquicentennial of the publication of the *Wealth of Nations* in 1926 was followed fifty years later by a full-scale celebration of the bicentennial event. On the former, see J. M. Clark et al., *Adam Smith, 1776–1926* (Chicago: University of Chicago Press, 1928). In connection with the latter, see T. W. Hutchison, "The Bicentenary of Adam Smith," *Economic Journal,* vol. 86 (September 1976), pp. 481–492; G. J. Stigler, "The Successes and Failures of Professor Smith," *Journal of Political Economy,* vol. 84 (December 1976), pp. 1199–1214; and the entire Winter 1976 issue of *History of Political Economy,* which contains papers on Smith by Ronald Meek, H. W. Spiegel, E. G. West, and others. A major part of the bicentennial was the publication by the University of Glasgow of Smith's complete works and correspondence, accompanied by a new biography by I. S. Ross and two volumes of critical essays edited by A. S. Skinner and T. Wilson.

Smith's theory of history and his development of systematic inquiry is examined by Andrew S. Skinner in "Economics and History—the Scottish Enlightenment," *Scottish Journal of Political Economy,* vol. 12 (February 1956); "Adam Smith: The Development of a System," *Scottish Journal of Political Economy,* vol. 23 (June 1976), pp. 111–132; and "Smith and Shackle: History and Epistemics," *Journal of Economic Studies,* vol. 12 (1985), pp. 13–20; by G. Bryson in *Man and Society: The Scottish Inquiry of the Eighteenth Century* (New York: A. M. Kelley, 1968); and by Ronald L. Meek in "Smith, Turgot, and the 'Four Stages' Theory," *History of Political Economy,* vol. 3 (Spring 1971), pp. 9–27. On a related issue, see S. Rashid, "Adam Smith's Interpretation of the History of Economics and Its Influence in the 18th and 19th Centuries," *Quarterly Review of Economics and Business,* vol. 27 (Autumn 1987), pp, 56–69. Smith's theory of property rights is the subject of a note by David E. R. Gay, "Adam Smith and Property Rights Analysis," *Review of Social Economy,* vol. 33 (October 1975), pp. 177–179.

The starting point of Smith's theory of economic development is the division of labor. Nevertheless, Smith seemed of two minds on the subject. He recognized its benefits in Book I and its limitations in Book V. For a discussion of the issues, see E. G. West, "Adam Smith's Two Views on the Division of Labor," *Economica,* vol. 31 (February 1964), pp. 23–32; and Nathan Rosenberg, "Adam Smith on the Division of Labor: Two Views or One?" *Economica,* vol. 32 (May 1965), pp. 127–140. For historical antecedents of the concept, see Vernard Foley, "The Division of Labor in Plato and Smith," *History of Political Economy,* vol. 6 (Summer 1974), pp. 171–191; and Salim Rashid, "Adam Smith and the Division of Labor: A Historical View," *Scottish Journal of Political Economy,* vol. 33 (August 1986), pp. 292–297. Alienation, the favorite theme of Karl Marx, has also been proposed as the concern of Adam Smith: see E. G. West, "The Political Economy of Alienation: Karl Marx and Adam Smith," *Oxford Economic Papers,* vol. 21 (March 1969), pp. 1–23; the critique of West by R. Lamb, "Adam Smith's Concept of Alienation," *Oxford Economic Papers,* vol. 25 (July 1973), pp. 275–285; and West's rejoinder, "Adam Smith and Alienation: A Rejoinder," *Oxford Economic Papers,* vol. 27 (July 1975), pp. 295–301. See also M. Fay, "The Influence of Adam Smith on Marx's Theory of Alienation," *Science and Society,* vol. 47 (Summer 1983), pp. 129–151. The concept of alienation arises again in J. P. Henderson, "Agency or Alienation? Smith, Mill and Marx on the Joint-Stock Company," *History of Political Economy,* vol. 18 (Spring 1986), pp. 111–131.

Smith's theory of economic development is explored by J. J. Spengler, "Adam Smith's Theory of Economic Development," *Science and Society,* vol. 23 (1959), pp. 107–132; by W. O. Thweatt, "A Diagrammatic Presentation of Adam Smith's Growth Model," *Social Research,* vol. 24 (July 1957), pp. 227–230; by V. W. Bladen, "Adam Smith on Productive and Unproductive Labor: A Theory of Full Development," *Canadian Journal of Economics and Political Science,* vol. 24 (1960), pp. 625–630; by Hla Myint, "Adam Smith's Theory of International Trade in the Perspective of Economic Development," *Economica,* vol. 44 (August 1977), pp. 231–248; by P. Bowles, "Adam Smith and the Natural Progress of Opulence," *Economica,* vol. 53 (February 1986), pp. 109–118; and by Gavin C. Reid, "Disequilibrium and Increasing Returns in Adam Smith's Analysis of Growth and Accumulation," *History of Political Economy,* vol. 19 (Spring 1987), pp. 87–106.

J. P. Henderson, "The Macro and Micro aspects of *The Wealth of Nations,*" *Southern Economic Journal,* vol. 21 (July 1954), pp. 25–35, presents a balanced overview of Smith's economics. For more detail on the micro issues of Smithian economics, see M. A. Stephenson, "The Paradox of Value: A Suggested Interpretation," *History of Political Economy,* vol. 4 (Spring 1972), pp. 127–139; David Levy, "Diamonds, Water and Z Goods: An Account of the Paradox of Value," *History of Political Economy,* vol. 14 (Fall 1982), pp. 312–322; H. M. Robertson and W. L. Taylor, "Adam Smith's Approach to the Theory of Value," *Economic Journal,* vol. 67 (June 1957), pp. 181–198; Ronald L. Meek, "Adam Smith and the Classical Concept of Profit," *Scottish Journal of Political Economy,* vol. 1 (June 1954), pp. 138–153; Sam Hollander, "Some Implications of Adam Smith's Analysis of Investment Priorities," *History of Political Economy,* vol. 3 (Fall 1971), pp. 238–264; P. E. Mirowski, "Adam Smith, Empiricism and the Rate of Profit in Eighteenth-Century England," *History of Political Economy,* vol. 14 (Summer 1982), pp. 178–198; R. F. Hébert and A. N. Link, "Adam Smith on the Division of Labor and Relative Prices," *History of Economics Society Bulletin,* vol. 9 (Fall 1987), pp. 80–84; David Levy, "Adam Smith's Case of Usury Laws," *History of Political Economy,* vol. 19 (Fall 1987), pp. 387–400; and C. E. Staley, "A Note on Adam Smith's Version of the Vent for Surplus Model," *History of Political Economy,* vol. 5 (Fall 1973), pp. 438–448.

A number of writers have explored Smith's views on specific public policy issues and on the role of government in general. For a cross section of such views, see Nathan Rosenberg, "Some Institutional Aspects of the Wealth of Nations," *Journal of Political Economy,* vol. 68 (1960), pp. 557–570; R. D. Freeman, "Adam Smith, Education, and Laissez-Faire," *History of Political Economy,* vol. 1 (Spring 1969), pp. 173–186; Warren J. Samuels, "The Classical Theory of Economic Policy: Non-legal Social Control," *Southern Eco-*

nomic Journal, vol. 31 (October 1973), pp. 123–137; G. J. Stigler, "Smith's Travels on the Ship of State," *History of Political Economy,* vol. 3 (Fall 1971), pp. 265–277; Donald Winch, "Science and the Legislator: Adam Smith and After," *Economic Journal,* vol. 93 (September 1983), pp. 501–520; and G. M. Anderson, W. F. Shugart II, and R. D. Tollison, "Adam Smith in the Customhouse," *Journal of Political Economy,* vol. 93 (August 1985), pp. 740–759.

On the relevance of Adam Smith's thought for the modern age, see S. Moos, "Is Adam Smith Out of Date?" *Oxford Economic Papers,* vol. 3 (June 1951), pp. 187–201; K. E. Boulding, "After Samuelson, Who Needs Adam Smith?" *History of Political Economy,* vol. 3 (Fall 1971), pp. 225–237; and R. H. Coase, "The Wealth of Nations," *Economic Inquiry,* vol. 15 (July 1977), pp. 309–325.

REFERENCES

Blaug, Mark. *Economic Theory in Retrospect,* 4th ed. London: Cambridge University Press, 1985.

Cantillon, Richard. *Essai sur la nature de la commerce en général,* H. Higgs (ed.). London: Macmillan, 1931 [1755].

Gray, Alexander. "Adam Smith," *Scottish Journal of Political Economy,* vol. 23 (June 1976), pp. 153–169.

Schumpeter, Joseph A. *History of Economic Analysis.* New York: Oxford University Press, 1954.

Smith Adam. *The Wealth of Nations,* Edwin Cannan (ed.). New York: Modern Library, 1937 [1776].

———. *The Theory of Moral Sentiments.* Indianapolis, Ind.: Liberty Classics, 1976 [1759].

CLASSICAL ECONOMIC ANALYSIS (I): UTILITY, POPULATION, AND MONEY

INTRODUCTION

Adam Smith did more to establish economics as a scientific discipline than any writer before him. He established the foundations of classical value theory and provided a meaningful blueprint for economic growth. He also breathed into political economy an underlying philosophy based on the doctrine of utility, or self-interest. The desire to improve one's position manifests itself in individual attempts to acquire benefits and avoid costs. For Jeremy Bentham (1748–1832), a younger contemporary of Smith, the doctrine came to be formalized in terms of the *pleasure-pain principle*. In his *Introduction to the Principles of Morals and Legislation* (1789), Bentham wrote with confidence:

> Nature has placed mankind under the governance of two sovereign masters, *pain* and *pleasure*. It is for them alone to point out what we ought to do as well as to determine what we shall do....The *principle of utility* recognizes this subjection...(p. 17).

The idea that self-interest was, if not the exclusive, at least the dominant influence on human activity gained ground very quickly in the eighteenth century. Smith was merely one in a long line of philosophers who espoused the principle. Also included in the line was David Hume, Smith's teacher and friend. Together they forged a philosophical framework that served as a touchstone for the new field of political economy.

THE PRINCIPLE OF UTILITY IN CLASSICAL ECONOMICS: JEREMY BENTHAM

From a policy standpoint there are two distinct ways in which the principle of utility (self-interest) has been interpreted. One rests on the belief in a *natural* identity of interests, the other on the belief in an *artificial* identity of interests. Adam Smith championed the natural identity thesis, which placed a great deal of confidence in natural order and harmony. He believed that the individual self-interests of human nature harmonize of their own accord in a free economy; consequently his basic prescription promoted essentially a laissez faire policy. Bentham, however, took a different tack. Although admitting that individuals are chiefly self-interested, Bentham denied any natural harmony of egoisms. Crime, for example, provides a case of self-interested behavior that violates the public interest. The very fact that crime existed was for Bentham sufficient proof that natural harmony did not. The central tenet of Bentham's philosophy, therefore, was that the interest of each individual must be identified with the general interest, and that it was the business of the legislator to bring about this identification through direct intercession. Thus it was in the form of the *artificial identity of interests* framework that Bentham first adopted the utility principle. His doctrine came to be known as *utilitarianism*.

On the surface, Bentham's doctrine bears a resemblance to the ancient Greek philosophy of hedonism, which also held that moral duty is fulfilled in the gratification of pleasure-seeking interests. But hedonism prescribes individual actions without reference to the general happiness. Utilitarianism added to hedonism the ethical doctrine that human conduct *should* be directed toward maximizing the happiness of the greatest number of people. "The greatest happiness for the greatest number" was the watch phrase of the utilitarians—those who came to share in Bentham's philosophy. Among them were such personalities as Edwin Chadwick (see Chapter 9) and the father-son combination of James and John Stuart Mill (see Chapter 8). This group championed legislation plus social and religious sanctions that punished individuals for harming others in the pursuit of their own happiness.

Bentham defined his principle in the following fashion:

> By the principle of utility is meant that principle which approves or disapproves of every action whatsoever, according to the tendency which it appears to have to augment or diminish the happiness of the party whose interest is in question...not only of every action of a private individual, but of every measure of government (*Principles of Morals and Legislation,* p. 17).

What is noteworthy about this declaration is the very minimal distinction Bentham made between morals and legislation. His self-conceived mission was to make the theory of morals and legislation scientific in the Newtonian sense. As Newton's revolutionary physics hinged on the universal principle of attraction (i.e., gravity), Bentham's theory of morals swung on the principle of utility. Newton's roundabout influence on the social sciences was felt in other ways as well. The nineteenth century was one with a passion for measurement. In the social sciences, Bentham rode the crest of this new wave. If pleasure and pain could be measured in some objective sense, then every legislative act could be judged on welfare considerations. This achievement required a conception of the general interest, which Bentham readily undertook to provide.

According to Bentham, the general interest of the community is measured by the sum of the individual interests in the community. The utilitarian approach was both democratic and egalitarian. It mattered not whether one was a pauper or a king—each individual interest was to receive equal weight in the measurement of the general welfare. Thus if something adds more to a peasant's pleasure than it subtracts from the happiness of an aristocrat, it is desirable on utilitarian grounds. Likewise, if government action of a certain kind enhances the happiness of the community more than it diminishes the happiness of some segment of it, intervention is thereby justified.

All of this presupposes a kind of "moral arithmetic," which Bentham saw as analogous to the mathematical operations required of Newtonian physics. The operations of moral arithmetic are not all of the same kind, however. The values of different pleasures are added for individuals, but the value of a given pleasure must be *multiplied* by the number of people who experience it, and the various elements that make up the value of each pleasure must also be multiplied by each other. One distinctly economic facet of this welfare theory lies in Bentham's choice of money as the measure of pain and pleasure. Money, of course, is subject to diminishing marginal utility as more of it is acquired, which Bentham recognized, though he did not explore the marginalist principle as thoroughly as some of his successors did. In other words, Bentham was more of a utilitarian than a marginalist. He therefore did not take part in the marginal-utility revolution that reoriented the general theory of value, although he influenced William Stanley Jevons (see Chapter 14), who did participate in the so-called revolution.

The Felicific Calculus

Bentham's attempt to measure economic welfare in the scientific sense took the form of the felicific calculus, or summing up, of collective pleasures and pains. As early as 1780, in his *Introduction to the Principles of Morals and Legislation* (p. 30), Bentham described the circumstances by which the values of pleasure and pain were to be measured. For the community, they consist of the following seven factors:

1 The intensity of pleasure or pain
2 Its duration
3 Its certainty or uncertainty
4 Its propinquity or remoteness
5 Its fecundity, or the chance it has of being followed by sensations of the same kind (i.e., pleasure followed by more pleasure, or pain followed by more pain)
6 Its purity, or the chance it has of not being followed by sensations of the

opposite kind (e.g., childbirth has a low index of purity because it represents a mixture of pain and pleasure)

7 Its extent, that is, the number of people who are affected by it

Bentham recognized that the fifth and sixth circumstances are not inherent properties of pain or pleasure itself but only of the act that produces pleasure or pain. Consequently, they enter only calculations of the tendency of any act or event to affect the community.

Calculations of Welfare   Bentham also carefully spelled out the mechanics by which welfare calculations were to be made. "To take an exact account, then, of the general tendency of any act, by which the interests of the community are affected," he exhorts, "proceed as follows":

> Begin with any one person of those whose interests seem most immediately to be affected by it: and take an account,
>
> **1** Of the value of each distinguishable pleasure which appears to be produced by it in the first instance.
>
> **2** Of the value of each pain which appears to be produced by it in the first instance.
>
> **3** Of the value of each pleasure which appears to be produced by it after the first. This constitutes the fecundity of the first pleasure and the impurity of the first pain.
>
> **4** Of the value of each pain which appears to be produced by it after the first. This constitutes the fecundity of the first pain and the impurity of the first pleasure.
>
> **5** Sum up all the values of all the pleasures on the one side, and those of all the pains on the other. The balance, if it be on the side of pleasure, will give the good tendency of the act upon the whole, with respect to the interests of that individual person; if on the side of pain, the bad tendency of it upon the whole.
>
> **6** Take an account of the number of persons whose interests appear to be concerned; and repeat the above process with respect to each. Sum up the numbers expressive of degrees of good tendency...in regard to...the whole: do this again with respect to each individual, in regard to whom the tendency of it is bad upon the whole. Take the balance; which, if on the side of pleasure, will give the general good tendency of the act...if on the side of pain, the general evil tendency with respect to the same community (*Principles of Morals and Legislation,* pp. 30–31).

Probably anticipating criticism of the impracticability of his welfare theory, Bentham admitted that he did not expect the felicific calculus to be followed pursuant to every moral judgment or legislative enactment. But he enjoined legislators and administrators always to keep the theory in view, for as close as the actual process of evaluation comes to it, the nearer it will be to an exact measure.

An Evaluation of Utilitarianism

There are several practical and analytical difficulties in Bentham's theory of welfare measurement, some which he recognized and some which he ignored.

One of the many problems that Bentham had to face was that of "interpersonal comparisons" of utility. One man's happiness, to paraphrase an old cliché, may be another man's poison. The fact that different individuals have different tastes, different incomes, different goals and ambitions, etc., makes comparisons of utility (gained or lost) between individuals illegitimate by any objective criteria. Bentham admitted this difficulty, but he felt that such comparisons must be made, or else social reform is impossible. His welfare theory is therefore subjective (i.e., normative) in content.

Another problem in Bentham's welfare theory concerns the weighting, if any, of qualitative pleasures. Do pleasures of the mind, for example, receive more or less emphasis than pleasures of the body? Bentham was unable to resolve this question, although he was aware of the difficulty. Like so many later economists, he resorted to money as the best available measure of utility, although money measures do not always register qualitative changes unambiguously.

One shortcoming of Bentham's welfare theory of which he was apparently unaware concerns the logical pitfall that economists call the *fallacy of composition*. The fallacy asserts that because something is true of a part, it is therefore true of the whole. In reference to Bentham, there may be a logical fallacy in the assertion that the collective interest is the sum of the interests of individuals. While the assertion may be true in some instances, it is not necessarily true in all.

A simple example may serve to illustrate this point. It is presumably in the general interest of American society to have every automobile in the United States equipped with all possible safety devices. However, a majority of individual car buyers may not be willing to pay the cost of such equipment in the form of higher auto prices. In this case, the collective interest does not coincide with the sum of the individual interests. The result is a legislative and economic dilemma. In other words, Bentham's basic assumption regarding welfare measurement may lead to inaccurate estimates of the general welfare.

On purely philosophical grounds, Bentham's view of human nature is essentially passive: people are "pushed" about by the search for pleasure and the avoidance of pain. Hence there are no "bad" motives or "moral" deficiencies; there are only "bad" calculations regarding pleasure and pain. Bentham did not think it wrong to make a bad calculation; it may be stupid, but presumably stupidity can be corrected by education. Indeed, the utilitarians placed a great deal of emphasis on education as a means of social reform.

Utilitarianism is also overly narrow in its approach to human behavior. Little or no room is given to behavioral motives other than the pursuit of pleasure and the avoidance of pain. But Bentham felt that the felicific calculus was a useful, if unoriginal, theory, despite its inherent difficulties. Individual pleasure-pain calculations may be made unconsciously, and yet they exist, Bentham affirmed. "In all this," he charged, "there is nothing but what the practice of mankind, wheresoever they have a clear view of their own interest, is perfectly comfortable to" (*Principles of Morals and Legislation*, p. 32).

Bentham's search for an exact, quantitative measure of utility was bound to prove futile, of course. Even to this day, welfare economists have never been able successfully to solve the problem of interpersonal utility comparisons in such a way as to derive truly objective criteria on which to base welfare decisions. Nevertheless, the influence of Bentham's philosophy was carried over through James Mill, a fellow utilitarian, to his son, John Stuart, particularly in the area of social reform. Even more important for the history of economic analysis, the felicific calculus provided a starting point for Jevons's more profound insights into the marginal-utility theory of consumer behavior (see Chapter 14).

Bentham's influence on economic policy was especially profound in the first decades following his death, when Edwin Chadwick and John Stuart Mill held high the banner of utilitarian reform. His approach to economics remains influential even today, however, having served to inspire contemporary extensions of neoclassical theory into such areas as the economics of crime and the economics of franchise bidding (see the Notes for Further Reading at the end of the chapter). In a general sense, Bentham proved to be the master innovator of institutional and administrative reforms designed to alter economic incentives in compliance with the general will.

THE PRINCIPLE OF POPULATION IN CLASSICAL ECONOMICS: THOMAS MALTHUS

If the principle of utility was one cornerstone of classical economics, the population principle was another. The writer who gave classical population theory its definitive statement was Thomas Robert Malthus (1766–1834). John Maynard Keynes called him the "first of the Cambridge economists," for it was at Cambridge that Malthus distinguished himself as an undergraduate in Jesus College. There Malthus prepared himself for a ministerial career. Despite a congenital cleft palate, he won prizes for his declamations in Greek, Latin, and English. He graduated in 1788 and took holy orders the same year, but he remained at Cambridge as a graduate fellow until 1804, at which time he married and thereby had to resign his fellowship, according to the rules of the College.

Malthus's father counted Jean-Jacques Rousseau and David Hume among his friends, both of whom are reputed to have been young Thomas's first visitors when he was an infant. As he grew older, Malthus was educated privately and learned to be an independent thinker, a trait that he later put to good use in establishing his theory of population. In 1798 Malthus published, anonymously, *An Essay on the Principle of Population as It Affects the Future Improvement of Society, with Remarks on the Speculations of Mr. Godwin, M. Condorcet, and Other Writers*. Anonymity, however, quickly gave way to general recognition, and in due course, Malthus's name became a household word.

The full title of the *Essay* hints at the motivation behind it. Malthus reacted against the extreme optimism of the philosophers Godwin and Condorcet. Inspired by the political euphoria of the French Revolution, these two philosophers forecast the elimination of social evils. They described a society devoid of war, crime, government, disease, anguish, melancholy, and resentment, where every man unflinchingly sought the good of all. Malthus's answer to the Godwin-Condorcet vision appears, in retrospect, to be deceptively simple: The biological capacity of man to reproduce will, if left unchecked, outstrip the physical means of subsistence, he stated, and in consequence render the perfectibility of human society impossible.

The first *Essay* was constructed largely in Malthus's own head. Afterward, and partly because of the furor it created, he began to add some empirical flesh to his bare-bones theory. The *Essay* went through subsequent editions in 1803, 1806, 1807, 1817, and 1826. Finally, it culminated in *A Summary View of the Principle of Population,* published in 1830. Despite numerous modifications through its several editions, however, the essential principle of the first *Essay* remained unchanged.

An Outline of the Theory

Malthus based his population principle on two propositions. The first asserted that "Population, when unchecked, increases in a geometrical progression of such a nature as to double itself every twenty-five years" (*A Summary View,* p. 238). Malthus attempted to add precision to this principle by basing it on population experience in the United States. Available statistics were unreliable, however, and provided little real empirical support for Malthus's first postulate. Consequently, he was careful to indicate that this doubling of population every twenty-five years was neither the maximum growth rate of population nor always necessarily the actual rate. But Malthus clearly asserted the existence of a potential growth rate of population that advanced in *geometric* progression.

Counterpoised to the first postulate was the second: Under even the most favorable circumstances, the means of subsistence (i.e., the food supply) cannot possibly increase faster than in arithmetic progression. The precision that Malthus lent to this second assertion was unfortunate, since the arithmetic progression of the food supply could not be supported by fact, not even as loosely as the first assertion could. Nevertheless, juxtaposition of the first two postulates led to recognition of the obvious discrepancy between the potential growth of population versus the food supply. In Malthus's own words: "The power of population being...so much superior, the increase of the human species can only be kept down to the level of the means of subsistence by the constant operation of the strong law of necessity, acting as a check upon the greater power" (*A Summary View,* p. 21).

This population dilemma posed both a theoretical and a practical question. The theoretical question centered on identification of the actual checks to population growth; the practical question concerned solutions to the problem, namely, which checks should be encouraged over others. Malthus discussed both questions, beginning with the identification problem.

Positive and Preventive Checks   The ultimate check on population growth is limited food supply. But there are others, and Malthus classified them into positive checks and preventive checks. The former, such as disease, increase the death rate, whereas the latter, such as contraception, lower the birthrate. Malthus himself favored neither contraception nor abortion as practical means to circumscribe population growth. In a carefully measured condemnation of the latter, he described abortion as "improper arts to conceal the consequences of irregular connection"!

The significance of Malthus's contribution lay in his ability to fashion the procreative tendency and the checks to it into a theoretical structure that focused attention on those forces tending to change the number of people on earth. Table 6-1 presents Malthus's population theory in summary form.

As theory, the population principle tells us that population will increase whenever the cumulative effect of the various checks is less than that of procreation, that it will decrease whenever the cumulative effect of the checks is greater than that of procreation, and that it will remain unchanged whenever the combined effects of the checks and of procreation are self-canceling.

Theoretical Limitations   Although the theory outlined in Table 6-1 is quite general, Malthus himself tended to view the outcome of the population-food supply struggle as inevitably leading to a subsistence economy. This view was unfortunate for two reasons: (1) as prophecy, it has proved to be wrong in many instances, and (2) it is not at all inherent in the theoretical structure devised by Malthus.

On the one hand, Malthus's population theory is neutral with respect to assumptions and conclusions. Given relevant empirical inputs for Table 6-1, the theory is capable of explaining all manner of population changes: growth, depopulation, or stagnation. On the other hand, Malthus inferred the actual attainment of a subsistence economy because the tendency to procreate would *in fact* dominate the cumulative effect of the checks in force. Malthus asserted that this consequence was inevitable, although, in fact, the advanced economies of the world have so far managed to avoid it.

TABLE 6-1
MALTHUS'S DISTINCTION BETWEEN POSITIVE
AND PREVENTIVE CHECKS

Positive checks (factors increasing deaths)	Preventive checks (factors reducing births)
War	Moral restraint
Famine	Contraception
Pestilence	Abortion

Does this mean as theory, Malthus's population principle is invalid? Not necessarily, for his theoretical structure is quite capable of yielding general conclusions regarding population and subsistence for different economies at different historical periods. What is required to make the theory operational in a predictive sense, however, is reliable information about the magnitude of the tendencies given prominence by the theory.

Malthus may also be faulted for overlooking other checks that might forestall his gloomy conclusion. For one thing, he failed to separate, conceptually, sex and procreation. Yet in a world of modern birth control techniques and other arts of family planning, the distinction is often made. Many families limit the number of their offspring for reasons other than financial ones, e.g., a desire for personal freedom and mobility or a career. One cannot discount altogether the "cosmetic motive" for birth control—too many children may damage the appearance, comfort, and well-being of the mother. These additional checks are capable of reducing the disparity between multiplication of the species and growth of the food supply.

A more serious shortcoming of Malthus's population theory was his tendency, shared by other classical writers, to underestimate the advance of agricultural technology. There was already the hint in the *Essay* that agriculture is subject to diminishing returns, a topic that Malthus later expanded in his theory of rent. As an economic law, however, diminishing returns hold only for a constant state of technology. And in the advanced economies rapid progress in technology has so far succeeded in forestalling the Malthusian specter. This does not, of course, deny the very real threat of subsistence in the underdeveloped world. There the Malthusian specter appears to be a genuine threat to the practical objective of economic growth and development.

EARLY MONETARY ISSUES

For a time at least Malthus's population theory seemed to settle an important question in classical economics, the question of the labor supply. After Malthus, population came to be the chief determinant of wages, and in subsequent explanations of labor's aggregate share of annual output emphasis was placed on the wages-fund concept. An issue that proved more difficult to settle was the monetary question, namely what effect, if any, money has on economic activity.

Preclassical Monetary Theory

From roughly 1650 to 1776, monetary theory consisted primarily of two strands of thought. One strand asserted that "money stimulates trade" and numbered among its proponents John Law, Jacob Vanderlint, and (Bishop) George Berkeley. This argument stressed the effect of money on output and employment, largely ignoring the possible relation between money and prices. The other strand was the quantity theory of money, which, as we have seen in

Chapter 3, concentrated on the relation between money and prices. The important contributors to the development of the quantity theory were John Locke, Richard Cantillon, and David Hume.

Like many early theories, the money-stimulates-trade argument was a useful first approximation. Underlying the theory was the idea that, given a volume of trade, there is an appropriate amount of money required for transactions purposes. Money is an important determinant of aggregate spending, which in turn determines the levels of output and employment. This theoretical progression is the element of truth in the money-stimulates-trade doctrine. But it does not go far enough, especially in two critical respects. First, as previously noted, it ignored the possible effects of money on the price level. And second, it overlooked the role of expectations in the decision-making process. This last matter sharply divides Keynes (see Chapter 19) from the money-stimulates-trade theorists of the seventeenth and eighteenth centuries. Unlike his forebears, Keynes did not assert that money holds the key to solving unemployment. However, like them, he saw money as the key to *explaining* unemployment.

Although we have already discussed the mechanics of the quantity theory of money in Chapters 3 and 4, we take this occasion to mention once again the name of David Hume (1711–1776), at whose hands the quantity theory of money took the form of its commonly accepted version. It was Hume who attempted a reconciliation of the money-stimulates-trade theory with the quantity theory of money. Moreover, it is in Hume's economic writings that the concept of neutral money emerges for the first time. As Keynes observed, "Hume had a foot and a half in the classical world" (*The General Theory,* p. 343n.).

Eighteenth-century attitudes toward money cannot be understood in a historical vacuum. The century opened with the monetary experiments of John Law, "who was inspired by the idea that an abundance of money is the royal road to wealth" (Rist, *History of Monetary and Credit Theory,* p. 103). After the collapse of Law's system, most of the enlightened men of that epoch— from Cantillon to Hume, from Quesnay and Turgot to Smith, and in the next century, from Thornton to Ricardo—de-emphasized the importance of money, insisting that labor and natural resources are instead the fundamentals of wealth. Paradoxically, the business community continued to believe in a metallic currency even while the theorists argued against it.

The eighteenth century was one in which Europe was ravaged by war; consequently there was a great deal of pressure on the economies of Europe to expand the money supply. Scarcely had forced paper currency been established in England at the close of the century when everybody began to ponder ways and means of returning as quickly as possible to metallic currency. There may be some lessons for the present in this past experience. Adam Smith clearly taught that the only things that count in the advancement of wealth are the resources nature provides for man's activity and the use he makes of them through his labor and inventions. But this is not enough. It must be kept in mind that human beings live in society and that society is based on a set of reciprocal exchanges. The greater part of these exchanges can only be effected after an interval of time, which introduces some uncertainty about the future. The goods that offer the best possibility of guarding against the uncertainties of time are precious, rare, durable, indestructible objects, such as gold. Such objects therefore necessarily play an important role in all human societies in which the future is a reality.

As a rule, economic analysis underestimates the place taken by the future in economic activity. The thought of the future is never far from the minds of the industrialist, merchant, and business person. They continually focus their vision on the future as regards prices, markets, and sources of supply and demand. Stable money is an important bridge between the present and the future. Only because of stable money (or in its absence other stable and precious objects) can persons wait, reserve their choices, and calculate their chances. Without it, they are completely afloat in a sea of uncertainty.

In the modern age, controversies over "hard money" versus paper currencies are rare, although this may be changing. What has been more durable as a theoretical issue is the controversy over money's "neutrality" or "non-neutrality." The neutrality of money refers to the fact that changes in the money stock have no effect on *relative* prices. In their zeal to discredit the mercantilist idea that money constitutes wealth, early monetary theorists gave the impression that money is a veil that hides the real forces of productivity, which alone account for genuine economic wealth. All that monetary changes do is change the *price level* in proportion to the change in money. Hume's exposition of this view is classic:

> If we consider any one kingdom by itself, it is evident, that the greater or less plenty of money is of no consequence; since the prices of commodities are always proportioned to the plenty of money.... It is a maxim almost self-evident, that the prices of everything depend on the proportion between commodities and money, and that any considerable alteration on either has the same effect, either of heightening or lowering the price...(*Writings on Economics,* pp. 33, 41).

It is one thing to isolate the effects of money changes on the price level while ignoring the concomitant effects on relative prices, but it is quite another to deny that monetary shocks have any effect whatsoever on relative prices. Not all early monetary theorists were naive in this regard. Cantillon (see Chapter 4) saw quite clearly the relative price effects of money, and Hume also worked out a domestic adjustment mechanism that described the short-run as well as the long-run effects of a change in money. He observed that an increase or decrease in money supply impacted upon employment, output, and productivity, as well as on prices (Mayer, "David Hume and Monetarism," p. 573). Finally, Gary Becker and William Baumol found virtually no support for the view that early monetary theorists unequivocally endorsed the "neutral money thesis." They thereby concluded that the whole idea was basically a "straw man" constructed for the convenience of neoclassical monetary theorists ("The Classical Monetary Theory," p. 376).

Classical Monetary Theory

Insofar as pure theory is concerned, most of the ground in monetary economics was broken in the eighteenth century. The nineteenth century had little more to do than adopt the monetary theory of Cantillon and Hume, which it did, sometimes adding more confusion than light.

Perhaps the best summary statement of the period's monetary thought was the Bullion Report of 1810. In the opening years of the nineteenth century the move to an inconvertible paper currency saw only a slight increase in the circulation of British bank notes and little change in exchange rates. But beginning in 1808 the increase in note issue began to make itself felt as prices climbed steadily and exchange rates fell. Certain sectors of the public expressed their concern, and early in 1810 Francis Horner, a member of Parliament, proposed in the House of Commons that a committee be appointed to investigate the high price of bullion. A number of witnesses were called to testify, after which a report, drawn up largely by Horner, William Huskisson, and Henry Thornton, was delivered to the House in June. It was not debated until the following year, however, when its conclusions were rejected.

The Bullion Report was the first official argument against discretionary monetary policy. It maintained that an excessive amount of note issue influenced the value of paper money and attributed the high price of bullion (inflation) to this cause. Somewhat paradoxically, the report maintained that the reigning British monetary problems were not occasioned by a lack of public confidence in paper money, although this was a widely held belief among the public. The committee's position in this regard may have been staked by Thornton, who had taken a similar position in his book published in 1802, *An Enquiry into the Nature and Effects of the Paper Credit of Great Britain*. By the time they reached the end of the report, however, the committee had practically reversed itself, for it concluded that the return to convertibility was the only way to "effectively restore general confidence in the value of the circulating medium of the kingdom" (Cannan, *The Paper Pound*, p. 70).

The Bullion Report served as a pretext for David Ricardo's (see Chapter 7) early pamphlets on monetary matters, which were published as commentaries on the report. In 1809, Ricardo published his "Treatise on the Price of Bullion," and in 1816, his "Proposals for an Economical and Secure Currency." In both works Ricardo reaffirmed the quantity theory of money and advocated a return to convertibility. The concept of *quantity* completely dominated Ricardo's monetary theory. He maintained that both declines and rises in the price level are regulated by changes in the quantity of money. The idea of money as a store of value seems not to have occurred to him. He makes no mention of the demand for money. Money is defined in the narrowest terms as a mere *regulator* of value. Ricardo either rejected or ignored the idea of money as a link between the present and the future by virtue of its imperishability and scarcity. His view of credit was also overly restrictive. For example, he did not think of checks as instruments of circulation (as Cantillon did) but as a means of economizing on the use of money. Since he did not regard checks as currency instruments, therefore they could not affect prices. Taken together, Ricardo's ideas on money had the effect of changing the quantity theory of money into the *Ricardian* theory of money. His formulation was so one-sided and restrictive that it led many later economists to regard with suspicion any theory of money or prices in which quantity plays a part.

One curiosum remains to be covered on this topic. Found among Ricardo's papers after his death and published in 1823 was his *Plan of a National Bank,* which furthered the notion that paper money is an efficient substitute for metallic money because it requires fewer resources to maintain. All that is necessary is to fix the quantity of paper money once and for all. Ricardo devised a plan for this whereby the state would be granted the monopoly issue of paper money and would only be able to issue new notes against a backing of new gold from abroad. An element of currency elasticity was introduced, however, by allowing the central bank to engage in open-market operations: it would buy government securities when it desired to increase the quantity of money and sell them when it desired to decrease the quantity of money. These purchases and sales were to be determined by changes in the exchange rate, which would reflect the relation between the value of paper money and its metallic counterpart. Thus it can be seen that the idea of such operations, while sometimes regarded as the height of modernism, is in fact very old. Moreover, it seems but a brief step from recognizing the legitimacy of such operations under a gold standard to the idea of a fully managed, fiat currency.

John Stuart Mill (see Chapter 8), who represented classical economics at the height of its influence, also accepted the quantity theory but added qualifications to it, some of which served to correct the Ricardian excesses. For one thing, Mill recognized (as did Cantillon and Hume) that the rigid conclusions of the quantity theory were based on the assumption of an equiproportionate distribution of new money relative to initial money holdings. Any other distribution would upset the strict proportionality between money and prices. Further, he believed that the strict quantity theory held only for metallic money and that:

> When credit comes into play as a means of purchasing, distinct from money in hand, we shall hereafter find that the connection between prices and the amount of circulating medium is much less direct and intimate, and that such connection as does exist no longer admits of so simple a mode of expression (*Principles of Political Economy,* p. 495).

Finally, Mill recognized that an increase in bank credit under conditions of full employment could drive the interest rate down.

By far the brightest light among the classical monetary theorists was Henry Thornton, the British banker and member of Parliament mentioned above in connection with the Bullion Report of 1810. Thornton made two important contributions to monetary theory: (1) the distinction between the natural rate of interest and the bank (loan) rate of interest and (2) the doctrine of "forced saving."

Regarding the first principle, Thornton correctly pointed out that the rate of return on invested capital (determined by thrift and productivity) regulates the bank interest rate on loans. If the bank rate is below the former, competition for business loans will drive the bank rate up; if the bank rate is above the former, the demand for bank loans will dry up, forcing banks to lower rates in order to make loans. Therefore, the question of determining the optimum quantity of bank loans depends on a comparison of the rate of return on capital (Thornton called this the "natural" rate) and the interest rate on bank loans. If investment and savings are determined by the real forces of thrift and productivity, then only a change in one or the other of these forces will shift the schedules depicted in Figure 6-1. In this model, SS' represents the supply of savings as a function of the interest rate. Likewise, II' represents the demand for investable funds also as a function of the interest rate. The intersection of SS' and II' determines the natural rate (r). In monetary equilibrium, the loan rate (i) will be equal to the natural rate. But if monetary equilibrium is disturbed by an increase in paper money, the interest rate on bank loans will be driven down, say to i' (because of an increase in loanable funds). At the same time, SS' and II' would remain unchanged unless there was a change in the

FIGURE 6-1
At monetary equilibrium, the loan rate is equal to the natural rate ($i = r$). With a monetary disturbance, the loan rate will diverge from the natural rate ($i \neq r$).

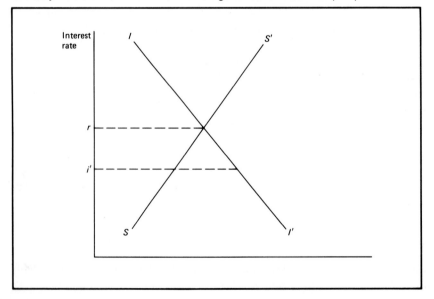

real factors of thrift and productivity, which would not be induced by a purely monetary phenomenon such as an increase in paper money.

Thus a gap would be created between the natural rate and the loan rate, and this gap would give rise to an insatiable demand for loans. The ensuing inflationary pressure would be eliminated only when the loan rate was again raised to its former level at r. In the process, however, prices would have climbed to a higher level. In this way, the quantity theory is vindicated: An increase in money leads to higher prices but no (long-run) change in the real interest rate.

Thornton's second contribution—the doctrine of forced saving—recognized that an increase in money brings about an increase in capital as well as an increase in prices. This would be the case as long as part of the new money went to entrepreneurs. If entrepreneurs converted this new money into capital, then output effects (forced capital accumulation) would accompany the higher prices associated with the increase in money; hence money would not be strictly neutral, as Hume maintained. In addition, Thornton suggested the possibility that an increase in bank notes under conditions of general unemployment would lead to an increase in output and employment rather than an increase in prices. Clearly, Thornton affirmed the neutrality of money only as a long-run proposition, and then only under certain circumstances.

CONCLUSION

The issues and concerns raised in this chapter combined to form the general backdrop against which classical economic analysis was staged in the nineteenth century. Self-interest became the dominant explanation of economic activity. Malthus's population theory entered economic analysis as an endogenous variable and became an integral part of the theory of income distribution. Finally, the quantity theory of money provided the analytical structure for understanding and explaining changes in the aggregate price level. With the exception of population theory, each of these propositions has remained within the corpus of mainstream economics. Population changes were subsequently relegated by neoclassical economics to the rank of exogenous variables, i.e., "outside" influences beyond the direct concern of the theorist.

Our review of each of these subjects has been necessarily brief and should not be construed as exhaustive. In particular, it is extremely difficult to render an unequivocal summary of classical monetary theory in terms of the neutral-money doctrine. Down to the present the quantity theory has remained one of the oldest and most durable ideas in economics. Modifications of it continued well into the neoclassical period and, after a brief Keynesian interlude, are continuing today (see Chapter 20).

NOTES FOR FURTHER READING

General references to Bentham and his ideas include J. L. Stocks, *Jeremy Bentham* (Manchester, England: Manchester University Press, 1933); C. W.

Everett, *Jeremy Bentham* (New York: Dell, 1966); D.J. Manning, *The Mind of Jeremy Bentham* (London: Longmans, 1900); and Elie Halévy, *The Growth of Philosophic Radicalism,* M. Morris (trans.) (London: Faber, 1928).

From the standpoint of economics, perhaps the best original source on Bentham is his *Economic Writings,* 3 vols., W. Stark (ed.) (London: G. Allen, 1952–1954). *The Works of Jeremy Bentham,* 11 vols., J. Bowring (ed.) (New York: Russell & Russell, 1962), is more complete but ranges far beyond economics to morals, philosophy, and jurisprudence.

Two opposing views of Bentham's felicific calculus are presented by Lionel Robbins, *Bentham in the Twentieth Century* (London: University of London, Athlone Press, 1965), and John Plamenatz, *The English Utilitarians,* 2d ed. (Oxford: Blackwell, 1958). On the same subject, see W. C. Mitchell, "Bentham's Felicific Calculus," *Political Science Quarterly,* vol. 33 (June 1918), pp. 161–183, reprinted in *The Backward Art of Spending Money* (New York: McGraw-Hill, 1937).

Other treatments include W. Stark, "Liberty and Equality, or: Jeremy Bentham as an Economist," *Economic Journal,* vol. 51 (April 1941), pp. 56–79, and vol. 56 (December 1946), pp. 583–608; Jacob Viner, "Bentham and J.S. Mill: The Utilitarian Background," *American Economic Review,* vol. 39 (March 1949), pp. 360–382; and T. W. Hutchison, "Bentham as an Economist," *Economic Journal,* vol. 66 (June 1956), pp. 288–306. Also interesting is P. A. Palmer's "Benthamism in England and America," *American Political Science Review,* vol. 35 (October 1941), pp. 855–871.

The standard reference on Malthus is James Bonar, *Malthus and His Work,* 2d ed. (New York: Macmillan, 1924). A more recent rendition is G. F. McCleary, *The Malthusian Population Theory* (London: Faber, 1953). Bonar, C. R. Fay, and J. M. Keynes combined efforts to write "A Commemoration of Thomas Robert Malthus," *Economic Journal,* vol. 45 (June 1935), pp. 221–234, on the occasion of the centenary of Malthus's death. Keynes was also lavish in his praise of Malthus in his *Essays in Biography* (New York: Norton, 1963).

For other appraisals, see Lionel Robbins, "Malthus as an Economist," *Economic Journal,* vol. 77 (June 1967), pp. 256–261; and R. L. Meek, "Malthus: Yesterday and Today," *Science and Society,* vol. 18 (Winter 1954), pp. 21–51. Noteworthy treatments of Malthus's population theory include S. M. Levin, "Malthus's Conception of the Checks to Population," *Human Biology,* vol. 10 (1938), pp. 214–234; S. M. Levin, "Malthus and the Idea of Progress," *Journal of the History of Ideas,* vol. 27 (January–March 1966), pp. 92–108; Kingsley Davis, "Malthus and the Theory of Population," in P. F. Lazarsfeld and M. Rosenberg (eds.), *The Language of Social Research* (New York: Free Press, 1955); J. P. Hubel, "The Demographic Impact of the Old Poor Law: More Reflections on Malthus," *Economic History Review,* vol. 33 (August 1980), pp. 367–381; J. M. Pullen, "Malthus on the Doctrine of Proportion and the Concept of the Optimum," *Australian Economic Papers,* vol. 21 (December 1982), pp. 270–285; J. M. Pullen, "Some New Information on the Rev. T. R. Malthus," *History of Political Economy,* vol. 19 (Spring 1987), pp. 127–140; P. Laslett, "Gregory King, Robert Malthus and the Origins of English Social Realism," *Population Studies,* vol. 39 (November 1985), pp. 351–362; and Sam Hollander, "On Malthus's Population Principle and Social Reform," *History of Political Economy,* vol. 18 (Summer 1986), pp. 187–235. The correspondence between Senior and Malthus on the subject of population is included in Senior's *Selected Writings on Economics* (New York: A. M. Kelley, 1966).

Monetary theory has an old and extensive history. On the preclassical period, see Douglas Vickers, *Studies in the Theory of Money: 1690–1776* (Philadelphia: Chilton, 1959); A. E. Monroe, *Monetary Theory before Adam Smith* (Cambridge, Mass.: Harvard University Press, 1923); William Letwin, *The Origins of Scientific Economics* (Garden City, N.Y.: Doubleday, 1964), which contains a reprint of Locke's early *Manuscript on Interest;* and Jacob Viner, *Studies in the Theory of International Trade* (New York: Harper & Row, 1937). Major individual performances among early writers are detailed by F. Cesarano, "Monetary Theory in Ferdinando Galiani's *Della Moneta,*" *History of Political Economy,* vol. 8 (Autumn 1976), pp. 380–399; A. H. Leigh, "John Locke and the Quantity Theory of Money," *History of Political Economy,* vol. 6 (Summer 1974), pp. 200–219; J. A. Weymark, "Money and Locke's Theory of Property," *History of Political Economy,* vol. 12 (Summer 1980), pp. 282–292; M. I. Duke, "David Hume and Monetary Adjustment," *History of Political Economy,* vol. 11 (Winter 1979), pp. 572–587; and T. Mayer, "David Hume and Monetarism" (see References).

Adam Smith's ideas on money and monetary theory, which have not been aired in this chapter, are the subject of David Laidler's "Adam Smith as a Monetary Economist," *Canadian Journal of Economics,* vol. 14 (May 1981), pp. 185–200. Bimetallism is discussed within a general equilibrium framework by C. N. Chen, "Bimetallism: Theory and Controversy in Perspective," *History of Political Economy,* vol. 4 (Spring 1972), pp. 89–112. An important nineteenth-century monetary economist was Thomas Tooke, whose ideas on the subject are explored by Arie Arnon, "The Transformation of Thomas Tooke's Monetary Theory Reconsidered," *History of Political Economy,* vol. 16 (Summer 1984), pp. 311–326. For an examination of classical monetary theory in light of contemporary debate over the desirability of reinstituting the gold standard, see David Glasner, "A Reinterpretation of Classical Monetary Theory," *Southern Economic Journal,* vol. 52 (July 1985), pp. 46–67. The evolution of the monetary rule espoused by modern monetarists has been traced to Jeremy Bentham and Henry Thornton by G. S. Tavlas in "Some Initial Formulations of the Monetary Growth Rate Rule," *History of Political Economy,* vol. 9 (Winter 1977), pp. 535–547. See also R. L. Hetzel, "Henry Thornton: Seminal Monetary Theorist and Father of the Modern Central Bank," *Federal Reserve Bank of Richmond Economic Review,* vol. 73 (July/August 1987), pp. 3–16.

David Ricardo's contributions to the theory of money and banking have been explored by J. C. W. Ahiakpor, "Ricardo on Money: The Operational Significance of the Non-neutrality of Money in the Short-Run," *History of Political Economy,* vol. 17 (Spring 1985), pp. 17–30; and by A. Arnon, "Banking between the Invisible and Visible Hands: A Reinterpretation of Ricardo's Place within the Classical School," *Oxford Economic Papers,* vol. 39 (June 1987), pp. 268–281, in which the latter argues that Ricardo paved the way for central banking.

Henry Thornton is perhaps the most interesting monetary theorist among the classical economists. His one major work, *An Enquiry into the Nature and Effects of the Paper Credit of Great Britain* (1802), has been reprinted, edited by F. A. Hayek (New York: Farrar & Rinehart, 1939). See also Hayek's "Note on the Development of the Doctrine of 'Forced Saving,'" *Quarterly Journal of Economics,* vol. 47 (November 1932), pp. 123–133. Ricardo's monetary theory is reviewed in R. S. Sayer's "Ricardo's Views on Monetary Questions," *Quarterly Journal of Economics,* vol. 67 (February 1953), pp. 30–49. For surveys of the field that take in more than the classical theories alone, see Charles Rist, *History of Monetary and Credit Theory* (see References), and F. W. Fetter, *Development of British Monetary Orthodoxy, 1797–1875* (Cambridge, Mass.: Harvard University Press, 1965).

REFERENCES

Becker, Gary, and William Baumol. "The Classical Monetary Theory: The Outcome of the Discussion," *Economica,* n.s., vol. 19 (November 1952), pp. 355–376.

Bentham, Jeremy. *An Introduction to the Principles of Morals and Legislation.* Oxford: The Clarendon Press, 1879 [1789].

Cannan, Edwin. *The Paper Pound of 1797–1821.* London: King, 1921.

Hume, David. *David Hume: Writings on Economics,* E. Rotwein (ed.). Madison, Wis.: The University of Wisconsin Press, 1970.

Keynes, J.M. *The General Theory of Employment, Interest and Money.* London: Macmillian, 1936.

Malthus, T. R. *An Essay on the Principle of Population and a Summary View of the Principle of Population,* A. Flew (ed.). Baltimore: Penguin, 1970.

Mayer, Thomas. "David Hume and Monetarism," *Quarterly Journal of Economics,* vol. 95 (August 1980), pp. 89–101.

Mill, J.S. *Principles of Political Economy,* W. J. Ashley (ed.). New York: A. M. Kelley, 1965 [1848].

Rist, Charles. *History of Monetary and Credit Theory,* Jane Degras (trans.). New York: Macmillan, 1940.

CLASSICAL ECONOMIC ANALYSIS (II): THE RICARDIAN SYSTEM AND ITS CRITICS

INTRODUCTION

We have seen that Adam Smith established the foundations of classical value theory and the first scientifically rigorous theory of economic growth. *The Wealth of Nations* caught the imagination of its readers, and political economy became a serious and timely topic of interest and debate. The book itself represented both a culmination of previous developments and a catalyst to future advances and refinements. One of those persons who "caught fire" on reading Smith's work was Ricardo.

David Ricardo (1772–1823) was the son of a Jewish immigrant stockbroker. With but a modicum of commercial education, Ricardo parlayed a modest stake into a sizable fortune by making shrewd investments in securities and real estate. In 1799, while on vacation and bored, he picked up Adam Smith's *Wealth of Nations* and soon became engrossed in its contents. Ten years later he began arguing economic questions in pamphlets and the press, an avocation that subsequently became a consuming intellectual pursuit. What ensured Ricardo's place in the history of economics was his ability to forge a general analytic system that yielded sweeping conclusions based on relatively few basic principles. His "system" was a monument to the process of deductive reasoning. Three principles were critical to Ricardo's analysis, each borrowed, as it were, from someone else. The three critical propositions were (1) classical rent theory, (2) Malthus's population principle, and (3) the wages-fund doctrine. Since the second and third propositions have already been examined in earlier chapters, we pause to review the first before proceeding to an explanation of the Ricardian system.

THE CLASSICAL DOCTRINE OF RENT

The first tract on rent that could be called "classical" in the sense that term is used here was written by James Anderson (1739–1808), a Scottish farmer and inventor of the "Scottish plough." In 1777, Anderson published a pamphlet that clearly stated the principle of diminishing returns, albeit in embryonic form. This was followed by the more or less independent, multiple discoveries of basically the same idea in 1815 by Sir Edward West, Malthus, Robert Torrens, and Ricardo. Space does not permit a detailed comparison of these different presentations at this point. We aim to concentrate on Ricardo's presentation because it is more relevant to the present context. However, it should be noted that Ricardo acknowledged his debt to both Malthus and West in this regard.

Role of the Corn Law

From Anderson to Ricardo, the immediate impetus for the development of the classical doctrine of rent was the Corn Law controversy, which emerged during the Napoleonic wars. Napoleon's embargo on British ports effectively kept foreign grain out of England. British farmers were forced to increase production of domestic grain in order to feed the population. And since costs of production were higher in England than abroad, the price of British grain rose. Between 1790 and 1810, British corn prices rose on the average 18 percent per year. Land rents also increased to the point where landlords developed a vested interest in continuing to restrict grain imports. The Corn Law passed by Parliament in 1815 effectively achieved this end. It was this question of agricultural protectionism and its effects on income distribution and economic growth that provided the stimulus for the development of classical rent theory.

Malthus began his tract by tracing the effects of increased cultivation on the price of grain:

> The cause of the high comparative money price of corn is its rich comparative real price, or the greater quantity of capital and labour which must be employed to produce it; and the reason why the real price of corn is higher and continually rising in countries which are already rich, and still advancing in prosperity and population, is to be found in the necessity of resorting to constantly poorer land...which require[s] a greater expenditure to work...[so that] the price rises in proportion (*An Inquiry into the Nature and Progress of Rent*, pp. 35–36).

> It follows...that the price of produce in every progressive country must be just about equal to the cost of production on land of the poorest quality actually in use; or to the cost of raising additional produce on old land, which yields only the usual returns of agricultural stock with little or no rent....It will always answer to any farmer who can command capital, to lay it out on his land, if the additional produce resulting from it will fully repay the profits of his stock, although it yields nothing to his landlord (*Inquiry*, p. 32).

In other words rent, which Ricardo defined as "payment for the original and indestructible powers of the soil," does not exist at the margin (i.e., the worst land in cultivation) and arises on better lands only when poorer lands are brought into use. Ricardo was more explicit:

> If all land had the same properties, if it were unlimited in quantity and uniform in quality, no charge could be made for its use, unless where it possessed peculiar advantages of situation. It is only, then, because land is not unlimited in quantity and uniform in quality, and because in the progress of population, land of an inferior quality, or less advantageously situated, is called into cultivation, that rent is ever paid for the use of it. When in the progress of society, land of the second degree of fertility is taken into cultivation, rent immediately commences on that of the first quality, and the amount of that rent will depend on the difference in the quality of these two portions of land (*The Works and Correspondence of David Ricardo*, I, p. 70).

In this passage, Ricardo identified rent at the *extensive* margin (i.e., when more land was taken into cultivation). But according to Ricardo, rent also arises because of diminishing returns on land of the same quality (i.e., the *intensive* margin). He observed:

> It often, and indeed commonly happens, that before...the inferior lands are cultivated, capital can be employed more productively on those lands which are already in cultivation. It may perhaps be found, that by doubling the original capital employed on...[this land], though the produce will not be doubled...it may be increased...[by something else], and that this quantity exceeds what could be obtained by employing the same capital, on [other] land.
>
> In such case, capital will be preferably employed on the old land, and will equally create a rent; for rent is always the difference between the produce obtained by the employment of two equal quantities of capital and labour (*Works*, I, p. 71).

The effect of the Corn Law was to force more intensive and extensive agriculture in England. What Ricardo showed was that diminishing returns existed at both the intensive margin (more inputs applied to the same land) and the extensive margin (the same inputs applied to different types of land). Table 7-1 helps to clarify some points in Ricardo's discussion of rent.

The first column in the table shows units of labor and capital, which are assumed to be added to production in fixed proportions (e.g., one man, one shovel). Lands of different fertility (but fixed amounts) are represented by different grades, such that No. 1 represents land of the highest fertility and Nos. 2 to 5 represent lands of lesser fertility, in descending order. The marginal product (MP) of capital and labor is defined as the change in total product resulting from the addition of one more capital-labor input to production. In conformance with the law of diminishing returns, marginal product declines as more inputs are added to each type of land. As conventionally defined, and in this context, diminishing returns to labor occur only on the *intensive* margin. But total product also declines as production moves out to poorer lands. At the *extensive* margin, decreasing total output is due to differences in fertility.

Using Ricardo's definition of rent as "the difference between the produce obtained by the employment of two equal quantities of capital and labour," we may identify from Table 7-1 the real rents paid at both the intensive and ex-

TABLE 7-1

Capital and labor	No. 1	(MP$_1$)	No. 2	(MP$_2$)	No. 3	(MP$_3$)	No. 4	(MP$_4$)	No. 5	(MP$_5$)
				Total and marginal products to types of land						
0	0		0		0		0		0	
1	100	(100)	90	(90)	80	(80)	70	(70)	60	(60)
2	190	(90)	170	(80)	150	(70)	130	(60)	110	(50)
3	270	(80)	240	(70)	210	(60)	180	(50)	150	(40)
4	340	(70)	300	(60)	260	(50)	220	(40)	180	(30)
5	400	(60)	350	(50)	300	(40)	250	(30)	200	(20)

tensive margins. Thus if only No. 1 land was cultivated, a real rent of 10 bushels would arise on it after the introduction of the second "dose" of capital and labor ($100 - 90 = 10$). Introduction of a third dose of capital and labor on No. 1 land would soon raise total rent on that land to 30 bushels ($100 - 80 + 90 - 80 = 30$), and so on. At the extensive margin, rent is the difference between output on the best land and the worst land in cultivation for equal amounts of capital and labor on each. Thus if, say, No. 1, No. 2, and No. 3 land each receive three doses of capital and labor, rent on No. 1 land would be 60 bushels ($270 - 210 = 60$), and rent on No. 2 land would be 30 bushels ($240 - 210 = 30$). As always, there would be no rent at the margin of the last land in use.

The information in Table 7-1 will easily give the optimum allocation of total expenditures among types of land, once information is known about the prices of inputs and outputs. Suppose the price per bushel of corn to be $1, so that the numbers in Table 7-1 are converted to revenues merely by placing dollar signs in front of them. It can easily be seen from the table that if the price of each dose of capital and labor (per production period) was $100, production would take place only on No. 1 land. But if the price of the input was $60 per dose, it would be profitable to extend production to the point where marginal revenue (MP × price of corn) equals marginal input cost ($60). This would entail extending production to No. 5 land, employing five units of capital and labor on No. 1 land, four on No. 2, three on No. 3, two on No. 4, and one on No. 5 (verify this in Table 7-1).

It should be pointed out that this theory explains agricultural rents *only*. In the classical theory of rent, land was assumed to have no alternative uses. Either it was used to produce a homogenous commodity called "corn," or it lay fallow. The amount of land used by the manufacturing sector was assumed to be of negligible value, and no analysis of rent was offered on such land. Since the problem attacked by Malthus and Ricardo was that of determining the distribution of total output between rent versus wages and profits, they ignored the manufacturing sector, where rents were (assumed) negligible, and concentrated fully on the major sector of the economy, agriculture. Their theory allowed capital and labor to be perfectly mobile, not only between parcels of land but also between manufacturing and agriculture. Land, however, was assumed merely to be brought into or out of agricultural production.

THE RICARDIAN SYSTEM

For reasons that we shall discuss below, Ricardo had a far greater impact on the future direction of economic theory than Malthus. But as theoretical antagonists, each played an important part in the development of the other's analytical system. Malthus saw a close and direct link between the general level of wages and the price of corn. He argued in favor of the Corn Law because he felt that free importation of grain would drive down domestic grain prices (and wages) and precipitate a depression. To Ricardo, however, the Corn Law signaled a rise in wages and a fall in profits and thus less capital accumulation and an end to economic growth. In answering Malthus, Ricardo constructed a most ingenious argument, built around the labor theory of value.

The Labor Theory of Value: Empirical or Analytical?

Few misconceptions in the history of economics have been perpetuated as extensively as the popular one concerning Ricardo's theory of value. The interpretation of the theory that lingers is that of a strict uncompromising labor theory of value. Yet there is little or no support in Ricardo's writings for this interpretation. Ironically, it was not Ricardo's critics (e.g., Malthus and Samuel Bailey) but his ardent disciples who were mostly responsible for the misinterpretation. We prefer to characterize Ricardo's theory of value as a "real-cost" theory, where, nevertheless, labor is the most important (empirical) factor.

The central problem posed by Ricardo in his *Principles of Political Economy and Taxation* was how changes occur in the relative income shares of land, labor, and capital and what effect these changes have on capital accumulation and economic growth. The determination of rent was an integral part of this problem, of course. But every theory of income distribution must rest on a theory of value, and Ricardo set out to modify Smith's value theory for his own use. Specifically, Ricardo perceived certain deficiencies in Smith's doctrine of "natural value." According to Smith, a rise in the price of one factor (e.g., wages) would increase the price of goods produced by that factor (labor). To Ricardo, this was a superficial analysis, especially if the change in value was to be more than a nominal price-level change.

Ricardo felt that with certain modifications, the labor theory of value provided the best general explanation of relative prices and that Smith's restriction of the labor theory to a "primitive economy" was unnecessary. To Ricardo, the relation between value and labor time expended in production was straightforward: "Every increase of the quantity of labor must augment the value of that commodity on which it is exercised, as every diminuation must lower it" (*Works*, I, p. 13). Although Ricardo never wavered from this basic position, he nevertheless added several qualifications necessary to make the theory more realistic. In this process, his theory of value ceased to be a pure labor theory. But Ricardo consistently sidestepped his own qualifications in subsequent analysis and policy and made use of a simple labor theory in order to reach general conclusions.

The first exception to the above rule that Ricardo allowed was in the case of nonreproducible goods. "There are some commodities," he maintained, "the value of which is determined by scarcity alone. No labour can increase the quantity of such goods, and therefore their value cannot be lowered by an increased supply." The value of a Renoir painting or a bottle of a 1929 Lafitte-Rothschild, to use Ricardo's words, "is wholly independent of the quantity of labor originally necessary to produce them, and varies with the varying wealth and inclinations of those who are desirous to possess them" (*Works,* I, p. 12). Quantitatively, this exception was unimportant to Ricardo, since "These commodities...form a very small part of the mass of commodities daily exchanged in the market."

More important qualifications of the labor theory of value were made respecting the role and importance of capital, which was treated as "indirect" or "embodied" labor. Here Ricardo distinguished between fixed and circulating capital. Circulating capital "is rapidly perishable and requires to be frequently reproduced," whereas fixed capital "is of slow consumption." Value will therefore increase as the ratio of fixed to circulating capital increases and as the durability of capital increases. This fact is demonstrated by Ricardo in the following passage:

> Suppose two men employ one hundred men each for a year in the construction of two machines, and another man employs the same number of men in cultivating corn, each of the machines at the end of the year will be of the same value as the corn, for they will each be produced by the same quantity of labour. Suppose one of the owners of one of the machines to employ it, with the assistance of one hundred men, the following year in making cloth, and the owner of the other machine to employ his also, with the assistance likewise of one hundred men, in making cotton goods, while the farmer continues to employ one hundred men as before in the cultivation of corn. During the second year they will all have employed the same quantity of labour, but the goods and machine together of the clothier, and also of the cotton manufacturer, will be the result of the labour of two hundred men, employed for a year; or rather, of the labour of one hundred men employed for two years; whereas the corn will be produced by the labour of one hundred men for one year, consequently if the corn be of the value of 500£ the machine and cloth of the clothier together, ought to be of the value of 1000£ and the machine and cotton goods of the cotton manufacturer, ought to be also of twice the value of the corn. But they will be of more than twice the value of corn, for the profit on the clothier's and cotton manufacturer's capital the first year has been added to their capitals, while that of the farmer has been expended and enjoyed. On account then of the different degrees of durability of their capitals, or, which is the same thing, on account of the amount of time which must elapse before one set of commodities can be brought to market, they will be valuable, not exactly in proportion to the quantity of labour bestowed

on them... but something more, to compensate for the greater length of time which must elapse before the most valuable can be brought to market (*Works,* I, pp. 33–34).

Ricardo's example clearly illustrates that he recognized the two ways in which capital affects the value of goods: (1) the capital used up in production constitutes an addition to the value of the product, and (2) the capital employed per unit of time must be compensated (at the going rate of interest). This recognition by Ricardo that *time* as well as labor is an important element of value constituted a genuine contribution to economics, for which he subsequently was given little, if any, credit.

From an analytical standpoint, then, it is clear that Ricardo based value on the real costs of labor and capital. His theory differed from Smith's in that it excluded rent from costs. But from an empirical standpoint, Ricardo held that the relative quantities of labor used in production are the major determinants of relative values. On the methodological front, Ricardo exemplifies the abstract, deductive reasoner. He preferred to base the principles of his analytical system on a single, dominant variable rather than on a number of lesser ones of dubious effect. To this end, he warned his readers (after noting the above effects of capital on value): "In the subsequent part of this work, though I shall occasionally refer to this cause of variation [i.e., time], I shall consider all the great variations which take place in the relative value of commodities to be produced by the greater or less quantity of labour which may be required from time to time to produce them" (*Works,* I, pp. 36–37). Ricardo, at least, was less open to the criticism leveled against some modern theoreticians, namely, the failure to state explicitly the assumptions underlying one's analytical constructs.

Despite its rigor, Ricardo's value theory contained several deficiencies. In the first place, his handling of qualitative differences in labor was unsatisfactory. Ricardo assumed that wage adjustments for qualitative differences in labor would occur in the marketplace and that once determined, the scale of differences would vary little. Since Ricardo was seeking a measure of market value in the first place, this is a circular argument. In the second place, the exclusion of rent from costs can be justified only if land has no alternative uses (which Ricardo assumed, unrealistically). Moreover, the Ricardian theory of value kept the role of demand restricted to a special class of (nonreproducible) goods. This is of course inadequate in the case where goods are not produced subject to constant average costs of production.

The Nature of Economic Progress: The Stationary State

In the Ricardian system the theory of value, reduced to Ricardo's level of simplification, plus the theory of rent, provided the key to the central problem of income distribution. It was, of course, necessary to relate the theory of value to the theory of prices in a complex economy. Ricardo did this by relating market price to the costs of production in the marginal (no-rent) firm. He noted:

The exchangeable value of all commodities, whether they be manufactured, or the produce of the mines, or the produce of the land, is always regulated, not by the less quantity of labour that will suffice for their production under circumstances highly favorable, and exclusively enjoyed by those who have peculiar facilities of production; but by the greater quantity of labour necessarily bestowed on their production by those who continue to produce them under the most unfavorable circumstances (*Works,* I, p. 73).

Ricardo recognized that there is no perfect measure of value, since any measure chosen varies with fluctuations in wages and profit rates. We have seen that different durabilities of capital and different ratios of fixed to circulating capital will affect market prices differently if wages change relative to profits. Thus Ricardo devised an analytical gimmick—the "average firm"—in which both the ratio of capital to labor and capital durability are assumed equal to the economy average. So armed, Ricardo was ready to solve the problem of income distribution and its changes over time.

Let us illustrate Ricardo's process utilizing the product information contained in Table 7-2. Suppose that three doses of labor and capital on a given farm produce 270 bushels of corn per year. Each labor input, by virtue of its advance from the wages-fund, constitutes an expenditure of circulating capital, whereas each capital input, through annual depreciation, constitutes an expenditure of fixed capital. Ricardo defined total profits as total revenue minus the sum of fixed and circulating capital expenditures incurred per production period. Now assume that the price per bushel of corn is $1, that the wage rate per worker is 10 bushels of corn and $10 of other necessities (the latter can be given in dollar terms because they are assumed to be produced under conditions of constant cost), and that the annual depreciation per unit of capital is $10. Profits on No. 1 land would be calculated as in Table 7-2.

If all land were equally fertile, profits could continue at the same rate. But with the progress of capital and population, cultivation must be extended to No. 2 land, where three doses of labor and capital produce only 240 bushels of corn. Technically, more labor and capital are now needed to produce the same output on No. 2 land as on No. 1 land. Therefore, the price of corn must rise to $1.125 (270/240 × $1.00 = $1.25). In Ricardo's system, this increase in the price of corn has the effect of raising money wages and aggregate rents and of lowering profits. The ensuing distributional pattern is illustrated in Table 7-3.

Table 7-3 shows what we learned earlier—that rent arises on No. 1 land

TABLE 7-2

Value of product	=	270 × $1	=	$270
Wage rate	=	(10 × $1) + $10	=	20
Wage bill	=	3 × $20	=	60
Depreciation	=	3 × $10	=	30
Total profit	=	$270 – $90	=	180
Rent			=	0

TABLE 7-3

	No. 1 land		No. 2 land	
Value of product	270 × $1.125	= $303.75	240 × $1.125	= $270.00
Wage rate	(10 × $1.125) + $10	= 21.25	(10 × $1.125) + $10 =	21.25
Wage bill	3 × $21.25	= 63.75	3 × $21.25	= 63.75
Depreciation	3 × $10	= 30.00	3 × $10	= 30.00
Profits	$303.75 – 93.75 – 33.75	= 176.25	$270 – 93.75	= 176.25
Rent		= 33.75		= 0

only when production with the same amount of capital and labor is extended to No. 2 land. The calculation of rent is, as Ricardo indicated, the value of the initial firm's output less the value of the marginal firm's output. The illustration can be extended to additional firms (i.e., types of land), of course, but the distributional effects of economic growth are already clear. Increased agricultural production leads to higher money wages but the same *real* wages. Ricardo assumed, via the population principle, that wage rates would be at subsistence levels in the long run. On the other hand, higher nominal wage rates and increasing aggregate rents place a two-way squeeze on profits. Although under competition profits are the same for all firms in a given industry, the inevitable tendency of profits is to decline as output increases. Eventually a minimum profit rate is reached at which new investment (i.e., additional capital accumulation) ceases. Ricardo described this as the "stationary state." Theoretically, this minimum profit rate is zero; practically, however, it may be slightly above zero.

The process that Ricardo described may therefore be restated as a paradox: The logical result of economic growth is stagnation! Ricardo's analytical system did not allow for technological progress, and it uncritically accepted the population principle; it may be attacked on both these grounds. But granting Ricardo's assumptions, it is a logically consistent system. In its final version, the stationary state arises in the following manner. The average wage rate is determined by the proportion of fixed and circulating capital (i.e., the wages-fund) to the population. As long as profits are positive, the capital stock is increasing, and the increased demand for labor will temporarily increase the average wage rate. But when wage rates rise above subsistence, the "domestic delights" come into play, and population increases. A larger population requires a greater food supply, so that, barring imports, cultivation must be extended to inferior lands. As this occurs, aggregate rents increase and profits fall, until ultimately the stationary state is reached.

RICARDO'S CRITICS: MALTHUS AND SENIOR

Within a short period after the appearance of Ricardo's *Principles,* a number of writers rallied to his doctrine and method. Perhaps the most able of these writers was John Ramsay McCulloch, a frequent contributor to Britain's most influential journal, *The Edinburgh Review*. Also conspicuous among this group were James Mill, the father of John Stuart (see Chapter 8), and Thomas DeQuincey. These men considered themselves Ricardians, and they faithfully sought to spread and defend the ideas of their master. But Ricardo did not enjoy the luxury of uncritical success. Two of his foremost critics in England were Thomas Malthus, with whom we are already familiar, and Nassau Senior, who became the first professor of political economy at Oxford University in 1825.

The Ricardo-Malthus Correspondence

From their first meeting in 1811, there was little of fundamental importance in political economy that Malthus and Ricardo agreed on. This fact is revealed in their lengthy correspondence with each other, which spanned two decades. Many disagreements were minor, but in 1815 their respective investigations of the Corn Law put them on opposite sides of the free-trade issue.

Corn-Law Controversy In Ricardo's system, rent is viewed as a *socially unnecessary payment* (i.e., a current payment made but not necessary to bring forth the available supply of land). Thus when land rents rise (as Ricardo argued they would under the Corn Law), they do so at the expense of profits. Since Ricardo saw profit as the engine that drove economic progress, he perceived in the Corn Law a threat to economic growth, and he therefore argued vigorously in favor of free trade.

Malthus, however, argued that higher corn prices were in the interests of the workers, since the workers' purchasing power was closely tied to the price of corn.[1] It was, as we noted earlier, common for classical writers on political economy to speak of "corn wages" in an attempt to describe real purchasing power. Therefore, a crucial question in the Corn Law debate was whether or not higher corn prices meant higher *real* wages. Ricardo thought not, and he argued accordingly. Malthus took the opposite stand and argued in favor of the Corn Law.

Their antagonism on this and other points of economics constituted merely the first of many famous disagreements that would ensue among future economists. George Bernard Shaw captured this element of economics in his wry comment: "If you took all the economists in the world and laid them end to end, they still wouldn't reach a conclusion." Are there no permanent truths in economics?

Obviously, economists do frequently disagree, much to the dismay of those individuals who find security in unanimity of opinion. However, as in the case of Malthus and Ricardo, disagreement is rarely based on theoretical principles

---

[1] For clarification on this point, see Grampp, "Malthus on Money Wages and Welfare."

but rather on interpretation, method, or policy. We have already seen that Malthus and Ricardo agreed on the basic theory of rent. Yet debates on interpretation, method, and policy leave considerable room for value judgments, which in turn reduce the frequency of unanimity among participants of the debate.

Economic Method   Equally illuminating on this point was the disagreement between Malthus and Ricardo on economic method, which found form in the Malthus-Ricardo debate on exchange value. Recall that Ricardo treated costs as the determinant of value but strove for simplification to the point where a single variable (i.e., labor) became the only significant one. Malthus, on the other hand, who was interested in economic principles "with a view to their practical application," insisted on incorporating Ricardo's cost analysis into a supply-and-demand framework. In this, Malthus was clearly on the right track, but his theory of value did not win out over Ricardo's. The reasons for this are not entirely clear. There were two aspects of the value question that Malthus addressed. The first was an explanation of exchange value; the second, an explanation of the *measure* of value.

According to Malthus, the principle of supply and demand determines what Adam Smith called "natural price" as well as market price. He defined *demand* as the will combined with the power to purchase and *supply* as the quantity of commodities for sale combined with the intention to sell them (*Principles,* p. 61). "But however great this will and these means may be among the demanders of a commodity," argued Malthus, "none of them will be disposed to give a high price for it, if they can obtain it at a low one; and as long as the means and competition of the sellers continue to bring the quantity wanted to market at a low price, the real intensity of the demand will not show itself" (*Principles,* p. 63). Malthus then correctly concluded that the causes of an increased price are "an increase in the number, wants, and means of the demanders, or a deficiency in the supply; and the causes which lower the price are a diminution in the number, wants, and means of the demanders, or an increased abundance in its supply" (*Principles,* p. 64).

Ricardo rejected this notion because he understood the term "demand" to mean something different. In fact, a comparative study of the works of both authors shows that Malthus and Ricardo often talked to each other at crosspurposes and that the whole confusion on the role of demand and supply could have been cleared up if they had each understood the difference between a change in quantity demanded (i.e., movement along a demand schedule) and a change in demand (i.e., shift of the schedule). However, the notion of supply and demand *schedules* had not yet found its way, explicitly, into economic analysis. For his part, Ricardo viewed Malthus's efforts as an undue concern with trivia. In two letters to Malthus, he wrote:

> If I am too theoretical (which I really believe is the case), you I think are too practical. There are so many combinations and so many operating causes in political economy that there is a great danger in appealing to experience in favor of a partic-

ular doctrine, unless we are sure that all the causes of variation are seen and their effects duly estimated (*Works,* VI, p. 295).

Our differences may in some respects, I think, be ascribed to your considering my book as more practical than I intended it to be. My object was to elucidate principles, and to do this I imagined strong cases that I might show the operation of those principles (*Works,* VIII, p. 184).

To be sure, there was also something else at work. Ricardo's theory of value was oversimplified and long run in its outlook, but it was the cornerstone on which the entire Ricardian system rested. To abandon it would lead to collapse of the whole analytical structure, something that Ricardo understandably resisted vehemently.

Compared with his views on the nature of exchange value, Malthus's ideas on the *measure* of value underwent many changes through his successive works. This fact indicates that he was not quite sure of his mind on the subject, a failing that intruded on other parts of Malthus's economics as well. In the final analysis, this wavering aspect of his thought presented a weak defense against the onslaught of Ricardo's relentless logic and may consequently explain why it was Ricardo, not Malthus, who carried the day in British classical economics.

Say's Law and Underconsumption   Having challenged the Ricardian theory of value, Malthus was not about to let up. He further questioned the Ricardian theory of profits. One major assumption of Ricardo's analysis was that the cost of producing food controls wages (directly) and profits (indirectly through the effect on wages). In the Ricardian system, higher corn prices lead to higher money wages and falling profits. Malthus, however, would not concede that higher food prices were the only or even the major reason for lower profits. Utilizing a Smithian distinction between "productive" and "unproductive" consumption, Malthus singled out insufficient aggregate demand as a source of weakening investment incentives and thus of lower profits.

Malthus's argument runs as follows. That part of production devoted to the "necessities of life" creates its own demand, whereas the demand for that part devoted to "convenience and luxuries" depends on the consumption habits of the "nonproductive" elements of society (e.g., the landlords). Since the landlords do not always spend their incomes like other groups in society (i.e., on consumption goods), it is possible that an oversupply of commodities might exist. What is required to guarantee a steady expansion of output and to eliminate an oversupply of goods is a sufficient level of "effectual demand," and this, Malthus thought, would not be guaranteed by the mere importation of cheap food.

In a letter to Ricardo, Malthus set forth his position on effectual demand:

Effectual demand consists of two elements, the power and will to purchase. The power to purchase may perhaps be represented correctly by the produce of the country whether small or great; but the will to purchase will always be the greatest, the smaller the produce compared with the population, and the more scantily the wants of society are supplied. When capital is abundant it is not easy to find new objects sufficiently in demand. In a country with little comparative capital the value of yearly produce may very rapidly increase from the greatness of demand. In short I by no means think that the power to purchase necessarily involves a proportionate will to purchase, and I cannot agree... that in reference to a nation, supply can never exceed demand. A nation must certainly have the power of purchasing all that it produces, but I can easily conceive it not to have the will (*Works,* VI, pp. 131–132).

The classical idea that Malthus attacked in this passage was the notion that in the process of production, exactly enough income is generated to purchase the output produced and that—barring hoarding—all the income so generated *will* be spent to purchase that output. Given currency by the French economist J. B. Say, this classical notion became known simply as "Say's law," which states that supply creates its own demand. Few notions were so completely assimilated into the mainstream of classical economics. Malthus's criticism of Say's law therefore indelibly marked him as a maverick among economists, a fact that nevertheless endeared him to that well-known pioneer of modern macro theory, John Maynard Keynes (see Chapter 19).

Although Malthus's assault on this bastion of classicism had little effect on orthodox economics before Keynes, it contains at least one major insight into the savings-investment decisions that so concerned Keynes at a later date. The insight concerns the idea of an optimum propensity to save. In several key passages from his *Principles,* Malthus affirmed this idea:

If consumption exceed production, the capital of a country must be diminished, and its wealth must be gradually destroyed from its want of power to produce; if production be in great excess above consumption, the motive to accumulate and produce must cease from the want of an effectual demand.... The two extremes are obvious; and it follows that there must be some intermediate point, though the resources of political economy may not be able to ascertain it, where, taking into consideration both the power to produce and the will to consume, the encouragement to the increase of wealth is the greatest (*Principles,* p. 7).

In other words, Malthus recognized that consumption expenditures represent demand and that savings represent potential demand (through investment), but that the latter by no means *guarantee* effective demand. In more modern jargon, ex post saving is always equal to ex post investment (a fact that Malthus apparently accepted), but ex ante saving need not always equal ex ante investment.[2] Thus Malthus argued the possibility of a general glut.

Malthus's criticism of Say's law was important for two reasons: (1) it contained a theory of output and employment that bore Keynesian trappings, and (2) it constituted a critique of Ricardo's theory of profit. Yet Malthus's analysis of aggregate saving was analytically stillborn, since he neither specified the market forces capable of maintaining the optimum rate of saving nor analyzed

---

[2] This point is explained further in the Keynesian context in Chap. 19.

the purely monetary causes of overproduction. As a consequence, Say's law was successfully defended by Ricardo and his followers, and it subsequently become a familiar cornerstone of classical economics.

Nassau Senior and the Emergence of "Scientific" Economics

In the nineteenth century there were three Englishmen whose works provided the main stepping-stones between Adam Smith and John Stuart Mill: Ricardo, Malthus, and Nassau Senior. Born in 1790 in Berkshire, Senior was the eldest son of the Vicar of Durnford. He was educated at Eton and later at Oxford, where he obtained a law degree in 1815, the year in which Malthus, West, Ricardo, and Torrens published their pamphlets on rent. Law practice did not suit Senior's temperament, however, and after some postgraduate work in political economy, he was named to the first endowed chair of political economy at Oxford in 1825. Appointed to various governmental commissions in the 1830s and 1840s, Senior was instrumental in shaping legislative reforms in education, factory conditions, and the Poor Law (see Chapter 9).

Chief among his published works was *An Outline of the Science of Political Economy,* first printed in 1836 and revised by Senior in 1850. *Political Economy* suffers from a lack of organization and consistency, and yet it is an important milestone in the history of economics, not only for its criticism of Ricardian economics but also for its original contributions. We shall examine those contributions under two major headings: (1) Senior's formulation of the scope and method of economic inquiry and (2) his important modifications of the Ricardian theories of value and costs.

Senior on Economic Method Senior was totally engrossed in that unexciting though necessary stage of development of any academic discipline: identifying basic principles and organizing them, along axiomatic lines, into a genuinely scientific framework. This qualifies him, in the view of Joseph Schumpeter, as the first "pure theorist" in economics. Certainly his subjective originality and his tireless attempts to unify and systematize economic theory entitle Senior to a more prominent place in the history of economics than he is generally accorded.

Senior began his *Political Economy* by defining the boundaries of economic inquiry. Political economy, he avowed, is "the science which treats of the nature, the production, and the distribution of wealth." He warned that other writers had used the term "political economy" in a much wider sense—to include government, for example—but that the outcome of their efforts had been decidedly unscientific. Economic inquiry was to be essentially *positive* (i.e., devoid of value judgments), in Senior's view, since the province of the economist is "not happiness, but wealth" (*Political Economy,* p. 2).

Senior clarified his methodological position in the following passage:

[The economist's] premises consist of a very few general propositions, the result of observation, or consciousness, and scarcely requiring proof, or even formal statement, which almost every man, as soon as he hears them, admits as familiar to his thoughts, or at least as included in his previous knowledge; and his inferences are nearly as general, and, if he has reasoned correctly, as certain, as his premises.

But his conclusions, whatever be their generality and their truth, do not authorize him in adding a single syllable of advice. That privilege belongs to the writer or statesman who has considered all the causes which may promote or impede the general welfare of those whom he addresses, not to the theorist who has considered only one, though among the most important, of those causes. The business of a Political Economist is neither to recommend nor to dissuade, but to state general principles, which it is fatal to neglect, but neither advisable, nor perhaps practicable, to use as the sole, or even the principal, guides in the actual conduct of affairs. . . . To decide in each case how far these conclusions are to be acted upon, belongs to the act of government, an act to which Political Economy is only one of many subservient Sciences (*Political Economy,* pp. 2–3).

The too ready confusion by many writers of the *science* of economics with the *art* of government was responsible, in Senior's view, for the unfavorable public prejudices in his day against political economy and political economists. Essentially, economics was to be an exercise in reasoning, not a fact-gathering expedition, and Senior was prepared to state the facts on which the general principles of economics rest in a few sentences, "and indeed in a very few words." The difficulty of mastering economics, according to Senior, lay not in observing and stating these few propositions but in reasoning from them correctly.

The Four Postulates Those "few sentences" to which Senior alluded took the form of four basic postulates, or axioms, on which economic theory is based. These propositions are presented here in his own words:

1 That every man desires to obtain additional wealth with as little sacrifice as possible

2 That the population of the world, or in other words, the number of persons inhabiting it, is limited only by a fear of a deficiency of those articles of wealth which the habits of the individuals of each class of its inhabitants lead them to require

3 That the powers of labour, and of the other instruments which produce wealth, may be indefinitely increased by using their products as the means of further production

4 That, agricultural skill remaining the same, additional labour employed on the land within a given district produces in general a less proportionate return, or, in other words, that though, with every increase of the labour bestowed, the aggregate return is increased, the increase of the return is not in proportion to the increase of the labour (*Political Economy,* p. 26).

The second and fourth postulates present, respectively, Senior's guarded affirmation of Malthus's population principle and the classic law of diminishing returns, but not without important modifications of each. Senior was willing to accept Malthus's population principle in the abstract, but he had little faith in its empirical validity. His main argument was that man's desire to better his position in the world is at least as important as his sexual desire and that by not realizing this, Malthus overlooked a strong, additional check on the growth of population.

Senior's optimism on the population question might also be linked to his interpretation of the laws of increasing and decreasing returns in industry and agriculture. In his fourth postulate, Senior rendered the law of decreasing returns more exact (in its modern sense) by adding the proviso that technology must be held constant. Ricardo undoubtedly recognized that the validity of this law rests on the constant-technology assumption, but he never explicitly stated it. In explaining his fourth postulate, however, Senior voiced his conviction that the normal state of affairs in industry is *increasing* returns. He based this view on the questionable assumption that labor skills tend to increase in some sort of relation to increased population and capital, a view that runs counter to the orthodox Malthusian doctrine but that was nevertheless accepted by a surprisingly large number of writers in Senior's day.

Our attention shall be focused on the first and third postulates, however, because in his elaboration of each, Senior advanced the classical and Ricardian theories of exchange value. In his discussion Senior also adumbrated a much improved theory of capital and interest.

Value and Costs   Senior's modifications of the Ricardian theory of value were more important, in an analytical sense, than those introduced by Malthus. His major departures from Ricardo include (1) an acceptance of the utility theory of value and (2) a critique of Ricardo's cost-of-production theory and the (classical) assumption of free competition.

Several continental writers in the first half of the nineteenth century (e.g., Say and Condillac) perceived the fact that utility is more than a mere condition of value, as Ricardo had stated, but a *cause* of value. However, they were unable to do anything analytically with this notion before Dupuit (see Chapter 12), and so utility theory accomplished nothing. Senior did better than others in this respect, and Léon Walras (see Chapter 16) correctly credited him with the notion of marginal utility.

The chief adversary of the labor theory of value in the nineteenth century was always the supply-and-demand theory. Malthus, for example, went right to it and concentrated on it exclusively. Senior also adopted it, but in general he handled the demand-supply discussion better than Malthus. The higher flight of Senior's discussion was due to his recognition not only of the importance of relative utility but also of the *interdependence* between relative utility and relative scarcity.

Having earlier defined economics as the science of wealth, Senior proceeded in his *Political Economy* to define wealth, value, and utility. Wealth, he affirmed, includes all goods and services that (1) possess utility, (2) are relatively scarce, and (3) are capable of being transferred. This definition is at once broader than Adam Smith's—because it includes services as well as physical output—and very modern: it recognizes the pivotal importance of both demand factors (utility) and supply factors (scarcity).

Senior's definition of value and utility are no less modern. Value is "that quality in anything which fits it to be given and received in exchange; or in other words, to be lent or sold, hired or purchased.'' And utility ''denotes no intrinsic quality in the things we call useful; it merely expresses their relations to the pains and pleasures of mankind'' (*Political Economy*, p. 7). Finally, the notion of diminishing marginal utility and its relation to relative scarcity were clearly set forth in Senior's discussion of human love of variety in consumption:

> Not only are there limits to the pleasure which commodities of any given class can afford, but the pleasure diminishes in a rapidly increasing ratio long before those limits are reached. Two articles of the same kind will seldom afford twice the pleasure of one, and still less will ten give five times the pleasure of two. In proportion, therefore, as any article is abundant, the number of those who are provided with it, and do not wish, or wish but little, to increase their provision, is likely to be great; and so far as they are concerned, the additional supply loses all, or nearly all, its utility (*Political Economy*, pp. 11–12).

What stands out in the above passage is Senior's clear recognition that both utility and scarcity *together* determine value. Surely Senior had in his grasp the key to unlock the classical paradox of value! Further progress in the first half of the nineteenth century was hampered, however, by the failure or unwillingness of British economists to apply the differential calculus to economic analysis. But in France, Cournot and Dupuit were soon to scale the heights of marginal analysis (see Chapter 12).

Senior on Monopoly   Ricardo's influence on Senior was considerable, even though they differed on several points. Senior maintained, for instance, that ''Of the three conditions of value, utility, transferableness, and limitation of supply, the last is by far the most important.'' His discussion of value was therefore colored by a concern for those forces that limit supply (i.e., affect costs of production), among which he regarded the existence of monopoly as crucial. Four degrees of monopoly are considered by Senior:

1 A monopoly in which the producer does not have exclusive producing powers but in which he has exclusive facilities that he may use indefinitely with equal or increasing advantage (as in the case where exclusive patents are necessary to produce a certain product).

2 A monopoly in which the monopolist is the only producer but in which, because of the uniqueness of the product, he cannot increase the amount of his produce (as in the case of certain French vineyards, where increased output is impossible without destroying the unique properties of the wine produced).

3 A monopoly in which the monopolist is the only producer and can increase indefinitely, with equal or increasing advantage, the amount of his produce (as in the case of book publishing, where the product is protected by copyright, and the relative cost of publication diminishes as the number of copies published increases).

4 A monopoly in which the monopolist is not the only producer but has peculiar facilities which diminish and ultimately disappear as output is increased. (This includes most cases of economic production, including agriculture, where land or fertility must ultimately run out as output is increased).

These four cases are important because the effect of each case on production costs either establishes or does not establish an upper and lower limit to market price and therefore opens the way for varying degrees of demand to determine price. In the first case, for example, market price comes closer to the seller's cost of production than any other monopolized commodity, since competition among sellers without the exclusive facility (e.g., patent) will tend to keep prices in line with their costs of production. The monopolist with the patent may, of course, enjoy pure profits, but is effectively barred from selling at a price above the nonpatented competition, although the actual price will depend on conditions of demand as well as on conditions of production.

The second case is that of completely inelastic supply, in which there is no upper limit on price save the level of demand, while the lower limit to price is equal to costs of production. The third case is the same as the first except that since the monopoly is absolute, there is no upper limit to price save that imposed by demand. The fourth case is the most general. It includes production under conditions of differential advantage and diminishing returns. This is really the Ricardian case, except that price depends not only on the production costs of the marginal firm but also on demand.

One has only to read Cournot (see Chapter 12) and Senior side by side to realize how loose the theory of monopoly was before 1838. Nevertheless, by classifying the major cases of value the way he did, Senior succeeded in reconciling Ricardo's analysis with the supply-demand theory. A review of Senior's four cases reveals that cost of production is the controlling criterion in some cases and that demand is the controlling criterion in others, but the two are always interacting. It is true that Senior, having gotten this far, did not push the supply-demand analysis as far as he could have in evaluating the factors of production, but he certainly made this task easier for those who were to follow.

Capital and Interest   Senior also extended Ricardo's real-cost analysis by adding the cost of "abstinence" to the cost of labor. In the somewhat paradoxical statement of his third postulate, Senior hinted at the fact that roundabout methods of production are more productive than direct methods in the long run, a fact that the Austrian economist Böhm-Bawerk (see Chapter 13) greatly clarified at a later date. "Roundaboutness" means postponing production of consumption goods by using labor and raw materials first to produce capital goods, which are then used along with labor and raw materials to produce *more* consumer goods than could have been produced in the first place with labor and raw materials alone. A classic example of increased efficiency from roundabout production might be drawn from the story of the fictional hero Robinson Crusoe. A person stranded on a deserted isle must face the economic necessity of securing food. Assuming that an island stream contains a bounteous supply of fish, the most direct method of production to adopt would be to catch fish by hand. However, if the person postponed fishing long enough to fashion a pole and hook or a bow and arrow (crude forms of capital goods), he or she would catch more fish at a faster rate than would be possible using the most direct, but least efficient, method.

Although the example is simple, the same principle holds when time is taken to accumulate more sophisticated capital equipment in advanced economies. By "abstinence" Senior meant refraining from current consumption in order to accumulate capital, or "intermediate" goods. This is the key to the third postulate: "that the powers of labour, and of the other instruments which produce wealth, may be indefinitely increased by using their products as the means of further production." But since capital goods do not satisfy consumer desires directly, there is a sacrifice involved in postponing consumption unless they received a reward. Senior's contribution to capital theory was to identify this reward for "abstinence" as interest, or the cost of waiting, during which time capital could be accumulated.

Senior's description of interest as a return to abstinence was his most original contribution to economics, and it soon became assimilated into the mainstream of economic theory. In it he surpassed Smith, Malthus, and Ricardo, and his analysis of capital and interest stood as the most complete in British economics until the time of Jevons (see Chapter 14). A retrospective view of Senior's performance must therefore conclude that all his contributions, though essentially modifications of Ricardo's analysis, were extremely important modifications for the future development of economics.

THE SUPREMACY OF RICARDIAN ECONOMICS

It is a curious phenomenon that although very little of pure Ricardian analysis remains in the mainstream of modern economics and very much of the analysis of Ricardo's early critics does, Ricardo's influence on other economic writers nevertheless remained paramount through much of the nineteenth century. Every major British economist in the nineteenth century, including John Stuart Mill (see Chapter 8) and Alfred Marshall (see Chapter 15), paid tribute to Ricardo. The fact that they did so while rejecting or reshaping some of his fundamental ideas in no way lessens the significance of their respect for him as an economic theorist. Always in a numerical minority, Ricardo and the Ricardians still carried the day in early British economics.

The reasons for this phenomenon had as much to do with the nature of the Ricardian opposition as with the aggressiveness of Ricardo's disciples. Malthus's writings, for example, belie a theoretical looseness and an intellectual vacillation that undoubtedly undermined their effectiveness as an alternative to Ricardo's. Even Senior, whose method and analysis were more rigid than Malthus's, darted and swerved on a number of minor theoretical points. Moreover, Senior's failure to connect his modifications of Ricardo with the question of income distribution probably had an unfavorable effect on the ability of those contributions to attract a wider audience. As a result, Ricardo was in the peculiar position of being able to use impeccable logic to defend his system and simultaneously destroy opposing arguments, which were often based on mere common sense. The fact that Ricardo could do so convincingly and endear himself to other economists tells us much about his vast intellectual powers and also about the kind of people economists admire.

Moreover, there is something very positive about Ricardo's performance that must be noted, for failure to understand this point constitutes a misappreciation of what economics, as a science, is really about. The point is simply this: Ricardo's tightly reasoned analytical system showed a methodological consistency that was not matched by his predecessors or his contemporaries but that was of paramount importance to the successful development of a fledgling science. Today it seems that Senior's overall performance, in fact, and his specific attempts to give economics a scientific foundation, would have been improbable, if not impossible, without the prior performance of Ricardo.

unexprience

SUMMARY: THE ELEGANT DYNAMICS
OF THE CLASSICAL SYSTEM

With the aid of W.J. Baumol,[3] whose analysis this section follows closely, we may summarize the essence of classical economics in fairly concise verbal and graphical terms. Those British economists who lived and wrote during and after the time of Malthus and before Mill constitute the group whose economics are summarized here. A *synthesis* is all that is attempted, since there certainly was no unanimity of views on all economic topics among members of the classical school.

The major concern of the classical writers was, of course, economic growth, or the transition from a progressive state to a stationary state. The less desirable *stationary* state was viewed as the inevitable outcome of economic history. Classical (Ricardian) economic analysis was therefore long run, based upon a few simple (sometimes questionable) assumptions from which sweeping generalizations about economic development were made. Key elements in the process were (1) the Malthusian population principle, (2) the principle of diminishing returns in agriculture, and (3) the wages-fund doctrine.

The fundamental argument of classical growth theory follows simple lines. In an expanding economy, the level of investment and wages is high and growing. Capital accumulation proceeds apace. But high wages induce population growth, and the consequent pressures on the food supply—coupled with a fixed, existing quantity of fertile land—lead to diminishing returns to capital and labor in agriculture and the necessity of utilizing inferior grades of land to feed a growing population. Consequently, costs of production increase and profits fall. Falling profits cause a decrease in accumulation and investment as the stationary state is approached. Actual arrival of the stationary state could be postponed indefinitely through a series of highly productive inventions, but no classical writer denied its inevitability in the long run.

---

[3] See *Economic Dynamics*, chap. 2.

The process described above may be viewed graphically as a movement toward the stationary state over time—decades or perhaps even centuries. Consider Figure 7-1. The size of the working population is measured on the horizontal axis. The vertical axis measures total product and total wages (in real terms) but does not include total rent, which Ricardo treated as a mere transfer of income from one class to another. Thus whenever profits fall—other things being equal—rents rise, and the stationary state is reached when profits fall to zero.

The slope of line OS in Figure 7-1 is equal to the ratio of total subsistence wage payments to the size of the working population (e.g., Y^*P^* divided by OP^*). Although there is little evidence that Ricardo—or, for that matter, any of the classical economists—consistently regarded the subsistence wage as a constant proportion of total output, Figure 7-1 assumes, for simplicity, that it is. Thus, at output level Y_1 and population P_1, the subsistence wage per worker would be equivalent to the ratio S_1P_1/OP_1. Likewise, at output and population levels Y_2 and P_2, respectively, the subsistence wage would be S_2P_2/OP_2. Moreover, since the level of subsistence as a proportion of output is assumed constant, $S_1P_1/OP_1 = S_2P_2/OP_2$.

Suppose now that we begin the analysis at an early stage of the classical economy, where population is small (say, OP_1) compared with other resources and where profits, the rate of accumulation, and wages are therefore all relatively high. The dynamic path to stationary-state equilibrium, it will be seen,

FIGURE 7-1
At population OP_1, total output is Y_1P_1 and total wages are S_1P_1. Profits of Y_1S_1 will increase the demand for labor and push wages up to Y_1P_1. Since wages are above subsistence at this level, population will increase to OP_2, thus tracing out the stepwise path to long-run equilibrium.

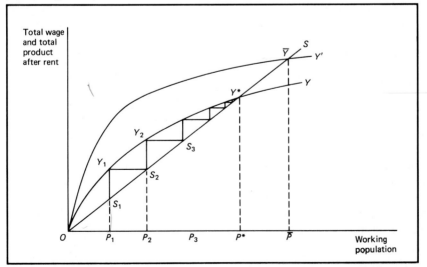

depends on the speed at which the population adjusts to changes in the level of market wages. At population OP_1, total output (after rent) would be Y_1P_1, and total wages would be S_1P_1. Given Ricardo's residual theory, total profits would equal Y_1S_1.

According to the wages-fund doctrine, the presence of accumulated profits leads to increased demand for labor, and the increased competition for labor eventually pushes wages up to Y_1P_1, at which point accumulation ceases, as profits are squeezed out. But since wages are above subsistence at Y_1P_1, population begins to increase (to OP_2), and wages eventually return to subsistence at S_2P_2.

Population is in only temporary equilibrium at OP_2, however, for the increase in population to that level is accompanied by an increase in output from Y_1 to Y_2, thus opening up profits again in the amount of Y_2S_2. This new accumulation causes wages and population to rise once again, thus tracing out the stepwise path in Figure 7-1. At population level P^*, the economy has reached the stationary state. Profits have disappeared from the system, wages are at the subsistence level, and rents on land of the highest fertility are at a maximum. In short, the dynamic working out of the classical theory—i.e., Malthusian population theory, diminishing returns in agriculture, the subsistence theory of wages, the classical theory of capital accumulation (the wages-fund doctrine), and the residual theory of profits—predicts a stationary-state equilibrium.

The long-run, stepwise adjustment path to stationary-state equilibrium in Figure 7-1 assumes that population adjustments take place fairly rapidly, although this may not actually be the case. In reality, therefore, the adjustment path may follow (from below) the total-product curve OY. If population expands slowly, for example, then long before it reaches OP_2 some profit may reappear, propelling the process onward and keeping wages up above subsistence and near the total-product curve OY.

Postponement of the stationary state is illustrated in Figure 7-1 by an increase in productivity, brought about, perhaps, by improvements in technology. This increased productivity shifts the total-product curve upward to OY' and moves the point of stationary equilibrium to the right, to point $\bar{Y}$.

In this way, the classical economists provided a sweeping analysis of the economic process. The method is essentially deductive, although the classical dynamics is based on several empirical hypotheses that may or may not have been valid at the time (e.g., the assumption that all saving is automatically invested). Moreover, at least one of the hypotheses—the population principle—contained noneconomic variables that in contemporary analysis would be relegated to an exogenous role. Nevertheless, the classical dynamics represented a bold and striking approach to the policy problems of the time.

NOTES FOR FURTHER READING

An excellent and thorough study of Ricardo is presented by Mark Blaug, *Ricardian Economics* (New Haven, Conn.: Yale University Press, 1958). An older, though not necessarily inferior, treatise is J. H. Hollander's *David Ricardo* (Baltimore: Johns Hopkins, 1910). Assistance in getting through the main parts of Ricardo's *Principles* is provided by Oswald St. Clair's *Key to Ricardo* (London: Routledge, 1957), which must be in virtually every economics library in the country.

The influence of Ricardo on his contemporaries can be traced through four excellent articles: S. G. Checkland, "The Propagation of Ricardian Economics in England," *Economica,* vol. 16 (February 1949), pp. 40–52; S. Hollander, "The Reception of Ricardian Economics," *Oxford Economic Papers,* vol. 29 (July 1977), pp. 221–257; R. L. Meek, "The Decline of Ricardian Economics in England," *Economica,* vol. 17 (February 1950), pp. 43–62; and F. W. Fetter, "The Rise and Decline of Ricardian Economics," *History of Political Economy,* vol. 1 (Fall 1969), pp. 370–387. On the rebirth of Ricardian economics in more modern dress, see J. R. Hicks and S. Hollander, "Mr. Ricardo and the Moderns," *Quarterly Journal of Economics,* vol. 91 (August 1977), pp. 351–370.

Ricardo's value theory has been the subject of ongoing review, criticism, and reinterpretation. See, for example, J. M. Cassels, "A Reinterpretation of Ricardo on Value," *Quarterly Journal of Economics,* vol. 46 (May 1935), pp. 518–532; S. C. Rankin, "Supply and Demand in Ricardian Price Theory: A Reinterpretation," *Oxford Economic Papers,* vol. 32 (July 1980), pp. 241–262; L. E. Johnson, "Ricardo's Labor Theory of the Determinant of Value," *Atlantic Economic Journal,* vol. 12 (March 1984), pp. 50–59; A. Burgstaller, "Demand and Relative Price in Ricardo: An Examination of Outstanding Issues," *History of Political Economy,* vol. 19 (Summer 1987), pp. 207–215; R. H. Timberlake, "The Classical Search for an Invariable Measure of Value," *Quarterly Review of Economics and Business,* vol. 6 (Spring 1966), pp. 37–44; C. Casarosa, "A New Formulation of the Ricardian System," *Oxford Economic Papers,* vol. 30 (March 1978), pp. 38–63; G. J. Stigler, "Ricardo and the 93% Labor Theory of Value," *American Economic Review,* vol. 48 (June 1958), pp. 357–367; and G. J. Stigler, "The Ricardian Theory of Value and Distribution," *Journal of Political Economy,* vol. 60 (June 1952), pp. 187–207. The latter two articles are reprinted in *Essays in the History of Economics* (Chicago: The University of Chicago Press, 1965). The connection between John Locke and Ricardo on the question of value is probed by Gunnar Myrdal, *The Political Element in the Development of Economic Theory* (London: Routledge, 1953).

The Ricardian theory of profits has been a lightning rod of controversy. See John Eatwell, "The Interpretation of Ricardo's Essay on Profits," *Economica,* vol. 42 (May 1975), pp. 182–187; Terry Peach, "David Ricardo's Early Treatment of Profitability: A New Interpretation," *Economic Journal,* vol. 94 (December 1984), pp. 733–751; Sam Hollander, "On a 'New Interpretation' of Ricardo's Early Treatment of Profitability," *Economic Journal,* vol. 96 (December 1986), pp. 1091–1097; R. Prendergast, "David Ricardo's Early Treatment of Profitability: A New Interpretation: A Comment," *Economic*

Journal, vol. 96 (December 1986), pp. 1098–1104; and Peach's reply to the critics, "Ricardo's Early Treatment of Profitability: Reply," *Economic Journal,* vol. 96 (December 1986), pp. 1105–1112. The most recent controversy about Ricardo was touched off, at least in part, by Sam Hollander's wholesale reinterpretation of Ricardo's economics, *The Economics of David Ricardo* (Toronto: University of Toronto Press, 1979).

For an investigation of more specific topics in Ricardo's writings, see C. S. Shoup, *Ricardo on Taxation* (New York: Columbia University Press, 1960); Hans Brems, "Ricardo's Long-Run Equilibrium," *History of Political Economy,* vol. 2 (Fall 1970), pp. 225–245; S. Hollander, "The Development of Ricardo's Position on Machinery," *History of Political Economy,* vol. 3 (Spring 1971), pp. 105–135; M. J. Gootzeit, "The Corn Laws and Wage Adjustment in a Short-Run Ricardian Model," *History of Political Economy,* vol. 5 (Spring 1973), pp. 50–71; and S. Hollander, "Ricardo and the Corn Laws: A Revision," *History of Political Economy,* vol. 9 (Spring 1977), pp. 1–47. For a mathematical exposition of Ricardo's theory by William Whewell (1794–1866), see J. L. Cochrane, "The First Mathematical Ricardian Model," *History of Political Economy,* vol. 2 (Fall 1970), pp. 419–431.

The contentious nature of Malthus and his singular position among his contemporaries is discussed in W. D. Grampp, "Malthus and his Contemporaries," *History of Political Economy,* vol. 6 (Fall 1974), pp. 278–304. See also M. B. Harvey-Phillips, "Malthus' Theodicy: The Intellectual Background to His Contribution to Political Economy," *History of Political Economy,* vol. 16 (Winter 1984), pp. 591–608. Some historians contend that there are two Malthuses in the history of economic thought: the Malthus of the *Essay on Population* and the Malthus of *The Principles of Political Economy.* An attempt to integrate the two can be found in J. J. Spengler, "Malthus' Total Population Theory: A Restatement and Reappraisal," *Canadian Journal of Economics and Political Science,* vol. 2 (February, May 1945), pp. 83–110, 234–264. Malthus's position on the Corn Law continues to be controversial. Grampp presents one view (see References), but a contrary interpretation is provided by J. J. Spengler, "Malthus the Malthusian vs. Malthus the Economist," *Southern Economic Journal,* vol. 24 (July 1957), pp. 1–11. An earlier view on the same subject is that of H. G. Johnson, "Malthus on the High Price of Provisions," *Canadian Journal of Economics and Political Science,* vol. 15 (May 1949), pp. 190–202. The impact of economic growth on the working classes is the subject of G. Gilbert's "Economic Growth and the Poor in Malthus' *Essay on Population,*" *History of Political Economy,* vol. 12 (Spring 1980), pp. 83–96.

Some insights into the workings of Ricardo's mind and his reactions to Malthus's *Principles* can be gained from a study of vol. 2 of the masterful Sraffa edition of Ricardo's *Works* (see References). This volume reproduces Ricardo's many notes and marginalia added to his personal copy of Malthus's *Principles.* On the value debate between the two authors, see also V. E. Smith, "Malthus' Theory of Demand and Its Influence on Value Theory,"

Scottish Journal of Political Economy, vol. 3 (October 1956), pp. 205–220; O. Pancoast, "Malthus versus Ricardo," *Political Science Quarterly,* vol. 58 (1943), pp. 47–66; and L. Castabile, "Natural Prices, Market Prices and Effective Demand in Malthus," *Australian Economic Papers,* vol. 22 (June 1983), pp. 144–170.

Several authors have explored Malthus's views on aggregate demand, economic growth, and business cycles. For a sampling, see W. A. Eltis, "Malthus's Theory of Effective Demand and Growth," *Oxford Economic Papers,* vol. 32 (March 1980), pp. 19–56; J. J. O'Leary, "Malthus and Keynes," *Journal of Political Economy,* vol. 50 (December 1942), pp. 901–919; same author, "Malthus' General Theory of Employment and the Post-Napoleonic Depression," *Journal of Economic History,* vol. 3 (1943), pp. 185–200; S. Hollander, "Malthus and the Post-Napoleonic Depression," *History of Political Economy,* vol. 1 (Fall 1969), pp. 306–335; L. A. Dow, "Malthus on Sticky Wages, the Upper Turning Point, and General Glut," *History of Political Economy,* vol. 9 (Fall 1977), pp. 303–321; same volume, S. Rashid, "Malthus's Model of General Gluts," pp. 366–383; and A. M. C. Waterman, "On the Malthusian Theory of Long Swings," *Canadian Journal of Economics,* vol. 20 (May 1987), pp. 257–270.

And now for the rest of the field. A fine portrait of Sir Edward West that goes beyond his contribution to classical rent theory is contained in W. D. Grampp, "Edward West Reconsidered," *History of Political Economy,* vol. 2 (Fall 1970), pp. 316–343. One economist whose ideas were picked up by Malthus and used against Ricardo was James Maitland (1759–1839), the eighth Earl of Lauderdale, whose *Inquiry into the Nature and Origin of Public Wealth* (1804) was a substantial analytical contribution even though it was considered highly unorthodox in its day. On the connection of Lauderdale and Malthus, see Morton Paglin, *Malthus and Lauderdale: The Anti-Ricardian Tradition* (New York: A. M. Kelley, 1961). Lauderdale has also been linked to Keynes. See Maurice Mann, "Lord Lauderdale: Underconsumptionist and Keynesian Predecessor," *Social Science* (June 1959), pp. 153–162; and P. Lambert, "Lauderdale, Malthus et Keynes," *Revue d'economie politique* (January–February 1966), pp. 32–56. For a wider sweep, see B.A. Corry, *Money, Saving and Investment in English Economics, 1800–1850* (New York: St. Martin's, 1962); and R. G. Link, *English Theories of Economic Fluctuations, 1815–1848* (New York: Columbia University Press, 1959).

A number of British writers set themselves against Ricardo, especially in regard to the theories of value and rent. Among them were Samuel Bailey, John Craig, Richard Jones, William F. Lloyd, Mountifort Longfield, and Robert Torrens. For the full force of these other arguments see R. M. Rauner, *Samuel Bailey and the Classical Theory of Value* (Cambridge, Mass.: Harvard University Press, 1961); B. W. Thor, "The Economic Theories of John Craig, a Forgotten Economist," *Quarterly Journal of Economics,* vol. 52 (August 1938), pp. 697–707; W. L. Miller, "Richard Jones's Contributions to the Theory of Rent," *History of Political Economy,* vol. 9 (Fall 1977), pp. 346–365; R.

M. Romano, "William Forster Lloyd—A Non-Ricardian," *History of Political Economy,* vol. 9 (Fall 1977), pp. 412–441; L.S. Moss, "Mountifort Longfield's Supply and Demand Theory of Price and Its Place in the Development of British Economic Theory," *History of Political Economy,* vol. 6 (Winter 1974), pp. 405–434; and L. Robbins, *Robert Torrens and the Evolution of Classical Economics* (New York: St. Martin's, 1958).

Some of Nassau Senior's previously unpublished writings have been collected under the title *Industrial Efficiency and Social Economy,* 2 vols., S. L. Levy (ed.) (New York: Holt, 1928). Levy also offers a favorable assessment of Senior in *Nassau W. Senior: The Prophet of Modern Capitalism* (Boston: Humphries, 1943). The standard reference on Senior is Marian Bowley, *Nassau Senior and Classical Economics* (London: G. Allen, 1937).

On his side, Ricardo had the faithful and tireless McCulloch, who defended Ricardo against all challengers. The standard work on McCulloch is D. P. O'Brien's *J. R. McCulloch: A Study in Classical Economics* (London: G. Allen, 1970). Finally, Say's law and its importance for classical macroeconomics is covered extensively in Thomas Sowell, *Say's Law* (Princeton, N.J.: Princeton University Press, 1972).

REFERENCES

Baumol, W. J. *Economic Dynamics,* 3d ed. New York: Macmillan, 1970.
Grampp, W. D. "Malthus on Money Wages and Welfare," *American Economic Review,* vol. 46 (December 1956), pp. 924–936.
Malthus, T. R. *An Inquiry into the Nature and Progress of Rent, and the Principles by Which It Is Regulated.* A reprint of economic tracts edited by J. H. Hollander. Baltimore: Johns Hopkins, 1903 [1815].
———. *The Principles of Political Economy, Considered with a View to Their Practical Application,* 2d ed. New York: A. M. Kelley, Publishers, 1951 [1836].
Ricardo, David. *The Works and Correspondence of David Ricardo,* 10 vols., P. Sraffa (ed.), with the collaboration of M. Dobb. London: Cambridge University Press, 1951–1955.
Senior, N. W. *An Outline of the Science of Political Economy.* New York: A. M. Kelley, Publishers, 1938 [1836].

CLASSICAL ECONOMIC ANALYSIS (III): JOHN STUART MILL

INTRODUCTION: WUNDERKIND AS CLASSICAL ECONOMIST

John Stuart Mill (1806–1873) was the remarkable son of a remarkable father. Born in London, he was the eldest son of James Mill, an economist, disciple of Jeremy Bentham, and author of the compendious *History of British India*. Not a man to be bound by social convention, James Mill undertook the education of his children when they were very young. In his *Autobiography,* John Stuart Mill recounts the unusual and exacting education he received at the hands of his father.

At the age of three he began to learn Greek, and by the age of eight he had read the works of the great Greek writers (Herodotus, Xenophon, Plato, and Diogenes) in that language. During the same period he was taught arithmetic by his father, while his *self*-education included a reading of the histories, among others, of Hume, Gibbon, and Plutarch, most of which were borrowed from Bentham's library by his father. At age eight he began to learn Latin and was responsible for teaching what he learned to his younger brothers and sisters.

When he was twelve, Mill embarked upon studies in logic, in both English and Latin prose. The following year he read Ricardo's *Principles* and submitted to his father's grilling questions on political economy. Of these latter studies, Mill later remarked: "I do not believe that any scientific teaching ever was more thorough, or better fitted for training the faculties, than the mode in which logic and political economy were taught to me by my father" (*Autobiography,* p. 20). At the tender age of fourteen, Mill's formal education was complete!

Perhaps humility cannot be taught, but Mill revealed a generous measure of it when he reflected on his unusual upbringing:

What I could do, could assuredly be done by any poor boy or girl of average capacity and healthy physical constitution: and if I have accomplished anything, I owe it, among other fortunate circumstances, to the fact that through the early training bestowed on me by my father, I started, I may fairly say, with an advantage of a quarter of a century over my contemporaries (*Autobiography,* p. 21).

In 1823, Mill joined his father in the service of the East India Company, and he remained with the company until his retirement in 1858. His mind kept teeming with ideas, however, and he frequently wrote articles on various philosophical and literary topics. His first major work, *A System of Logic,* published in 1843, was favorably received and ran to several editions, as did his very successful *Principles of Political Economy,* which appeared in 1848. These two works assured Mill's reputation as one of the outstanding thinkers of his day. They were followed, in fairly rapid succession, by *On Liberty* (1859), *Considerations of Representative Government* (1861), *Utilitarianism* (1863), *Auguste Comte and Positivism* (1865), and *The Subjection of Women* (1869).

As a political and social thinker, Mill touched four main areas: (1) the problem of method in the social sciences, (2) the clarification of the (Benthamite) principle of utility, (3) individual freedom, and (4) the theory of representative government. It is, however, to his economic contributions that we now turn.

Mill's Intellectual "Transition"

In view of the rigors of Mill's early education, it is not surprising that at the age of twenty he suffered a prolonged period of mental depression, during which it appeared to him that none of the goals in life for which he had been trained were capable of bringing true happiness. He became aware of certain inadequacies in his upbringing.

Exposure to the Romantics In an attempt to develop his own "internal culture," Mill turned to the works of the romantic poets Coleridge and Wordsworth and to the ideas of the French philosophers of the Enlightenment. The writings of the poets, especially, not only gave Mill solace in his depression but also, because of their antagonism to political economy, induced him to rethink certain ideas on the subject.

Coleridge and Wordsworth were later followed by the literary critics Carlyle,[1] Dickens, and Ruskin in their reaction against the encroaching industrialism and materialism of Victorian England. In industrialism they saw a decline of the sensibilities and quality of life, and they held political economy—the *science of industrialism*—to blame for fostering the social erosion they observed. In claiming to be protectors of the old order, the romantics denied

---

[1] Having read Malthus on population, it was Carlyle who dubbed economics "the dismal science."

the efficacy of scientific inquiry. Moreover, they failed to see that economists do not necessarily give their stamp of approval to the existing order when they seek to analyze and explain social events. Few economists of the day even sought to refute such bland criticism. Mill, however, was the exception.

Mill and Comte During his mental crisis, Mill also read the works of Auguste Comte, the French philosopher and student of Henri Saint-Simon (see Chapter 10). Comte espoused a general *science of man.* Political economy was to be subsumed under this general science, which Comte named *sociology.*[2] Charging that political economy as a deductive science lacked empirical and historical relevance, Comte called for a new method as well as a new ordering of the social sciences. The new method was called *positivism,* by which Comte meant empiricism, or induction.

Mill reacted to these diverse criticisms by reconstructing the philosophical and methodological foundations of his own positions on political economy as a separate discipline. He was sympathetic to Comte's attempts to construct a general science of man, but he nevertheless defended economics as a separate science. He also moved closer to Comte's position on scientific method, but he consistently defended the Ricardian approach as inherently useful to a *social* science.

According to Mill, in the social arena the empirical, or inductive, method could not be relied on solely, since causes of social phenomena are often complex and interwoven and effects are not easily distinguishable from one another. Mill viewed deduction as a desirable check on the errors of casual empiricism. But deduction need not lead to dogmatic acceptance of ideas and theories that cannot be supported by fact. Thus facts are a desirable check to pure deduction. In short, Mill achieved a delicate balance between the inductive-deductive extremes in economic method.

The Structure of Mill's Inquiry into Economics

Reflecting this delicate balance, it is characteristic of Mill's *Principles of Political Economy* that in matters of theory, he reaffirmed and enlarged the Ricardian framework, while simultaneously incorporating new ideas and new supportive evidence on numerous matters of political economy. Of all books on economics, Mill's *Principles* was one of the most widely read and widely employed. Used as a text for almost sixty years (until replaced by Marshall's), it was and is a complete treatise on classical economic theory, economic policy, and social philosophy.

Character and Aim of the Principles The character and aim of the work are best described by Mill himself:

---

[2] Sociology today, as a separate discipline, has become much more specialized than Comte's original vision of it. To Comte, sociology was to be an all-embracing study of humans, including economics, psychology, anthropology, history, and the like.

For practical purposes, Political Economy is inseparably intertwined with many other branches of Social Philosophy. Except on matters of mere detail, there are perhaps no practical questions, even among those which approach nearest to the character of purely economical questions, which admit of being decided on economical premises alone. And it is because Adam Smith never loses sight of this truth; because, in his applications of Political Economy, he perpetually appeals to other and often far larger considerations than pure Political Economy affords—that he gives that well-grounded feeling of command over the principles of the subject for purposes of practice.... It appears to the present writer that a work similar in its object and general conception to that of Adam Smith, but adapted to the more extended knowledge and improved ideas of the present age, is the kind of contribution which Political Economy at present requires (*Principles,* pp. xxvii–xxviii).

Thus the dual character of his work—theory and applications—was noted at the outset by Mill, and he clearly set out to summarize and synthesize all economic knowledge of the day.

Mill's methodological eclecticism gave the *Principles* a unique flavor. Through his contact with Comte and the Saint-Simonians, he came to assert the now famous dichotomy between economic laws of production and the social laws of distribution. The former, according to Mill, are unchangeable; they are governed by natural laws. These laws, which had been so well described by Ricardo and his followers, are the proper province of economics in the narrow sense—as a separate science. But the laws of distribution, Mill insisted, are not determined by economic forces alone. They are, instead, almost entirely a matter of human will and institutions, which themselves are the product of changing values, mores, social philosophies, and tastes. The laws of distribution are therefore malleable, and their full explanation and understanding lie not merely in economic inquiry but in the historical laws that underlie economic progress.

Much of Comte's thought concerned the discovery of these historical laws. His celebrated view of history expressed in the "law of three stages" asserts that the human intellect, in progressing, passes through three separate and distinct stages: (1) the *theological* stage, in which human behavior and other phenomena are attributed to a deity or to "magic"; (2) the *metaphysical* stage, in which the essence, or "nature," of a thing is substituted for divine personalities (e.g., natural law as an explanatory device); and finally (3) the *positive* stage, in which introspective knowledge is eliminated and the scientific method is employed in finding "truth." Comte attributed all social and economic progress to the perfection of the human intellect as it passes through these three stages.

While we do not wish to debate the logical adequacy of these historical laws here, the important thing, as far as Comte's influence on other writers is concerned—including Mill—is the idea of relativity. The five divisions, or books, of Mill's *Principles* amplify the distinction between the immutable laws of production and the relative laws of distribution. The economics of production, value, and exchange are generally confined to Books, I, II, and III of the *Prin-*

ciples, whereas Mill's social views are aired in Book IV ("Influence of the Progress of Society on Production and Distribution") and Book V ("On the Influence of Government").

Mill on Production   A fundamental appreciation of Mill's ideas on production might be obtained from reviewing Ricardo's *Principles* as well as the (minimal) post-Ricardian refinement on that topic. The key roles in economic progress played by productive and unproductive labor, Say's law, capital accumulation, the Malthusian population doctrine, and the wages-fund doctrine are all presented with great clarity. Mill, as Ricardo and all the classical economists had done generally, assigned a crucial role to capital and to capital accumulation. He attached great importance to his "five fundamental propositions respecting capital," which restated the classical theory of economic progress.

In the classical tradition, Mill argued that, given Say's law, employment and increased levels of output are dependent on the accumulation and investment of capital. Part of the investment in capital, the result of saving, is required to tide labor over a discontinuous production period. Although he later seemed to recant this idea, Mill revealed a clear understanding of the wages-fund doctrine:

> There can be no more industry than is supplied with materials to work up and food to eat. Self-evident as the thing is, it is often forgotten, that the people of a country are maintained and have their wants supplied, not by the produce of present labour, but of past. They consume what has been produced, not what is about to be produced. Now, of what has been produced, a part only is allocated to the support of productive labour; and there will not and cannot be more of that labour than the portion so allotted (which is the capital of the country) can feed, and provide with the materials and instruments of production (*Principles,* p. 64).

Unemployment of resources—other than as a temporary state of affairs—was not considered possible because of Say's law. Contrary to the Malthusian position, saving would automatically be turned into another form of spending (i.e., investment), and a general glut of goods from underconsumption was impossible. Mill, in short, never considered that there could be a lack of aggregate demand in the economic system.

Mill on Economic Growth   Mill's clearest exposition of classical economics was in the area of economic development. Like Ricardo, he believed one of the factors limiting economic growth to be diminishing returns to agriculture. Another limit was a declining incentive to invest. In general, however, Mill focused upon the crucial variables of capital accumulation, population growth, and technology. Combining them with diminishing returns to agriculture, Mill devised a clear discussion of the classical theory of economic development.

Like Ricardo before him, Mill believed that the economy, owing to diminishing returns and falling incentives to invest, was being propelled from a *progressive* state to a *stationary* state (see Chapter 7). But alone among the classical economists, Mill did not believe that the stationary state was undesirable, since, as we shall see, it provided the necessary condition for his program of social reform. Mill believed that once the stationary state was reached, problems of equity in distribution could be evaluated and social reforms could proceed apace. Apart from his views on distribution, however, Mill's statement of the dynamics of classical production theory achieved a depth of clarity and understanding of classical dynamics that was never surpassed by any other writer affiliated with the classical school.

Mill's Theoretical Advances

In spite of Mill's clarity on the issue of classical production theory, it is tempting to assign him the role of a sophisticated synthesizer of little theoretical originality. Many historians of economics have maintained exactly this point of view. Unfortunately, this assessment could not be more unfair; as one important historian of thought has maintained, it would be difficult to point to a writer of greater theoretical originality than Mill.[3]

The purpose of this section is to elaborate on a few of Mill's more important theoretical contributions. Though Mill himself did not emphasize the importance of these theoretical ideas (the theory of joint supply is found in a footnote, for example), they nonetheless indicate that he was more of a bridge between classical and neoclassical analysis than has commonly been perceived.

Supply and Demand   The first clear British contribution to static equilibrium price formation in the modern sense was developed by John Stuart Mill. Utilizing purely verbal analysis, he advanced the theory of equilibrium price on several fronts. Mill fully recognized the analytical necessity of abstracting and simplifying the principles underlying the functional relation between price and quantity demanded and supplied. He noted, for example, that "in considering the exchange value scientifically, it is expedient to abstract from it all causes except those which originate in the very commodity under consideration" (*Principles*, p. 438). The outcome of Mill's abstractions was a correct formulation of demand and supply as *schedules* showing the functional relation between price and quantity demanded and supplied, *ceteris paribus*.

Noting the terminological confusion that previous writers had exhibited, Mill proposed that the proper mathematical relation to express demand and supply is an *equation*, not a *ratio*, as had so often been supposed in economic literature:

> A ratio between demand and supply is only intelligible if by demand we mean quantity demanded, and if the ratio intended is that between the quantity demanded and the quantity supplied. But again, the quantity demanded is not a fixed quantity, even

[3] See G. J. Stigler's interesting and still timely article, "The Nature and Role of Originality in Scientific Progress," *Economica* n.s., vol. 22 (November 1955), pp. 293–302.

at the same time and place; it varies according to the value; if the thing is cheap, there is usually a demand for more of it than when it is dear (*Principles,* p. 446).

The idea of a *ratio,* as between demand and supply, is [therefore] out of place, and has no concern in the matter: the proper mathematical analogy is that of an *equation.* Demand and supply, the quantity demanded and the quantity supplied, will be made equal. If unequal at any moment, competition equalizes them, and the manner in which this is done is by an adjustment of the value. If the demand increases, the value rises; if the demand diminishes, the value falls: again, if the supply falls off, the value rises; and falls if the supply is increased (*Principles,* p. 448).

Mill thus broke the circularity contained in most early formulations of value-and-demand theory. Misunderstanding of the correct nature of demand, for example, could lead to the allegation that demand depends in part on value but that value is determined by demand. Given Mill's distinction, however, if "demand increases" (or decreases) is read as a rightward (leftward) *shift* in demand, Mill's compact statement is almost entirely analogous to modern explanations of the mechanics of price changes. He therefore presented a perfectly adequate distinction between price-determined and price-determining changes in demand and supply. Mill's performance in this regard was not equaled in England until Fleeming Jenkin presented a graphical exposition on supply and demand in his 1870 essay, *On the Graphical Representation of Supply and Demand.* Mill was, moreover, one of Alfred Marshall's most important sources on the subject.

Joint Supply   Another contribution of great subsequent importance to value theory was Mill's development of the theory of jointly supplied goods. Although Marshall is often given credit for the invention of the concept (he simply added the graphics), Mill stated the principle concisely in his chapter entitled "Some Peculiar Cases of Value":

It sometimes happens that two different commodities have what may be termed a joint cost of production. They are both products of the same operation, or set of operations, and the outlay is incurred for the sake of both together, not part for one and part for the other. The same outlay would have to be incurred for either of the two, if the other were not wanted or used at all. There are not a few instances of commodities thus associated in their production: for example, coke and coal-gas are both produced from the same material, and by the same operation. In a more partial sense, mutton and wool are an example: beef, hides, and tallow: calves and dairy produce: chickens and eggs. Cost of production can have nothing to do with deciding the value of the associated commodities relatively to each other. It only decides their joint value. The gas and the coke together have to repay the expenses of their production, with the ordinary profit. To do this, a given quantity of gas, together with the coke which is the residuum of its manufacture, must exchange for other things in the ratio of their joint costs of production. But how much of the remuneration of the producer shall be derived from the coke, and how much from the gas, remains to be decided. Cost of production does not determine their prices, but the sum of their prices (*Principles,* pp. 569–570).

The Problem   The question raised by Mill in this regard is: Given a single cost function, how are profits from the two separate productions to be allocated to the jointly produced goods? Calculation of profits presupposes, of course, that prices can be determined for separate commodities. Mill's directions for determining an equilibrium were explicit:

> Equilibrium will be attained when the demand for each article fits so well with the demand for the other, that the quantity required of each is exactly as much as is generated in producing the quantity required of the other. If there is any surplus or deficiency on either side; if there is a demand for coke, and not a demand for all the gas produced along with it; or *vice versa;* the values and prices of the two things will readjust themselves so that both shall find a market (*Principles*, p. 571).

The Solution   Mill's solution to the joint-supply problem may be restated as follows: In the case where goods are produced jointly in fixed proportions, the equilibrium price of each product must be such as to clear *its* market, *subject to the condition that the sum of the two prices equals their* (average) *joint costs.* His apparently complete understanding of this special aspect of competitive pricing, without benefit of mathematical analysis, seems incredible today.

It should enhance our understanding of this complex problem to examine Marshall's graphics of the theory of joint supply. These graphics are found in a footnote to Chap. 6, Book V, of Marshall's *Principles of Economics.* In Figure 8-1, a joint-supply, or *average-cost,* function for steers is labeled *SS'.* The total demand for steers is represented by demand curve *DD'*, which is the vertical summation of the separate demands for beef and hides. The demand function for beef is depicted in Figure 8-1 as *dd'*, and so the demand for hides may be easily derived by vertically subtracting the demand for beef from the total

FIGURE 8-1
At competitive equilibrium *ON,* the price of beef (*NF*) is determined by the intersection of *ss'* and *dd'*, and the price of hides (*GF*) is determined by subtracting *NF* from the total supply function.

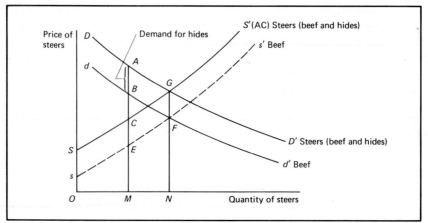

demand for steers. Thus at total quantity *OM* of steers produced, *MB* represents the demand price for beef and *BA* represents the demand price for hides.

A special type of *supply curve* can be derived for beef, moreover. It is obtained by subtracting the demand price for hides from the supply price of the composite output, steers. As we have seen, the demand price for hides at quantity *OM* is equal to *BA*. Subtracting *BA* from the total supply function yields a derived supply price for beef at quantity *OM* of *ME* and thus a supply price for hides of *EC*. Following this procedure, the dashed supply function for beef (*ss'*) can be traced for each quantity.

Competitive equilibrium, as Mill clearly understood, is achieved when *ON* steers are produced. At quantity *ON*, the price of beef (*NF*) is achieved by the intersection of the supply-and-demand curves for beef (*ss'* and *dd'*). The price of hides is similarly determined (*GF*). The competitive market for both goods is in equilibrium when the quantity *ON* is produced.[4] Several interesting characteristics of the Mill-Marshall model should be noted. An increase in the *demand* for one of the goods—say, hides—increases the *supply* of the other (in this case beef) and thus lowers its price. Second, an increase in average cost (*SS'*) raises the price of both the jointly produced goods. Moreover, these two results, as well as the construction of the Mill-Marshall analysis, depend upon an assumption of fixity in the proportions of goods produced; i.e., an increase in steer production implies a proportionate increase in the production of beef and hides. Other models may be constructed on nonproportionality assumptions, of course.

The subsequent importance of Mill's theory of joint supply is fairly clear. It has seen much use in general economic analysis, specifically in the areas of transportation and public-utility economics. More recently it has been used in public-goods models and in problems involving the supply of by-products, such as pollution. Mill's joint-supply theory was, in sum, a contribution of great significance for economic analysis.

The Theory of Reciprocal Demand   Mill extended his deep understanding of supply and demand into the area of international values. Citing Ricardo as the premier writer on the issue of comparative costs and advantage, Mill proceeded to construct a model that included both cost *and* demand determinants of international values and the terms of trade. Again, Mill used merely verbal exposition (Edgeworth and Marshall once more provided the graphics), but there is perhaps no better evidence of his analytical powers than his model of the equation of international demand.

Mill set out his ideas on trade in his *Essays on Some Unsettled Questions of Political Economy* but repeated the essentials of his argument in his *Principles* (Book III, Chap. 18). Abstracting from transport costs and technological change, Mill built a two-country (England and Germany), two-commodity

---

[4] Note that at this point the sum of the two prices (*NF* + *FG*) equals their joint costs of production, *NG*.

(cloth and linen) model in order to investigate international price determination. Mill stated his law of reciprocal demand concisely:

> The produce of a country exchanges for the produce of other countries, at such values as are required in order that the whole of her exports may exactly pay for the whole of her imports. This law of International Values is but an extension of the more general law of Value, which we called the Equation of Supply and Demand.... The value of a commodity always so adjusts itself as to bring the demand to the exact level of the supply.
>
> But all trade, either between nations or individuals, is an interchange of commodities, in which the things that they respectively have to sell constitutes also their means of purchase: the supply brought by the one constitutes his demand for what is brought by the other. So that supply and demand are but another expression for reciprocal demand: and to say that value will adjust itself so as to equalize demand with supply, is in fact to say that it will adjust itself so as to equalize the demand on one side with the demand on the other (*Principles*, pp. 592–593).

The Edgeworth-Marshall Exposition   Mill amplified his theory with an elaborate numerical example, but an economy of exposition may be achieved by utilizing a graphic interpretation of reciprocal demand popularized by Edgeworth and Marshall. In Figure 8-2 the lines *OP, OP'*, etc., represent the alternative international price lines that might face England and Germany. They express the price of cloth in terms of linen or the price of linen in terms of cloth, i.e., the "terms of trade." The flatter the *OP* curve, the cheaper linen

FIGURE 8-2
At the international price line *OP'*, quantity OC_0 of cloth will trade for quantity OL_1 of linen; however, at the price line *OP*, a larger quantity of linen OL_0 may be obtained for the same amount of cloth OC_0.

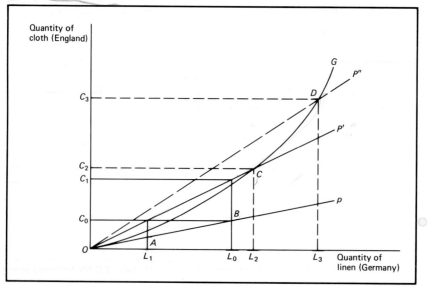

is in terms of a given quantity of cloth and the more dear cloth is in terms of linen. The point can easily be established with respect to Figure 8-2. Quantity OC_0 of cloth will trade for quantity OL_1 of linen assuming price line OP'—i.e., at a ratio of OL_1/OC_0—but quantity OC_0 will trade for OL_0, a ratio of OL_0/OC_0, given price line OP. Obviously, the line OP represents a *lower* price of linen in terms of cloth than price line OP' does, because a larger quantity of linen may be obtained for the same amount of cloth.

Now assume some fixed quantity of linen, say OL_0. The price of cloth in terms of linen is given as a ratio OC_0/OL_0 along price line OP or as OC_1/OL_0 along OP'. Clearly the price of linen becomes dearer in terms of cloth (more cloth for a given amount of linen) as the price line becomes more vertical (a movement from OP to OP', for example). Thus it is clear that if England is trading the good on the vertical axis (cloth) for the German good (linen) on the horizontal axis, England would get better terms of trade with a clockwise rotation of the price line and Germany's position would improve with a counterclockwise rotation. When England's terms of trade improve, Germany's deteriorate, and vice versa. In other words, a lowering of the price of linen in terms of cloth raises the price of cloth in terms of linen. It should be clear that a movement *along* any given price line—say, at points A and B in Figure 8-2—connotes the *same* price ratio of cloth to linen and linen to cloth.

Mill Once Again   With a concept of the price line in hand, we may now turn to Mill's analysis. Mill viewed the trading of goods as a "real-goods" trade. As he noted, "the supply brought by the one constitutes his demand for what is brought by the other. So that supply and demand are but another expression for reciprocal demand." Mill's statement may be illustrated in Figure 8-2. At price OP' of cloth/linen, Germany will demand OC_2 of cloth but will simultaneously *supply* OL_2 of linen. At a lower price of cloth, represented by price line OP'', Germany will increase its demand for cloth to OC_3. Simultaneously, Germany will supply an increased amount, OL_3, of linen.

A demand for cloth is thus expressed by a supply of linen. By varying price and connecting such points as C and D, a curve OG can be traced out. It is called a *reciprocal-demand curve*, but it is not a demand curve constructed in the usual sense. That is, it does not relate prices of a good to the quantity of that good demanded. Rather, it expresses the international demand for a good *in terms of the amounts of another good that a country would be willing to supply in trade.* Manifestly, the amounts of linen that Germany would be willing to supply in trade depend upon the cost of producing linen in Germany, the cost of producing cloth in relation to the cost of producing linen in Germany,[5] and the overall demand for linen and cloth in Germany. In short, many market factors lie behind Mill's reciprocal-demand functions.

[5] Note that given price line OP in Figure 8-2, Germany will not demand any of England's cloth. OP represents a high price of cloth in terms of linen. At such a high price of cloth, Germany would produce and supply cloth to its domestic market.

Mill's Reciprocal Demand A summary of Mill's theory requires a second figure, 8-3, which reproduces Germany's demand function of Figure 8-2 and also one for England, OE (constructed in the manner described for Germany). As Mill indicated, trade will take place at such prices as are required to make the value of imports equal the total value of exports, *simultaneously,* for each party to the trade. If the value of exports does not equal the value of imports to both England and Germany simultaneously, price adjustment will take place to bring the equilibrium about. This extension of the more general law of supply and demand is graphically expressed in Figure 8-3. Given price OP', Germany would be willing to supply OL_0 linen for AL_0 cloth. But demand-and-supply conditions in England are such that the quantity OL_0 of linen would be demanded at a much lower price, OP'', of cloth (higher price of linen). England, in other words, would be willing to supply L_0B of cloth for OL_0 linen. But at price OP'', Germany would not be willing to give OL_0 of linen for L_0B of cloth. Clearly, international demands and supplies are not in equilibrium at either price OP' or price OP''.

What happens? As Mill carefully noted, prices (international values) will adjust so as to bring demands and supplies into equilibrium. Indeed, it is the

FIGURE 8-3
Price level OP is an equilibrium price level because the quantity of cloth supplied by England, C^*, equals the quantity of cloth demanded by Germany, and the quantity of linen supplied by Germany, L^*, equals the quantity of linen demanded by England.

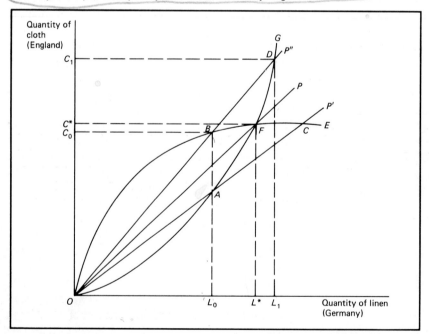

disequilibrium of supply and demand that brings about the price adjustment. At price OP', for example, England would demand a greater quantity (represented at point C) of linen than OL_0 or what Germany would be willing to supply. Similarly at price OP'', Germany would demand a larger quantity of cloth than L_0B, the amount that England would supply. Thus demand-and-supply disequilibrium forces an adjustment.

Prices will adjust until the price line becomes OP in Figure 8-3. At point F, the reciprocal-demand curves OG and OE intersect. The economic meaning of the intersection is that at price OP of cloth/linen or linen/cloth, the quantity supplied of cloth by England, C^*, equals the quantity of cloth demanded by Germany, C^*. Simultaneously, the quantity of linen supplied by Germany, L^*, equals the quantity of linen demanded by England, L^*. The value of exports equals the value of imports for both nations. It is a price adjustment or alteration in the terms of trade that brings this equilibrium about.

General Equilibrium in Exchange   Figure 8-3 may also be used to demonstrate Mill's understanding of general equilibrium in exchange. The model described in Figure 8-3 is in fact a general equilibrium model not unlike that formalized by Léon Walras more than two decades later (see Chapter 16). Mill's ingenuity can perhaps best be seen by converting the reciprocal demand curves of Figure 8-3 into more conventional demand and supply curves, as drawn in Figures 8-4a and 8-4b. Recall that the offer curves of Germany and England are both demand *and* supply curves. Consider Germany's curve, OG, in Figure 8-3. Offer curve OG traces out the amount of linen Germany would supply for given quantities of England's cloth at alternative given price ratios. As the price of linen rises (which is equivalent to a fall in the price of cloth), Germany is willing to give more linen for more cloth. In equilbrium at price P in Figure 8-3, Germany gives the quantity L^* for quantity of cloth C^*. At a *higher* price of linen (a lower price of cloth) given by price ratio P'', Germany would supply more linen, L_1, if it received a greater quantity of cloth, C_1, in return.

Figure 8-4a summarizes these observations in terms of supply and demand curves expressed not in money prices but in the real prices designated by the ratios of exchange. At the high price P'' for linen (expressed in terms of the ratio of cloth to linen) Germany would be willing to supply L_1 of linen but England would demand only L_0 of linen. Clearly, at price P'' there is an excess supply of linen in terms of the desires of demanders and suppliers of linen. Market pressures would then exist for the price of linen (in terms of cloth) to fall.

Viewed from a general equilibrium perspective, however, it is clear that Germany's supply of linen is *also* the mirror image of its demand for cloth. Similarly, England's demand for linen also represents its supply of cloth. These "mirror-image" relations are reproduced in Figure 8-4b, which contrasts the demand and supply of cloth in terms of the real price of cloth. A high price of linen in terms of cloth means a low price of cloth in terms of linen. At

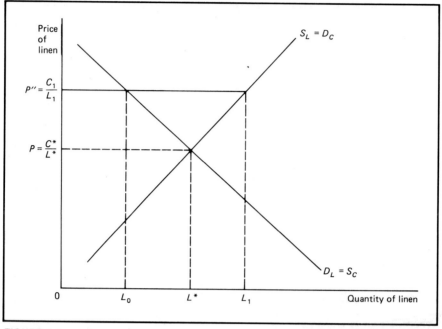

FIGURE 8-4a
An excess supply of linen will bring down the price of linen (in terms of cloth) to an equilibrium level where quantities demanded of linen and cloth will be equal to quantities supplied of linen and cloth.

the price ratio P'', the quantity demanded of cloth in Germany is C_1 while the quantity of cloth that England is willing to supply is C_0. (All information may be transferred directly from Figure 8-3 to Figures 8-4a and 8-4b.) As previously noted, the supply curve of cloth also summarizes the demand curve for linen, and the demand curve for cloth is the supply curve for linen. At the low price of cloth in terms of linen, pressure for a rise in price exists since the quantity demanded of cloth exceeds the quantity supplied. Thus, twin pressures exist simultaneously in the linen and cloth markets. Reduction in linen price means an increase in cloth prices. Price changes occur until both markets clear simultaneously. Excess demand in one market *must* imply excess supply in the other. This idea is the basis for understanding how markets are interrelated in general equilibrium, i.e., simultaneous equilibrium in all markets of an exchange economy.

Mill's "Neoclassical" Contributions While Mill was unquestionably the "grand master" and repository of earlier classical thought, his role as a creative theorist who pointed the way to neoclassical economic analysis has often been totally neglected. His high performance in demand theory, including the "peculiar" case of joint supply and demand, places him in a direct line to

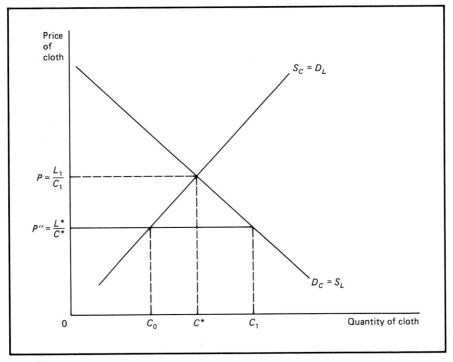

FIGURE 8-4*b*
An excess demand for cloth will drive up the price of cloth (in terms of linen) to an equilibrium level where quantities demanded of linen and cloth will be equal to quantities supplied of linen and cloth.

Alfred Marshall (Chapter 15). Indeed, the issues raised by conditions of joint supply have formed the basis of important contemporary branches of economic theory, including the theory and practice of economic regulation and the conditions surrounding the demands for public goods.

But Mill's purely theoretical achievement goes even beyond Marshallian economics. His verbal model of reciprocal demand in the theory of international trade, which has been depicted here graphically, was an outstanding and unique theoretical achievement. The role of price adjustments in establishing conditions of reciprocal equilibrium in several markets simultaneously was not a central theme in economic analysis until the neoclassical period and beyond. This advance places Mill one step ahead of Léon Walras, who later built a system of economic analysis upon this simple and profound idea. In conception (if not in formalization and development) general equilibrium theory could justly be termed "Millian" as well as "Walrasian." In short, Mill's incisive contributions to value theory mark him as a bold and original pioneer during the high time of classical economics. Rather than view him as a slavish imitator/ synthesizer of classical economics, Mill might justly be viewed as an important transitional figure from the classical age to the era of Marshallian *and* Walrasian neoclassicism.

Mill's Normative Economics

Although he is most frequently regarded as the last great classical economist, Mill lived through the period of nineteenth-century intellectual and socialist criticism of classical economics (see Chapter 10). Being the sensitive, humane individual and fiercely independent thinker that he was, Mill could not help but be affected by this criticism. In fact, he often took even the most bizarre socialist critics more seriously than they deserved. For a time, he was almost a Saint-Simonian, although in his later life he found difficulties in the Saint-Simonian doctrine too elusive to resolve. Nevertheless, Mill was sympathetic to the *ideals* of socialism, if not the critical analysis of the socialist writers. In a word, John Stuart Mill was a zealot in the matter of social reform, but in a way that would preserve and enhance individual freedom and dignity as much as possible.

It is this humanistic concern for greater equality of wealth and opportunity that sets Mill apart from other classical economists. Once again, Mill performed a delicate balancing act. His deftness as a theoretician is keenly displayed in the first three books of the *Principles;* his élan as a reformer permeates the last two books. The last two books emphasize *applications* of political economy for the improvement of humanity, and Mill made it clear where he stood on the relation of theory versus practice in economics. He once wrote to a friend: "I regard the purely abstract investigations of political economy...as of very minor importance compared with the great practical questions which the progress of democracy and the spread of socialist opinions are pressing on" (*Letters,* I, seminar 170). It should be noted, however, that Mill never lost sight of the importance of theory as the proper foundation, or framework, for issuing policy statements.

The last two books of the *Principles,* then, unlike the first three, are teleological (goal-oriented). They reveal Mill's concern for such social reforms as wealth redistribution, equality of women, rights of laborers, consumerism, and education.

The Stationary State   Part of the teleological orientation of Books IV and V of the *Principles* was the concept of the stationary state, which Mill viewed as a precondition for lasting social reform. Here Mill broke with the Ricardian tradition. Ricardo viewed the stationary state primarily as a theoretical construct and thus as useful in demonstrating the possible outcome of certain analytical principles in the theory of economic growth. But to Mill, the stationary state became almost a kind of utopia, in which, having achieved affluence, the state could get on with solving the problems that really matter—namely, equality of wealth and opportunity.

In Book IV, Mill attacked the idea of wealth accumulation for the mere sake of accumulation, and he announced his break from the classical tradition:

> I cannot...regard the stationary state of capital and wealth with the unaffected aversion so generally manifested towards it by political economists of the old school. I am inclined to believe that it would be, on the whole, a very considerable improvement on our present condition. I confess I am not charmed with the ideal of life held out by those who think that the normal state of human beings is that of struggling to get on...(*Principles*, p. 748).

In other places, too, Mill sounds remarkably modern; almost in league with those economists who denounce economic growth for its own sake.[6] There is also a word of caution from Mill's pen for those who would "improve" society by first tearing it down:

> It is only in the backward countries of the world that increased production is still an important object: in those most advanced, what is economically needed is a better distribution, of which one indispensable means is a stricter restraint on population. Levelling institutions, either of a just or unjust kind, cannot alone accomplish it; they may lower the heights of society, but they cannot, of themselves, permanently raise the depths (*Principles*, p. 749).

The above passage indicates, at the end, Mill's conviction that true social reform does not consist merely in the destruction of oppressive institutions. Rather it consists in

> ...the joint effect of the prudence and frugality of individuals, and of a system of legislation favoring equality of fortunes, so far as is consistent with the just claim of the individual to the fruits, whether great or small, of his or her own industry (*Principles*, p. 749).

Wealth Redistribution   One means favored by Mill to achieve the goal of greater equality was the redistribution, not of income, but of wealth. The distinction between the two is not trivial. John Stuart Mill believed, as his father did, that individuals should be allowed to "reap the fruits of their own industry," which is to say that every man has a right to the income he *earns*. But neither father nor son looked favorably on the accumulation of wealth as an end in itself. Both held that beyond a certain limit, further material gains are frivolous. In the younger Mill, this aversion to overaccumulation took the form of a proposal to limit the size of bequests. Mill established his own norms as follows:

> Were I framing a code of laws according to what seems to me best in itself, without regard to existing opinions and sentiments, I should prefer to restrict...what any one should be permitted to acquire, by bequest or inheritance. Each person should have power to dispose by will of his or her whole property; but not to lavish it in enriching some one individual, beyond a certain maximum, which should be fixed sufficiently high to afford the means of comfortable independence. The inequalities

---

[6] Most vocal among modern economists who have joined this chorus are John Kenneth Galbraith (*The Affluent Society,* New York: Houghton-Mifflin, 1958) and E. J. Mishan (*The Costs of Economic Growth,* London: Staples, 1967).

of property which arise from unequal industry, frugality, perseverence, talents, and to a certain extent even opportunities, are inseparable from the principle of private property, and if we accept the principle [as Mill did] we must bear with these consequences of it: but I see nothing objectionable in fixing a limit to what any one may acquire by the mere favour of others; without any exercise of his faculties, and in requiring that if he desires any further, he shall work for it (*Principles*, pp. 227–228).

Clearly, what Mill advocated was a world in which people would be free from the pressing demands of economic necessity and open to improvements in the quality of life. This latter notion he shared with the romantic poets, although he denounced their criticism of political economy. It and the asceticism Mill revealed in seeking to limit individual fortunes are normative propositions, not analytical ones. But they reveal the deep, philosophical humanism of a great theoretician in economics as well as a great philosopher.

On the opportunities for personal development (along nonmarket lines) in the stationary state, Mill was emphatic:

It is scarcely necessary to remark that a stationary condition of capital and population implies no stationary state of human improvement. There would be as much scope as ever for all kinds of mental culture, and moral and social progress; as much room for improving the Art of Living, and much more likelihood of its being improved, when minds ceased to be engrossed by the art of getting on (*Principles*, p. 751).

Government and Laissez Faire   A major part of Mill's normative economics concerns the proper role and influence of government, a topic he took up in Book V of the *Principles*. He began by distinguishing between the necessary functions of government and its optional functions. The necessary functions "are either inseparable from the idea of government or exercised habitually and without objection by all governments" (*Principles*, p. 796). Other functions, however, are not universally accepted, and there is room for controversy as to whether or not governments should exercise them.

This distinction between necessary and optional functions is important only insofar as it enabled Mill to minimize discussions of the former and concentrate on the latter. Mill's list of necessary government functions includes the power to tax, coin money, and establish a uniform system of weights and measurements; protection against force and fraud; the administration of justice and the enforcement of contracts; the establishment and protection of property rights, including determination of the use of the environment; protection of the interest of minors and mental incompetents; and the provision of certain public goods and services, such as roads, canals, dams, bridges, harbors, lighthouses, and sanitation.

Mill followed his discussion of government activity in these areas with a lengthy digression on the economic effects of all manner of taxes, direct and indirect. His treatment of such questions was exhaustive and has been little surpassed in the many years that have elapsed since. Nevertheless, it is a detour that threatens the continuity of Mill's narrative in Book V on the proper grounds for government action. Returning to that subject in the final chapter of the *Principles,* Mill placed the burden of proof on those who would advocate government intervention. He himself stood squarely in the classical tradition by reaffirming the maxim that laissez faire should be the rule and that any departure from it, "unless required by some great good, is a certain evil."

But although Adam Smith was less doctrinaire on the matter of government interference than he is generally made out to be, John Stuart Mill was even less so. The key to Mill's philosophical position on the limits of the laissez faire principle lies in his recognition that government interference under capitalism *could be required by some great good.* Thus Mill was able to list several exceptions to the doctrine of laissez faire without compromising on the basic principle. His exceptions would allow government intervention in the areas of consumer protection, general education, preservation of the environment, selective enforcement of "permanent" contracts based on future experience (e.g., marriage), public-utility regulation, and public charity.

In short, Mill recognized, and in some cases enunciated for the first time, the majority of popular exceptions to laissez faire that have become an integral part of modern capitalism, at least in the United States. The various watchdog agencies of government (e.g., the Food and Drug Administration), state-supported education, the Environmental Protection Agency, divorce laws and courts, regulatory commissions (e.g., the Federal Power Commission, the Federal Aviation Administration, and the Federal Communications Commission), and welfare legislation in the United States have all been inspired by a kind of Millian desire to make capitalism fairer and more humane. The specific details of Mill's policy concerns and proposals are considered in Chapter 9.

In fairness to Mill, he was very explicit about the caveats the state should employ in instituting such measures, and he would not necessarily approve of all existing amendments to the institutions of capitalism. Nevertheless, it is his willingness to make such amendments that underlines the transitional nature of his works and thoughts and that marks Mill as very much a modern economist.

Mill and His Influence

John Stuart Mill was undoubtedly a product of his intellectual environment, but he was also a molder of it. Fully within the classical tradition, he devoted his intellectual efforts to a synthesis and improvement of economic knowledge at a time when economics as a science was beset on all sides by romantic, social, and methodological criticism. He enriched economic theory by his own analytical contributions, and he did not hesitate to issue normative proclamations to point the way for practical applications of economic knowledge. To his credit, Mill never confused the two branches of economics—theory and policy—and yet he skillfully displayed the interconnections between the two. Wherever Mill asserted his normative views, he warned his readers of their arbitrariness. Yet even while doing so, he revealed a spirit of disinterested inquiry by carefully presenting both the advantages and the disadvantages of a given proposition or course of action.

His influence on other economists and social thinkers was deep and long-lasting. In his own century, Mill's concern for fundamental questions and his multifaceted brilliance as economist, philosopher, and logician insulated him against the attacks of lesser minds. Indeed, Mill's legacy remains. As is true of most great thinkers, his questions have proved more durable than his answers. In this chapter we have concentrated on Mill's theoretical performance, with mere side glances at his policy proposals. In the next we shall see how Mill's ideas on policy became part of the political landscape.

THE DECLINE OF CLASSICAL ECONOMICS

Classical economics was, of course, never without its critics. The Malthusian population doctrine and the differential-rent theory, for example, underwent frequent attacks by radicals, socialists, and reformers throughout the nineteenth century. But in an 1869 issue of the *Fortnightly Review* a curious event took place within the classical orthodoxy of Great Britain that shook the foundations of the classical theoretical system. John Stuart Mill recanted the wages-fund doctrine.

The Wages-Fund Revisited

The wages-fund doctrine held that at the end of a production period, a given stock of circulating capital is advanced to laborers to tide them over the next production period. This stock of capital is determined by many variables, including the productivity of labor and capital in previous periods, the amount of investment in previous periods, and so forth. In crude terms, the doctrine indicated that at a macroeconomic level, the average wage rate over a productive period would be given by dividing the stock of capital by the number of laborers. Thus, in *real terms,* a maximum real wage (that is, all the goods consumed by laborers) is determined at the beginning of the production period. Properly stated, and given the assumption of a discrete time period of production in the economy, the wages-fund doctrine forms an integral, and indeed an inextricable, part of the dynamics of the classical system (see Chapter 7).

Confusions Surrounding the Doctrine   Numerous confusions always surrounded the wages-fund doctrine. One of them concerns the introduction of money wage payments, which customarily stand as the proxy for real wages. If the fund is understood as a money amount, then the amount going to labor could indeed be elastic and variable. The stock of real wage goods on hand is nonaugmentable (at a given time), irrespective of the amount or variability of money wages paid. Money wages, then, are not the "capital" of the wages-fund theory. Even Adam Smith, who provided early and otherwise clear statements of the wages-fund theory, was not immune to the problem. As Frank Taussig has pointed out with reference to Smith's statements of the doctrine:

Sometimes, indeed most commonly, this "stock" is conceived in terms of money or as consisting of funds in the hands of the immediate employer. Sometimes the money payments are described as of no essential importance, as only steps toward the distribution of real wages. The uncertainty and confusion which thus showed itself in Adam Smith continued to appear in almost all the discussions of wages for fully a century after his time (*Wages and Capital*, p. 145).

Micro Theory versus Macro Theory Another difficult problem concerned the attempt, by both defenders and critics of the wages-fund, to read a *microeconomic* theory of wage determination into statements of the doctrine. For example, Francis A. Walker, an American critic of the concept, was led to argue that the wages-fund doctrine ignored the varying productivity of workers and therefore did not explain varying wage returns between different types of laborers or between laborers of different countries (e.g., East Indians and Englishmen). Walker had much company in this criticism. Unfortunately, and in spite of misuse on the part of its proponents, the wages-fund doctrine was designed only as a rough-and-ready *macroeconomic* argument. It was not until the development of the marginal-productivity theory decades later that a satisfactory explanation of individual wage determination was approached.

Mill's Recantation[7]

All the main elements of the classical wages-fund doctrine were present in Mill's *Principles,* including the assumption of a point-input-point-output production process. Mill assumed that the present remuneration of labor was the consequence of *past* applications of capital and labor, and he believed that a proportion of total output was destined for labor in advance of production. He further perceived and applied the doctrine at an *aggregate* level and in *real* terms. This constitutes his *theoretical* view of the doctrine.

By 1869, Mill had altered his views on the wages-fund doctrine, and there has been a great deal of controversy as to why he did so. Several explanations deal exclusively with considerations other than Mill's theoretical views. Since Mill recanted the doctrine on the occasion of his review of a book by W.T. Thornton, one reason given for the recantation is his friendship with Thornton. Another explanation given is Mill's late but deep involvement in social reform. A third reason often cited is the combined influence on Mill of his wife, Harriet Taylor, and of the philosopher Auguste Comte. While none of these influences should be discounted completely, it seems clear from a close examination of Mill's writings that by 1869 he had changed his theoretical view of the wages-fund. It is on this last matter that attention will be focused in this chapter.

The central issue in the recantation concerned the fixity of the fund ear-

---

[7] This section follows closely the argument presented by R. B. Ekelund, Jr., "A Short-Run Classical Model of Capital and Wages: Mill's Recantation of the Wages Fund," *Oxford Economic Papers,* vol. 28 (March 1976), pp. 66–85.

marked for the payment of labor. The idea of a fixed fund in the short run implied that in the aggregate, workers could claim no more in wage payments than an amount that would exactly deplete the fund. Thus the doctrine of the wages-fund was frequently used to demonstrate the futility of efforts by labor unions to raise their aggregate compensation. The long run was a different matter—no classical economist argued that the fund was fixed over the long run. However, some advanced the argument that if labor unions were too aggressive in pushing their claims, profit expectations would decline, so that in the future less capital would flow into the fund, thereby reducing real wages somewhere down the road. In later life, Mill became sympathetic to labor unions, and this may have been the impetus that led him to reexamine the concept of the wages-fund, in particular the subject of its short-run fixity.

In his 1869 review of Thornton's book *On Labour,* Mill undid the fixity assumption. Of the aggregate amount that is spent on wages, Mill asserted only that there is some upper limit. He wrote:

> ...there is an impassable limit to the amount which can be so expended; it cannot exceed the aggregate means of employing classes. It cannot come up to those means; for the employers have also to maintain themselves and their families. But, short of this limit, it is not, in any sense of the word, a fixed amount ("Thornton on Labour and Its Claims," p. 516).

Mill's argument advanced to the point that he divided the employer-capitalist's means into two parts: his capital and his income on that capital. While the former is usually equated in classical economic nomenclature with the wages-fund, Mill argued that the capitalist could add to that amount by discretionary reductions of his income. The capitalist, in other words, might respond to exogenous variables (e.g., union pressure, different profit expectations, etc.) in such a way that he voluntarily reduced expenditures on himself and his family in order to spend more on labor. In this way, Mill apparently thought that labor unions might be able to redistribute income in favor of the workers. Unfortunately, Mill's argument did not distinguish between money wages and real wages, nor between short-run and long-run effects. Consequently, his recantation does not rest on a sound theoretical footing.

A Short-Run Wages-Fund Model In order to expose the deficiencies of Mill's recantation, we shall place it in the context of a short-run wages-fund model that rests on the usual classical assumptions. Those assumptions are:

1 Production takes place within a point-input-point-output production process.

2 The entire output of the economy is composed of fixed capital, wage goods, and capitalist consumables. There is, moreover, no transference of demands between markets; i.e., wage earners do not transfer demands to capitalist consumables and vice versa.

3 Production in all industries is marked by a constant ratio of fixed to circulating capital.

4 Perfect competition (i.e., constant costs of production) exists everywhere.

5 The money supply is fixed for the term in question.

6 Population and productivity remain unchanged during the period in question.

Under these assumptions, the aggregate stock of goods in real terms during any period, say t_1, is determined by past production and cannot be increased during t_1. In real terms, consumption and investment decisions are made at the beginning of the period (i.e., the end of t_0) and the entire stock of goods is depleted by the end of the period, albeit at different rates of use. For example, consider Figure 8-5, where the total stock of goods at the end of t_0 is represented by OY_0, divided so that OM_0 is equal to fixed capital (e.g., machinery), M_0W_0 is equal to wage goods available for purchase by workers, and W_0Y_0 is equal to capitalist consumables. This tripartite division conforms to Mill's representation. Under the usual assumptions of the wages-fund theory, these various stocks are used up during the production period, so that at the end of t_1, each has fallen to zero.

Now let us examine the effects of a decision by the capitalist to reduce his own real income (W_0Y_0) in order to spend more on labor, the prospect Mill raised in his recantation. The effects of this redistribution of income are carried through in Figures 8-6a and 8-6b. The former depicts the market for goods that are bought by workers, the latter the market for goods purchased

FIGURE 8-5
The total stock of goods available (OY_0) at the end of period t_1 diminishes to zero.

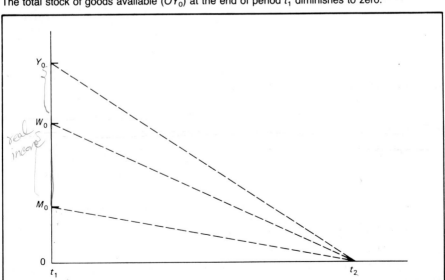

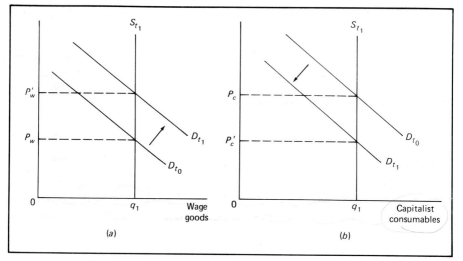

FIGURE 8-6
As the demand for wage goods increases from D_{t_0} to D_{t_1}, prices will rise from P_w to P'_w. In the long run, the entry of new firms will shift supply, causing prices to fall back to P_w. A similar effect will occur in the capitalist consumables market, in which a leftward supply shift will force prices back up to P_c. Over time, the quantities in both markets will also adjust.

by capitalists. Under the rigid supply conditions of the wages-fund model, output in each period is fixed and determined by the previous period. Thus the supply curves in Figures 8-6a and 8-6b are vertical lines. A voluntary reduction in real income by capitalists will cause the demand for capitalist consumables to shift to the left, lowering the average price of such goods from P_c to P'_c. *Pari passu*, an increase in workers' real income will shift the demand for wage goods to the right, thereby raising the average price of those goods from P_w to P'_w.

The conclusion of this analysis is that under the assumptions of the classical wages-fund doctrine, the effects of any reallocation of funds by capitalists in favor of labor are solely upon prices in the two markets. Furthermore, given a constant money stock and velocity, the price changes in the two markets will be proportionate in opposite directions, so that the aggregate price level will not be affected. More important from the standpoint of the laboring classes, the increase in money wages occasioned by the transfer of income from the capitalist class produces a price increase in wage goods that offsets the rise in money wages. Real wages remain unaffected by the transfer. Since Mill implied that workers would be better off under such a transfer, it seems clear that he confused real wages with money wages.

Long-Run Adjustments The nature of the long-run adjustments that would accompany the kind of income redistribution just considered does not hold any brighter prospects for permanent increases in real wages. Given price changes in the two markets traced above, higher profits in the wage-goods industry would signal new firms to enter whereas lower profits in the capitalist-consumables market would encourage some firms to exit. These long-run changes can be envisioned by shifting the vertical supply curve to the right in Figure 8-6a and to the left in Figure 8-6b. Under constant-cost conditions, price would tend to return to P_w in Figure 8-6a and to P_c in Figure 8-6b. The adjustments in each market might be lengthy, but the tendency would be for prices to return to their former level before the income transfer Mill suggested. The point that Mill seemed to forget (or deny) in his 1869 recantation is that in the classical world, permanent increases in real wages are traceable to real factors only, such as improvements in technology or some other increase in worker productivity. Mill seems to have been victimized by the idea that aggregate welfare can be improved by taking income from one group and giving it to another, an idea that seems to die hard, as witnessed by contemporary American and British experience with government-forced attempts to redistribute income.

Cairnes's Last Stand

to restore & rank, reputations, etc.

In 1874, J.E. Cairnes, in the face of the attacks by Longe and Thornton and of Mill's recantation, attempted to rehabilitate the wages-fund doctrine and to revive classical theory. In *Some Leading Principles of Political Economy Newly Expounded*, Cairnes defended the validity of the doctrine. The real issue was not the determinacy or indeterminacy of the fund, but simply what the capitalist qua capitalist did in the real world. Cairnes did not view the capitalist as setting aside a *specific* amount for wages, but as long as he acted as a capitalist and made investments, a wages-fund would exist.

Determinants of the Fund Cairnes went into great detail on the determinants of the individual capitalist's investment, and he specifically mentioned the amount of his total means, the capitalist's time preference, and the opportunity for making a profit. The investment determinants for society as a whole parallel Mill's, i.e., the "effective desire of accumulation" and the extent of the field for investment. Total investment, which includes investment in fixed capital and raw materials, does not give an accurate understanding of the wages-fund, however, and so Cairnes was led to investigate the *proportion* of wages to total capital. Here he made some incisive statements. The proportion of wages to total capital, Cairnes maintained, is determined by three factors: (1) the nature of national industries, or the economy's production function; (2) the total capital of the country; and (3) specifically the supply of labor.

On the first point Cairnes was very clear. As he noted:

> If, for example, his [the capitalist's] purpose is to engage in cotton or woollen manufacture, a very large proportion of his whole capital will assume the form of buildings, machinery, and raw wool or cotton...of fixed capital and raw material, which would leave a correspondingly small proportion available for the payment of wages (*Some Leading Principles*, p. 170).

Other things being equal, in agricultural nations, where labor inputs are large, one would expect a large proportion of total capital to go to labor. But given the state of the economy's production function, the price of inputs determines factor shares. Supply-and-demand conditions for inputs obviously affect input prices, and Cairnes believed that the demand for labor was inelastic, since presumably investment was predetermined by other factors. Shifts in the supply of labor, however, were inversely related to the size of the wages-fund, though Cairnes thought that such shifts were only minor influences on the size of aggregate wages.

Clearly Cairnes was into an explanation of the state of wages over time. Ignoring the discrete production period assumption, Cairnes looked to the growth or decline of aggregate capital and to the nature of national industries as prime variables in the determination of wages. In this matter he adapted to the Ricardian position that a growth in fixed capital relative to total capital would cause profits and investment to fall over time. Technology would forestall the stationary state, but the latter would arrive nonetheless. The long-run prospects for laborers were bleak unless, of course, they saved and became part of the entrepreneurial class.

Cairnes's discussion of the long run is perfectly consistent with classical positions on the wages-fund, but his defense of the doctrine broke down when he turned (again following Mill) to a discussion of the trade union issue. Unfortunately, at this juncture Cairnes fell into Mill's error of identifying the fund with a money amount. This problem is implicit in Cairnes's statement that:

> If beyond the amount actually spent on wages at any given time there be an indefinite margin of wealth which workmen by judicious combination may conquer; then it is evident Trades-Unionism has a great field before it, and workmen will naturally and properly look to this agency as the principal means of improving their condition (*Some Leading Principles*, p. 214).

This "indefinite margin of wealth" is clearly a money amount in the hands of capitalists.

In short, wages can be higher or lower only within limits. Subsistence, of course, sets the lower limit. If union demands go beyond the upper limit, entrepreneurial investment will cease, and the fund will decline. But when profits are within these limits, union leaders can bargain successfully.[8]

Cairnes's Impact on Classical Economics Where does Cairnes's defense leave the wages-fund doctrine? In terms of the short run, Cairnes would have to *deny* that wages are fixed, since he viewed the fund as a money amount. In real-goods terms, of course, the fund is fixed as of any moment, and given the discrete time period of production assumption, the average wage is fixed over the period. Critics and defenders of the doctrine simply failed to come to grips with a correct, albeit naive, theoretical construct.

---

[8] It is interesting that Cairnes believed the United States, a "progressive" society, was ripe for unionization since profits were above minimum. By contrast, he thought Great Britain was approaching the stationary state.

As a believer in the classical stationary state, Cairnes was very pessimistic concerning the long-run outcome of the condition of the laboring classes, especially in Great Britain. The declining rate of profit and the growth of land rent were the limits to progress. As he noted:

> Against these barriers Trades-Unions must dash themselves in vain. They are not to be broken through or eluded by any combination, however, universal, for they are barriers set by nature herself (*Some Leading Principles,* p. 283).

However, Cairnes was not totally devoid of suggestions for labor. First, he admonished labor for squandering higher real wages on larger populations, and he urged "self-restraint," as Malthus had. Second, laborers should attempt to become part of the capitalist class by saving to augment the fund.

The laborer must learn to save, and Cairnes offered an empirical example of how this might be done. Calculating that £120 million was spent on alcoholic drinks per year, Cairnes attributed the largest portion of the expenditure to laborers. (He offered the further judgment that three-fourths of it was both physically and morally injurious to them.) Thus Cairnes concluded that half of this sum could be saved and channeled into labor cooperatives. Though such massive investment would go far toward improving labor's position in income distribution, Cairnes was not especially sanguine concerning his proposals. With typically Victorian disdain he noted:

> What workmen have to overcome in order to engage effectively in cooperative industry is, first, the temptation to spend their means on indulgences generally pernicious, and which at all events may without detriment be dispensed with; and, secondly, the obstacles incident to their own ignorance and generally low moral condition (*Some Leading Principles,* pp. 289–290).

Indeed, by identifying the fund with a money amount, Cairnes expanded the confusion established by Mill and by the doctrine's critics. Many of his other writings on distribution (his adherence to a residual theory of wages rather than profits, for example) are similarly marred by confusion. The decline of classical economics was thus in evidence, not only because a competitive theory (marginalism) was in ascendance, as we shall soon see, but also because important members of the tradition misinterpreted some of its fundamental precepts. J.E. Cairnes, although he made advances in other areas (particularly in scientific methodology), may have undermined the theoretical tradition he fought so energetically to protect.

DID CLASSICAL ECONOMIC THEORY EVER DIE?

Mill's recantation of the wages-fund doctrine and the subsequent confusion that it caused in the ranks of the classical orthodoxy is but one factor among a host of other possible explanations for the decline of classical economics. The rise of marginalism (see Chapters 12 to 14) is often cited as a causal factor of this decline, as is the fast-swelling ranks during the nineteenth century of historicist and socialist critics of economic orthodoxy (see Chapter 10). Great policy debates, such as those over free trade, the rent issue, and trade unions, also played a role in the questioning of classical theory, especially in England and America. Unquestionably, all these developments played a role in the decline of classical economics as an ongoing paradigm.

Economists in the last third of the nineteenth century appeared to be asking questions that the classical theoretical system could not answer satisfactorily, if at all. The policy conclusions of classical theory simply were not acceptable to the majority of social scientists.[9] Individual (microeconomic) behavior became the issue of the day, and economic analysis advanced in a new direction.

Can classical economics, then, have died in any meaningful sense? Though it is often easier to view intellectual history in terms of sharp breaks with past ideas, such a view would do a serious disservice to the classical economists and to their theoretical structure. Old theories do not die, and unlike old soldiers, they do not even fade away. For instance, Alfred Marshall, the great neoclassical contributor to microeconomics, was very adamant in his admiration for, and use of, Ricardo's theory of cost in formulating partial-equilibrium analysis. Moreover, contemporary economists, in struggling with the problems of economic development in underdeveloped nations, have returned on occasion to the simple analytics of classical dynamics. In other words, not only did classical ideas work themselves into neoclassical economics, but the whole construction is still being used.

Achievements of the Classical School

As economic analysis, classical economics was cogent and logically correct. While its assumptions encompassed many broad and challengeable generalizations, its sweeping logic was elegant. Perhaps no one described better the transition from the classical to the neoclassical era in theory than Alfred Marshall. He noted:

> The change may, perhaps, be regarded as a passing onward from that early stage in the development of scientific method, in which the operations of Nature are represented as conventionally simplified for the purpose of enabling them to be described in short and easy sentences, to that higher stage in which they are studied more carefully, and represented more nearly as they are, even at the expense of some loss of simplicity and definiteness, and even apparent lucidity (*Principles of Economics*, p. 766).

Few episodes in the history of economic thought match the achievements of the classical economists in discovering and formulating the operations of an entire economic system. In addition, they established the method upon which modern economic reasoning is based. Although the assumptions of classical economics were in fact simplistic, the goal of the classical economists was

---

[9] There were exceptions, of course. The American social critic Henry George, in his popular book *Progress and Poverty* (1879), rejected the wages-fund doctrine while recasting the Ricardian theory of differential land rents into a policy of urban-site value taxation.

nothing less than global analysis of entire economies. One might legitimately wonder whether such large ends would or could be sought by contemporary economists. "Progress" and the quest for technical accuracy have probably robbed us of the will, but the classical theoretical structure remains as an inspiration for such an attempt.

NOTES FOR FURTHER READING

Insights into Mill's life and unusual upbringing are contained in frank detail in J. S. Mill, *Autobiography* (New York: Columbia University Press, 1924), which was originally published in 1873, the year of Mill's death, in accordance with his wishes. In addition, see Alexander Bain, *John Stuart Mill, A Criticism: With Personal Recollections* (London: Longmans, 1882); Herbert Spencer et al., *John Stuart Mill: His Life and Works* (Boston: Osgood and Co., 1873); W. L. Courtney, *Life of John Stuart Mill* (London: Secker & Warburg, 1954); and Bertrand Russell, "John Stuart Mill," in *Portraits from Memory and Other Essays* (London: G. Allen, 1956).

Mill's thought is multidimensional, covering such fields as logic, philosophy, and economics. His contributions to the field of logic are epoch-making. One can do no better in this respect than to start with Mill himself. See J. S. Mill, *A System of Logic* (London: Longmans, Green, 1884); and same author, "On the Logic of the Moral Sciences," in H. M. Magid (ed.), *A System of Logic* (Indianapolis: Bobbs-Merrill, 1965). Mill's classic essays, "On Liberty," "Utilitarianism," and excerpts from "Considerations on Representative Government," have been edited and reprinted by Marshall Cohen in *The Philosophy of John Stuart Mill* (New York: Modern Library, 1961). See also R. P. Anschutz, *The Philosophy of John Stuart Mill* (London: Oxford University Press, 1953). At one stage of his life, Mill was attracted by the positivist philosophy of Auguste Comte. See, for example, J. S. Mill, *Auguste Comte and Positivism* (London: Lippincott, 1865); and his correspondence with Comte, *Lettres inédites de John Stuart Mill à Auguste Comte* (Paris: Felix Alcan, 1899), available only in French. R. B. Ekelund and Emilie Olsen, "Comte, Mill and Cairnes: The Positivist-Empiricist Interlude in Late Classical Economics," *Journal of Economic Issues*, vol. 7 (September 1973), pp. 383–416, explore the impact of Comte's positivism on Mill and Cairnes. A further source of information on Mill's methodology is J. K. Whitaker, "John Stuart Mill's Methodology," *Journal of Political Economy*, vol. 83 (October 1975), pp. 1033–1050.

Turning to Mill's economics in the more narrow sense, several general works are noteworthy. Almost everything written on Mill by other economists has been collected under the editorship of John C. Wood, *John Stuart Mill: Critical Assessments* (London: Croom Helm, 1987). Pedro Schwartz, *The New Political Economy of John Stuart Mill* (Durham, N.C.: Duke University Press, 1973), reviews Mill's views on economic policy, demonstrating the relevance of Mill's thought for contemporary capitalism. The indefatigable Sam

Hollander, *The Economics of John Stuart Mill* (Toronto: University of Toronto Press, 1985), has undertaken, in two volumes, a wholesale reinterpretation of Mill's economics in which he advances the controversial claim that there was no real intellectual break between classical and neoclassical (i.e., Marshallian) economics.

G. J. Stigler defends Mill's originality as an economist in "The Nature and Role of Originality in Scientific Progress," *Economica,* vol. 22 (November 1955), pp. 293–302, reprinted in Stigler's *Essays in the History of Economics* (Chicago: University of Chicago Press, 1965). Other assessments of Mill in the large picture of economics include V. W. Bladen, "John Stuart Mill's *Principles:* A Centenary Estimate," *American Economic Review,* vol. 39, suppl. (May 1949), pp. 1–12; James Bonar, "John Stuart Mill, the Reformer: 1806–73," *Indian Journal of Economics,* vol. 10 (April 1930), pp. 761–805; W. D. Grampp, "Classical Economics and Moral Critics," *History of Political Economy,* vol. 5 (Fall 1973), pp. 359–374; Neil de Marchi, "The Success of Mill's *Principles,*" *History of Political Economy,* vol. 6 (Summer 1974), pp. 119–157; same author, "Mill and Cairnes and the Emergence of Marginalism in England," *History of Political Economy,* vol. 4 (Fall 1972), pp. 344–363; and J. P. Platteau, "The Political Economy of John Stuart Mill, or, the Coexistence of Orthodoxy, Heresy and Prophecy," *International Journal of Social Economics,* vol. 12 (1985), pp. 3–26. A. L. Harris discusses Mill's ideas on freedom in two articles: "J. S. Mill on Monopoly and Socialism," *Journal of Political Economy,* vol. 67 (December 1959), pp. 604–611; and "Mill on Freedom and Voluntary Association," *Review of Social Economy,* vol. 18 (March 1960), pp. 27–44. See also, Elynor D. Davis, "Mill, Socialism, and the English Romantics: An Interpretation," *Economica,* vol. 52 (August 1985), pp. 345–358.

The standard treatment of Mill's theory of international trade and reciprocal demand is Jacob Viner, *Studies in the Theory of International Trade* (New York: Harper, 1937), pp. 535–541. Mill's terms-of-trade argument was expanded by F. Y. Edgeworth in his *Papers Relating to Political Economy,* vol. 2 (London: Macmillan, 1925), pp. 340*ff.;* more recently by N. Kaldor, "A Note on Tariffs and the Terms of Trade," *Economica,* vol. 7 (November 1940), pp. 377–380; and again by H. G. Johnson, "Optimum Tariffs and Retaliation," *Review of Economic Studies,* vol. 21 (1953–1954), pp. 142–153. The possibility of "multiple equilibriums" in international trade and of Mill's alleged attempts to rule them out is discussed in two papers, one by D. R. Appleyard and J. C. Ingram, "A Reconsideration of the Addition to Mill's 'Great Chapter,'" *History of Political Economy,* vol. 11 (Winter 1979), pp. 459–476; and the other by J. S. Chipman, "Mill's Superstructure: How Well Does It Stand Up?" *History of Political Economy,* vol. 11 (Winter 1979), pp. 477–499. See also the reply to Appleyard and Ingram that follows Chipman in the same issue.

Mill's rendition of Say's law may well have derived from his father, James Mill. On this matter, see B. Balassa, "John Stuart Mill and the Law of

Markets," *Quarterly Journal of Economics,* vol. 73 (May 1959), pp. 263–274; and the comment by L. C. Hunter in the same journal, vol. 74 (May 1960), pp. 158–162. A clarification of Say's law has been attempted by W. J. Baumol, "Say's (At Least) Eight Laws, or What Say and James Mill May Have Really Meant," *Economica,* vol. 44 (May 1977), pp. 145–162; but see also W. O. Thweatt, "Baumol and James Mill on 'Say's' Law of Markets," *Economica,* vol. 47 (November 1980), pp. 467–470.

On other specific aspects of Mill's economics, see L. C. Hunter, "Mill and Cairnes on the Rate of Interest," *Oxford Economic Papers,* vol. 11 (February 1959), pp. 63–97; J. H. Thompson, "Mill's Fourth Fundamental Proposition: A Paradox Revisited," *History of Political Economy,* vol. 7 (Summer 1975), pp. 174–192; Sam Hollander, "J. S. Mill on 'Derived Demand' and the Wage Fund Theory Recantation," *Eastern Economic Journal,* vol. 10 (January–March 1984), pp. 87–98; W. C. Bush, "Population and Mill's Peasant-Proprietor Economy," *History of Political Economy,* vol. 5 (Spring 1973), pp. 110–120; M. E. Bradley, "Mill on Proprietorship, Productivity, and Population: A Theoretical Reappraisal," *History of Political Economy,* vol. 15 (Fall 1983), pp. 423–429; Sam Hollander, "Dynamic Equilibrium with Constant Wages: J. S. Mill's Malthusian Analysis of the Secular Wage Path," *Kyklos,* vol. 37 (1984), pp. 247–265; same author, "The Wage Path in Classical Growth Models: Ricardo, Malthus and Mill," *Oxford Economic Papers,* vol. 36 (June 1984), pp. 200–212; and V. R. Smith, "John Stuart Mill's Famous Distinction between Production and Distribution," *Economic Philosophy,* vol. 1 (October 1985), pp. 267–284. An interesting exchange on Mill's "utility" theory is contained in the following papers: M. Bronfenbrenner, "Poetry, Pushpin and Utility," *Economic Inquiry,* vol. 15 (January 1977), pp. 95–110; M. S. McPherson, "Liberty and the Higher Pleasures: In Defense of Mill," *Economic Inquiry,* vol. 18 (April 1980), pp. 324–318; and the rejoinder by Bronfenbrenner, "Liberty and Higher Pleasures: A Reply," *Economic Inquiry,* vol. 18 (April 1980), pp. 319–320.

The wages-fund controversy and Mill's role in it were first capably summarized by F. W. Taussig, *Wages and Capital* (New York: Appleton, 1896; reprinted 1968, New York: A. M. Kelley). Marshall's student and successor, A. C. Pigou, discusses the grounds of Mill's famous recantation in "Mill and the Wages Fund," *Economic Journal,* vol. 57 (June 1949), pp. 171–180. William Breit, "Some Neglected Early Critics of the Wages Fund Theory," *Southwestern Social Science Quarterly,* vol. 48 (June 1967), pp. 53–60, probed the early criticisms of the theory, and then examined the "first round" of the famous controversy, in which Longe, Thornton, and Mill figured prominently, in "The Wages Fund Controversy Revisited," *Canadian Journal of Economics and Political Science,* vol. 33 (November 1967), pp. 523–528. Scott Gordon concentrates on the latter phase of the controversy in "The Wage-Fund Controversy: The Second Round," *History of Political Economy,* vol. 5 (Spring 1973), pp. 14–35. The interpretation of Mill's recantation utilized in this chapter is based on R. B. Ekelund, "A Short-Run Classical Model of Capital and

Wages: Mill's Recantation of the Wages Fund," *Oxford Economic Papers,*vol. 28 (March 1976), pp. 66–85, which has sparked a controversy of its own. For more on this subject, see J. Vint, "A Two Sector Model of the Wage Fund: Mill's Recantation Revisited," *British Review of Economic Issues,* vol. 3 (Autumn 1981), pp. 71–88; T. Negishi, "Mill's Recantation of the Wages Fund: Comment," *Oxford Economic Papers,* vol. 37 (March 1985), pp. 148–151; and Ekelund, "Mill's Recantation Once Again: Reply," *Oxford Economic Papers,* vol. 37 (March 1985), pp. 152–153. Yet another controversy has swirled around the issue of whether Mill used a "Malthusian" argument in support of trade unions. Arguing in favor of such a view, E. G. West and R. W. Hafer, "J. S. Mill, Unions, and the Wages Fund Recantation: A Reinterpretation," *Quarterly Journal of Economics,* vol. 92 (November 1978), pp. 603–619, have challenged Ekelund's interpretation of Mill's recantation, but see the response by R. B. Ekelund and W. F. Kordsmeier, "J. S. Mill, Unions, and the Wages Fund Recantation: A Reinterpretation-Comment," *Quarterly Journal of Economics,* vol. 96 (August 1981), pp. 531–541.

Space constraints have limited our discussion of J. E. Cairnes to his participation in the wages-fund controversy. Careful study of Cairnes's methodology, however, would still repay contemporary students. In this regard see M. D. Bordo's interesting paper "John E. Cairnes on the Effects of the Australian Gold Discoveries, 1851–73: An Early Application of the Methodology of Positive Economics," *History of Political Economy,* vol. 7 (Fall 1975), pp. 337–359.

REFERENCES

Cairnes, J. E. *Some Leading Principles of Political Economy Newly Expounded.* London: 1874.

Marshall, Alfred. *Principles of Economics,* 8th ed. London: Macmillan, 1964 [1890].

Mill, J. S. "Thornton on Labour and Its Claims," *Fortnightly Review* (May, June 1869), pp. 505–518, 680–700.

———. *Letters of John Stuart Mill,* 2 vols., H. S. R. Elliot (ed.). London: Longmans, 1910.

———. *Autobiography of John Stuart Mill.* New York: Columbia University Press, 1924 [1873].

———. *Principles of Political Economy,* W. J. Ashley (ed.). New York: A. M. Kelley, Publishers, 1965 [1848].

Taussig, F. W. *Wages and Capital.* New York: A. M. Kelley, Publishers, 1968 [1896].

Thornton, W. T. *On Labour: Its Wrongful Claims and Rightful Dues, Its Actual Present and Possible Future.* London: 1869.

ECONOMIC POLICY IN
THE CLASSICAL PERIOD

INTRODUCTION

In the twentieth century the visibility and prestige of economists have grown in proportion to their ability to translate economic theory into economic policy. Contemporary economists are advisers to governments, members of policymaking institutions (e.g., the Federal Reserve System), and researchers in various "think tanks" (e.g., the American Enterprise Institute) that prepare analyses of current economic issues. In some cases, notably Greece and West Germany, professional economists have risen to the highest leadership positions.[1]

In much the same fashion, eighteenth- and nineteenth-century economists, both amateur and professional, strove to bring economic theory to bear on all manner of public-policy issues. Indeed, early economists such as Smith, Malthus, and Ricardo seemed to have little interest in economics apart from its potential influence on policy. As we have seen in earlier chapters, Ricardo, Malthus, and Senior were in the thick of debates over the Corn Laws and welfare (Poor Law) reform. Smith's *Wealth of Nations* and Malthus's *Essay on Population* were largely policy tracts aimed against mercantilist measures and extreme optimism, respectively.

---

[1] The direct impact of economists upon public policy will be discussed again in Chap. 24. In the United States economists have long had a direct impact upon politicians, but that impact was institutionalized in 1960 by the establishment of an official Council of Economic Advisers. Economists' ability to sway or direct public policy in this context is, as we shall see, of questionable magnitude.

203

This chapter extends the perception of classical economics as a motive force in the formation of economic policy by examining the policy prescriptions of three of the most influential personalities of the time, Nassau Senior, John Stuart Mill, and Sir Edwin Chadwick. Senior occupied a position of prominence as Drummond Professor of Political Economy at Oxford University, and was frequently called upon as a consultant to the British government. Mill was not only the leading theoretical economist of his day, but also a member of Parliament and a strong voice for certain Benthamite reforms. Chadwick, who was Bentham's last secretary before the latter's death in 1832, was a career civil servant in the British government who spearheaded sanitation and other reforms. The policy views of these three individuals are especially pertinent to an understanding of how classical theoretical and philosophical views intruded on practical policy measures. Senior, Mill, and Chadwick not only forged novel and creative solutions to the problems they perceived in British society, but also anticipated many issues that have emerged in twentieth-century America. Before turning to their important ideas, let us consider the condition of "laissez faire" in England from about 1830 to 1865.

Laissez Faire in Theory and Practice

The changing institutional constraints facing individual competitors over the sixteenth and seventeenth centuries in England ultimately ended the vast regulatory system called mercantilism (see Chapter 3). By 1640 or so, economic regulations that restricted competition were in retreat as authority shifted from the monarch to Parliament and the courts. The high time of laissez faire in Great Britain was the seventeenth century to the last quarter of the nineteenth century. The philosophical arguments in *The Wealth of Nations* opened people's eyes to the economic benefits of a system of natural liberty and probably accelerated the trend of deregulation, but it is difficult to argue that they *caused* deregulation, since that trend was noticeable at least a century before Smith penned his great works in philosophy and economics.

Peel and Gladstone: The Political Environment

Politically speaking, the retreat of mercantilism was never complete. Some regulations were repealed, others remained in effect but were unenforced, still others remained in effect and *were* enforced. Among the latter were various import tariffs, including the Corn Laws, and a system of economic relief to the indigent, known as the Poor Laws. As England moved into the nineteenth century, its reform agenda included various new industrial regulations that were implemented at the same time that Parliament gradually dismantled the remaining artifacts of feudal and mercantilist controls. Side by side with the dismantling of mercantilism, moreover, arose a professional bureaucracy of civil servants, which ultimately took over the implementation and development of much "social" legislation in the nineteenth century.

The first important intervention of the post-mercantilist era was the Factory Act. Actually a series of acts rather than a single piece of legislation, the first Factory Act (1802) concerned the labor of pauper children. A new act in 1819, sponsored by Sir Robert Peel, regulated hours and conditions of children's employment. A third act (1833), sponsored by Lord Althorp and drafted mainly by Sir Edwin Chadwick, placed controls on the employment of children in England's vast textile industry. Although revised and amended several times, these acts contained minimal provisions for enforcement. Nevertheless, the Factory Acts are regarded as landmark social legislation. They were not the only examples of active government involvement in the economy. The final dominance of industrial over agricultural interests, the rapid development of new forms of transportation after 1830, and the urban congestion ushered in by the machine age and the factory system all created intense pressures for new social and economic legislation.

On net balance, however, the age was a victory for laissez faire and economic freedom in the sense that marginal gains for free trade were consistently being made in micro markets *and* marginal constraints on public institutions were gradually and progressively put in place. Two particularly notable constraints on government typified the age of nineteenth-century laissez faire. The first was a fairly rigid adherence to a monetary gold standard. Such a standard, when observed, denies the government access to the printing press (fiat money) and therefore restrains the amount of government spending for war or social programs.[2] Although England had suspended the gold standard at various times in its history due to the exigencies of war, it nevertheless continued a tradition through the first half of the nineteenth century of maintaining the discipline of a monetary gold standard. After the fiscal strain of the Napoleonic wars, for example, the Bank of England restored strict convertibility in 1821, and by 1844 further restrictions cut off the treasury from automatic access to the bank.

The second important restriction on government during the heyday of classical economics was the limits placed by a conservative government (under the leadership of Prime Minister Peel and Chancellor of the Exchequer Gladstone) on the amount and types of taxation government could levy. William Gladstone in particular promoted a number of policies designed to produce a balanced withdrawal of government from the private sector. Among these policies were repeal of the Corn Laws (accomplished in 1846), reduction of income taxes, and the prohibition of sales and excise taxes. The calculated effect of Gladstonian policies of public finance was less government and a practical realization of laissez faire, but in this context laissez faire consisted mainly of

---

[2] The use of the printing press to finance wars is a practice spanning the ages from ancient civilizations to contemporary times. For example, the Vietnam war was financed in large measure by bond sales of the U.S. Treasury to the Federal Reserve System, a practice that contemporary "monetarists" see as the underlying cause of increasing inflation rates in the late 1960s and 1970s. The United States abandoned the gold standard in 1934 and, in 1971, severed all connections between gold and monetary expansion.

legal limitations on the tax base available to the government.[3] The state would necessarily be kept small in terms of its sphere of influence because it could not "afford" to intervene on a large scale. This is the kind of social, political, and economic background against which Senior, Mill, and Chadwick operated.

NASSAU SENIOR ON CHILD LABOR AND THE FACTORY ACTS

Beginning in 1814, the British Parliament passed a series of increasingly stringent acts regulating the employment of children, adolescents (those under eighteen years of age), and adult women. Early legislative efforts were modest, but in 1833 the first effective act was passed under the sponsorship of Lord Althorp. Althorp's Act banned employment of children under nine years of age and restricted the hours and conditions of work for those between the ages of nine and eighteen. The act also provided an enforcement mechanism, which had been missing from earlier factory acts. Reformers generally hailed Althorp's Act as a great step forward in social policy. Nassau Senior, economist and consultant administrator, was at the center of the discussion concerning this early capitalist reform measure, and his role in this timely debate gives us insight into the policy implications of classical economics.

Senior's "Last Hour"

Senior was called upon by the British government to assess the economic implications of the Factory Acts. He accepted the general provisions of Althorp's Act but argued that given the cost structure of the typical textile mill (England's chief industry of the period), further reductions of hours worked would eliminate the margin of profit. His argument proceeded along the following lines. The cotton industry was competitive, and the average net profit per firm was 10 percent. Senior took this as the normal rate of return in the industry. Senior's research uncovered the fact that the average firm in the industry was spending £4 on fixed capital (plant and equipment) for every £1 on working capital (raw materials). Thus he argued that a reduction in the workday by one hour would reduce variable costs (and output) but not reduce fixed costs. In effect, the work reduction would force plant and equipment to be idle, and increase the fixed-cost burden per unit of output (because output would fall but fixed costs would not). Senior felt that because of the disproportionate share of fixed costs in the total costs of manufacturing, the increase in per-unit costs by reducing the workday would wipe out the normal rate of return of the textile mills.

---

[3] Baysinger and Tollison ("Chaining Leviathan: The Case of Gladstonian Finance") argue that the inauguration of Gladstonian financial and economic policies in mid-nineteenth-century England marked an "official" end of mercantilism. The question of when mercantilism actually declined, however, depends on how the terms "mercantilism" and "laissez faire" are defined and understood.

Until recently, Senior's argument has been evaluated chiefly on the quality of his empirical research, which has been found lacking by most writers. But there is a sound analytical principle in Senior's analysis that must be taken to heart. He argued that restrictions on labor contracts that render capital idle reduce the marginal efficiency of capital, thereby diminishing the efficiency of resource allocation. Writing in 1843, Senior made it clear that a legislated reduction in the marginal efficiency of capital (which lowers the rate of return on capital investment below what could be earned in other industries) would cause higher-cost producers to leave the industry, thereby reducing employment and granting a competitive advantage to foreign producers not subject to legislated restrictions (*Industrial Efficiency and Social Economy*, p. 309). In other words, Senior advised Parliament that the Factory Acts functioned to hand foreign competitors an increased share of the domestic textile market, an important lesson that is not without relevance for contemporary debates regarding international competition. We must conclude that there is merit in Senior's analysis even though his argument that elimination of the "last hour" of work would destroy normal profit is incorrect (indeed, it has often been the subject of ridicule by contemporary writers).

Senior's Interest-Group Theory of Economics

A more subtle aspect of Senior's analysis of the Factory Acts has been largely ignored, and this aspect seems to foreshadow a contemporary development in economic theory, namely the theory of public choice (see Chapter 24). Senior recognized that Althorp's Act imposed an economic loss on the parents of children under nine who could no longer work in the textile mills, and a similar loss on the parents of children between the ages of nine and thirteen whose hours were restricted by the act. He also noted a corresponding gain on the part of workers (or their parents) over thirteen. This led him to question the motives of those seeking to restrict the length of the workweek. He concluded that the factory acts were not inspired by the "public interest" so much as the interest of the (adult male) factory operatives who sought to raise their own wages. In a closely reasoned passage, Senior argued:

> [The workers'] original object was to raise the price of their *own* labour. For this purpose the spinners, who form...a very small...but a powerful body among them, finding that they could not obtain a limitation of the hours of work to ten by combination, tried to effect it through the legislature. They knew that Parliament would not legislate for adults. They got up therefore a frightful, and (as far as we have heard and seen) an utterly unfounded picture of the ill treatment of the children, in the hope that the legislature would restrain all persons under 18 years old to ten hours, which they knew would, in fact, restrict the labour of adults to the same period (*Selected Writings*, p. 19).

Analytically, what lies at the heart of this issue is whether or not young workers and female workers were in direct competition with adult male workers for jobs and pay. While this issue has not been settled by contemporary historians of economic thought, strong evidence exists to support the position that child labor and female labor were *substitutes* for adult male labor rather than complements. (Senior himself treated them mostly as complements, and probably erred in doing so.) Technological advances (e.g., invention of the spinning mule, etc.) were making it possible for adolescents and women to enter the work force by reducing the physical exertion required on the job. The same technological advances threatened to unemploy the spinners (mostly adult males), who possessed the necessary brawn and had acquired the necessary skills under the earlier technology. Senior was alert to the interest-group pressures and interpreted the movement toward a ten-hour workweek on the basis of small-group interests. Threatened by gradual reductions in wages and employment due to technological advance in the textile industry, spinners supported "ten hours" legislation. Unable to get a ten hours bill passed, they tried indirectly to reduce the elasticity of demand for their services by lobbying against the employment of children, adolescents, and females.

For the historical record, the spinners were successful in achieving their objectives. The Factory Act of 1833 led to a significant reduction in child labor. The number of workers under fourteen years of age in the textile industry was reduced by 56 percent between 1835 and 1838, and this reduction occurred while overall employment within the industry was growing rapidly. Flush with this success, the adult male textile operatives gained additional restrictions on the hours and work conditions of females in the Factory Act of 1844.

While the "correct" interpretation of this historical episode involving the British Factory Acts remains controversial, Senior's role in the policy debates of his day is enlightening in several respects. For one thing, it reveals in a meaningful way how economic theory can be brought to bear on important social issues. For another, it pits the informed economist against the less-informed (at least in economics) social reformers who frequently agitate for change. Whether right or wrong in all parts of his analysis, Senior showed that he was alert to the lessons of Adam Smith—namely that the self-interest axiom applies to coalitions of private-interest groups and to politicians as well as to businessmen.

DISTRIBUTIVE JUSTICE AND LAISSEZ FAIRE: SOCIAL AND ECONOMIC POLICIES OF J. S. MILL

John Stuart Mill, economist and member of Parliament, was in the vanguard of those espousing progressive policies regarding education, welfare, trade unions, and the equality of women. Mill's wider concern for long-term distributive justice was the hall-mark of his social thought, which also bore the indelible imprint of the economist. The mechanism that triggered Mill's reform proposals was the arrangement of proper incentives to desirable ends. Mill's sociological and philosophical treatment of society's "ends" underwent considerable change over time, but his reform proposals were consistently grounded in "market" measures. That is to say, Mill recognized the nature and importance of economic incentives as a guide to human action,

Nature and Scope of Economic Policy

Mill's *Principles of Political Economy* (1848) accomplished a twofold objective. On the one hand, it presented a more complete and systematic set of economic principles than that contained in Ricardo's important work. On the other, it extended economic analysis explicitly into the area of social reform. It is this last idea that especially distinguished Mill's work as an economist.

Mill was an ardent defender of liberty, but he kept an ever watchful eye on the conditions of the poor. Committed to both commercial and individual freedom, Mill would sometimes countenance exceptions to the former in order to nurture the latter. In his view, personal liberty required equality of *opportunity,* not equality of income or talents. Thus he noted that

> ...many, indeed, fail with greater efforts than those with which others succeed, not from difference of merits, but differences of opportunities; but if all were done which it would be in the power of a good government to do, by instruction and by legislation, to diminish this inequality of opportunities, the difference of fortune arising from people's own earnings could not justly give umbrage (*Principles,* Robson (ed.), p. 811).

To Mill the crucial thing for liberty is that individuals should "all start fair," and it was a central role of government to establish social and economic policies that prompted equality of opportunity.

Mill divided government interferences into two types: (1) "authoritative" interventions that prohibit or restrict market forces and (2) "supportive" interventions that augment market forces. These two types of interventions might also be thought of in terms of the concepts of ex ante and ex post. Ex ante equality refers to those interventions designed to ensure that individuals start fairly; i.e., all runners begin at the same mark. Ex post equality refers to those interventions such as taxation that attempt to impose some criterion of fairness in the actual outcome of social processes involving risk and uncertainty. Both types of equality may result from the same social policy,[4] but in general this division is useful for analyzing Mill's several policy positions.

Mill on Taxation and Poverty

Like Adam Smith before him, Mill was a general advocate of proportional taxation. He stressed "equality of sacrifice," but he also expressed great concern

---

[4] In golf, for example, handicapping is used to equalize competition in the sense of making the contest more equal at the start, but the data for handicapping are derived from average scores in previous contests. In the same sense, taxation over time blends the ex ante and ex post concepts of equality. Mill brilliantly made this point in an essay on "Endowments" (*Essays,* p. 628).

for the effects of taxation on the condition of the poor. Mill sponsored three different tax policies aimed at alleviating poverty: a tax exemption on certain incomes, the inheritance tax, and certain sumptuary restrictions.

The Income Tax To Mill, the least objectionable of all taxes was a "fairly assessed" income tax. He wished tax rates to be proportional at all income levels, with a built-in exemption for all incomes below a certain amount. In 1857 he suggested that this minimum be set at £100, although the controlling factor must be whatever amount is required to purchase the "necessaries of the existing population." Mill advanced the argument one stage further by defending a low tax rate on the next increment of income (between £100 and £150) on the grounds that existing indirect taxes were regressive and fell hardest on individuals earning between £50 and £150 (*Principles,* Robson (ed.), p. 830).[5] Mill's proposal does not constitute a minimum-income program because it does not guarantee everyone an income of £100; it merely exempts from taxation those at incomes below this level. Mill sought to build into the tax system individual incentives to work. The exemption was important in removing marginal disincentives to earn among the poorest classes of society.

By the same reasoning, proportional taxes were preferable to progressive income taxes. Mill noted:

> To tax the larger incomes at a higher percentage than the smaller, is to lay a tax on industry and economy; to impose a penalty on people for having worked harder and saved more than their neighbors. It is not the fortunes which are earned, but those which are unearned, that it is for the public good to place under limitations (*Principles,* Ashley (ed.), p. 808).

Inheritance and Excise Taxes Mill saw inheritance taxes as a means to redress extreme inequalities of wealth and to encourage a situation in which all start fairly. He argued that "inheritance and legacies, exceeding a certain amount, are highly proper subjects for taxation: and that the revenue from them should be as great as it can be made without giving rise to evasions, by donation *inter vivos* or concealment of property, such as it would be impossible adequately to check" (*Principles,* Ashley (ed.), p. 809). Mill did not object to the principle of graduation (higher rates on larger amounts) in the matter of inheritance taxes as he did in the matter of income taxes. The difference was a matter of incentives, and of earned versus unearned wealth.

Taxation in general is a means to redistribute wealth, and in his day Mill

---

[5] Although he believed that, in principle, proportional income taxes would be the most equitable, Mill was not eager to place sole reliance on income taxes as a source of government revenue. Tax evasion, fraud, and improper conduct in collection would inevitably result when income taxes were strictly enforced. "Commercial dishonesty," he pointed out, was "the certain effect of Sir Robert Peel's income tax; and it will never be known for how much of that evil product the tax may be accountable, or in how many cases a false return was the first dereliction of pecuniary integrity" (*Essays,* p. 702). In spite of these weighty objections, Mill justified an income tax so that the rich would pay their share of taxation.

thought that indirect taxes, such as taxes on commodities, bore disproportionately on the poor, especially since many such duties were on "necessities." He advocated selective discrimination in setting import duties and excise rates so that the burden of taxation would not fall unduly on the poor. He did not question the appropriateness or legitimacy of these levies, but he objected to their relative burden:

> The duties which now yield nearly the whole of the customs and excise revenue, those on sugar, coffee, tea, wine, beer, spirits, and tobacco, are in themselves, where a large amount of revenue is necessary, extremely proper taxes; but at present grossly unjust, from the disproportionate weight with which they press on the poorer classes.... It is probable that most of these taxes might bear a great reduction without any material loss of revenue (*Principles*, Robson (ed.), p. 872).

Revenue requirements were even to be tempered with principles of distributive justice in Mill's theory of taxation.

Mill's concern that the poor enjoy equality of opportunity also explains his support of sumptuary taxes, especially those on "snob" goods. He declared that expenditure by the rich not "for the sake of the pleasure afforded by the things on which the money is spent but from regard to opinion, and an idea that certain expenses are expected from them, as an appendage of station... is a most desirable subject of taxation" (*Principles*, Ashley (ed.), p. 869).

Taking all these proposals together and recognizing the financial requirements of the state, Mill sought to promote equality of opportunity by providing incentives to work, by reducing the regressive burden of indirect taxes on the poor, and by compensating for the latter with a high and progressive inheritance tax. Mill's integrated approach to economic policy thus suggested a poverty program utilizing tax relief. Income distribution consistent with equality of opportunity could and should be altered, in Mill's view, by legislative power. But indirect support through tax relief was not sufficient in itself. Mill designed a more direct form of support as well.

The Poor Laws and Welfare Reform

Mill's combination of social justice, belief in the allocative merits of economic incentives, and laissez faire convictions are evidenced in his opinions on the Poor Laws. He thought it "right that human beings should help one another; and the more so, in proportion to the urgency of the need..." (*Principles*, Robson (ed.), p. 960). He supported the findings of the Royal Commission on Poor Law Reform (which included Nassau Senior and Edwin Chadwick) on the grounds that the absence of relief would have grave social consequences for the disabled poor—the blind, the aged, the sick, the very young, and so forth. The problem was to design a system of relief that would care for the destitute but discourage the able-bodied from becoming wards of the state. This was clearly a matter of structuring economic incentives. Mill wrote in the *Monthly Repository* of 1834:

The condition of a pauper must cease to be, as it has been made, an object of desire and envy to the independent labourer. Relief must be given; no one must be allowed to starve; the necessaries of life and health must be tendered to all who apply for them; but to all who are capable of work they must be tendered on such terms, as shall make the necessity of accepting them be regarded as a misfortune.... To this end, relief must be given only in exchange for labour, and labour at least as irksome and severe as that of the least fortunate among independent labourers ("The Proposed Reform of the Poor Laws," p. 361).

Efficiency of this able-bodied army of paupers could only be obtained within the workhouses, since the decentralized program of parish relief was fraught with inefficiencies and outright bribery. Mill felt that the parish relief system imposed "fatal consequences" on the industry and prudence of the poor, whereas the workhouse offered "the means by which society may guarantee a subsistence to every one of its members, without producing any of the fatal consequences to their industry and prudence" that the outdoor parish relief system provided ("Lord Brougham's Speech," p. 597).

Social justice may have been at the root of Mill's support for the Poor Laws, but he did not take a leading role in their establishment. Mill was most definitely concerned, however, with the design of an optimum system to alleviate, and ultimately eliminate, poverty. The total thrust of his writings and correspondence on this issue reflects a lifelong concern with the means of achieving three interrelated goals pertaining to poverty and income distribution—aid for the destitute, provision of the right kind of work incentives for the able-bodied unemployed, and use of government policy as a vehicle for altering income distribution. Whether anyone today would defend Mill's means to attain these goals is less important than the recognition that he attempted to blend a concept of social justice with market economics.

Income Redistribution in Theory and Practice

Mill's 1845 essay "The Claims of Labour" outlined a program for public policy that exemplified clearly the distinction in economics between "normative" and "positive" that he had made in his earlier work, *On Logic*. Noting the gathering momentum of socialist agitation for income redistribution, Mill affirmed the desirability of policies that redistribute income to the poor. Once again, however, he asserted that the question was one of means, not ends. Mill was not impressed by the proposals of the socialists and the romantics. For the most part, they sought to improve the condition of the poor by merely raising wages—a program Mill found dangerous because its advocates refused to attach population sanctions to their wage proposals. Given human nature and the incentives that would be established by these proposals, Mill concluded that an increase in the birthrate would wipe out the gains in wages. What was needed was a change in the living habits of the working class. Noted Mill: "If the whole income of the country were divided among them in wages or poor-rates, still, until there is a change in [laborers] themselves, there can be no lasting improvements in their outward condition'' (*Essays*, p. 375). Mill had nightmarish visions of large classes of people becoming dependents of the state, citing the Irish and French experiences in this regard (*Later Letters*, p. 44). He regarded welfare dependence as a most pernicious form of evil and, unhappily, a lesson that the poor learn more easily than any other.

Having rejected socialist and romantic proposals for income redistribution as being at odds with the nature of human beings, Mill championed instead a system of self-help based on education and positive economic incentives. Like Bentham, he advocated public education. Although the measure was defeated by the House of Lords in 1834, Mill supported Chadwick's proposal that government pay for the education of pauper children. He construed education as learning in the broad sense, and he customarily backed changes that would cultivate ''a taste for capitalist values'' among the laborers. One such measure was a plan of government loans to the poor for improving their living accommodations. Mill was sensitive to the fact that government aid is often useful, and sometimes necessary, to start improvement programs that, once in place, are able to keep themselves going without further help.

Indeed, this idea is consistent with Mill's support of a minimum income for the laboring poor. Public assistance can always be a tonic rather than a sedative, Mill argued,

> ...provided that the assistance is not such as to dispense with self-help, by substituting itself for the person's own labour, skill and prudence, but is limited to affording him a better hope of attaining success by those legitimate means. This accordingly is a test to which all plans of philanthropy and benevolence should be brought, whether intended for the benefit of individuals or of classes, and whether conducted on the voluntary or on the government principle (*Principles*, Robson (ed.), p. 961).

Mill was not willing to place full confidence in private charity, however, because he considered it uneven in its bestowal of benefits. Besides, Mill argued, poverty has external effects (i.e., costs) on the wider community (e.g., crime, mendicity) and so should be solved by public policy rather than by private charity.[6]

In addition to the positive measures discussed above, Mill recommended the removal of present discouragements to the poor. He chided government for failing to build the right kind of economic and legal incentives into the social structure. Specifically, he charged that it was the government's responsibility to remove every restriction, every artificial hindrance, that legal and fiscal systems place on attempts of the poor to advance their own improvement. Among these items Mill suggested a remedy of defects in the common law of partnership, which made impractical a fair trial of the joint-stock experiments of the poor. Even more interesting is Mill's proposal to revamp the tax system

---

[6] A ''free rider'' problem would exist when no private individual has any incentive to provide charitable contributions because he assumes that others would. This is, for instance, the classic argument for government's provision of national defense.

on land transactions. The Stamp Office took a toll on land transactions of the smallest amount, whereas legal fees were the same for all sizes of transactions. The result was a reduction of incentives to invest on the part of the poor peasant. Should the poor manage to save, Mill argued, economic constraints within the legal system meant that no investment outlets were open for their savings. The land tax system was therefore of negative value in establishing opportunities for redistribution.

In sum, Mill wished to implement, through government policy, a minimum-income plan that utilized market forces to maintain work incentives. He clearly believed that the "low moral condition" of the poor could be affected positively in the face of public assistance, provided that "while available to everybody, it leaves to everyone a strong motive to do without it if he can" (*Principles,* Robson (ed.), p. 961).

UTILITARIAN AS ECONOMIC POLICYMAKER: THE POLITICAL ECONOMY OF SIR EDWIN CHADWICK

There is some disagreement about the extent to which J. S. Mill was a collectivist, but it is clear that he was greatly influenced by the political thought of Jeremy Bentham. He defended private property, personal liberty, and decentralized government, even though he sometimes seemed willing to compromise these ends to the utilitarian ethic of the greatest good for the greatest number. His friend and ally, Edwin Chadwick, bowed more deeply at the utilitarian altar, and his persistence as the quintessential bureaucrat produced many far-reaching effects on British social and economic policy. In a phrase, Chadwick had his insistent fingers in practically every interventionist pie between 1830 and 1890.

Chadwick's domineering personality made him hated by many and feared by some, but one could hardly question his boundless energy. Actively involved in the design and implementation of English social and economic legislation for over thirty years, Chadwick is credited as the driving force behind improvements in the Poor Laws, water supply, drainage, sewage treatment, public health, civil service, school architecture, education of pauper children, and many other programs. With Bentham, he was also the leading proponent of a "competitive principle" that has enjoyed a resurgence in our own day. Unlike Mill, however, he had few credentials as a "serious economist." In keeping with this, his biographers have approached him as a lawyer and civil servant. Be that as it may, it would be almost impossible to find anyone in the nineteenth century who saw more clearly the variety and kinds of economic problems that confront the modern policymaker.

Law and Economics

Chadwick was trained in law, but he forsook the life of a barrister for a career in the civil service. He was sympathetic to Bentham's "world view" and, in particular, to his theory of legislation that was grounded in utilitarianism. He was also versed in Ricardian economics. This intellectual heritage reinforced Chadwick's conviction that individual initiative is the mainspring of social progress. Throughout his life he remained a vocal defender of this principle and often advocated change in the existing social structure in order to preserve the free play of individual initiative.

What Chadwick brought to Benthamism was an administrative genius that bridged the gap between utilitarian theory and bureaucratic practice. Bentham's theory of legislation was based on a rejection of Adam Smith's doctrine of the *natural* identity of private and public interests and its replacement with institutional devices to bring about an *artificial* identity of interests. His idea was to arrange obligations and punishments in such a way that the incentive to effect public harm through private action or enterprise was removed, or at least, diminished. But the practical implementation of this idea required a clear conception of the public interest. Bentham's personal view that the public interest is the summation of individual interests was fraught with analytical difficulties because it involved interpersonal-utility comparisons (see Chapter 6). By contrast, Chadwick defined the public interest in terms of economic efficiency: Anything that reduced economic waste was found to be in the public interest. Under this banner, Chadwick advocated sweeping administrative reforms in the provision of both private and public goods.

Perhaps an example will serve to illustrate Chadwick's approach to institutional reforms through incentive-manipulation. Put in charge of improving sanitation and thereby reducing the mortality of British criminals transported to Australia, Chadwick noted that the British government paid a flat fee to the ship's captain for each convict who embarked from a British port. The captains, of course, found that they could maximize profits by taking on as many prisoners as could be safely carried without endangering the ship and by minimizing expenses (food and drink, etc.) on the prisoners en route. Survival rates among the prisoners under this incentive system were as low as 40 percent, humanitarian pleas for improved sanitation notwithstanding. After a quick assessment of the situation, Chadwick changed the payment system so that the ship's captain received a fee for each live convict that *disembarked* in Australia. Within a short time the survival rate increased dramatically to 98½ percent ("Opening Address"). All that was needed was to give the ships' captains an incentive to protect the health of their cargo—thus creating an artificial identity between the public interest (i.e., the safety of the prisoners) and the private interests (i.e., the profit of the shipper).

Economics of Crime, Courts, and Police   Bentham's utilitarianism also provided the psychological foundation for Chadwick's theory of human behavior, which surfaced in his 1829 proposal that a municipal police force be established in the city of London. Chadwick's report on police, prepared for Sir

Robert Peel's[7] Select Committee, was a brilliant tour de force of Benthamite principles and an effective vehicle for showcasing Chadwick's "preventive principle," which was to become the base for so many of his later reforms. According to this principle, the surest way to reduce waste is not to alleviate inefficiencies after the fact but to keep them from occurring in the first place. Chadwick was a fanatic on the principle of prevention, and he always implied that preventive measures were generally accompanied by large pecuniary economies.

Criminal Behavior Chadwick was an avid believer in the primacy of statistical research, and he commonly conducted "field inquiries" on the nature of problems that required administrative solutions. His direct questioning of criminal offenders produced the following behavioral profile: thieves, he learned, are impatient with steady labor, dislike physical exertion, enjoy leisure, are not easily deterred by the threat of punishment, and value the prospect of "uninterrupted" success. In sum, Chadwick believed criminals made rational choices based on pecuniary gain in regard to their "career" selection. Typical of the responses Chadwick got from his field inquiries was the retort of one Frenchman to the question of why he chose a life of crime. Reported the convict, "I keep myself within bounds of moderation: yet as a thief, I realise eighteen francs a day. But at my trade as a tailor I only earn three. I put it to you—would *you* be honest only on that?" ("Précis," p. 391).

Chadwick concluded that individuals calculate the expected benefits and costs of committing illegal acts, and that for any given booty obtained, the *expected* gain will be smaller the higher the probabilities of apprehension and conviction. He did not reject the earlier claim by Bentham and others that there are tradeoffs between the severity of punishment and its certainty, but Chadwick's research denied the importance of severe punishment as a strong deterrent to crime. His empirical studies convinced him of two important facts: (1) that existing police administration and jurisprudence placed the risk costs associated with crime at very low levels, although the punishments were very severe; and (2) that a high probability of capture and conviction was the stronger deterrent to crime.

Police Effectiveness Chadwick consistently argued that crime prevention was the joint responsibility of police *and* the public, but he directed his attention to administrative reforms that would make the police a more efficient preventive force. His proposals confronted the subjects of police compensation, administrative economies, and technological innovation.

Chadwick saw a close connection between the quality of law enforcement and the compensation of enforcers. He found that police wages were so low in

---

[7] British policemen to this day are called "bobbies" in honor of Sir Robert, who successfully established a metropolitan police force in 1829—over many strenuous objections.

Britain as to encourage as many thefts of high-valued property as possible, "in order that large rewards may be offered for its recovery" ("Preventive Police," p. 254). A solution to the wage problem was to base police wages on productivity, but Chadwick was unable to devise an operational procedure for doing so because of an inability to measure the real services of prevention. As a second-best solution he suggested an adjustment of wages based on the comparison of crimes committed in one police jurisdiction with those committed in other jurisdictions where property was similarly situated. Distortions caused by discrepancies between actual and reported crimes or in the rate of reporting crimes would, of course, remain in such a system, and, as Chadwick recognized, only improvements in the collection and accuracy of crime data could correct these deficiencies.

On most matters of administrative economy Chadwick was a centralist. He consistently harped on the desirability of a centralized bureau for collecting and disseminating crime data, including descriptions of stolen property. Within the ranks of traditional police organization, he challenged specialization and division of labor as principles of preventive efficiency. Chadwick argued that where deterrence is the objective, maximum efficiency will be promoted by the geographical dispersion of preventive "inputs." It is physically easier to extinguish fires (and thereby reduce property loss) if detection and extinction occur soon after combustion. Consolidation of police and fire-preventive agents would therefore place more preventive agents in the field and consequently reduce the time lag in detecting and extinguishing fires. Chadwick drove home his point with the force of a scientific rule: "The force of one man for fire service at half a mile is worth four men at three quarters of a mile, worth six men at a mile, and worth eight men at a mile and a half" ("Police and the Extinction of Fires," p. 426). An additional benefit of consolidation would be improved efficiency in the detection of arson. Chadwick viewed this as no small consequence, since reliable estimates put the number of intentional fires in the London metropolis at one-third of the total.

Some of Chadwick's proposals for raising the probability of capture of criminals were innovative without being technological in the sense of requiring improved capital. For example, he favored replacing uniformed officers with plainclothesmen and varying the rounds of patrolmen to keep potential thieves off guard. He also advocated the use of more and better streetlights as a deterrent to crime. But in one fantastic insight, Chadwick anticipated the use of the patrol car in modern law enforcement. He described his modest proposal as follows:

As a Commissioner of inquiry into the organization of a general force, I have proposed a patrol by a tricycle worked by two men abreast, armed with revolvers. The patrol with the tricycle would be regulated to be worked at eight miles an hour instead of three. There would be no footfall to be heard, and the patrol would be silent for all suburban districts. If there are any men perceived at night with a trap that takes to flight, the tricycle patrol may put on extra speed which will keep them in sight or overtake them, for the tricycle has now attained a possible speed of eighteen miles an hour. The difficulties of escape from two men would be enormously increased ("Tricycles," p. 435).

The Economics of Justice Among the costs imposed on lawbreakers is not only the probability of capture but also the probability of conviction. Chadwick recognized that the probability of punishment is not a single value in each case but rather is the compound result of a series of separate probabilities that arise at each stage of the judicial procedure. Besides the chance of being discovered, pursued, or detected (which is governed by the state of police), Chadwick cited:

1 The chance, if detected and apprehended, of being indicted
2 The chance of error in framing the indictment
3 The chance of dismissal of a bill of indictment by the grand jury
4 A number of contingent chances in the trial process, e.g., exclusion of evidence, the quality of witnesses, lawyers, judges, and juries

Chadwick's most vicious attack on existing institutions was on the grand jury system. He labeled it "the stronghold of perjury," a system that gives to delinquents "all the chances (of escape) arising from the ignorance and want of skill both in the jurymen and the witness" ("Preventive Police," p. 298). He estimated that criminals go free more often because of a lack of expertise among jurors than improper action taken by judges, and he called for the elimination of the grand jury system as one way of raising costs to the guilty without simultaneously raising the probability of convicting the innocent.

In addition to reforms that would streamline court procedures, Chadwick favored institutional arrangements that would lower the individual costs of prosecuting crimes or of providing information necessary to court proceedings. Streamlining of court procedures in itself lowers the cost of providing information, since the major cost to witnesses is the time spent in court testimony. Chadwick cited other costs to crime victims as well—delays caused by restricting judicial hearings to only one jurisdiction or judge, and the mistreatment of some witnesses by judges. His overall approach to procedural reforms was in this, as in all cases, fundamentally economic. He declared: "We should bear in mind that simplicity, expedition, certainty, and freedom from expense, are the most desirable qualities for penal as well as other procedure" ("Preventive Police," p. 294).

Public Health and the Value of Time

Although Chadwick was the undisputed leader of the overall public-health movement in nineteenth-century England, the basic feature of his proposed reform of the sanitation system involved the distribution of water. The existing system required consumers to bear the cost of transporting water from distribution point to home because they were required to purchase water from central locations. The purchase price of water was low but the full cost was high because of the substantial time spent hauling water to the point of use. Chadwick's analysis of the situation identified the opportunity cost of time. He pointed out that "if the labourer or his wife or child would otherwise be employed, even in the lowest paid labour or in knitting stockings, the cost of fetching water by hand is extravagantly high" ("Report on the Sanitary Condition of the Labouring Population," p. 142).

Chadwick recognized that the *full* cost of water was the sum of its purchase price plus the opportunity wage rate per hour times the number of hours it took to fetch the water for home use. To provide the appropriate economic incentive for improved personal hygiene, he called for a reduction in the full cost of water by having it home-delivered. Once again, the solution to a public problem required the creation of an artificial identity of interest. The desired (public) result of home sanitation could be ensured by the proper structuring of economic incentives. Also important is the fact that Chadwick recognized the value of time and added this as a relevant variable in the formulation of economic policy.

Institutional Forms of Competition

The idea that the function of politics and the judiciary consists of altering the institutional structures of society so as to induce self-interested individuals to behave in a way conducive to the public good is a decidedly Benthamite notion. There is a certain "despotic" flavor to this view because the practice of Benthamite politics is facilitated best by concentrating the ownership and control of property rights in the hands of a central authority.[8] Chadwick almost seemed to view centralized control as a prerequisite for eliminating waste, and he was so committed to this principle that he reformulated the notion of competition to accommodate it to the exigencies of central authority.

After thirty years of investigating, designing, and reformulating a myriad of public policies, Chadwick consolidated his views on the proper mode of government interventions and presented them in a "position paper" to the Royal Statistical Society. Citing the coexistence of "sound and unsound" principles of competition, Chadwick contrasted the orthodox view (which assumed large-numbers rivalry among firms in a share-the-market context) with his "new" concept of competition that assumed rivalry among several bidders to win an *exclusive* right to serve the entire market. Chadwick labeled the former notion "competition within the field" and the latter "competition for the field." Describing his sustained support for the latter principle, Chadwick declared:

> As opposed to that form of competition [within the field], I proposed as an administrative principle, competition "for the field," that is to say, that the whole field of

---

[8] It is precisely on this point that Mill and Chadwick parted company on the matter of economic policy. Chadwick was a centralist, whereas Mill came to distrust the centralized concentration of power.

service should be put on behalf of the public for competition—on the only condition on which efficiency, as well as the utmost cheapness, was practicable, namely the possession, by one capital or by one establishment, of the entire field, which could be most efficiently and economically administered by one, with full securities towards the public for the performance of the requisite service during a given period ("Results of Different Principles," p. 385).

Chadwick had an early notion of "public goods"—those that provide benefits external to the immediate user—and it is to the production of these goods that he sought most vigorously to apply the principle of competition within the field. The attempt to implement or enforce a competitive system based on decentralized property rights was judged wasteful by Chadwick, so he proposed an alternative system. Government, representing society, would buy out competing suppliers and let out contracts, through a bidding process, for the exclusive right to supply the public good. Chadwick termed this principle "contract management."

In more modern dress, the Chadwick principle can be explained in terms of Figure 9-1. The negatively sloped cost curves are those of a public utility, transportation firm, or natural monopoly. The profit-maximizing monopolist would produce a quantity Q_p and sell it at price P_p. Chadwick's point is that given certain conditions and alternative property rights assignment, the existence of natural monopoly need not imply monopoly price and profits. Specif-

FIGURE 9-1
In the absence of price and/or quantity contract specifications, average cost will increase from AC to AC', resulting in a transfer of welfare from the monopolist to society by $GP_p BF$. If the government specifies some quantity Q_A to be supplied, bidding will continue until price reaches P_A.

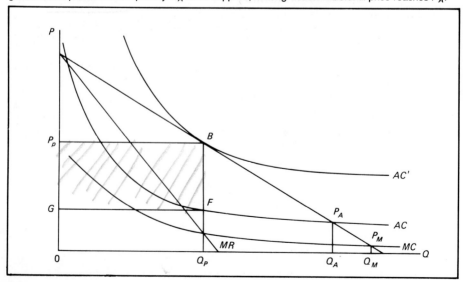

ically, given that an elastic supply of competitive bidders exists and that the costs of bidder collusion are high enough, the government could purchase the small number of competing firms and let out for bid the exclusive right to supply the good or service in question.

A number of institutional and contractual arrangements are possible in this context. The government may or may not provide fixed plant and capital equipment. The contract period may be of fixed duration, or it may be reopened at the discretion of the government. Certainty and/or perfect information may or may not be assumed on the part of all or some parties. For example, treatment of windfall gains and losses may be made part of the model. Solutions will, of course, vary according to the nature of the assumptions made.

Some possible solutions may be shown with the aid of Figure 9-1. Let us assume that certainty and perfect information exist on the part of the government and the bidders and that the government supplies the fixed capital. The problem, then, is to investigate how the nature of the contract specifications alters the solution. Clearly, if the maximum bid is made by suppliers to the government in the absence of price and/or quantity contract specifications, the solution remains unaltered, except for a transfer of welfare from the monopolist to society. Such a transfer is depicted in Figure 9-1 by the amount GP_pBF. It would in effect raise the average cost to the successful supplier to AC', resulting in a Chamberlinian "tangency solution" (see Chapter 18) between AC' and the demand curve at price P_p.

The more usual case—the one that Chadwick featured in the example of railroads—is the situation in which the government contractually specifies some minimum quantity (and/or quality) to be offered and lets potential suppliers engage in a bidding process. If it is assumed that the government contractually specifies some quantity Q_A to be supplied, bidding will proceed to price P_A, at which only normal profits are being earned. The important point is that Chadwick's principle makes the attainment of a "competitive" solution (where average revenue equals average cost and economic profit is zero) a possibility through public ownership and private operation. All this implies that the competitive bidding process, given altered property-rights assignment, might approximate at least some of the results of the orthodox model of competition, where competition is defined as a market structure of many rival, independent firms. Whether or not this is a practical result depends on numerous institutional forces, including the mode of consolidation, design of contracts, cost of acquiring information, and so on.

Chadwick's Policy Proposals: Applications of Contract Management

Water Supply Chadwick's investigation into the conditions of water supply and public health in London revealed that the problem was one of natural monopoly.[9] Thus he regarded competition within the field as inappropriate. He found the field of service currently divided among seven separate companies, several of which had become multiform monopolies, duplicating one another's facilities, so that two or three sets of pipes ran down many streets, doling out insufficient supplies of water of inferior and often unwholesome quality. Chadwick estimated that consolidation under the principle of contract management could save £100,000 per year, which could then be used for exploration and development of new water supplies.

Chadwick noted that municipal gas companies in the city of Paris competed under an almost identical situation of natural monopoly. There a government study into the cost and supply conditions of several independent gas companies found the charges excessive. The city then undertook consolidation according to Chadwick's principle, with the result that customer charges declined 30 percent, the quality of gas supplied improved, and the value of shareholders' assets was raised by 24 percent ("Results of Different Principles," p. 388). Chadwick presented additional evidence of two gas companies in northern England whose prime cost of supplying gas dropped by almost two-thirds after effecting the kind of consolidation he championed.

His proposed administrative reform of London water was rejected, Chadwick claimed, owing to the vigorous protests of vested interests. As if to get the last word, Chadwick asserted that retention of the traditional form of competition over the decade of the 1850s burdened consumers with higher prices, stockholders with unsafe returns, and the public with inadequate improvements in water quality and delivery systems.

Railroads   In the 1860s, Chadwick became the leading British proponent of the nationalization of railroads. His argument did not support government *operation* of the railways but rather consolidation under the principle of contract management. In Chadwick's view, railroads were a natural monopoly characterized by disunity of management and wasteful competition. However, he was unwilling to allow a coincidence of ownership and administration. On the surface, he appeared to be in the best tradition of laissez faire when he argued that "the Government is utterly incapable of any direct management of manufactures, or of anything else of an administrative character" ("On the Proposal That the Railways Should Be Purchased by the Government," p. 202). At the same time, however, his proposal called for concentration of authority in the hands of a central administration. By 1860, moreover, Chadwick could cite the government's successful implementation of a contract management scheme for the provision of postal services.

Funerals   Chadwick's proposed applications of the principle of contract management did not stop with the waste engendered by natural monopoly.

---

[9] A natural monopoly is said to exist when it is technically more efficient to have a single producer or enterprise. In some cases, the survival of a single firm is the natural outcome of competition among several firms.

High information and search costs to consumers often provide a source of imperfect competition. Chadwick recognized this fact in his analysis of the funeral markets in London and Paris. Once again he proposed contract management as a solution.

Relying on earlier research, Chadwick estimated that in London there were between 600 and 700 undertakers available to perform roughly 120 funerals per day, so that there were about six undertakers competing for each funeral. Although the market situation outwardly appeared competitive on the supply side, Chadwick identified certain characteristics on the demand side that altered the degree of competitiveness:

> ...under the circumstances of the occurrence of deaths, there being no time to seek about or to make inquiries to enable the parties to make a selection upon any comparison of charges, the service is practically a monopoly. The expense to the survivors of all classes above the class of pauper, and in particular to the most respectable class of mechanics, forms a grievous addition to the evils and inflictions of bereavement by death; and although the charges made are exorbitant, the character of the service rendered is in every respect of a low and objectionable character, and befitting an inferior religious and social condition ("Results of Different Principles," p. 388).

Beyond these circumstances, monopoly charges for funeral services encouraged "home funerals," which led to health and sanitary hazards.

Parliament ignored Chadwick's proposals, but on the Continent, particularly in the cities of Munich, Frankfurt, Berlin, and Paris, implementation of his principle had gone far in mitigating or eliminating these evils. Regulated charges of interment in Paris (while not an ideal system because the charges included a tax for support of public worship) are illustrative of the benefits he thought to be derived from competition for the field:

> In Paris, and also in some other cities of the Continent, at intervals of terms of years sufficient for the renewal of carriages, establishments, &c., the entire field of service for the interment of the dead is put to competition, for contracts to render the funeral service at scales of material, decoration and attendance, conformable to the habits and wishes of different classes of society, divided into nine classes, and the range of expense is from 15s. to 145£.... Under this system of competition for the field where it prevails on the Continent, the public have a superior service, and a wider range of choice, as well as much protection to survivors not afforded in this country ("Results of Different Principles," pp. 389–390).

Pursuing the matter further, Chadwick estimated the total cost of 28,000 interments in Paris at £80,000 in 1843, while the estimated cost of 45,000 interments in London, under competition within the field, was £626,000. Chadwick concluded that under the French rate structure London funerals would have cost £166,000, a saving of £460,000, which he attributed directly to the uniform rate. Thus, monopoly power created by high information costs could be eliminated, or at least mitigated, by use of the principle of contract management.

CONCLUSION

By attempting to analyze events and prescribe economic policy in their own age, classical writers such as Senior, Mill, and Chadwick, along with earlier thinkers such as Malthus and Ricardo, set the stage for policy developments in the twentieth century. Although times have changed, many of the problems confronting capitalist economies today were faced by England over a century ago. It should therefore come as little surprise that today's economists and other social scientists are rethinking many older problems, in some cases retracing their steps, albeit with the aid of more advanced analytical and research techniques.

The classical economists were forced to deal with the consequences of emerging forms of industrial and market competition. Where markets failed in providing optimal results (e.g., melioration of poverty, personal hygiene, convict deaths, "wasteful" duplication, etc.), it became obvious that legal and legislative changes could be effected to provide incentives to achieve "more desirable" social and economic solutions. The difference between economists as policymakers, then as now, lies mainly in the kind and amount of interventions deemed necessary or, indeed, optimal. The differences between Mill and Chadwick in particular are instructive on this issue.

Both Mill and Chadwick were in the Benthamite tradition and both supported government interventions. As early as 1832, Mill was justifying legislative interventions based on externalities and the "free rider" principles. A critical difference between him and Chadwick, however, is that Mill remained skeptical of consolidating political and economic power in a central authority. Chadwick tended to see externalities everywhere, and he offered no practical limit to this extension of central authority. Though Mill was sympathetic to some of Chadwick's proposed reforms, he refused to endorse them all, especially if they held out the prospect of increased centralization. Like Chadwick, Mill believed that incentives and competitive pressures should be built into socioeconomic institutions for the betterment of humankind. At the same time, he could not reconcile extensive government ownership and control of the means of production with the traditional, Smith-inspired theory of competitive capitalism.

Perhaps more than his contemporaries, J. S. Mill embraced the advent of representative democracy and its recourse to the state for equality of circumstances. He looked to a new compromise between humans and their environment and trusted that education and his country's libertarian heritage would operate in such a way that all citizens might come to share both liberty and property in a more equitable way. Chadwick, on the other hand, shared very little of this trust.

NOTES FOR FURTHER READING

Lionel Robbins's *The Theory of Economic Policy in English Classical Political Economy* (London: Macmillan, 1965) provides a good general introduction to classical economic policy. Robbins's interpretations are pristine and get to the heart of important matters. For example, on Mill's so-called socialist leanings he writes: "Mill is very typical. It is this vision of the future, rather than that of central collectivisim, which has usually captured the fancy of lovers of liberty who, for one reason or another, have wished to transcend the society based on private property and the market" (p. 160). Also see Robbins's comments on the contrast between the precision suggested by Bentham's "felicific calculus" and the rough-and-ready *marginal* alterations in economic policies actually recommended by Bentham's disciples (p. 181). Another valuable introduction to classical economic theory is D. P. O'Brien's *The Classical Economists* (Oxford: Clarendon Press, 1975). Chapters 6, 9, and 10 are especially good, as are the bibliographies that follow them. Also see the valuable set of essays edited by A. W. Coats, *The Classical Economists and Economic Policy* (London: Methuen, 1971). For the view that Bentham was a collectivist and Mill essentially a Benthamite, see J. B. Brebner, "Laissez-Faire and State Intervention in Nineteenth Century Britain," *Journal of Economic History,* vol. 8, suppl. (1948), pp. 59–73. On the influence of economists on nineteenth-century legislation, see two contributions by F. W. Fetter: "The Influence of Economists in Parliament on British Legislation from Ricardo to John Stuart Mill," *Journal of Political Economy,* vol. 83 (October 1975), pp. 1051–1064; and the somewhat longer treatment *The Economists in Parliament, 1780–1868* (Durham, N.C.: The Duke University Press, 1979).

The medieval and philosophical origins of the concept of laissez faire are discussed by Jacob Viner, "The Intellectual History of Laissez-Faire," *Journal of Law & Economics,* vol. 3 (October 1960), pp. 45–69. Contributors to the romantic and literary criticism of economics that had some impact on Mill are reviewed by W. D. Grampp, "Classical Economics and Moral Critics," *History of Political Economy,* vol. 5 (Fall 1973), pp. 359–374. There is an extensive literature dealing with individual policy issues in classical economics. On the Factory Acts in particular, see K. O. Walker, "The Classical Economists and the Factory Acts," *Journal of Economic History,* vol. 1 (1941), pp. 170–191; L. R. Sorenson, "Some Classical Economists, Laissez Faire, and the Factory Acts," *Journal of Economic History,* vol. 12 (1952), pp. 101–117; D. P. O'Brien, *The Classical Economists* (mentioned above), pp. 277–279; and Mark Blaug, "The Classical Economists and the Factory Acts—A Reexamination," *Quarterly Journal of Economics,* vol. 72 (May 1958), pp. 211–226; and on a related topic, see W. D. Grampp, "The Economists and the Combination Laws," *Quarterly Journal of Economics,"* vol. 93 (November 1979), pp. 501–522. In his analysis of the Factory Act of 1833, H. P. Marvel, "Factory Regulation: A Reinterpretation of Early English Experience," *Journal of Law & Economics,* vol. 20 (October 1977), pp. 379–402, concluded that "this innovation in industrial regulation was not enacted and enforced solely out of compassion for the factory children. It was, instead, an early example of a regulated industry controlling its regulators to further its own interests." Thus Marvel describes the very same process of rent seeking in representative democracy that we elaborated in Chapter 3. The implication is that other forms of early nineteenth-century social controls may also constitute examples of rent seeking, although these other forms have not yet been subjected to such analysis. For a similar conclusion, see Clark Nardinelli, "Child Labor and the Factory Acts," *Journal of Economic History,* vol. 15 (1980), pp. 739–755. The public-choice ramifications of Senior's analysis of the Factory Acts are explored by G. M. Anderson, R. B. Ekelund, Jr., and R. D. Tollison, "Nassau Senior as Economic Consultant: The Factory Acts Reconsidered," *Economica,* vol. 56 (February 1989), pp. 71–81. On the confused issue of Senior's "last hour" analysis, see Orace Johnson, "The 'Last Hour' of Senior and Marx," *History of Political Economy,* vol. 1 (Fall 1969), pp. 359–369; and J. B. DeLong, "Senior's 'Last Hour': Suggested Explanation of a Famous Blunder," *History of Political Economy,* vol. 18 (Summer 1986), pp. 325–333. On education, see E. G. West, "Private versus Public Education, A Classical Economic Dispute," *Journal of Political Economy,* vol. 72 (October 1974), pp. 465–475; same author, "Resource Allocation and Growth in Early Nineteenth-Century British Education," *Economic History Review,* vol. 23 (April 1970), pp. 68–95; and Margaret O'Donnell, *The Educational Thought of the Classical Political Economists* (London: University Press of America, 1985). On classical views of "appropriate" policy toward emergent corporate forms of business organization, see C. E. Amsler, R. L. Bartlett, and C. J. Bolton, "Thoughts of Some British Economists on Early Limited Liability and Corporate Legislation," *History of Political Economy,* vol. 13 (Winter 1981), pp. 774–793. On the issues of agrarian economic organization and population incentives see W. C. Bush, "Population and Mill's Peasant-Proprietor Economy," *History of Political Economy,* vol. 5 (Spring 1973), pp. 110–120.

J. S. Mill's many policy views are featured in the masterful and very accessible collection of his writings in the Toronto series. See especially Mill's *Essays on Economics and Society* (see References). There is some debate as to whether Mill was in the vanguard of those supporting progressive policies regarding income distribution, the equality of women, trade unions, public education, and welfare programs. The argument for this proposition was suggested by P. Schwartz, *The New Political Economy of J. S. Mill* (Durham, N.C.: The Duke University Press, 1972). The same view is enlarged by R. B. Ekelund, Jr., and R. D. Tollison, "The New Political Economy of J. S. Mill: The Means to Social Justice," *Canadian Journal of Economics,* vol. 9 (May 1976), pp. 213–231. E. G. West, "J. S. Mill's Redistribution Policy: New Political Economy or Old?" *Economic Inquiry,* vol. 16 (October 1978), pp. 570–586, presents the contrasting view that Mill was a Victorian moralist, a blatant Malthusian with regard to the prospects of the poor and an elitist supporter of labor unions; but see the rejoinder by Ekelund and Tollison that follows West's article. Readers are left to make their own decision in this regard.

Notwithstanding the debate over the "newness" of Mill's policy views, Pedro Schwartz has made a very good case for his conclusion that the critiques of laissez faire by Cairnes, Sidgwick, Marshall, and Pigou would have been unthinkable without Mill's earlier efforts. Concludes Schwartz: "From Mill stemmed the neo-classical (one might say, the Cambridge) tradition of critical evaluation of the working of the market" (*The New Political Economy,* mentioned above, p. 151). More than once Mill argued that interventions were necessary in the case of natural monopoly. As an advocate of government ownership of waterworks (production and distribution) and gas companies, Mill argued for municipal purchase and administration of these companies where possible. As Schwartz has shown with respect to Mill's views on the regulation of the London water supply, however, Mill was very concerned that a centralized board not be given power to consolidate water services. See P. Schwartz, "John Stuart Mill and Laissez-Faire: London Water," *Economica,* vol. 23 (February 1966), pp. 71–83. In spite of his earlier advocacy of centralization in the case of the Poor Law administration, Mill (under the possible influence of de Tocqueville) came to distrust centralized concentration of authority. Provision of telegraph and railway services may have been an exception. See the Appendix to R. B. Ekelund and E. O. Price's "Sir Edwin Chadwick on Competition and the Social Control of Industry: Railroads," *History of Political Economy,* vol. 11 (Summer 1979), pp. 213–239.

The distinction between Bentham's "artificial" identity of interests and Smith's "natural" identity of interests is discussed by Elie Halévy, *The Growth of Philosophical Radicalism,* Mary Morris (trans.) (Boston: Beacon Press, 1955). Chadwick's role in the history of public administration is well known. The astonishing range of social causes in which Chadwick involved himself is outlined in his massive vita. See R. A. Lewis, *Edwin Chadwick and the Public Health Movement, 1832–1854* (London: Longmans, 1952), pp. 380–395. Chadwick's participation in Poor Law reform made him one of the most hated public figures of his day, and his personality did not ease the situation. Lewis, in what seems a majority opinion, describes him as follows: "He was a bore, a really outstanding specimen of bore in an age when the species flourished. He was too keenly aware of his own merits; while, on the other hand he had no patience with fools, and his definition of a fool was a very wide one, taking in, as it did, nearly everybody who disagreed with him. With a wholesome suspicion of power wielded by others he managed to combine a boundless confidence in the benefits of power in his own strong hands, and every scheme drawn up by Edwin Chadwick seemed to contain a provision at some point for giving more power to Edwin Chadwick.... He stirred up a great deal of mud, and it is a tribute not a reproach that so much of it was thrown back at him by his critics." For another biographical treatment of Chadwick, see S. E. Finer, *The Life and Times of Sir Edwin Chadwick* (London: Methuen, 1952).

Although Chadwick was the quintessential economic policymaker of the nineteenth century, relatively little has been written of his policy exploits by economists. Some notable exceptions are R. A. Lewis, "Edwin Chadwick and the Railway Labourers," *Economic History Review,* vol. 3 (1950), pp. 107–118; R. F. Hébert, "Edwin Chadwick and the Economics of Crime," *Economic Inquiry,* vol. 16 (October 1977), pp. 539–550; and Ekelund and Price,

"Chadwick on Competition and Social Control," (see above). The only full-scale economic interpretation of Chadwick's policy views is in a doctoral dissertation by E. O. Price, Contributions of Sir Edwin Chadwick to Economic Policy, unpublished Ph.D. dissertation (College Station: Texas A & M University, 1979).

After a long hiatus, the Bentham-Chadwick plan of contract management has been recast as the "Chicago Theory of Regulation." Harold Demsetz, "Why Regulate Utilities?" *Journal of Law & Economics,* vol. 11 (October 1968), pp. 55–65, explicated a principle of competition whose origin he attributed to Edwin Chadwick, but see W. M. Crain and R. B. Ekelund, "Chadwick and Demsetz on Competition and Regulation," *Journal of Law & Economics,* vol. 19 (April 1976), pp. 149–162.

It is important to note that practical implementation of the "Chadwick plan" may engender many problems not anticipated by Chadwick or his modern defenders. Critics argue that the design and implementation of optimal contracts may present as many as or more difficulties than those found in more traditional forms of regulation. See, for example, V. P. Goldberg, "Regulation and Administered Contracts," *Bell Journal of Economics,* vol. 7 (Autumn 1976), pp. 426–448. The problems of contract management vary with the technical and competitive characteristics of the industry and must be developed in the context of case study. For an interesting example of the latter, see O. E. Williamson, "Franchise Bidding for Natural Monopolies—In General and with Respect to CATV," *Bell Journal of Economics,* vol. 7 (Spring 1976), pp. 73–104.

An appreciation of Chadwick's incredible foresight and creativity in the policy analysis of economic problems can be gleaned from the comparison of his views on crime with the "latest word" by economists on the subject. See Hébert, "Chadwick and the Economics of Crime" (see above); G. S. Becker, "Crime and Punishment: An Economic Approach," *Journal of Political Economy,* vol. 76 (March/April 1968), pp. 169–217; G. S. Becker and G. J. Stigler, "Law Enforcement, Malfeasance, and Compensation of Enforcers," *Journal of Legal Studies,* vol. 3 (January 1974), pp. 1–18; and G. J. Stigler, "The Optimum Enforcement of Laws," *Journal of Political Economy,* vol. 78 (May/June 1970), pp. 526–536.

REFERENCES

Baysinger, Barry, and Robert Tollison. "Chaining Leviathan: The Case of Gladstonian Finance," *History of Political Economy,* vol. 12 (Summer 1980), pp. 206–213.
Chadwick, Edwin. "Preventive Police," *London Review,* vol. 1 (1829), pp. 252–308.
———. *Report on the Sanitary Condition of the Labouring Population of Great Britain,* M. W. Flinn (ed.). Edinburgh: Edinburgh University Press, 1965 [1842].
———. "Results of Different Principles of Legislation and Administration in Europe; Of Competition for the Field, as Compared with Competition within the Field of Service," *Royal Statistical Society Journal,* vol. 22 (1859), pp. 381–420.

————. "Opening Address," *Journal of the Royal Statistical Society of London,* vol. 25 (1862).

————. "On the Proposal That the Railways Should Be Purchased by the Government," *Journal of the Society of Arts,* vol. 9 (February 1866), pp. 203ff.

————. "The Police and the Extinction of Fires," in B. W. Richardson (ed.). *The Health of Nations: A Review of the Works of Edwin Chadwick,* vol. 2. London: Longmans, 1887.

————. "Précis of Preventive Police," in B. W. Richardson (ed.), *The Health of Nations: A Review of the Works of Edwin Chadwick,* vol. 2. London: Longmans, 1887.

————. "Tricycles for Police," in B. W. Richardson (ed.), *The Health of Nations: A Review of the Works of Edwin Chadwick,* vol. 2. London: Longmans, 1887.

[Mill, J. S.] "Lord Brougham's Speech on the Poor Law Amendment Bill" *Monthly Repository,* vol. 7 (1834), p. 597.

[Mill, J. S.] "The Proposed Reform of the Poor Laws," *Monthly Repository,* vol. 8 (1834), p. 361.

Mill, J. S. *Principles of Political Economy,* W. J. Ashley (ed.). New York: A. M. Kelley, Publishers, 1965 [1848].

————. *Principles of Political Economy,* in J. M. Robson (ed.), *Collected Works,* vols. 2 and 3. Toronto: University of Toronto Press, 1966 [1848].

————. *Letters of John Stuart Mill,* 2 vols., H. S. R. Elliot (ed.), London: Longmans, 1910.

————. *Essays on Economics and Society,* in J. M. Robson (ed.), *Collected Works,* vols. 4 and 5. Toronto: University of Toronto Press, 1967.

————. *The Later Letters of John Stuart Mill, 1848–1873,* in F. E. Mineka and D. N. Lindley (eds.), *Collected Works,* vols. 14–17. Toronto: University of Toronto Press, 1972.

Senior, N. W. *Industrial Efficiency and Social Economy,* vol. 2. New York: Henry Holt, 1928.

————. *Selected Writings on Economics.* New York: A. M. Kelley, 1966.

PART **THREE**

REACTIONS AND ALTERNATIVES TO CLASSICAL THEORY IN THE NINETEENTH CENTURY

JOHN MAYNARD KEYNES   KARL MARX   ALFRED MARSHALL   WILLIAM STANLEY JEVONS   ADAM SMITH

CHAPTER 10

SOCIALISTS AND HISTORICISTS

INTRODUCTION

Between the appearance of Adam Smith's pioneer work in 1776 and John Stuart Mill's capstone performance in 1848, several events of tremendous social, political, and economic significance occurred. The American Declaration of Independence, written the same year in which Smith's *Wealth of Nations* was published, marked the birth of a new nation and its launch on the drive to economic self-sufficiency. On the Continent, the impact of the sweeping social reorganization that followed the French Revolution was felt throughout Europe. Coincident with these two upheavals was the steady rise of industrialism and the factory system in England, continental Europe, and America.

The factory system ushered in major transformations in the social and economic landscape. Many contemporary writers feel that the working class bore the chief costs of these changes in the form of economic dislocation and urban congestion. Critics of the period arose to question the benefits of industrialization and the validity of an analytical system that sought to explain the consequences and momentum of the new industrial society. Thus the nineteenth century was an intellectual battleground of sorts for literary, methodological, and to a lesser extent analytical skirmishes in the social sciences.

Not every country was a battleground to the same degree. England and the Continent, for example, were separated intellectually as well as geographically. Great Britain has had a long tradition of individualism at least since the time of John Locke. This was reflected in England's parliamentary government (limited monarchy), which existed alongside the absolute monarchies of Europe in the eighteenth and early nineteenth centuries. Tempered by Edmund Burke's conservative views of social change, British individualism and libertarianism escaped the social upheavals of the French Revolution and culminated, in the economic sphere, in the now familiar writings of Adam Smith and the classical economists.

Continental thought, by contrast, was greatly influenced by Cartesian rationalism, which rejected material things in the search for inner truth. Continental philosophers of the eighteenth and early nineteenth centuries placed more emphasis on group, rather than individual, activity. Rousseau, for example, thought that property rights were conducive to individual and social progress but that there were desirable social uses of property. And Hegel viewed freedom not in the Lockian sense, as a relation between individual and group, but in terms of *associations* with others: family, church, and state. It is not surprising, therefore, that the first attacks on classical political economy were devised on shores other than Great Britain's.

With the exception of Rousseau, all the great philosophers of the French Enlightenment viewed history as an endless progression of humans toward reason and truth. In the economic arena, this view seemed justified by the rapid expansion of production and productive capacity in the first half of the nineteenth century. But the same rapid advances were not made in the social realm. The working class generally received low wages, worked long hours, and toiled under the poorest conditions. Hence throughout the nineteenth century, there were attempts to "socialize" economics by champions of the working class.

Closely connected with the rise of socialist ideas was a current of thought that appeared near the end of the eighteenth century and became distinctive in the first half of the nineteenth: the idea that society evolves, or progresses, through a succession of stages, each superior to the former. This idea appeared first as a theory of history; it later became a theory of economics as well.

Pioneering this new approach was the French philosopher Condorcet (1743–1794). He believed that historical development is subject to general laws and that the task of the historian is to discover those laws by which humans progress "toward truth and well-being." Condorcet called for a new science, based on history, "with which to predict the progress of the human species, to direct it and to accelerate it." This new science was to be empirical, not rationalistic. "Observations on what man has been and on what he is today," wrote Condorcet, "lead immediately to the ways of assuring and accelerating the further progress for which man's nature permits him to hope" (*Esquisses d'un tableau historique des progres de l'esprit humain*, p. 4).

Sparked in part by the rationalist philosophy of the Enlightenment, the French Revolution and its aftermath proved that reason alone could not bring about social perfection, as the rationalists had formerly assumed. Thus Condorcet looked upon the errors of the past, and especially of the Revolution, as part of a transitional stage on the path to social perfection. In studying the epochal nature of history, Condorcet clearly perceived the fact that the development of social progress is more uneven than the development of knowledge. He attributed the lag in social development to the fact that history, until that time, had always been the history of *individuals* rather than the history of the *masses*. Consequently, the needs and well-being of society had been sacrificed to those of a few people. Condorcet sought to rectify this by making history the study of the masses. He therefore originated two important themes that in some measure underlie almost all nineteenth-century criticism of capitalism: the idea of "natural" laws of historical development and the "collectivist" view of history as a study of the masses.

SAINT-SIMON, SISMONDI, AND LIST: EXAMPLES OF EUROPEAN EVOLUTIONARY THOUGHT

The idea of progressive "stages" in historical and economic development was expanded, first by Henri Saint-Simon and then by Simonde de Sismondi and Friedrich List. Taken together, their writings provide a cross-sectional illustration of the historical evolutionary approach to economic development. Each contributed to the development of that approach in his own way.

Saint-Simon: Prophet of Industrialism

Claude Henri de Rouvroy Comte de Saint-Simon (1760–1825) was both an eccentric and a prophet. Born into the French nobility, Saint-Simon claimed to be a descendant of Charlemagne, who allegedly appeared to him while he was imprisoned during the French Revolution. By Saint-Simon's account, Charlemagne charged him with a great mission: to save the French Republic in the wake of the French Revolution. Saint-Simon certainly held no modest view of his own importance. He is said to have instructed his servant to awaken him each day with the following adjuration: "Arise, Monsieur le Comte, you have great things to do today."

Despite his eccentricity, however, Saint-Simon frequently revealed keen analytical insight into social and economic processes. He succeeded in founding a school of followers, and he influenced a number of important thinkers, including Auguste Comte, Karl Marx, and John Stuart Mill.

Reason and the Identity of Class Interests   In economics, Saint-Simon's influence was more on method than on analysis. As indicated above, he developed an evolutionary theory of history, which his secretary, Auguste Comte, later refined into the popular "three-stage" theory of history. Basically, Saint-Simon's own investigation of history revealed a juxtaposition of *two* contradictory social systems. The first (pre-Revolutionary France) was based on military force and the uncritical acceptance of religious faith; the second (France after the Revolution) was based on industrial capacity and the voluntary acceptance of scientific knowledge. To Saint-Simon, science and industry were the hallmarks of the modern age, and his major concern was to reorganize society so as to remove all barriers to the development of both. In increased production lay the future welfare of society, he felt. Accordingly, "the production of useful things is the only reasonable and positive end that political societies can set themselves" (*Oeuvres de Saint-Simon et d'Enfantin*, XVIII, p. 13).

Although this is the same welfare concept accepted by the classical economists, Adam Smith had shown how it could be accomplished outside politics by general reliance on the principle of self-interest. In contrast, Saint-Simon found the key to increased production in *reason* and in the identity of *class interests*. His singular distrust of self-interest was buttressed by his discovery in the study of history of a growing commonality of interests that accompanied the advance of civilization. He therefore felt that economic cooperation and industrial organization would result spontaneously from the progress of society. Saint-Simon declared:

> All men are united by the general interests of production, by the need they all have for security in work and liberty in exchange. The producers of all lands are therefore essentially friends. Nothing stands in the way of their uniting, and the coalition of their efforts is the indispensable condition if industry is to attain the ascendency it can and should enjoy (*Oeuvres*, XIX, p. 47).

Social Reorganization   The chief goal of Saint Simon's new order was to increase the control of humans over things, not over people. Hence, the "control" implied in his proposed organizational structure is not government in the traditional sense but rather *industrial administration*. Saint-Simon was very antagonistic toward government as we know it and its interference in the industrial sphere. "Government always harms industry when it mixes in its affairs," he wrote; "it harms it even in instances where it makes an effort to encourage it" (*Oeuvres*, XVIII, p. 186).

Despite his zealous and persistent plea for reorganization, however, Saint-Simon was rarely explicit or even consistent on the specific nature of industrial organization in the modern age. This lack of consistency in his various programs of reorganization probably attests to his own unsettled mind on the optimum social organization in an industrial society, but it also reflects his conviction that the most appropriate form of organization is historically relative, and hence subject to change.

What Saint-Simon clearly did advocate was that the technical expertise of artists, scientists, and industrial leaders be formally recognized and utilized in the conception and planning of public works designed to increase social welfare. Top-priority items on Saint-Simon's list of public works were the construction of roads and canals, drainage projects, land clearance, and the provision of free education.

In his plan for an "industrial parliament" Saint-Simon outlined a program of economic organization that would utilize the talents of the scientific and industrial elite. This industrial parliament, patterned after the British government, would consist of three bodies. The first (the Chamber of Invention) would be composed of 300 members: 200 civil engineers, 50 poets, 25 artists, 15 architects, and 10 musicians. Its primary duty, according to Saint-Simon, would be to draw up a plan of public works "to be undertaken in order to increase

France's wealth and to improve the condition of its inhabitants'' (*Oeuvres,* XX, p. 51). The second assembly (the Chamber of Examination) would also consist of 300 members, the majority being mathematicians and physical scientists. Its job would be to evaluate the feasibility and desirability of projects proposed by the first chamber and also to develop a master plan for public education. Finally, a third assembly (the Chamber of Execution) of unspecified number would include representatives of each branch of industry. The third chamber was the most important in the overall plan. It would exercise veto power over all projects proposed and approved by the Chambers of Invention and Examination, and it would also levy taxes.

Some later writers have interpreted Saint-Simon's industrial parliament as a blueprint for a fully planned economy. However, Saint-Simon himself confined the concept of centralized planning only to the production of public works, and in this he was not outside the classical economic tradition. Adam Smith, for example, had noted that government should provide:

> ...those public institutions and those public works, which, although they may be in the highest degree advantageous to a great society are, however, of such a nature, that the profit could never repay the expense to any individual or small number of individuals, and which it therefore cannot be expected that any individual or small number of individuals should erect or maintain (*The Wealth of Nations,* p. 681).

Saint-Simon nevertheless went beyond classical economics in other respects. He struck a distinctly Keynesian note, for example, when he argued that government should, if necessary, provide employment for the able-bodied and assistance for the disabled.

In the end, Saint-Simon's major departure from classical economic liberalism was his distrust of self-interest as a guiding force and his insistence that it be replaced by cooperation and the identification of class interests. Where the production of private goods was concerned, Saint-Simon advocated merely a loose confederation of professional associations, ''more or less numerous and connected...to permit their formation into a generalized system by being directed toward a great common industrial goal'' (*Oeuvres,* XXII, p. 185). This ''common industrial goal'' was, of course, increased output. Industrial associations could contribute to economic efficiency in production by sharing knowledge and technology among their members. Saint-Simon gave no indication that the interests of these associations would be in conflict with those of society at large. On the contrary, he consistently avowed that all men had a stake in the outcome of the production process. Nevertheless, Saint-Simon did add certain qualifications to his proposals. He insisted, for example, that new forms of social and economic organization

> ...must conform directly to the interests of the greatest majority of the population; they must be considered as a general political consequence deduced from the divine moral principle; *all men must regard themselves as brothers; they must concern themselves with helping one another* (*Oeuvres,* XXII, pp. 116–117).

In his later years, Saint-Simon's writings took on a more religious tone, and his followers eventually modified his doctrine almost beyond recognition. It was they who developed a social doctrine called (somewhat inappropriately) *Saint-Simonism*, which in most respects little resembled the ideas of the master. The Saint-Simonians were often men of skill and genius—a few had a hand in the construction of the Suez Canal—but they were also zealots in the extreme. Some appeared unrestrained in their pursuit of physical pleasures, and one small band of Saint-Simonians even attracted, by their frequent orgies, the attention and condemnation of a French society inclined to be extremely liberal in such matters.

Nevertheless, Saint-Simon himself seems to have accurately charted the future direction of capitalism in many important respects. He seems, for example, to have fully anticipated the advent of the corporate society and its social implications—a theme upon which the modern economist John Kenneth Galbraith (see Chapter 17) has frequently elaborated.

Simonde de Sismondi: Critic of Capitalism

Born in Geneva and trained as a historian, J. C. L. Simonde de Sismondi (1773–1848) acquired practical experience in business and finance in France while he was very young. He later became one of the first and foremost critics of classical economic theory and method in the nineteenth century. In so doing, he laid much of the ground-work for the method of analysis later advanced by the German historical school (see below).

Sismondi the Critic   Examining the effects of the industrial revolution with the historian's eye, Sismondi observed that economic cooperation, the hallmark of the guild system, gave way under the industrial regime to conflicts of interest between labor and capital. Moreover, he found that improvements in living conditions among the workers lagged seriously behind the tremendous increases in wealth wrought by the machine age. Unrestrained competition, instead of increasing social welfare, led to universal rivalry, large-scale production, and oversupply. The latter, in turn, precipitated commercial crises and depression.

Some fifty or more years before Marx, Sismondi anticipated the class struggle between labor and capital that was to distinguish Marxian economics. Whereas Saint-Simon believed that economic cooperation and organization were the inevitable outcome of the advance of civilization, Sismondi blamed the class struggle on the institutions of capitalism. But unlike Marx, Sismondi did not see class struggle as a permanent phenomenon. It was merely the result of existing social institutions and could be eliminated through appropriate changes in those institutions. What escaped Sismondi, moreover, was the realization of precisely which factors constitute the driving force of historical development.

One of Sismondi's most telling attacks on classicism concerned machinery.

In general, classical economists viewed the introduction of machinery as beneficial since it improved economic efficiency, lowered costs of production and product prices, and thus increased consumer welfare. Sismondi, on the other hand, while recognizing the cost-reducing advantages of machinery, felt that such benefits did not justify the harm incurred by technological unemployment. The introduction of labor-saving machinery displaces workers. Moreover, since machinery is expensive, it is usually concentrated in the larger firms, so that many small manufacturers are driven out of business. According to Sismondi, since each individual so unemployed is a consumer who finds his income drastically reduced while more machines simultaneously produce more output, overproduction and economic crisis inevitably follow. Sismondi's conclusion does *not* necessarily follow, however. He was either unable to see or unwilling to admit that the growth of output frequently creates additional employment opportunities.

It is important to note that Sismondi's criticism was not aimed at machinery per se but at the social organization that allowed workers to be subjected to the vagaries of competition. About this he was explicit:

> Every invention in the arts, which has multiplied the power of man's work, from that of the plough to the steam engine, is useful....Society had made progress only through such discoveries; it is through them that the work of man has sufficed for his needs....It is not the fault of the progress of mechanical science, but the fault of the social order, if the worker, who acquires the power to make in two hours what would take him twelve to make before, does not find himself richer, and consequently does not enjoy more leisure, but on the contrary is doing six times more work than is demanded (*Nouveaux principes d'économie politique,* I, p. 349).

Sismondi on Theory and Method Sismondi's disagreement with classical economics was based less on theoretical principles than on its method, aims, and conclusions. While Nassau Senior (see Chapter 7) strove to remove all normative elements from economics so as to render it scientific, Sismondi viewed economics as a subset of the science of government. Thus while Saint-Simon was willing to replace government with industrial administration, Sismondi viewed government and economics as inseparable. To Sismondi, economics was a moral science: "The physical well-being of man, insofar as it can be the work of his government, is the object of political economy" (*Nouveaux principes,* I, p. 8). A science that concerns itself solely with the means of increasing wealth without studying the purpose of such wealth was, in Sismondi's view, a "false science."

In a subtle attack on the theory of self-interest, Sismondi pointed out that in the struggle to achieve personal gain, not every individual force is equal. Hence, "Injustice can often triumph...being backed by public force which is believed to be impartial, but which, in fact, without examining the cause, always places itself on the side of the stronger" (*Nouveaux principes,* I, p. 408). Furthermore, Sismondi argued that in the social arena, exercise of individual self-interest does not always coincide with the general interest. His poignant example illustrating this point seems especially relevant today:

> It is to the interest of one to rob his neighbor, and it is to the interest of the latter to let him do it, if he has a weapon in his hand, in order not to be killed; but it is not to the interest of society that one should use force and the other should give in. The entire social organization presents to us at every step a similar compulsion, not always with the same sort of violence, but always with the same danger of resistance (*Nouveaux principes,* I, p. 200).

Sismondi especially attacked the abstract, deductive method of the Ricardian school, preferring instead the comparative, historical method. His telling description of economics is both an indictment of classical economics and a clarification of his own method:

> It is not founded on dry calculations, nor on a mathematical chain of theorems, deduced from some obscure axioms, given as incontestable truth....Political economy is founded on the study of man and men; human nature must be known, and also the condition and life of societies in different times and in different places. One must consult the historian, and the travellers; one must look into one's self; not only study the laws, but also know how they are executed; not only examine the tables of exportation and importation, but also know the aspect of the country, enter the bosom of families, judge the comfort or suffering of the mass of the people, verify great principles by observation of details, and compare ceaselessly science with daily practical life (*De la richesse commerciale,* I, p. xv).

In other words, Sismondi clearly perceived the complexity of the industrial era, and he felt that the few abstract theories of the classical economists were inadequate for the modern age. He held the classical theorists culpable for drawing too many loose observations in England alone, without regard to other countries. The conclusions of classical economic theory, which were frequently held as absolute principles, were therefore considered spurious by Sismondi. Moreover, he strongly protested the tendency of the abstract theorists to reduce habits and customs to calculations. Finally, Sismondi criticized "those who wished to see man isolated from the world, or rather who considered abstractly the modifications of his existence, and always arrived at conclusions that are belied by experience" (*Études sur l'économie politique,* I, p. 4).

In sum, Sismondi the historian was interested in those periods of transition that encompass the exit from one regime and the entrance to another. In practice, he was concerned with ameliorating the condition of the proletariat (a term he coined) during this transition. He may be said to have originated the line of inquiry that the French call *économie sociale* ("social economy"). Sismondi influenced a number of writers who were not outright socialists but who recognized the evils of unrestrained laissez faire. These writers, along with Sismondi, sought some happy halfway house that would retain the principle of individual liberty as much as possible.

In retrospect, Sismondi's criticism of the classical school was somewhat justified, but his reason was marred by a logical flaw. In his theory of over-production, Sismondi reasoned that if increased production is to be useful, it must always be *preceded* by increased demand. He did not admit the possibility that increased production could itself *create* additional demand. Sismondi's interest in political economy was nevertheless summed up in his theory of economic crises and his concern for their effects on the working class.

Friedrich List and the National System of Political Economy

Friedrich List (1789–1846), son of a German leatherworker, forsook an academic career to become active in German politics. In 1819, he became leader of the General Association of German Manufacturers and Merchants and the very soul of the movement to confederate the German states.

The economic and political unity that characterized much of Europe in the first half of the nineteenth century was totally absent from Germany. The peace treaty that ended Germany's participation in the Napoleonic wars left that country divided into thirty-nine different states, most of which were individual monarchies economically and politically isolated from one another. Such isolation was primarily the result of a complex system of interstate tariffs that impaired the free and easy exchange of goods. At the same time, however, no import duties existed. Thus British surplus products (and those of other countries) found their way into German markets, where they were offered at extremely low prices.

Under these circumstances, the very existence of German manufacturing and mercantile interests was threatened, and by the 1830s there arose among the German states a general clamor for economic unity and uniform tariffs. It was this movement that consumed List's interests and energy.

Protectionism and the Stages of Economic Development   In his analysis of national systems of political economy, List applied a method of inquiry originated by Saint-Simon: the idea that an economy must pass through successive stages before it reaches a "mature" state. The historical stages of development detailed by List were: (1) barbaric, (2) pastoral, (3) agricultural, (4) agricultural-manufacturing, and (5) agricultural-manufacturing-commercial. Like Sismondi and Saint-Simon, List was as much interested in the transition between stages of economic development as in the end result. He felt that passage through the first three stages would be brought about most speedily by free trade between states and nations but that economies in transition between the last two stages required economic protection until the final stage was reached. Free trade was warranted once again, however, when the final stage of development was attained, "in order to guard against retrogression and indolence by the nation's manufacturers and merchants" (*The National System of Political Economy*, pp. 143ff).

By List's classification and testimony, only Great Britain had attained the final stage of economic development. While the Continental and American nations struggled to reach this apogee, however, cheap British imports were thwarting the development of domestic manufacturing. List felt that until all nations reached the final stage in their development, international competition could not exist on an equal footing. Thus he favored protective tariffs for Germany until its greatest national economic power was attained.

It is important to note that List was not an outright protectionist; rather, he felt that protection was warranted only at critical stages in history. His writings are replete with examples borrowed from history and experience showing that economic protection is the only way for an emerging nation to establish itself. List felt that the American experience offered vindication of his views, and he of course found ready support among United States protectionists, particularly Alexander Hamilton and Henry Carey.

List's Criticism of Classical Economics List strongly opposed the absolutist, cosmopolitan tendencies of the classical economists. They derived principles, he maintained, which were then assumed to hold for all nations and all times. By contrast, List's theory and methodology were strongly nationalistic and historical. His theory of stages in economic development, for example, was calculated to demonstrate the insufficiency of classical economics to recognize and reflect the variety of conditions existing in different countries and, most especially, in Germany.

Like Sismondi, List subordinated economics to politics in general. In his view, it was not enough for the statesman to know that the free interchange of products will increase wealth (as demonstrated by the classical economists); he must also know the ramifications of such action for his own country. Thus List argued that free trade that displaces either population or domestic industry is undesirable. Moreover, List would not sacrifice the future for the present. He maintained that the crucial economic magnitude in economic development is not wealth (as measured by exchange values) but *productive power*. In his own words, "The power of producing wealth is...infinitely more important than the wealth itself" (*The National System of Political Economy*, p. 108). Thus economic resources must be safeguarded so that their future existence and development are assured. This view constitutes further justification for List's protectionist arguments; it also lies at the root of the popular "infant-industry" argument[1] in support of protective tariffs.

For List, the ultimate goal of economic activity should be national development and the accretion of economic power. In this, he (as Marx was to do later) perceived industry as more than the mere result of labor and capital. Rather, he conceived industry as a *social* force that itself creates and improves

---

[1] This argument, known to every student of international trade, maintains that specific tariffs are justified in order to protect new and emerging industries from ruinous foreign competition until such time as a level of productive efficiency is reached that will enable the industry to meet foreign competition.

capital and labor. In addition to effecting present production, industry gives an impetus and a direction to future production. Therefore, List recommended the introduction of industry into underdeveloped countries even at the expense of temporary loss.

List's originality in economic theory and method consisted in his systematic use of historical comparison as a means of demonstrating the validity of economic propositions and in his introduction of new and useful points of view in contradistinction to the economic orthodoxy of classical liberalism. In stretching the dynamic fabric of classical economic growth by representing economic development as a succession of historical stages, he provided a methodological rallying point for the economists of the German historical school. Thus List may appropriately be considered the forerunner of that school.

THE UTOPIAN SOCIALISTS: OWEN, FOURIER, AND PROUDHON

Although socialism is a vibrant force in contemporary life, the concept itself is very vague. The word "socialism" usually conjures up a number of meanings: public ownership of economic enterprise, subjugation of individual freedom, elimination of private property, conscious direction of economic activity, and so on. In practice, socialism is rarely the clear-cut alternative to capitalism it is often held out to be. Every capitalist economy today possesses some socialist elements or institutions and vice versa. Moreover, many past writers who are today called "socialist" can be differentiated from one another on the basis of significant (often frequent) philosophical differences. There is, however, sufficient common ground among such writers to distinguish them from the classical economists. This is particularly true of that group of writers often referred to as the *utopian socialists*.[2] The utopians regarded capitalism as irrational, inhumane, and unjust. They repudiated the idea of laissez faire and the doctrine of harmony of interests. They were all optimistic concerning the perfectibility of humans and the social order through the proper construction of the social environment.

The Grand Experiment of Robert Owen

Born in obscurity of Welsh parents, Robert Owen (1771–1858) rose to considerable fame and fortune before his thirtieth year. As he worked his way up the ladder of success in the textile industry, Owen observed the changes in economic and social life wrought by the rapid introduction of machinery. The mechanical marvels of Arkwright (spinning frame), Crompton (spinning mule), and Hargreaves (spinning jenny) helped make Owen a wealthy man; but their impact also turned Owen's attention to the plight of the textile worker.

---

[2] Marx used this phrase in order to distinguish his theory of socialism from other theories not based on dialectical materialism. It is debatable whether Marx's own theory was significantly less utopian than the theories he disdained; nevertheless the phrase is useful in a categorical sense.

Owen did not believe that individual suffering among workers was a necessary condition for the accumulation of wealth. He challenged the predominant social view that poverty was the just consequence for the sins of the working class. In *A New View of Society* (1813) he turned traditional social theory upside down by maintaining that an individual's character is formed *for* him and not *by* him.

In short, Owen maintained that the poor are wretched because they are poor; they are not poor because they are wretched! Improve a man's social environment, Owen argued, and you improve the man. This one precept was the central and innovational feature of Owen's social philosophy, but he embellished it considerably with the statement of what he called his "true principles." Owen set forth these true principles as follows in his *Report to the County of Lanark* in 1821:

1 Character is universally formed *for* and not *by* the individual.

2 *Any* habits and sentiments may be given to mankind.

3 The affections are *not* under the control of the individual.

4 Every individual may be trained to produce far more than he can consume, while there is sufficiency of soil left for him to cultivate.

5 Nature has provided means by which populations may be at all times maintained in the proper state to give the greatest happiness to every individual, without one check of vice or misery.

6 Any community may be arranged, on a due combination of the foregoing principles, in such a manner as not only to withdraw vice, poverty, and, in a great degree, misery from the world, but also to place *every* individual under such circumstances in which he shall enjoy more permanent happiness than can be given to *any* individual under the principles which have heretofore regulated society.

7 That all the assumed fundamental principles on which society has hitherto been founded are erroneous, and may be demonstrated to be contrary to fact.

8 That the change which would follow the abandonment of these erroneous maxims which bring misery to the world, and the adoption of principles of truth, unfolding a system which shall remove and forever exclude that misery, may be effected without the slightest injury to any human being (cited in Morton, pp. 58–59).

The proving ground for Owen's social theories was New Lanark Mills in Scotland, the management of which Owen commenced in 1800, shortly after his marriage to the proprietor's daughter. The work force at New Lanark was known as an intemperate and immoral lot, given to frequent bouts of debauchery and drunkenness. But Owen did not approach his management position at New Lanark as just another job. He hoped to prove his theory that a change in social environment would change the workers' character. More important in the economic sense was Owen's conviction that a contented work force would be an efficient one. At New Lanark, Owen restricted the labor of children and devoted much time to their education. He also improved housing conditions for the workers and their families, raised wages, shortened work hours, and made other provisions to enrich the lives of the community's inhabitants.

Owen's investment in human character at New Lanark must be regarded as a success. To the amazement of his fellow industrialists, Owen's mills continued to earn substantial profits after the introduction of reforms. Despite the social and economic success of New Lanark, however, Owen was eventually forced out of the venture by partners who resented his program. This convinced him that private initiative could not be relied on to bring about lasting social and economic reform. In a retrospective view of his grand experiment, Owen said:

> Private initiative would give to the laboring poor neither education nor employment, for the children of commerce have been trained to direct all their facilities to buy cheap and sell dear; and consequently, those who are the most expert and successful in this wise and noble art are, in the commercial world, deemed to possess foresight and superior achievements, while such an attempt to improve the moral habits and increase the comfort of those whom they employ are termed wild enthusiasts (cited in Beer, I, p. 165).

As a result, Owen advocated a larger role for government. He sought laws on factory reforms, aid to the unemployed, and, eventually, a national system of education. He lived to see a second social experiment at New Harmony, Indiana, fail within three years of its establishment, but unfortunately he did not live to see many of his suggested reforms legislated into action. In this, Owen was clearly ahead of his time, for most of the reforms he championed are now commonplace in industrial societies.

The Shattered Dream of Charles Fourier

In his saner moments Charles Fourier (1772–1837) was more than a little eccentric; in his wilder moments he was probably only slightly less than insane. In between, he revealed a mastery of the smallest detail and an uncanny power for predicting future developments. Like Saint-Simon and List, Fourier believed that civilization passes through certain stages of development, though no one took his theory seriously. His vision of the world almost sounds like a prolonged hallucinogenic "trip": Nineteenth-century France was allegedly in the fifth stage of advancement, having passed through (1) confusion, (2) savagery, (3) patriarchism, and (4) barbarity. After passing through two more stages, it would eventually approach the upward slope of harmony—the final stage of utter bliss—which would last for 8,000 years. Then, however, history would reverse itself, and society would regress through each stage back to the beginning.

In apocalyptic fashion, Fourier detailed the earthly changes that would accompany harmony: six new moons would replace the one in existence; a halo, showering gentle dew, would circle the north pole; the seas would turn to Kool-Aid; and all the violent or repulsive beasts of the earth would be replaced by their opposites: antilions, antiwhales, antibears, antibugs, and antirats would be not only commonplace but also serviceable to humankind. To top it all off, the life span of humans in the harmonic stage would stretch to 144 years, five-sixths of which would be devoted to the unrestrained pursuit of sexual love (Fourier was a crafty old bachelor as well as a childishly enthusiastic visionary!).

It is tempting to dismiss all this as the pure frenzy of a madman, except for one thing: Fourier had a plan for reorganizing society that, despite its fantastic character, captured the imagination of others who shared his distress over the evils of capitalism. His plan, moreover, was a forerunner of the twentieth-century commune.

What Fourier proposed was a multiplicity of "garden cities" (*phalanstères*) modeled after a grand hotel, where, ideally, fifteen hundred people would live in common. No restrictions would be placed on human liberty. Fourier did not believe in income redistribution of the leveling kind; maintained that income inequality and poverty "are of divine ordination, and consequently must for ever remain, since everything that God has ordained is just as it ought to be" (*Nouveau monde industriel*, 1848, cited in Gide and Rist, p. 256).

Nor did he object to private property per se, only to its *abuse*, as when income is earned without work. Thus each resident of the hotel would be able to purchase accommodations suitable to his or her individual tastes and pocketbook. Economic production in the *phalanstère*, however, would be undertaken collectively. Cooperation would replace unrestrained self-interest. Individual property was not to be extinguished but transformed into fully participating common-stock shares of the *phalanstère*. Fourier promised high returns to wealthy capitalists who invested in his scheme, but no one ever did. Profits were to be divided exactly as follows: four-twelfths to capital, five-twelfths to labor, and three-twelfths to ability (i.e., management).

The main evil of capitalism, according to Fourier, was the conflict of individual interests. Hence the *phalanstère* was designed to eliminate conflicts of interest by making each member a cooperative *owner* as well as a wage earner. Each member would draw his or her share of income not only as a laborer but also as a capitalist (shareholder) and manager (each cooperative member had a voice in the management of the *phalanstère*).

Economies would be achieved in the *phalanstère* by communal living, which would offer the maximum of comfort at a minimum cost. Household tasks would, moreover, be undertaken collectively, thereby eliminating much individual drudgery. Dirty work would be farmed out to children, who have always taken a "preverse" delight in getting themselves filthy. In general, adults would do only work they enjoyed, and a kind of friendly competition would ensue in the form of contests to see who did his or her job best.

Perhaps it is easy to see why Fourier's plan appealed to other dreamers as well—if such a place could actually exist and, more importantly, persist, who indeed would not want to live there? Unfortunately, Fourier's ideas had much less practical influence than Owen's, although the cooperative movement owes a debt to Fourier as well. He died a tragic figure, nevertheless, having spent his last few years waiting at home during advertised hours for wealthy capitalists to come to him and finance his fantastic scheme. No one ever did.

Proudhon: "Scholastic Anarchist"

Pierre Joseph Proudhon (1809–1865) is usually considered a French socialist, although he was equally as vehement in his criticism of the socialism he knew as in his criticism of capitalism. The two most distinguishing features of his thought include a desire to remove all authority and an almost medieval concern for economic justice in exchange. These two characteristics have been combined in our designation of Proudhon as a "scholastic anarchist."

Proudhon's Criticism of Authority Proudhon was above all a libertarian. In 1840 he published an attack on private property that gained for its author both notoriety and charges of conspiracy against the state.[3] Proudhon's work was entitled *What Is Property?* and his answer was: Property is theft! He defended his position accordingly:

> If I were asked the following question: What is slavery? and I should answer in one word, *It is murder*, my meaning would be understood at once. No extended argument would be required to show that the power to take from a man his thought, his will, his personality, is a power of life and death; and that to enslave a man is to kill him. Why then to this other question: What is property? may I not likewise answer, *It is robbery*, without the certainty of being misunderstood; the second proposition being no other than a transformation of the first (cited in Manuel and Manuel, p. 363).

Despite his invectives against property, Proudhon did not wish to eliminate private property, for he was not opposed to ownership per se. Rather, he was opposed to the attributes of property: unearned income in the form of rent, interest, or profit. Proudhon, like Saint-Simon, felt strongly that all men should work. He himself had no choice. His whole life was spent in abject poverty.

In another major work, Proudhon complained that the French Revolution of 1789 had lost its direction and concentrated merely on *reforming* the political hierarchy, when it should have swept it away. Political powers always tend toward centralization, he argued, and thence toward tyranny. Proudhon had a passion for liberty—he wanted liberty to be absolute, everywhere, and forever. This passion was nevertheless rooted in a strong desire for social order.

In places, Proudhon sounds almost Saint-Simonian, although he generally deprecated Saint-Simon's ideas. On anarchy, for example, Proudhon wrote:

> To live without government, to abolish all authority, absolutely and unreservedly, to set up pure *anarchy* seems to [some] ridiculous and inconceivable, a plot against the Republic and against the nation. What will these people who talk of abolishing government put in place of it? they ask.

---

[3] In his conspiracy trial, Proudhon was acquitted by a council of judges who were so confounded by his mild manner and abstruse arguments in his own defense that they declared him "an economist, not an anarchist; a man of meditation, not of revolution." Even the stoic Proudhon found the judges' declamation amusing, as he later confided to a friend.

> We have no trouble in answering. It is industrial organization that we will put in place of government.... In place of laws, we will put contracts.... In place of political powers, we will put economic forces. In place of the ancient classes of nobles, burghers, and peasants, or of business men and working men, we will put the general titles and special departments of industry: Agriculture, Manufacture, Commerce, etc. In place of public force, we will put collective force. In place of standing armies, we will put industrial associations. In place of police, we will put identity of interests. In place of political centralization, we will put economic centralization.
>
> Do you see now how there can be order without functionaries, a profound and wholly intellectual unity? (*General Idea of the Revolution in the Nineteenth Century,* cited in Manuel and Manuel, p. 371).

Also like Saint-Simon, Proudhon placed his faith in a higher order of social unity than that provided by the existing social structure. Truth and reality are essentially historical, he declared, and progress is inevitable. Science, rather than authority, holds the key to the future, and it, rather than self-interest, is alone capable of establishing social harmony. In the *General Idea of the Revolution in the Nineteenth Century,* Proudhon wrote:

> What no monarchy, not even that of Roman emperors, has been able to accomplish; what Christianity, that epitome of the ancient faiths, has been unable to produce, the universal Republic, the economic Revolution, will accomplish, cannot fail to accomplish. It is indeed with political economy as with the other sciences: it is inevitably the same throughout the world: it does not depend upon the fancies of men or nation: it yields to the caprice of none.... Truth alone is equal everywhere: science is the unity of mankind. If then science, and no longer religion or authority, is taken in every land as the rule of society, the sovereign arbiter of interests, government becoming void, all the legislation of the universe will be in harmony (cited in Manuel and Manuel, pp. 374–375).

The classical economists, too, had proclaimed the cosmopolitan nature of political economy and opposed excessive government intervention in the economic world. Proudhon was very attracted to this doctrine because it offered a kind of protection of individual freedom, which he was seeking. Unlike the socialists he knew, Proudhon wished to preserve economic forces and economic institutions. At the same time, however, he wished to suppress existing conflict between these forces.

Thus property should not be eliminated, according to Proudhon, but universalized—everyone should have property, and this would be the greatest guarantee of liberty. He saw no role for the state in dividing up property, however. Instead, Proudhon thought this would be achieved through a process of rationalization, or enlightenment. His thought was always evolutionary rather than revolutionary.

Proudhon on Justice and Exchange Despite his affinity for the classical creed, Proudhon refuted the arguments of the classical economists so that their position would not be confused with his own. He detected a false promise in classical liberalism that aborted its conclusions. Classical economic liberalism relied upon the price mechanism to accomplish social ends, and Proudhon was convinced that the price mechanism was just as oppressive as law and government.

In essence, Proudhon's rejection of classical liberalism turned on one of the assumptions of the classical system. Classical economists assumed a more or less equal diffusion of economic power, whereas Proudhon saw the price mechanism as oppressive because of the extremely unequal diffusion of market power. The law of supply and demand, he claimed, is a "deceitful law...suitable only for assuring the victory of the strong over the weak, of those who own property over those who own nothing" (*On the Political Capacity of the Working Classes,* cited in Ritter, p. 121).

Presumably, Proudhon would admit the market as a method of organizing society if everyone had an equal chance to benefit from the vagaries of supply and demand. But he did not believe that all traders were equally subject to the market; hence the market could not fulfill its promise of protection for each individual's freedom to pursue his or her own goals.

In retrospect, Proudhon's criticism of economic liberalism seems unfair, since what he objected to was monopoly, not competition. In fact, he gloried in the latter. While the market itself is oppressive, Proudhon declared competition "the spice of exchange, the salt of work. To suppress competition is to suppress liberty itself" (*General Idea of the Revolution,* cited in Ritter, p. 123). Competition encourages creativity and on that account should be maintained. The task of the economist, as Proudhon saw it, was to create a more appropriate environment for competition so that its salutary effects could be recognized.

Proudhon's ideal world is one in which individuals are perfectly free to bargain with one another for all the things they want. It is a mutual society where respect, rather than authority, provides the glue that holds the social fabric together. The bargaining relation "imposes no obligation on its parties but that which results from their personal promise...it is subject to no external authority....When I bargain for some good with one or more of my fellow citizens, it is clear that then it is my will alone that is my law" (*General Idea of the Revolution,* cited in Ritter, p. 124).

In order to protect bargainers from being exploited by their rivals, Proudhon sought to equalize their power. It was with this in mind that he proposed the universalization of property and the creation of interest-free loans for all customers. To protect against trade stalemates that might result from the leveling of power relations, Proudhon encouraged social diversity, which in turn is encouraged by competition and is consistent with individual liberty. Social diversity tends to avoid economic deadlocks by increasing the incentive of traders to compromise. Nonmarket disputes (e.g., over ideology), moreover, cannot arise under true mutualism.

This mutualism of Proudhon's is another tendency that he shared with Saint-Simon. Neither trusted the egoistic practice of self-interest to spontaneously establish social harmony. Saint-Simon, however, suggested replacing traditional government with a hierarchy of experts who are best able to discern and provide for the public interest. Proudhon eschewed all forms of law, government, and hierarchy in favor of the mutualist norm of commutative justice. The duty of all bargainers in Proudhonian exchange is to give goods to one another of equal real value. Thus Proudhon would impose the same basic rule of trade as Aristotle or Aquinas (see Chapter 2). The problem with such maxims of trade (as we have seen) is that their purely subjective nature does not guarantee the viability of mutual exchange. In fairness to Proudhon, he recognized this shortcoming of his theory of exchange, but he never could adequately resolve it in a manner consistent with his other principles of liberty.

HISTORICISM

Figuratively speaking, the kind of criticism surveyed to this point put chinks in the armor of classical economics without seriously wounding the corpus of economic theory. To some extent nineteenth-century economics was a victory of reason over sentiment, although it should be pointed out that in the end, legitimate criticism tends to modify economic doctrine, even if the path to modification is long and labyrinthian. One form of methodological criticism did make significant inroads into economics, however—the historical movement that gathered steam and influence during the second half of the nineteenth century.

There were two nineteenth-century variants of historicism that impacted on economics. The German variant was prior to its English counterpart and to some extent had a different influence. German historicism constituted a milder form of criticism in the nineteenth century than Marxian economics; therefore it appears in this chapter as a backdrop to Marx's singular performance in the social sciences. The British variant of historicism was not unrelated to its German strain, but its impact was more forcefully felt on neoclassical British economics and on American institutionalism (see Chapter 17). Consequently, a more thorough discussion of British historicism is reserved for a later chapter.

Among other issues, the historicists raised the question of whether economics could be studied apart from the political, historical, and social milieu, an issue that is still debated among certain social scientists. Both William S. Jevons (see Chapter 14) and Alfred Marshall (see Chapter 15) made important concessions to the historicist point of view. Moreover, a number of the organizers of the American Economic Association (founded in 1886), in particular Richard T. Ely, its first secretary, were educated in Germany under the aegis of the historicists. The significance of the movement, therefore, should not be taken lightly, even if the major methodological issues raised by the historicists (regarding induction and deduction) were sometimes based on a misunderstanding of logical processes.

THE GERMAN HISTORICAL SCHOOL

The German historical school is often divided into two groups of writers: the "older" and less extreme school, and the "younger" school, whose views on method were more extreme and uncompromising. The older group of writers is traditionally represented by Wilhelm Roscher, its founder, Karl Knies, and Bruno Hildebrand; the younger group is dominated by the tenacious Gustav Schmoller.

Dating the origin of ideas is always a difficult (if not impossible) business, and the case of economic historicism is clearly no exception. While writers who combined an interest in economic subjects with historical research may be found throughout the history of ideas, it is clear that a coterie of them were grouping intellectually from the beginning of the fourth decade of the nineteenth century in Germany (Roscher began his historical research as early as 1842).

Several reasons exist for the subsequent supremacy of the historicist movement in Germany. First, a more favorable environment allowed historical economics to embed itself. Theoretical economics had never become firmly entrenched in Germany. As Professor Schumpeter remarked, theory in that country was an alien plant that had been transplanted by hands that were by no means especially skillful.

Second, continental, and particularly German, philosophy had always stressed an "organic" approach, as contrasted to an individualistic approach, to philosophical and social problems. Thus men of the caliber of Roscher, Knies, and Hildebrand, spurred partly by the philosophy of Hegel and by the organic jurisprudence of Frederick Karl von Savigny, were drawn into the search for a broad omnibus of economic and cultural laws that would explain the world aound them. A strained interpretation of Roscher, for example, is not required in order to find Hegelian ideas on history, which Hegel viewed as a continuous unfolding of self-revealed purpose in phenomena external to individuals. Hegel's stress upon evolving ideas as the motive force for changes in social organization is implicit in most of the German radical literature, including the historicist movement. It figures centrally in Friedrich List's doctrine of the succession of states, for example, which was developed as early as 1845. Indeed, Hegelian philosophy permeated practically all aspects of German social thought in the nineteenth century, including that of Marx and the romantics.

Wilhelm Roscher

It is unfortunate that time and a dubious reputation have cast a shadow over the mass of historicist literature. Most historians of thought pass over it in silence, while others pause to make jest over the famous (and pointless) *methodenstreit*, literally "battle of methods," between Schmoller and the leader of the Austrian school, Carl Menger (see Chapter 13). This neglect is particularly regrettable in the case of the representative and founder of the older school, Wilhelm Roscher.

Roscher was born at Hanover in 1817, and from 1835 to 1839 he studied jurisprudence and philosophy at the universities of Göttingen and Berlin. As head of the historical school, he taught at the University of Leipzig (from 1848), where he was professor of political economy. Although Roscher began his work on economic history and the historical method as early as 1838, his magnum opus was the *Principles of Political Economy (System des Volkswirtschaft),* first published in 1854.

The *Principles* reveals Roscher as a scholar of the first magnitude. In addition to writing an encyclopedic work, which encompasses all of the topics of, say, J.S. Mill's classical treatise, Roscher showed an ability as a historian of economic thought without peer in the nineteenth century. Not the least of the book's singular features is the fact that it was written as an elucidation of the historical method in economics.

As has been suggested above, the historical method attempts to combine organic, biological analysis and statistics of all kinds in order to discover the laws of the phenomenon at issue. These laws, at least in Roscher's formulation, were always *relative* to an ever-changing set of institutions. Unlike Schmoller and the more extreme historicists, Roscher did not wish to totally abandon Ricardian economics but rather to *supplement* and complete it. In a brilliant discussion of the Ricardian method, Roscher noted:

> That which is general in Political Economy has, it must be acknowledged, much that is analogous to the mathematical sciences. Like the latter, it swarms with abstractions....It also, always supposes the parties to the contract to be guided only by a sense of their own best interest, and not to be influenced by secondary considerations. It is not, therefore, to be wondered at, that many authors have endeavored to clothe the laws of Political Economy in algebraic formulae. [But]...the advantages of the mathematical model of expression diminish as the facts to which it is applied become more complicated. This is true even in the ordinary psychology of the individual. How much more, therefore, in the portraying of national life!...The abstraction according to which all men are by nature the same, different only in consequence, is one which, as Ricardo and von Thünen have shown, must pass as an indispensable stage in the preparatory labors of political economists. It would be especially well, when an economic fact is produced by the cooperation of many different factors, for the investigator to mentally isolate the factor of which, for the time being, he wishes to examine the peculiar nature. All other factors should, for a time, be considered as not operating, and as unchangeable, and then the questions asked, What would be the effect of a change in the factor to be examined, whether the change be occasioned by enlarging or diminishing it? But it never should be lost sight of, that such a one is only an abstraction after all, for which, not only in the transition to practice, but even in finished theory, we must turn to the infinite variety of real life (*Principles,* pp. 104–105).

Roscher's warnings about the abstract method have been repeated in our own time (see Leontieff, pp. 1–7). But Roscher was not willing to embrace economics as simply a set of normative, value-loaded prescriptions. Rather, in distinguishing between studies of "what is" and "what should be," Roscher clearly eschewed *normative* analysis and studies of ideal systems in his study of economics, alleging that such systems are transitory and conflicting, taking as their base different natures and social configurations.

Roscher sought to describe "what has been" and how national or social life "came to be so." As he put the matter:

> Our aim is simply to describe man's economic nature and economic wants, to investigate the laws and the character of the institutions which are adapted to the satisfaction of these wants, and the greater or less amount of success by which they have been attended. Our task is, therefore, so to speak, the anatomy and physiology of social or national economy (*Principles,* p. 111).

Within this scenario, Roscher expected to discover broad laws of historical development of which, as already noted, the Ricardian theory was only a small part. He wished, in short, to discover nothing less than the laws of socioeconomic development with which he could compare existing stages within and between nation-states.

The advantages of Roscher's method, if achieved, are obvious. He argued that "once the natural laws of Political Economy are sufficiently known and recognized, all that is needed, in any given instance, is more exact and reliable statistics of the facts involved to reconcile all party controversies on questions of the politics of public economy."

Further, the historical method would ideally secure, amid an ocean of ephemeral opinions, "a firm island of scientific truth, as universally recognized as truth as are the principles of mathematical physics by physicians of the most various schools."

To these ends Roscher (together with Knies and Hildebrand) devoted his lifework. In a prolific stream of publications, which included the 1,000-page *Principles,* Roscher set out to discern the nonseparability of economics from other phenomena. But the plain truth is that in treating the *theory* of most of the traditional topics selected—money, values, wages, etc.—Roscher presented analyses that would compare favorably with those in Mill's *Principles* (he incorporated Jevons's contributions to utility and statistics in the later edition). What was different about Roscher's work was an incredible display of historico-statistical virtuosity aimed at enlarging upon and elucidating the received economic theory.

Thus Roscher took side excursions into the construction of price indexes and, with the history of prices, into economic institutions and topics including slavery, the church, money (paper and specie), luxury, profits, insurance, population, international trade, and protection. Many of these accounts still repay careful reading, but despite Roscher's best efforts, not to mention his obviously considerable mental talent, he (and this also holds true for Knies and Hildebrand) was unable to establish any laws of historical development. He was, in short, unable to reorient the method of economics.

Gustav Schmoller

Instead of appreciating the beautiful sunset of Roscher's *Principles,* younger German economists mistakenly identified it as a sunrise. Although many writers dived into the ocean of historical research, none came close to the notorious Gustav Schmoller, leader of the younger school.

Schmoller, pushing Roscher's historicism to extremes, argued that all received economic analysis, mainly Ricardian, was not only useless but pernicious (since it led to social conclusions that were presumably not to Schmoller's taste). Schmoller drew up sharp lines of demarcation in the debate over method: he contrasted the method of the classical economists and the neoclassical Austrians (especially Menger), who were defending and employing what he regarded as abstract deductive argument, with the historico-inductive method of the German school.

Schmoller seriously proposed that received theory be completely discarded, owing to the unrealism of assumptions, to the degree of theoretical abstraction, and to the neglect of interrelated and relevant facts. The resultant gap would ultimately be filled by historical laws of development, laws that Schmoller attempted to discuss in numerous publications, including his elephantine *Grundrisse der Allgemeine Volkswirtschaftslehre* (roughly, *Outline of General Economic Theory*), the most massive attempt in the literature to capture historical laws in a systematic treatise.

Published between 1900 and 1904, Schmoller's *Grundrisse* was, as Wesley Mitchell once remarked, a "book of beginnings." Schmoller, it must be emphasized, did not believe that the determinants of the laws of history were simple, as in the Malthusian system. In other words, rather than reduce these laws to simple explanatory theories, Schmoller utilized a historical and ethnological approach to such topics as medieval institutions (especially the guild system), urban development, banking, and industry studies. As Schumpeter noted, the Schmollerian economist was essentially a historically minded sociologist. An attempt was made to study economics organically. Economic issues were not simply logical issues but took on the broadest possible context.

While the older school of German historicists questioned the absolutism of economic theory, the younger school rejected theory altogether. In the extreme to which Schmoller took the doctrine, historicism was antirationalist. It refused to derive general rules from reason, insisting instead on observing and recording the unique in its infinite historical variation. Thus it offered no principles to guide or restrain human action. Historicism was a well without a spring to feed it.

Such theoretical antagonism was bound to stir up controversy sooner or later, and when it came, the controversy was hottest and heaviest in Germany. The first blow in the famous *methodenstreit* (battle of methods) was struck by the Austrian economist Carl Menger (see Chapter 13) at a time when historicism was nearing high tide. In 1883, Menger published a book on methodology that confronted the fundamental problems of procedure in the social sciences and attempted to vindicate the rights of theoretical analysis while putting

Schmoller's school in its proper place. Schmoller struck back in an unfavorable review of the book. Menger took the offensive again in a pamphlet entitled the *Errors of Historicism* (1884), which elicited a predictable rebuttal from Schmoller. These events not only provoked much ill will but also unleashed a flood of literature that took decades to subside.

It is not our intention to delve deeply into the intricacies of this famous quarrel, which involved personalities and intellectual preferences as well as methodological substance. Much of the fight amounted to tilting at windmills, since it was an argument over precedence and the relative importance of theory versus history. Although the entire episode may yet prove a fertile ground for historians of economic thought to plow, we tentatively agree with Schumpeter's judgment that "since there cannot be any serious question either about the basic importance of historical research in a science that deals with a historical process or about the necessity of developing a set of analytic tools by which to handle the material, the controversy, like all such controversies, might well...have been wholly pointless (*History of Economic Analysis,* p. 814).

CONCLUSION

During the nineteenth century many diverse ideas were launched that affected economics as a discipline and challenged the hegemony of British economic thought and analysis. The first half of the century, particularly, witnessed a substantial number of salvos leveled at classical economics. Some observers may feel that the criticisms of evolutionists, radicals, and reformers were on target; yet it is not easy to gauge their full effect on economic analysis even in retrospect. It is clear, however, that what was missing in all the intellectual ferment of the nineteenth century was a truly scientific "engine of analysis." Near the middle of the century one writer undertook to fill this void. His name was Karl Marx.

It is significant that German historicism and Marxian economics were outgrowths of the same root of Hegelian philosophy. Hegel considered history the proper approach to the science of society, a theme sounded loudly by Marx as well as the historicists. Hegel's peculiar view of liberty, however, was submission to the authority of the state, a view Marx did not share. As we shall see in the next chapter, Marx's theory anticipated the withering away of the state. Most of the German historicists, however, exalted the nation and the work of the government; they were better Hegelians than Marx in this regard.

On the practical side, German historicists promoted a "social policy" of ameliorating the condition of the working class. They envisioned a kind of "people's capitalism" in which workers obtained a proprietary interest in industry. Their views were therefore compatible with the welfare state that Bismarck undertook when he came to power in Germany near the turn of the century. It was on the intellectual front that their failures were most obvious. Not only did they fail to discover the laws of historical development; they also failed in their attempt to establish a historical method. Although they strongly supported fact-finding, their quantitative data were not assembled in such a way as to verify economic theory but rather to speak for themselves. This was a futile undertaking because there can be no meaningful measurement without theory.

The question of balance between theory and facts is a delicate one, however, no less so today than it was a century ago. A clear implication of the historicist doctrine is that some theories might be "empty" in the sense that they have no empirical foundation or content. Roscher, perhaps more than any member of the German historical school, seemed aware of the symbiotic nature of theory and facts. He noted:

> It is evident, that, of statistics in general, economic statistics constitute a chief part, and precisely the part most accessible to numerical treatment. As these economic statistics need to be always directed by the light of Political Economy, they also furnish it with rich materials for the continuation of its structure, and for the strengthening of such foundations as it already has. They are, moreover, the indispensable condition of the application of economic theorems to practice (*Principles*, pp. 94–95).

Not so very long ago a similar concern was expressed by Wassily Leontieff in his presidential address to the American Economic Association. Leontieff warned that "the weak and all too slowly growing empirical foundation [of economics] clearly cannot support the proliferating superstructure of pure, or should I say, speculative, economic theory" ("Theoretical Assumptions and Nonobserved Facts," p. 1). It is almost as though Leontieff (who has since become a Nobel laureate) was warning that contemporary economic theory may yet have to pay dearly for neglecting the saner and less extreme messages of the historicist doctrine.

NOTES FOR FURTHER READING

Three articles in particular form a useful backdrop for this chapter. See W. D. Grampp, "Classical Economics and Its Moral Critics," *History of Political Economy,* vol. 5 (Fall 1973), pp. 359–374; T. E. Kaiser, "Politics and Political Economy in the Thought of the Ideologues," *History of Political Economy,* vol. 12 (Summer 1980), pp. 141–160; and C. C. Ryan, "The Friends of Commerce: Romantic and Marxist Criticisms of Classical Political Economy," *History of Political Economy,* vol. 13 (Spring 1981), pp. 80–94. General surveys of socialist thought deserving of attention are Alexander Gray, *The Socialist Tradition: Moses to Lenin* (London: Longmans, 1946); G. D. H. Cole, *A History of Socialist Thought,* 5 vols. (New York: St. Martin's, 1953–1960); and George Lichtheim, *The Origins of Socialism* (New York: Praeger, 1969). Gray is particularly strong on the economic aspects of socialist thought, and Lichtheim concentrates on socialist thought before Marx. Robert Heilbroner's ever-popular *Worldly Philosophers,* 4th ed. (New York: Simon and Schuster, 1972), contains a delightful chapter on the utopian socialists.

A noteworthy survey of evolutionist ideas is presented in Henryk Grossman's two-part article "The Evolutionist Revolt against Classical Economics," *Journal of Political Economy,* vol. 51 (October, December 1943), pp. 381–390, 506–522. Part I discusses the ideas of Condorcet, Saint-Simon, and Sismondi; part II treats the ideas of James Steuart, Richard Jones, and Karl Marx.

Saint-Simon is given considerable space in Elie Halévy's *Era of Tyrannies,* R. K. Webb (trans.) (Garden City, N.Y.: Anchor Books, Doubleday and Company, Inc., 1965), and is the subject of a full-scale treatment both by Emile Durkheim, a sociologist, in *Socialism and Saint-Simon,* A. W. Gouldner (ed.) and C. Sattler (trans.) (Yellow Springs, Ohio: Antioch Press, 1958), and by Frank Manuel, a historian, in *The New World of Henri Saint-Simon* (Cambridge, Mass.: Harvard University Press, 1962). E. S. Mason has pointed out the relevance of Saint-Simon's ideas to twentieth-century capitalism in "Saint-Simonism and the Rationalisation of Industry," *Quarterly Journal of Economics,* vol. 45 (August 1931), pp. 640–683. Some of the same themes are underlined by Niles Hansen in "Saint-Simon's Industrial Society in Modern Perspective," *Southwestern Social Science Quarterly,* vol. 47 (December 1966), pp. 253–262. Most of Saint-Simon's published works are in French; however, a number of translations appear in *Social Organization, the Science of Man, and Other Writings,* F. M. H. Markham (ed.) (New York: Harper & Row, 1964), which also contains a useful introduction. Another source of English translations is *The Doctrine of Saint-Simon: An Exposition. First Year, 1828–1829,* G. G. Iggers (trans.) (Boston: Beacon Press, 1958). F. A. Hayek offers a distinctly unsympathetic treatment of Saint-Simon and his ideas in *The Counter-Revolution of Science: Studies in the Abuse of Reason* (New York: Free Press, 1955).

A collection of Sismondi's essays appears in *Political Economy and the Philosophy of Government* (New York: A. M. Kelley, Publishers 1965 [1847]), but some of his works (e.g., *Nouveaux principes*) have never been translated into English. Another selection of texts available in English translation appears in Henry W. Spiegel (ed.), *The Development of Economic Thought* (New York: Wiley, 1952, pp. 253–268). On Sismondi as an economist, see Mao-Lan Tuan, *Simonde de Sismondi as an Economist* (New York: Columbia University Press, 1927); and Thomas Sowell, "Sismondi: A Neglected Pioneer," *History of Political Economy,* vol. 4 (Spring 1972), pp. 62–88. V. I. Lenin sought to refute Sismondi's ideas in *A Characterization of Economic Romanticism* (Moscow: Foreign Languages Publishing House, 1951 [1897]).

Friedrich List's ideas were readily received by American protectionists in the nineteenth century, but the American position had already been staked out much earlier by Alexander Hamilton in his *Report on the Subject of Manufactures* (1791), which has been reprinted in A. H. Cole (ed.), *Industrial and Commercial Correspondence of Alexander Hamilton* (New York: A. M. Kelley, Publishers, 1968). Margaret E. Hirst, *Life of Friedrich List and Selections from His Writings* (London: Smith, Elder and Co., 1909), includes excerpts

from List's *Outlines of American Political Economy,* which was written on behalf of the American protectionists during List's visit to the United States. Additional references to List's works can be found in Henry W. Spiegel, *The
Growth of Economic Thought* (Englewood Cliffs, N.J.: Prentice-Hall, 1971).

The most important writings of Robert Owen are contained in *A New View
of Society and Other Writings* (New York: Everyman's Library, Dutton,
1927). The standard biography is Frank Podmore, *Robert Owen: A Biography*
(New York: Appleton, 1906). E. R. A. Seligman's *Essays in Economics* (New
York: Macmillan, 1925) contains an essay entitled "Owen and the Christian
Socialists."

Many of Fourier's writings have not been translated into English, although
exceptions are to be found in *Design for Utopia: Selected Writings of Charles
Fourier,* Julia Franklin (trans.) (New York: Schocken Books, 1981), and *The
Utopian Vision of Charles Fourier: Selected Tracts on Work, Love, and Pas-
sionate Attraction,* J. Beecher and R. Bienvenu (eds. and trans.) (Boston: Bea-
con Press, 1971). Good coverage of Fourier's ideas is provided in N. V.
Riasanovsky, *The Teachings of Charles Fourier* (Berkeley: University of
California Press, 1970); E. S. Mason's "Fourier and Anarchism," *Quarterly
Journal of Economics,* vol. 42 (1928), pp. 228–262, repays a careful reading,
even at this late date.

Several works of Proudhon have now been translated, including *What Is
Property?,* B. R. Tucker (trans.) (New York: H. Fertig, 1966); *General Idea of
the Revolution in the Nineteenth Century,* J. B. Robinson (trans.) (London:
Freedom Press, 1923); and part of *The Philosophy of Poverty,* which appears
under the title *System of Economic Contradictions: or the Philosophy of Poverty,* B. R. Tucker (trans.) (Princeton, Mass.: B. R. Tucker, 1888). A group of
articles on banking and other topics make up Proudhon's *Solution of the Social Problem,* Henry Cohen (ed.) (New York: Vanguard, 1927). Biographical
information is included in George Woodcock's *Pierre-Joseph Proudhon* (New
York: Macmillan, 1956) and in J. H. Jackson's *Marx, Proudhon and European
Socialism* (New York: Macmillan, n.d.), which also details the relation between the two leading socialists of the mid-nineteenth century.

Other articles on Proudhon present diverse views, ranging from J. S.
Shapiro's "Pierre Joseph Proudhon: Harbinger of Fascism," *American Historical Review,* vol. 50 (July 1945), pp. 714–737, to Dudley Dillard's "Keynes
and Proudhon," *Journal of Economic History,* vol. 2 (May 1942), pp. 63–76.
The latter compares Proudhon favorably with Keynes. For an early example of
utopian, anarchistic thought in America, see B. N. Hall, "The Economics of
Josiah Warren, First American Anarchist," *History of Political Economy,* vol.
6 (February 1974), pp. 95–108.

T. W. Hutchison discusses German historicism, both the "older" and
"younger" schools, in his *Review of Economic Doctrines, 1870–1929,* (Oxford: The Clarendon Press, 1953); chaps. 8 and 12 and again in "Some Themes
from Investigation into Method," in J. R. Hicks and W. Weber, *Carl Menger
and the Austrian School of Economics* (London: Oxford University Press,

1973). On Schmoller and the later historicists, see Ben B. Seligman, *Main Currents in Modern Economics,* chap. 1 (New York: Free Press, 1962); and W. C. Mitchell, *Types of Economic Theory,* chap. 19 (New York: A. M. Kelley, 1969). Mitchell's assessment of the *methodenstreit* is especially interesting. For a different and more modern view of the famous controversy, see Sam Bostaph, "The Methodological Debate between Carl Menger and the German Historicists," *Atlantic Economic Journal,* vol. 6 (September 1978), pp. 3–16. A sympathetic view of the historical school and its contributions, in particular the positive accomplishments of a single member of the younger school, is presented by A. Schweitzer in "Typological Method in Economics: Max Weber's Contribution," *History of Political Economy,* vol. 2 (Spring 1970), pp. 66–99. It is very difficult to lead the non-German-speaking, nonmethodologically minded through the morass of arguments that collectively constitutes the *methodenstreit.* The Mengerian position was reiterated by E. Böhm-Bawerk in "The Historical vs. the Deductive Method in Political Economy," *Annals of the American Academy of Political and Social Science,* vol. 1 (October 1890), pp. 244–271. J. A. Schumpeter provides a useful and perceptive overview of the stage and its actors in his *History* (see References), pp. 800–824. Finally, those interested in methodology should consult Felix Kaufman's *Methodology of the Social Sciences* (New York: Oxford University Press, 1944). A sympathetic treatment of the German historical school that concentrates on the group's contributions to the theory of economic policy and pattern modeling is contained in H. K. Betz, "How Does the German Historical School Fit?" *History of Political Economy,* vol. 20 (Fall 1988), pp. 409–430.

REFERENCES

Beer, Max. *A History of British Socialism,* 2 vols. London: G. Allen, 1953.

Condorcet, Marquis de Marie-Jean. *Esquisses d'un tableau historique des progres de l'esprit humain.* Paris: 1795.

Gide, Charles, and Charles Rist. *A History of Economic Doctrines from the Time of the Physiocrats to the Present Day,* 2d ed., R. Richards (trans.). Boston: Heath, 1948.

Leontieff, Wassily. "Theoretical Assumptions and Nonobserved Facts." *American Economic Review,* vol. 61 (March 1971), pp. 1–7.

List, Friedrich. *The National System of Political Economy,* S. S. Lloyd (trans.). New York: Longmans, 1928 [1841].

Manuel, F. E., and F. P. Manuel (eds.). *French Utopias: An Anthology of Ideal Societies.* New York: Free Press, 1966.

Morton, A. L. *The Life and Ideas of Robert Owen.* New York: Monthly Review Press, 1963.

Ritter, Allan. *The Political Thought of Pierre-Joseph Proudhon.* Princeton, N.J.: Princeton University Press, 1969.

Roscher, Wilhelm. *Principles of Political Economy.* New York: 1878 [1854].

Saint-Simon, Henri. *Oeuvres de Saint-Simon et d'Enfantin,* 47 vols. Aalen: Otto Zeller, 1963.

Schumpeter, J. A. *History of Economic Analysis,* E. B. Schumpeter (ed.). New York: Oxford University Press, 1954.

Sismondi, J. C. L. Simonde de. *De la richesse commerciale, ou principes d'économie politiques appliquées à la legislation du commerce*, 2 vols. Geneva: 1803.

———. *Nouveaux principes d'économie politique*, 2d ed., 2 vols. Paris: Delaunay, 1827.

———. *Études sur l'économie politique*, 2 vols. Paris: 1836.

Smith, Adam. *The Wealth of Nations*, Edwin Cannan (ed.). New York: Modern Library, 1937.

CHAPTER 11

KARL MARX AND "SCIENTIFIC SOCIALISM"

INTRODUCTION

Although he was spurred by the same social concerns as writers discussed in the preceding chapter, Karl Marx commands separate treatment for two main reasons: (1) He fashioned an entire system of scientific thought largely on his own, and (2) he is unquestionably one of the most influential writers in all of economics and in the western world. Indeed, his spirit is more alive today in the hearts and minds of human beings than it was in the last century, when Marx toiled long hours over his many manuscripts.

This chapter examines Marx's contributions to economics, while recognizing that they are intricately bound to his views of history and society. It therefore attempts to explore all three insofar as is necessary to aid our understanding of the Marxian system.

MARX'S LIFE AND WORKS

The man whose ideas changed half the world was born at Trier, Prussia, in 1818. He was the son of middle-class Jewish parents who later converted to Christianity. Marx's youth was spent happily enough—he was popular with his playmates and enjoyed an unusually pleasant relationship with his father. At the age of seventeen, young Marx entered the University of Bonn as a law student. Although he had a sharp mind, Marx's application to his studies suffered from the distractions of youth. He attended class rarely, and he seemed during his first year at Bonn to sow a great many wild oats. Consequently, his first year as an undergraduate at Bonn was also his last. Disappointed with his son's academic performance, Marx's father withdrew him from the school the following year and enrolled him at the University of Berlin, where the "party-school" atmosphere of the University of Bonn was totally absent. During the continuance of his training in jurisprudence and political economy at Berlin, Marx came under the influence of Hegel and Feuerbach, whose ideas helped shape his own views of history, religion, and society.

Having completed his Ph.D. dissertation at the University of Jena in 1841, Marx moved back to Bonn, hoping to secure a teaching position at the university he had formerly attended. He abandoned this hope in 1842 and assumed the editorship of the *Rheinische Zeitung,* a German newspaper in which he could air his somewhat unorthodox ideas and indulge his desire to acquaint himself with the literature of the French socialists. Strict censorship imposed on the *Rheinische Zeitung* in 1843 led to Marx's resignation as editor. After a June wedding to his childhood sweetheart (Jenny von Westphalen), he moved to Paris and undertook the founding of a new journal—the *Deutsch-Französische Jarbucher.* All the while Marx continued to write, though mostly on philosophical topics. It was in Paris, however, that he began a systematic study of economics, especially of Smith and Ricardo. There, too, he studied the materialist philosophers, including Locke, he became acquainted with Proudhon, and he began to distill most of his major ideas. His most active literary decade was yet to come, but in 1844 Marx wrote a number of manuscripts, which were later collected and published as *Economic and Philosophic Manuscripts of 1844.*

Meanwhile, Marx was without honor in his own country. The Prussian government declared him guilty of treason in 1844 for his articles in the *Jarbucher,* thus making it impossible for him to return to his homeland. The following year, under instigation from Prussia, France also expelled Marx. He fled to Brussels, where, in due course, his *Theses on Feuerbach* (1845), *The German Ideology* (1846, with Engels), and *The Poverty of Philosophy* (1847) were published—the last a scathing critique of Proudhon's earlier *Philosophy of Poverty.* In 1847 Marx gave a series of lectures, which were later published as *Wage Labour and Capital* (1849). *The Communist Manifesto* followed in 1848, and in 1849 Marx and his family settled in London, where he was to stay for the rest of his life, most of which was spent writing and studying economics in the library of the British Museum. In 1851, Marx entered a ten-year period as occasional contributor to the *New York Daily Tribune,* whose fees helped to sustain his family's meager existence.

Beginning in 1857, a veritable sea of ink spewed from Marx's pen. In that year alone he prepared a lengthy critique of political economy that was to serve as an outline for his later magnum opus. Now known as the *Grundrisse,* these manuscripts were undiscovered and unpublished until the World War II period. *A Contribution to the Critique of Political Economy* was begun in 1858 and finished the following year. By 1863, Marx had also completed *Theories of Surplus Value.* The first volume of *Capital* appeared in 1867, but Marx died in 1883, before the second and third volumes could be published. The latter appeared under the editorship of Marx's lifetime friend and collaborator,

Friedrich Engels. Engels himself died in 1895, only a year after the publication of the third and final volume of *Capital*.

The details of Marx's personal life reveal the disconsolateness of all kinds of adversity, including abject poverty and tormenting political exile. Certainly, Marx could be bitter about his personal trials. He made no effort to hide his bitterness when, near the end of his life, he wrote acidly: "I hope the bourgeoisie will remember my carbuncles all the rest of their lives!" It is no surprise, then, that Marx is frequently portrayed as a sullen, brooding genius. But this characterization obscures one of the most remarkable things about the man—his extraordinary success, despite adversity, in the personal relationships that matter most. His love for his wife, and hers for him, was enduring and uncompromising. His children adored him as he, too, had loved and admired his own father. Carbuncles notwithstanding, Karl Marx had, by several criteria, a very fruitful life.

OVERVIEW OF THE MARXIAN SYSTEM

What one finds in Marx's mature thought is a theory of historical processes, based on material and economic forces and culminating in social and economic change of the existing order. In contrast to the overt, intellectual specialization of a later day, Marx's thought ranged over philosophy, history, and economics. As a philosopher and historian he was steeped in, but not a part of, the German tradition. As an economist he was likewise steeped in, but not a part of, the British classical tradition.

Hegel, Feuerbach, and German Philosophy

The dominant figure in German philosophy during the nineteenth century was Georg Hegel (1770–1831), whose ideas influenced not only Marx but also the German historicists (see Chapter 10). For Marx, at least, the fascinating aspect of Hegel's philosophy was his theory of progress. According to Hegel, history holds the key to the science of society. History is not a sequence of accidental occurrences or a collection of disconnected stories; rather, it is an organic process guided by the human spirit. It is not smoothly continuous, but instead is the outcome of opposing forces. Progress obtains, according to Hegel, when one force is confronted by its opposite. In the struggle, both are annihilated and are transcended by a third force. This so-called dialectic has frequently been summarized, conceptually, by the interplay of "thesis," "antithesis," and "synthesis." Following Hegel, historical progress occurs when an idea, or thesis, is confronted by an opposing idea, or antithesis. In the battle of ideas, neither one remains intact, but both are synthesized into a third; this is how all general knowledge, as well as history, advances.

As Marx matured, he criticized Hegel on several grounds, but he nevertheless adopted the Hegelian dialectic. He modified it, however, in light of Ludwig Feuerbach's doctrine of materialism. Feuerbach was no less a

Hegelian than Marx, but in his *Essence of Christianity,* written ten years after Hegel's death, he extended Hegel's concept of "self-alienation" in a radical direction. Feuerbach added "materialism"—the idea that humans are not only "species beings," as Hegel asserted, but also sensuous beings and that sense perception must therefore become the basis of all science. According to Feuerbach, all history is the process of preparing humans to become the object of "conscious," rather than "unconscious" activity.

In religion Feuerbach saw one area where unconscious activity predominates. Religion is the mere projection of idealized human attributes onto an otherworldly object (i.e., God). This supernatural object is then worshipped by humans as all-powerful, all-knowing, and all-perfect. As a self-proclaimed "realist," Feuerbach considered religion unreal. He regarded the attributes of the divinity as nothing more than the *idealized* attributes of humans, which, of course, cannot be realized in this imperfect world. In other words, religion makes life bearable. Humans are willing to accept their imperfect, earthly existence only because they unconsciously promise themselves perfection in another world. To Feuerbach, it was obvious why religion is such a universal phenomenon.[1]

In view of this analysis, Feuerbach perceived religion as a form of self-alienation. He and Marx both used the term "alienation" to refer to a process—and a result—of converting the products of individual and social activity into something apart from themselves, both independent of them and dominant over them. However, Feuerbach confined his analysis to the way in which humans alienate themselves in religion and in philosophy, whereas Marx applied the concept to all manner of political and economic activity, including the very institutions of capitalism. In Marx, for the first time, the state joins hands with God as an alien being. It derives its power and its existence from the fact that human beings are either incapable or unwilling to face head-on the problems that confront them in daily social interaction with one another. Over time, this monolithic structure called the "state" increases its power over people's lives, simply because they allow it to do so.

Marx's Economic Interpretation of History

With the above background we can now begin to appreciate the innovational character of Marx's thought. Grafting Feuerbach's materialism to Hegel's dialectic, Marx developed a "dialectical materialism," which he then extended to the economic realm. Marx considered the prime mover of history to be the way in which individuals make a living, that is, the way in which they satisfy their material needs. This is important because unless their material needs are satisfied, human beings would cease to exist. In Marx's words, "Men must

---

[1] Marx's acceptance of this view underlies his description of religion as "the opiate of the masses."

be able to live in order to 'make history,'" therefore, "The first historical act is...the production of the means to satisfy these needs, the production of material life itself" (*The German Ideology,* cited in *Writings of the Young Marx,* p. 419).

Production, of course, is not only a historical act but an economic one as well, and it is part of the uniqueness of Marx that he clearly understood and appreciated the interrelations between economics and history. In fact, Marx's identification and exposition of production as the focal and driving force from among the mutually conditioning forces of production, distribution, exchange, and consumption are what distinguished his own economics from that existing up to his time. In Marx, economics became the *science of production.*

Production is a social force insofar as it channels human activity into useful ends. But Marx asserted that methods of production help to shape human nature itself. In one of his earlier works he wrote:

> The way in which men produce their means of subsistence depends first of all on the nature of the actual means they find in existence and have to reproduce. This mode of production must not be considered simply as being the reproduction of the physical existence of the individuals. Rather it is a definite form of activity of these individuals, a definite form of expressing their life, a definite *mode of life* on their part. As individuals express their life, so they are. What they are, therefore, coincides with their production, both with *what* they produce and with *how* they produce. The nature of individuals thus depends on the material conditions determining their production (*The German Ideology,* cited in *Precapitalist Economic Formations,* p. 121).

Marx recognized, as Adam Smith did, that the development of productive forces in every economy depends upon the degree to which the division of labor is carried. But unlike Smith, Marx saw a conflict of interests as the logical outcome of the progressive division of labor. The division of labor leads first to separation of industrial and commercial labor from agricultural labor and hence to separation of town and country. Next it leads to the separation of industrial from commercial labor, and finally to a division among workers within each kind of labor. Thus further conflict arises: individual interests contradict community interests, and each worker becomes "chained" to a specific job. Eventually humans' labor becomes an alien power, opposed to them and enslaving them.

Out of this conflict between individual interests and community interests Marx saw the emergence of the state as an independent power, a power divorced from the real interests of the individual and the community. Yet the state owes its being to the social classes already determined by the division of labor. Each class in power seeks to promote its own interest as the general community interest. However, the community perceives this class interest as an alien force over which it has no control.

The situation becomes intolerable when two conditions are fulfilled: First, the great mass of humanity must be rendered propertyless while simultaneously being confronted with the contradiction of an existing world of wealth and culture. Both these factors presuppose a great increase in productive power and a high degree of its development, as under mature capitalism. Second, the development of productive forces must be universal. As a practical premise, the phenomenon of the "propertyless" class must be of worldwide proportions; otherwise, revolution and communism could exist only as local events, not as universal realities.

Static versus Dynamic Forces in Society

What Marx called the "forces of production," developed in the modern age through division of labor, are essentially dynamic. They consist of land, labor, capital, and technology, each of which is constantly changing in quantity and/ or quality as a result of changes in population, discovery, innovation, education, and so on. In the course of production of their social life, however, humans enter into certain "definite relations that are indispensable and independent of their will, relations of production which correspond to a definite stage of development of their material productive forces." These "rules of the capitalist game" are essentially static and consist of two types: *property* relations and *human* relations. Property relations exist between people and things; human relations exist between people. According to Marx, it is the sum total of these relations that constitutes the economic structure of society and upon which is superimposed a legal and political superstructure corresponding to definite forms of social consciousness. Every aspect of the socioeconomic structure owes its origin to the relations of production simply because institutions exist in order to make humans conform to the relations of production.

Figure 11-1 provides a simple schematic summary of Marx's theory of society. As the division of labor is pushed to its logical conclusion, labor becomes increasingly fragmented. The ensuing conflicts of interest are further aggravated by the institution of private property, which ensures the splitting up of accumulated capital among different owners and thus the division between capital and labor. In terms of Figure 11-1, the dynamic *forces* of production come into conflict with the static *relations* of production. Once this conflict reaches a sufficient pitch, class struggle and revolution occur, and the pyramid of society tumbles, from top to bottom.

Marx succinctly summarized the dynamic process of social change determined by the forces of production in his preface to *A Contribution to the Critique of Political Economy:*

> The mode of production of material life determines the character of the social, political, and spiritual processes of life. It is not the consciousness of men that determines their existence, but on the contrary, their social existence that determines their consciousness. At a certain stage of their development, the material forces of production in society come in conflict with the existing relations of production, or—what is but a legal expression for the same thing—with the property relations within which they have been at work before. From forms of development of the forces of production these relations turn into their fetters. Then comes the period of social revolution. With the change of the economic foundation the entire immense superstructure is more or less rapidly transformed.

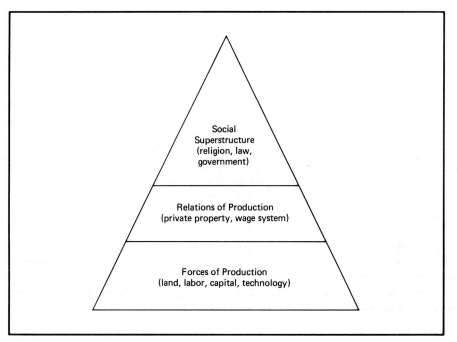

FIGURE 11-1
Marx's "social pyramid," in which the structure of society owes its origin to the basic facts of economic production.

No social order ever disappears before all the productive forces, for which there is room in it, have been developed; and new higher relations of production never appear before the material conditions of their existence have matured in the womb of the old society.... The bourgeois relations of production are the last antagonistic form of the social process of production—antagonistic not in the sense of individual antagonism, but of one arising from conditions surrounding the life of individuals in society; at the same time the productive forces developing in the womb of bourgeois society create the material conditions for the solution of that antagonism (*Critique of Political Economy*, pp. 20–21).

All this is, of course, more than a theory of economics; it is a theory of history, politics, and sociology as well. However, Marx's greatest work, *Capital*, is clearly an analysis of capitalism, not of socialism or communism. Nevertheless, a full understanding of the dynamics of that analysis would be extremely difficult were one not first aware of the Marxian theory of how social change comes about.

MARX'S EARLY WRITINGS ON CAPITALIST PRODUCTION

The Economic and Philosophical Manuscripts of 1844

Shortly after he moved to Paris in 1843, Marx began a critical study of political economy. In 1844, he completed several manuscripts, which were apparently

intended to be a major part of a forthcoming book. The book never material-
ized, however, and the manuscripts lay unpublished for more than eighty
years. When a full edition of these extant works was published in 1932 under
the title *Economic and Philosophic Manuscripts of 1844,* the occasion generated much excitement among Marxian scholars and some reinterpretation of
Marx's later works. Contrary to some interpretations, we find a basic continuity between Marx's early writings and *Capital,* although by the time he
wrote the latter, Marx had abandoned the metaphysical concepts that he had
initially acquired from the German philosophers in favor of a more empirical
analysis.

The central theme of the *Manuscripts* is that history, especially under modern capitalism, is the saga of alienation in people's lives as producers and that
communism, achieved through a revolution against private property, is the final escape from alienation. Although he had not worked out the labor theory of
value, Marx already expressed in the *Manuscripts* the idea that labor is the
source of all wealth. The empirical observation is also there that the worker
gets only a small part of this wealth, barely enough to continue working. The
lion's share of the product of labor goes to the capitalist, and this leads to a
bitter struggle between capital and labor. In this struggle the aim of the capitalist, who has all the advantages, is to keep wages to a minimum. Labor becomes a mere commodity under capitalism, and all human relations are soon
reduced to money relations. In these relations, the capitalist inevitably is enriched at the expense of the worker, who lives at a subsistence level.

In an early analysis of profit, also found in the *Manuscripts,* Marx noted a
trend toward monopoly concentration of capital into fewer and fewer hands.
This trend leads to an increase in total profits and an increase in the total misery of the working class. Marx theorized that eventually the contradictions
within the capitalist system would lead to its demise, thus opening the way for
humans to become truly free. All these ideas reappear in Marx's more mature
works, although, as might be expected, they are worked out with more precision and detail there.

What the *Manuscripts* of 1844 do not contain is a penetrating analysis of the
real contradictions of capitalism—one must look to *Capital* for that. But they
do contain a fairly mature statement of methodological criticism aimed at political economy. The following passage is an example:

> Political economy proceeds from the fact of private property, but does not explain it
> to us. It expresses in general, abstract formulas the *material* process through which
> private property actually passes, and these formulas it then takes for *laws.* It does
> not *comprehend* these laws—i.e., it does not demonstrate how they arise from the
> very nature of private property. Political economy does not disclose the source of
> the division between labour and capital, and between capital and land. When, for
> example, it defines the relationship of wages to profit, it takes the interest of the
> capitalists to be the ultimate cause; i.e., it takes for granted what it is supposed to
> explain. Similarly, competition comes in everywhere [but] it is explained from ex-
> ternal circumstances. As to how far these external and apparently accidental cir-
> cumstances are but the expression of a necessary course of development, political

economy teaches us nothing...to it, exchange itself appears to be an accidental fact. The only wheels which political economy sets in motion are *greed* and the *war amongst the greedy—competition (Manuscripts,* pp. 106–107).

Clearly, Marx criticized economists for not explaining (understanding?) the underlying *causes* of capitalism; in his view it was simply not enough to understand the mere workings of markets. One must also know how the market mechanism came about and where it was going. Marx felt it essential to grasp the connection between, as he put it: "private property, avarice, and the separation of labour, capital, and landed property; between exchange and competition, value and the devaluation of men, monopoly and competition, etc.; the connection between this whole estrangement and the money system."

Moreover, Marx attempted in the *Manuscripts* to criticize political economy on the basis of *real social contradictions* that he had empirically observed. The basic contradiction underlined by Marx is that "The worker becomes all the poorer the more wealth he produces...[he] becomes an ever cheaper commodity the more commodities he creates." The devaluation of workers, in other words, proceeds in direct proportion to the increasing value of commodities, and in the process workers confront the objects of their labor (commodities) as things outside themselves, things that, once completed, they have no control over or ownership of—as *alien* things, a power independent of its producer. This idea, of course—that labor is by its very nature the externalizing of a human capacity—Marx got from Hegel. But he now criticized economics for concealing the alienation inherent in the nature of labor by not considering the direct relation *between the worker and production.* This relation, so assiduously analyzed by Marx, is the hallmark of Marxian economics and is the feature that distinguishes it from classical economics.

The Grundrisse (1857–1858)

The *Manuscripts* of 1844 represent an initial foray into economic criticism by the young Marx. They do not have the polish or incisiveness of the later *Capital.* But in the ensuing years, Marx perfected the tools of analysis that he inherited from the classical economists. By 1858 he had accumulated a number of manuscripts that collectively might be considered an outline and draft version of the technical arguments later used in *Capital.* This collection of papers, only recently brought to light and published during World War II, bears the title *Grundrisse der Kritik der Politischen Ökonomie (Outlines of the Critique of Political Economy).* Only fragments of the *Grundrisse* have been translated into English, but they reveal some things that are not included in *Capital,* such as a discussion of precapitalist systems and a study of the interrelations of the component parts of capitalism (e.g., production, distribution, exchange, and consumption).

Marx criticized his predecessors in economics for their basically ahistorical view of production. In the *Grundrisse,* he sought to relate the process of production to the stage of social development in society. He particularly took issue with Mill's position that production—as opposed to distribution—is subject to immutable laws independent of history (see Chapter 8). His own view, of course, was that production takes place within a social context and can be undertaken only by social individuals and at a certain stage of social development. Moreover, every form of production creates its own legal relations and forms of government. Marx concluded that the so-called general conditions of production espoused by the classical economists were nothing more than abstract concepts that together did not make up any real stage in the history of production.

These abstract concepts make it possible, in Marx's view, for economics to deal with the true nature of capitalist production. The true nature of capitalist production involves the study of labor as basic to production, the analysis of the historical bases of capitalist production, and examination of the fundamental conflict between bourgeoisie and proletariat. In the *Grundrisse*, Marx began to weave together these ideas. He perfected the labor theory of value and the theories of surplus value and of money. The following year, in *A Contribution to the Critique of Political Economy*, Marx developed the thesis that the conflict between the development of the productive forces and the relations of production provides the driving force of social revolutions. Thus by 1860, the foundation was set for Marx's crowning achievement, the first volume of which appeared in 1867.

THE NATURE OF CAPITALISM

The purpose of much of the foregoing has been to establish that by the time Marx was ready to write *Capital*, he had certain clear-cut objectives in mind—objectives that were consistent with his dialectical view of history. Specifically, Marx had to show (1) how the commodity form of market exchange leads to class conflict and exploitation of the labor force, (2) how the commodity system will eventually fail to operate because of its own inherent contradictions, and (3) why the class conflict under capitalism, unlike class conflicts under earlier economic systems, should ultimately result in rule by the formerly exploited class rather than by a new ruling class.

Marx understood capitalism to be an economic system in which people make a living by buying and selling things (i.e., commodities). According to Marx, four properties distinguish commodities. Commodities are (1) useful, (2) produced by human labor, (3) offered for sale in the market, and (4) separable from the individual who produced them. In *Capital*, Marx set out to analyze the production and distribution of commodities. Such an explanation would indeed be empty without a theory of value, and Marx, who was well grounded in classical economics, turned to Smith and Ricardo on this point.

The Labor Theory of Value

After a careful review of classical economic literature and an intellectual process of logical exclusion, Marx arrived at *labor* as the essence of all value. To him, value was an *objective* property of each and every commodity. It therefore had to be rooted in something more substantial than the "superficial" market forces of supply and demand. In fact, Marx could not have been impressed by purely subjective valuations (by utility comparisons, for example), since philosophically he was a materialist and therefore held that material relations alone determine value. He also believed that these relations determine value *prior* to the determination of price, so that price reflects merely a value caused by the purely objective element common to all commodities—labor.

Contradiction in Classical Value Theory? We have seen that classical economics contained not one but two theories of exchange value: the short-run determination of price by supply and demand and the long-run theory of "natural price," or cost of production. Marx sensed the contradiction in this. The theory of natural price holds that price is invariant in the long run, whereas even casual observation reveals that market prices fluctuate constantly. Now if such fluctuations are the result of mere chance, then so too are economic crises, and Marx's theory of dialectical materialism collapses. Marx, of course, saw things differently. In *Wage Labour and Capital* he wrote: "It is solely in the course of these fluctuations that prices are determined by the cost of production. The total movement of this disorder is its order" (*The Marx-Engels Reader*, p. 175).

Such statements are characteristic of Marx's dialectic, but they are puzzling to the uninitiated reader. "What does he mean?" we ask. The answer is that Marx recognized, as did the classical economists, that under competition market prices do not fluctuate at random but must revolve around a definite point. If the selling price of a commodity falls below its cost of production, its producer is forced out of business. If the selling price exceeds the cost of production, excess profits arise, which attract competitors and lead temporarily to overproduction, so that price falls. Consequently, the point around which competitive market price fluctuates is cost of production, which to Marx meant labor costs. Thus he saw value as being determined not by the "laws of the market" but by production itself.

The matter has been summed up effectively in another way by Murray Wolfson, a prominent Marxian scholar. Wolfson notes that market prices are ideal (i.e., subjective) estimates of the ratios of exchange by potential buyers and sellers. But competition forces these ideal estimates to conform to the material reality of the labor consumed in their production. One might, of course, explain prices directly by the interaction of these ideal estimates until the subjective valuations are in equilibrium. However, Marx's materialism requires a different explanation. The direction of causation cannot be from the *ideal* valuation to the *objective* exchange ratio. A scientific explanation must go from material to ideal. Marx's labor theory of value is consequently distinguished from earlier labor theories because it is firmly rooted in materialist philosophy.

Wages and Capital Having settled on an objective labor theory of value, Marx had to face the same kind of problems that Ricardo faced: (1) If labor is the essence of exchange value, what is the exchange value of labor, and (2) how is the value of goods produced by machinery determined? The answer to the first problem entails a theory of wages; the answer to the second entails a theory of capital.

Marx unfolded the first problem this way. The value of labor power may be divided into an amount necessary for the subsistence of labor and an amount over and above that. The former, which Marx called "socially necessary labor," determines the exchange value of labor itself—its wage. The latter, termed "surplus value," is appropriated by the capitalist. Marx made it clear that capitalism could not exist unless the worker produced a value greater than his or her own subsistence requirements:

> If a day's labor was required in order to keep a worker alive for a day, capital could not exist, for the day's labor would be exchanged for its own product, and capital would not be able to function as capital and consequently could not survive.... If, however, a mere half-day's labor is enough to keep a worker alive during a whole day's labor, then surplus value results automatically...(*Grundrisse*, p. 230).

This surplus value does not arise in exchange, but in production. Thus the aim of production, from the capitalist's standpoint, is to get surplus value out of each worker. This is what Marx meant by the "exploitation of labor." Exploitation exists because the extra value contributed by labor is expropriated by the capitalist. Surplus value arises not because the worker is *paid less* than he is worth but because he *produces more* than he is worth. Since this extra amount is expropriated by the owners of land and capital, surplus value may be regarded as the sum of the nonlabor shares of income (i.e., rent, interest, and profit).

Marx considered the principle of surplus value to be his main achievement. Certainly it is an integral part of the central theme of class conflict and revolution. Under capitalism, two classes emerge, with one class being forced to sell its labor power to the other in order to earn a living. This contractual arrangement transforms labor into a commodity alien to the worker. Without the difference between labor's exchange value (subsistence) and its use value (value of labor's output), the capitalist would have no interest in buying labor power, and hence it would not be salable. So the ingredients for social conflict are inherent in capitalism—alienation and polarization of classes.

Ricardo had proffered labor as the best *measure* of value, though not necessarily as the sole *cause* of value. Marx went further than Ricardo in this respect; he saw labor as both the measure and the cause of value. Moreover, he held that only labor—not machines—can produce surplus value. How, then, does one value machinery? Marx's answer is that machines are "congealed labor" and therefore equal in value to the cost of the labor that produced them. This answer denies the fact that machines are productive in themselves and should therefore be valued in excess of the labor that has gone into their production. Nevertheless, Marx was so committed to the labor theory of value that he either ignored this objection or relegated it to minor importance.

The "Great Contradiction"   A more serious objection to the labor theory arose from Marx's critics in the form of what has since become known as the "great contradiction." The contradiction is posed as follows: If the exchange value of commodities is determined by the labor time they contain, how can this be reconciled with the empirically observed fact that the market prices of these commodities frequently differ from their labor values? Or to put it another way: We know that competition guarantees a uniform rate of profit throughout the economy. Yet even in a competitive economy the ratio of capital to labor differs among industries. With a Marxian theory of value (i.e., labor alone creates surplus value), profits should be higher in labor-intensive industries, but empirically this is not the case. Thus, since capital/labor ratios differ while the rate of profit remains uniform, it cannot be true (Marx's critics argued) that value is determined by payments to labor alone.

Although the evidence is that Marx anticipated this problem early in his writings, the celebrated answer to his critics is contained in the third volume of *Capital,* published posthumously. Marx maintained that the problem is resolved by the theory of the competition of capitals, which asserts that competition between firms and industries will tend to establish a uniform rate of profit for all firms engaged in production. When this average profit is added to the (different) costs of production in different industries, the individual deviations of market prices from true (labor) values tend to cancel out (in the aggregate).

Some Marxian Definitions   Before analyzing Marx's solution to the great contradiction in detail, it is necessary to clarify some of his technical terms. In solving the valuation problem, Marx employed the following terminology:

Constant capital (c)	= charges on fixed capital (i.e., depreciation plus the cost of raw-material inputs)
Variable capital (v)	= total wages paid to labor
Outlay (k)	= cost of production (excluding profit), or $c + v$
Surplus value (s)	= contribution of workers for which they are not paid, or excess of gross receipts over the sum of constant and variable capital
Rate of surplus value (s')	= ratio of surplus value to variable capital employed, or s/v
Rate of profit (p')	= ratio of surplus value to outlay, or $s/(c + v)$
Organic composition of capital (O)	= ratio of capital to labor employed in production

In contemporary terms it could be said that GNP $= c + v + s$ and NNP $= v + s$.

The Transformation Problem   Marx attempted to resolve the great contradiction by employing the illustration reproduced below as Table 11-1. His analysis and discussion rest on three major assumptions: (1) different commodities are produced with different organic compositions of capital (i.e., different capital/labor ratios) and use up constant capital at different rates in production; (2) for convenience, the rate of surplus value is taken to be 100 percent; and (3) competition will tend to equalize the rate of profit among industries at the "average rate," that is, the ratio of aggregate surplus value to aggregate outlay.

Marx noted that the organic composition of capital in any single industry will depend on the technical relation of labor power to other means of production. But for purposes of illustration, the ratios of constant capital to variable capital in Table 11-1 are arbitrarily chosen. Five different commodities are represented in column 1, each produced with different capital/labor ratios, as revealed in column 2. Commodity A, for example, is produced with 80 units of constant capital and 20 units of variable capital. For simplicity assume that 80 and 20 are dollar expenditures so that the heterogeneous units of "capital" and "labor" can be summed to determine outlay in each of the five industries. It can be noted, therefore, that outlay equals $100 in each industry and that the aggregate outlay of the simple economy is $500. Column 3 shows the units of constant capital used up in the production process for each of the five industries. The dollar cost of each commodity is determined in column 4 by adding wage costs (variable capital) to column 3. Land is left out of the illustration as a means of production but can easily be accommodated along with constant capital. Column 5 shows surplus value in each industry, entered at 100 percent of expenditures on variable capital. Column 6 reveals the "true" value of each

TABLE 11-1
TRANSFORMATION OF VALUES INTO PRICES

(1) Commodity	(2) Capitals	(3) Capital used up	(4) Cost	(5) Surplus value	(6) Labor value	(7) Average profit	(8) Sales price	(9) Deviation of price from value†
A	80c+20v	50	70	20	90	22	92	+ 2
B	70c+30v	51	81	30	111	22	103	− 8
C	60c+40v	51	91	40	131	22	113	−18
D	85c+15v	40	55	15	70	22	77	+ 7
E	95c+5v	10	15	5	20	22	37	+17
Total	500*	202	312	110	422	110	422	0

*This total includes a combination of "stocks" and "flows" (c + v) and is used to determine the average profit in column 7.

†Although the sales price (column 8) and labor value (column 6) differ for each commodity column 9 shows that the algebraic sum of individual differences is zero.

commodity according to Marx's labor theory. The values in this column are determined by adding each row in column 4 to each row in column 5.

According to Marx, the cost of a commodity differs from its sales price by the average amount of profit, which is added to cost (column 4) in order to determine the sales price (column 8). Column 7 is the average profit for each industry and is uniform across industries because of the law of competition. The profit rate in Marxian terms is $s/(c + v)$, or $110/500 = 0.22$, which, when multiplied by the outlay in each industry ($100), yields the dollar amounts shown in column 7. A comparison of columns 8 and 6 shows that market price differs from labor value for each commodity, as the critics contended, but column 9 reveals that the algebraic sum of the individual differences is zero. Marx concluded: "The deviations of prices from values mutually balance one another by the uniform distribution of the surplus value, or by the addition of the average profit of 22 percent of advanced capital to the respective cost-price of the commodities" (*Capital,* III, p. 185).

This transformation of values into prices supports Marx's contention that in the aggregate, labor is the true source of value, and in his preface to the third volume of *Capital,* Engels touted it as a triumph over Marx's critics. The truth is, however, that few economists today are willing to accept the transformation problem as a valid substantiation of the labor theory of value. Ingenious as it is, Marx's solution still denies that machinery is productive over and above the amount of labor congealed in it, a view that modern economists refuse to accept.

Although much attention has been concentrated in this section on the mechanics of value theory, it should be noted that this subject was of relatively minor importance to Marx, who was more interested in the construction of a quasi-Ricardian model of the development of an entire socioeconomic system. The narrower subject of value theory gained importance after Marx's death because of an emphasis on price determination in neoclassical economics. It is interesting to note, however, that debates over the transformation problem have been most furious among neoclassical economists rather than among neo-Marxians.

The Laws of Capitalist Motion

We have yet to describe in detail the dynamics of Marx's theory—what he called "the laws of capitalist motion"—which would eventually sound the death knell of capitalism. A major departure from classical economics is contained in Marx's emphasis on technological change as the driving force of his social dynamics. Adam Smith was a preindustrial writer who understood progress in terms of rational human behavior rather than in terms of technical advance. David Ricardo had very limited industrial experience; it was never his intention to recast political economy as a theory of technological change. If anything, he saw the economic problem of society as an agricultural one. John

Stuart Mill was more open to the prospects of technological change, and yet he did not allow it the central role in his theory that Marx did in his.

Marx described five laws, or general tendencies, inherent in capitalism. Each stemmed from the dynamic nature of the economy, and each was rooted in the conflict between the dynamic "forces of production" and the static "relations of production."

The Law of Accumulation and the Falling Rate of Profit Under capitalism, all business people try to acquire more surplus value in order to increase their profit. Surplus value is, by definition, derived from labor. Thus we might expect capitalists to seek out labor-intensive production methods in order to maximize their profits. In fact, however, they continually strive to substitute capital for labor. The incentive to do so is spelled out by Marx in *Capital:*

> Like every other increase in the productiveness of labour, machinery is to cheapen commodities, and, by shortening the portion of the working day, in which the labourer works for himself, to lengthen the other portion that he gives, without equivalent, to the capitalist. In short, it is a means for producing surplus value (*Capital,* I, p. 405).

The individual capitalist can profitably substitute capital for labor because it takes time to adjust to new methods of production. The first capitalist to introduce labor-saving machinery will therefore be able to produce at lower costs than his or her rivals and yet sell at a price determined in the market by the prevalence of less mechanized firms.

However, what is true for the individual is not true for all. If every capitalist introduces more machinery, the organic composition of capital is increased; surplus value falls, and so does the average rate of profit. (Verify this from Table 11-1.) Hence the collective effect of each capitalist's drive to accumulate more capital and more profit tends to drive down the average rate of profit.

Another reason why the rate of profit may fall over time is that workers may push for higher wage rates. If realized, this prospect will drive up production costs, while prices will still be determined by "socially necessary labor." Ricardo also recognized this prospect, but he felt that such a development would be checked by the Malthusian population trap. But Marx was no Malthusian. Instead, he maintained that population is culturally and socially determined. Therefore, higher wages will not necessarily be forced down again by rapid population growth.

The Law of Increasing Concentration and the Centralization of Industry The drive for profit described above eventually and inevitably leads to a greater substitution of capital for labor and transforms small-scale industry into large-scale enterprises with a more marked division of labor and far greater capacity for output. This increase in production and productive capacity, Marx felt, would lead to general overproduction, thus driving prices down to the point where only the most efficient producers would survive. The less efficient firms would be driven out of business by the above circumstances, their assets being gobbled up by the survivors. Consequently, industry would become more and more centralized, and economic power would be increasingly concentrated in the hands of a few.

The Law of a Growing Industrial Reserve Army   The dynamic change that accompanies technological innovation and capital-labor substitution has a drastic effect on the working class—unemployment. In the passage below, note how Marx turns the division of labor that Smith hailed as an economic blessing into a curse:

> The self-expansion of capital by means of machinery is directly proportional to the number of workers whose means of livelihood have been destroyed by this machinery. The whole system of capitalist production is based upon the fact that the worker sells his labour power as a commodity. Thanks to the division of labour, this labour power becomes specialised, is reduced to skill in handling a particular tool. As soon as the handling of this tool becomes the work of a machine, the use-value and the exchange-value of the worker's labour power disappear. The worker becomes unsalable, like paper money which is no longer legal tender. That portion of the working class which machinery has thus rendered superfluous...either goes to the wall in the unequal struggle of the old handicraft and manufacturing industry against machine industry, or else floods all the more easily accessible branches of industry, swamps the labor market, and sinks the price of labour-power below its value (*Capital,* I, p. 470).

This displacement of workers by machines creates a "growing industrial army of unemployed," one of the inherent contradictions Marx saw within capitalism. As the foregoing discussion illustrates, this unemployment is of two types: (1) technological unemployment (caused by the substitution of machinery for labor) and (2) cyclical unemployment (caused by overproduction, which in turn is caused by increasing concentration and centralization).

The Law of Increasing Misery of the Proletariat   As the industrial reserve army grows, so does the misery of the proletariat. In addition, capitalists generally seek to offset a falling rate of profit by lowering wages, imposing longer workdays, introducing child and female labor, and so forth. All this contributes to the absolute misery of the working class.

The first effect of widespread use of machinery is to bring women and children into the labor force, for slight muscular strength can be amplified by the use of machines. Instead of selling only his own labor power, therefore, the worker is forced to sell that of his wife and children. In Marx's words, the worker "becomes a slave trader." Such exposure to the rigors of factory life leads to high child mortality rates and to moral degradation among women and children, and Marx sought to confirm these facts by citations from public-health reports in Britain.

As the most powerful means for shortening the working time required to produce a commodity, the machine also becomes the most powerful means for prolonging the workday, so that the capitalist can appropriate more surplus value. Moreover, specialized and costly machinery left idle even for short periods is expensive to capitalists, so they strive to minimize the length of idle machine time. According to Marx, the result is longer workdays, less leisure time, and more misery for the laborer. Longer workdays and intensification of work effort sap the strength and longevity of the working class.

From a historical standpoint, this seems the least valid of Marx's arguments. In strictly economic terms, Marx's doomsday prophecy has not been fulfilled. Of course it is unclear whether the working class has made great economic strides *because* of Marx's influence or *despite* his prediction of increasing misery. At any rate, his formulation of the increasing-misery doctrine does not lend itself readily to empirical testing. Orthodox Marxians have attempted to reconcile actual working conditions with this part of Marx's theory by asserting that the *relative* misery of the working class has increased—they point to the dehumanizing effects of today's automated production, increasing alienation and polarization of workers, ethnic minorities, and so on.

The Law of Crises and Depressions   In a very modern fashion, Marx linked the explanation of business cycles to investment spending. He noted that capitalists will invest more at some times than at others. When the army of unemployed grows and wages fall, capitalists will tend to hire more labor and invest less in machinery and equipment. But when wages rise, as we have seen, capitalists will substitute machines for workers, bringing about unemployment and depressed wages. This causes periodic crises. Marx's crisis theory is part of his intention to demonstrate the increasing-misery doctrine. Thus the mere *occurrence* of crises was not enough; he also had to show capitalism's susceptibility to crises of increasing severity. He did this by stressing the never-ending drive of the capitalist for accumulation.

In Marx, increasing misery is related to unemployment, which in turn is a consequence of the capitalist's efforts to accumulate capital, as outlined above. This drive to accumulate is, in turn, self-contradictory and is in fact a major cause of economic crises because it leads to the *overproduction of capital*. To quote Marx:

> As soon as capital would have grown to such a proportion compared with the labouring population, that...the increased capital produces no larger, or even smaller, quantities of surplus-value than it did before its increase there would be an overproduction of capital. That is to say, increased capital $C + \Delta C$ would not produce any more profit...there would be a strong and sudden fall in the average rate of profit...due to a change in the composition of capital...(*Capital*, III, pp. 294–295).

This falling average rate of profit would signal the impending crisis. Over time, these crises would become more severe; that is, they would affect more people (because of increases in population over time) and last longer. Moreover, according to Marx, there would be a tendency toward *permanent* depression because the industrial reserve army gets larger as the crises become more severe. The logical outcome of such a tendency is social revolution. Eventually the proletariat must unite, throw off their chains, and take over the means of production.

The End of Capitalism and Beyond

According to Marx, the classical economists misrepresented the economic system insofar as they considered money a mere medium of exchange. Commodities rarely trade for other commodities directly; instead, they are sold for money, which is then used to purchase other commodities. Symbolically, the classical representation of production and exchange is C-M-C', where C stands for commodities and M stands for money. But Marx held that in a capitalist economy, the process is M-C-M', where $M' \hbar M$. In other words, money (capital) is accumulated to purchase (or produce) commodities, which are then sold for an even greater sum of money. M' is M plus profit (surplus value), and ultimately the drive to accumulate, as we have seen, produces the kind of internal contradictions that lead to the demise of the economic system.

Marx's writings firmly establish this belief in a world revolution, although he rarely discussed the nature of the postcapitalist world. We know that the "new" society was to be a communist one in which bourgeois private property would no longer exist. Marx speaks of

> ...communism as the *positive* transcendence of *private property,* or *human self-estrangement,* and therefore as the real *appropriation of the human* essence by and for man; communism therefore as the complete return of man to himself as a *social* (i.e., human) being—a return become conscious, and accomplished within the entire wealth of previous development. This communism, as fully developed naturalism, equals humanism, and as fully developed humanism equals naturalism; it is the *genuine* resolution of the conflict between man and nature and between man and man— the true resolution of the strife between existence and essence, between objectification and self-confirmation, between freedom and necessity, between the individual and the species. Communism is the riddle of history solved, and it knows itself to be this solution (*Manuscripts,* p. 135).

In *The Communist Manifesto,* Marx spoke of communism as a revolutionary new mode of production, and he described the general characteristics applicable to this new mode:

1 Abolition of property in land and application of all rents of land to public purposes.

2 A heavy progressive or graduated income tax.

3 Abolition of all right of inheritance.

4 Confiscation of the property of all emigrants and rebels.

5 Centralization of credit in the hands of the state, by means of a national bank with state capital and an exclusive monopoly.

6 Centralization of the means of communication and transport in the hands of the state.

7 Extension of factories and instruments of production owned by the state, the bringing into cultivation of wastelands, and the improvement of the soil generally in accordance with a common plan.

8 Equal liability of all to labor. Establishment of industrial armies, especially for agriculture.

9 Combination of agriculture with manufacturing industries; gradual abolition of the distinction between town and country by a more equitable distribution of the population over the country.

10 Free education for all children in public schools. Abolition of children's factory labor in its present form. Combination of education with industrial production, etc.

This ten-point program raises a number of questions as to implementation and operation, but Marx never broached the subject. Obviously he saw his task as the *analysis* of capitalism and its internal contradictions, and apparently he preferred to leave the building of new societies to others. Consequently, after Marx's death the door was left ajar for considerable controversy and disagreement over the *applied* aspects of his political economy. The bitter battle near the turn of the century between moderate Marxian revisionists, such as Eduard Bernstein, and the more militant Leninists attests to the inability of Marx's theory to give a clear course of action deducible from the theory itself. Bernstein admirably summed up the genius and the pitfalls of Marx's writings this way:

> A dualism runs through the whole monumental work of Marx...the work aims at being a scientific inquiry and also at proving a theory laid down long before its drafting. Marx had accepted the solution of the Utopians in essentials, but had recognized their means and proofs as inadequate. He therefore undertook a revision of them, and this with the zeal, the critical acuteness, and love of truth of a scientific genius....But as Marx approaches a point when that final aim enters seriously into question, he becomes uncertain and unreliable....It thus appears that this great scientific spirit was, in the end, a slave to a doctrine (*Evolutionary Socialism,* pp. 209–210).

THE LEGACY OF MARX

Marx has had a profound influence on the twentieth century, and it is a testimonial to his far-ranging intellect that this influence has surpassed the boundaries of economics alone. Even within the discipline of economics, however, Marx's influence has reached far beyond the small group of economists who are Marxist in the strict sense—people such as Paul Sweezy, Maurice Dobb, Paul Baran, and Ernest Mandel, to name a few. Any economist who reasons from the primacy of production in explaining economic relations may be said to have felt the influence of Marx. The same can be said for those who embrace the dialectical method, whether or not they accept the ultimate conclusions of Marx's analysis.

In Marx's time, the dialectical method of thought, especially Hegelian, permeated the Continent, whereas the English-speaking world was more influenced by the empiricism of Locke and Hume. The consequence is that scientific thought in general has been empirical in nature while social, political, and theological thought, especially with its roots on the Continent, has tended to be dialectical in nature. This has led to very different perspectives, which explains the observed lack of understanding and tolerance between the different bodies of thought.

Modern Marxists have ostensibly rallied around the essential core of humanism in Marx's thought. The complexities of mass production and the "third world" deprivation of various groups and nations have made the kind of alienation Marx described seem very real to a large segment of society. Even those who decry the necessity of violent revolution for meaningful social change are often spurred by a Marx-like humanism to seek alternative forms of social reform. In the end, this may prove to be the most durable part of Marx's legacy to the world.

NOTES FOR FURTHER READING

The standard source of biographical information on Marx is Franz Mehring's *Karl Marx: The Story of His Life,* Edward Fitzgerald (trans.) (London: G. Allen, 1936). Two other sources worth mention are E. H. Carr's *Karl Marx: A Study in Fanaticism* (London: Dent, 1934) and Robert Payne's more recent *Marx* (New York: Simon & Schuster, 1968). The personal side of Marx is explored by Edmund Wilson in *To the Finland Station* (Garden City, N.Y.: Doubleday, 1940). See also David McLellan, *Karl Marx* (New York: Viking, 1975).

Ernest Mandel has written several interpretative works on Marx's economics. *An Introduction to Marxist Economic Theory* (New York: Pathfinder Press, 1970) is a brief and highly readable introduction to Marxian economics for student and professor alike. *The Formation of the Economic Thought of Karl Marx,* Brian Pearce (trans.) (New York: Monthly Review Press, 1971), is more difficult but nevertheless very instructive. Finally, Mandel's two-volume work, *Marxist Economic Theory,* Brian Pearce (trans.) (New York: Monthly Review Press, 1968), challenges the most ardent Marx enthusiast. For another view on the development of Marx's economics, see Roman Rosdolsky, *The Making of Marx's "Capital"* (London: Pluto Press, 1977). The impact of Marx's ideas, both as originally propounded and as interpreted and reformulated down to the present time, is the subject of David McLellan (ed.), *Marx: The First 100 Years* (New York: St. Martin's Press, 1983).

The development and continuity of Marx's thought has been discussed by a number of other writers, both in regard to Marx's overall thought and in regard to specific aspects of his analytical system. See, for example, Murray Wolfson, "Three Stages in Marx's Thought," *History of Political Economy,* vol. 11 (Spring 1979), pp. 117–146, in which he argues that Marx was successively an empiricist, a humanist, and a materialist, and that his conception of the ideal society changed with each successive stage. The following articles stress Marx's early thought on various aspects of his mature theory: J. E. Elliot, "Continuity and Change in the Evolution of Marx's Theory of Alienation: From the *Manuscripts* through the *Grundrisse* to *Capital*," *History of Political Economy,* vol. 11 (Fall 1979), pp. 317–362; Allen Oakley, "Aspects of Marx's *Grundrisse* as Intellectual Foundations for a Major Theme in *Capital*," *History of Political Economy*, vol. 11 (Summer 1979), pp. 286–302; and Arie Arnon, "Marx's Theory of Money: The Formative Years," *History of Political Economy*, vol. 16 (Winter 1984), pp. 555–576. Arnon shows, for example, how Marx's monetary theory evolved from a Ricardian starting point but wound up on the side of Thomas Tooke, against Ricardo. Suzanne Brunhoff, *Marx on Money*, M. J. Goldbloom (trans.) (New York: Urizen Books, 1976), presents a mature view of Marx's monetary theory, which Arnon supplements by his historical work. For more on the subject of Marx's monetary theory, see Don Lavoie, "Marx, the Quantity Theory, and the Theory of Value," *History of Political Economy*, vol. 18 (Spring 1986), pp. 155–170, who accuses Marx of being a "closet" quantity theorist; and Murray Wolfson, "Comment: Marx, the Quantity Theory, and the Theory of Value," *History of Political Economy*, vol. 20 (Spring 1988), pp. 137–140, who elaborates the dualism in Marx's thought that underlies Lavoie's interpretation.

The influence of classical economics on Marx's thought and the extent to which his analysis emulated earlier economists has been a subject of repeated attention. See G. S. L. Tucker, "Ricardo and Marx," *Economica*, vol. 28 (August 1961), pp. 252–269; and B. Belassa, "Karl Marx and John Stuart Mill," *Weltwirtschaftliches Archiv*, vol. 83 (1959), pp. 147–163. Although the answer seems obvious on the surface, the question of how close Marx's value theory was to Ricardo's continues to crop up. One important source of ideas on Marx's theory of value is I. I. Rubin, *Essays on Marx's Theory of Value* (Toronto: Black Rose Books, 1972). The proposition that labor alone is the source of surplus value is explored by S. Merrett, "Some Conceptual Relationships in *Capital*," *History of Political Economy*, vol. 9 (Winter 1977), pp. 490–503. S. Groll, "The Active Role of 'Use Value' in Marx's Economic Analysis," *History of Political Economy*, vol. 12 (Fall 1980), pp. 336–371, advances the unconventional view that demand played an important role in Marx's theory of value and that Marx's concept of demand is closer to modern theory than to Ricardo's. J. S. Dreyer, "The Evolution of Marxist Attitudes toward Marginalist Technique," *History of Political Economy*, vol. 6 (1974), pp. 48–75, explains how marginalist techniques of pricing have crept into Marxian economics. The subject of value in Marxian economics continues to draw attention and to spur revision. For some recent attempts, see S. Bowles and H. Gintis, "The Marxian Theory of Value and Heterogeneous Labour: A Critique and Reformulation," *Cambridge Journal of Economics*, vol. 1 (1977), pp. 173–192; Ian Steedman, "Heterogeneous Labour, Money Wages, and Marx's Theory," *History of Political Economy*, vol. 17 (Winter 1985), pp. 551–574, who concludes that Marx's concept of abstract labor is of little or no use and that his concept of value is essentially no different from the classical concept of a quantity of labor; and David Leadbeater, "The Consistency of Marx's Categories of Productive and Unproductive Labour," *History of Political Economy*, vol. 17 (Winter 1985), pp. 591–618, who defends Marx's use of the categories and finds them consistent and effective for analyzing the determinants and limitations of capitalist accumulation.

Although the phrase "laws of capitalist motion" is uniquely Marxian, Marx drew freely upon classical economics, especially in formulating those "laws" relating to the behavior of profits and wages. On Marx's profit theory, see Angus Walker, "Karl Marx, the Falling Rate of Profit and British Political Economy," *Economica,* vol. 38 (November 1971), pp. 362–377; M. A. Lebowitz, "Marx's Falling Rate of Profit: A Dialectical View," *Canadian Journal of Economics,* vol. 9 (May 1976), pp. 232–254; and S. Groll and Z. B. Orzech, "Technical Progress and Values in Marx's Theory of the Decline in the Rate of Profit: An Exegetical Approach," *History of Political Economy,* vol. 19 (Winter 1987), pp. 591–614, which challenges the dominant view that Marx attributed the falling rate of profit to changes in the organic composition of capital.

Marx's wage and employment theories are matters of continuing debate. On Marx's conviction that overproduction would be a frequent occurrence under capitalism, see B. Shoul, "Karl Marx and Say's Law," *Quarterly Journal of Economics,* vol. 71 (November 1957), pp. 611–629. Immiserization (Marx's term for the worsening conditions of the proletariat) may spring from a number of causes: low wages, long hours, unemployment, alienation, exploitation, and so forth. M. Wolfson, Z. B. Orzech, and S. Hanna, "Karl Marx and the Depletion of Human Capital as Open-Access Resource," *History of Political Economy,* vol. 18 (Fall 1986), pp. 497–514, have explored the possibility of exploitation in terms of external costs rather than in terms of Marx's main theoretical formulation based on the labor theory of value. They conclude that there may be more exploitation in the former sense than in the latter. The causes of immiserization, and the historical accuracy of Marx's prophecy that it will increase over time, are discussed by T. Sowell, "Marx's 'Increasing Misery' Doctrine," *American Economic Review,* vol. 50 (March 1960), pp. 111–120; F. M. Gottheil, "Increasing Misery of the Proletariat: An Analysis of Marx's Wage and Employment Theory," *Canadian Journal of Economics and Political Science,* vol. 28 (February 1962), pp. 103–113; R. L. Meek, "Marx's Doctrine of Increasing Misery," *Science and Society,* vol. 26 (1962), pp. 422–441; and D. Furth, A. Heertje, and R. Van Der Veen, "On Marx's Theory of Unemployment," *Oxford Economic Papers,* vol. 30 (July 1978), pp. 253–276.

The possible link between immiserization and the Malthusian population problem is the subject of a series of recent papers in the *American Economic Review*. W. J. Baumol, "Marx and the Iron Law of Wages," *American Economic Review,* vol. 73 (May 1983), pp. 303–308, touched off the debate by claiming that Marx did not subscribe to the view that wage levels must fall toward subsistence under mature capitalism, a position emphatically rejected by Sam Hollander, "Marx and Malthusianism: Marx's Secular Path of Wages," *American Economic Review,* vol. 74 (March 1984), pp. 139–151; but defended by M. D. Ramirez, "Marx and Malthusianism: Comment," *American Eco-*

nomic Review, vol. 76 (June 1986), pp. 543–547. Reacting to the Baumol/ Ramirez versus Hollander debate, A. Cottrell and W. A. Darity, Jr., "Marx, Malthus, and Wages," *History of Political Economy,* vol. 20 (Summer 1988), pp. 173–190, have taken the middle ground—they argue that Baumol/Ramirez fail to establish that Marx rejected the falling-wage doctrine but that Hollander went too far in ascribing to Marx the consistent position that wages must be driven downward. Cottrell and Darity find that immiserization of the proletariat need not be linked to a secular decline in real wages. Outside of this debate, but on the same general subject, Michael Perelman, "Marx, Malthus, and the Organic Composition of Capital," *History of Political Economy,* vol. 17 (Fall 1985), pp. 461–490, advances the notion that Marx viewed the "Malthusian problem" as merely one of the many internal contradictions of capitalism.

The sparks of controversy have been ignited once again by Sam Hollander, on yet another issue, namely whether or not Marx's economics may be characterized as general equilibrium theory. Hollander argues the affirmative in "Marxian Economics as 'General Equilibrium' Theory," *History of Political Economy,* vol. 13 (Spring 1981), pp. 121–155; but his claim has been challenged by Dusan Pokorny in "Karl Marx and General Equilibrium," *History of Political Economy,* vol. 17 (Spring 1985), pp. 109–132, who finds no textual evidence in Marx to support Hollander's claim.

The most famous critique of Marx's economics in the nineteenth century, designed to be the definitive repudiation of Marxian analysis, was launched by the Austrian economist Eugen Böhm-Bawerk, *Karl Marx and the Close of His System,* Paul Sweezy (ed.) (New York: A. M. Kelley, 1949). Joining Böhm-Bawerk in his attack on Marx was the Russian economist Ladislaus von Bortkiewicz, "The Transformation of Values into Prices in the Marxian System," reprinted in the volume by Böhm-Bawerk referred to above; and same author, "Value and Price in the Marxian System," *International Economic Papers,* no. 2 (1952). Together, these works touched off a long debate, which is still raging, on the validity of Marx's solution to the "transformation problem." The following works represent a cross-section of the issues in this protracted debate: J. Winternitz, "Values and Prices: A Solution of the So-Called Transformation Problem," *Economic Journal,* vol. 58 (June 1948), pp. 276–280; K. May, "Value and Prices of Production: A Note on Winternitz's Solution," *Economic Journal,* vol. 58 (December 1948), pp. 596–599; F. Seton, "The Transformation Problem," *Review of Economic Studies,* vol. 24 (June 1957), pp. 149–160; and R. Meek, "Some Notes on the Transformation Problem," *Economic Journal,* vol. 66 (March 1956), pp. 94–107.

After a brief hiatus, the debate was revived in 1971 by Paul Samuelson, "Understanding the Marxian Notion of Exploitation: A Summary of the So-Called Transformation Problem between Marxian Values and Competitive Prices," *Journal of Economic Literature,* vol. 9 (June 1971), pp. 399–431. Samuelson's article drew additional comment from Joan Robinson and Martin Bronfenbrenner in the December 1973 issue of the same journal. Furthermore, the debate continued with interpretations and commentary by William J. Baumol and Michio Morishima and a "final word" by Samuelson in the March

1974 issue of the *Journal of Economic Literature*. Nevertheless, see the article by Allen Oakley, "Two Notes on Marx and the 'Transformation Problem,'" *Economica*, vol. 43 (November 1976), pp. 411–418.

Surprisingly little has been written about Marx's vision of communism or about the relative economic merits of socialism versus competition from a strictly Marxian perspective. Perhaps this is because Marx spent far more time analyzing the weaknesses of capitalism than sketching out the postcapitalist society. Several articles skirt these issues. See J. E. Elliot, "Marx and Contemporary Models of Socialist Economy," *History of Political Economy*, vol. 8 (Summer 1976), pp. 151–184; same author, "Marx and Engels on Communism, Scarcity, and Division of Labor," *Economic Inquiry*, vol. 18 (April 1980), pp. 275–292; and same author again, "Marx and Schumpeter on Capitalism's Creative Destruction: A Comparative Restatement," *Quarterly Journal of Economics*, vol. 95 (August 1980), pp. 45–68. T. W. Hutchison, "Friedrich Engels and Marxian Economic Theory," *Journal of Political Economy*, vol. 86 (April 1978), pp. 303–320, suggests that Engels's contributions to Marx's economics are much more important than has been generally recognized, specifically Engels's account of the essential functions of the competitive-price mechanism. See also O. Horverak, "Marx's View of Competition and Price Determination," *History of Political Economy*, vol. 20 (Summer 1988), pp. 275–298, who tries to bring Marx's theory of competition into sharper relief by contrasing it with the neoclassical concept of competition. Finally, Joan Robinson, *Essay on Marxian Economics* (London: Macmillan, 1966), attempts to reconcile Marxian and orthodox economics. Among other things, she contends that Marx's argument regarding the fate of capitalism does not depend crucially on the labor theory of value.

REFERENCES

Bernstein, Eduard. *Evolutionary Socialism: A Criticism and Affirmation*, E. C. Harvey (trans.). New York: Schocken Books, 1965.

Marx, Karl. *A Contribution to the Critique of Political Economy*, S. W. Ryazanskaya (trans.). Moscow: Progress Publishers, 1970.

———. *Capital*, Ernest Untermann (trans.) and F. Engels (ed.), 3 vols. Chicago: Charles Kerr, 1906–1909.

———. *Grundrisse der Kritik der Politischen Ökonomie*, 2 vols. Berlin: Dietz-Verlag, 1953.

———, and F. Engels. *The Communist Manifesto*, Samuel Moore (trans.). Chicago: Regnery, 1954.

———. *Economic and Philosophic Manuscripts of 1844*, Martin Milligen (trans.) and D. J. Struik (ed.). New York: International Publishers, 1964.

———. *Precapitalist Economic Formations*, J. Cohen (trans.) and E. J. Hobsbawm (ed.). New York: International Publishers, 1965.

———. *Writings of the Young Marx on Philosophy and Society*, L. D. Easton and K. H. Guddat (eds. and trans.). Garden City, N.Y.: Anchor Books, Doubleday, 1967.

———. *The Marx-Engels Reader*, R. C. Tucker (ed.). New York: W. W. Norton, 1972.

Wolfson, Murray. *A Reappraisal of Marxian Economics*. New York: Columbia University Press, 1966.

PART FOUR

MICROECONOMICS IN EUROPE AND ENGLAND

JOHN MAYNARD KEYNES   KARL MARX   ALFRED MARSHALL   WILLIAM STANLEY JEVONS   ADAM SMITH

CHAPTER 12

MICROECONOMICS IN FRANCE: COURNOT AND DUPUIT

INTRODUCTION

In Chapter 7 we considered a classical macro model that was, in the main, suggested by Ricardo and other classical writers. This model utilized the basic tenets of classical economic theory (population doctrine, wages-fund theory, etc.) to make deductions and generalizations concerning aggregate output, income distribution, and population. Although Ricardo's was the first spirited explanation of abstract methods in political economy, great strides of a different sort in the establishment of formal economic analysis were being made outside Britain in the first half of the nineteenth century. The subject of these other efforts was not the macroeconomic variables of income, output, population, profits, and wages (as distributive shares) but rather the behavior of microeconomic quantities such as the prices, quantities offered and demanded, and profits connected with *specific* commodities or services. Theories concerning the effects of various forms of economic organization (monopoly, for example) upon prices and outputs were under consideration, as were ideas respecting the effects of transport costs, rents, and transport pricing schemes on the location of industries. Important tenets of public finance and welfare economics were advanced in this period, and the theory of price discrimination and product differentiation took root. When viewed in retrospect, the era was one of the most fecund in the history of economic analysis.

The major purpose of Part Four is to outline some of the pre-Marshallian contributions to economic theory, with special emphasis on continental advances outside England. Chapters 12 and 13 deal with selected European and American contributions, and Chapter 14 treats an important benchmark in the development of analysis in England—Jevons's 1871 presentation of utility theory. The first two writers under review were French contemporaries, Cournot and Dupuit.

COURNOT (1801–1877)

Antoine-Augustin Cournot, one of the most original minds ever to attack economic theory, led a life filled with tragedy and disappointment. Born in 1801 in Haute-Saône, France, Cournot received his initial training at local schools before entering the École Normale in Paris at the age of twenty, where he continued mathematical studies. Throughout his youth, Cournot indulged an insatiable appetite for books (scientific and otherwise) in spite of an ominous (and ultimately fulfilled) presentiment of impending blindness. When the École Normale disbanded, Cournot remained in Paris, where, after a period of relative poverty, he obtained work as the secretary to one of Napoleon's generals, Marshall Gouvion Saint-Cyr. He completed his doctorate (at the University of Paris) during this period (1823 to 1833) and came into contact with leading intellectuals of the day, many of them physical scientists and engineers. During his tenure as a university student, Cournot published several mathematical articles as well as the military memoirs of his employer.

Cournot's papers on mathematics attracted the attention of the great physicist and statistician Poisson, who helped him secure a position as professor of mathematics at Lyons in 1834. Here Cournot taught differential calculus and completed the initial work on his book on probability *(Exposition de la théorie des chances et des probabilités)*. The next year Cournot was appointed school superintendent of Grenoble, and within a few months he assumed additional responsibilities as Inspector General of Education (succeeding Ampère, who is known to all students of electrical science). In 1838, Cournot married and also published his seminal work on microeconomics, *Recherches sur les principes mathématiques de la théorie des richesses (Researches into the Mathematical Principles of the Theory of Wealth)*. He was also made a traveling inspector general of education, based in Paris.

Trouble with his vision forced Cournot to spend a leave of absence in Italy in 1844. He became superintendent of the Dijon Academy in 1854, where he remained until his retirement in 1862. Throughout this period and during his retirement in Paris, Cournot continued to publish books on social philosophy and on economic questions. Probably as a result of his piecemeal loss of sight, the character of his work altered. His two later books on economics, *Principles de la théorie des richesses* and *Revue sommaire des doctrines économiques,* published in 1863 and 1877, respectively, do not employ mathematics to treat economic questions, and they do not add significantly to Cournot's original work on economic theory *(Recherches)*. Cournot died suddenly in 1877, but, sadly, almost no one had yet noticed his work on economic theory, with a few important exceptions such as Léon Walras. He would probably be more than a little surprised and pleased at the course of microeconomic analysis in the post-1877 period because his impact and influence permeate to the very core of modern economic theory.

Cournot on Method

Cournot's ideas on the proper method in political economy are of great importance in assessing his role in theory development. In defense of the use of mathematics as a shorthand for expressing complex ideas, Cournot evaluated the earlier efforts of Smith, Say, and Ricardo:

> There are authors, like Smith and Say, who, in writing on Political Economy, have preserved all the beauties of a purely literary style; but there are others, like Ricardo, who, when treating the most abstract questions, or when seeking great accuracy, have not been able to avoid algebra, and have only disguised it under arithmetical calculations of tiresome length. Any one who understands algebraic notation, reads at a glance in an equation results reached arithmetically only with great labor and pains (*Mathematical Principles,* p. 4).

In a brilliant defense of mathematical investigation, moreover, Cournot's chief criticism of past writers was "They imagined that the use of symbols and formulas would have no other end than that of leading to numerical calculations" and they did not see that the object of mathematical analysis was to "find relations between magnitudes which cannot be estimated numerically and between *functions* whose law is not capable of being expressed by algebraic symbols." This view of method persists in his later works also. "Science," Cournot wrote in 1863, "is not obliged to await empirical laws...in order to draw certain and useful consequences from general characteristics which they can supply, or certain relationships which can exist between them and upon which reason, alone, sheds light." Thus Cournot championed the use of mathematics, specifically differential and integral calculus, in expressing arbitrary functions, with the restriction that certain conditions be met. An example, familiar to all students of economics, may make Cournot's method clearer.

One of Cournot's great achievements was to have discovered the law of demand *(loi de débit)*. As most students know, the law of demand states that quantity demanded is a function of price, or $D = F(P)$. Quantity demanded is, of course, related to a number of other variables (income, wealth, and the like), but these are assumed constant when drawing up an individual demand schedule. When one of the nonprice determinants alters, the whole demand *curve* shifts, which connotes a change in demand. A change in quantity demanded occurs when price changes, all other determinants remaining constant. Cournot understood perfectly the value of analysis of the *ceteris paribus* assumption, or "other things equal." This is evident in his *Principles de la théorie des richesses,* where he noted that the law of demand

> ...rests essentially on population, on the distribution of wealth, on general well-being, on tastes, on the habits of the consuming population, on the multiplication of markets, on the extension of the market resulting from transport improvements. All these conditions relative to demand remain the same; if we suppose that production

conditions change (i.e., that costs rise or fall, that monopolies are restricted or suppressed, that taxes are increased or lightened, that foreign competition is prohibited or allowed) prices will vary and the corresponding variations in demand, provided that prices are actually raised, will serve for the construction of our empirical tables. If, to the contrary, prices change because the law of demand has itself changed, due to a change in causes which no longer influence production but consumption, the construction of our tables will be made impossible, since they must show how demand changes by virtue of a change in price and not by virtue of other causes.[1]

It is clear that Cournot identified the law of demand with the modern conception of a demand function; likewise, his change in "demand" corresponds to the modern usage of a change in "quantity demanded." This method of analysis is so common today that the modern theorist would not think of expressing complex ideas in verbal form alone, but Cournot pioneered mathematical and graphical approaches when verbal expression was the only tack of the theorist.

A further and legitimate question might be raised: What kind of theory did Cournot seek to develop with mathematical tools? Was the theory he contemplated chimerical or out of touch with reality, as so many argue of economic theory today? The answer to these questions reveals the brilliantly dual nature of Cournot's approach to method. Cournot conceived of an economic analysis to be *grounded* in empirical observation and in facts. The point may be illustrated by returning to Cournot's pioneering concept of the law of demand.

Having rejected utility as a foundation for his demand function, Cournot presented what was basically an empirical approach to demand. The title of the chapter on demand in the original *Recherches, "De la loi du débit,"* or "The Law of Sales," hints at this empirical approach, and Cournot quite explicitly gave his demand function an empirical definition. He noted: "Sales or demand (for to us these two words are *synonymous* and *we do not see for what account theory need take into consideration a demand which is not followed by a sale*)...increase when price decreases." He acknowledged that prices and the law of demand could fluctuate in the period of a year, and he defined his curve to relate *average* annual price P with $F(P)$, "the quantity sold *annually* in the country or in the market under consideration." Hence, $D = F(P)$ is a curve connecting time-series data on sales and the prices at which these sales are realized.

Thus Cournot's theoretical specification of demand (negatively sloped, continuous) resulted from his own observation and from simplifications and observations of the relations between price and quantity. Theory may then be lifted from these facts and manipulated in order to arrive at deductions based on certain assumptions. But theory was to be derived and specified in the first instance from actual observed facts and not from caprice. The tools, so de-

---

[1] Quotations without page references in this chapter are from unpublished translations made by the authors of this text. Original French texts are cited in References at the end of the chapter, but English titles are substituted for the French where translations exist.

rived, possess a usefulness and a generality that far transcend the empirical facts from which they were born. It was part of Cournot's genius to have been able to recognize and explain these methods of theory and model construction.

Cournot's Micro Models

Cournot turned this method into the creation of numerous models of firm behavior based upon the demand curve. We shall consider two of these models: (1) the monopoly model and (2) the duopoly (two producers) model. Cournot's major contributions may then be evaluated.

Monopoly Model In Chap. 5 of the *Researches,* Cournot turned to an analysis of profit maximization by a proprietor of a mineral spring that has just been found to possess salubrious qualities known to no other. Sale of a *single* liter of the water might fetch as much as 100 francs, but, as Cournot demonstrated, the monopolist will not charge the highest price he could get for the water. Rather, he will adjust his price so as to maximize net receipts. Cournot demonstrated mathematically that, in the case of zero costs, the monopolist would maximize *gross* receipts. Assuming a demand function $D = F(p)$ and also assuming the demand curve is always negatively sloped (i.e., $dD/dp \setminus 0$), the proprietor will adjust p such that total revenue, $pF(p)$, is at a maximum. Cournot demonstrated that this occurs when marginal cost equals marginal revenue (or when the slope of a profit function, $\pi = TR - TC$, equals zero). In the case of zero costs, a maximum occurs when marginal revenue equals zero.

Cournot's monopoly model may be viewed graphically (see Figures 12-1*a* and 12-1*b*. Assume the linear demand curve in Figure 12-1*a* to represent Cournot's law of demand. (Ignore curve *MC* for the present.) The (zero-cost) proprietor will adjust his sales of mineral water such that he sells quantity Q_n at price P_n since at quantity Q_n the addition to total revenue (marginal revenue) is equal to the addition to total cost (marginal cost). That is, $MR = MC$ at quantity Q_n. Alternatively, but equivalently, the zero-cost proprietor simply maximizes total revenue, as seen at quantity Q_n in Figure 12-1*b*. In the zero-cost case, the *TR* curve *becomes* the profit function π_0.

Cournot's monopoly model of a mineral-springs proprietor burdened with positive costs of production clearly uncovered the "marginal principle," which is the central organizing principle of economic theory. To put the problem in the form of a question, when the monopolist faces costs of production, what price would he charge and what quantity would he sell to maximize profits? Cournot solved the problem in a straightforward fashion. Assuming that $\phi(D)$ was equal to the cost of making a number of liters equal to D, Cournot's profit equation becomes $\pi = pF(p) - \phi(D)$.) Profit maximization requires that the slope of the profit function equal zero—or, in Cournot's notation, that $D + dD/dp \{ p - d[\phi(D)]/dD \} = 0$. In plainer language, profit maximization takes place where $MR - MC = 0$. As Cournot put it, "Whatever may be the

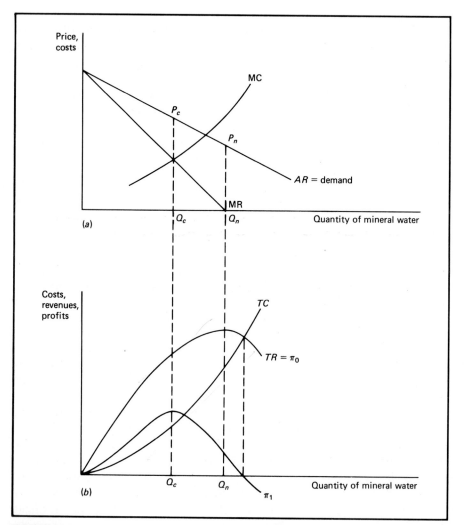

FIGURE 12-1
In a zero-cost situation, the firm will sell Q_n at P_n. With positive costs, quantity Q_c will be sold at P_c, following the marginal principle. Note that at Q_c, the profit function π_1 is at a maximum.

abundance of the source of production, the producer will always stop when the increase in expense exceeds the increase in receipts" (*Mathematical Principles*, p. 59).

In reference to Figure 12-1*a*, Cournot established that profits are at a maximum where $MR = MC$. Output produced will be Q_c, and price will be P_c; further, Q_c will be lower and P_c will be higher than in the case of zero costs. Alternatively, Cournot's monopoly theory might be interpreted as in Figure 12-1*b*, which reproduces the total cost, total revenue, and profit function relevant to the mineral-springs proprietor. The proprietor will cease production at Q_c in

Figure 12-1*b*, where the profit function π_1 is at a maximum (Cournot included a second condition—that the slope of the profit function be zero at Q_c and, further, that profits decline with *either* increases or decreases in quantity). Note that the mineral spring is not operated to maximize gross returns at Q_n but to maximize *net returns* at Q_c. The geometrically inclined reader will determine that at Q_c, the *slope* of the *TC* function is equal to the *slope* of the *TR* function, or $MC = MR$, as in Figure 12-1*a*. Cournot's development of the theory of monopoly would, in short, compare most favorably with that of any modern textbook writer, for it is precisely Cournot's theory that modern writers on monopoly are explicating.

Cournot's Duopoly Analysis   Perhaps the most famous theory developed by Cournot relates to the introduction of an additional seller of mineral water. In a profoundly original theoretical conception, Cournot laid the groundwork for many other ideas of importance to economics, such as imperfect competition (see Chapter 18) and the theory of games. Although Cournot's theory of duopoly (two sellers) was later altered and refined (notably by the Englishman Francis Y. Edgeworth and the French mathematician Joseph Bertrand), nothing can mask Cournot's brilliant and original insight.

Cournot considered two sellers, A and B, who both know the total (aggregate) demand curve for their perfectly homogeneous product, mineral water. Otherwise, they are completely uninformed about each other's policies, to the extent that A thinks that B will keep his quantity constant no matter what A does, and B thinks the same thing about A's quantity. Further, both sellers continue to make this assumption no matter how much experience they have *to the contrary*. In the language of duopoly, this assumption is called *a conjectural variation of zero*, i.e., a conjecture that B will have no output reaction to A's actions. Cournot further assumed that either A or B could supply all the output of mineral water and, moreover, that mineral-water production is costless. He analyzed the problem of output and price determination both mathematically and graphically in the *Researches,* but our discussion will be in graphical terms.

In order to analyze the duopoly problem, Cournot developed a new tool of graphical analysis, the *reaction curve,* one of which is reproduced in Figure 12-2.

Figure 12-2 depicts a concave reaction function *AA*, which reveals A's choice of outputs with respect to B's choice of outputs. Specifically, it shows the outputs firm A will select in order to *maximize profits,* given B's selection of outputs. For example, if B selects output Ob_0, A—in order to maximize profits—will want to charge a certain price for an output Oa_0. If, on the other hand, B produces quantity Ob_1, A will be led by the motive of profit maximization to produce a lower quantity Oa_1, and so on for all other quantities B might produce. Whatever quantity B chooses, moreover, A *thinks* that it will be permanent, and so A acts to maximize his or her profits.

What quantity will A and B end up producing? Clearly, the problem cannot

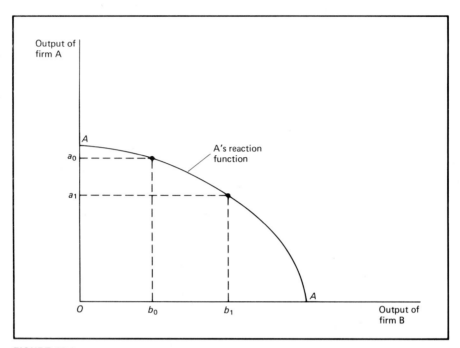

FIGURE 12-2
A's reaction curve describes the profit-maximizing output level for A given each level of output that B chooses. Thus when B chooses to produce b_0, A will maximize profits by producing a_0.

be solved without adding B's reaction function indicating the kind of responses B will make to A's output. The two functions are combined in Figure 12-3, where B's reaction function is defined in the same manner as A's was above.

Suppose B decides to produce some output—say, Ob_0—on the assumption that A will keep output at level Oa_0. B would then be maximizing his or her profits at output Ob_0. On the assumption that B would hold output at level Ob_0, A would maximize profits by producing output Oa_1. Such a move would cause B to reassess the situation and to increase his output to Ob_1, which maximizes *his or her* profits on the assumption that A will keep output at Oa_1. However, the assumption proves unfounded (though B, or A, is assumed never to catch on), and the process of output variation to maximize profits goes on as traced by the arrows in Figure 12-3.

Point E (Figure 12-3) represents an equilibrium solution for firms A and B, i.e., one to which they will always return if moved away. At point E the duopolists both share profits (Cournot expressed this amount mathematically) and charge a common price that is lower than the price that would obtain under simple monopoly (a fact that Cournot himself noted) but higher than the one that would be charged under competition, with many sellers. Cournot was quick to point out that collusion between the two competitors would result in production of monopoly output and a two-way split of monopoly profits. But

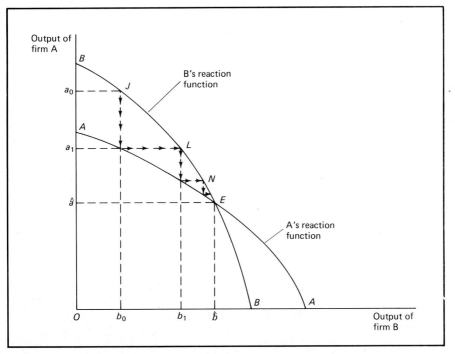

FIGURE 12-3
Beginning at point J (when B's output is b_0), the arrows trace the path to stable equilibrium (point E) through successive output adjustments by A and B.

Cournot expressed duopoly output precisely: it would be two-thirds the output produced if the market were competitive. In fact, his general expression for output was that it would be $n/n + 1$ times competitive output. Thus if there were five sellers, quantity sold would be five-sixths of competitive output. If there were 2,000 sellers, output would clearly approach the competitive amount. In this manner Cournot related his duopoly theory to the competitive model.

Cournot: An Evaluation

Besides duopoly theory, Cournot provided many other important theoretical insights. Among them were (1) a clear statement of the simple competitive model; (2) a very advanced model of composite and derived demand (for copper and zinc to produce brass); and (3) last but not least, a full-blown discussion of the *stability* of various economic equilibriums, which considers the possibility of mild variations in quantity and price. (The reader may gain some notion of the third issue by *reversing* the reaction curves *or* by switching the labels of the axes in Figure 12-3.) Cournot's book was, in short, filled with new ideas.

Still, Cournot's contributions to method and to monopoly-duopoly theory have dominated the attention of theorists. And these ideas, especially those related to duopoly, have attracted several critics. As previously mentioned,

Edgeworth and Bertrand tinkered with Cournot's duopoly model, altering many of his assumptions. Why, for example, should a duopolist consider the quantity and not the price of his rival constant? More pointedly, how can A (for example) continue to assume that B's output will remain constant in spite of *repeated* evidence to the contrary? What if there were an output limit on one or both of the duopolists? And so on.

Many of these issues have been resolved, of course, but it is part of the continuing fascination of Cournot's model that the solution of one issue brings up two more. Oligopoly models, bilateral bargaining, and alternative assumptions concerning conjectural variation in modern game theory have been suggested by Cournot-like models. His simple model was, and continues to be, the font of many ideas in economic theory. Such powerful ideas surely place him among the first rank of economic theorists. But even more, Cournot possessed a grand vision of what economic theory could be—a box of tools, rooted in empiricism, which would constitute the organizing principles in analyzing myriad economic problems. This cognizance, so tragically ignored by his contemporaries, carried him to a pinnacle of achievement seldom reached in the history of economic theory.

JULES DUPUIT (1804–1866)

While Cournot was working out the foundations of microeconomics, a venerable French institution—the School of Civil Engineering—was about to produce a man who would combine micro tools with a theory of utility to establish the foundations of welfare economics, public finance, and public-goods theory. Like Cournot, this famous French engineer thought of economics as an avocation, not a profession, and although he possessed a fine technical education, he brought keen practical insight to an analysis of economic problems.

Arsine-Jules- Émile-Juvenal Dupuit was born on May 18, 1804, in Fossano, Italy, when the region was ruled by France. At the age of ten, Dupuit returned with his parents to France. There he continued his education in the secondary schools at Versailles, at Louis-le-Grand, and at Saint-Louis, where he finished brilliantly by winning a physics prize in a large competition.

Dupuit was accepted to the French School of Civil Engineering (the École des Ponts et Chaussées) in 1824, and in 1827 he was put in charge, in the department of Sarthe, of an engineering district that encompassed roadway and navigation work. He was married in 1829 and was made first-class engineer in 1836, two years before Cournot published the *Researches*.

Dupuit concerned himself with problems of economic interest throughout his illustrious career as an engineer. He conducted experiments on the deterioration of roadways, which resulted in his *Essay and Experiments on Carriage Hauling and on the Friction of Rotation* (1837). A subsequent contribution on the same subject earned him a gold medal, awarded as a result of an engineers' ballot. As a result of his engineering activities, Dupuit was eventually decorated with the Legion of Honor on May 1, 1843.

The floods of the Loire in 1844 and 1846 occasioned Dupuit's *Theoretical and Practical Studies on the Movement of Running Water* (1848), and his classic *Floods: An Examination of the Means Proposed to Prevent Their Return,* published in 1858, was another attack on the same problem. In 1850, Dupuit was called to municipal duty in Paris as director and chief engineer, a job in which he studied municipal water distribution and supervised the construction of sewers. In December of 1855, Dupuit was named Inspector-General of Civil Engineering. He was, in short, one of the most distinguished engineers in France at the time. But political economy was Dupuit's hobby and the object of his passionate attention, and his career as an engineer was no more remarkable than his career as an economist. Unfortunately, a projected book entitled *Political Economy Applied to Public Works,* to which Dupuit referred as early as 1844, was never brought to completion (death intervened in 1866). With the exception of the short plea for free trade, *Commercial Freedom,* published in 1861, Dupuit's reputation as an economist must stand with a considerable number of journal contributions to economic policy and theory.

Dupuit's Unique View of Economics

Dupuit's special insights into economic analysis were the combined result, on the one hand, of his technical and scientific training in calculus and functions and, on the other, of his keen observation and utilization of the mountain of statistics on public-works revenues and costs gathered by himself and his fellow engineers. Dupuit had read Smith, Ricardo, and J. B. Say, the French expositor of classical economics. However, Dupuit's economics marks a clear departure from the old school. French economists of the day, Pelagrino Rossi and Joseph Garnier in particular, influenced Dupuit's opinions on classical, *macro* issues. But the one writer who could have helped him most in the area of micro analysis—Cournot—was apparently unknown to him. And, at one point, both lived and worked in Paris simultaneously!

Dupuit's contributions relate primarily to his engineering interests. In the words of one of his biographers, "Political economy, which attracts at every turn the engineer's interest, had also been the object of his constant study, and he was no less learned in that science than in that of public works." But it was the *combination* of these interests that produced Dupuit's special genius for theory and concept formation. Specifically, Dupuit combined three elements to produce analytical tools: (1) subjects of economic interest and importance; (2) relevant, observed facts and statistics abstracted from these subjects; and (3) mathematical analysis—deductive logic and graphical depiction—to organize and reorganize relations suggested by these facts and statistics. Theories, so derived, could be confronted with new facts and data for confirmation or alteration.

So conceived, Dupuit's method treated political economy as a combined science of reason and observation. Cournot also combined the two, but with far less emphasis on empirical grounding and its correspondence to theory.

Unorganized statistics are, of course, meaningless. As Dupuit noted, "To better see the facts, to better observe them, one must clarify them by light of reason." But "empty theories," i.e., those having no empirical referent in the real world, are far more ludicrous. So Dupuit's whole effort was directed toward a real-world problem—measuring public utility, the *social welfare* produced by public goods and services. In keeping with this aim, he made seminal discoveries in the theoretical areas of marginal utility, demand, consumers' surplus, simple and discriminating monopoly, and marginal-cost pricing. These ideas, which are all related to the optimum price and output policies of public goods, will be considered in turn.

Marginal Utility and Demand

Dupuit was the first economist to present a cogent discussion of the concept of marginal utility and to relate it to a demand curve. Fully utilizing his powers of observation and abstraction, Dupuit was able to show, as early as 1844, that the utility that an individual (and a collection of individuals) obtains from a homogeneous stock of goods is determined by the use to which the last units of the stock are put. In doing so, he clearly pointed out that the marginal utility of a stock of some particular good diminishes with increases in quantity. From observation Dupuit established that each consumer "attaches a different utility to the same object according to the quantity he can consume." He illustrated his point with a practical example of a technological improvement in water distribution to a town (in his essay "On Utility and Its Measure"):

> Water is distributed in a city which, situated on a height, could procure it only with great pains. There was then such a value that the hectoliter per day was 50 francs by annual subscription. It is quite clear that every hectoliter of water consumed in these circumstances has a utility of *at least* 50 francs.

Dupuit suggested that each unit of a given quantity of water will have a different utility. But why should each increment of the same commodity possess a different utility? Dupuit continued his argument, supposing that as a result of the installation of pumps, costs of production for water drop by 20 francs:

> What happens? First, the inhabitant who consumed a hectoliter will continue to do so and will realize a benefit of 20 francs on his first hectoliter; but it is highly probable that this lower price will encourage him to increase his consumption; instead of using it parsimoniously for his personal use, he will use it for *needs less pressing, less essential,* the satisfaction of which is *worth more than 30 francs,* since this sacrifice is necessary to obtain water, but is worth *less than 50,* since at this price he relinquished this consumption ("On Utility and Its Measure").

Each increment of the same commodity carries a different utility because additional units will allow "less pressing, less essential" needs to be met. The additional utility derived from additional units of the same commodity must decline.

Extending the example, Dupuit supposed that when the price fell to 20 francs, the individual would demand 4 hectoliters "to be able to wash his house every day; give them to him at 10 francs, he will ask for 10 to be able to water his garden; at 5 frs. he will ask for 20 to supply a water font; at 1 franc he would want 100 to have a continuous flow," and so on. It is the least pressing need for a commodity, not the most pressing need, that defines the exchange value of the *entire* stock of goods. Dupuit's argument can be conveniently summarized as in Figure 12-4.

Assume that the consumer is originally in equilibrium when the price of water is at p_1 and the quantity taken is q_1. Now assume with Dupuit that the price of water falls to p_2. At the lower price for water the individual is in disequilibrium at point c. The marginal utility of the last unit of the consumer's existing stock is greater than the now-lower marginal utility of water represented by the lower price. In terms of price, what the consumer would pay for q_1 of water is greater than the price he or she *must* pay for quantity q_1. The same quantity of water (q_1) could be bought at a lower total expenditure, but Dupuit assumed that the consumer would not do this. Attached to each incremental unit of water between quantity q_1 and quantity q_2 is a marginal satisfaction greater (albeit diminishing) than that which would obtain for the incremental unit corresponding to price p_2. Thus in an effort to maximize total satisfaction, the individual will increase purchases of water up to, but not beyond, quantity q_2.

As suggested by the labeling of the vertical axis (marginal utility = price) of

FIGURE 12-4
As the price of water declines from p_1 to p_2, the consumer will begin to satisfy less pressing wants. Therefore the consumption of water will increase from q_1 to q_2.

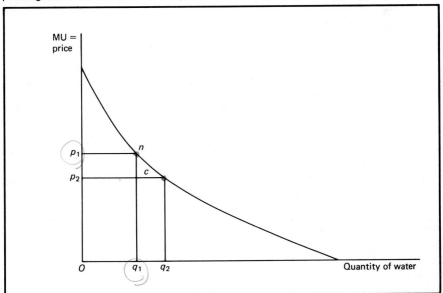

Figure 12-4, the marginal-utility curve is Dupuit's demand curve (*courbe de consommation*), and although most of his examples are concerned with transportation and communication, he considered the same laws to apply to all goods and services. He provided explicit directions in his article entitled "Tolls," which appeared in the 1852–1853 French *Dictionary of Political Economy*, on the manner in which a demand curve should be constructed:

> If, in a table of two columns, one inserts in the first all the prices, from 0, the one which corresponds to the greatest consumption, up to the price that stops all consumption, and in the second, regarding the price, the corresponding quantity consumed, we will have the exact representation of what we call the law of consumption.

Dupuit constructed such a demand curve in 1844, six years after Cournot's *Researches* was published, in a paper entitled "On the Measurement of the Utility of Public Works."

Like Cournot, Dupuit gave the equation for the curve of consumption as $y = f(x)$ or, alternatively, $Q_d = f(p)$. Additionally, Dupuit (as Léon Walras and other economists were to do later) placed the independent variable, price, on the x axis and the dependent variable, quantity, on the y axis. Modern microeconomic diagrams, following Alfred Marshall's practice, reverse this procedure because Marshall treated marginal-demand price as a function of quantity (see Chapter 16). Dupuit's construction is reproduced as Figure 12-5. Dupuit described his construction as follows:

> If... [we supposed that] along a line *OP* the lengths *Op*, *Op'*, *Op"*... represent various prices for an article, and that the verticals *pn*, *p' n'*, *p"n"*... represent the number of articles consumed corresponding to these prices, then it is possible to construct a curve *Nn'n"P* which we shall call the curve of consumption. *ON* represents the quantity consumed when the price is zero, and *OP* the price at which consumption falls to zero ("On the Measurement of the Utility of Public Works," p. 106).

It is obvious that this curve is identical in conception to that of Figure 12-4; that is, Dupuit's demand curve is a marginal-utility curve. Dupuit made his meaning clear, with reference to Figure 12-5, by stating that "The utility of... *np* articles is at least *Op* and... for almost all of them the utility is greater than *Op*."

The relation that Dupuit posited between price, marginal utility, and quantity was, he thought, a "fact of experience" that "has been verified statistically." It was, in addition, a theory of powerful originality, for in linking the demand curve with utility it established a new approach to economic inquiry—welfare economics. Specifically, Dupuit agreed that the total area under the demand curve of Figure 12-5 (area *OPN*) represents the total utility produced by the commodity. At some price—say, *Op"*—there is some amount that consumers would be *willing* to pay for the commodity over and above what they must pay. The amount that they *must* pay is represented by area *Op"n"r"* in Figure 12-5, and it represents the firm's receipts (ignore for the present the

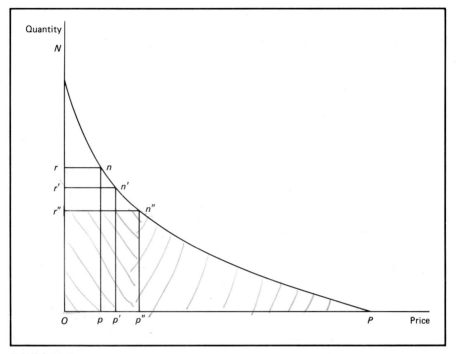

FIGURE 12-5
The area inside *OPN* represents the total utility derived from a commodity having the demand curve *PN*. At price *Op*, consumers pay an amount equal to *Ornp* and receive a surplus utility equal to *nPp*.

other price-output combinations). In the case of zero costs (that described in Figure 12-5) areas *Op"n"r"* may be called "producers' surplus" or "producers' rents." The amount that consumers would be willing to pay over and above what they must pay is area *p"n"P*. In Dupuit's terms this is "utility remaining to consumers," and in modern terms it is called "consumers' surplus." Dupuit's numerical examples (see the following section) of these concepts will illustrate their importance and will at the same time demonstrate Dupuit's advances in monopoly and price discrimination.

Consumers' Surplus, Monopoly, and Discrimination

In the course of his economic writings, Dupuit was led to investigate some of the factors that give rise to monopoly pricing. Conditions existing in the French railroad companies were of particular interest to him, and as scores of later economists were to show, he pointed out that "the interest of ordinary capitals is regulated by the law of supply and demand...while the means of transportation are monopolies." Thus, generally speaking, "ways of communication," or forms of transportation, are sheltered from competition.

He illustrated the point by a comparison between the economic principles that determine house rents and those affecting transport rates. Exorbitant rents for lodging, according to Dupuit, could not exist for very long, since "If it was known that house rental yields a revenue superior to the rental of other capitals, speculation would focus very quickly on the construction of houses and equilibrium would be established." Thus the entry and exit process prohibits monopoly rents over the long run in houses, but as Dupuit indicated, this freedom to enter the railroad industry is inhibited by certain factors indigenous to that industry. Enormous amounts of capital, in the first instance, restrict the possibility of entry to a limited number of persons. Also, because of the uniqueness of the first enterprise, a "new one can survive only at the expense of the first and...the profit which is sufficient for one is not sufficient for two."

The analytical contribution to monopoly theory emerged when Dupuit addressed himself to the principles on which the simple monopolist, as constituted above, behaves. He uncovered the rule of monopoly profit maximization in the course of his discussion of the effects on utility of tolls and transport charges. Table 12-1, reproduced from an 1849 article, is useful in illustrating Dupuit's early conception of this well-known principle.

The data in Table 12-1 refer to a tariff or rate that a monopoly railroad may charge for passage. Here Dupuit was considering the case of an unregulated monopolist free to charge a rate that would maximize profits. His monopolist was a profit maximizer, for "If the road or bridge or canal is private property, the owner company has only one aim, and that is to get the largest possible income from the toll." Thus the monopolist facing the demand schedule of Table 12-1 with no costs of production would charge a rate of 5 francs in order to

TABLE 12-1
A MONOPOLY DEMAND AND UTILITY CALCULATION

Tariff	Number of passengers	Utility	Yield of the toll	
			Gross	Net
0	100	445	0	−200
1	80	425	80	−80
2	63	391	126	0
3	50	352	150	50
4	41	316	164	82
5	33	276	165	99
6	26	234	156	104
7	20	192	140	100
8	14	144	112	84
9	9	99	81	63
10	6	69	60	48
11	3	36	33	27
12	0	0	0	0

maximize profits or gross receipts. The example was then extended to the monopolist with costs of production when Dupuit supposed that the "cost of traction" could be represented by 2 francs per unit of passage. These traction costs may be identified with variable costs, and in this case, as Dupuit correctly pointed out:

> The rate which maximizes net yield is not the same as that which maximizes gross yield. The latter rate was 5, the former is 6, and it would grow indefinitely with the cost. It follows that when traction cost diminishes, the toll must diminish to yield maximum receipts ("On Tolls and Transport Charges," p. 20).

Dupuit correctly stated the principle of profit maximization in terms of net revenue and pointed out that if the *level* of traction costs increased, the profit-maximizing tariff would increase and output would decrease. The net receipts, additionally, are net only of variable expenses. Fixed costs, such as "certain administrative expenses, interest on construction expenditures, etc.," must also be covered in the long run. Consequently, Dupuit's net receipts are not long-run profits, as are his gross receipts (without costs of production). Dupuit, referring to what is our Table 12-1, said that "If fixed costs were more than 104 [francs] and it were possible to charge only one uniform rate, the railroad would be a losing proposition with any tariff."

In addition to an analysis of profit maximization, Dupuit's early treatment of monopoly contained another important analytical tool, which was later used by Alfred Marshall. Specifically, both investigations posited a relation between monopoly revenue and consumers' surplus, given, of course, the constancy of the marginal utility of money. Making an implicit identification of the demand curve with a utility function, Dupuit supplied a utility calculation for his railroad example (see column 3, Table 12-1). In this case the price that maximized net revenue would be a tariff of 6 francs, and the total utility (consumers' surplus, producers' surplus, and costs) produced by this tariff would be 234 francs.

According to Dupuit, total utility always breaks down into three parts: lost utility, producers' surplus, and consumers' surplus. At the 6-franc tariff the total utility of 234 francs divides as follows. The lost utility equals 52 francs, the total variable costs of carriage (fixed costs are assumed nonexistent). The producers' surplus is identical to the net receipts of 104 francs. The consumers' surplus is the residual of 78 francs. The sum of the three parts equals 234, the total utility associated with 26 passengers (from Table 12-1).

If we momentarily depart from Dupuit's presentation and assume that the fixed cost is exactly 104, then monopoly revenue disappears. In the short run the 104 francs accruing to the owner of the railway is of the nature of an economic rent (i.e., producers' surplus) on fixed investment, but as Dupuit succinctly pointed out, these fixed costs must ultimately be met by the monopolist. Thus, under the assumption that the fixed costs are 104 francs there would be no monopoly revenue. A consumers' surplus is produced, however, in the amount of 78 francs.

Price Discrimination and Welfare: Numerical Analysis   Dupuit recognized that consumers' surplus could be diminished or increased by a policy of price discrimination. These possibilities are explored in Tables 12-2 and 12-3. Table 12-2 utilizes the same demand data as Table 12-1 but assumes a fixed cost of 110 francs. The notable change is that there now exists no single tariff that will maximize profit; a tariff of 6 francs will, however, minimize losses. Profits are nevertheless possible if *price discrimination* is allowed. Suppose 14 passengers could be induced by some means of differentiation to pay a tariff of 8 francs while 12 continued to pay 6. The same 26 passengers would then yield a gross revenue of 184 francs and a profit of 22 francs. The consumers' surplus, however, would decline from 78 to 50 francs.

Table 12-3 shows these results and the effects of various other combinations of dual pricing. Using the dual price (4,7) as an example, Dupuit's calculations are obtained as follows. From Table 12-2 we know that 41 passengers are willing to buy tickets at a price of 6 francs. Dupuit assumed it possible to distinguish 20 passengers from this group who would be willing to pay a price of 7 francs for the journey. In this case discrimination would yield gross receipts of 224 francs $[(20 \times 7) + (21 \times 4)]$. Subtracting total costs of 192 francs leaves net receipts to the monopolist of 32 francs. The consumers' surplus is calculated as the difference between total utility and gross receipts, a value of 92 francs.

Discrimination: Dupuit's Graphics

Dupuit also expressed these ideas graphically. In Figure 12-6, suppose *OM* is the profit-maximizing price. The utility produced by the commodity or service depicted by the demand curve of Figure 12-6 would be distributed in the following manner: the monopoly revenue would equal the area *OMTR;* the consumers' surplus (or the utility remaining to consumers, in Dupuit's terminology) would equal area *TMP;* finally, the lost utility, *utilité perdue,* would equal the triangle *RTN.*

TABLE 12-2
MONOPOLY DEMAND, UTILITY, AND COSTS

Tariff	Number of passengers	Total utility	Costs			Revenue	
			Variable	Fixed	Total	Gross	Net
0	100	445	200	110	310	0	−310
1	80	425	160	110	270	80	−190
2	63	391	126	110	236	126	−110
3	50	352	100	110	210	150	−60
4	41	316	82	110	192	164	−28
5	33	276	66	110	176	165	−9
6	26	234	52	110	162	156	−6
7	20	192	40	110	150	140	−10
8	14	144	28	110	138	112	−26
9	9	99	18	110	128	81	−47
10	6	69	12	110	122	60	−62

TABLE 12-3
THE TWO-CLASS TARIFF

	Single Tariff (6)	Two-class tariff				
	(6)	(6, 8)	(5, 10)	(4, 7)	(3, 7)	(2, 6)
Number of passengers	26	(12,14)	(27,6)	(21,20)	(30,20)	(37,26)
Total utility	234	234	276	316	352	391
Gross revenue	156	184	195	224	230	230
Total costs	162	162	176	192	210	236
Net revenue	−6	22	19	32	20	−6
Consumers' surplus	78	50	81	92	122	161

Under conditions of competition this lost utility would result from scarcity of resources. However, since Dupuit assumed zero costs of production, lost utility in his example can only be attributable to restrictions of output under monopoly. The significance of Dupuit's theory of price discrimination is that he showed how economic welfare could be increased (i.e., lost utility could be reduced) by differential pricing. As he pointed out with reference to Figure 12-6:

> When the consumers can be placed in several categories [via separating markets or differentiating products or services] each of which attributes a different utility to the same service, it is possible, by a certain combination of taxes, to increase the product of the toll [the sum of consumers' surplus and monopoly revenue] and to diminish the loss of utility ("On the Measurement of the Utility of Public Works," p. 108).

Thus if the monopolist faced with the demand curve of Figure 12-6 was able to increase the total quantity sold to Or via discrimination, the *total utility* (the sum of consumers' surplus and monopoly revenue in the no-cost case) would equal the area $OPnr$, which is greater than $OPTR$ by $RTnr$. The increase in monopoly receipts would clearly depend on the number of submarkets that the monopolist would be able to establish and invade. As Dupuit correctly pointed out:

> If from among the pn consumers at price Op you can distinguish the number pq who would consume at the price OM, and from among the latter the number Mq' who would consume at price Op', and can oblige them by various combinations to pay those prices, then the yield of the tax will be the sum of the three rectangles $Ornp + pqTM + Mq'n'p'$; the utility to consumers [consumers' surplus] will be the three triangles $nqT + Tq'n' + n'p'P$; while the loss of utility is merely that due to the lowest tax, the triangle Nrn ("On the Measurement of the Utility of Public Works," pp. 108–109).

Monopoly profits under discrimination (assuming no costs) have increased considerably over those that result from the simple monopoly price OM. Specifically, profits have been augmented by $Mp'n'q' + Rqnr$, and it is important to note that they could have been increased *without* increasing output above that established under the simple monopoly output OR. In other words, price discrimination could affect the distribution of welfare without affecting the total utility produced. But Dupuit believed that discrimination was desirable *only* if

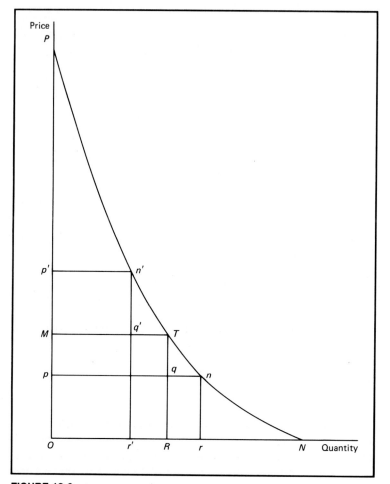

FIGURE 12-6
In addition to price *OM,* a lower price, *Op,* will enlarge the seller's revenue
and the consumers' surplus by reducing lost utility. A higher price, *Op',* will
enlarge the seller's revenue but lower the consumers' surplus.

it increased quantity over that obtained under a single-price, simple monopoly
system, for only in that event would *utilité perdue* be reduced.

With respect to Figure 12-6, Dupuit knew that output would increase if only
one of the markets could be served at the simple monopoly price but more
than one could be served with price discrimination. The market in which price
Op' is charged would have been served in any event, given the simple monopoly profit-maximizing price *OM.* But the relatively weaker market delineated
by price *Rq* would not have been entered at the simple monopoly price *OM.*
Dupuit's implicit suggestion that output would increase (by *Rr*) if discrimination allowed the monopolist to enter markets not entered at the simple monop-

oly price was only much later given scientific treatment by A. C. Pigou and Joan Robinson (see Chapter 18). Yet it is certainly clear that Dupuit, as early as 1844, was at the threshold of output analysis under discrimination, which finally yielded to Robinson's expert treatment almost a century later.

Benefit-Cost Analysis: The Early Application of Price Theory to Public Goods

Although Dupuit is generally given credit for having been the first writer to analyze the optimum provision of public goods and public works from a welfare standpoint, recent research has proved that he was but one of a long line of French engineer-economists interested in these problems. The French engineers Joseph Minard and Henri Navier, for example, were working on similar questions long before Dupuit. Nevertheless, Dupuit's invention of the marginal-utility function enabled him to give much improved estimates of the benefits derived from governmentally supplied goods, and it is his formulation that has inspired contemporary research on these issues.

Dupuit's general rule for the provision of public goods—highways, water distribution, public transport, etc.—was that the government should provide these goods if a pricing scheme could be devised such that the total annual cost associated with the good could be covered while producing some "net utility." In other words, the good should be provided if the *marginal* annual receipts of an enterprise could cover the *marginal* costs (including capital costs) to be amortized annually over a specified number of years.

His theory of optimum provision may be illustrated utilizing the model of price discrimination developed above. Dupuit's analysis of discrimination was completely general in its description of the pricing technique. Specifically, he recognized that a public monopoly, in contrast to a private monopoly, may follow a policy of constrained discrimination. In Dupuit's view, government ownership finds its *raison d'être* in society's decisions concerning the distribution of real income. If the public interest is an overriding consideration in the conduct of a service or in the provision of a good, the government would operate the enterprise in such a manner as to maximize the consumers' surplus. The consumers' surplus produced by a pricing system, which is of no importance to a private monopolist, is of prime importance to a government that concerns itself with the distribution of income. As Dupuit noted:

> By varying the price or differentiating it in various manners, the three parts of total utility assume variable proportions at each other's expense.
>
> The conduct of a monopoly raises a series of important questions.... Is the largest possible profit to be earned? Is the yield to be a fixed sum and the loss of utility reduced to a minimum? ("On Tolls and Transport Charges," p. 31).

The government would likely seek to maximize the consumers' surplus under the full-cost constraint, which Dupuit presumably invoked as an allocative criterion. This could be accomplished by using a single price, and in several examples the single price was suggested. However, Dupuit did not eschew the value of a policy of price discrimination by a government-operated monopoly.

One important instance where discrimination was recommended to a government monopoly was the hypothetical example described by Table 12-3. Assuming profit maximization, Dupuit pointed out that "The tariff (4, 7) yields decidedly more than the others and that is the one which a private company would adopt." (This profit-maximizing two-class tariff nevertheless results in an improvement in the consumers' surplus over the simple monopoly rate of 6; output would increase, and average [simple] price would decline as well.) The two-class tariff does not maximize consumers' surplus, however, and should the government assume ownership of the enterprise, some sort of alternative pricing scheme could be established. Considering such a policy and its effect on consumers' utility, Dupuit pointed out with reference to Table 12-3:

> The tariff (2, 6) maximizes utility [net utility, or producers' surplus and consumers' surplus], though it does involve the railway in a loss of 6; but this loss can be avoided by raising the second-class price just a little above 2, which would reduce utility to about 260 and passengers to 60. This is the tariff which the government would adopt, *because it would cover all costs.* The railway operated by a private company would serve only forty-one passengers and give them a utility of 92; if operated by the government, it would serve 60 passengers and give them a utility of about 160 ("On Tolls and Transport Charges," pp. 22–23).

Thus Dupuit's pricing tool provided a frame for the analysis of the effects of discriminating monopoly under alternative property and institutional arrangements. His early and original insights into welfare theory, nurtured as they were by an economic and empirical tradition among French engineers, have provided the necessary backdrop against which an important and fruitful area of modern economics is being enacted. The clear enunciation and application of the utility principle and the demonstration that society's welfare could be improved by public action in a private economy when conditions of competition are not ubiquitously effective leave Dupuit unchallenged as the most important early precursor of modern doctrine and practice in the area.

A NOTE ON ENGINEERS IN THE HISTORY OF ECONOMICS

The material of this chapter demonstrates that the economic theory of the firm, with many of its analytical accoutrements, was on its way before 1850 in the writings of certain French economists. Profit maximization in competitive, monopoly, and duopoly models was analyzed in elegant fashion by Cournot. Dupuit's discovery of marginal utility balanced the presentation of microeconomics and directed emphasis toward consumer theory and welfare economics. Yet both these writers worked outside the mainstream of economic thought, even on the Continent. Neither received adequate attention or fair treatment by their contemporaries, which suggests in part that their contributions were ahead of their time. But their fates as economists probably also rest in part on the peculiar system of French education and the niche occupied by each writer within that system.

Although the subject is too complicated to go into in great detail here, it should be noted that for centuries there have been two varieties of higher education in France: the universities and the *grandes écoles*. The latter are establishments of higher learning of limited size, usually concentrating on training of a functional and highly specialized nature. The earliest and most durable of the *grandes écoles* were established to train engineers, and it is still the case that an engineer who graduates from a French *grande école* generally benefits from a high social status and has access to jobs of great responsibility and high pay. Moreover, these *grandes écoles* have always been linked very closely with the state, even more so since the time of Napoleon.

Both Cournot and Dupuit were products of the *grandes écoles,* Cournot of the École Normale and Dupuit of the École des Ponts et Chaussées. It is ample testimony to the rigor of the technical training they received that both men were able to accomplish so much in a field that had up to their time been virtually untouched by mathematics. The remarkable thing, however, is that theirs were not isolated performances. At the École des Ponts et Chaussées in particular, an impressive oral and written tradition in economic inquiry had accumulated since its establishment in 1747. By the 1830s, Henri Navier (1785–1836), Joseph Minard (1781–1870), and Charlemagne Courtois were plumbing the depths of public economics by establishing benefit-cost frameworks for the evaluation of public works. It was they, in fact, who initiated the kind of inquiry that spurred Dupuit to the heights of marginal analysis.

The influence of the *grandes écoles* eventually reached beyond France. In 1830, Charles Ellet, an American engineering student, began a two-year period of study at the École des Ponts et Chaussées, where he eagerly absorbed the lessons of Navier and Minard. Back in America, Ellet initiated important theoretical studies on the subjects of price discrimination, demand and monopoly, and the economic determination of market areas. Jacob Viner ranked Ellet "with Cournot and Dupuit as a pioneer formulator of the pure theory of monopoly price in precise terms" (*The Long View and the Short,* p. 388). The French econo-engineering tradition continued, moreover, after 1850. In the second half of the century, two other students of the École des Ponts et Chaussées shone brightly. Emile Cheysson (1836–1910) brilliantly illuminated many aspects of microeconomic theory within a framework of analysis evocative of modern econometrics, and Clement Colson (1853–1939) extended the French genius for applied microeconomics into the present century, especially in regard to the economics of transportation.

The special genius of French engineers was recognized by such giants among economists as Alfred Marshall. In his *Industry and Trade* (p. 117), Marshall observed that

Frenchmen are specially fitted for certain large enterprises by their talent for engineering. From early times French cathedrals and fortifications, French roads and canals have borne evidence to high creative faculty. Since the Revolution the engineering profession has been held in special honour in France: there is perhaps no other country in which the ablest lads are so generally inclined towards it.

Yet it wasn't only French engineers who contributed to economic analysis in the nineteenth century. In Germany, Wilhelm Launhardt (1832–1918), a railway engineer, made important contributions to the theory of monopoly pricing, to industrial location and market-area analysis, and to welfare economics. An Austrian engineer, Wilhelm Nördling, constructed empirical cost curves for the Austrian railways in 1886. Finally, in England, two especially able engineers, Dionysius Lardner and Fleeming Jenkin, carried the graphical representation of supply, demand, and profit maximization to the heartland of classical economics. Their efforts in this regard, perhaps more than any other factor, convinced William Stanley Jevons (see Chapter 14) that classical economic theory had outlived its usefulness and should give way to a new paradigm of economic analysis.

One important observation to be derived from a survey of applied economics in the nineteenth century, therefore, is that a significant number of original and important contributions to microeconomics were made by men cut from the cloth of the engineer rather than the cloth of the philosopher.

The writers discussed in this chapter were mainly *practitioners* (students who feel that economic theory is abstract, unrealistic, and insipid may be heartened by this fact). Their interest in, and concern with, practical problems sprang from the daily necessity of getting things done. And because their contributions lay outside the mainstream of economic theory, they did not always find receptive audiences among economists for their ideas. Practitioners, to be sure, have little time for the metaphysical aspects of value and distribution. They must solve practical problems, usually in a hurry. Perhaps it is not surprising, therefore, that a perusal of the best economic writings of the engineers of the nineteenth century is in many respects more enlightening and more rewarding than a study of the best writings of the nineteenth-century economists.

This does not suggest that nineteenth-century economists did not do topflight work in economic theory. This book is full of examples to the contrary. Rather, it suggests that economists may have much to learn from developments in related fields of inquiry. Insularity of ideas within professions or specialties may, in other words, be very costly to the progress of ideas. Since the time of Adam Smith, economists and other scientists have practiced the Smithian dictum of specialization and division of labor in pursuing theoretical advance. The rewards have indeed been bounteous. But even Smith was vividly aware of the disadvantages of overspecialization. Today's economists cannot afford to be any less aware of the dangers of intellectual overspecialization and the insularity of ideas that frequently accompanies it.

NOTES FOR FURTHER READING

Although Cournot's microeconomics has received a great deal of attention from twentieth-century theorists, a very small number of assessments of his work exist in English. For those who read French, however, the most comprehensive and recent work on Cournot is by Claude Ménard, *La formation d'une rationalité économique: A. A. Cournot* (Paris: Flammarion, 1978). A review of Ménard's book, in English, by R. F. Hébert appears in the *History of Economic Thought Newsletter,* vol. 23 (Autumn 1979), pp. 21–23. Other French sources are Emile Callot, *La philosophie biologique de Cournot* (Paris: 1960); Georges Loiseau, *Les doctrines économiques de Cournot* (New York: 1970); F. Bompaire, *Le principe de liberté économique dans l'oeuvre de Cournot et dans celle de l'École de Lausanne* (Paris: 1931); and two articles by René Roy, "L'Oeuvre économique d'Augustin Cournot," *Econometrica,* vol. 7 (April 1939), pp. 134–144; and "Cournot et l'école mathematique," *Econometrica,* vol. 1 (1933), pp. 13–22. An interesting account of Cournot's life is given by A. J. Nichol, "Tragedies in the Life of Cournot," *Econometrica,* vol. 6 (July 1938), pp. 193–197; and by Irving Fisher, "Cournot and Mathematical Economics," *Quarterly Journal of Economics,* vol. 12 (January 1898), pp. 119–138, 238–244.

The empirical nature of Cournot's demand theory is documented in C. L. Fry and R. B. Ekelund, Jr., "Cournot's Demand Theory: A Reassessment," *History of Political Economy,* vol. 3 (Spring 1971), pp. 190–197. Perhaps the clearest discussion of the Cournot, Bertrand, and Edgeworth solutions to the duopoly problem is presented by Fritz Machlup in his *Economics of Sellers' Competition* (Baltimore: Johns Hopkins, 1952). Game theory, which derives partly from Cournot's conjectural assumption, was brilliantly established by John von Neumann and Oskar Morgenstern in *The Theory of Games and Economic Behavior* (Princeton, N.J.: Princeton University Press, 1953 [1943]).

The economic writings of Dupuit are composed largely of journal contributions in the *Annales des Ponts et Chaussées* and in the *Journal des Économistes.* A collection of Dupuit's major articles (in French), published in Italy under the editorship of Mario de Bernardi, is entitled *De l'Utilité et sa mesure: Écrits choisis et republies* (Torino: La Riforma Sociale, 1934). Two of these articles are in published translation (see the References).

Dupuit's contributions to utility theory and to other facets of economic analysis are assessed in the following works: G.J. Stigler, "The Development of Utility Theory," *Journal of Political Economy,* vol. 58 (August, October 1950), pp. 307–327, 373–396, reprinted in Stigler, *Essays in the History of Economics* (Chicago: The University of Chicago Press, 1965); R. W. Houghton, "A Note on the Early History of Consumer's Surplus," *Economica,* n.s., vol. 25 (February 1958), pp. 49–57; R. B. Ekelund, Jr., "Jules Dupuit and the Early Theory of Marginal Cost Pricing," *Journal of Political Economy,* vol. 76 (May–June 1968), pp. 462–471; R. B. Ekelund, Jr., "A Note on Jules Dupuit and Neoclassical Monopoly Theory," *Southern Economic Journal,* vol. 25 (January 1969), pp. 257–262; R. B. Ekelund, Jr., "Price Discrimination and Product Differentiation in Economic Theory: An Early Analysis," *Quarterly Journal of Economics,* vol. 84 (May 1970), pp. 268–278; and R. B. Ekelund, Jr., and W. P. Gramm, "Early French Contributions to Marshallian Demand Theory," *Southern Economic Journal,* vol. 36 (January 1970), pp. 277–286. The early French tradition in public finance, of which Dupuit was a part, is discussed in two articles by R. B. Ekelund, Jr., and R. F. Hébert: "Dupuit and Marginal Utility: Context of the Discovery," *History of Political Economy,* vol. 8 (Summer 1976), pp. 266–273; and "French Engineers, Welfare Economics and Public Finance in the Nineteenth Century," *History of Political Economy,* vol. 10 (Winter 1978), pp. 636–668. Also on Dupuit, see Alan Abouchar, "A Note on Dupuit's Bridge and the Theory of Marginal Cost Pricing," *History of Political Economy,* vol. 8 (Summer 1976), pp. 274–277; and R. B. Ekelund, Jr., and Y. N. Shieh, "Dupuit, Spatial Economics and Optimal Resource Allocation: A French Tradition," *Economica,* vol. 53 (November 1986), pp. 483–496. The history of the concept of consumer surplus, beginning with Dupuit's seminal contribution, is traced up to the first half of this century by R. B. Ekelund, Jr., and R. F. Hébert, "Consumer Surplus: The First Hundred Years," *History of Political Economy,* vol. 17 (Fall 1985), pp. 419–454.

The recurrent theme in Ellet's work is that business decision making could and should be based on mathematically derived principles, which Ellet called "the Laws of Trade." See Charles Ellet, Jr., *An Essay on the Laws of Trade in Reference to the Works of Internal Improvement of the United States* (New York: A. M. Kelley, 1966); and same author, "The Laws of Trade Applied to the Determination of the Most Advantageous Fare for Passengers on Railroads," *Journal of the Franklin Institute,* vol. 30 (1840), pp. 369–379. With few exceptions, Ellet has been passed over by historians of economic thought. The notable exceptions are C. D. Calsoyas, "The Mathematical Theory of Monopoly in 1839: Charles Ellet, Jr.," *Journal of Political Economy,* vol. 58 (April 1950), pp. 162–170; an unpublished dissertation by C. H. Shami, *Charles Ellet, Jr., Early American Economist and Econometrician 1810–1862: An Analytical Exposition of His Theories* (New York: Columbia University, 1968); R. B. Ekelund, Jr., and D. L. Hooks, "Joint Demand, Discriminating Two-Part Tariffs and Location Theory: An Early American Contribution," *Western Economic Journal,* vol. 10 (March 1972), pp. 84–94; and C. R. Bell, "Charles Ellet, Jr., and the Theory of Optimal Input Choice," *History of Political Economy,* vol. 18 (Fall 1986), pp. 485–495.

The lively interest in applied economic questions at the École des Ponts et Chaussées is amplified by examining the contributions of a number of its famous students. See R. B. Ekelund, Jr., and R. F. Hébert, "Public Economics at the École des Ponts et Chaussées: 1830–1850," *Journal of Public Economics,* vol. 2 (July 1973), pp. 241–256. Besides Ellet, who was enrolled at the Ecole as an *externe,* R. D. Theocharis, "C. Courtois: An Early Contributor to

Cost-Benefit Analysis," *History of Political Economy,* vol. 20 (Summer 1988), pp. 265–274, has added the name of Charlemagne Courtois to the list of pioneering engineer-economists.

Emile Cheysson's contributions to economics have been analyzed by R. F. Hébert in several articles: "Emile Cheysson and the Birth of Econometrics," *Économies et Sociétés,* vol. 20 (October 1986), pp. 203–222; "A Note on the Historical Development of the Economic Law of Market Areas," *Quarterly Journal of Economics,* vol. 86 (November 1972), pp. 563–571; "Wage Cobwebs and Cobweb-Type Phenomena: An Early French Formulation," *Western Economic Journal,* vol. 11 (December 1973), pp. 394–403; and "The Theory of Input Selection and Supply Areas in 1887: Emile Cheysson," *History of Political Economy,* vol. 6 (1974), pp. 109–113. Wilhelm Nördling's statistical research on railway cost curves is preserved in Elizabeth Henderson's translation, "Note on the Cost of Railway Transport," *International Economic Papers,* no. 10 (1960), pp. 64–70. Cheysson incorporated Nördling's statistics into his "econometric" model of railway profit maximization.

Except for those who read German, the contributions of the railway engineer Wilhelm Launhardt remain virtually inaccessible. Before his untimely death in 1986, Professor Klaus Hennings of the University of Hannover (where Launhardt spent his teaching career) was working on Launhardt's papers with the intent to publish an analysis of the German engineer's contributions. We do not know whether Hennings's researches have been completed or published, however. A translation of a brief extract from Launhardt's *Mathematische Begrundung der Volkwirtschaftslehre* is included in W. J. Baumol and S. M. Goldfeld (eds.), *Precursors in Mathematical Economics: An Anthology* (London: London School of Economics and Political Science, 1968). For those who read German, Erich Schneider, "Bemerkungen zu einer Theorie der Raumwirtschaft," *Econometrica,* vol. 3 (1935), pp. 70–105, provides an exposition of Launhardt's contributions to location theory.

British engineers who helped pioneer advances in nineteenth-century microeconomics include Dionysius Lardner and Fleeming Jenkin, who both fit into the story of William Stanley Jevons (see Chapter 14). Lardner's book, *Railway Economy,* resides in the library at the École des Ponts et Chaussées, but it is not known whether there was any direct filiation between French and English engineers on microeconomic ideas. D. L. Hooks, "Monopoly Price Discrimination in 1850: Dionysius Lardner," *History of Political Economy,* vol. 3 (Spring 1971), pp. 208–223, explores Lardner's contribution to the theory of monopoly price and the concept of demand for a product over economic distance. Jenkin's economic writings have been collected and reprinted under the title *The Graphic Representation of the Laws of Supply and Demand, and Other Essays on Political Economy, 1868–1884* (London: London School of Economics and Political Science, 1931). For an assessment of Jenkin and his work, see A. D. Brownlie and M. F. L. Prichard, "Professor Fleeming Jenkin, 1833–1885: Pioneer in Engineering and Political Economy," *Oxford Economic*

Papers, vol. 15 (November 1963), pp. 204–216. An excellent commentary on both Lardner and Jenkin is provided by R. M. Robertson, "Jevons and His Precursors," *Econometrica,* vol. 19 (July 1951), pp. 229–249.

REFERENCES

Cournot, A. A. *Principes de la théorie des richesses.* Paris: Librarie Hachette, 1863.

————. *Researches into the Mathematical Principles of the Theory of Wealth,* N. T. Bacon (trans.). New York: A. M. Kelley, Publishers, 1960 [1838].

Dupuit, Jules. "On the Measurement of the Utility of Public Works," in R. H. Barback (trans.), *International Economic Papers,* no. 2. London: Macmillan, 1952, pp. 83–110 [1844].

————. "On Tolls and Transport Charges," in E. Henderson (trans.), *International Economic Papers,* no. 11. London: Macmillan, 1962, pp. 7–31 [1849].

————. "Tolls," in Charles Coquelin (ed.), *Dictionnaire de l'économie politique,* vol. II. Paris: Guillaumin, 1852–1853.

————. "On Utility and Its Measure," *Journal des Économistes,* 1st ser., vol. 35 (July–September 1853), pp. 1–27.

Marshall, Alfred. *Industry and Trade,* 3d ed. London: Macmillan, 1920.

Viner, Jacob. *The Long View and the Short: Studies in Economic Theory and Policy.* New York: Free Press, 1958.

CHAPTER 13

MICROECONOMICS IN VIENNA: MENGER, WIESER, AND BÖHM-BAWERK

INTRODUCTION

German economics in the nineteenth century may be viewed in the literal sense, as contributions emerging from the native sons of Germany, or it may be treated as the collective wisdom of economists who expressed themselves in the German language. In the literal sense, the peak analytical performances in the nineteenth century were relatively few, although powerfully original. Several key German writers anticipated the marginalist revolution in economic analysis, and their work is on a par with Cournot and Dupuit. J. H. von Thünen, H. H. Gossen, and H. K. von Mangoldt contributed to an analytical tradition that was rich in theoretical insight but was underappreciated by the German historical school (see Chapter 10). As the historicists gained the upper hand in the universities of late nineteenth-century Germany, the seat of analytical economics shifted to Austria, a country politically apart from Germany, but joined to its sister state by a common language and culture.

This chapter deals primarily with the economics of the three writers who together made up the Viennese school. The founder of this group was Carl Menger (1840–1921). He was joined by two younger but able disciples: Friedrich Wieser (1851–1926) and Eugen Böhm-Bawerk (1851–1914). Together they established a systematic approach to economic analysis that survives today as an alternative to mainstream (i.e., Anglo-American) neoclassical economics. Many of their students and their students' students have become prominent twentieth-century economists, especially Joseph Schumpeter (see Chapters 21 and 24), Ludwig von Mises (see Chapter 21), Friedrich Hayek (see Chapter 21), Fritz Machlup, Gottfried Haberler, and Oskar Morgenstern (see Chapter 22).

In order to stress the continuity of Germanic ideas, we turn first to the pioneers—those writers who blazed the way for theoretical economics in Germany and Austria. The contributions of von Thünen, Gossen, and Mangoldt form an analytical backdrop for the Viennese school.

VON THÜNEN

Johann Heinrich von Thünen (1783–1850) was a successful farmer and brilliant theorist who worked in isolation on his agricultural estate in Mecklenburg, Germany. He understood, as few economists have before or since, the proper relation between theory and facts—which is the hallmark of any scientific investigation. It was this characteristic of his thought that endeared him to Alfred Marshall (see Chapter 15), who claimed to have "loved [him] above all my masters" (*Memorials,* p. 360). One of the things Marshall learned from von Thünen was how to apply the principle that all forms of expenditure should be carried to the point at which the product of the last unit equals its cost: the total product is maximized only when resources are allocated equimarginally.

Von Thünen is credited with a number of important and original anticipations of modern economic theory, such as the concepts of economic rent, diminishing returns, opportunity costs, and the marginal-productivity theory of wages. Above all else, however, he was a pioneer in the economic theory of location; so we will examine his contribution to marginal analysis primarily in that context.

Like Ricardo, von Thünen recognized that differences in the cost of producing agricultural products result from utilization of land of different quality and location (i.e., distance from a central selling point). But whereas Ricardo focused on differences in soil fertility, von Thünen concentrated his analysis on differences in land location. At the same time, he recognized that those products that are bulky in relation to value are more costly to transport than those that are less so and that some farm products cannot stand a long period in transit because of their perishability.

The problem, therefore, was to devise the best (most profitable) system of land utilization. Von Thünen's solution was so carefully worked out that he rightfully deserves the distinction of being called the father of location theory in economics. His argument was couched in a theoretical construction, or model, which has the following characteristics. A large town (market) is situated in the center of a fertile plain that has neither canals nor navigable rivers. The only means of conveyance is by horse-drawn wagon or a similar means of transport. All land within the plain is of equal fertility, and there are no other comparative advantages of production between plots. At a considerable distance from the city, the plain ends in an uncultivated wilderness. The town draws its produce from the plain, the inhabitants of which it supplies with manufactured products. There is no trade with the outside world.

A model developed by Melvin Greenhut shows how the boundaries of production are determined for two competing crops once the costs of production and transportation are known. In Figure 13-1 assume that O is the central market point in the middle of a homogeneous plain. OA is the cost of producing a dollar's worth of potatoes and $A'S$ is the cost of transporting the potatoes over a distance of OJ miles. Similarly, $A''T$ and OK represent an identical cost and distance in the opposite direction. AS and AT show the gradual increase in transport costs (and total costs) as the distance from O increases. On the other hand, OB represents the cost of producing a dollar's worth of wheat, and $B'M$ ($B''N$) represents its transport cost for distance OX' (OX). The freight rate is assumed to be higher on potatoes than on wheat because the former yields a greater bulk per acre than the latter.

Von Thünen's assumption of a uniform, homogeneous plain implies that labor and capital are equally productive at all locations and that the cost of production per acre of output is everywhere the same. From Figure 13-1 it will be seen that at a distance beyond OL, the delivered cost of a dollar's worth of potatoes (cost line AS) exceeds the delivered cost of a dollar's worth of wheat (cost line BM). Therefore, producers of potatoes will tend to locate to the west of L and to the east of H, whereas wheat producers will locate to the east of L and to the west of H.

Furthermore, if transport costs are the same in every direction, OL becomes the radius of a circle within which potato production will take place. In other words, von Thünen's model gives us the least-cost location for each crop within the isolated state. It also illustrates the principle of equimarginal allocation. Resources should be allocated to potato production only up to the point where the cost of producing a dollar's worth of potatoes equals the cost of producing a dollar's worth of wheat. Finally, the model can be generalized to include more than two crops.

Von Thünen's theory deals with the classical problem in location analysis, namely, the location of producers over an area that serves consumers at a cen-

FIGURE 13-1
The delivered cost of a dollar's worth of potatoes (AS or AT) exceeds the delivered cost of a dollar's worth of wheat (BM or BN) to the east of L and to the west of H. Therefore potato producers will locate in the OL and OH regions, and wheat will be grown in the LX' and HX regions.

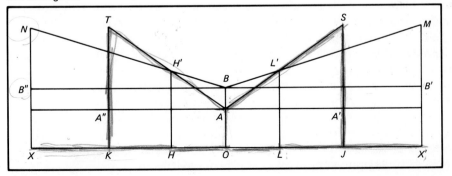

tral point. Although its assumptions are restrictive, it nevertheless marked a significant beginning in locational analysis and in mathematical economics. Moreover, Greenhut has shown that the analysis is not limited to agricultural locations but can be adapted to the locational decision of manufacturing concerns as well.

GOSSEN

The first writer who developed a full-fledged theory of consumption grounded in the marginal principle was Hermann Heinrich Gossen (1810–1858), also a native of Germany. He served as a tax assessor for the Prussian government but had retired from this position by the time he wrote his one great work in 1854, a book entitled *Development of the Laws of Human Relationships and of Rules to Be Derived Therefrom for Human Action.* Despite its author's high expectations, the book passed almost unnoticed. In bitter disappointment, Gossen recalled all of the unsold copies from the publisher (who had published it on commission only) and destroyed them. Afflicted with tuberculosis soon afterward, Gossen died in 1858, convinced that his ideas, original and valuable as they were, would never bring honor to his name. So ended in personal tragedy a life that had much to give theoretical economics but that received even less recognition than the life of the pioneer Cournot.

Technically speaking, Gossen's work is of a piece with that of Dupuit, Jevons, Walras, and, to a somewhat lesser extent, Menger. Yet more than anyone else—with the possible exception of Jevons—Gossen's economics seems to be rooted in an attempt to mathematicize Bentham's hedonic calculus. Gossen viewed economics as the theory of pleasure and pain, or, more specifically, how people as individuals and as groups may realize the maximum of pleasure with the minimum of painful effort. He insisted that mathematical treatment was the only sound way to handle economic relations and applied this method throughout his work to determine maxima and minima.

Gossen's book was organized in two parts of about equal length. The first, devoted to pure theory, has attracted the most (belated) attention for its early formulation of the two laws that have come to bear Gossen's name. Gossen's first law formulated the principal of diminishing marginal utility and gave it graphical expression. His second law described the condition for utility maximization: to maximize utility a given quantity of a good must be divided among different uses in such a manner that the marginal utilities are equal in all uses. Also in this first part of his work are Gossen's laws of exchange (accompanied by complicated geometrical representation) and his theory of rent. The second part of his book is devoted to applied theory, including the "rules of conduct pertaining to desires and pleasures" and the refutation of certain "social errors" concerning education, property, money, and credit. Philosophically, Gossen was a utilitarian and a classical liberal; that is, he was opposed to government intervention, especially in those instances when individual initiative and free competition suffice as guiding principles of the economic order.

The neglect of Gossen's work was a setback for the progress of economic theory. He was rediscovered by Jevons in 1879, but only after independent discoveries of the same magnitude had been made in economics by Jevons, Menger, and Walras. Important contributions to the subjective theory of value and the marginal principle preceded Gossen's, of course (Dupuit's contribution appeared a decade earlier, for example), but no work carried either idea as far as Gossen did until after 1870. His bitter disappointment at the neglect of his work was understandable, but it must be noted that Gossen was naive in an almost childlike way. He openly proclaimed that his work did for economics what Copernicus had done for astronomy—a somewhat pretentious claim that Léon Walras (see Chapter 16) nevertheless took for understatement. But then we must remember Walras's own disappointment when he did not receive the Nobel Peace Prize after putting his own name in nomination. As for Gossen, perhaps the most encouraging thing that can be said of his personal tragedy is that the future was on his side.

VON MANGOLDT

Hans Karl Emil von Mangoldt (1824–1868) had an advantage over von Thünen and Gossen insofar as he operated from an academic base. Having received his doctorate in 1847 from the University of Tübingen, he then studied for two years under Roscher's supervision at the University of Leipzig and for a short time with Georg Hanssen[1] at the University of Göttingen. In between he pursued a journalistic career that he was forced to abandon in 1854 because of his liberal beliefs. Mangoldt got permission to teach on the basis of his first book, a study of entrepreneurial profits, published in 1855. Seven years later he was elected to the chair vacated by Karl Knies at the University of Freiburg. In 1863, he published his second book, an *Outline of Economics,* a small treatise that had its origin in Mangoldt's lecture notes but nevertheless contained some highly original theoretical innovations. T.W. Hutchison called it "a distant infant cousin of Marshall's *Principles*" (*Review of Economic Doctrines,* p. 134).

Mangoldt's theoretical work is divided into two parts. As noted, his first book (1855) developed the theory of profit and the role of the entrepreneur. This book shows the combined influence of Roscher and von Thünen (through Hanssen). It was probably inspired in part by the challenge of socialism, which induced Mangoldt to take a fresh look at how factor rewards are distributed. Mangoldt was one of a few early writers who separated the entrepreneur from the capitalist and linked entrepreneurial profit to risk taking. Specifically, he characterized entrepreneurial profits as the reward for a range of activities, including finding particular markets, clever acquisition of productive agents,

---

[1] Georg Hanssen (1809–1894) held a faculty position at Göttingen where he was known primarily for his empirical work, but he also did much to draw attention to the work of von Thünen.

skillful combination of factors of production on the right scale, successful sales policy, and in the final analysis, innovation. Frank Knight found Mangoldt's profit theory "a most careful and exhaustive analysis" (*Risk, Uncertainty and Profit*, p. 27).

The second part of Mangoldt's work (the *Outline*) consists of a reworking of the main parts of economic theory from a curiously ambiguous perspective, one that combined aspects of classical and neoclassical analysis. Despite this ambiguity, the list of original contributions by Mangoldt is fairly impressive, considering the fact that Mill's *Principles* represented the state of the discipline in Mangoldt's day. This list includes a "Marshallian" treatment of supply and demand, embryonic notions of elasticity and economies of scale, a discussion of multiple equilibriums, the generalization of von Thünen's (marginal productivity) principle of distribution (especially a generalized concept of rent), and a graphical analysis of price formation under conditions of joint supply and demand.

Mangoldt's subjective theory of value must be added to the small but growing list of such treatments before 1871, but the subjective viewpoint did not permeate his analysis as it did the later work of the Austrians. In fact, even though Menger knew of Mangoldt's work, he seemed to be little influenced by it. As regards von Thünen and Gossen, from whom Menger could have profited, they seemed to be altogether unknown to him. The German economists Menger showed greatest familiarity with were mostly, but not exclusively, historicists. They included Hermann, Hildebrand, Hufeland, Knies, Rau, Roscher, Schäffle, and Storch. Consequently, the purpose of this section has not been to link von Thünen, Gossen, and Mangoldt with the Austrian school in any overt sense but merely to indicate the depth and breadth of Teutonic economic thought in the nineteenth century. In this manner, the stage is set for an appreciation of the Austrian contribution. We wish to note, however, that a retrospective view of the contributions of early German theorists gives new force and meaning to Alfred Marshall's statement that "the most important economic work that has been done on the Continent in this century [19th] is that of Germany" (*Principles*, p. 66).

CARL MENGER (1840–1921)

Life and Methödenstreit

The fundamental details of Menger's life can be set forth simply. He was born in 1840 in Galicia, then part of Austria, and he came from a family of Austrian civil servants and army officers. Menger studied law at the universities of Prague and Vienna, and in 1867 he turned to economics, perhaps because of an interest in stock market prices (he covered the stock market for a time as a writer for the Vienna *Zeitung*). Menger published his carefully written *Grundsätze* (translated as *Principles of Economics*) in 1871, and his fame soon began to spread. He received an appointment to the University of Vienna, where he stayed until his retirement in 1903, and between 1876 and 1878 he served as tutor to Crown Prince Rudolf.

At first blush, Menger appears to have been the epitome of the devoted and uncomplicated academic. But in fact he was the leader of a veritable theoretical revolution, the founder of a school of thought, and a verbal scrapper par excellence against what he regarded as the excesses of German historicism.

In his latter role, Menger was a major protagonist in the *methödenstreit* (method struggle) with historicist Gustav Schmoller (see Chapter 10). Menger achieved a certain fame by attacking Schmoller in 1883 *(Untersuchungen über die Methode des Sozialwissenschaften)* and by defending the Austrian approach of concentrating upon the subjective, atomistic nature of economics. Emphasizing all-important *subjective* factors, Menger defended self-interest, utility maximization, and complete knowledge as the grounds upon which economics must be built. Aggregative, collective ideas could not have adequate foundation unless they rested upon individual components.

Schmoller defended the historical method as the only method relevant for analyzing the social organism. In Schmoller's view, the Austrians, by focusing upon the individual's behavior under constraints, were leaving out the most important things—dynamic institutions. In the end, the debate became personal and, in consequence, pointless. Schmoller and his followers (effectively, it would seem) boycotted Austrian professors at German universities, and it was a long while before Germany produced theorists of the first rank. In the end, however, the steady influence of Menger's *Principles*[2] and the work of the disciples he attracted began to overcome historicist criticism, and the controversy ended with the Austrians winning. Austrian economics picked up adherents in England (William Smart and James Bonar), and the day was eventually won by subjective utility analysis. We now turn to the hub of Austrian theory, Menger's *Principles*.

Menger and Economizing Man

Menger began his investigation into value theory with a lengthy and systematic discussion of goods. He distinguished goods from what he called "useful things." In order for a thing to possess goods character, four conditions had to be met simultaneously: (1) the thing must fulfill a human need, (2) it must have properties that would render it capable of being brought into a causal connection with the satisfaction of the need, (3) there must be a recognition of this causal connection, and (4) there must be command of the thing sufficient to direct it to the satisfaction of the need. If one of these conditions was missing, all a person would have was a useful thing.

Menger also distinguished goods by order. Goods of the first order are ca-

---

[2] Ironically, Menger dedicated his *Principles* to Wilhelm Roscher, founder of the older historical school. As noted in Chap. 10, Roscher was far less extreme in his critique of economic theory than Schmoller.

pable of satisfying human needs directly, while higher-order goods (capital, production goods) derive goods character from their ability to produce lower-order goods. Higher-order goods can satisfy human needs only indirectly, for as Menger pointed out with reference to the production of bread, "What human need could be satisfied by a specific labor service of a journeyman baker, by a baking utensil, or even by a quantity of ordinary flour?" (*Principles,* pp. 56–57).

In further setting out laws governing goods character, Menger emphasized the *complementarity* of higher-order goods. Higher-order goods' satisfaction of needs requires command over complementary goods of higher order. An individual, for example, may have everything he or she needs to make bread except yeast. In consequence, other higher-order things lose goods character. (If these items are involved in the production of a number of goods, they do not lose goods character because of the absence of yeast.)

An interesting passage in which Menger related the causal connection between first-order goods and higher-order goods relates to tobacco. Suppose, with Menger, that because of a change in tastes, the demand for tobacco disappeared (much to the delight of the American Cancer Society). What would be the consequence? According to Menger:

> If, as the result of a change in tastes, the need for tobacco should disappear completely, the first consequence would be that all stocks of finished tobacco products on hand would be deprived of their goods-character. A further consequence would be that the raw tobacco leaves, the machines, tools, and implements applicable exclusively to the processing of tobacco, the specialized labor services employed in the production of tobacco products, the available stocks of tobacco seeds, etc., would lose their goods-character. The services, presently so well paid, of the agents who have so much skill in the grading and merchandising of tobaccos in such places as Cuba, Manila, Puerto Rico, and Havana, as well as the specialized labor services of the many people both in Europe and in those distant countries, who are employed in the manufacture of cigars, would cease to be goods (*Principles,* p. 65).

It is the causal sequence, i.e., the notion that the value (and goods character) of first-order goods is transmitted or imputed to higher-order goods, that so typifies Austrian economics. Menger also emphasized a basic complementarity and interdependence of all goods we consume, and he formed the basis for constrained utility maximization by his statement, "The most complete satisfaction of a single need cannot maintain life and welfare." This complementarity, which Menger so belabored with respect to consumption, was also, as we shall see, carried over to production by the Austrians.

Economic Goods and the Valuation Process

After a very detailed analysis of a good, Menger set out to show how humans, on the basis of a knowledge of available supply and demand, direct the available quantities of goods to the greatest possible satisfaction. In Menger's view, the origins of human economy were coincident with the origins of economic goods. *Economic goods* are defined as those whose requirements are greater than the available supply. *Noneconomic goods,* conversely, are those, such as air or water, whose supply exceeds requirements. And here Menger makes an interesting point—that the basis for property is the protection of ownership of economic goods. (Communism, by contrast, is founded upon noneconomic relations.) Of course, there is nothing inherent in goods that makes them economic or noneconomic; their character can change with changes in supply or requirements.

According to Menger, a good is said to have value if economizing humans perceive that the satisfaction of one of their needs (or the greater or lesser completeness of its satisfaction) depends on their command over the good. Utility is the capacity of a thing to satisfy human needs, and—provided the utility is recognized—it is a prerequisite of goods character. Menger carefully pointed out that noneconomic goods may also possess utility since the subjective valuation between use and need (one's need for air or water, for instance) relates to a specific quantity; use value is a characteristic of only economic goods since it presupposes scarcity.

Menger's distinctions call to mind Smith's water-diamond dilemma. Smith, it will be recalled, was puzzled by the fact that water, which has so much value in use, has no value in exchange, while diamonds, which have practically no value in use, are exchanged at high prices. Menger argued that both water and diamonds undisputedly possess utility, the difference being that diamonds are scarce relative to the demand for them. Further, the subjective valuation between use of, and need for, water could not be related to a specific quantity, and water therefore cannot possess use value. Use value presupposes scarcity, and economic goods alone possess use value.

The Equimarginal Principle

Although Menger was preceded by Gossen, he presented one of the first clear discussions of the equimarginal principle of welfare maximization. He first emphasized that satisfactions have different degrees of importance to people:

> The maintenance of life depends neither on having a comfortable bed nor on having a chessboard, but the use of these goods contributes, and certainly in very different degrees, to the increase of our well-being. Hence there can also be no doubt that, when men have a choice between doing without a comfortable bed or doing without a chessboard, they will forgo the latter much more readily than the former (*Principles*, p. 123).

This is the subjective factor in an economizing individual's valuation process, i.e., the extent to which different satisfactions have different degrees of importance. Menger also emphasized that within the same class of goods, satisfactions may vary in importance. The point is that people try to satisfy the more urgent needs before the less urgent, but they will *combine* the more complete satisfaction of more pressing wants with the lesser satisfaction of less pressing wants.

TABLE 13-1
THE THEORY OF VALUE

I	II	III	IV	V	VI	VII	VIII	IX	X
10	9	8	7	6	5	4	3	2	1
9	8	7	6	5	4	3	2	1	0
8	7	6	5	4	3	2	1	0	
7	6	5	4	3	2	1	0		
6	5	4	3	2	1	0			
5	4	3	2	1	0				
4	3	2	1	0					
3	2	1	0						
2	1	0							
1	0								
0									

Menger illustrated his theory with the use of numbers, shown above in Table 13-1. The Roman numerals depict ten classes of wants, with want III less urgent than want II, want IV less urgent than want III, and so on. Menger assumed that an individual is able to rank satisfactions and to assign number indices to them (cardinal ranking). Thus the individual can say that consumption of the first unit of commodity I (food) yields 10 units of satisfaction, while the first unit of commodity V (say, tobacco) gives but 6. Further, satisfactions from consuming, say, goods IV and VII (or any other two goods) are independent. Some other resource (other than goods I to X) is being used, moreover, to obtain units of these ten goods, and additional unit amounts of each commodity may be obtained with an equal expenditure of the resource (for convenience, we call this other resource "money," and we assume that the unit price of all goods is $1).

An economizing person, according to Menger, would behave in the following manner. If the individual possessed scarce means in the amount of $3 and spent it all on the commodity of highest importance (1), he or she would obtain 27 units of satisfaction. The individual would, however, seek to combine satisfactions obtained from commodities I and II. Buying 2 units of commodity I and 1 unit of commodity II, the individual would obtain 28 units of satisfaction. With, say, $15 at his or her command, the individual would allocate expenditures so that, at the margin, the satisfaction obtainable from commodities I through V would just equal 6, as can easily be verified from Table 13-1.[3] Thus Menger established an equimarginal principle. That is, given scarce means (dollars, in our example), the individual will arrange his or her various con-

[3] The reader may be wondering what the economizing individual would do if he or she possessed $16 rather than $15. Another expenditure of $1 would yield only 5 units of satisfaction, and satisfactions would then *not* be equal at the margin. Unless units of all commodities were infinitely divisible (an assumption of mathematical continuity), the individual would be in disequilibrium. The result is a consequence of Menger's discrete ordering.

sumptions so that at the margin, satisfactions are equal. In doing so, Menger's economizing individual, like that of Jevons, maximizes total satisfaction.

Menger, in rather Germanic prose, described an objective, concrete factor in the valuation process:

> Accordingly, in every concrete case, of all the satisfactions secured by means of the whole quantity of a good at the disposal of an economizing individual, only those that have the least importance to him are dependent on the availability of a given portion of the whole quantity. Hence the value to this person of any portion of the whole available quantity of the good is equal to the importance to him of the satisfactions of least importance among those assured by the whole quantity and achieved with an equal portion (*Principles,* p. 132).

Thus it is the least urgent satisfaction obtainable from a given stock of goods that gives value to that good. For example, imagine a given quantity of water available to an individual. He or she puts the available stock to many uses, from the most urgent (maintaining life) to the least (watering his or her flower garden). The determination of the value of any portion of water is in this case objective—it is in its least important use, gardening. Any given portion of the good could stand for any other portion, of course.

In extending value theory, Menger also considered the impact of differences in the quality of goods on their value. Like Jevons, moreover, he presented a theory of exchange and its limits, concluding that under certain cases, "If command of a certain amount of A's goods were transferred to B and if command of a certain amount of B's goods were transferred to A, the needs of both economizing individuals could be better satisfied than would be the case in the absence of this reciprocal transfer" (*Principles,* pp. 177–178). His examples of isolated exchange are copious, eschew mathematical expression, and are often cumbersome. In addition, Menger analyzed the effects of competitive and monopoly structures upon price. Like Jevons, but unlike Dupuit, he did not relate utility (satisfactions, in Menger's terms) to the demand curve. Thus, along with Jevons, he ignored consumers' surplus. Yet a survey of Menger's overall contributions to utility and value theory reveals a contribution of clear originality in breadth and in choice of exposition. It remains to take a brief look at Menger's important development of the concept of imputation.

Imputation and Factor Values

One of Menger's most interesting and important contributions relates to his attempt to value higher-order goods (productive resources). *Opportunity cost* is clearly understood in relation to the value of final goods to Menger's economizing individual. The value of a particular good to an individual is equal, in Menger's words, "to the importance he attaches to the satisfactions he would have to forgo if he did not have command of it." But Menger applied an opportunity cost concept to the valuation of higher-order goods as well.

Menger's valuation experiments are best understood by means of a simple example.

Suppose a given amount of labor (*a*), capital (*b*), and land (*c*) combine to produce some output (*x*). Upon what does the value of any unit of productive resources—say, a unit of labor—depend? The value of a unit of labor is determined by the net loss of satisfaction resulting from the reduction in final output attributable to the unit of labor. The reduction in output depends, of course, on the degree to which the productive resources are substitutable. Productive relations may generally be of two sorts: (1) *variable proportions,* in which the proportions of different higher-order goods can be altered to produce a given output, and (2) *fixed proportions,* in which a fixed amount of one resource must be combined with a fixed amount of another resource to produce a given output. An example of the former might be the ability to alter proportions of fertilizer and land to produce a given amount of agricultural output. Fixed-proportion relations might be typified by the necessary proportions of hydrogen and oxygen to produce water. Menger clearly understood the importance of both types of productive relations and their significance for the valuation of higher-order goods, and, unlike Wieser and Böhm-Bawerk, he emphasized the very wide range within which proportions could be varied.

Returning to our example, how would Menger evaluate a unit of labor? He gives explicit directions:

> Assuming in each instance that all available goods of higher order are employed in the most economic fashion, the value of a concrete quantity of a good of higher order is equal to the difference in importance between the satisfactions that can be attained when we have command of the given quantity of the good of higher order whose value we wish to determine and the satisfactions that would be attained if we did not have this quantity at our command (*Principles,* pp. 164–165).

In the case of variable proportions, the reduction in a unit of labor *a* would mean that the output of *x* (x^0) would be reduced, say, to some x^1. The remaining labor, capital, and land still produce *x*. The value of the unit of labor would then be the difference in total satisfaction when x^0 was produced and when x^1 was produced (or $x^0 - x^1$). Menger's theory might be characterized as a *marginal-value-productivity* theory of input valuation.

If productive relations are arranged in rigidly fixed proportions, on the other hand, the reduction of a unit of labor would mean that no *x* would be produced. Would the value of a unit of labor (or of any of the other inputs), then, be the whole output of *x?* Assuming that resources are originally combined to produce goods for a maximum of satisfaction, a recombination of the remaining labor, capital, and land could produce a *different* good—say, *y*—but it would result in lower total satisfaction. Thus Menger reasoned that the value of a unit of labor would be the difference between total satisfaction when the unit was used to produce *x* (x^0) and total satisfaction when all resources but that unit were used to produce some other good, *y*. Unfortunately, it is difficult to develop a concept of marginal productivity under such circumstances, and

Wieser and Böhm-Bawerk all but ignored Menger's insistence on the applicability of variable proportions. Wieser, however, significantly enriched certain of Menger's ideas on value and on the valuation of higher-order goods. It is to these developments that we now turn.

FRIEDRICH VON WIESER (1851–1926)

Friedrich von Wieser was born in Vienna in 1851 of aristocratic parents. At the age of seventeen he entered the University of Vienna to study law. After graduating in 1872, Wieser was briefly employed in government service, although his strong intellectual interests attracted him to academics once more, this time to a study of economics. With a travel grant and along with his boyhood friend (and later brother-in-law), Eugen von Böhm-Bawerk, Wieser studied economics at the universities of Heidelberg (under Karl Knies), Jena, and Leipzig. Already much impressed with Menger's *Principles,* Wieser, while in Germany, wrote a seminar paper on value that formed the foundation for his later ideas. In 1884, he was appointed a professor of economics at the German University in Prague. In 1903, Wieser inherited Menger's position at the University of Vienna. He became Minister of Commerce in 1917, but (owing to the collapse of the Austro-Hungarian Empire) later returned to teaching. A man of far-ranging intellect, Wieser maintained his broad interests by extensive writing on numerous topics and by creating, in his own home, a forum for artistic and intellectual communication (he was a great fan of the opera).

Wieser's most important theoretical work was *Natural Value* (*Der natürliche Werth*), published in Vienna in 1889. His vast interests led him to undertake a work that melded economic theory and institutional analysis, *Social Economics,* which was written as the invited theoretical volume in the massive *Grundriss der Sozialökonomik* under the editorship of Max Weber. J. A. Schumpeter's *Economic Doctrine and Method,* which later became the *History of Economic Analysis,* was written as the methodological volume in the series.

In his later years, Wieser's interests turned to sociology, and on the basis of an exhaustive analysis of numerous societal organizations, he published his great sociological study and last work, *Das Gesetz der Macht* (1926). Although Wieser possessed an incredible range of interests, his major one was economics, and he is famous chiefly for his extensions of Menger's ideas on utility, value, and input-output valuations. Unfortunately, however, the emphasis placed upon his purely theoretical ideas has clouded interest in his later and seminal work, *Social Economics.* Thus the following discussion will attempt to balance both aspects of Wieser's contribution. We begin with a discussion of some of the major theoretical ideas of *Natural Value.*

Value Theory

Some of the most interesting and important contributions to Austrian value theory were made by Wieser, including his invention of the term "marginal utility" (*Grenznutzen*). Wieser's basic statement of the general law of value expanded upon Menger's earlier model. With the aid of an arithmetic example, Wieser explained the law:

(I) Goods	0	1	2	3	4	5	6	7	8	9	10	11
(II) Prices	0	10	9	8	7	6	5	4	3	2	1	0
(III) Total utility	0	10	19	27	34	40	45	49	52	54	55	55
(IV) Total value	0	10	18	24	28	30	30	28	24	18	10	0
(V) Total utility minus total value	0	0	1	3	6	10	15	21	28	36	45	55

Ascending branch   Descending branch

The first line depicts the number of goods purchased at alternative prices listed on the second line of Wieser's example (he called these prices "units of value"). Total utility from consuming alternative quantities is calculated by adding up successive units of value. For example, when the individual is consuming 2 units of the commodity, total enjoyment is 19 utility units, the sum of 1 unit at 10 and 1 unit at 9. The addition of a third unit of consumption adds a marginal utility of 8 for a total of 27 units. Note that Wieser, as Dupuit had earlier, identified price of the goods (or units of value) with marginal utility.

Line IV of the example presents the calculation of total value or receipts, that is, price multiplied by the quantity of goods sold (line I times line II). Given the negatively sloping demand function, total receipts rise first, reach a maximum, and then decline. Line V shows the value lost from indifference, and it is the difference between total utility and total receipts. Menger had argued that it is the use to which the *last* unit of a stock of goods is put that represents the value of any unit of a homogeneous stock. Wieser now argued that the total value of the stock increases by *less* than the price paid for *additional* units of the good. In adding the second unit of the stock, for example, the individual experiences a 9-unit increase in total utility, but now both units possess a valuation of 9. Since it is the marginal unit that represents value to the consumer, he or she would be unwilling to pay more than 9 for both units. In a competitive market, moreover, only one price for homogeneous goods can prevail. Thus total *receipts* will increase as long as the incremental addition to total utility exceeds the incremental loss. Wieser called this situation (purchases of goods 0 to 5 in his numerical example) the "upgrade" (or ascending) branch of value, and the opposite situation the "downgrade" (or descending) branch of value.

The Antinomy of Value: Graphics Though Wieser did not use one, a simple graphical model will illustrate these elementary but crucial points. Figure 13-2a depicts total receipts and total utility, while Figure 13-2b depicts corresponding demand, marginal-revenue, and marginal-utility functions. As quantity consumed increases between 0 and x, both total value and total utility rise, and marginal revenue is positive (but declining). These movements characterize the upgrade of value. Beyond quantity x, total utility continues to rise be-

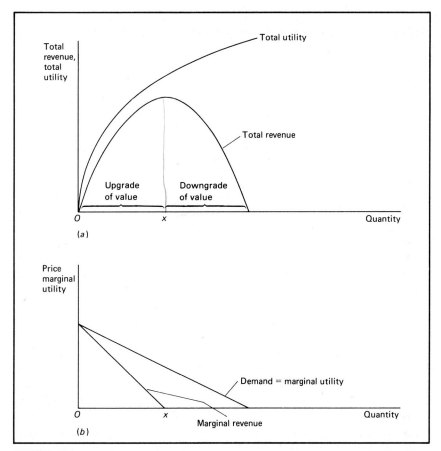

FIGURE 13-2
The upgrade of value is over the range where total utility and total revenue are rising and marginal revenue is positive. The downgrade of value is over the range of output where total utility is still rising but total revenue is declining and marginal revenue is negative.

cause marginal utility is still positive, but total receipts begin to decline (marginal revenue is negative).[4]

What conclusions did Wieser draw from these aspects of his value theory? Though he thought that for the most part society's production was on the upgrade of value—that is, total receipts and utility increasing together—he nevertheless noted the antinomy (opposition) between exchange value and utility in the downgrade. In the downgrade (for quantities greater than x in Figures 13-2a and 13-2b) total utility is still rising when total receipts are falling. Rea-

---

[4] It might be worthwhile to compare Wieser's model with Dupuit's (see Chap. 12) on these points.

sons for the antinomy between value and utility were clearly set forth by Wieser:

> In every self-contained private economy utility is the highest principle; but, in the business world, wherever the providing of society with goods is in the hands of undertakers who desire to make a gain out of it, and to obtain a remuneration for their services, exchange value takes its place. The private entrepreneur is not concerned to provide the greatest utility for society generally; his aim is rather to obtain the highest value for himself—which is at the same time his highest utility. Utility approves itself as the first principle in the entrepreneur's economy; but, just because of this, in the conflict between exchange value and social utility, it is exchange value which is victorious,—so far at least as the entrepreneur has power to act according to his own interest (*Natural Value*, p. 55).

Wieser was, of course, describing the deleterious effects of monopoly on social utility. The antinomy held only insofar as the entrepreneur possessed economic power. Under free competition, as Dupuit indicated earlier, social utility will be maximized, and no antinomy between value and utility will exist. In fact, Wieser concluded that the "economic history of our own time is rich in examples which prove that competition can press prices far on the down grade of exchange value."

But what of those cases where competition did not prevail? Though he believed that those instances were too few to justify a socialist economic organization, Wieser advocated "selected" governmental interferences, which we shall encounter in connection with our discussion of his later work, *Social Economics*. Wieser, however, noted another important breakdown in the services of exchange value in a real economy. In a self-contained, idealized economy, value in use depends upon utility, and goods are produced according to the rank of their value. Exchange value is, in this case, the measure of personal acquisition.

In a real economy, exchange value depends not only upon utility but upon purchasing power as well. Exchange value in the real world does *not* necessarily measure value in use, or utility. In such a world, production is determined not only by "simple want" but also by the superior means of a part of the populace. Cognizant of the radical implications of applying utility theory to a real economy, Wieser clearly noted:

> Instead of things which would have the greatest utility, those things are produced for which the most will be paid. The greater the differences in wealth, the more striking will be the anomalies of production. It will furnish luxuries for the wanton and the glutton, while it is deaf to the wants of the miserable and the poor. It is therefore the distribution of wealth which decides how production is set to work, and induces consumption of the most uneconomic kind: a consumption which wastes upon unnecessary and culpable enjoyment what might have served to heal the wounds of poverty (*Natural Value*, p. 58).

The disparity of purchasing power between demanders leads to still another anomaly. The price of some commodities, e.g., bread, is determined by the valuation of the weakest buyers, ordinarily the poorest. Wealthy people, on the other hand, do not have to pay their maximum demand price for bread, but only that price determined by the weakest buyer's valuation. Wieser claimed, "It is only where the rich compete among themselves for luxuries...that they pay according to their own ability, and are measured according to their own personal standard." Real-world prices, in other words, do not ordinarily reflect the marginal-utility valuations that would exist if the marginal utility of purchasing power were the same for all individual demanders (such a state would not require equality of income distribution).

Natural Value   In order to bring these ideas into focus, Wieser constructed an idealized model of value as it would exist in a communistic state. Natural value would exist where goods were valued simply by the relation between the amount of the stock and marginal utilities. It would not be disturbed by "error, fraud, force, change," or the existence of private property and the consequent disparities in purchasing power. Utility, or value in use, would be the sole guide to the allocation of scarce resources in the production of goods. Production decisions would be determined by highest marginal-utility valuations and not by fragmented income distribution.

Although Wieser's model is at a high level of abstraction, he came to a most important practical conclusion from considering it. The conclusion, which has been all too slowly learned by communist countries, was that goods and factor prices play a crucial role in determining an optimum allocation of scarce resources. Land rent is a case in point. As Wieser noted:

> Land rent is, perhaps, the formation of value that is most frequently attacked in our present economy. Now I believe our examination will show that, even in the communistic state, there must be land rent. Such a state must, under certain circumstances, calculate the return from land, and must, from certain portions of land, calculate a greater return than from others: the circumstances upon which such a calculation is dependent are essentially the same as those which to-day determine the existence of rent, and the height of rent. The only difference lies in this, that, as things now are, rent goes to the private owner of the land, whereas, in a communistic state, it would fall to the entire united community (*Natural Value*, pp. 62–63).

Thus the formation of natural value, even in a communistic state, requires a market-system allocation. Rents and "natural" returns to all factors had to be paid in order to ensure an economic distribution of resources. These returns, however, did not have to be privately received, and they could be taxed away by government.[5]

In sum, Wieser's analysis of value uncovered the fact that the formation of value was a neutral phenomenon. An understanding of natural value did not provide evidence either for or against a socialist organization of society (presumably the case had to rest upon other grounds). It was the foundation for

---

[5] Henry George, an American economist, said as much in his *Progress and Poverty* (1879). George advocated the taxation of urban site rents in order that "productive" factors (labor and capital) might be encouraged.

exchange value in *all* societies, irrespective of the fact that natural value was overlaid with many other factors (such as controls, regulations, fiat, vast differences in purchasing power, and monopoly). Wieser was the first economist to point out the generality of the theory of utility valuation and, explicitly, the usefulness of the market system in allocating resources irrespective of social organization.

Factor Valuation: Wieser's Theory of Imputation

Wieser much admired Menger's earlier treatment of imputation and clearly built his system of input and output valuation upon it, although he discovered a critical weakness in his mentor's approach. Menger had argued that the value of a complementary good in production might be determined by removing it from the combination producing the output where the input's marginal productivity is highest. In the case of fixed proportions, removal of one of the inputs required the recombination of the others to produce a different product. The value of the removed factor (which Menger termed the "share dependent upon cooperation") was then determined by the difference in value terms between the old product (with the removed factor) and the alternative product (made with the remaining inputs). The problem, as Wieser plainly saw, was that *overvaluation* was possible.

Wieser's simple example makes his criticism clear. Suppose the total value produced by three inputs in their best alternative (highest-marginal-utility product) is 10 units of value. Taking away one of the inputs and recombining the other two might generate a product with 6 units of value. The value of the removed input is then 4. The problem, which Wieser recognized, was that all the inputs could be valued in the same way, giving 12 as the sum of their separate values. But their value in combination was only 10! Consequently, Menger's method could lead to overvaluation of inputs.

The Simultaneous Solution   As an alternative method, Wieser suggested that the productive contribution of the input be the modus operandi of the valuation process. As Wieser put it, "The deciding element is not that portion of the return which is lost through the loss of a good, but that which is secured by its possession" (*Natural Value*, p. 85). In order to arrive at this deduction, Wieser assumed that all production goods (inputs) are actually employed in an optimum fashion. Returning to Menger's example, he assumed that resources are combined in fixed proportions (although he clearly recognized the existence of variable proportions in the real world). A hunter, for example, depends upon both rifle and cartridge to kill a tiger that is about to spring on him or her. Valued together, Wieser argued, the value of rifle and cartridge is the success of the shot. Taken singly, however, the value of each cannot be calculated. As Wieser pointed out, there are two unknowns (x and y) and one equation, $x + y = 100$, where 100 is the value of the successful result.

With more unknowns than equations, the problem cannot be solved. But

Wieser's ingenious solution was to determine the contribution of combined productive factors in every industry and to set this contribution out in equations. As he directed:

It is possible not only to separate these effects approximately, but to put them into exact figures, so soon as we collect and measure all the important circumstances of the matter; such as the amount of the products, their value, and the amount of the means of production employed at the time. If we take these circumstances accurately into account, we obtain a number of equations, and we are in a position to make a reliable calculation of what each single instrument of production does (*Natural Value*, pp. 87–88).

As an example of his calculation of the contribution of cooperating productive inputs, Wieser presented three industry equations with three unknown input values:

$$x + y = 100$$
$$2x + 3z = 290$$
$$4y + 5z = 590$$

Here x, y, and z are productive inputs, and the right-hand side of the equality is the total value produced by the *combined* inputs (the combinations are, of course, fixed). Solving simultaneously, the values of the inputs are determined: $x = 40$, $y = 60$, and $z = 70$. Each input is thus ascribed a definite share in producing total value. Wieser's productive contribution, in other words, is that portion of the total return that is attributed to an individual productive element. These values, in a simultaneous system, exactly exhaust total product.

Resource Allocation   Importantly, Wieser's simultaneous solution may be viewed in a slightly different manner, one that illustrates the Austrian view of the whole valuation process. The issue might be put in the form of a question: Assuming that resources are properly allocated and that the system is in equilibrium (as we did in the equations above), what is the value of each input, and how are resources allocated?[6] Given that an input is used in the production of a number of final or consumer goods, its value will be determined by the *least* valuable good that it produces. This value is determined at the margin, by the marginal utility of the last unit of the least valuable good the input is producing. Input value is imputed, and the value of the input, thus derived, establishes the opportunity cost of utilizing it in all other industry productions requiring it. Given fixed-proportions production functions in all industries and

---

[6] Wieser referred to these inputs as "cost means" of production. He contrasted these cost means with cost-specific means of production. Cost-specific means are those inputs that are scarce or those that are suited only to the production of one product or a limited number of products. Cost means of production, on the other hand, are distributed over the entire productive process. As a general rule, Wieser thought that labor and capital should be regarded as cost means, while land should usually be classed as specific means.

the rational (profit-maximizing) allocation of resources, the supplies of all other goods utilizing the input will be determined. Given the marginal utilities for these other goods, values are determined.

It is important to note that Wieser's (the Austrian) solution to the problem of input and output valuation is not like that found in the typical text on the principles of economics or like that set forth in Marshall's *Principles,* for that matter. Rather than developing the determinants of demand and supply and showing their combined role in determining value, Wieser (and the Austrians generally) emphasized the role of the marginal utility of final goods as the primary determinant of value. Supply had no independent role to play in establishing values. Inputs are valued in cause-and-effect fashion by imputation. Through opportunity cost, values of inputs and outputs are determined in the entire system.[7]

In sum, the marginal utility of final output is presented as the *source* of value by Austrian economists. In addition, they discovered a very special kind of input productivity theory, one that might best be described as a marginal-utility-product theory of input valuation. In other words, the value of an additional unit of input applied to production was determined by the marginal utility of the additional units produced ($MUP_i = MP_i \times MU_x$) rather than by the traditional marginal-*value* product, which is found by multiplying the marginal *revenue* to the firm by the marginal product of the input ($MVP_i = MP_i \times P_x$). However one views the Austrian approach in contrast to the traditional Marshallian system, it is clear that the Austrian value theory reached a high point in Wieser's *Natural Value.* Wieser's explication of the system must, in sum, rank as one of the high theoretical achievements of the Austrian school.

Wieser's *Social Economics:* Institutional Aspects of Austrian Economics

In addition to his seminal theoretical pursuits, Friedrich von Wieser was a man of catholic intellectual interests and resources. As a student in the gymnasium, he was especially attracted to history and sociology, being greatly influenced by the writings of Herbert Spencer and Count Leo Tolstoy. Tolstoy's "history of the anonymous masses," as exemplified in *War and Peace,* influenced him particularly. Wieser was attempting to explain existing social relations and social forces through a study of the broad splashes of history, but he finally concluded that economic forces, more than any other, played the dominant role in social evolution. The result was, of course, his *Natural Value,* discussed in the previous sections.

---

[7] It has been argued that, in one sense at least, this system is circular since it assumes the thing to be proved. The content of this argument is that one begins by assuming an optimum distribution of resources and then, via opportunity cost, one "explains" value and the optimum distribution of inputs. The interested reader should consult G. J. Stigler's *Production and Distribution Theories* on this point.

Wieser's thought was never deflected from his early concerns about the economic determinism of history, and although a long period of scientific investigation upon the nature and determination of value intervened, he returned to his first interest toward the end of his life. Most importantly, however, he returned to an analysis of economic society armed with an elaborate and refined subjective value theory. Wieser's carefully measured excursion into economic sociology resulted in his *Theorie der Gesellschaftlichen Wirtschaft (Social Economics)*, which appeared in 1914 on the eve of World War I. The book is an amazing tour de force filled with remarkably prophetic insights into the nature of contemporary economic processes and directions of analysis, but, unfortunately, the attention of most historians of thought has been drawn solely to Wieser's theoretical contributions.

The purpose of this section is to focus upon Wieser's theory of social economics, which was, in all essentials, a theory of economic welfare. Specifically, Wieser's welfare theory stemmed from a comparison of the determinants of value in an ideal state (simple economy, in his terms) and actual conditions resulting from the historical evolution of economic and sociological phenomena. The evolution of economic society was determined, in Wieser's view, by certain characteristics of human nature, and most especially by the elements of power and leadership as they develop in the individualistic social economy. The interesting result of these developments was a stratification of economic, political, and social relations and—following the principle of stratification—a fragmentation of utilities and prices. Drawing upon his theory of social development, Wieser was able to offer normative evaluations and prognoses concerning the development of the economic system and, specifically, to place business and labor "power blocs" at center stage.

Individualism, Institutions, and the Economic Process

Although Menger showed an early interest in the evolution of economic institutions (e.g., money and markets), Wieser made a concerted effort to integrate the theory of institutions with economic analysis. Despite his concern with collective goals (e.g., economic welfare), Wieser adopted the individualistic approach, explicitly rejecting the collective approach.

> What valid substitute may we offer for the individualistic theory of society? In its naive formulation it has become inadequate. But one cannot get away from its fundamental concept, that the individual is the subject of social intercourse. The individuals who comprise society are the sole possessors of all consciousness and of all will. The "organic" explanation (Marxian-Hegelian), which seeks to make society as such, without reference to individuals, the subject of social activity, has patently proved a failure (*Social Economics*, p. 154).

Thus for Wieser the individual is the root of all decisions, and decisions are always made in the face of constraints. Institutions enter economic analysis by defining the constraints on individual decision making. Menger had expressed the judgment that the most useful social institutions are those that evolve without conscious design. Wieser added that institutions, whether the result of conscious or unconscious design, become part of the economic process once they take their place in the social structure. In the final analysis, Wieser's economics is a bridge between the ideas of Menger and Veblen (see Chapter 17).

In Wieser's view the individual maximizes his or her utility subject to the constraints developed by ever-changing institutions, which are the collective results of individual human action. At any time the socioeconomic system has a dynamic, historical dimension that is shaped by past actions. Individuals create and destroy institutions over time. The long evolution of the institutions of any real society (as opposed to the "rarefied" state of natural value) begins with individuals diverse in abilities and natural endowments. As institutions take form, they take on a kind of power to constrain individuals in recognizable and in unrecognizable ways. These constraints are the "natural controls" of freedom to which subsequent generations are born into. Systems of property rights, contracts, laws, morals, and financial structure are all institutions of this sort, as are the behavior patterns and habits of social classes. True freedom consists of the individual's recognition that such controls lead to his or her further development, progress, and preservation.

These so-called natural controls can, of course, run amuck if society comes under the grip of tyrannical rulers. Put another way, although controls and institutions stamp every age and establish constraints on individuals, such constraints are malleable—they can and do change over time. For this reason, Wieser made an explicit appeal to leadership, which he conceived as a kind of economic, political, and moral "entrepreneurship." Leadership implies changes in all institutions, but good leaders will bring favorable change whereas bad leaders will bring unfavorable change. In other words, history is not unidimensional—it can as easily move backward as it can move forward.

A critical point of Wieser's economics is that it is economic theory that illuminates sociology, not sociology that illuminates economic behavior. Individuals are, simply, and in all things, maximizers of utility under constraints. Institutions establish the constraints and therefore indirectly determine the collective level of utility in society. Wieser's entire thought may be interpreted within this central, organizing principle.

Wieser's Welfare Theory Long before John Kenneth Galbraith, with whom the idea has been associated, Wieser argued for the establishment of labor unions as a countervailing force in the labor market. Monopolies in the product markets and monopolies in the input markets exhibited only external similarities, and whereas product monopolies are opposed to unorganized consumers, "The union is pitted against entrepreneurs who are themselves monopolistically organized as regards the demand for labor." Unorganized labor is, in terms of modern price theory, monopolistically and monopsonistically "exploited"; i.e., the workers do not receive the full value of their marginal products. Wieser believed that laborers should organize and use the strike as a defensive weapon against monopoly-monopoloid (and monopsony) structures. Contrasting unions and union activity with the theoretical results of the Austrian theory of value, Wieser found that the best that laborers can hope to achieve is their full marginal productivity. Unions are necessary where market imperfections exist on the product and resource sides of markets. Further, Wieser noted that competitive input price will be approximated in the presence of countervailing power:

> When a union enforces a wage-rate that allows the full marginal productivity, it has won a considerable success for its members. It counteracts the unhealthy consequences of the over-competition of unorganized workers on wages, as well as defeating agreements between entrepreneurs to control wages. The union compels the entrepreneurs to agree to the price that would be established by an effective competition of demand (*Social Economics,* pp. 377–378).

In addition to active unionization, Wieser also called for an expanded role for the state in fostering the spirit of the social economy. Where the supposed results of unbridled freedom do not obtain in the economy, as Wieser put it, "The state alone has a call to protect the weak." Further, the state must be recognized as an "indispensable factor in the national economic process." Essentially and broadly, the role of the state is to increase economic welfare in the face of power and capitalistic domination and vis-à-vis historically justified rights to private property. Utility theory must serve as the basis for the state's assessment of economic power. Specifically, Wieser favored energetic state regulation and/or control of imperfectly competitive firms whenever the profits of "mammoth capital" were unearned, e.g., realized without the efforts of true and enlightened leadership. Wieser proffered examples of unearned profits such as urban rents raised by the increase of population and rural ground rents for large, landed estates, in addition to abuses in founding stock companies and in stock exchange speculation.

In addition to the regulation of the social economy, the state was to undertake certain projects that would produce only a small marginal exchange value, but that—when the public's interest is taken into account—would be productive of great total utility. Most "social goods," including means of transportation (such as railroads and canals), fall into this category. For such projects, Wieser suggested a type of benefit-cost analysis that would account for the utility produced by externalities in the private economy. Market valuations, in short, may be misleading, and it is part of the legitimate function of the state to seek out and to encourage by subsidy or ownership projects productive of high total utility.

Wieser believed that the state should *not* attempt to redress all the inequalities in income and property via progressive taxation, but he found that a rationale for progressive taxation could be developed within the doctrine of diminishing marginal utility. In other words, the government should consider the "gradations of personal value that are the expression of inequalities of income and property'' in its tax policy. Progressive taxation, in addition, had its analogy in the private economy in the theory of price discrimination, which approximates a levy based on ability to pay, as, for example, railroad tariffs. The state, in some small measure, via progressive taxation, approaches the social equalization of use-value calculation in the economy. To go beyond a progressive tax on income—say, progressive wealth or property taxes—would violate the private spirit of Wieser's social economy.

The Relevance and Impact of Wieser's Normative Economics   Wieser's *Social Economics* was nothing less than a normative program of economic policy based upon Austrian economic theory and upon a theory of power. Whereas the evolutionary character of the economic system appeared as a leitmotif in Marshall's *Principles,* it played the starring role in the mature thought of Wieser. His distrust of the static-equilibrium analysis of classical and neoclassical economics was clear in his statements concerning the role of the theorist:

> The theorist must always start from the static assumption. It yields most readily to his idealizing method. Dynamic relationships cannot be clearly defined in his thinking until after the static conditions have been fully apprehended (*Social Economics,* p. 457).

Nonetheless, classical theory was, in the main, a theory of economic development, and Wieser seemed to be calling for a return to a similar analysis, although his benchmark was not the classical theory of distribution but rather the Austrian version of neoclassical utility and distribution theory. In addition, Wieser's view of the economic process was Darwinian, and he envisioned no approach to the stationary state.

Alfred Marshall's development of welfare economics, as we shall see in Chapter 15, was established within a framework of static equilibrium analysis, and he utilized the demand curve and consumers' surplus as measures of welfare. Marshall was, of course, well aware of some of the deficiencies of static equilibrium analysis, and he was careful to provide caveats throughout the *Principles.* But Wieser's was an even more striking departure in that he clearly juxtaposed a theory of power-oriented evolution with a framework of static utility analysis. Wieser then drew conclusions concerning the effects of power upon welfare. The existence of monopoly (monopoloid firms) in product and resource markets—and the resultant stratification of utilities, prices, and incomes—could be condemned, as could other institutions inhibiting welfare maximization. The potential inherent in countervailing power waxed large in his analysis of labor bargaining, antitrust intervention, and international trade. Wieser recognized that the idealized classical and neoclassical models missed some very important and fundamental developments in the economy, namely, the emergence of powerful, large-scale enterprise, not necessarily characterized by the model of pure monopoly. Thus, in contrast to other neoclassical theorists, Wieser attempted to analyze the workings of a modern economy. A similar method was undertaken by other economists of the period, including the early institutionalists, but Wieser's genuine originality lies in the combination of Austrian utility theory with an evolutionary theory of institutions. He created a normative role for economic theory in general, and specifically for utility theory. The result was of a different cast from that of Marshall or Pigou, but it was a theory of welfare nonetheless.

The policy proposals drawn from Wieser's welfare analysis were prophetic of directions taken by contemporary economic policy. Rather than refine the equilibrium conditions necessary for static welfare maximization, Wieser discounted the value of a highly refined ideal system to policy and proceeded to what might be termed a second-best solution. The relevance of Wieser's late work to contemporary economic policy is enhanced by his ever-present desire to remain within the confines of a system of private property. His importance, which exists apart from the scientific contributions of *Natural Value*, lies in the solutions he suggested to the paradox that obtains between property and the maximization of utility.

EUGEN BÖHM-BAWERK (1851–1914)

Eugen Böhm-Bawerk, brother-in-law and friend of Friedrich von Wieser, was the third of the great founders of Austrian economics. A large number of writers place Böhm-Bawerk in the pantheon of capital theorists, and some even evaluate him as the premier capital theorist. Surely his impact upon neoclassical and postneoclassical theorists, such as Knut Wicksell and Friedrich Hayek, has been of vast importance. But Böhm-Bawerk enjoyed a variety of achievements besides being a principal developer of Austrian capital theory.

Born in Brünn, Austria, in 1851, Böhm-Bawerk was the son of a highly placed government official. He entered government service briefly after graduating from the law school at the University of Vienna, but he soon was attracted to a study of economics. Along with Wieser, Böhm-Bawerk launched his economic studies in Germany, where he worked under the German historian Karl Knies. He was appointed professor of economics at the University of Innsbruck in 1881, and there he completed his first book, which concerned the value of patents as abstract, legal claims. In 1884, Böhm-Bawerk published the first volume of his three-volume magnum opus, collectively entitled *Capital and Interest (Kapital und Kapitalzins)*. The first volume is entitled *History and Critique of Interest Theories* (1884), the second (and very likely the most important) is *The Positive Theory of Capital* (1889), and the third, which is a collection of appendixes to the third edition of *The Positive Theory of Capital,* is entitled *Further Essays on Capital and Interest* (1909–1912). All these important works have been translated into English.

In addition to his writings, Böhm-Bawerk distinguished himself as a statesman. In 1889 he was called to the Ministry of Finance for the purpose of preparing taxation and currency reform. He was named Austrian Minister of Finance for the first time in 1895, again in 1897, and for the final time in 1900. His tenure in the position is associated with great stability and progress in Austrian financial management, a goal Böhm-Bawerk achieved without being associated with any political party. In 1904, he resigned and resumed his academic writing and teaching at the University of Vienna.

Though Böhm-Bawerk was a tireless scholar, his work was often interrupted by civil duties. Much of it was rushed into print; unfortunately, this was especially true of *The Positive Theory of Capital*. Thus his work has been criticized as incomplete or ambiguous. There is small doubt that it is difficult reading for one at any level of expertise. But, even though he may have been overenthusiastic about his old professor's work, Schumpeter was moved to compare Böhm-Bawerk to Ricardo and to declare that his *Positive Theory of Capital* "was an effort to scale the greatest heights that economics permits, and that the achievement actually reached a level where only a few lofty peaks are to be found."

Other historians of economic thought would not agree with Schumpeter, and presumably Professor Stigler could be placed in this camp (see his *Production and Distribution Theories*, p. 227). Irrespective of these contrasting opinions, Böhm-Bawerk's influence upon later economists (as Stigler willingly admits) outstripped even that of Menger and Wieser. Moreover, especially in the area of capital and interest theory, Böhm-Bawerk's fame persists. Many contemporary capital theorists believe, not without some justification, that neoclassical capital theory finds its roots in Böhm-Bawerk. Whatever the merits of these opposing views, it is clear that Böhm-Bawerk is a worthy candidate for our study of the history of economic analysis. We begin with a brief excursion into his lucid exposition of the role of subjective factors in establishing exchange value, after which his theory of capital and interest will be considered.

Subjective Value and Exchange

Along with Wieser, Böhm-Bawerk was an early adopter of Menger's value theory. Moreover, he adopted most of Wieser's advances over Menger's treatment, and he utilized the opportunity cost concept (as Wieser had in 1884) in discussions of the Austrian system for the pricing of inputs and outputs.

Böhm-Bawerk, in short, did not make significant advances in value theory over what had been done by his friend and colleague, Wieser. His assumptions are, for the greatest part, identical to those made by Wieser, including the ones concerning fixed-proportions production functions, an imputed theory of input (and output) valuation, and an assumption of rigidly fixed supplies of the inputs.[8] Böhm-Bawerk contributed interesting nuances on themes originally developed by Menger and Wieser, to be sure, but he did not appreciably advance this area of Austrian economics.

---

[8] Böhm-Bawerk mentions an interesting exception to rigidly fixed supplies in *The Positive Theory of Capital*. Adopting Jevons's theory of labor supply, he admitted that the disutility of work might enter as an independent determinant of input supply. But he minimized this independent determinant on the grounds that Jevons's theory requires a piece-rate system, which, Böhm-Bawerk's casual empiricism told him, was unimportant in the modern economy.

TABLE 13-2

	Strong buyers						Weak buyers			
Buyers	A_1	A_2	A_3	A_4	A_5	A_6	A_7	A_8	A_9	A_{10}
Valuation of	$300	$280	$260	$240	$220	$210	$200	$180	$170	$150
one horse	$100	$110	$150	$170	$200	$215	$250	$260		
Sellers	B_1	B_2	B_3	B_4	B_5	B_6	B_7	B_8		
	Weak sellers						Strong sellers			

One of Böhm-Bawerk's most interesting and successful variations on the subjective-value theme is of prime importance, however, both for its clarity and for its ingenuity. It is Böhm-Bawerk's discussion of how different subjective valuations affect buyers and sellers in their determination of price or objective value. The example could—with profit—be used today to illustrate the underlying subjective factors in exchange.

In *The Positive Theory of Capital*, Böhm-Bawerk demonstrated the determination of price with two-sided competition. His famous example is that of ten buyers and eight sellers of horses in a free market. All the horses offered for sale are assumed of equal quality, and all candidates for the exchange possess perfect knowledge of the market situation.

Böhm-Bawerk set up a table conveying a picture of ten buyers ($A_1 \rightarrow A_{10}$) and eight sellers ($B_1 \rightarrow B_8$) of horses and the degree of *subjective* valuation by each party to the exchange with respect to horses.[9] An adaptation of Böhm-Bawerk's table is presented here as Table 13-2.

From the table we see that buyer A_1 places a $300 subjective valuation on a horse and that he will demand a horse at any price *at or below* $300. Similarly, seller B_6, for example, places a $215 valuation on the horse he has for sale, meaning that he will sell his horse *at or above* $215. As a convention, we shall identify the strength of buyers as *decreasing* from A_1 to A_{10}, and the strength of sellers as *increasing* from B_1 to B_8. Thus seller B_1 is the weakest in that he places the lowest of the minimum subjective evaluations upon horses, and buyer A_{10} is the weakest in that he has the *lowest* of the maximum subjective valuations upon horses.

How is exchange value determined? At a bid of $150, what situation would prevail in the market? At $150 all ten willing buyers remain in the market, but only three willing sellers; that is, because of subjective evaluations, only sellers B_1, B_2, and B_3 would be willing to offer one horse each at an exchange value of $150. Obviously, the market does not clear since there are ten buyers and only three sellers at $150.

[9] Note that Böhm-Bawerk expressed the subjective valuations of buyers and sellers in terms of *objective* dollar valuations, without alluding to some of the possible theoretical problems raised thereby.

As price rises above $150, however, the horse market begins to adjust. Weaker buyers—those with lower subjective evaluations—are eliminated from the market, and as price rises, sellers are added. At a price of $210, for example, four buyers have been eliminated from the trading (buyers A_7 to A_{10}), and a total of five sellers are included. But can a price of $210 be a market-clearing price? Clearly not, since at $210, six buyers ($A_1$ to A_6), but only five sellers (B_1 to B_5), are willing to trade.

If price rises by $5 to $215, would an equilibrium be possible? Unfortunately, although buyer A_6 is dropped from the bargaining, a price of $215 *adds* seller B_6. Thus at a price of $215 there are five buyers but six sellers. The market cannot clear at $215.

By now the problem should be obvious. How might one drop buyer A_6 from exchange without simultaneously including an additional seller (in this case B_6)? The answer is simple. Price must rise above $210 to exclude A_6, but not as high as $215, so that B_6 is not included. Thus, given the data of Table 13-2, the price limits will be set as follows: price must be greater than $210 but less than $215. A price of $213 or any intermediate value would therefore clear the market.

Böhm-Bawerk put his finger on one of the determining factors in exchange value, the influence of *marginal pairs* of buyers and sellers in determining price. Successful buyer A_5 and seller B_5, coupled with unsuccessful buyer A_6 and seller B_6, are the main characters in price determination. One might phrase it in another (but a little more confusing) manner. It is the evaluations of the weakest of successful buyers (A_5) and the strongest of successful sellers (B_5) coupled with the evaluations of the strongest of unsuccessful buyers (A_6) and the weakest of unsuccessful sellers (B_6) that set the limits to exchange value.

Thus Böhm-Bawerk established that it is these marginal pairs of buyers and sellers—and these marginal pairs alone—that determine price. Outside these limits, buyers and sellers might be added indefinitely without affecting equilibrium price. The addition of buyers or sellers with subjective evaluations *within* the limits set by the marginal pairs has the effect of narrowing the limits set to price. An infinitely large addition of buyers and sellers would make the supply and demand functions look like the typical and smooth Marshallian ones we see today. But Böhm-Bawerk wished to emphasize the discrete and discontinuous nature of the functions (imagine or draw up stair-step demand and supply functions from the data of Table 13-2). Real-world market situations, in Böhm-Bawerk's view (and in the typical Austrian assumptions), were not characterized by smooth and continuously differentiable demand and supply functions, including infinite numbers of buyers and sellers. Rather, in the Austrian view, any practical exchange situation included only a finite number of traders, and the discrete nature of buyer and seller evaluations had to be accounted for. This typically Austrian assumption is a large point of contrast with the prevailing Marshallian view, which assumes continuity. The latter (and prevailing) approach is far easier to deal with mathematically, which might account for some of its success. But Böhm-Bawerk would question the assumptions of the Marshallian view and would argue instead that in any practical, real-world situation, these assumptions do not hold and economic analysis might as well account for the fact.

Irrespective of the relative merits of these two opposing views of the world, it is clear that the Austrians had a point. But, further, it was Böhm-Bawerk who best explicated the nature of price determination in a world of discrete numbers of buyers and sellers. The role of subjective evaluations in exchange, moreover, was never more clearly described. Though Menger and Wieser had worked out the essentials of Austrian value theory, it was left for Böhm-Bawerk to clarify the process of exchange.

Capital Theory

Perhaps the most important contribution made by Böhm-Bawerk was his elegant introduction of *time* considerations into economic analysis. His central and simple premise was that the production of final (consumers') goods takes time and that roundabout methods of producing these goods are more productive than direct methods. Though roundabout methods are more productive (an advantage), they are also time consuming (a disadvantage).

Böhm-Bawerk's view was that original means of production (raw materials, resources, labor) could be used in immediate production (as Robinson Crusoe did, for instance) or could be used to produce capital (which he called "produced means"), which, when accumulated and combined with labor, would then produce consumers' goods. Böhm-Bawerk thought that the latter method was more effective; further, he believed that the longer the productive period was (which means a more roundabout and capital-intensive method), the higher the total product would be. Time itself becomes an input, and the length of the production period of consumers' goods is itself a variable.

These points are illustrated in Figure 13-3. Time is measured on the horizontal axis, and total product (Q) is measured on the vertical axis. The production period in Figure 13-3 is represented on the time axis. Period tt'' is longer than period tt', for instance, and period tt''' is greater than period tt''. Total output, as is obvious from Figure 13-3, grows absolutely with the extension of the period of production. Marginal output, it must be noted, declines with these extensions.

What happens when the production period is extended? In other words, why did Böhm-Bawerk argue that longer periods are more productive? As the production period grows in length, more capital is used, the ratio of capital to labor increases, and final output is enlarged, albeit at a decreasing rate.

The Discontinuous Production Period The similarities of Böhm-Bawerk's model to the classical wages-fund doctrine are more than superficial. Böhm-Bawerk considered a discontinuous production period of variable length, however, whereas the classical production period was discontinuous but of fixed

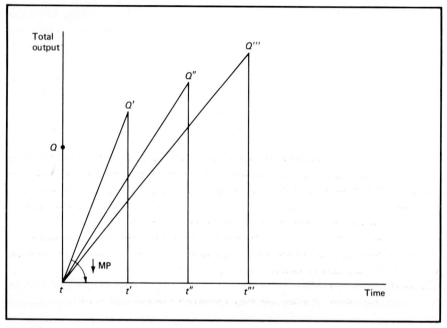

FIGURE 13-3
As "roundaboutness" increases from t to t', etc., total output also increases, but at a
decreasing rate. The slope of the ray tQ' is the marginal product of capital during period tt'.

duration. Although the immediate determinant of the length of the production
period is the same in Böhm-Bawerk's model as the classical wages-fund doctrine, Böhm-Bawerk made a close investigation of the interest rate, which was
the major determinant of the size of the subsistence fund. Before turning to
this relation, however, it is important that we consider a major problem encountered in Böhm-Bawerk's statement of the production period.

Böhm-Bawerk's period-of-production model is characterized by continuous
inputs and point outputs. That is, inputs are being added in a flow, but outputs
"ripen" at some discrete point in time. The important question that immediately arises concerns the length of the production period. At one point Böhm-
Bawerk suggested that an absolute period of production might be used. The
essential problem with its use soon became obvious, however. Assume, for
example, that a point output produced today is a silver drinking cup. What is
the absolute period of production? Conceivably, the silver input used in producing the cup might have been mined in Roman times. The concept of determining a production period for any point output is therefore ridiculous.

Böhm-Bawerk thus proposed an alternative approach, the average production period, in which inputs are weighted according to their proximity to point
outputs. Inputs are weighted by the number of periods used, and the sum of
these weighted inputs is then divided by the number of inputs in order to obtain an average production period.

Unfortunately, Böhm-Bawerk's second approach contains some grave deficiencies. One of the chief objections is rather obvious. Inputs are simply not homogeneous, and there are no provisions in Böhm-Bawerk for making them so except his assumption that they are. Second, and perhaps more importantly, there is the question of assigning the proper "period" weights. Is output attributable to the most recent inputs or to inputs in a more distant past? Although these problems were serious, Böhm-Bawerk retained the assumption of an average period of production as a workable theoretical constraint.[10]

The Interest Rate   Another of Böhm-Bawerk's achievements was his clear explanation of the interest rate. He regarded interest as a payment for the use of capital, and capital, as we have seen, means intermediate products (i.e., roundaboutness). As roundaboutness usually means longer time engaged in production, so interest must be related to time in some logical way. Böhm-Bawerk based his interest theory on *positive time preference:* the fundamental proposition that present goods are worth more than future goods. He offered three "proofs" for this fundamental proposition.

The first cause capable of producing a difference in value between present and future goods derives from the pressing nature of present wants. As Böhm-Bawerk noted, we are not indifferent to the future, but we live in the present. Future wants are almost always perceived as less pressing than immediate wants. In general, people find themselves in one of two circumstances. Those who are less well provided for in the present than in the future judge present goods to be more valuable. Those who find themselves better provided for in the present than they are likely to be in the future still have command over future goods by the possession of present goods (especially money) which they can store up as a reserve for the future.

The second cause for the difference in value between present and future goods is that people systematically undervalue future wants and the means to satisfy them. Here Böhm-Bawerk's argument rests on three corollaries: (1) since we can't know the future with certainty, the imaginary picture that we construct of our future wants will always be fragmentary and incomplete; (2) most people suffer from a general lack of willpower—faced with the choice between "now" and "then," few will postpone gratification of a present want; and (3) given the uncertainty and shortness of human life, people do not wish to postpone something which they may never get to enjoy.

The third cause for the difference in value between present and future goods is the technical superiority of present goods over future goods as a means of satisfying human wants. This corollary rests on the principle of roundaboutness earlier established by Böhm-Bawerk. It simply recognizes that present goods (including money) can be entrained in production *sooner* than future goods, so that the flow of output that will emerge from intermediate

---

[10] One of Böhm-Bawerk's "students" in capital theory, Knut Wicksell, at first adopted the average period of production but later abandoned it as unworkable.

products will always be larger if started now than if started at some future time.

Of these three causes, Böhm-Bawerk placed the greatest emphasis on the third, which he claimed was independent of the other two and, moreover, was capable of explaining positive time preference on its own. More protracted methods of production are always more productive than less protracted methods of production, and therein lies the technical superiority of present goods. From this general discussion, it was a fairly short leap to the idea that interest is the premium people pay for present goods over future goods. From the perspective of the lender, of course, interest is the compensation required to postpone the higher enjoyment conveyed by present goods. It is noteworthy that Böhm-Bawerk's theory of interest and capital is deeply rooted in the subjectivism of Austrian value theory in general. Indeed, it was on this basis that he distanced himself most from the classical approach to the subject. With a few notable exceptions (e.g., Lauderdale and Senior) classical economic theory treated capital as subservient to labor because it was itself the product of labor. This idea (which was also held in the extreme by Karl Marx) proved to be a major stumbling block to meaningful analytical progress in the theory of interest. The fault of classical interest theory is that it refused to admit that capital was productive apart from labor. Senior saw the error of this argument, but he remained a "classical" economist by encasing his new insights within the cost-of-production theory of value. Thus, Böhm-Bawerk, who credited Senior with overturning certain false ideas about capital and interest, also criticized him for neglecting time preference and opportunity costs, two cornerstones of the new subjectivism. In the final analysis, however, Böhm-Bawerk used Senior's foundation to build a new edifice rather than scrap all past ideas to begin anew.

POSTSCRIPT

The analytical performance of the Austrians, and indeed of all the neoclassical writers, amplifies at least one important point. Their ideas demonstrate that the dawning of neoclassical analysis was a lengthy process. Microanalysis was born in several countries and in the writings of quasi-isolated individuals, most of whom did not even belong to the contingent of academic economists. If anything, neoclassical economics was an international invention greatly nurtured by contributors from allied fields. But the pace of microanalytic work quickened in the early 1870s, and the noontime of the neoclassical age was about to arrive in the writings of Léon Walras and Alfred Marshall, among others. We shall turn to these developments presently in the following chapters.

NOTES FOR FURTHER READING

For an overview of German economics in the nineteenth century, see T. W. Hutchinson, *Review of Economic Doctrines, 1870–1929,* chap. 8. Von Thünen's work is accessible in the English language in two separate volumes:

the first is vol. 1 of von Thünen's *Isolated State,* Carla Wartenberg (trans.) and Peter Hall (ed.) (Oxford: Pergamon, 1966); vol. 2 of *The Isolated State* has been translated by B. W. Dempsey in *The Frontier Wage* (Chicago: Loyola University Press, 1960). Various assessments of particular aspects of von Thünen's economics include but are not limited to E. Schneider, "Johann Heinrich von Thünen," *Econometrica,* vol. 2 (January 1934), pp. 1–12, reprinted in H. W. Spiegel (ed.), *The Development of Economic Thought* (New York: Wiley 1952); A. H. Leigh, "Von Thünen's Theory of Distribution and the Advent of Marginal Analysis," *Journal of Political Economy,* vol. 54 (December 1946), pp. 481–502; H. L. Moore, "Von Thünen's Theory of Natural Wages," parts I and II, *Quarterly Journal of Economics,* vol. 9 (April, July 1895), pp. 291–304, 388–408; Colin Clark, "Von Thünen's *Isolated State,*" *Oxford Economic Papers,* n.s., vol. 19 (November 1967), pp. 370–377; B. F. Kiker, "Von Thünen on Human Capital," *Oxford Economic Papers,* n.s., vol. 21 (November 1969), pp. 339–343; H. D. Dickinson, "Von Thünen's Economics," *Economic Journal,* vol. 79 (December 1969), pp. 894–902; and A. Grotewold, "Von Thünen in Retrospect," *Economic Geography,* vol. 35 (October 1959), pp. 346–355. Mark Blaug provides a useful guide to von Thünen's life and influence in his introduction to a new Italian translation of von Thünen's *Isolated State,* included in the IRPET Classics of the Regional Science Series.

Léon Walras's effusive praise of Gossen is evident in "Walras on Gossen," translated and reproduced in Spiegel, *Development of Economic Thought* (see above), pp. 471–488. Other secondary sources on Gossen are as rare as a first edition of his *Entwicklung,* but see the preface to W. S. Jevons, *The Theory of Political Economy,* 2d ed. (London: Macmillan, 1879); and M. Pantaleoni, *Pure Economics,* T. B. Bruce (trans.) (London: Macmillan, 1898). Also see H. W. Spiegel, "Gossen," *International Encyclopedia of the Social Sciences,* vol. 6, pp. 209–210; and W. Jaffé, "The Normative Bias of the Walrasian Model: Walras versus Gossen," *Quarterly Journal of Economics,* vol. 91 (August 1977), pp. 371–388.

Translations of Mangoldt's works have been made in dribs and drabs. See Mangoldt, "The Exchange Ratio of Goods," *International Economic Papers,* vol. 11 (1962), pp. 32–59; "On the Equations of International Demand," *Journal of International Economics,* vol. 5 (1975), pp. 55–97; and "The Precise Function of the Entrepreneur and the True Nature of Entrepreneur's Profit," in F. M. Taylor (ed.), *Some Readings in Economics* (Ann Arbor, Mich.: Wahr, 1907), pp. 34–49. The most serviceable secondary sources on Mangoldt are E. Schneider, "Hans von Mangoldt on Price Theory: A Contribution to the History of Mathematical Economics," *Econometrica,* vol. 28 (1960), pp. 380–392; and K. H. Hennings, "The Transition from Classical to Neoclassical Economic Theory: Hans von Mangoldt," *Kyklos,* vol. 33 (1980), pp. 658–682.

For an excellent critical review of the thought of Menger, Wieser, and Böhm-Bawerk, see G. J. Stigler's *Production and Distribution Theories,* chaps. 6–8 (see References); and T. W. Hutchison's *Review of Economic Doc-*

trines, 1870–1929, chaps. 9–12 (see References). Also valuable is J. A. Schumpeter's *History of Economic Analysis,* (New York: Oxford University Press, 1954) pp. 843–855, 924–932. On Menger's founding role of the Austrian school, see Frank Knight's introduction to the Dingwall translation of Menger's *Principles;* "Hayek on Menger," in Spiegel (ed.), *Development of Economic Thought* (see above), pp. 526–567; H. S. Bloch, "Carl Menger: The Founder of the Austrian School," *Journal of Political Economy,* vol. 48 (June 1940), pp. 428–433; and J. A. Schumpeter, *Ten Great Economists* (New York: Oxford University Press, 1951), which contains essays on Böhm-Bawerk and Wieser as well as on Menger. The entire issue of the *Atlantic Economic Journal,* vol. 16 (September 1978), is devoted to papers on Menger and Austrian economics. See especially the papers by Moss, Kirzner, and Lachmann.

On the development of utility theory in general, see G. J. Stigler, "The Development of Utility Theory," *Journal of Political Economy,* vol. 58 (August–October 1950), reprinted in *Essays in the History of Economics* (Chicago: The University of Chicago Press, 1965); Jacob Viner, "The Utility Concept in Value Theory and Its Critics," *Journal of Political Economy,* vol. 33 (August–September 1925), pp. 369–387, 638–659, reprinted in *The Long View and the Short* (New York: Free Press, 1958); R. S. Howey, *The Rise of the Marginal Utility School, 1870–1889* (Lawrence, Kans.: The University Press of Kansas, 1960); Emil Kauder, *A History of Marginal Utility Theory* (Princeton, N.J.: Princeton University Press, 1965); and the entire issue of *History of Political Economy,* vol. 4 (Fall 1972), especially the articles by Blaug, Howey, Streissler, Stigler, and Shackle. A most important article for understanding the differences between the three cofounders of the marginal utility tradition is W. Jaffé, "Menger, Jevons, and Walras De-homogenized," *Economic Inquiry,* vol. 14 (December 1976), pp. 511–524. See also W. N. Butos, "Menger: A Suggested Interpretation," *Atlantic Economic Journal,* vol. 13 (July 1985), pp. 21–30. Two useful sources of information on Menger's "institutional" economics include A. M. Endres, "Institutional Elements in Carl Menger's Theory of Demand: A Comment," *Journal of Economic Issues,* vol. 18 (September 1984), pp. 897–902; and G. P. O'Driscoll, Jr., "Money: Menger's Evolutionary Theory," *History of Political Economy,* vol. 18 (Winter 1986), pp. 601–616.

Wieser's social economics is described in vol. II of W. C. Mitchell's *Lecture Notes on Types of Economic Theory* (New York: A. M. Kelley, Publishers, 1969) and in R. B. Ekelund, Jr., "Power and Utility: The Normative Economics of Friedrich von Wieser," *Review of Social Economy,* vol. 28 (September 1970), pp. 179–196. An instructive description of Wieser's system (and of the Austrian system generally) of input and output pricing may be found in chap. 12 of M. Blaug's *Economic Theory in Retrospect,* 4th ed. (London: Cambridge University Press, 1985). The Austrian system also spread to England. See William Smart, *An Introduction to the Theory of Value* (New York: A. M. Kelley, Publishers, 1966).

Böhm-Bawerk's theory of capital and interest has been the subject of continual debate among economic theorists. In fact, it was the subject of a debate in the *Quarterly Journal of Economics* between Böhm-Bawerk and J. B. Clark in the 1890s and early 1900s. The debate is summarized in an unpublished doctoral dissertation by David E. R. Gay entitled *Capital and the Production Process: A Critical Evaluation of the Böhm-Bawerk-Clark Debate and Its Relation to Current Capital Theory* (College Station: Texas A & M University, 1973). An overview of Böhm-Bawerk's period-of-production model based on a subsistence fund and its role in capital theory is presented in Donald Dewey, *Modern Capital Theory* (New York: Columbia University Press, 1965), and F. A. Lutz, *The Theory of Capital,* chap. 1 (London: Macmillan, 1965). The mechanics of Böhm-Bawerk's theory of interest is analyzed graphically and mathematically by Robert Dorfman, "A Graphical Exposition of Böhm-Bawerk's Interest Theory," *Review of Economic Studies,* vol. 26 (February 1959), pp. 153–158; J. Hirshleiffer, "A Note on the Böhm-Bawerk/Wicksell Theory of Interest," *Review of Economic Studies,* vol. 34 (April 1967), pp. 191–200; and D. E. R. Gay, "The Aggregate Factor-Price Frontier in Böhm-Bawerk's Period of Production Capital Model: A Graphical Derivation," *Eastern Economic Journal,* vol. 3 (July 1975), pp. 205–211. It should be noted, at least in passing, that Böhm-Bawerk's protégé, Knut Wicksell, attempted a clarification of the theory of capital along Böhm-Bawerk's lines in his *Value, Capital and Rent* (New York: A. M. Kelley, 1970). A. M. Endres, "The Origins of Böhm-Bawerk's Greatest 'Error': Theoretical Points of Separation from Menger," *Journal of Institutional & Theoretical Economics,* vol. 143 (June 1987), pp. 291–309, explores Böhm-Bawerk's departure from Menger.

In addition to everything else, Böhm-Bawerk was a formidable historian of thought. His *History and Critique of Interest Theories,* first published in 1884, is a masterpiece, unmatched in its subject area. The first English translation, by William Smart, appeared in 1890, and the work has been retranslated by George D. Huncke and Hans F. Sennholz (South Holland, Ill.: Libertarian Press, 1959). Along with Wieser, Böhm-Bawerk was interested in the sociology of power and its effects upon production and exchange. In this regard, see his "Control of Economic Law," in R. Mez (trans.), *Shorter Classics of Eugen von Böhm-Bawerk,* vol. I (South Holland, Ill.: Libertarian Press, 1962) [1914]. See also Emil Lederer, "Social Control versus Economic Law: An Old Dogma and a New Situation," *Social Research,* vol. 51 (Spring/Summer 1983), pp. 91–110.

The Austrian tradition spread through a second generation of writers. Numerous scholars, including Oskar Morgenstern and Joseph Schumpeter, were touched by the Austrian point of view, but F. A. Hayek and Ludwig von Mises, in particular, spread Austrian economics. See Hayek's *Individualism and Economic Order* (Chicago: The University of Chicago Press, 1948), which is a collection of his most important early journal articles, including his contributions to the socialist economics controversy, to the philosophy of economic science, and to monetary theory. Two works of von Mises are of special interest: *Human Action: A Treatise on Economics* (New Haven, Conn.: Yale University Press, 1949), which is a summary statement of Mises's views on a wide range of topics, including epistemological problems of economics and social science, socialist economics, monetary theory, public finance, and labor economics; and *Socialism: An Economic and Sociological Analysis* (New Haven, Conn.: Yale University Press, 1951), in which von Mises presents a detailed analysis of key problems of economic and social organization that must be solved by a socialist state, with special emphasis on property-rights structures and economic calculation. *Socialism* also contains a brief historical sketch of the differences between the main socialist movements and of their historical development.

REFERENCES

Böhm-Bawerk, Eugen. *The Positive Theory of Capital,* in George D. Huncke (trans.), *Capital and Interest,* vol. II. South Holland, Ill.: Libertarian Press, 1959 [1889].

Greenhut, M. L. *Plant Location in Theory and Practise.* Chapel Hill, N.C.: The University of North Carolina Press, 1956.

Hutchison, T. W. *A Review of Economic Doctrines, 1870–1929.* Oxford: Clarendon Press, 1953.

Knight, F. H. *Risk, Uncertainty and Profit.* New York: Harper & Row, 1965 [1921].

Marshall, Alfred. *Principles of Economics,* 2d ed. London: Macmillan, 1891.

————. *Memorials of Alfred Marshall,* A. C. Pigou (ed.). London: Macmillan, 1925.

Menger, Carl. *Principles of Economics,* James Dingwall and Bert F. Hoselitz (trans.), Glencoe, Ill.: Free Press, 1950 [1871].

Stigler, George J. *Production and Distribution Theories: The Formative Period.* New York: Macmillan, 1941.

Wieser, Friedrich. *Natural Value,* A. Malloch (trans.) and William Smart (ed.). New York: Kelley and Millman, 1956 [1889].

————. *Social Economics,* A. Ford Hinrichs (trans.). New York: A. M. Kelley, Publishers, 1967 [1914].

CHAPTER 14

MICROECONOMICS IN ENGLAND: WILLIAM STANLEY JEVONS

INTRODUCTION

The climate of economic opinion in England was of a distinctly stormy nature in the late 1850s, the 1860s, and the 1870s. Mill's recantation of the wages-fund doctrine in the *Fortnightly Review* in 1869 (see Chapter 8) was thought by many to be the death knell of classical economics. But, in truth, the reasons for the decline of credence in the classical paradigm may be lain at many doors. An interest in labor problems, socialist and "progressive" philosophies, and Darwinian evolutionist ideas, as well as the historicists' reactions to classical political economy (see Chapter 10) and Mill's eleventh-hour misgivings about laissez faire, all contribute to an explanation of the milieu into which utility theory was introduced in England. If widespread dissatisfaction with an old paradigm is, as many intellectual historians believe, the prerequisite for the emergence of a fundamentally new (but not necessarily contradictory) system of thought, then a ready explanation for the emergence of Jevons's *Theory of Political Economy* in 1871 is at hand.

WILLIAM STANLEY JEVONS (1835–1882)

William Stanley Jevons was one of the most interesting and enigmatic characters in the history of British economic thought. A man of rare (often esoteric) powers of analysis, he was also one of the most practical professional economists who ever lived. Although his ideas were profound and original, he left no student followers of consequence, and this in spite of the fact that he held a major university post in political economy (at Manchester).

Jevons was born in England in 1835 and was raised in an educated (but nonacademic) Unitarian environment in which economic and social problems were often discussed. Still, Jevons's early training was technical (including mathematics, biology, chemistry, and metallurgy), and the subjects and tools of his early education permeated his entire intellectual career.[1] Financial problems and a remunerative job offer as assayer at the Sydney Mint led Jevons to interrupt his training and move to Australia at the age of eighteen. He remained there for five years, during which time, his biographer J. M. Keynes claims, he was struck with all the original ideas on economics that he later developed and expanded in England.

With his interest in political economy awakened, Jevons returned to England in 1859 to continue his studies at the University of London, where he obtained a degree in 1865. This early period was especially fecund for Jevons. In 1862, in several communications to the British Association, he outlined (1) the skeletal structure of utility theory (*Notice of the General Theory of Political Economy*) and (2) the scenario for his statistical studies of fluctuations (*On the Study of Periodic Commercial Fluctuations, with Five Diagrams*), both of which are discussed in this chapter. In 1863 Jevons published a book entitled *Pure Logic* (one of the most significant and presently neglected areas of his interests), and in 1865 he published *The Coal Question*, a book that brought him to prominence in economic circles.

The Coal Question was based upon a questionable analogy between the role of corn in Malthus's theory of population and that of coal in the industrial progress of Britain. Nevertheless, the book attracted a good deal of attention in political and intellectual circles, including that of Prime Minister Gladstone. From this point onward, Jevons's interests fluctuated from pure logic to economics and back again. His economic interests ran the gamut from statistical analyses of prices and gold (and significant institutional studies of money markets) to pure theory and commercial fluctuations, of which his well-known sunspot theory was one (*The Solar Period and the Price of Corn* [1875]). In 1871 his greatest finished work on economic theory, *Theory of Political Economy*, was published; the book was based upon his early ideas on utility theory communicated to (but ignored by) the British Association in 1862.

In 1876, after numerous bouts of nervous and physical exhaustion (at the age of thirty-six he was obliged to give up all work for a time), Jevons left Manchester for a professorship in political economy at University College in London. Renewed ill health and a desire to complete a massive *Principles of Economics* forced him to resign this post in 1880. Unfortunately for the state of economics, this last work was never completed (although fragments remain). In August 1882 an enfeebled Jevons, just short of his forty-seventh birthday, drowned while on holiday on the south coast of England.

---

[1] A lifelong music lover, Jevons became enchanted, following an early devotion to Beethoven, with the "experimental" music of Berlioz and Wagner, who he believed were writing the "music of the future." His knowledgeable and laudatory descriptions of the innovative nature of these composers are clear evidence that the quest for rearrangement and changes in form was a deeply engrained habit of his thought. It is interesting to note that Jevons's early conviction about his own genius and originality almost exactly parallels Wagner's.

Jevons's untimely death deprived the world of an original economic mind. But this assessment has been formed mostly in retrospectives of his work. As noted above, Jevons left no serious students. In addition, Alfred Marshall assumed a disappointingly ungenerous attitude toward him. J. M. Keynes calculated that by 1936 only 39,000 copies of Jevons's *nine* major works in economics and logic had been sold! How might one account for the distinctly mediocre impact of one whose powers of originality have been favorably compared to Marshall's? Keynes gave us an interesting retrospective:

> What sort of man was Jevons in himself? There is no strong personal impression of him which has been recorded, and 54 years after his death it is not easy to find a definite imprint on the minds of the few now left who knew him. My belief is that Jevons did not make a strong impression on his companions at any period of his life. He was, in modern language, strongly introverted. He worked best alone with flashes of inner light. He was repelled, as much as he was attracted, by contact with the outside world. He had from his boyhood unbounded belief in his own powers; but he desired greatly to influence others whilst being himself uninfluenced by them. He was deeply affectionate towards the members of his family but not intimate with them or with anyone ("William Stanley Jevons," pp. 545–546).

Seldom has an economist been more candid concerning himself and his powers than Jevons was in 1858 in a letter to his sister Henrietta (who was reading Smith's *Wealth of Nations* at the time):

> There are a multitude of allied branches of knowledge connected with man's condition; the relation of these to political economy is analogous to the connection of mechanics, astronomy, optics, sound, heat, and every other branch more or less of physical science, with pure mathematics. I have an idea, which I do not object to mention to you, that my insight into the foundations and nature of the knowledge of man is deeper than that of most men or writers. In fact, I think that it is my mission to apply myself to such subjects, and it is my intention to do so. You are desirous of engaging in the practically useful; you may feel assured that to extend and perfect the abstract or the detailed and practical knowledge of man and society is perhaps the most useful and necessary work in which any one can now engage.... There are plenty of people engaged with physical science, and practical science and arts may be left to look after themselves, but thoroughly to understand the principles of society appears to me now the most cogent business (*Letters and Journal*, p. 101).

Even at an earlier age Jevons was sure that he would revolutionize the science of economics, but, paradoxically, he was often filled with self-doubt and apparent inconsistencies. Intractable aloofness and even profound loneliness were part of his character. Very early in his life Jevons recognized that he was not possessed of "personal power" or the ability to use "manners, language, persuasion, to accomplish an end." But he admittedly did nothing to remedy this "great deficiency" in his personality. On the contrary, he seemed to enjoy it. In a revealing letter from Australia to his beloved sister Lucy, Jevons bragged that, with one "slight exception," he had never gone to a party and that he had at last succeeded in "impressing upon all friends the fact that it is

no use inviting me." And in the same letter, Jevons defended his own aloofness as a way of life:

> I cannot say of course that my disposition for reserve and loneliness was originally
> intentional on my part; it probably originated in bashfulness, which other people
> think, and which, no doubt, is, a very silly thing. Yet I ascribe to this disposition
> almost everything I am, and believe that a certain amount of reserve and solitude is
> quite necessary for the information of any firm and original character. This is in fact
> almost self-evident, for if any one were brought up in continual intercourse with the
> thoughts of a number of other people, it follows almost necessarily that his thoughts
> will never rise above the ordinary level of the others.... Solitude, no doubt, pro-
> duces one class of minds and characters, and society another; the latter may give
> quickness of thought and some other showy qualities, but must tend to interrupt
> longer and more valuable trains of thought, and gradually destroy the habit of fol-
> lowing them, while solitude promotes reflection, self-dependence, and originality.
> These, I believe, I possess to a greater or less extent, and I therefore, on principle,
> do not altogether regret that my habits have been as you know them (*Letters and
> Journal*, pp. 85–86).

Jevons apparently never regretted his "habits," for they carried over into his
later academic life. Keynes quotes Jevons's less famous colleague, Professor
Herbert Foxwell, as saying that " 'There never was a worse lecturer, the men
would not go to his classes, and he worked in flashes and could not finish anything thoroughly,' and then after a pause with a different sort of expression
[Foxwell continued], 'the only point about Jevons was that he was a genius.' "
A look at Jevons's entire lifework bears out Foxwell's opinion. Jevons's legacies to economics are indeed fragmentary, but they are the leavings of genius.

THE THEORY OF VALUE

Jevons's major thrust in economic theory was the foundation of utility analysis. From this foundation he constructed a theory of exchange and a theory of
labor supply and capital. Many of these ideas, which were expressed chiefly in
his *Theory of Political Economy*, were not new. Indeed, Jevons very generously noted that many of the features of his economic theory had been developed before by others. Two of his most important precursors were Dionysius
Lardner, who developed a theory of the firm in his *Railway Economy* of 1850,
and Fleeming Jenkin, who established a graphical presentation of the laws of
supply and demand in 1870. Nevertheless, many of Jevons's theoretical contributions were original and of the first rank. His discovery of marginal utility
was made independently of all other writers, and thus reflects his original cast
of mind.

Utility Theory

The actual discovery of utility theory, and specifically marginal-utility theory,
was made by Jules Dupuit, as we have seen in Chapter 12. There had been
essentially adventitious statements of the same principle by Nassau Senior,

William Lloyd, and Montifort Longfield. Dupuit, however, had developed the theory in an empirical milieu and had based his argument on empirical facts. Jevons, although possibly looking to the practical concerns of Lardner for inspiration, at least based his reasoning partially on physiological theory. In this connection Jevons specifically noted the Weber-Fechner studies of stimulus and response.

In his establishment of utility theory, Jevons's background in science and scientific measurement was much on his mind. Economics to Jevons was fortunate in that some of its important quantities (prices and so forth) were capable of exact measurement. He had early and unbounded faith in the future of mathematics and statistics as indispensable aids to discovery in economics. Yet he placed a *subjective* maximand—utility—in the starring role in economic analysis. Jevons admitted that the calculus of pleasure and pain (or utility theory) had subjective features, although he expressed hopes that the *effects* of utility might somehow be ascertained. In 1871 he wrote:

> A unit of pleasure or of pain is difficult even to conceive; but it is the amount of these feelings which is continually prompting us to buying and selling, borrowing and lending, labouring and resting, producing and consuming; and *it is from the quantitative effects of the feelings that we must estimate their comparative amounts.* We can no more know nor measure gravity in its own nature than we can measure a feeling; but, just as we measure gravity by its effects in the motion of a pendulum, so we may estimate the equality or inequality of feelings by the decisions of the human mind (*Theory of Political Economy,* p. 11).

Immediately, then, Jevons acknowledged that one could, at best, obtain only ordinal *estimates* of the quantity around which the entire economic system revolves. In his *Theory,* Jevons noted that utility is basically introspective, and he recognized explicitly that interpersonal comparisons from one individual or group to another are impossible (although he may have failed to heed his own warnings in the concept of a "trading body," as we shall see). Nevertheless, despite all these difficulties, Jevons set out the new core of economics in utility terms.

Marginal Utility   Following Bentham's lead (see Chapter 6), Jevons maintained that the value of pleasure and pain varies according to four circumstances: (1) intensity, (2) duration, (3) certainty or uncertainty, and (4) nearness or remoteness. Jevons discussed each of these at length. Pain is simply the negative of pleasure, and in individual calculations the algebraic sum (i.e., net pleasure) is the meaningful quantity. Like Bentham before him, Jevons injected a probabilistic element into economic analysis when he discussed the ways in which the uncertainty of future events and future "anticipated feelings" affect behavior. In one especially telling passage, Jevons suggested how time preference and anticipation permeate economic quantities:

> The cares of the moment are but ripples on the tide of achievement and hope. We may safely call that man happy who, however lowly his position and limited his possessions, can always hope for more than he has, and can feel that every moment of

exertion tends to realize his aspirations. He, on the contrary, who seizes the enjoyment of the passing moment without regard to coming times, must discover sooner
or later that his stock of pleasure is on the wane, and that even hope begins to fail
(*Theory*, p. 35).

This all-important element was nevertheless omitted from Jevons's theory of
utility.

Jevons asserted that maximizing pleasure is the object of economics, or, in
his own words, humans seek to procure the "greatest amount of what is desirable at the expense of the least that is undesirable." However, it is necessary to make this proposition more objective by attaching it to something more
concrete, such as *commodities*.

Jevons defined a commodity as an "object, substance, action, or service
which can afford pleasure or ward off pain," and he denoted the "abstract
quality whereby an object serves our purposes, and becomes entitled to rank
as a commodity." Eschewing any pretensions of direct measurability, Jevons
claimed that behavior would reveal utility and preferences and that the investigator would not make value judgments. As he clearly noted, "Anything
which an individual is found to desire and to labour for must be assumed to
possess for him utility." Thus flagpole sitters, astronauts, kamikaze pilots,
heroin addicts, and suicides might simply be regarded as maximizing utility
(under certain constraints, of course).

Jevons's formal analysis of utility relates commodities, as defined above, to
utility. His theory of marginal utility is basically simple and straightforward. It
may be explained and illustrated with the aid of the elementary arithmetic and
graphs used by Jevons himself. Unlike any of his predecessors, Jevons clearly
specified that a utility function is a relation between the commodities an individual consumes and an act of individual valuation. Utility is not, in sum, an
intrinsic or inherent quality that things possess. Instead, utility has meaning
only in the act of valuation.

Jevons's vast improvements over Bentham's performance consist in the following features of his formal utility analysis: (1) his clear distinction between
total utility and marginal utility, (2) his discussion of the nature of marginal
utility, and (3) his establishment of the equimarginal principle, as it relates to
alternative uses of the same commodity and to choices *between* commodities.
Jevons unlocked Adam Smith's water-diamond paradox in distinguishing between total utility and what Jevons called the "degree of utility." The latter
may be regarded as the same as marginal utility. Both total and marginal utilities were related to the quantities of goods possessed, and only to those quantities.

Graphical Analysis   Using a simple algebraic notation, Jevons's utility
function is expressed as $U = f(X)$, to be read as "the utility of commodity X
(food) is a function of the quantity of X the individual holds." It should be
noted that all other goods are left out of the picture; i.e., it may be assumed
either that they are nonexistent or that their quantities are held constant. As-

suming that one could add tiny portions of food to the individual's store—that is, "continuously," in the language of arithmetic—one might derive a utility function as depicted in Figure 14-1a. Here the total utility of food (the quantities of other things held constant) may be seen to rise as quantities are added up to X_0, reach a maximum at that point, and then decline. But the utility of an *additional* unit of food, which Jevons called the "degree of utility," *declines* as units of food are added to the individual's consumption. Arithmetically, Jevons wrote du/dx, to be read as "the ratio of a small change in utility to a

FIGURE 14-1
Total utility rises continuously up to X_0 units of food, but marginal utility declines continuously as additional units of food are consumed per unit of time.

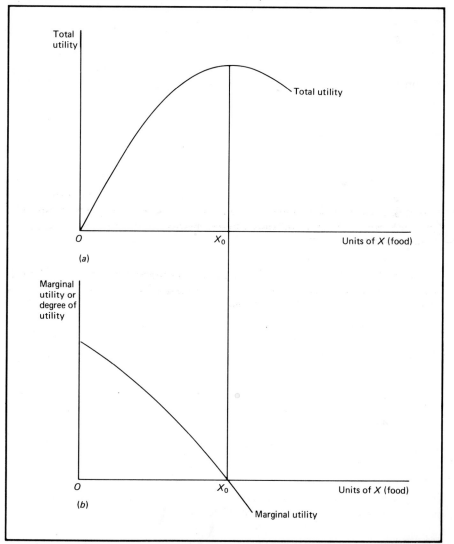

small change in X (food)." Figure 14-1b, which is derived from Figure 14-1a, demonstrates this idea. Further, he assumed that the marginal utility (used synonymously with "degree of utility") of food was declining after the very first unit taken, although he was undoubtedly aware that this might not always be the case. *Jevons's law* may then be stated as follows: The degree of utility for a single commodity varies with the quantity possessed of that commodity and ultimately decreases as the quantity of that single commodity increases.

The Equimarginal Principle Jevons presented a clear understanding of the *individual's* maximizing behavior in discussing a person's allocation of any given commodity among alternative uses. If an individual starts with a fixed stock S of a commodity X and the *uses* of that commodity are represented by x and y, then the stock must be divided up between those uses such that $S = x + y$. Now Jevons, in effect, asks the question: How does an individual decide how to allocate his fixed stock among the two uses? The answer is simple and intuitively reasonable. The quantity of X should be allocated to the two uses so that the increase in utility from adding an additional unit of X in use x just equals the increase in utility from adding an additional unit of X in use y. In Jevonian terms, the equimarginal condition implies that

$$\frac{du}{dx} = \frac{du}{dy} \quad \text{or} \quad MU_x = MU_y$$

where MU_x stands for the degree of utility of commodity X in use x, and similarly for y.

The equimarginal principle, first clearly explained by Jevons, also holds for the allocation of scarce, fixed means (say, income) among all goods in the individual consumer's budget. If x represents number of beers and z represents packs of cigarettes, then the consumer will allocate scarce income y such that the $MU_x = MU_z$, assuming that beers and cigarettes are the same price and that all y is expended on these two goods. A more general formulation of the equimarginal principle, one that does not appear in Jevons but that accounts for different prices of n goods, is the one familiar to every student of basic economics:

$$\frac{MU_x}{P_x} = \frac{MU_z}{P_z} = \frac{MU_n}{P_n}$$

Further, in order to ensure that all income is allocated among the individual's consumptions (which could include a savings account), an additional condition is expressed:

$$P_x X + P_z Z + \cdots + P_n N = Y$$

where $P_x X$ represents the individual's expenditure on X, $P_z Z$ represents the expenditure on Z, etc. The sum of all these expenditures equals income Y. Although Jevons did not work out the details, his argument underlies the whole development of the theory of individual maximization behavior, which is at the core of contemporary theory.

Jevons's Theory of Exchange

Utilizing the theory of utility discussed in the previous section, together with a *law of indifference,* Jevons developed a theory of exchange—that is, an explanation of why and how goods trade between individuals in a market. Jevons's law of indifference states that in any free and open market, at any one time, there cannot be more than one price for the same (homogeneous) commodity.

At this point Jevons introduced the "trading body," a concept that, as we shall see, is not without some difficulties. By a trading body Jevons meant "any body of either buyers or sellers," which runs the gamut from individuals to an entire population. Every trading body, moreover, "is either an individual or an aggregate of individuals, and the law in the aggregate must depend upon the fulfillment of the law in the individuals." Neglecting, for the moment, any problems with the concept, let us assume, with Jevons, that there is one trading body (A) possessing a stock of beef (*a*) and another (B) possessing a stock of corn (*b*). How does exchange take place? Jevons gives, as usual, a graphical and symbolic treatment.

Let the marginal-utility functions for corn and beef be represented as in Figure 14-2, which we here adapt, with slight alterations, from Jevons's own diagram.

FIGURE 14-2
At all points to the left of *m*, A receives a net gain in utility by exchanging beef for corn, whereas at all points to the right of *m*, B receives a net gain of utility by exchanging corn for beef.

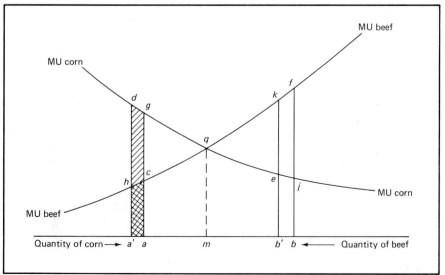

Let an increase (decrease) in the quantity of corn (beef) be read from left to right on Figure 14-2 and an increase (decrease) in the quantity of beef (corn) be read from right to left in the same figure. Units of both commodities must be represented by equal lengths, of course.

Consider trading body A and assume that it holds a quantity a' of corn. An *increase* in A's holding of corn, represented by the little line $a'a$, simultaneously represents a decrease in A's holdings of beef. But the important point is that A *gains* by the trading of beef for corn. Why? Because it would gain more utility by acquiring corn than it would lose by giving up beef. Specifically, with reference to Figure 14-2, A would gain area $a'hca$, for a *net gain* of area $hdgc$.

A would continue to trade until equilibrium is reached at point m, which represents, in this simple case, the intersection of the marginal-utility curves. B does the same. (It is left for the reader to trace out B's maximizing behavior.) At m, no further gains from trade can be realized by either trading body, and trade ends.[2] Thus Jevons concluded that freedom of exchange, projecting these results, must be to the advantage of all. Laissez faire thus received a boost from this aspect of utility theory.

Theory of Labor

One of Jevons's most interesting applications of utility theory was to the theory of *labor supply*. With labor, as with all other activities, two quantities were of primary importance to Jevons in explaining behavior: cost incurred and utility gained (proxies for pain and pleasure). Jevons defined labor as "any painful exertion of mind and body undergone partly or wholly with a view of future good." The reader may object that most people at least claim to like their work. Jevons, however, was thinking of some concept of *net* pain, i.e., a balance of the painfulness and the pleasure of working. He also implicitly assumed that workers were on a piecework system and that they could alter the amount of work performed. This latter assumption, except perhaps over a long-run period, does not present a very accurate picture of present conditions or even of those that obtained in Jevons's time. Nevertheless, his idea has some applicability wherever the conditions he assumed are existent.

In analyzing the work decision, Jevons focused upon three quantities: net pain from work, amount of production, and amount of utility gained. Graphi-

---

[2] Jevons also expressed the condition arithmetically. If we let MU_a^A represent the final degree of utility of trading body A for commodity a (corn) and so on, then Jevons's equilibrium equations of exchange may be expressed as

$$\frac{MU_a^A}{MU_b^A} = \frac{MU_b^B}{MU_b^B} = \frac{b \text{ (total quantity of beef retained)}}{a \text{ (total quantity of corn retained)}}$$

cally, the combination of these quantities may be analyzed as in Figure 14-3. In a piecework system the worker's real wage and income depend on his or her rate of production. The curve *pq* may be regarded as the degree of utility weighted by the worker's production or output. The *reward* for labor, in other words, may be regarded as the product of the rate of production and the degree of utility. The *costs* of labor are represented by the curve traced out by *ed*. Here Jevons assumed that the act of beginning work is onerous (getting up in the morning for some of us?) and produces net *pain*. But as work continues, it becomes more and more pleasurable on balance, until a point is reached where painfulness begins to overwhelm the pleasure of working. Thus the net-pain-of-labor curve peaks out and turns downward, becoming negative.

A significant point that Jevons made is that the worker will stop producing when the net pain of working is equivalent to the degree of utility of the real wages produced. That occurs at point *m* in Figure 14-3. At point *m*, where the cost of working *md* (net pain) equals the reward from working *mq* (the utility reward), the worker would cease work. To go beyond this point would bring greater costs than rewards. Thus Jevons established a theory of labor supply based upon his notions concerning utility.

Jevons as a Pure Theorist

Our investigation of some of Jevons's purely theoretical ideas is necessarily incomplete. His theory of rent and his productivity theory of capital and interest have not come within our purview. However, our discussion of his utility ap-

FIGURE 14-3
In this analysis based on hedonic calculus, a worker will offer labor services in the amount *Om*, because at that point the cost of working, *md*, equals the reward of work, *mq*.

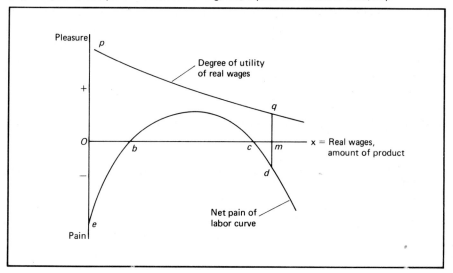

proach to value, exchange, and labor should leave little doubt in the reader's mind that Jevons was an innovative, original thinker.

Although utility theory revolutionized value theory, Jevons's own ideas on exchange value were curiously lopsided. Though he never relied upon supply and demand curves, he was—from the work of Fleeming Jenkin—undoubtedly aware of their role in value determination. For example, he noted that "Our theory is perfectly consistent with the laws of supply and demand; and if we had the functions of utility determined, it would be possible to throw them into a form clearly expressing the equivalence of supply and demand."

But despite the fact that he said, "The laws of supply and demand are thus a result of what seems to me the true theory of value or exchange," he zeroed in almost exclusively upon *utility* as the source of value. Thus we have Jevons's well-known catena:

> Cost of production determines supply;
> Supply determines final degree of utility;
> Final degree of utility determines value.

Labor value, and presumably the value of *all* inputs, is determined by the utility or value of the product and not vice versa. Independent alterations in supply due to alterations in costs of productive inputs are not taken into account. Supply of goods, as in the theory of exchange shown in Figure 14-2, is presumed *fixed*.

Jevons's independent discovery of utility analysis led him to neglect the earlier cost-of-production emphases of classical writers, including Smith, Ricardo, and Mill. Indeed, Jevons believed that utility theory effectively refuted the labor theory of value, which he (erroneously) identified as *the* sole determinant of value in Ricardo's *Principles*. What Jevons failed to recognize in his economic analysis was that supply and demand *mutually* determine prices. Fleeming Jenkin had suggested as much in 1870 or earlier, but it was Alfred Marshall's (see Chapter 15) great achievement to have clearly recognized and elaborated upon the co-impact of independently determined supply and demand upon price determination.

In spite of this fundamental criticism of his value theory, Jevons's decision *not* to formally link demand curves with marginal-utility curves has been lauded by many economists, most notably by Léon Walras (see Chapter 16). As we have seen, Jevons looked forward to the day when these "functions of utility" could be empirically determined, at least in an ordinal (ranking) sense. But until that day, he was unwilling to link demand and utility functions in partial equilibrium, as Dupuit had done before him and as Marshall was later to do.

For the demand curve of even a single *individual* to represent a utility measure (i.e., for price and marginal utility to be equated, as was the case in Dupuit—see Figure 12-4), very restrictive assumptions must be imposed. The marginal utility of money must be held constant with respect to the prices or quantities of all other goods; goods in the consumer's budget must be assumed to be unrelated; etc. These conditions are not apt to be met in any real-world case, and it is to Jevons's credit that he recognized this important point.

True to his ambivalent nature, however, Jevons erred in a related matter. Recall that he had defined a trading body as any body of buyers and sellers. Presumably, as we discovered in connection with the theory of exchange, he believed that an aggregate degree-of-utility function could be constructed in order to analyze trade. Such a construction is manifestly illegitimate, however, since it would require the summing up of different individuals' degree-of-utility functions for some good. Since incomes, tastes, and preferences vary, there is no reason to expect that the MU's of these individuals would be comparable. The fact that Jevons required only ordinal ranking is of no help to him in this dilemma. An interpersonal summation of rankings would not avoid the problem.

Thus many ambiguities are contained in Jevons's theoretical apparatus. His analysis of utility was pathbreaking, and it was an essential key to value theory, but his voyage into microeconomic analysis lacked the sophistication and the completeness of Marshall's. Still, many pioneering bits of analysis are contained in his *Theory of Political Economy.* One might speculate that had he lived to complete his projected *Principles,* Jevons might have left economic science far richer; however, as it stands, his contributions to pure theory, though piecemeal, were solid. Keynes (who was perhaps Alfred Marshall's greatest student) described Jevons's *Theory* as "simple, lucid, unfaltering, chiselled in stone where Marshall knits in wool."

JEVONS AND STATISTICAL SCIENCE

Jevons's pioneering efforts in utility analysis were more than matched by his efforts in empirical and statistical science. In 1862, after publishing early works on scientific meteorology, Jevons set out to apply scientific principles to commercial statistics.[3] His first paper, entitled "On the Study of Periodic Commercial Fluctuations," was forwarded along with his earliest theoretical paper to the meeting of the British Association in 1862. In it Jevons analyzed variation in the following variables: average rate of discount, 1845 to 1861 and 1825 to 1861; total number of bankruptcies, 1806 to 1860; average price of government bonds, 1845 to 1860; and average price of wheat, 1846 to 1861. Jevons presented his data diagrammatically, and concluded that data should be arranged in such a way as to best elucidate the most interesting aspects for the purposes of the investigator. As an early discoverer of *seasonal fluctuations,* Jevons noted:

> Every kind of periodic fluctuation, whether daily, weekly, monthly, quarterly, or yearly must be detected and exhibited, not only as a subject of study in itself, but because we must ascertain and eliminate such periodic variations before we can cor-

---

[3] Most of Jevons's statistical studies were collected after his death by his wife, Harriet, and published by his friend Foxwell. These studies can be found in Jevons's *Investigations in Currency and Finance.*

rectly exhibit those which are irregular or non-periodic, and probably of more interest and importance (*Investigations,* p. 4).

Thus Jevons offered various explanations for the seasonal fluctuations in his various data, applying the process of scientific abstraction used in his theoretical work.

Price Series and Index Numbers

One of Jevons's most important statistical papers was "A Serious Fall in the Value of Gold Ascertained and Its Social Effects Set Forth" (1863). In it Jevons wished to apply the general proposition "that an article tends to fall in value as it is supplied more abundantly and easily than before" to the then-recent gold discoveries in Australia and California. The French economist Michel Chevalier had predicted such a fall, but others, including Newmarch and McCulloch, had doubted that it would occur.

In order to understand Jevons's achievement better it must be recognized that economists of this period had only vague and ambiguous notions of what a fall in value was. Thus Jevons had to begin with an introductory lesson in logic applied to statistics. He had to explain the meaning of an average rise of prices, and, most importantly, the method of constructing price indices. In this latter effort, he was clearly a pathbreaker. He discussed at length the compilation of price tables, computation of arithmetic and geometric means, the problem of weighting, and the selection of the sample commodities. Then with statistics gathered from various periodicals, including *The Economist,* the *Gazette,* and *The Times,* Jevons constructed an average annual price of thirty-nine commodities for the years 1845 to 1862. After assessing the statistics and painstakingly plotting them, he concluded:

> It is hardly necessary to draw attention to the permanent elevation of prices since 1853.... The lowest average range of prices since 1851 has indeed happened in the last year 1862; but prices even then stood 13 percent above the average level of 1845-50.... *Examine the yearly average prices at any point of their fluctuations since 1852, and they stand above any point of their fluctuations before then within the scope of my tables.* There is but one way of accounting for such a fact, and that is by supposing a very considerable permanent depreciation of gold (*Investigations,* pp. 44-45).

Jevons also discussed the depreciation of silver and the *rate* of fall in the value of gold, relating the total fall in gold value to the quantity in use.

Finally, Jevons investigated the *effects* of gold depreciation (price increase) on debtors, creditors, and various other classes. Throughout he displayed a keen practical knowledge of credit institutions and commerce. He concluded that creditors, those injured by gold depreciation, have no equitable claim to compensation, but he failed to discuss the distributional effects of gold depreciation. He recognized, however, the *indirect* effects of gold discovery, such as the creation of new colonies, the dissemination of the English people and language, and the reanimation of commerce.

Several years later Jevons continued and expanded his statistical study of price movements in "The Variation of Prices and the Value of the Currency Since 1782," published in the *Journal of the Statistical Society of London* (June 1865). In this paper Jevons expanded his index number methods by reducing data from Tooke and Newmarch's *History of Prices* into price indexes of all commodities and individual classes of commodities. He evaluated the theoretical foundations of all commonly used price indexes, favoring the geometric mean over Laspeyres's arithmetic mean and the harmonic mean. On the merit of these alternative calculations, Jevons observed, "It is probable that each of these is right for its own purposes when these are more clearly understood in theory" (*Investigations*, p. 114). The geometric mean presented some calculational advantages, such as the facility to correct results by the continual use of logarithms. Also, Jevons wanted a ratio that would *underestimate* variations by comparison with Laspeyres's arithmetic mean.

As in his previous paper, Jevons meticulously explained his construction of the index from Tooke's data, including methods for "correcting" the data over various intervals and for the classifications of commodities. For example, the price data between 1800 and 1820 had to be corrected to reduce prices and their variations to a gold standard, because the Bank of England sponsored a paper standard during this period (see Chapter 6). The quality of Jevons's study, in short, was extremely high, and the results, multiple price indexes between 1782 and 1865, mark the most important early attempt at systematic price indexing in economic literature. Jevons's instinct for order and his readiness to raise questions concerning the quality of his raw data and his statistical methods make his contributions to price-index construction not only above the level of his time but considerably in advance of it.

Sunspots and Commercial Activity

Jevons's romance with statistical investigations unfortunately carried him to the most fanciful and, unfortunately, the most ridiculed idea of his life, the explanation of commercial crises on the basis of the periodic alteration of spots on the sun. The "sunspot theory" integrated Jevons's earlier work on prices with his lifelong interest in astronomical and meteorological phenomena. In "The Solar Period and the Price of Corn" (1875), he put the matter succinctly:

> If the planets govern the sun, and the sun governs the vintages and harvests, and thus the prices of food and raw materials and the state of the money market, it follows that the configurations of the planets may prove to be the remote causes of the greatest commercial disasters (*Investigations*, p. 185).

Jevons's meteorological research had convinced him that the sunspot period was 11.11 years in length. Parts of James E. Thorold Rogers's great work, *A History of Agriculture and Prices in England,* had begun to appear, giving Jevons a source of raw data. But in 1875, Jevons did not believe that the information he had in hand justified a firm belief in a *causal* relation between sunspots and commercial activity. Still, in noting that the electric telegraph was a favorite dream of sixteenth- and seventeenth-century physicists, Jevons pointed out:

> It would be equally curious if the pseudo-science of astrology should, in like manner, foreshadow the triumphs which precise and methodical investigations may yet disclose, as to the obscure periodic causes affecting our welfare when we are least aware of it (*Investigations*, p. 186).

In 1878 Jevons returned to the subject of sunspots with renewed vigor, first in a paper to the British Association ("The Periodicity of Commercial Crises and Its Physical Explanation") and then in an article in *Nature* ("Commercial Crises and Sun-Spots"). Jevons was convinced by new evidence that the duration of the sunspot cycle was 10.44 years instead of 11.11, a dating that more closely correlated with the commercial cycle of crises. The coincidence was just too much for Jevons, and he lunged to a conclusion:

> I can see no reason why the human mind, in its own spontaneous action, should select a period of just 10.44 years to vary in. Surely we must go beyond the mind to its industrial environment. Merchants and bankers are continually influenced in their dealings by accounts of the success of harvests, the comparative abundance or scarcity of goods; and when we know that there is a cause, the variation of the solar activity, which is just of the nature to affect the produce of agriculture, and which does vary in the same period, it becomes almost certain that the two series of phenomena, credit cycles and solar variations, are connected as effect and cause (*Investigations*, p. 196).

Unfortunately, Jevons appeared to have let a coincidence drag him into an untenable and rigid position. How were alterations in harvests *transmitted* into commercial cycles? Although he had dealt with European experience in the earlier paper, Jevons now argued that the impact on money and commercial markets in England was *through* foreign trade with India and the Orient. Periodic crises in Indian harvests would alter prices of raw produce and the nature of England's trade balance. In his 1875 paper, Jevons had emphasized the "psychic" determinants—optimism, despondency, panic, etc.—of the trade cycle, and he had tried to relate them to oscillations in the price of food. Now Jevons abandoned these psychic effects in the "transmission mechanism" and emphasized merely the *coincidence* of high prices in India and commercial crises in England. But Jevons himself noted the major problem with such an argument: that if the *cause* of commercial crises in England was the high price of agricultural produce in India, a lag between high prices and crises would be expected or even required. None could be observed. In short, some explanation of the relation or transmission was needed, but Jevons offered none. His theory drawn from his study of the available data was simply incomplete. Astronomers returned to a 11.11-year sunspot cycle, moreover, and while the idea probably had some merit in primarily agrarian societies, it is now believed that the determinants of the trade cycle are far more complex than Jevons (or other early writers) thought.[4]

In spite of the "sunspot episode," Jevons's overall statistical work deserves very high marks. The scientific spirit of the attempt to discuss the causes of economic phenomena permeates Jevons's empirical work, and his study of price series will forever stand as a monument and as an example to those concerned with economics and empiricism.

JEVONS'S PREFACE OF 1879 AND THE INTERNATIONAL SPREAD OF ECONOMIC IDEAS

Jevons's contributions to economic theory and statistics are almost matched by his role in the *spread* of economic analysis. Seldom has a writer been more generous in acknowledging the priority of other writers, both previous and contemporary, on points of analysis. Perhaps this statement should begin, "Seldom has a British writer," since, as was mentioned in Chapter 10, Wilhelm Roscher and other continentals were astute in acknowledging their antecedents and contemporaries. Nevertheless, the tenacity of Jevons in ferreting out past and present colleagues of all nations is remarkable and important in the history of economic analysis.

In May of 1874 a correspondence began between the French economic theorist Léon Walras (see Chapter 16) and Jevons. Walras published his *Elements of Political Economy* in that year, setting out a framework of general equilibrium and utility analysis. Interested in propagating these ideas, Walras initiated a monumental correspondence with a large number of economists from all over the world. The result of that correspondence, among other mutual benefits, was the establishment of a list of "mathematico-economic" works originally drawn up by Jevons but amended by Walras. Jevons, in the preface to his second edition of 1879, described this list:

> With the progress of years, however, my knowledge of the literature of political economy has been much widened, and the hints of friends and correspondents have made me aware of the existence of many remarkable works which more or less anticipate the views stated in this book. While preparing this new edition, it occurred to me to attempt the discovery of all existing writings of the kind. With this view I drew up a chronological list of all the mathematico-economic works known to me, already about seventy in number, which list, by the kindness of the editor, Mr. Giffen, was printed in the *Journal of the London Statistical Society* for June 1878 (*Theory*, p. xix).

Jevons forwarded this list to all the leading economists of the time, and Walras had it published in the *Journal des Économistes*.

In his 1879 preface and in the annotated list of mathematico-economic writ-

---

[4] It is interesting to note here that another famous scientist, Newton, spent years trying to convert base metals into gold.

ings, Jevons brought to the attention of other economists the theoretical efforts of Cournot, Dupuit, Ellet, Gossen, both Léon Walras and his father, Auguste, von Thünen, Jenkin, and Lardner, together with a host of other lesser-known writers, such as Cesare Beccaria, Lang, Bordas, Minard, and Boccardo. Many of these writers remain virtually unknown today, and some deservedly so, but at the seed time of neoclassical analysis the recognition and critical evaluation of the work of other theorists were of profound importance.

In the process of classifying and identifying earlier writings, Jevons confronted the fact that his own work was not very original. Cournot had pioneered in mathematical expression; Cournot, Lardner, and Dupuit in the theory of the firm; and Dupuit and Gossen in utility theory, the latter going so far as to establish clearly the equimarginal principle. But in spite of the obvious disappointment Jevons must have felt on making these discoveries, he exerted a herculean effort to identify and popularize earlier and contemporary writers on economic analysis. In doing so, he set a sterling example of what a scholar should be, and at the same time he encouraged an open-door policy on economic ideas, which vastly enriched the neoclassical tradition in England and elsewhere.[5]

POSTSCRIPT: THE IMPORTANCE OF JEVONS

Jevons might well be described as the "complete economist." While he personally vacillated between thinking of himself as a genius and as a failure, his economic work, although admittedly tentative as regards theory, was of consistent and genuine high quality. His seminal investigations in statistics, as well as in formal economic analysis—not to mention the scholarly thrust of his entire performance—were in themselves formidable.

But the range, originality, and uncommon deftness with which he handled all areas of economic inquiry set him apart from most modern *academic* contributors to the field. Marshall, who also possessed these qualities to a very high degree, was practically the last major British theorist to possess a wide breadth of powers. The explanation might lie in the insularity in economic theory that has occurred in economic circles in post-Marshallian days. No longer are many theorists experienced in the nuts and bolts of empiricism, such as keeping and calculating statistics. Jevons, on the other hand, was constantly tinkering with statistics on price and commercial fluctuations, as he had learned to do in Australia with meteorological data. Modern theorists also tend to dismiss other areas related to economics whose subject matter appears irrelevant or pedestrian or where much data gathering is going on. Jevons, on the other hand, appealed to the theory of the lever in mechanics to support his utility-based equations of exchange.

---

[5] T. W. Hutchison, in an interesting paper on the international flow of ideas, "Insularity and Cosmopolitanism in Economic Ideas," suggests that this new door was slammed shut in England mainly by the hegemony and dominance of Marshall's *Principles*. After 1890, in other words, insularity, if not downright chauvinism, again characterized British economic thought.

Many modern economic theorists wish economics to be a science, and some endlessly develop different nuances and variations of nuances upon *received* economic theory. But theory per se is not science, and others point out that the *factual* foundation is simply insufficient to support modern economic analysis, not to mention the speculations drawn from it. Certain theorists desire scientific economic analysis, but they refuse to follow the (admittedly lengthier) methods adopted by all other successful sciences.

It is doubtful whether such a transformation could be accomplished very rapidly, but for those who would try, the experience and lifework of Jevons can certainly stand as a shining example (as can the nonacademic work of Dupuit, Ellet, Lardner, and von Thünen). Jevons's biographer, Keynes, noted that Jevons could claim unnumbered progeny in the "black arts of inductive economics." But with characteristic vision, Keynes added that "The scientific flair which can safely read the shifting sands of economic statistics is no commoner than it was." Keynes's statement is no less accurate today than it was when he made it, but one might legitimately question whether this lack of flair is due to a dearth of abilities, as Keynes suggests, or, in part at least, to the insular and overspecialized education and orientation of economic theorists.

NOTES FOR FURTHER READING

The best source on Jevons is Jevons himself. Few economists have led more interesting, albeit short, lives. Furthermore, Jevons had few peers as an observer of life and a commentator on ideas. His *Letters and Journal,* capably edited by his wife, Harriet, is a must in gaining an appreciation of Jevons's incisive views on every conceivable subject from himself to science, music, statistics, political economy, and a multitude of other topics. In letters to his sister Lucy, his brother Herbert, and many others, Jevons chronicled his sojourn in Australia and his travels to the United States in 1859. These letters also tell of his growing interest in social science and of his decision to apply mathematics to economics. His life and entire career are laid bare in his correspondence with members of his family and with other economists, including his friends H. S. Foxwell and Léon Walras. We now also have an excellent collection entitled *Papers and Correspondence of William Stanley Jevons,* R. D. C. Black (ed.) (New York: A. M. Kelley, 1977). For additional biographical material, see H. W. Jevons, "William Stanley Jevons: His Life," *Econometrica,* vol. 2 (July 1934), pp. 225–231; and H. S. Jevons, "William Stanley Jevons: His Scientific Contributions," *Econometrica,* vol. 2 (July 1934), pp. 231–237.

Jevons's *Theory of Political Economy, Coal Question,* and *Investigations in Currency and Finance* are indispensable in reconstructing his contributions to economic theory and statistics. His theories of labor, capital, rent, and interest are forthrightly analyzed by G. J. Stigler in *Production and Distribution Theories: The Formative Period* (New York: Macmillan, 1941). On Jevons's methodology, see his trenchant essay entitled "Economic Policy," read before Section F (on statistics) of the British Association for the Advancement of Science, reprinted in R. L. Smyth (ed.), *Essays in Economic Method* (New York: McGraw-Hill, 1962).

The best single secondary source on Jevons is still J. M. Keynes's "William Stanley Jevons, 1835–1882," written on the occasion of the centennial of Jevons's birth and reprinted in Keynes's *Essays in Biography* (London: Macmillan, 1933). See also Lionel Robbins, "The Place of Jevons in the History of Economic Thought," *The Manchester School of Economics and Social Studies,* vol. 7 (1936), pp. 1–17; and R. D. C. Black, "W. S. Jevons and the Foundation of Modern Economics," *History of Political Economy,* vol. 4 (Fall 1972), pp. 364–378. Also by Black, see "Jevons, Marginalism and Manchester," *The Manchester School of Economics and Social Studies,* vol. 40 (March 1972), pp. 2–8. This entire issue of *The Manchester School* contains a compendium of papers devoted to Jevons on the 100th anniversary of the publication of his *Theory of Political Economy.* On a narrower topic, the affiliation of Jevons and the eminent astronomer George Darwin, see K. H. Hennings, "George Darwin, Jevons and the Rate of Interest," *History of Political Economy,* vol. 11 (Summer 1979), pp. 199–212.

The academic and intellectual milieu in England before and after Jevons is the subject of discussion by S. G. Checkland, "Economic Opinion in England as Jevons Found It," *The Manchester School of Economics and Social Studies,* vol. 19 (May 1951), pp. 143–169; N. B. deMarchi, "The Noxious Influence of Authority: A Correction of Jevons's Charge," *Journal of Law & Economics,* vol. 16 (April 1973), pp. 179–190; and T. W. Hutchison, "The Marginal Revolution and the Decline and Fall of English Classical Political Economy," *History of Political Economy,* vol. 4 (Fall 1972), pp. 442–468.

Cournot's influence on Jevons's theory of demand is probed by Sam Bostaph and Y. N. Shieh in "W. S. Jevons and Lardner's *Railway Economy,*" *History of Political Economy,* vol. 18 (Spring 1986), pp. 49–64, which also serves as an excellent introduction to Lardner's work. The same authors further amplify this theme in "Jevons's Demand Curve," *History of Political Economy,* vol. 19 (Spring 1987), pp. 107–126, which contrasts Jevons's performance with that of Fleeming Jenkin. Finally, a new interpretation of Jevons's formulation of value theory is given by R. B. Ekelund, Jr., and Yeung-Nan Shieh in "Jevons on Utility, Exchange, and Demand: A Reassessment," *Manchester School of Economics and Social Studies,* vol. 57 (March 1989), pp. 17–33. Ekelund and Shieh argue that Jevons worked out certain partial *and* general equilibrium concepts independently of Marshall and Walras and that he was far more creative in both of these areas than is commonly thought.

Jevons's mathematical approach to microeconomic theory originally met with stiff resistance. Margaret Schabas, "Some Reactions to Jevons' Mathematical Program: The Case of Cairnes and Mill," *History of Political Economy,* vol. 17 (Fall 1985), pp. 337–354, maintains that Cairnes and Mill first stood together against the use of mathematics in economic theory, but eventually came around to Jevons's position. Jevons's early and skillful attempts to introduce statistical techniques to economic analysis are appraised by J. Aldrich, "Jevons as Statistician: The Role of Probability," *Manchester School of Economics and Social Studies,* vol. 55 (September 1987), pp. 233–256, who concludes that although Jevons did not contribute materially to the development of theoretical statistics per se, he set the pattern for the economist as consumer of statistical techniques.

REFERENCES

Hutchison, T. W. "Insularity and Cosmopolitanism in Economic Ideas, 1870–1914," *American Economic Review,* vol. 45 (May 1955), pp. 1–16.

Jevons, W. S. *Theory of Political Economy.* New York: Kelley and Millman, 1957 [1871].

————. *Letters and Journal,* H. A. Jevons (ed.). London: Macmillan, 1886.

————. *Investigations in Currency and Finance,* H. S. Foxwell (ed.). London: Macmillan, 1909.

Keynes, J. M. "William Stanley Jevons, 1835–1882: A Centenary Allocution on His Life as Economist and Statistician," *Journal of the Royal Statistical Society,* vol. 99 (1936), pp. 516–548.

ALFRED MARSHALL AND THE DEVELOPMENT OF PARTIAL-EQUILIBRIUM ANALYSIS

INTRODUCTION

The foundations of neoclassical economics were clearly established in England and on the Continent by 1870, as the abundance of evidence presented in the last three chapters suggests. These distinguished contributors paved the way for the seminal and cohesive works of Alfred Marshall (1842–1924) and Léon Walras (1834–1910)—the twin founders of modern neoclassical analysis. Fundamental differences in the scope and method in the approach of these two writers are detailed in the following chapters and will help to place each in perspective. Since there is a clear progression between the ideas of Jevons and Marshall, however, we begin our discussion of neoclassicism with Marshall.

MARSHALL'S LIFE AND WORKS

Alfred Marshall, son of a bank cashier, was born in Clapham, England, in 1842. His ancestors were mostly clerics, and Alfred's father, William, was no less evangelical, despite a secular career at the Bank of England. William Marshall was, in fact, a no-nonsense disciplinarian who frequently pushed his intelligent—though overworked—son to his mental and physical limits. It was not at all uncommon for him to drill Alfred on his schoolwork until almost midnight. Later, Alfred Marshall recalled that only annual summer visits to a distant aunt saved him in his youth from mental and physical exhaustion.

At prep school Marshall acquired the name "Tallow Candles" for his pallor, ill dress, and overwrought appearance. He did not make friends easily, and his two most enjoyable intellectual pursuits—mathematics and chess— were forbidden by his authoritarian father. In 1861, a rebellious Marshall refused a scholarship at Oxford (which would have led to the ministry) because, as he put it, he could not abide further study of dead languages. His father, on the other hand, could not afford to send Marshall to college on his own. So, with the financial aid of a wealthy uncle, Marshall enrolled at Cambridge, where he not only indulged his taste for mathematics but also distinguished himself as an honor student.

Marshall's passion for mathematics served him well in two respects. Initially, he viewed his mathematical studies as an expression of independence from his domineering father. Also, because he received a modest income from tutoring in mathematics, Marshall was able to repay his uncle and support himself at Cambridge. Later he wrote: "Mathematics had paid my arrears. I was free for my own inclinations" (Pigou, *Memorials of Alfred Marshall*, p. 5).

Those inclinations ultimately led him to political economy in 1867, but only after several detours. Marshall described his roundabout path to economics:

> From Metaphysics I went to Ethics, and thought that the justification of the existing condition of society was not easy. A friend, who had read a great deal of what are now called the Moral Sciences, constantly said: "Ah! if you understood Political Economy you would not say that." So I read Mill's *Political Economy* and got much excited about it. I had doubts as to the propriety of inequalities of opportunity, rather than of material comfort. Then, in my vacations I visited the poorest quarters of several cities and walked through one street after another, looking at the faces of the poorest people. Next, I resolved to make as thorough a study as I could of Political Economy (Pigou, *Memorials*, p. 10).

Having thus chosen economics as his field, Marshall approached the study of that subject with a personal dedication that he maintained till the end—a dedication that in no small measure accounts for his sizable contributions to economic analysis.

While his father still hoped in vain that his son would take holy orders, Marshall instead took a bride, in 1877. His marriage to Mary Paley, a former student of his and lecturer at Newnham College, forced him—as had been the case with Malthus—to resign his fellowship at Cambridge. The Marshalls left Cambridge for Bristol, where both husband and wife lectured on political economy at newly founded University College. There, too, they collaborated on the *Economics of Industry, which was first published in 1879.*

Their years at Bristol were spent happily enough, save for an extended period of illness on Marshall's part. In 1884, however, a faculty position at his former school opened up, and a recovered Marshall returned to Cambridge. There the Marshalls spent the rest of their years in what Alfred Marshall called "a small cultured society of great simplicity and distinction."

Fifty years of writing by Alfred Marshall produced eighty-two publications, including books, articles, lectures, conferences, and testimony (before three Royal Commissions). His immensely popular and influential *Principles of Economics* (1890) has gone through nine editions to date; *Industry and Trade* (1919), through five editions; and *The Economics of Industry* (1879), through two editions and ten printings. Only his *Money, Credit and Commerce* (1923) has not appeared in multiple editions, and this is because it was published a mere year before Marshall's death.

All his biographers agree, however, that Marshall's impact on economics cannot be measured by his publications alone. Much more important for the progress of economic theory was his practice of transmitting his original ideas to a generation of able students long before those ideas appeared in print. The strong oral tradition that Marshall began at Cambridge constitutes an extremely important chapter in the history of economic analysis, particularly in monetary theory (see Chapter 20).

As early as 1888, Herbert Foxwell wrote of Marshall: "Half the economic chairs in the United Kingdom are occupied by his pupils, and the share taken by them in general economic instruction in England is even larger that this" (*Quarterly Journal of Economics*, vol. 2, p. 92). Indeed, a list of Marshall's students reads like a *Who's Who* of British economists in the early twentieth century. In addition to the more renowned J. M. Keynes (see Chapter 19), there were A. C. Pigou, Joan Robinson (see Chapter 18), and D. H. Robertson, to name a few. These students nurtured the "Cambridge tradition" begun by Marshall, and they extended it in many directions.

Marshall's incessant delay in putting his ideas into print was a frequent source of frustration to students and friends alike. To his credit, Marshall was an extremely cautious and meticulous writer who hesitated to publish anything until he had thought through the implications of its content and perfected its presentation. The result was elegant and lasting contributions to economic analysis, but contributions more often than not published after the bloom of novelty had wilted. Keynes cites the extreme example of Marshall's monetary theories—which had been a part of the Cambridge tradition for several decades before finally finding their way into print in 1923 (in *Money, Credit and Commerce*).

The same caution caused Marshall to be a late expositor of marginal-utility analysis, although historical evidence indicates that he derived the principle of marginal utility independently of, and at about the same time as, Jevons, Menger, and Walras. In one sense, however, Marshall stood above Jevons and Walras. His training in mathematics established him as a much better mathematician. Yet his approach to the use of mathematics in economics remained circumspect. In his youth he had translated the works of Ricardo and Mill into mathematical symbols, but apparently he did so as a mere personal convenience. Later, in the preface to his famous *Principles*, Marshall justified the mathematics-as-convenience approach:

> The chief use of pure mathematics in economic questions seems to be in helping a person to write down quickly, shortly and exactly, some of his own thoughts for his own use....It seems doubtful whether anyone spends his time well in reading lengthy translations of economic doctrines into mathematics, that have not been made by himself (*Principles*, pp. x–xi).

In the *Principles,* Marshall confined his use of diagrams and other mathematical notations to footnotes and appendixes so as not to allow his mathematics to detract from his economics. He was interested above all in plain communication—with businessmen as well as with students. Moreover, he was acutely aware that overreliance on mathematics "might lead us astray in pursuit of intellectual toys, imaginary problems not conforming to the conditions of real life: and, further, might distort our sense of proportion by causing us to neglect factors that could not easily be worked up in the mathematical machine" (Pigou, *Memorials,* p. 84).

Had Marshall in fact foreseen the subsequent development of mathematical economics in all its intensity, he might have wished to publish his own rules on the subject in a more conspicuous place than in a letter to his friend and colleague, Arthur Bowley. On February 27, 1906, Marshall wrote, somewhat retrospectively:

> I had a growing feeling in the later years of my work at the subject that a good mathematical theorem dealing with economic hypotheses was very unlikely to be good economics: and I went more and more on the rules—(1) Use mathematics as a shorthand language, rather than as an engine of inquiry. (2) Keep to them till you have done. (3) Translate into English. (4) Then illustrate by examples that are important in real life. (5) Burn the mathematics. (6) If you can't succeed in 4, burn 3. This last I did often (Pigou, *Memorials,* p. 427).

Marshall's doubts as to the usefulness of the techniques of theoretical mathematics and statistics should not, however, be misinterpreted. He continuously counseled deep historical and statistical knowledge of any matter under investigation. He considered command of empirical facts a prerequisite to reasonable conclusions. In sum, Marshall was a master economist because he possessed a *combination* of talents. Keynes best underscored Marshall's gifts when he wrote:

> His mixed training and divided nature furnished him with the most essential and fundamental of the economist's necessary gifts—he was conspicuously historian and mathematician, a dealer in the particular and the general, the temporal and the eternal, at the same time (Pigou, *Memorials,* p. 12).

Finally, Marshall was an economist's economist—an acknowledged and undisputed leader of colleagues and students alike. His view was that economics "is a field needing the co-operative work of many men with many different bents of mind." Like his contemporary Walras, Marshall helped advance the professionalization of economics. The difference was that Marshall was able to exert his influence from the firm footing of a long-standing tradition at Cambridge University, whereas Walras was forced to operate from a lonely outpost in Switzerland.

MARSHALL AND HIS METHOD

It is in the way Marshall viewed things that we find some of his most interesting and enduring contributions to economic science. The key to Marshall's partial-equilibrium approach to economic theory and to applied economics, in other words, is contained in his statements on method. Although the Marshallian method is a composite of several interrelated ideas, we shall look at the topics separately. First, we shall consider Marshall's definition of economics and of an economic law; next, we shall describe his brilliant conception of the role of time in economic analysis; and finally, we shall discuss the relation of Marshall's concept of time to markets and market periods. The way is then paved for a discussion of his famous conception of competitive equilibrium.

In the first place, Marshall viewed the science of economics in about 1890 as merely an extension—really a *continuation*—of the ideas espoused by Adam Smith. He clearly indicated his belief that neoclassical economics was merely an elaboration or a modern version of old classical doctrines. A new age and new problems changed the *emphasis* of economic analysis, but Marshall believed that the relatively simple analyses of Ricardo and Mill could bear scrutiny. The change in emphasis was the extension of the microeconomic branch of economic science occurring at the time. But how did Marshall view economic science?

Again and again, throughout the *Principles,* Marshall explicated his conception of economic science. In defining the scope and purpose of his book, he noted in the preface to the first edition that:

> In accordance with English tradition, it is held that the function of the science is to collect, arrange and analyse economic facts, and to apply the knowledge, gained by observation and experience, in determining what are likely to be the immediate and ultimate effects of various groups of causes; and it is held that the Laws of Economics are statements of tendencies expressed in the indicative mood, and not ethical precepts in the imperative. Economic laws and reasonings in fact are merely a part of the material which Conscience and Common-sense have to turn to account in solving practical problems, and in laying down rules which may be a guide in life (*Principles,* pp. v–vi).[1]

Marshall's method, then, rests essentially upon refined common sense. Economic science is but the working out of common sense refined by organized analysis and reason. Facts and history are essential to the economic theorist, of course, but as Marshall himself noted, "Facts by themselves teach nothing." Regularities and tendencies of human actions, given institutional and ethical constraints, must be observed and extracted from historical and empirical data. Analysis, in this view, is shorthand for common sense: if given suf-

---

[1] Marshall, however, unlike certain writers in the classical tradition, did not adhere to an extreme view of economic man, i.e., one uninfluenced by altruistic motives. Indeed, one of the unique characteristics of his book is that Marshall *is* willing to take ethical forces, if they occur with sufficient regularity within economic classes, into account.

ficient regularities, it allows general rules or theories to be developed and applied in particular situations.

Complexity in human actions, in which Marshall claimed to find regularity, is one of the central reasons many historical and other heterodox thinkers rejected traditional economic analysis. Aware of the vulnerability of economic theory on this plane, Marshall provided brilliant defenses. In Book I he compared the abstract method of economics with that of the physical and natural sciences:

> Economic laws are statements with regard to the tendencies of man's action under certain conditions. They are hypothetical only in the same sense as are the laws of the physical sciences: for those laws also contain or imply conditions. But there is more difficulty in making the conditions clear, and more danger in any failure to do so, in economics than in physics. The laws of human action are not indeed as simple, as definite or as clearly ascertainable as the law of gravitation; but many of them may rank with the laws of those natural sciences which deal with complex subject-matter (*Principles*, p. 38).

Economic theory, Marshall thought, was facilitated in that the economic facts of human behavior could be segmented from general facts. Economics was concerned with *measurable motives,* that is, money and prices. Though not a perfect measure, "With careful precautions money affords a fairly good measure of the moving force of a great part of the motives by which men's lives are fashioned" (*Principles*, p. 39).

Time and *Ceteris Paribus*

Roughly, then, Marshall's method consisted of commonsense abstraction from economic facts and behavior utilizing general analysis and reason. The science of economics resulting from the application of this method, moreover, had the twin purposes of knowledge for its own sake and use in practical questions. But of what, precisely, did this method consist? If nature's riddles are complex and the human mind is limited, as Marshall avers, how specifically are we to acquire knowledge about economic subjects? With direct application to any market, for example, how are we adequately to analyze prices and profits when tastes, income, technology, and costs are continuously changing through time?

Time enters the analysis of economic facts and quantities at every step, and it was perhaps one of Marshall's greatest contributions to take into account its importance. Even better, he worked time into his entire *method* of approaching economic analysis, noting at the start that it was the "centre of the chief difficulty of almost every economic problem" (*Principles*, p. *vii*). Within his famous discussion of normal demand-and-supply equilibrium, Marshall clearly explains how time is to be handled in economic analysis:

> The element of time is a chief cause of those difficulties in economic investigations which make it necessary for man with his limited powers to go step by step; breaking up a complex question, studying one bit at a time, and at last combining his par-

tial solutions into a more or less complete solution of the whole riddle. In breaking it up, he segregates those disturbing causes, whose wanderings happen to be inconvenient, for the time in a pound called *Ceteris Paribus*. The study of some group of tendencies is isolated by the assumption *other things being equal:* the existence of other tendencies is not denied, but their disturbing effect is neglected for a time. The more the issue is thus narrowed, the more exactly can it be handled: but also the less closely does it correspond to real life. Each exact and firm handling of a narrow issue, however, helps towards treating broader issues, in which that narrow issue is contained, more exactly than would otherwise have been possible. With each step more things can be let out of the pound; exact discussions can be made less abstract, realistic discussions can be made less inexact than was possible at an earlier stage (*Principles,* p. 366).

Thus Marshall proposed to handle the problem of continuous change (time) through the judicious use of *ceteris paribus* assumptions, or conditioning clauses. Other writers had *implied* "other things being equal" in constructing theories, but it was Marshall's genius that explicated and utilized the method in cost-of-production analysis and in all of value theory.

Market Periods, Competition, and the Price of Fish: Time in Analysis *Ceteris paribus,* necessitated by inevitable effects of time upon economic quantities, is a most useful fiction for modern microeconomics. The manner in which Marshall integrated time and *ceteris paribus* into economic theory is perhaps best explained by using one of his own examples—the market for fish.

Marshall considered three hypothetical circumstances or problems that would affect the fishing trade. First, there are very quick changes, such as vagaries of the weather, which effect very short-term fluctuations in the price of fish. Second, Marshall posited changes of moderate length, such as an increase in the demand for fish owing to a cattle plague of some duration. Finally, he formulated a long-period problem for the fishing trade over a whole generation, perhaps caused by a change in tastes.

When considering short-run market conditions, the very quick day-to-day changes in demand and supply can be neglected. Temporary changes in the catch of fish, in the weather, or in the availability of substitutes or complements for fish obviously cause temporary oscillations around what Marshall called the *normal* short-term price of fish. Very short-term shifts in supply and demand—some of them canceling out—can easily be imagined. But the key to understanding Marshall's method lies in the relation between changing demand and production conditions through time and the concept of normal price. In order to get a clear understanding of Marshall's method, we must first look at the effects of time upon the production conditions of the firm (a fishing firm is our example).

The Short Run Marshall posited the existence of a *representative,* or average, firm operating in a competitive market. The concept is ambiguous, even by Marshall's own definition: "Our representative firm must be one which has had a fairly long life, and fair success, which is managed with normal ability, and which has normal access to the economies, external and internal, which belong to that aggregate volume of production; account being taken of the class of goods produced, the conditions of marketing them and the economic environment generally'' (*Principles*, p. 220). Mark Blaug attributes this invention to Marshall's ''restless quest for realism,'' but in fact the representative firm ''is an abstraction; it is neither an arithmetic average, nor a median, nor even a modal firm. It is representative, not with respect to size, but with respect to average costs'' (*Economic Theory in Retrospect*, p. 391). Aside from the difficulties associated with the concept, such a firm might be depicted as in Figure 15-1*a*. (Neglect for the moment the curves of Figure 15-1*b*.) Specifically, the short-run production conditions of the representative fishing firm are depicted in Figure 15-1*a*. In the short run (one or two years in Marshall's fishing example) the ability of the fishing industry to supply fish is not indefinitely expansible. To the firm depicted in Figure 15-1*a*, this limit to additional production is represented by the rising marginal- and average-cost functions beyond quantity q_i. The fishing firm, in other words, cannot alter all its inputs in a short period of time, and some of its inputs must be regarded as fixed. It takes time, for example, to build new boats and to train a new and larger generation of fishermen. The firm can, of course, increase other inputs. In the

FIGURE 15-1
A short-run increase in market demand from *DD* to *D'D'* raises the market price from *P* to *P'* and industry output from *Q* to *Q'*. Each firm will earn economic profits because the average revenue *P'* exceeds average costs *C* at quantity *q'$_i$*. In the long run, as new firms enter the industry, the supply curve will shift to the right, from *SRS* to *SRS'*, pushing the equilibrium price back to *P*, but there will be more output, *Q''*.

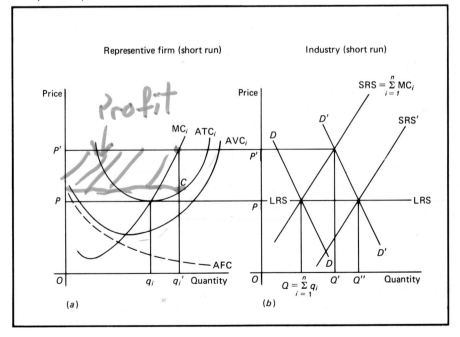

short run, then, which assumes the existence of fixed or quasi-fixed capacity, there is a distinction to the firm between average total costs and average variable costs, as variable inputs are added. The difference between average total cost and average variable cost is average fixed cost, which declines over the whole range of output (the dashed function in Figure 15-1*a*). A difference between the *AVC* and *AFC* functions of Figure 15-1*a* is not relevant in a period where all inputs may be varied, and the average total cost of adding inputs is equivalent to the average variable cost.

It is also important to note the reason why the average-cost functions of Figure 15-1*a* are U-shaped. As variable inputs—say, fishermen or nets—are added to the "plant" capacity of fishing boats, returns in the form of the number of fish caught per unit of input increase. Average costs, both total and variable, decline. But as variable units are added, average productivity of those inputs in terms of fish caught will decline beyond a point. The average *cost* of supplying fish, therefore, declines over a range of output but must inevitably rise. Likewise, the marginal cost to the fishing firm, that is, the change in total cost as output is increased one unit, may at first fall but must inevitably rise. Clearly, as a result of a simple law of arithmetic, marginal cost must equal both average variable costs and average total costs when the latter are at a minimum.

Now let us concentrate on Marshall's long-run–short-run distinction in *demand* conditions. Marshall posited an increase of moderate length in the demand for fish due to a cattle plague. His use of time in production and *ceteris paribus* enabled him to predict price and output in the fish market during the period. Having impounded in *ceteris paribus* the variations that *do* affect the fishing industry but that affect it too slowly to have an appreciable influence in the short run, Marshall focused attention on the factors that would affect the market for fish given a short-run increase in demand. Marshall argued that in the short run:

> We give our full attention to such influences as the inducements which good fishing wages will offer to sailors to stay in their fishing homes for a year or two, instead of applying for work on a ship. We consider what old fishing boats, and even vessels that were not specially made for fishing, can be adapted and sent to fish for a year or two. The normal price for any given daily supply of fish, which we are now seeking, is the price which will quickly call into the fishing trade capital and labour enough to obtain that supply in a day's fishing of average good fortune; the influence which the price of fish will have upon capital and labour available in the fishing trade being governed by rather narrow causes such as these. This new level about which the price oscillates during these years of exceptionally great demand will obviously be higher than before. Here we see an illustration of the almost universal law that the term normal being taken to refer to a short period of time, *an increase in the amount demanded raises the normal supply price* (*Principles*, p. 370).

The example perfectly illustrates Marshall's method. Very short-run and long-run factors affecting the fishing trade are ignored or assumed constant, while those influences having direct bearing on the market over the relevant time period are given full play in explaining market price and quantity. Operational time, not clock time, is at the center of the analysis. The "capital and labour available in the fishing trade" are obviously a function of different variables in the short and long run since it takes time to construct new capacity and to induce additional workers to enter the fishing trade. In consequence, normal supply price will differ in both periods, as we shall see presently.

Competitive Equilibrium Marshall's method and his simple model of short-run competitive equilibrium may be easily illustrated with the aid of the graphical analysis of Figure 15-1. The fishing-industry curves are depicted in Figure 15-1b, where the positively sloped short-run supply function (*SRS*) is, under purely competitive conditions, simply the horizontal summation of all the marginal-cost curves of the firms constituting the industry. The industry demand function for fish is originally assumed to be *DD*, and industry equilibrium exists at the intersection of *SRS* and *DD* with equilibrium values of price and output at P and Q (the sum of the quantities produced by all the firms). The representative firm is a price taker under competitive conditions. We assume that, before the disturbance, price P, or average revenue, is equal to minimum average total costs of production, and that total costs ($q_i \times ATC$) equal total revenue ($q_i \times P$). Thus no economic profits exist in the industry before the alteration in demand.

Now consider Marshall's supposition that a cattle plague causes an apparently temporary increase in the demand for fish to $D'D'$. After a period of adjustment (during which demand price exceeds supply price), the price of fish rises to P' and industry output rises to Q', which is the summation of the now larger outputs (q'_i) of the individual firms. The firms are maximizing profits at output q'_i since marginal cost is equal to marginal revenue (in competition, price is equal to marginal revenue). Thus the short-term *normal* supply rises with an increase in the demand for fish, as Marshall explained.

The important point is that, given sufficient information on the part of potential competitors, a price of P' could not ordinarily persist in the fish market. Economic *profits* are being earned by each firm since average revenue (P') exceeds average cost (C) at quantity q'_i. If the increase in fish demand becomes permanent because of a change in tastes, as Marshall assumed it did, then normal supply price will be governed by a different set of causes. In short, a permanent long-term increase in the demand for fish engenders long-term production adjustments for firms in the industry. Economic profits are the signal that, under competition, a long-term adjustment will take place. The nature of the adjustment could vary, however, and in a brilliant and typically Marshallian passage, Marshall described the possibilities:

> The source of supply in the sea might perhaps show signs of exhaustion, and the fishermen might have to resort to more distant coasts and to deeper waters, Nature giving a Diminishing Return to the increased application of capital and labour of a given order of efficiency. On the other hand, those might turn out to be right who think that man is responsible for but a very small part of the destruction of fish that

is constantly going on; and in that case a boat starting with equally good appliances and an equally efficient crew would be likely to get nearly as good a haul after the increase in the total volume of the fishing trade as before. In any case the normal cost of equipping a good boat with an efficient crew would certainly not be higher, and probably be a little lower after the trade had settled down to its now increased dimensions than before. For since fishermen require only trained aptitudes, and not any exceptional natural qualities, their number could be increased in less than a generation to almost any extent that was necessary to meet the demand; while the industries connected with building boats, making nets, etc. being now on a larger scale would be organized more thoroughly and economically. If therefore the waters of the sea showed no signs of depletion of fish, an increased supply could be produced at a lower price after a time sufficiently long to enable the normal action of economic causes to work itself out: and, the term Normal being taken to refer to a long period of time, the normal price of fish would decrease with an increase in demand (*Principles,* pp. 370–371).

Long-Run Conditions Returning to Figure 15-1, consider Marshall's second possibility, i.e., that additional capital and labor applied to the fishing trade would yield a proportionate increase in the catch. Economic profits might cause firms to react in several ways: existing firms might increase their scale of operations to produce greater output, and/or new fishing firms might join the market. If for convenience we eliminate the first possibility, the short-run industry supply curve will shift to the right with the entry of new firms, to *SRS'*. Since we are assuming that the normal cost of "equipping a good boat with an efficient crew" remains the same as at lower levels of total output, the representative firm's cost functions do not shift. After *all* adjustments take place, the market is again in long-term equilibrium with zero economic profits at price *P* but at a higher level of output. The long-run supply price of fish is constant (at *P* in Figure 15-1), and the long-run supply function (*LRS*) may be traced out by connecting the two intersections of supply and demand after all adjustments have taken place. If the *LRS* function is horizontal, as in Figure 15-1, we say that fishing is a *constant-cost industry*. Proportionate increases in inputs of capital and labor yield proportionate increases in output of fish.

Actually, we have been assuming that the fishing firm was in long-run equilibrium *before* the increase in demand took place. Figure 15-1*a* does not depict a long-run equilibrium for the firm, however. The long-run situation of the representative firm after all adjustments have taken place is as shown in Figure 15-2. Since there are no *fixed* costs in the long run, all costs to the firm are variable. This is reflected in Figure 15-2 by the fact that there is no distinction between average total cost and average variable cost. The long-run average-cost curve is commonly called an "envelope" or a "planning" curve, and it was first developed by Jacob Viner, not by Marshall (see the Notes for Further Reading at the end of this chapter). The envelope curve is really drawn as a series of tangencies of many possible short-run curves. Only one of these short-run curves (*SRAC_i*) is tangent at the point of minimum long-run average cost (point *A* in Figure 15-2). It is the same average cost (*ATC*) we assumed in

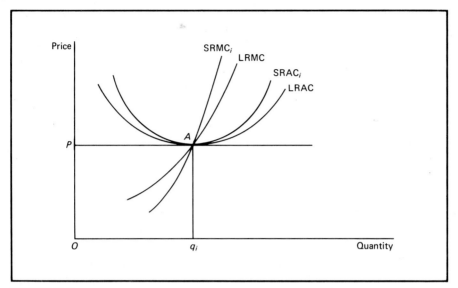

FIGURE 15-2
Long-run equilibrium for the firm is where the lowest point of the *LRAC* and a particular
SRAC curve are tangent to the market price.

Figure 15-1*a*. Given price P_0, the representative fishing firm will produce output q_i. At this long-run equilibrium for the firm, quantity q_i is produced with an
optimum scale of plant, i.e., at minimum long-run average costs. Quantity q_i is
also an optimum rate of output in that the scale of plant represented by $SRAC_i$
is utilized at its most efficient level, i.e., at minimum costs. The important
point is that competition and freedom of entry-exit in the fishing industry guarantee that output (given the cost conditions assumed) will be produced at minimum long-run average costs.

Thus a review of Marshall's fishing example yields insights into his method
encompassing time-period analysis and *ceteris paribus* assumptions. We have
further utilized it as a springboard for a discussion of Marshall's concept of
competitive equilibrium and market adjustment. So far we have considered
only the commonest representation of competitive market adjustment, the
constant-cost case. We now turn to two other cases alluded to by Marshall in
his discussion of adjustment in the fishing trade, i.e., the increasing- and
decreasing-cost-industry cases. We shall see that the latter concept was the
more important and controversial since it shaped some of Marshall's other
ideas, especially those on welfare economics, as well as shaping the course of
twentieth-century microeconomics.

INDUSTRY SUPPLY AND THE ECONOMICS OF PRODUCTION

It is a simple matter to demonstrate the two other long-run supply conditions
implied by Marshall in his example of the fishing trade. Unfortunately, some of

the concepts usually associated with these supply conditions are not clear in the *Principles* and caused difficulties for the theory of competition, as we shall see in Chapter 18. Graphically, however, cases of increasing and decreasing cost may be depicted simply. Consider Figures 15-3 and 15-4, for example, in which only industry curves are taken into account.

Increasing and Decreasing Costs

In the increasing-cost case, contrary to the one described by Figure 15-1, the firm's cost curves rise as industry output expands. That is, with reference to Figure 15-3, the *LRS* function is positively sloped. Full long-run adjustment to the increase in demand (from *D* to *D'*) will take place only at higher costs (at *B*). In the fishing example, for instance, Marshall noted the possibility that the supply of fish in the sea might become somewhat depleted, so that fishermen would have to resort to fishing in more distant areas. Such activity would become more costly in that proportionate applications of homogeneous capital and labor would yield less than proportionate returns in the catch.

But Marshall noted a more interesting possibility—that of a downward-sloping long-run supply function for the industry. With reference to Figure 15-4, decreasing *LRS* implies that additional output will be produced at lower costs to the firm. Here, an increase in demand (from *D* to *D'*), which increases firm output, causes the short-run supply function (*SRS'*) to intersect the new demand curve at a price lower than at the previous output level. The firm's average-cost curves shift with increased output, and in the fishing-trade exam-

FIGURE 15-3
Increasing long-run supply costs result when a representative firm's unit costs rise as a consequence of output expansion to meet an increase in market demand.

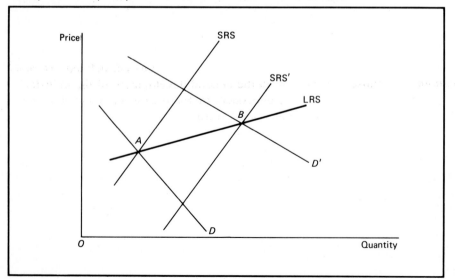

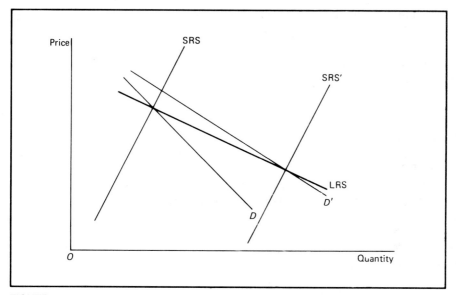

FIGURE 15-4
Decreasing long-run supply results when a representative firm's unit costs decline as a consequence of output expansion to meet an increase in market demand.

ple, Marshall suggested that reduced input prices are the cause. Better organization and larger operations in boatbuilding and net making mean that factor prices to the fishing firm would be lower. Thus the long-run industry supply of fish would be negatively sloped as in Figure 15-4.

Internal and External Economies   Although Marshall did not develop a full-blown theory of a firm's cost functions,[2] he discussed two types of economies in production that might explain industry supply behavior. Specifically, he divided economies associated with increased production into two types: those external to the firm and those internal to the firm. Marshall defined *external economies* as those "dependent on the general development of the industry" and *internal economies* as those dependent on the organization and efficiency of the management within the individual firms.

Internal economies from an increase in output are those stemming from the division of labor and improved use of machinery within the firm. Much specialized machinery can be utilized only in large units, so that full economic efficiency of both capital and labor can be attained only with increases in production. As output expands, long-run average cost declines, but after some level of output, average cost must again rise owing to inefficiencies of man-

---

[2] In his famous paper entitled "Cost Curves and Supply Curves" (see Notes for Further Reading at the end of this chapter), Jacob Viner developed the envelope, or long-run, cost curve for the firm.

agement and the difficulties of marketing the product. Internal economies and diseconomies are simply an explanation for the typical U-shaped long-run average-cost curve.

External economies occurring with increased output, as Marshall identified them, are production economies external to the firm but internal to the industry. Marshall linked external economies to the location of industry, but his discussion produced very few examples. Most are associated in some way with the location of industry. Among others, Marshall mentions the following external economies from the agglomeration of firms in a given locale:

1 Better information and skills
2 Availability of skilled labor
3 Economies in the use of specialized machinery

In explaining the first, Marshall (somewhat grandiloquently) noted that, after an industry has chosen a locale, "The mysteries of the trade become no mysteries; but are as it were in the air, and children learn many of them unconsciously." In addition, he wrote:

> Good work is rightly appreciated, inventions and improvements in machinery, in processes and the general organization of the business have their merits promptly discussed: if one man starts a new idea, it is taken up by others and combined with suggestions of their own; and thus it becomes the source of further new ideas. And presently subsidiary trades grow up in the neighborhood, supplying it with implements and materials, organizing its traffic, and in many ways conducing to the economy of its material (*Principles,* p. 271).

Second, Marshall argued that localized industry provided a "constant," orderly market for skilled and specialized labor. Presumably, industries are attracted to regions where scarce labor inputs (in the firm's production functions) are readily available. Simultaneously, of course, labor is attracted to regions where the demand for its services is high. As the industry "grows up" in a given area, the availability of specialized labor is expanded and enhanced.

Marshall suggested that as an industry grows up, economies in the use of specialized machinery become realizable. He also hinted that the growth of supportive, subsidiary industries creates external economies for firms within the industry. To use Marshall's words again:

> The economic use of expensive machinery can sometimes be attained in a very high degree in a district in which there is a large aggregate production of the same kind, even though no individual capital employed in the trade be very large. For subsidiary industries devoting themselves each to one small branch of the process of production, and working it for a great many of their neighbors, are able to keep in constant use machinery of the most highly specialized character, and to make it pay its expenses, though its original cost may have been high, and its rate of depreciation very rapid (*Principles,* p. 271).

External Economies, Graphically Considered As in Figure 15-1, the costs and revenues of the representative firm are depicted in Figure 15-5a, and the

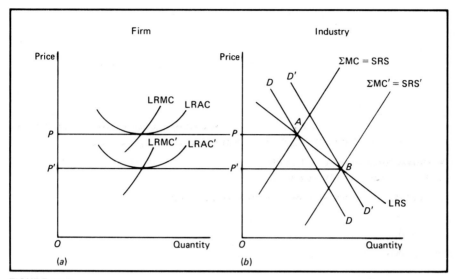

FIGURE 15-5
A short-run increase in market demand, from *DD* to *D'D'*, causes expansion of output by
existing firms and attracts new firms to the industry. The presence of external economies
lowers the *LRAC* and *LRMC* of each firm, and the result is a long-run downward-sloping
supply curve (*LRS*).

industry curves are shown in Figure 15-5b. Initial industry and firm equilibriums occur at price *P,* formed by the intersection of short-run industry supply
curve *SRS* (which equals ΣMC) and industry *DD.* If we assume that demand
increases to *D'D'*, short-term economic profits accrue to firms constituting the
industry (note that these profits are not shown in Figure 15-5, but the process
is totally analogous to that described in reference to Figure 15-1). Each firm's
rate of output is increased (as always, up to the point where price equals marginal cost of production), but profits signal the entry of new firms into the market. As new firms enter, external economies are engendered. The economies,
which shift the *long-run* cost curves of each of the firms downward, are, by
definition, external to each of the firms but internal to the industry.

Thus the positions of the long-run cost curves of the firm are *not* independent of changes in industry output, as they are in the constant-cost case.[3] With
reference to Figure 15-5, the firm's long-run cost curves shift downward to
LRAC' and *LRMC'* when new firms enter the industry. A new industry equilibrium is reached at price *P'* (point *B*), where short-run supply *SRS'* (or $\Sigma MC'$) is
equal to the new industry demand *D'D'*. Connection of the loci of the two equilibrium sets of price and quantity (represented at points *A* and *B* in Figure 15-5)

---

[3] We skirt the more complex question of whether the representative firm's rate of output (q_i in
Figure 15-1a) will be larger, smaller, or the same with changes in industry output.

traces out a downward-sloping long-run industry supply curve.[4] The decreasing function *LRS* appears to represent the analytical substance of what Marshall meant by the term "decreasing-cost industry," although there could be some debate on the issue. Clearly, the concept is fraught with difficulties, not only in interpretation but also in substance. However, far from being simply a theoretical curiosity, Marshall's discussion of external economies and decreasing costs is of prime importance on several counts. First, the limitations of his partial-equilibrium method are bared by the concept of the decreasing-cost industry. Second, a whole new area of micro analysis—the study of imperfect competition—was initiated in the 1920s and 1930s through a questioning of the compatibility of decreasing costs with the theory of competition.[5] Before discussing Marshall's analytical use of his alternative-cost assumptions, it will be instructive to look at each of these issues briefly.

Long-Period Supply: Analytical Difficulties

The limits of Marshall's method—which he clearly understood—are revealed in the case of external economies and decreasing costs. We have argued that the long-period supply function, as depicted in Figure 15-5*b,* is negatively sloped as a result of external economies. One might argue that the long-run costs curves of the firm shift downward because of a fall in input prices with increases in industry output. Unfortunately, as Blaug has suggested (*Economic Theory in Retrospect,* p. 381), such reasoning merely shifts the explanation a step away. Why, for instance, do input prices fall? If the fall is due to external economies in the supplying industries, we are still at pains to describe the nature of these economies. Consequently, we have left a fall in input prices off our list of external economies.

But even when we are confronted with the list Marshall described (better use of machinery, better methods, etc.), we encounter difficulties. Specifically, it becomes extremely doubtful whether partial-equilibrium analysis, such as that described by Figure 15-5, can handle the problem. The long-run supply curve is drawn up on the assumption that technology is constant. A change in technology would cause a *shift* in the curve. In the list of external economies given by Marshall, it would be difficult to find a single economy that did not, in some way, alter technology. This is especially true as the period considered lengthens.

One important question related to the analysis, then, concerns the reversibility of the long-run supply curve. Economies and/or technological ad-

---

[4] The short-run supply functions of Figure 15-5*b* are positively sloped, nevertheless, since they are the sum of positively sloped firms' marginal-cost functions.

[5] Marshall's concept of external economies and diseconomies was generalized by his student A. C. Pigou into a theory relating to "uncompensated services or disservices." Pigou also related these externalities to competitive market failure, but the force of his arguments has been considerably diluted by the modern theory of externalities developed by Frank Knight and Ronald Coase (see text below and Notes for Further Reading at the end of this chapter).

vances in an industry are ordinarily not destroyed when demand declines in that industry. Therefore, the long-run industry supply curve (as in Figure 15-5) would not be reversible. If economies are not reversible and alterations in technology are involved, partial-equilibrium analysis may be used only as a very rough approximation in explaining prices and conditions in the market. It is essentially noteworthy that Marshall himself recognized and pinpointed the difficulties. As he incessantly warned:

> Violence is required for keeping broad forces in the pound of *Ceteris Paribus* during, say, a whole generation, on the ground that they have only an indirect bearing on the question in hand. For even indirect influences may produce great effects in the course of a generation, if they happen to act cumulatively; and it is not safe to ignore them even provisionally in a practical problem without special study. Thus, the uses of the statical method in problems relating to very long periods are dangerous; care and forethought and self-restraint are needed at every step. The difficulties and risks of the task reach their highest point in connection with industries which conform to the law of Increasing Return; and it is just in connection with those industries that the most alluring applications of the method are to be found (*Principles,* footnote, pp. 379–380).

But, significantly, Marshall was unwilling to throw out the baby with the bath water. Noting that it is true that his method treated "variables *provisionally* as constants," he correctly indicated that it is also the case that his method is the only one "by which science has ever made any progress in dealing with complex and changeful matter, whether in the physical or moral world" (*Principles,* footnote, p. 380).

A second point concerns the compatibility of decreasing-cost conditions and the existence of competitive equilibrium. Far from being a matter of esoteric interest, this issue engendered debate that was a major factor leading to the development of the theory of imperfect competition in the 1930s.[6] Briefly stated, can perfect competition coexist with external economies and decreasing costs? A moment's reflection clearly reveals that it cannot. Given that the firm's long-run cost curves are inversely related to industry output (as would exist at least for increases in output when external economies are present), any firm would have the incentive to purchase all other firms. Any single firm would wish to *internalize* the external economies within the industry. A monopoly, with multiplant production, would be the likely outcome. Clearly, one must choose between the theory of competitive equilibrium and the theory of decreasing costs. The recognition of this fact by several of Marshall's students led to the extensive development in the twentieth century of a theory of imperfect competition.

Thus far we have examined Marshall's theory of competitive equilibrium, a theory that characterizes his partial-equilibrium method. We have also examined his discussion of external economies and decreasing cost, as well as some

---

[6] See the related discussion in Chap. 18.

of the theoretical difficulties that these concepts present. Before returning to these concepts and to the analytical use to which Marshall put them, we must look at another side of his massive contribution to competitive analysis, i.e., the theory of demand and consumers' surplus.[7]

DEMAND AND CONSUMERS' SURPLUS

In our discussion of competitive equilibrium we have assumed the existence of an industry demand function. Just what is a demand function, how is it constructed, and what is it used for? Marshall, more than any other economic theorist before or since, provided lengthy, though not always clear, answers to these questions. He was influenced, perhaps even to a large extent, by the demand analyses of Cournot and Dupuit, and it is clear that J. S. Mill's formulation of demand theory (see Chapter 8) left its mark. As we have seen, Marshall added a clear graphical treatment of Mill's concepts of joint supply and reciprocal demand. But in the case of demand theory, Marshall enlarged the concept significantly—so significantly, in fact, that the adjective "Marshallian" is often used to denote a whole tradition in demand theory. One of the reasons for Marshall's great emphasis upon demand in his *Principles,* of course, was to counteract the classical emphasis on costs of production as the sole determinant of value.

Marshall's Demand Curve Specification

Marshall stated the law of demand in the following manner: "There is then one general law of demand: The greater the amount to be sold, the smaller must be the price at which it is offered in order that it may find purchasers; or, in other words, the amount demanded increases with a fall in price, and diminishes with a rise in price" (*Principles,* p. 99). However, Marshall, unlike most of his predecessors, recognized that before one can draw up a demand schedule, a number of assumptions must be specified. We state these at the outset.

Marshall's *ceteris paribus* assumptions in gauging the functional relation between price and quantity demanded may be summarized as follows:

1 The time period for adjustment
2 The subject's tastes, preferences, and customs
3 The amount of money (income or wealth) at the subject's command
4 The purchasing power of money
5 The price and range of rival commodities

Time in Demand Analysis As he did in the case of his treatment of cost, Marshall applied his *ceteris paribus* method to demand theory. The role of

---

[7] Some of Marshall's contributions to value theory have already been treated. See Chap. 8 for the Mill-Marshall theories of joint supply and reciprocal demand.

time is again of primary interest. Time is a necessary element in demand theory, "for time is required to enable a rise in the price of a commodity to exert its full influence on consumption" (*Principles*, p. 110). As we have seen in the example of the fishing trade, time is related to taste changes. Taste for fish, in Marshall's example, was related to use. A cattle plague of some duration caused a change in the taste for fish in the long term. Marshall then related taste changes to use. But in *drawing up* the demand curve, Marshall was faced with a serious problem: If time is required to obtain the full effects on quantity demanded of a price change, is it not also the case that protracted use of the commodity might not alter tastes for it (and thus alter one of the bases upon which a demand schedule is drawn up)? As Marshall expressed the problem:

> Thus while a list of demand prices represents the changes in the price at which a commodity can be sold consequent on changes in the amount offered for sale, *other things being equal;* yet other things seldom are equal in fact over periods of time sufficiently long for the collection of full and trustworthy statistics. There are always occurring disturbing causes whose effects are commingled with, and cannot easily be separated from, the effects of that particular cause which we desire to isolate. This difficulty is aggravated by the fact that in economics the full effects of a cause seldom come at once, but often spread themselves out after it has ceased to exist (*Principles*, p. 109).

As he did in his theory of supply, Marshall noted the devilish problems that the element of time introduces into the theory of demand. His solution was to specify a parameter in demand theory for the time period of adjustment. Alteration of the time period of adjustment (say, the duration of the cattle plague) could change the demand curve significantly, and a specification of the period for which the demand function is drawn up is essential. Marshall clearly expressed the need for placing human tastes or customs, as well as the price of closely related goods, in his pound of *ceteris paribus:*

> The demand prices in our list are those at which various quantities of a thing can be sold in a market *during a given time and under given conditions.* If the conditions vary in any respect the prices will probably require to be changed; and this has constantly to be done when the desire for anything is materially altered by a variation of custom, or by a cheapening of the supply of a rival commodity, or by the invention of a new one (*Principles*, p. 100).

The Income Parameter   More than any other parameter, the income parameter has found alternative interpretations in post-Marshallian literature on demand. When the price of a good falls, two things happen. First, the good is cheaper relative to all other goods in the consumer's budget, and the consumer will substitute that good for others (the *substitution effect* of a price change); and second, the consumer's real income rises as the purchasing power of money increases, causing the consumer to buy more of all *normal* goods in his or her budget (the *income effect* of a price change).[8] The introduction of an income effect shifts or rotates the demand function, holding only money income constant with every price change. Thus Marshall had to indicate the kind of income he wished to hold constant along the demand curve. Although one can find statements that offer a contrary interpretation, in the main it appears that he wished to neglect alterations in the purchasing power of money. In his analysis of marginal diminishing price, Marshall stated the assumed constancy of the purchasing power of money (or income) as follows:

> The larger the amount of a thing that a person has the less, other things being equal (i.e., the purchasing power of money and the amount of money at his command being equal), will be the price which he will pay for a little more of it: or in other words his marginal demand price for it diminishes (*Principles,* p. 95).

Marshall explicitly noted the necessity for correcting for changes in both the purchasing power of money and real income or prosperity. Whether the Marshallian demand curve falls into the category of the modern constant-money-income or the modern constant-real-income formulation depends on the interpretation given to the assumed constancy of the purchasing power of money and the importance that is attached to it. According to Friedman's interpretation, the only way the purchasing power of money can remain constant as the price of the good under analysis changes is for the subject to be compensated by changes in money income or countermovements in the prices of other goods he or she consumes to maintain the constancy of real income in utility terms ("The Marshallian Demand Curve," pp. 463–465). According to the traditional interpretation, Marshall's assumption of the constancy of the purchasing power of money is a simplifying assumption that is, in rigorous terms, inconsistent with the rest of his formulation (Hicks, *The Theory of Wages,* pp. 38–41).

Viewed in retrospect, both interpretations appear correct, though each refers to a different point on Marshall's continuum of levels of abstraction. The possibility of two distinct interpretations results from Marshall's failure to distinguish explicitly at what point on his continuum of levels of abstraction he was operating in various facets of his analysis. In the theoretical formulation of the demand curve, Marshall's formulation fits the constant-real-income classification, and the Friedman interpretation appears valid. In practical applications such as consumers' surplus, the constant-money-income interpretation, which assumes that Marshall simply neglected changes in the purchasing power of money, seems more appropriate. The apparent ambiguity, which is encountered in Marshall's *Principles,* can often be resolved by remembering that his book was intended not only to be an exposition of economic analysis but also to be of use in the real world.

---

[8] A normal good is one whose consumption increases as income increases (steak, for example); consumption of an inferior good (hamburger, perhaps) declines as income increases.

Consumer's Surplus

In the category of operational concepts (i.e., those that are useful in the real world), perhaps none is assigned more importance in Marshall's *Principles* than the notion of a consumer's surplus. Commensurate with the position Marshall gave the concept, much ink has been used in debates over the issue in post-Marshallian literature. The use of Marshall's measure has been in and out of favor with economists, and it is certain that there are many difficulties connected with it. Whether Marshall's measure (or refurbishments of his measure) surmounts these difficulties is not really relevant. Certainly a measure of the benefits produced by goods (and particularly by public goods in cost-benefit calculations) is required for real-world decisions. Clearly, moreover, a consumer's surplus exists irrespective of whether a Marshallian demand curve measures it correctly. Marshall finally utilized the concept in the most interesting applications of analysis to real-world problems (e.g., monopoly and taxation) contained in the *Principles*.

The concept of a consumer's surplus originated not with Marshall but with Jules Dupuit (see Chapter 12). Marshall, however, named and developed the concept. He described consumer's surplus as follows:

> The price which a person pays for a thing can never exceed, and seldom comes up to that which he would be willing to pay rather than go without it: so that the satisfaction which he gets from its purchase generally exceeds that which he gives up in paying away its price; and he thus derives from the purchase a surplus of satisfaction. The excess of the price which he would be willing to pay rather than go without the thing, over that which he actually does pay, is the economic measure of this surplus satisfaction. It may be called consumer's surplus (*Principles*, p. 124).

Marshall, in explicating this concept, provided a numerical example.

The Case of Tea A consumer's demand schedule for an unimportant commodity (in the sense that it accounts for a small portion of his expenditures), such as tea, is posited. The demand schedule is reproduced as follows:

Price of tea per pound (shillings)	Quantity demanded
20	1
14	2
10	3
6	4
4	5
3	6
2	7

Let us suppose that the consumer purchases 1 pound of tea at a price of 20 shillings. This proves, according to Marshall, that the consumer's total enjoyment or satisfaction derived from consuming that pound is "as great as that which he could obtain by spending 20s. on other things" (*Principles*, p. 125).

Now suppose that the price falls to 14 shillings. The buyer could still purchase 1 pound of tea, obtaining a surplus satisfaction of 6 shillings or a consumer's surplus of *at least* 6 shillings. But if he buys an additional pound, the utility of this additional amount must be at least equivalent to 14 shillings. Thus he now obtains for 28 shillings a quantity of tea that is worth at least 34 shillings (20 shillings + 14 shillings) to him. The consumer's surplus, in Marshall's calculation, is at least 6 shillings.

We may view the situation graphically as in Figure 15-6, which depicts the consumer's demand for tea. Successive price declines clearly increase the surplus utility that the individual receives from consuming tea, so that when the price has fallen to 2 shillings, he buys 7 pounds, which "are worth to him not less than 20, 14, 10, 6, 4, 3, and 2s. or 59s. in all." This sum of 59 shillings measures the total utility to the consumer (*utilité absolue*, in Dupuit's terms) of the 7 pounds of tea. But the consumer must pay only 14 shillings for 7 pounds, so that he receives a sum of utility equivalent to (at least) 45 shillings from consuming 7 units of tea. Marshall identified this amount as consumer's surplus.

FIGURE 15-6

As price declines from 20 shillings to 2 shillings, the total utility of the consumer increases to a value of 59 shillings (20 + 14 + 10 + 6 + 4 + 3 + 2). Since the consumer must pay only 14 shillings for 7 pounds, his consumer surplus is equivalent to 45 shillings.

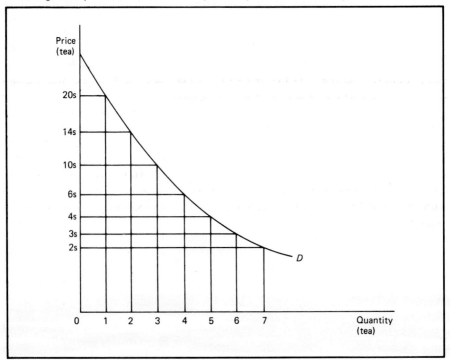

The Marshallian Measure   The concept of a consumer's surplus is clear, but large problems enter when an area under the Marshallian demand curve is used to represent the surplus. An example will clarify this. Let us suppose that the demand curve of Figure 15-6 is Marshallian in the sense that it is drawn up under the assumptions listed earlier in this chapter. It will be recalled that one of those assumptions is the constancy of the purchasing power of money. But as price falls for our consumer of tea, the purchasing power of his or her money will surely increase. An increase in the purchasing power of money is equivalent to an increase in the consumer's real income. The problem is, of course, that as real income increases (or as the purchasing power of money income increases), the marginal utility of real income *decreases,* just as the marginal utility of any good decreases with quantity increase. This means, with respect to the consumption of tea, that a shilling is not a shilling in utility terms as the consumer moves down his or her demand curve. The marginal utility of shillings is not the same when the consumer is buying 1 pound at 20 shillings as when he is buying 7 pounds at 2 shillings. Marshall expressed the consumer's surplus in money terms, but the units of money (say, 45 shillings when 7 pounds at 2 shillings are consumed) do not carry the same *utility* value because the real income of the consumer is altered. Without getting into unnecessary complexities, the Marshallian (constant-money-income) demand curve will either overestimate or underestimate the surplus.

Marshall sought to avoid the problem of explicitly assuming that the marginal utility of money (income) was constant, or approximately so. In fact he selected tea, an "unimportant" commodity, for the very reason that real-income changes would be of the second order of small quantities, neglectable because of their smallness. But in any rigorous theoretical treatment of consumers' surplus dealing with important commodities, the problem arises. Some modern theorists, as noted earlier, argue that the genuine Marshallian demand curve was a constant-real-income function. If so, his discussion of the measurement of consumer's surplus appears consistent with his specification of the demand function. Compensation in some form, such as an alteration in money income or a change in the prices of nonrelated commodities, would fill the bill. In empirical estimates, as opposed to purely theoretical tinkering, other types of compensations are required. After all, Marshall's purpose in developing the notion of consumer's surplus was primarily to provide "an aid in estimating roughly some of the benefits which a person derives from his environment" (*Principles,* p. 125).

Before turning to some of the applications that Marshall made of his analysis, it would be well to note briefly one other important problem encountered in his treatment of demand and utility.[9] The source of the problem is this: though Marshall wrote of *consumer's* surplus, he developed market demand

---

[9] Some (but not all) of the problems of utility measurement are avoided by using ordinal (indifference-curve) analysis. The ordinal approach requires the consumer to indicate more or less satisfaction rather than to make a numerical specification in cardinal (1, 5, 20, etc.) terms.

curves that summed up the functions of many individuals and attempted to determine *consumers'* surplus. We might call it the "problem of the apostrophe"—when demands (as utility functions) of many individuals are added up, we speak of consumers' surplus and treat the monetary value of the surplus as a utility value. But clearly, individuals' income, tastes, and preferences must differ, so that 5 pounds of tea at 4 shillings for individual A is not equivalent in *utility* to 5 pounds at 4 shillings for individual B. To be sure, money demands can be added up to form market demand curves, but illegitimate interpersonal comparisons of utility are involved when these money amounts (areas under the market demand curve) are used to express utility. Nevertheless, certain assumptions could be invoked (such as equal income of the separate demanders) that would make approximations more plausible. Importantly, Marshall was aware of most of the difficulties. But, after acknowledging them, he proceeded to put his imperfect approximation to use in discussions of monopoly and optimum public policies of taxation and subsidization.

MARSHALL ON OPTIMUM PRICING AND MONOPOLY

Utilizing a market demand curve as an approximation of the utility produced by a commodity, Marshall embarked upon a theoretical excursion that admitted government interference in free markets in order to promote maximum social satisfaction. Coupling his marginal-utility and demand curve with the theories of long-run supply developed in this chapter, Marshall sought to determine whether the government could tax or subsidize industries to improve welfare. He considered the welfare effects of taxes and "bounties" (subsidies) on industries characterized by decreasing, increasing, and constant long-run supply functions.

The Increasing-Cost Case

Marshall considered the effects of taxing or subsidizing an increasing-cost industry in graphical terms. Figure 15-7 reproduces his argument. Output for the increasing-cost industry originally takes place at quantity *OH* (and at price *OC*), where demand curve *DD'* intersects industry supply *SS'*. Consumers' surplus at quantity *OH* and price *OC* equals the area under the demand curve at that quantity (or *ADOH*) less the amount that consumers actually pay for quantity *OH* (or *OCAH*). Consumers' surplus is then seen as the area (approximate triangle) *CDA (ODAH−OCAH)*. Now suppose that the government enacts a per-unit tax on production in the amount *TA* per unit of output. The effect of this tax would be to shift the supply curve (which, remember, is the summation of the firm's marginal-cost functions) to the left by the amount of the tax. In our case, the supply function decreases to *ss'*. After the tax is levied, the quantity of the commodity sold is reduced to *Oh,* and price is raised to *Oc* (determined at the intersection of *ss'* and *DD'*). Now consumers pay *Ocah* for a quantity of the commodity that yields them *ODah* in utility. Consum-

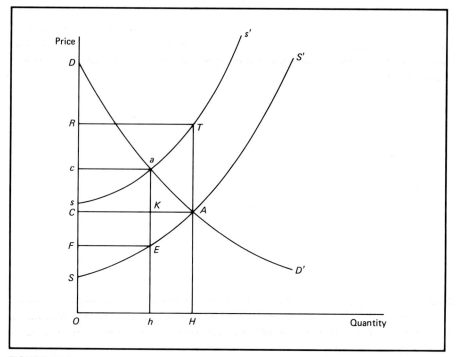

FIGURE 15-7
At initial equilibrium *A*, consumers' surplus is the area *CDA*. A per-unit tax in the amount
TA will reduce consumers' surplus to the area *cDa* and bring in tax revenue in the amount
FcaE. Since the area *FCKE* is greater than the triangle *aKA*, the government will increase
welfare by spending the tax proceeds on public goods.

ers' surplus is reduced to an amount *cDa*. The government's proceeds from
the tax are equal to the amount of the tax *aE* (= *TA*) multiplied by the output
produced after the tax, *FE* (= *Oh*): proceeds are equivalent to rectangle
FcaE.

Marshall was concerned with the question of the welfare effects of the tax
on consumers' surplus. The loss in consumers' surplus owing to the tax is
equal to *CcaA*. Assuming that government expenditures are exactly equivalent
in utility terms to the utility removed by the tax, government receipts exceed
the loss in consumers' surplus. The loss in consumers' surplus *not* accounted
for by the government's revenue is equal to triangle *aKA*. The gain in government revenue not accounted for by the loss in consumers' surplus is equal to
FCKE. Thus the two areas to be compared in this case are *FCKE* and *aKA*. If
FCKE exceeds *aKA* (as it does in Figure 15-7), then the government could increase welfare by taxation.[10]

---

[10] As Blaug pointed out in his *Economic Theory in Retrospect* (p. 388), the argument does not
necessarily hold when losses in producers' surplus are included.

Conversely, Marshall concluded that subsidization of an increasing-cost industry would cause a reduction in welfare. This point may also be demonstrated with reference to Figure 15-7, assuming that *ss'* is the original supply curve and that price and quantity are originally *Oc* and *Oh,* respectively. Should the government subsidize the industry in the amount *TA* (or *aE*) per unit, the supply function would shift rightward toward *SS'*, increasing equilibrium output and price to *OH* and *OC*. The total amount of the subsidy required will be the unit amount *TA* multiplied by the new equilibrium quantity produced, *OH* (or *CA*). It is equivalent to the area *CRTA*. Consumers' surplus increases by *CcaA* when output increases from *Oh* to *OH*. The increase in consumers' surplus is clearly *less* than the total subsidy. Marshall thus demonstrated that—on utility grounds, at least—increasing-cost industries should not be subsidized in order to increase welfare.

Subsidies and Decreasing Costs

In a second, more interesting case, Marshall argued that—on theoretical grounds—decreasing-cost industries should be subsidized in order to promote maximum well-being. The essentials of the argument are often heard in discussions today of electrical utilities and other utilities that are assumed to be characterized by decreasing costs. Marginal-cost pricing in, and subsidization of, such utilities is closely related to Marshall's concepts.

Figure 15-8 graphically demonstrates that welfare may be increased by subsidizing decreasing-cost industries. Assume that the original industry supply and demand functions are *DD'* and *ss'*, establishing price *Oc* and output *Oh*. Now, what if the government decided to subsidize the industry in order to increase total output to *OH?* The subsidy required for the effect would equal *TA* (or *aE*) per unit of output. The supply curve would, in effect, shift downward to *SS'*, and at the new equilibrium *OH* would be produced at price *OC*. Consumers' surplus increases from *cDa* (at output *Oh*) to *CDA* (at output *OH*), an increase of *CcaA*. The total subsidy, as in the increasing-cost example of Figure 15-7, is equal to the per-unit amount of *TA* multiplied by the number of units sold, *OH* (= *CA*), or a total subsidy equal to area *CRTA*. For the subsidy to create an increase in welfare, it is necessary that the increase in consumers' surplus *CcaA* be greater than the government's subsidy *CRTA*. This will be the case, referring to Figure 15-8, since area *KTA* is less than area *RcaK*. Marshall, then, demonstrated that welfare could be improved by subsidizing decreasing-cost industries.[11]

Constant-cost industries, of the kind described in Figure 15-1, were to be neither taxed nor subsidized. Given Marshall's assumptions, it is demonstrated that welfare would decline if either policy were enacted on industries of constant costs.

---

[11] He also showed that welfare would be reduced if these industries were taxed.

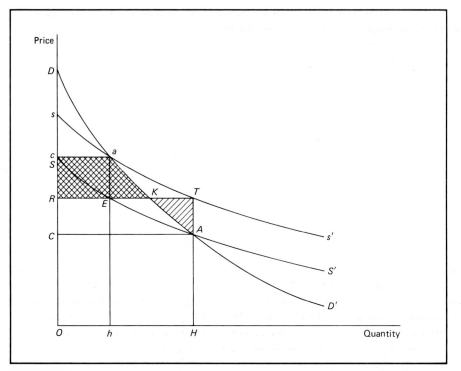

FIGURE 15-8
A subsidy in the amount of *TA* per unit of output will increase consumers' surplus from
cDa to *CDA*. Since the increase in consumers' surplus exceeds the cost of the subsidy,
consumer welfare is increased.

Some of the theoretical problems associated with Marshall's use of the demand curve as a welfare measure have already been discussed. But it is to
Marshall's credit that he pointed out a particularly important one where taxation and subsidization are involved. In his words, the "doctrine of maximum
satisfaction...assumes that all differences in wealth between the different parties concerned may be neglected, and that the satisfaction which is rated at a
shilling by one of them, may be taken as equal to one that is rated at a shilling
by any other" (*Principles*, p. 471). Any statement imputing utility levels to individuals or groups is, strictly speaking, nonscientific. In the tax-subsidy analysis, there are clearly gainers and losers. Is the utility lost by the losers (those
taxed) greater than, equal to, or less than the utility received by the gainers
(consumers of decreasing-cost-industry products)? A positive or negative answer to the question requires a value judgment, and Marshall did not flinch
from making a few, one of which was that "The happiness which an additional
shilling brings to a poor man is much greater than that which it brings to a rich
one" (*Principles*, p. 474). When speaking of policies in which there are gainers
and losers, some such assumption must be made, and Marshall was, *as a first
approximation*, ready to make it.

In Marshall's treatment of the doctrine of maximum satisfaction, we have more examples of the dichotomy between his theoretical and operational concerns. The theory and its conclusions are tentative in that they require certain nonscientific assumptions concerning the adding up of utilities of gainers and losers. But Marshall proceeded anyway, issuing warnings all along the way and concluding that his propositions "do not by themselves afford a valid ground for government interference." In his own view, he simply identified a problem, noting that much remained to be done, especially in the area of statistical estimates of supply and demand. The problem of devising policies to maximize welfare did, in fact, engender a great deal of interest among Marshall's students and others in the Cambridge tradition, though progress has been piecemeal and meager.[12] But Marshall was asking important questions, always with a view to the applications of economic analysis.

Monopoly and Economic Welfare

One other important example of Marshall's concern for the usefulness of utility theory can be found in the area of simple monopoly analysis. He went to great lengths in his chapter on monopoly to point out the implications of a distinction, originally stated by Jules Dupuit (see Chapter 12), between monopoly revenue and consumers' surplus. Again, as in the case of the consumers'-surplus argument, Marshall enlarged the analytical value of the tool by probing the implications of the monopolist's net revenue. Specifically, Marshall showed that because of various economies of scale and the ability to finance technological improvement, both associated with monopoly market structure, "The supply schedule for the commodity, if not monopolized, would show higher supply price than those of our monopoly supply schedule" (*Principles,* pp. 484–485). Marshall went further and stated that if the monopolist had unlimited command over capital, equilibrium quantity under free competition would be less than that for which the demand price is equal to supply price under monopoly.

On some of the most interesting pages of the *Principles,* Marshall analyzed the possibility of a short-run "altruistic entrepreneur" who might regard a gain in consumers' surplus as coequal with a gain in monopoly revenues. The money sum of consumers' surplus and monopoly revenue he called "total benefit." In another variant of Marshall's approach, the theory of "compromise benefit," the monopolist would calculate and maximize the sum of (1) monopoly revenue to be obtained at any given price and (2) some percentage (one-half, one-third, etc.) of the corresponding consumers' surplus. More importantly, Marshall thought that this principle could be applied by a government interested in increasing the consumers' welfare in the community supply of

---

[12] The problem of empirical identification of increasing- and decreasing-cost industries was tackled by A. C. Pigou, J. H. Clapham, and D. H. Robertson, with small success. The problem of scientific estimation of welfare or "benefit" transfers has beguiled many economists, who have had even less success (see Notes for Further Reading at the end of this chapter).

public goods (e.g., bridges, water, and gas), although he strongly indicated that it should do so only under the constraint of equating total revenue with total costs. But, ever practical, Marshall pointed out:

> Even a government which considers its own interests coincident with those of the people has to take account of the fact that, if it abandons one source of revenue, it must in general fall back on others which have their own disadvantages. For they will necessarily involve friction and expense in collection, together with some injury to the public, of the kind which we have described as a loss of consumers' surplus...(*Principles*, p. 488).

In the limiting case of government ownership or operation there would be no compromise; consumers' surplus would be maximized subject only to the provision that full costs be covered.

Thus, on the issues of governmental policy toward business, Marshall's utility theory (coupled with his theoretical views on long-run supply functions) led him to some rather unorthodox and even radical suggestions. Although the type of utility theory upon which his analysis is based has been largely out of favor for many years, the problems Marshall attacked (determining optimum public policies toward market enterprise) are still very much with us. It is noteworthy, moreover, that his analyses of these problems are still as cogent as most of those proffered by contemporary political economists.

The Case of Externalities

One of these applications that has loomed large in contemporary economic analysis concerns the general area of "externalities," property rights, and "market failure." Marshall's discovery and elaboration of the concept of external economies proved to be fertile ground for the development of new theoretical principles in the field of public economies.

Above we saw that Marshall identified something called "external economies," by which the effects of certain types of industry development and expansion lowered the cost curves of firms within industries—a positive "externality" to the firm.

Apart from Marshall's very practical identification of an externality, a philosophical tradition of welfare maximization stemming from Benthamite utilitarianism (see Chapter 6) continued through J. S. Mill and through one of Marshall's older contemporaries, Henry Sidgwick. In this tradition, providing the greatest good for the greatest number *solely* through market means contained a hitch. The market might "fail" in that some activities could produce positive or negative externalities that could not be charged to (in the case of negative externalities) or paid to (when the effects were positive) the initiator of the externality. An example of negative externalities might be a steel factory belching smoke and slag into the surrounding area, damaging houses, lungs, and drinking water downstream. Conversely, one may plant a garden that neighbors might enjoy but for which no practical means of charging can be devised. We are all familiar with such cases.

The point to make is that Marshall's protégé and handpicked successor at Cambridge (in 1910), A. C. Pigou, greatly expanded this idea and proposed a "neoclassical," "Marshallian" solution. In 1912 in his *Wealth and Welfare* and in an expanded "second edition" entitled *The Economics of Welfare* (1920), Pigou discussed the possibility of market failure. Assume the existence of a negative externality such as pollution of a stream. The marginal *social* costs of such productions exceed the marginal *private* costs to the polluting firm (by an amount equal to the marginal pollution damage).

Consider Figure 15-9, which depicts the marginal private cost, marginal social cost, and demand curves for such an activity. If the polluting firm is not made to bear social costs, the *MPC* curve is relevant to its decision making. Quantity Q_0 is produced, and society is forced to bear marginal pollution costs of AP_0. There is "too much" output of this good from society's point of view.

Pigou's solution was to impose a *tax* on the offending industry so that the *MSC* curve would be the perceived cost of production to the firm. In this case, the firm would bear the *full* cost of producing this good and output would be restricted to Q_1 (with an increased price). Taxes and subsides were Pigou's— and as we have seen—Marshall's method of addressing market failures of the negative or positive sort. In this framework, Pigou contemplated an *expanded* role for government, in the form of legislative or regulatory action.

FIGURE 15-9
If the polluting firm can ignore the social cost of production, it will produce output Q_0, forcing society to bear the cost AP_0. One way to raise the marginal private cost to the level of marginal social cost is by taxing the polluting firm according to the difference between *MSC* and *MPC*.

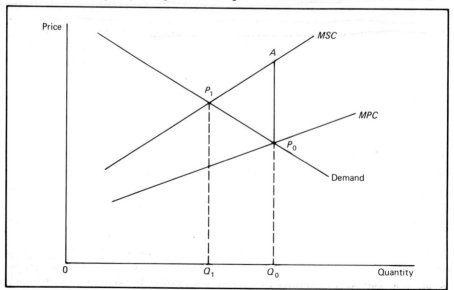

In one of the single most significant contributions to contemporary economic analysis, Ronald Coase challenged Pigou's assumption that externalities
are undirectional in nature. In "The Problem of Social Cost," published in
1960, Coase emphasized the two-way nature of externalities. The stream pol-
luters would not have created an externality if there had been no downstream
settlement. A cigarette smoker could not cause an externality if individuals did
not put themselves in his or her proximity. Coase thus emphasized the *reciprocal* nature of externalities and argued that Pigou's solution of government
legislative interference was faulty on several counts. If, for example, the costs
of transacting and bribing were low, the market itself could solve the problem
of downstream pollution described above. The pollutees could bribe the pol-
luters to reduce pollution, or the polluter could bribe the pollutees to accept it.
Either way, an efficient use of society's resources would be had *without government interference*. In this and other cases, Coase argued that if the judicial
system makes a proper assignment of liabilities (to the low-cost participant to
the externality), market forces and incentives may be sufficient to generate efficient solutions to these problems. The presence of externalities, in other
words, provides no *prima facie* case for governmental interferences of a legislative type (such as the Occupational Safety and Health Administration or
the Environmental Protection Agency in the United States). With this important digression in mind, let us now return to the mainstream of our discussion
on the market allocation of resources.

MARSHALL ON ELASTICITY, INPUT DEMAND, AND THE
OPTIMUM ALLOCATION OF RESOURCES

We now turn to a final and less settled area of Marshall's contribution—inputs
(derived input demand) and the efficient distribution of resources. In order to
gain a fuller appreciation for Marshall's achievement in these areas, we must
first consider his definition of elasticity.

Elasticity

In a contribution of genuine importance, Marshall described and categorized
the concept of elasticity of demand. The idea was not unique with him
(Fleeming Jenkin had alluded to it in 1870), but as usual, he enlarged the concept greatly, making it his own. As Marshall put it, "The *elasticity* (or *responsiveness*) of demand in a market is great or small according as the amount demanded increases much or little for a given fall in price, and diminishes much
or little for a given rise in price" (*Principles*, p. 102). Elasticity, an idea now so
familiar to every student of introductory economics, is defined simply as the
percentage change in quantity demanded divided by the percentage change in

price. Algebraically, $N_D = [\Delta Q_D/Q_D] \div [\Delta P/P]$.[13] Demand is considered elastic if N_D is greater than 1, inelastic if less than 1, and of unit elasticity if equal to 1.

Marshall enclosed his seminal discussion of the determinants of elasticity within numerous practical examples. Basically, he argued that, *ceteris paribus,* demand is more *elastic:*

1 The greater the proportion of an individual's total budget that expenditures on the commodity represent (salt, for instance, is a necessity and also represents a small expenditure for both rich and poor people)

2 The longer the price change is in effect (time again)

3 The larger the number of substitutes

4 The larger the number of uses to which the commodity can be put

For good measure, Marshall included much discussion of elasticity differences between rich, middle-class, and poor buyers. In a passage clearly revealing his Victorian preoccupation with classes, he noted, concerning the effect of acquired tastes on the demand for meat:

> In the ordinary working class districts the inferior and the better joints are sold at nearly the same price: but some well-paid artisans in the north of England have developed a liking for the best meat, and will pay for it nearly as high a price as can be got in the west end of London, where the price is kept artificially high by the necessity of sending the inferior joints away for sale elsewhere (*Principles,* p. 107).

And, in a cunning observation, Marshall noted that "Part of the demand for the more expensive kinds of good is really a demand for the means of obtaining a social distinction, and is almost insatiable" (*Principles,* p. 106).

The usefulness of final demand elasticity estimates, made possible by Marshall's brilliant discussion of the concept, is fairly obvious in budget analysis and all aspects of consumption theory. But, as will become apparent, Marshall extended the notion of elasticity *and* its usefulness from consumer demand to include the demand for factor inputs (labor, capital, land). We now turn to that contribution.[14]

Factor Demand

The study of factor demand (derived demand) and factor-demand elasticity was presumably initiated by Marshall, who was subsequently followed by A. C. Pigou and John R. Hicks. However, at least by the eighth edition of the *Principles,* Marshall credited both Böhm-Bawerk and Irving Fisher with related developments, and it seems fairly clear that Cournot was tinkering with a similar concept as early as 1838.

---

[13] Marshall also applied the basic concept to supply. Later, a "cross-elasticity" concept was developed. Cross-elasticity is defined as the responsiveness of the quantity demanded of a commodity A to a change in price of another commodity B.

[14] The following discussion relies largely on the treatment of factor demand in S. C. Maurice, "On the Importance of Being Unimportant" (see References).

Marshall's discussion of the determinants of derived-factor-demand elasticity is found chiefly in Book V, Chap. 6, of the *Principles,* entitled "Joint and Composite Demand, Joint and Composite Supply" (and in his mathematical notes XIV and XV, pp. 852–854). In his characteristic way, Marshall made no effort to treat a general theoretical situation. Instead, he used homely examples involving plasterers employed in housing construction and knife handles used in making knives. Chapter 6 involves plasterers, and the footnote and the math notes involve knives and handles.

In another of his characteristic ways, Marshall did not make his underlying assumptions specific. Yet he did make one explicit statement that subsequent writers apparently overlooked, a statement that places Marshall somewhat outside the frame of analysis followed by writers who built on his discussion. Hicks, R. G. D. Allen, and others interested in derived demand have almost uniformly assumed long-run competitive equilibrium. Marshall, on the other hand, wrote that:

> The period over which the disturbance extends being short, and the causes of which we have to account as re-adjusting demand and supply being only such as are able to operate within that short period...we should notice that, referring as it does to short periods, it is an exception to our general rule of selecting...cases in which there is time enough for the full long-period action of the forces of supply to be developed (*Principles,* p. 382).

In the model involving plasterers' labor, Marshall seems generally to assume variable-proportions production, or something very much like it. But he was as undecided in this area as the Austrian Menger (see Chapter 13). He does say that "A temporary check to the supply of plasterers' labour will cause a *proportionate* check to the amount of building...." This statement, in itself, indicates fixed proportions, at least as far as plasterers' labor is concerned. Nonetheless, in the text Marshall seems to imply variable factor proportions, but his results seem to follow only with an assumption of fixed proportions.

Variable proportions enter chiefly through commodity demand, i.e., through a change in the product. "Again, an increased difficulty in obtaining one of the factors of a finished commodity can often be met by modifying the character of the finished product," wrote Marshall. "Some plasterers' labour may be indispensable; but people are often in doubt how much plaster work it is worthwhile to have in their houses, and if there is a rise in its price they will have less of it" (*Principles,* p. 386).

Whether proportions are fixed or not, Marshall stated the fundamental law of derived demand as follows: "The demand schedule for any factor of production of a commodity can be *derived* from that for the commodity by subtracting from the demand price of each separate amount of the commodity the sum of the supply prices for corresponding amounts of the other factors."

The Blade-Handle-Knife Model Blades and handles are used in fixed proportions to make knives. Knowing the supply of blades and the demand for knives, the problem that Marshall posed was that of determining the derived demand for handles. He treated the problem both graphically and mathematically. Marshall's graphic model is reproduced as Figure 15-10. This figure, which is related to the Mill-Marshall joint-supply model, is constructed similarly to Figure 8-1.

Here the demand for knives DD' is given, as are the supply functions for knives and handles SS' and ss', respectively. Now the problem is to derive a demand function for handles, and Marshall uses the following conventions. Take a quantity OM of knives. MP is the demand price for OM knives. The supply price of OM knives is MQ, and the supply price of the handles for OM knives is Mq. The difference, Qq, is the supply price of OM blades. Now in order to obtain the demand price for handle inputs (to produce quantity OM), Marshall simply subtracted the supply price of blades (Qq) at OM from the demand price for knives (MP) at OM. A demand price Mp (MP-Qq) is thus obtained for handles. Qq, of course, equals Pp. An identical procedure is followed for all other quantities of knives, and a demand function dd' for handles may be traced out. The demand price for blades is simply the difference between the total-knife-demand price and the derived-demand price for handles. The supply price for blades is given *objectively* by the difference between the two supply functions SS' and ss'.

Equilibrium, in the model described by Figure 15-10, takes place when quantity OB of knives is produced at price BA. The derived demand for handles dd' intersects the handle supply function at a, and the equilibrium price

FIGURE 15-10
At equilibrium A, the price of handles, Ba, is determined by the intersection of ss' and dd', and the price of blades, aA, is determined by subtracting Ba from the supply of knives.

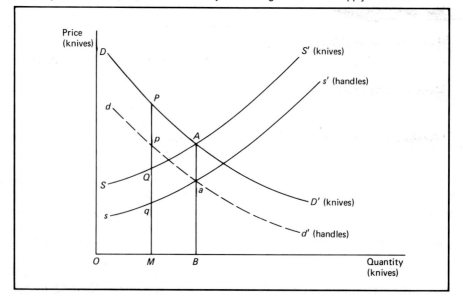

paid for handles is Ba. A price Aa, moreover, is paid for blades in equilibrium. (Obviously, $Ba + aA = BA$.) The demand for any input can be derived, then, if one knows the supply prices of the other factors and the demand for final output. But Marshall went further and devised a formula and a set of rules for calculating the *elasticity* of derived demand.

Marshall's Laws of Factor-Demand Elasticity   Marshall's formula for derived demand may be expressed in modern dress as it was by Martin Bronfenbrenner:

$$E_{DH} = \frac{S_H E_{SB} E_{DK}}{E_{SB} + E_{DK} (1 - S_H)}$$

where the elasticity of factor demand is defined as positive. In the above equation E_{DH} is the elasticity of demand for handles, S_H is the proportion of total cost accounted for by handles, E_{SB} is the elasticity of supply of blades, and E_{DK} is the elasticity of demand for knives.

Whether referring specifically to blades or handles or to a more general model, all factors other than the one in question are collapsed into a single factor. Following both his literary reasoning and his mathematical presentation, Marshall stated his famous "four rules" governing the elasticity of derived demand (*Principles,* p. 385). Marshall stated his rules of derived-demand elasticity in an indirect and circumspect manner, using, as was his custom, many examples. For clarity and precision, it is much better to use Pigou's reformulation of Marshall's rules (*The Economics of Welfare,* pp. 682–685). The listing of rules follows Marshall (*Principles,* pp. 385–386) rather than Pigou, however:

Marshall's first law: "The demand for anything is likely to be more elastic, the more readily substitutes for that thing can be obtained."

Marshall's second law: "The demand for anything is likely to be more elastic, the more elastic is the demand for any further thing which it contributes to produce."

Marshall's third law: "The demand for anything is likely to be less elastic, the less important is the part played by the cost of that thing in the total cost of some other thing, in the production of which it is employed."

Marshall's fourth law: "The demand for anything is likely to be more elastic, the more elastic is the supply of the co-operant agents of production."

In general, Marshall's laws have held up under the scrutiny of his students and members of the Cambridge school. Forty-two years elapsed between the first edition of his *Principles* (1890) and the appearance of Hicks's *Theory of Wages* (1932). In the interim, it seems, the only significant reference to the elasticity of derived factor demand was Pigou's reformulation of Marshall's laws. In an appendix to *The Theory of Wages* entitled "The Elasticity of Derived Demand," Hicks undertook a systematic reevaluation of Marshall's laws of derived input demand. In this important book, Hicks was the first to develop the concept of the elasticity of substitution (although it was presented almost simultaneously and quite independently by Joan Robinson). Hicks defined the elasticity of substitution as the proportional change in the capital/labor (or any two inputs) ratio relative to the change in the marginal rate of technical substitution, output held constant.

Adding this coefficient of substitution, Hicks analyzed Marshall's four laws mathematically in the appendix to *The Theory of Wages.* All but Marshall's third law, concerning input elasticity and relative shares, were confirmed. Hicks found that under a rising supply price of other factors, Marshall's third law holds if and only if the elasticity of the commodity demand exceeds the elasticity of substitution (since Marshall assumed zero elasticity of substitution, he was correct). That is, it is "important to be unimportant" if and only if consumers can substitute in consumption more readily than producers can substitute in production.

There has been considerable controversy since then concerning this final point, i.e., the importance of being unimportant. All this demonstrates that Marshall's contribution has been considered to be of the highest level of importance by leading post-Marshallian theorists. Furthermore, it illustrates another area of active theoretical concern that Marshall established in the *Principles of Economics.*

Resource Allocation and the Distribution of Product

In his theory of derived demand Marshall represented input proportions as fixed, though he created the case as a first approximation. His statements are not well organized, but Marshall adhered to a marginal-productivity theory of distribution, at least in the short run. It remained for Joan Robinson to clarify the analysis of input markets (see Chapter 18), though Marshall, at various points in the *Principles,* indicated that for the most efficient allocation of resources, all inputs should be hired up to the point where their marginal product equals their marginal cost. The productivity of each agent of production is subject to diminishing returns. As Marshall summed up his famous "principle of substitution":

> Every agent of production, land, machinery, skilled labour, unskilled labour, etc., tends to be applied in production as far as it profitably can be. If employers, and other businessmen, think that they can get a better result by using a little more of any one agent they will do so. They estimate the *net product* (that is *the net increase of the money value of their total output after allowing for incidental expenses*) that will be got by a little more outlay in this direction, or a little more outlay in that; and if they can gain by shifting a little of their outlay from one direction to another, they will do so.
>
> Thus then the uses of each agent of production are governed by the general conditions of demand in relation to supply: that is, on the one hand, by the urgency of all the uses to which the agent can be put, taken together with the means at the command of those who need it; and, on the other hand, by the available stocks of it. And equality is maintained between its values for each use by the constant tendency to shift

it from uses in which its services are of less value to others in which they are of greater value, in accordance with the principle of substitution (*Principles,* pp. 521–522).

In a number of chapters (Book VI, Chaps. 1–13), replete with practical examples, Marshall described the returns to the several factors of production. Rent was a return to inputs absolutely fixed in supply and without alternative opportunities, but Marshall also identified a "quasi-rent." Quasi-rent, in Marshallian terms, is a return to *temporarily* fixed factors devoted to production in the short run. It is of the nature of "sunk capital." As George Stigler pointed out, Marshall's statement is "merely another way of saying that only prime or variable costs are price-determining in the short run" (*Production and Distribution Theories,* p. 95). In the long run, returns to these fixed investments must be covered by market price, or capital will exit the industry. Only in the short run, in other words, is quasi-rent (the difference between total cost and variable cost) not a necessary payment in order to have output produced.

Marshall's treatment of the returns to labor is perhaps the most interesting part of his discussion of distribution. The demand for labor depended upon its marginal productivity, as the demand for any factor input. But the conditions governing the supply of labor differed markedly in the two market periods. In the short run Marshall adopted a theory of labor supply very much like the one developed by Jevons (see Chapter 14). Jevons had focused on the intersection of the marginal disutility of labor and the marginal utility of real income (represented by the marginal utility of the money wage). As in Jevons's model, laborers stop working when the marginal utility of their wage is equal to the marginal disutility of work. Although there were exceptions, Marshall believed that as a general rule, the supply of labor was positively related to the reward for labor in both long-run and short-run situations.

Marshall held that labor supply in the *long run* was governed chiefly by the cost of producing labor. If this were correct, wages would tend to subsistence, as several classical writers had suggested. But in view of the fact that wages were not at subsistence in England, Marshall found it necessary to explain why wages were higher than the cost of producing labor. Thus he insisted that both the mental *and* the physical powers of the worker had to be maintained. Three types of worker expenditures were identified: those for strict necessities, those for conventional necessities, and those for habitual comfort. The first type consists simply of those required for physical maintenance, such as expenditures for food, shelter, and clothing. Expenditures for conventional necessities are for items that are not strictly necessary for health and strength but are necessary socially. The third type—expenditures required for habitual comfort—reflects Marshall's belief (stated early in the *Principles*) that the tastes and habits of consumers, in this case laboring consumers, are altered over time.

Marshall pointed out additional peculiarities or rigidities in the labor market. In the first instance, the profit motive does not act in the same manner with labor or with other factors. Those who pay the cost of production (parents, for example) do not reap the rewards. Parents, moreover, would presumably educate in occupations in which the reward in proportion to expense is greatest. But the lag between investment and return is quite long, often fifteen to twenty years. Prediction over a period of this length is often impossible. Incomes of parents differ, moreover, which means that expenditures (or investments) in rearing and educating labor will be significantly different. These and other rigidities explained, according to Marshall, the widely differing observed wage rates in England at the time.

Profits and interest, the returns to entrepreneurship and capital, were similarly explained. The demand for capital, which is subject to diminishing returns, is its marginal productivity, and Marshall clearly indicated (*Principles*, p. 520) that it would be utilized up to the point where its marginal value product equaled the rate of interest. But in the long run, assuming a perfectly competitive system, the real return to capital would be determined by its cost of production.

The payment of profits is a payment for business ability, which in the long run is determined by cost of production. There is an important point here, however. In the case of any of the factors of production, it is through the business person's own ability that demand is made effective. The business person represents the demand or marginal-productivity schedules. But no one hires the entrepreneur. Rather, it is all society that demands goods. Society, in other words, makes demand effective by offering prices. Although part of the entrepreneur's skills may be inherited, in which case part of his or her returns are rent, acquired skills are, in fact, a cost of production. Thus Marshall concluded that, in the long run, costs of production determine the return to, and the supply of, *all* factors of production.

Marshall's treatment of distribution relied heavily on his Anglo-Saxon heritage in that area, and it is particularly reminiscent of Smith's and Ricardo's handling of the question. It may well be that he placed too much emphasis on cost of production as an explanation for factor returns, as did his academic forebearers. His discussion is also often criticized for general lack of vigor, which is undoubtedly the case.

All this notwithstanding, Marshall was perhaps never so close to practical wisdom as when he analyzed, through numerous examples, the reasons for wage and profit differentials or the impact of risk on rate of return. His practical knowledge of business behavior and actual markets was phenomenal, all of which makes his discourse on distribution one of the most enjoyable and profitable parts of the *Principles*.

MARSHALL IN RETROSPECT

Alfred Marshall's *Principles* was, in a significant sense, a benchmark in the development of the discipline of economics. But as we have seen, a number of important writers contributed to the corpus of neoclassical micro analysis before the publication of Marshall's classic work. Cournot, Dupuit, Jevons, and Walras, to mention only the most seminal contributors, antedated Marshall's concerns. On separate points of doctrine (e.g., consumers' surplus, demand, monopoly, joint supply, and marginal productivity), Marshall's inventions were clearly upstaged by the aforementioned writers and by J. S. Mill as well. Objectively, on a doctrine-by-doctrine basis, Marshall does not rank extremely high on originality, although it is true that many ideas may have been developed independently by him.

Upon what basis, then, does Marshall's great (and largely untarnished) reputation lie? As in the case of Adam Smith, his fame is due principally to the fact that he wrote a book that caught the academic spirit of the time and that he did so, it must be emphasized, by directing his appeal to the intelligent layman. In modern parlance, he "put it all together"; i.e., Marshall synthesized classical and neoclassical analyses of cost and utility, producing one cogent engine of economic analysis.

But, as we have seen, Marshall was much more than merely a synthesizer. His partial-equilibrium method was used as a glue that bound all the various branches of theory together. The use of conceptual time, which was at the heart of this method, was a massive and original contribution to modern economic theory and policy. In addition to numerous original theoretical inventions, Marshall never touched a "received" concept without extending or improving it.

There is little doubt that Marshall was a great theorist, but we tend to lose sight of the fact that he was also a very practical man. A probable reason for the subsequent emphasis on the theoretical aspects of his work is that Marshall's students (whose names almost form a litany of great twentieth-century British theorists) chose to work on and refine the theoretical concepts of the *Principles*. In other words, there appears to be a large and unfortunate gap between Marshall's interests in economics and those of the Marshallians, his students and followers. The Marshallians viewed their task as clarifying and developing the *analytical* areas of the *Principles,* while simultaneously ignoring and dismissing the practical context in which Marshall encased his ideas. Thus Marshall has usually been accused of making ambiguous statements of certain theoretical ideas. But many of these criticisms are misdirected, for they fail to treat Marshall's theory as he often treated it himself—as a tool for attacking practical social and economic problems. As has been indicated in the present chapter, an understanding of the several levels of abstraction he used in dealing with demand curves might have forestalled the protracted debate over the nature of the formal specification of demand in the *Principles*. Marshall's "ambiguities," moreover, have not seemed to force theorists to view all sides of economic questions, as he strove to do.

If Marshall were alive today, his quest for an economic analysis that could be used in practical economic problems might even lead him to characterize the theoretical developments that sprang from the *Principles* as "overelaborate." The complex process of mathematizing economic analysis, which the discipline has been undergoing for several decades, appears alien to the concept of the nature and purpose of economics. Marshall demanded empirical, or at least imaginable, referents to all his analytical tools. Many twentieth-century theorists of high reputation—some claiming to be disciples of Marshall—have been equally as adamant in demanding none.

Marshall, of course, was always ready to point out the gaps and deficiencies in his analytical constructs. But suggested *applications,* making allowance for the analytical deficiencies, were also part and parcel of his conception of the nature of economics. He would probably be the first to laud the development of theoretical improvements, but he would as surely criticize the insularity that many contemporary theorists cultivate between themselves and actual events. The kernel of Marshall's genius lay in his ability to learn from economic and social problems and, in turn, to contribute toward their solution.

NOTES FOR FURTHER READING

The secondary literature on Marshall and his ideas is enormous and growing. On Marshall himself, the best single source is J. M. Keynes, "Alfred Marshall," *Economic Journal,* vol. 34 (September 1924), pp. 311–372, reprinted in Keynes's *Essays in Biography* (London: Macmillan, 1933). Also reprinted from the *Economic Journal,* vol. 54 (June 1944), pp. 268–284, in Keynes's *Essays* is a memoir on Marshall's wife, "Mary Paley Marshall (1850–1944)." R. H. Coase, "Alfred Marshall's Mother and Father," *History of Political Economy,* vol. 16 (Winter 1984), pp. 519–527, rounds out the family portraits. The *Memorials of Alfred Marshall,* edited by his student A. C. Pigou (see References), should not be missed. For later assessments of Marshall's work by Marshallians, see G. F. Shove, "The Place of Marshall's Principles in Economic Theory," and C. W. Guillebaud, "The Evolution of Marshall's *Principles,*" both appearing in the *Economic Journal,* vol. 52 (December 1942), pp. 294–329, 330–349. T. W. Hutchison's *Review of Economic Doctrines 1870–1929,* chap. 4 (Oxford: Clarendon Press, 1953), contains a brief interpretive account of Marshall. A. W. Coats provides an excellent overview of British thought and thinkers in the Marshallian period in "Sociological Aspects of British Economic Thought," *Journal of Political Economy,* vol. 75 (October 1967), pp. 706–729.

Along related lines, see E. F. Beach, "Marshallian Methodology," *International Journal of Social Economics,* vol. 14 (1987), pp. 19–26. In recent years, David Reisman has been attempting, with mixed results, to reassess Marshall's economic thought in the broad areas of economic theory, economic growth, and economic policy. In particular, see Reisman's *The Economics of Alfred Marshall* (London: Macmillan, 1986) and *Alfred Marshall: Progress and Politics* (New York: St. Martin's Press, 1987).

An excellent and detailed overview of Marshall's contributions to analysis may be found in chaps. 9 and 10 of Mark Blaug's *Economic Theory in Retro-*

spect (see References). Milton Friedman's essay entitled "The Marshallian Demand Curve" (see References) offers a persuasive case for identifying the Marshallian demand curve with a constant-purchasing-power-of-money assumption. Other Marshallian writers, such as Hicks, disagree. See the classic paper by J. R. Hicks and R. G. D. Allen, "A Reconsideration of the Theory of Value," *Economica,* n.s., vol. 1 (February, May 1934), pp. 52–76, 196–219. See also M. J. Bailey's comment on Friedman's paper, "The Marshallian Demand Curve," *Journal of Political Economy,* vol. 62 (June 1954), pp. 255–261. For a sketch of developments related to the Marshallian demand curve, see R. B. Ekelund, E. G. Furubotn, and W. P. Gramm, *The Evolution of Modern Demand Theory,* chap. 2 (Boston: Heath, 1972). Marshall's "Giffen paradox," which posits the possibility of a *positively* sloped demand curve, is analyzed by G. J. Stigler in "Notes on the History of the Giffen Paradox," *Journal of Political Economy,* vol. 55 (April 1947), pp. 152–156. But for a recent assessment of Stigler's position, see William P. Gramm, "Giffen's Paradox and the Marshallian Demand Curve," *The Manchester School of Eonomic and Social Studies,* vol. 38 (March 1970), pp. 65–71.

The firm's envelope or planning curve, which simplifies Marshall's long-run analysis, was developed by Jacob Viner in his classic paper, "Cost Curves and Supply Curves," *Zeitschrift fur Nationalökonomie,* vol. 3 (September 1931), pp. 23–46. Marshall's fiction of the representative firm is severely criticized in Lionel Robbins, "The Representative Firm," *Economic Journal,* vol. 38 (September 1928), pp. 387–404. The whole area of Marshall's theories of production and distribution is brought under skillful and critical review in chap. 4 of Stigler's *Production and Distribution Theories.* On the suffusion of Marshall's time period method into his theory of distribution, see H. M. Robertson's "Alfred Marshall's Aims and Methods Illustrated from His Treatment of Distribution," *History of Political Economy,* vol. 2 (Spring 1970), pp. 1–64. Likewise, see G. L. S. Shackle, "Marshall's Accommodation of Time," in *Epistemics and Economics* (London: Cambridge University Press, 1972); and P. C. Dooley, "Alfred Marshall: Fitting the Theory to the Facts," *Cambridge Journal of Economics,* vol. 9 (September 1985), pp. 245–255. Marshall's fundamental contribution to time-period analysis in market exchange is also the subject of P. L. Williams, "A Reconstruction of Marshall's Temporary Equilibrium Pricing Model," *History of Political Economy,* vol. 18 (Winter 1986), pp. 639–653. In the same broad vein, see J. M. Gee, "Marshall's Views on 'Short-Period' Value Formation," *History of Political Economy,* vol. 15 (Summer 1983), pp. 181–205; and O. F. Hamouda, "On the Notion of Short-Run and Long-Run: Marshall, Ricardo and Equilibrium Theories," *British Review of Economic Issues,* vol. 6 (Spring 1984), pp. 55–82. Marshall's theory of exchange has also been reviewed by D. A. Walker, "Marshall's Theory of Competitive Exchange," *Canadian Journal of Economics,* vol. 2 (November 1969), pp. 590–597. The following two articles by D. A. Walker on Marshall's long-run and short-run concepts of labor supply should be read in tandem: "Marshall on the Long-Run Supply of Labor,"

Zeitschrift für die Gesamte Staatswissenschaft (October 1974), pp. 691–705; and "Marshall on the Short-Run Supply of Labor," *Southern Economic Journal,* vol. 41 (January 1975), pp. 429–441.

The related issues of external economies and increasing returns (decreasing costs) have probably been responsible for more debate than any others discussed in Marshall's *Principles.* As we saw in the text of the present chapter, A. C. Pigou translated the concept of external economies into a divergence between marginal social costs and marginal private costs. The important connection between Pigou's welfare economics and the earlier work of Henry Sidgwick is established by Margaret G. O'Donnell in "Pigou: An Extension of Sidgwickian Thought," *History of Political Economy,* vol. 11 (Winter 1979), pp. 588–605. The Pigovian solution was to levy a tax (or a subsidy in the opposite case) on the industry. In 1924, however, Frank Knight challenged Pigou's discussion on several crucial points, demonstrating that competition does not lead to excessive investment as Pigou (and others) had alleged. See Knight, "Some Fallacies in the Interpretation of Social Costs," *Quarterly Journal of Economics,* vol. 38 (August 1924), pp. 582–606. The modern Coasian criticism has created an entirely new area of economics—the economics of property rights. A good place to start in this vast literature is the survey by E. G. Furubotn and S. Pejovich, "Property Rights and Economic Theory: A Survey of Recent Literature," *Journal of Economic Literature,* vol. 10 (December 1972), pp. 1137–1157.

On the subject of consumers' surplus and particularly Marshall's role in its development, see P. C. Dooley, "Consumer's Surplus: Marshall and His Critics," *Canadian Journal of Economics,* vol. 16 (February 1983), pp. 26–38; and R. B. Ekelund, Jr., and R. F. Hébert, "Consumer Surplus: The First Hundred Years," *History of Political Economy,* vol. 17 (Fall 1985), pp. 419–454.

The question of the existence and, indeed, of the usefulness of the concepts of industries of constant, increasing, or decreasing returns was raised by J. H. Clapham in a delightful paper, "Of Empty Economic Boxes," *Economic Journal,* vol. 32 (September 1922), pp. 458–465, and D. H. Robertson extended the criticism of the concept in "Those Empty Boxes," *Economic Journal,* vol. 34 (March 1924), pp. 16–31. The incompatibility of competitive equilibrium and a condition of decreasing costs (increasing returns), which led partly to the development of the theory of imperfect competition, was brought out in a brilliant paper by Piero Sraffa, "The Laws of Returns under Competitive Conditions," *Economic Journal,* vol. 36 (December 1926), pp. 535–550. The Viner, Knight, Clapham, Pigou, Robertson, and Sraffa papers mentioned here are reprinted in *Readings in Price Theory,* George J. Stigler and Kenneth E. Boulding (eds.) (Homewood, Ill.: Irwin, 1952).

Marshall as "historicist-evolutionist" and the influence of Darwin on his thought are discussed by the prominent sociologist Talcott Parsons in two classic papers: "Wants and Activities in Marshall," *Quarterly Journal of Economics,* vol. 46 (November 1931), pp. 101–140; and "Economics and Sociology: Marshall in Relation to the Thought of His Time," *Quarterly Journal of Eco-*

nomics, vol. 46 (February 1932), pp. 316–347. On this important issue, see Marshall's own statements in "The Old Generation of Economists and the New," *Quarterly Journal of Economics,* vol. 11 (January 1897), pp. 115–135, reprinted in *Memorials of Alfred Marshall.* Several writers have continued to explore this nebulous idea up to the present time. See, for example, A. A. Awan, "Marshallian and Schumpeterian Theories of Economic Evolution: Gradualism vs. Punctualism," *Atlantic Economic Journal,* vol. 14 (December 1986), pp. 37–49; and A. L. Levine, "Marshall's Principles and the Biological Viewpoint: A Reconsideration," *Manchester School of Economic and Social Studies,* vol. 51 (September 1983), pp. 276–293.

For more evidence of Marshall's sociology and his tendency to blend it with his economics, see T. Levitt, "Alfred Marshall: Victorian Relevance for Modern Economics," *Quarterly Journal of Economics,* vol. 90 (August 1976), pp. 426–444; M. A. Pujol, "Gender and Class in Marshall's Principles of Economics," *Cambridge Journal of Economics,* vol. 8 (September 1984), pp. 217–234; R. M. Tullberg, "Marshall's Tendency to Socialism," *History of Political Economy,* vol. 7 (Spring 1975), pp. 75–111; A. Petridis, "Alfred Marshall's Attitudes to the Economic Analysis of Trade Unions," *History of Political Economy,* vol. 5 (Spring 1973), pp. 165–198; and J. D. Chasse, "Marshall, the Human Agent and Economic Growth: Wants and Activities Revisited," *History of Political Economy,* vol. 16 (Fall 1984), pp. 381–404. The latter explores the relations Marshall developed between income distribution, the standard of living, and economic growth.

The growing professionalism of economics in his day and particularly Marshall's contribution to it are the subjects of J. Maloney, "Marshall, Cunningham and the Emerging Economics Profession," *Economic History Review,* vol. 29 (August 1976), pp. 440–451; and R. F. Hébert, "Marshall: A Professional Economist Guards the Purity of His Discipline," in *Critics of Henry George,* R. V. Andelson (ed.) (London: Associated University Presses, 1979). Finally, some of the best and most interesting recent work on Marshall is that of John K. Whitaker, especially on the matter of the early development of Marshall's thought. See Whitaker's "Alfred Marshall: The Years 1877 to 1885," *History of Political Economy,* vol. 4 (Spring 1972), pp. 1–61; and "Some Neglected Aspects of Alfred Marshall's Economic and Social Thought," *History of Political Economy,* vol. 9 (Summer 1977), pp. 161–197. Professor Whitaker has also edited two volumes containing the early writings of Marshall: *The Early Economic Writings of Alfred Marshall, 1867–1890* (New York: Free Press, 1975).

REFERENCES

Blaug, Mark. *Economic Theory in Retrospect,* 4th ed. London: Cambridge University Press, 1985.

Coase, Ronald. "The Problem of Social Cost," *Journal of Law and Economics,* vol. 3 (October 1960), pp. 1–44.

Friedman, Milton. "The Marshallian Demand Curve," *Journal of Political Economy,* vol. 57 (December 1949), pp. 463–495.

Hicks, John R. *The Theory of Wages.* London: Macmillan, 1932. Revised 1968.

———. *Value and Capital,* 2d ed. London: Oxford University Press, 1946.

Marshall, Alfred. *Principles of Economics,* 8th ed. London: Macmillan, 1920.

Maurice, S. C. "On the Importance of Being Unimportant: An Analysis of the Paradox in Marshall's Third Rule of Derived Demand," *Economica,* vol. 42 (November 1975), pp. 385–393.

Pigou, A. C. *Wealth and Welfare.* London: Macmillan, 1912.

———. *The Economics of Welfare.* London: Macmillan, 1920.

——— (ed.). *Memorials of Alfred Marshall.* London: Macmillan, 1925.

Stigler, George J. *Production and Distribution Theories.* New York: Macmillan, 1941.

CHAPTER 16

LÉON WALRAS AND THE DEVELOPMENT OF GENERAL-EQUILIBRIUM ANALYSIS

INTRODUCTION: A STUDY IN CONTRAST

As Alfred Marshall represented the dominant figure in English postclassical economics at the turn of the century, so Léon Walras was the leading force among continental economists. The collective impact of Léon Walras (1834–1910) and Alfred Marshall (1842–1924) upon twentieth-century economists and economic analysis would be difficult to overestimate. The framework of contemporary mainstream developments in microeconomics, general-equilibrium analysis, and many other areas where a theoretical superstructure is required (monetary theory, for instance) is either Walrasian or Marshallian in character. For these reasons and for many others, Walras and Marshall are rightfully regarded by a large part of the profession as two of the most important economic theorists who ever lived.[1]

Although Marshall's contributions were reviewed in detail in the previous chapter, it is appropriate in a discussion of Walras's ideas to contrast certain fundamental differences between these two giants of neoclassical economic analysis. Although they were contemporaries, Walras was the elder statesman, in terms of both age and priority of discovery. But it is the scope and method of their respective theoretical achievements that provide the most instructive forms of contrast.

---

[1] This statement is not meant to imply that Walras and Marshall were the only contributors to the neoclassical paradigm. The small army of writers considered in Chaps. 12 through 14 were of a neoclassical ilk, and indeed the neoclassical age (c. 1870 to 1920) produced other great economists (e.g., Knut Wicksell and a whole Swedish tradition, F. Y. Edgeworth, P. H. Wicksteed, V. Pareto, and I. Fisher), some of whom will be considered subsequently in this book. However, Walras and Marshall are of such significance as to deserve special treatment.

419

It would be difficult to imagine two more dissimilar and diverse contributors to the mainstream of contemporary economic analysis than these two titans of the profession. Their great works—Walras's *Elements of Pure Economics* (1874) and Marshall's *Principles of Economics* (1890)—published almost twenty years apart, each had a resounding impact on economics. Each work, like each man, was different.

Partial Equilibrium versus General Equilibrium

In the first place, both writers were concerned essentially with the *microeconomic* foundations of price formation. That is, they—along with Cournot, Dupuit, and others before them—viewed the equilibrating process of prices and quantities as the result of market exchange (though, as we shall see, their views of the method of price and quantity adjustment differed). The essential difference between Walras and Marshall centers on the scope of the subject under analysis. Marshall, and practically all writers on microeconomics before him, utilized a convention in dealing with particular markets that is now called *partial-equilibrium analysis*. Walras, on the other hand, developed a broader and more complex method of looking at markets called *general-equilibrium analysis*.

The important distinction between Marshall and Walras on this point is basically simple, though a more complex discussion of general equilibrium may be found later in this chapter. Fundamentally, when one is considering a market in Marshallian partial-equilibrium terms, one is considering that market in quasi isolation. For instance, take the market for any commodity—such as orange juice. In both Marshallian and Walrasian views, the equilibrium price and quantity of orange juice are determined by the intersection of the demand function and the supply function (Walras called the latter an "offer curve"). Where these writers differed was in regard to the *determinants* of the supply and demand curves and the *mechanics* of market equilibrium.

In his specification of the individual demand function for orange juice, Marshall would make demand a function not only of the price of orange juice but also of the price of oranges, the prices of substitutes and complements for orange juice, and the income and tastes of the consumer. All the other factors influencing the demand for orange juice (the prices of distantly related goods, market interactions vis-à-vis changes in the price of orange juice, etc.) are held constant or ignored altogether. Thus Marshall used a large measure of *ceteris paribus* assumptions in dealing with individual and market demands for any particular good. He did likewise with his specification of individual and market supply curves. Marshall therefore wished to ignore or to hold in abeyance seemingly unrelated or distantly related determinants of the price and quantity of any particular good so that the main features of the individual market could be isolated for examination. This partial-equilibrium method had been employed before Marshall by Jenkin, Cournot, and Dupuit, among others.

Walras, on the other hand, attacked the value problem in another manner.

He was more interested in the *interdependencies* that exist between markets. In his view, these interrelations exist because the valuation process necessarily occurs in all markets simultaneously. Walras asserted that any one who has not maximized his or her satisfactions will have excess demands (to be defined below) for some goods, including orange juice, and excess supplies of others. The object of exchange is to maximize satisfaction, which to Walras meant disposing of excess supplies in order to eliminate excess demands. Therefore, every act of exchange influences the values of all goods in the economic system. Likewise, Walras viewed the production and input side of economic activity as interrelated. Indeed, the interdependence of the entire system of production *and* consumption was the subject of Walras's *Elements*.

How, then, would Walras describe the market for orange juice? He would argue that Marshall's *ceteris paribus* assumption was simply inappropriate because other things are not equal. Rather, the whole system is interconnected, so that an increase in demand for orange juice necessarily means that there are excess suppliers of other goods in the system. Consequently, any price change in orange juice will have further effects on other markets (e.g., haircuts) that react back on the orange-juice market and produce further changes. These basic interconnections of all markets, which Marshall chose to ignore, constitute the heart of Walras's system. Thus at an abstract, theoretical level, Walras argued that an analysis of the market for orange juice—in isolation from all variables in the system—was inappropriate.[2] In contrast to Marshall's partial-equilibrium approach, Walras's method is a general-equilibrium approach.

Some Doctrinal Antagonism over Method

All this is not to imply that Marshall and Walras were unaware of—or incapable of using—each other's system. In fact, Marshall, in elaborating Mill's doctrine of reciprocal demands (see Chapter 8), produced an elegant two-commodity, two-country general-equilibrium model for the determination of international values. In his *Principles,* however, he selected partial-equilibrium analysis as the appropriate method for dealing with selected markets in a complex world. Even so, he never denied the correctness of Walras's system.

Walras, on the other hand, was adamant—even rude—in pointing out what he perceived to be Marshall's major errors. Although Walras was not opposed to the use of demand curves for *particular* goods, he objected to the use of such curves if they excluded the interdependencies of utilities and demands for all goods. He also vehemently rejected the tacit identification of marginal utility with demand, a practice that Dupuit had originated. In fact, Walras's salvos were often directed jointly at Dupuit and Marshall.

---

[2] This is true irrespective of the fact that Walrasians are forced to utilize partial-equilibrium conventions in dealing with practical questions.

In a letter to his Italian contempory Maffeo Pantaleoni, for example, Walras pointed out that in the analysis of exchange he considered demand functions containing many independent variables and that this was the basic difference between his own concept of demand and those of Dupuit, Marshall, and two prominent Austrian theorists, Rudolph Auspitz and Richard Lieben (*Correspondence*, letters 379 and 465). Walras identified Marshall's demand formulation with that of Dupuit (see Chapter 12), and he held that Dupuit and Marshall illegitimately attempted to explain demand curves in terms of (marginal) utility curves. As for his own role in value theory, he considered himself to have been the first to show the interactions between Cournot's demand apparatus (without utility accoutrements) and Jevons's theory of the final degree of utility (see Chapters 12 and 14). Yet most of Walras's objections to the Dupuit-Marshall demand theory were ill-founded, for in this instance he failed to appreciate the convenience (and usefulness) of the *ceteris paribus* convention in partial-equilibrium theory.

Curiously, Walras was almost always in a pique when speaking of Marshall. He seemed always ready to find merit in other continental economists' work but, with the exception of Jevons, English writers were often the object of biting attack. For example, Walras exempted Jevons and Gossen from his partial-equilibrium indictment since they did not attempt to deduce demand curves from utility curves. But he called Marshall the "great white elephant of political economy" and attacked him and his brilliant colleague F. Y. Edgeworth for jealously and obstinately attempting to defend Ricardo's and Mill's theory of price (*Correspondence*, letter 1051).

Part of the problem lies, of course, in the fact that Walras and Marshall developed their analyses and wrote their respective books for two very different audiences. Marshall's avowed purpose in writing the *Principles* was to inform the intelligent lay person, and particularly the business person, of the fundamental tools and uses of economic analysis. Consequently, most of the formal analysis contained in the book appears either in footnotes or in appendixes. Walras, on the other hand, was clearly writing for his professional colleagues. The mathematics of the *Elements* into which Walras encased his theory was indeed formidable, and it is doubtful whether more than a handful of leading world theorists in 1874 readily digested it (Marshall was probably one of them). Surely these differences are fundamental in understanding the relative acceptance of the two works by the profession. What is not so easy to understand, perhaps, is an almost total lack of communication between Marshall and Walras. In spite of their cultural and theoretical differences, however, it is of crucial importance to become acquainted with the ideas of the men who have come to be appreciated as two of history's greatest economic theorists.

LÉON WALRAS: SKETCH OF HIS LIFE AND WORK

Léon Walras was born in 1834 in the province of Normandy, France. He retained the citizenship of his birthright even though he spent most of his adult life in another country. Like John Stuart Mill, he was reared in the household of an economist, though his early education was not nearly so rigorous as Mill's. Nevertheless, his father, Auguste, was the only teacher of economics he knew. Later, Walras was to stand on the shoulders of his father in many matters of economic policy, but in economic theory he reached new heights of originality.

Auguste Walras had been a classmate—and possibly an admirer—of Cournot at the École Normale Supérieure in Paris. Consequently, while Cournot was tumbling into obscurity as an economist, Léon Walras was mastering a copy of the *Mathematical Principles of the Theory of Wealth* handed him by his father. Subsequently, it was Léon Walras, more than any other writer, who called the world's attention to the pioneering work of Cournot. Despite his brilliance, Cournot had retreated from the problem of general-equilibrium analysis, declaring it beyond the powers of mathematical analysis. Walras not only proved Cournot wrong on this point but now is also generally acknowledged as the founder of general-equilibrium analysis.

There was little indication in Walras's youth that he would become a great economist. He received an ordinary education, taking two baccalaureate degrees—one in letters and one in science. Yet he flunked the mathematics section of the entrance exam to the École Polytechnique—France's preparatory school for civil engineers. Perhaps it was just as well, for he showed little interest in subsequent engineering studies undertaken at the École des Mines— an engineering school of lesser rank than the École des Ponts et Chaussées where Dupuit had excelled. In 1858 he turned to literary pursuits, publishing a mediocre novel in that year and a hardly more noteworthy short story the following year. As if admitting his own shortcomings as a *littérateur*, Walras promised his father, in 1858, that he would make economics his life work. Before he could obtain an academic position in his chosen field, however, he found time to father twin girls out of wedlock, edit a short-lived monthly review, and work for a railroad company and two banks. He was nevertheless studying economics in his spare time and doing some writing on the subject.

Walras's unpopular ideas—which in his youth were approximately the same as his father's (both favored land nationalization, mathematical economics, and a subjective theory of value, in contrast to Ricardo's cost-of-production theory)—kept him from securing an academic post in France, but in 1870 he was finally named—over the objections of three-sevenths of the selection committee—to a professorship in the faculty of law[3] at what later became the University of Lausanne (Switzerland). There Walras prospered intellectually, if not economically. He was never financially secure until his marriage to a rich widow in 1884, his first wife having died five years earlier. But at Lausanne he began the feverish activity that eventually led to the publication of all his best-known works.

---

[3] Lausanne followed the practice common in France (the result of a reorganization plan of Napoleon's) of offering all economics courses in the major universities in the school of law.

In 1874 and 1877 he published the two parts of his *Éléments d'économie politique pure,* a seminal work on the marginal-utility theory of value and on general-equilibrium analysis. This was followed, in 1881, by the *Théorie mathématique de bimétallisme* and, in fairly rapid succession, by the *Théorie mathématique de la richesse sociale* (1883) and the *Théorie de la monnaie.* Walras had always planned to write two systematic treatises on applied economics and social economics to accompany his 1874 work on pure theory, but his strenuous pace at Lausanne had sapped much of his energy by 1892. He quit teaching in that year and later was content to publish his collected papers (rather than the systematic works he had earlier envisioned) under the respective titles *Études d'économie sociale* (1896) and *Études d'économie politique appliquée* (1898).

In the heyday of his career at Lausanne, Walras corresponded with just about every economist of any repute throughout the civilized world. In part, he did so out of frustration, for his law students at the university showed little interest in, or concern with, economics. Deprived of stimulating colleagues or students (at least in economics), Walras followed the practice of sending all his prepublished manuscripts to other economists for critical review. This practice eventually blossomed into a very active and voluminous correspondence.

Intellectual frustration was not the only likely cause of Walras's tireless correspondence. The written record of that correspondence reveals his fervent zeal to persuade, beseech, cajole, or otherwise enlist the aid of other economists in spreading the mathematical method of analysis as it applied to economic theory. Regardless of his motives, Walras succeeded on a large scale in advancing the international dissemination of ideas so essential to rapid progress in any science.

In sum, Walras cast a broad shadow over the entire field of economics. His forte, of course, was pioneering new frontiers in economic analysis. In the words of William Jaffé, his main biographer:

> This was the achievement of Walras, a lonely, cantankerous savant, often in straitened circumstances, plagued with hypochondria and a paranoid temperament, plodding doggedly through hostile, uncharted territory to discover a fresh vantage point from which subsequent generations of economists could set out to make their own discoveries (*International Encyclopedia of the Social Sciences,* p. 452).

He had a keen sense of the importance of building strong foundations on which other advances could be erected. In a cunning assessment of his own approach to scientific inquiry, Walras wrote to Étienne Antonelli: "If one wants to harvest quickly, one must plant carrots and salads; if one has the ambition to plant oaks, he must have the sense to tell himself: my grandchildren will owe me this shade."

WALRAS AND MARSHALL AND THE MARKET ADJUSTMENT MECHANISM

Perhaps one of the most instructive contrasts between Walras and Marshall concerns the so-called law of markets. This is called the "adjustment mechanism'' in microeconomic discussions of markets. Closely related to the method of adjustment to equilibrium of supply and demand are the concepts of excess demand and stability of equilibrium in the Walrasian and Marshallian systems. Because they are closely related, all these items will be treated together, though the concept of excess demand will be extended in the following section on general equilibrium.

Price Adjustments versus Quantity Adjustments

The basic difference between Walras and Marshall, with regard to the market adjustment mechanism, is that Walras regarded *price* as the adjusting variable when markets are in disequilibrium whereas Marshall focused upon *quantity* as the adjusting variable. Stated symbolically and somewhat naively, Walras viewed demand and supply equations (or functions) in the following form:

$$Q_{d_x} = f(p_x) \tag{16-1}$$

$$Q_{s_x} = f(p_x) \tag{16-2}$$

Marshall, on the other hand, viewed functional relations the other way around:

$$D_{p_x} = f(q_x) \tag{16-3}$$

$$S_{p_x} = f(q_x) \tag{16-4}$$

Both these formulations require some explanation. First, the demand and supply equations are said to be "functions" since, in Walras's case, quantity demanded and quantity supplied of some commodity x—the left-hand side of equations (16-1) and (16-2)—are said to be functions (f) of the price of x—the right-hand side of equations (16-1) and (16-2). Marshall, in contrast, related the demand and supply price of some commodity x to the quantity of x demanded and supplied.

The variable described in parentheses on the right-hand side of all equations is called the *independent* variable (or *price* in Walras's case, and *quantity* in Marshall's). Changes in the independent variable cause the *dependent* variable—the left-hand side of equations (16-1) to (16-4)—to take on different values. Simply stated, Walras indicated that quantity demanded and supplied depends in some way upon *prices,* whereas Marshall indicated that demand price and supply price depend in some way upon the *quantity* of the good.[4]

The importance of this basic difference in the specification of demand-and-supply relations may be clarified graphically, as in Figure 16-1. In Figure 16-1*b* the supply and demand functions for some good are depicted, and price is as-

---

[4] Obviously, we are neglecting a host of other independent variables in the demand-and-supply relations, such as income, prices of substitutes and complements (indeed *all* other goods in Walras), utility, the production function, and prices of inputs. Some of these simplifications will be dropped in the following section on Walrasian general equilibrium.

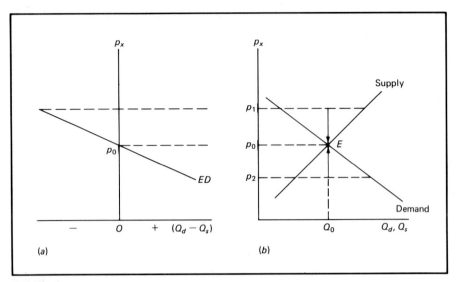

FIGURE 16-1
If market price is too high for equilibrium (for example, p_1), negative excess demand (i.e.,
excess supply) will drive price down toward its equilibrium value. If price is too low for
equilibrium, excess demand will drive price upward toward its equilibrium value.

sumed to be the independent variable.[5] Conceptually, one might imagine presenting demanders and suppliers with a list of prices to which they are to express the quantities they would supply and demand at alternative prices. Point
E in Figure 16-1b represents the equilibrium price and quantity that competition will produce in the market. If, for some reason, price were established
below equilibrium, say at p_2, quantity demanded at that price would exceed
quantity supplied, and a shortage would result. This shortage induces competition among buyers, which in turn bids up price. As price rises, some demanders are excluded from the market, and some sellers are included. There are
market forces, in other words, causing price and quantity to return to the equilibrium point E. Similarly, should price happen to be above equilibrium, a surplus of the good would result, and competition among suppliers would *lower*
price, thereby increasing the number of demanders in the market and decreasing the number of suppliers. In other words, price is the adjusting force (the
independent variable), and, further, the price mechanism, given a displacement from equilibrium, causes a return to the equilibrium. For this reason, the
system described in Figure 16-1 is said to be *stable* in the Walrasian sense.

[5] It is customary (except in economics) to display a two-variable function with the independent
variable always on the horizontal axis. Thus a literal depiction of Walrasian functions would display price on the horizontal axis. Through force of habit, economists generally portray price on
the vertical axis, even when it is assumed to be the independent variable, as in this case. This
modern eccentricity is undoubtedly due to the practice of Marshall, who displayed the variables as
shown in Fig. 16-1b. However, Marshall adhered to accepted practice, since he considered *quantity* to be the independent variable, not price (see the discussion below).

Walras's Excess-Demand Function   Stability can be described, alternatively, in terms of a concept of excess demand. Excess demand is defined simply as the difference between quantity demanded and quantity supplied at any given price, or symbolically as $ED = (Q_d - Q_s)$. An excess-demand schedule can be drawn up as in Figure 16-1a, which traces out these differences. For example, the excess demand at price p_1 is a *negative* amount since $Q_d - Q_s$ at that price is negative. Thus a negative excess demand can be regarded as positive excess supply. Excess demand is zero at the equilibrium price and positive at prices below equilibrium. The important point is that for stability in a Walrasian system, the *ED* function must be *negatively sloped,* as in Figure 16-1.

Now let us look at the adjustment mechanism and stability properties in Marshallian terms, as depicted in Figure 16-2. Figure 16-2 again reproduces the situation one normally expects to enounter in real markets, i.e., a positively sloped supply function and a negatively sloped demand curve, the same as those shown in Figure 16-1. The conceptual difference between Walras and Marshall is that Marshall would draw the demand and supply curves by presenting a list of alternative quantities to suppliers and demanders and asking them to list maximum demand prices that would be given for those quantities and minimum supply prices at which those quantities would be produced. The adjustment that takes place in the market (when demand and supply are not in equilibrium) is not a price adjustment, as Walras assumed, but a quantity adjustment.

The Marshallian quantity adjustment can be analyzed with reference to Figure 16-2. Assume that quantity for some reason is less than the equilibrium quantity Q_0. Quantity Q_1, for example, is less than Q_0, but at quantity Q_1, de-

FIGURE 16-2
If output is below its equilibrium value (for example, Q_1), the presence of economic profits will encourage greater output. If output exceeds its equilibrium value, the ensuing economic losses will encourage lower output.

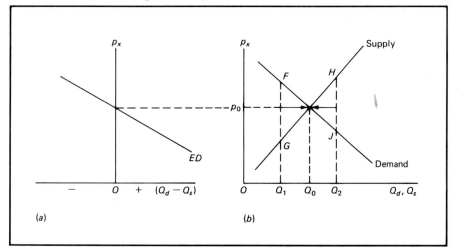

(a)

(b)

mand price (represented by point F on the demand curve) is greater than supply price (represented by point G on the supply curve). In Marshallian terms, when $D_p > S_p$, firms in the competitive industry are earning economic profits. Output will therefore increase, bringing the market back into equilibrium at E.[6] Similarly, if output should exceed the equilibrium level, as at quantity Q_2 in Figure 16-2, supply price for that output (represented by point H) will be greater than demand price (point J), and economic losses will induce firms to reduce output. Equilibrium is reestablished at Q_0. Thus, as the arrows in Figure 16-2 indicate, the Marshallian equilibrium is stable. Given disequilibrium, in other words, underlying forces in the system will guarantee a return to equilibrium. Likewise, in terms of the excess function developed in reference to Walrasian equilibrium demand, the Marshallian functions are seen to be stable.[7] Given positively sloped supply curves and negatively sloped demand functions, Marshallian *and* Walrasian stability each require a negatively sloped excess-demand function such as that in Figures 16-1 and 16-2.

Backward-Bending Supply

Perhaps the most interesting aspect of the Walrasian-Marshallian adjustment process relates to the problem of backward-bending supply curves.[8] Two examples readily come to mind. First, as practically all mercantile writers clearly perceived (see Chapter 3), the supply curve of labor might bend backward (see Figure 3-1) if workers trade off additional income from work for more leisure, so that they actually work less at higher wages. A second example of backward-bending supply may be drawn from markets for foreign exchange in international finance. Under certain conditions, in the presence of an inelastic demand for imported goods, the supply of foreign exchange may be backward-bending (for details, see Allen, "Stable and Unstable Equilibrium in the Foreign Exchanges"). The point of this discussion is that a possibility exists that negatively sloped supply-and-demand intersections might occur in real-world markets. Given this possibility, stability of equilibrium in both Walrasian and Marshallian terms takes on new dimensions, as the following discussion demonstrates.

Assume a market (say, for labor) in which the demand curve intersects only the backward-bending portion of the supply curve. This state of affairs is described in Figure 16-3, where at the demand price p_0, quantity demanded

---

[6] The increase in output occurs for two reasons: (1) existing firms increase output, and (2) there is an entry of new firms in the industry.

[7] Actually, to be consistent, some excess-price function should be developed in Figure 16-2a. For convenience, however, the inverse of the Marshallian supply and demand functions is taken so that a Marshallian excess-demand function can be compared with the one generated from Walrasian equilibrium. Marshall himself never bothered to do this, however.

[8] A proposed resolution of the difference between Walras and Marshall on the question of stability and backward-bending supply functions is offered by Milton Friedman and by Peter Newman (see Notes for Further Reading at the end of this chapter).

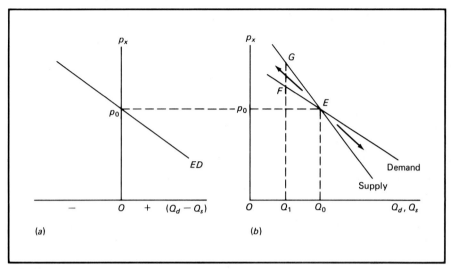

FIGURE 16-3
The market described in (b) is stable in a Walrasian sense (i.e., price is the independent variable), but unstable in a Marshallian sense (i.e., quantity is the independent variable).

equals quantity supplied. In sum, a negatively sloped excess-demand function, such as those encountered in Figures 16-1 and 16-2, is obtained. Clearly the system is stable in Walrasian terms since a price displacement from equilibrium engenders competitive forces that will guarantee a return to it.

The system described in Figure 16-3 is *unstable* in Marshallian terms. This can be verified by assuming some quantity Q_1 that is less than the equilibrium quantity Q_0. At Q_1, supply price G is clearly greater than demand price F. In that event Marshall envisioned economic losses and a *reduction* in output supplied. Any reduction in output from Q_1 in Figure 16-3 would magnify the divergence between demand and supply. Equilibrium, in short, would never be reached. Any departure from point E would be followed by explosive market disturbances if Marshallian adjustments take place. In the case described in Figure 16-3, then, a negatively sloped excess-demand function implies Walrasian stability but Marshallian instability!

Little imagination is required in order to understand the stability properties when the labeling of the demand and supply curves of Figure 16-3 is reversed. In this case the demand curve would intersect the supply curve from above. The excess-demand function corresponding to these curves would be positively sloped. The system would be unstable in the Walrasian sense because at all prices above equilibrium price p_0, quantity demanded would exceed quantity supplied. Price would rise because of the forces of competition, pushing the system further from equilibrium. However, Marshallian adjustment in this case would produce stability, since at quantities below equilibrium quantity Q_0, demand price would exceed supply price and thus produce a return to equilibrium. In sum, the positively sloped excess-demand function (which ac-

companies negatively sloped supply and demand schedules) expresses instability in Walras's system and stability in Marshall's. Stability (in terms of excess demand) is symmetrical in both systems for normally sloped demand and
supply schedules, but asymmetrical when demand and supply curves are both
negatively sloped.

Market Stability

At first blush the issue of stability might seem obscure and difficult, if not simply irrelevant. It might be argued, for instance, that the issue of unstable markets vanishes in the face of market experience. If by "unstable markets" we
mean price and quantity "explosions" away from equilibrium, then little empirical evidence on the existence of such phenomena exists. Although instability has not been observed in real-world markets, the question of instability is
far from being irrelevant. Perhaps real-world constraints (futures markets and/
or arbitrage in international finance) prevent markets from exploding. Further,
if markets are presumed to be stable, it is nevertheless of real importance to
discern the *process* by which equilibrium is displaced and the manner in which
it is restored. Though the question of market equilibrium is, strictly speaking,
a different matter from that of stability, the adjustment processes of Walras
and Marshall coupled with their analyses of stability and instability force attention on the problem.

"Cobweb" Theorems When a dynamic element is introduced into the
static processes of Walras and Marshall, alternative conditions for stability
must be derived. The so-called cobweb theorem, well known to agricultural
economists since it applies principally to goods with long production processes, is one such model. Lagged-variable models of the cobweb type have
many crucial implications for stability in real-world agricultural markets.[9]

The practical importance of stability in markets has probably been overshadowed by an academic interest in stability. Contemporary economic theorists, following the lead of Walras and Marshall, have demonstrated a persistent interest in discussing the stability properties of their analytical models. It
has not been considered enough to describe a model. Rather, it is important to
show that the model has properties that make it viable and stable. Many of the
most important contributions to modern macroeconomic and monetary theory,
for example, deal with displacement of market equilibrium and the process by
which equilibrium is restored.

---

[9] Evidence indicates that the complexities of cobweb-type models may not have escaped earlier economists of the nineteenth century. (See R. F. Hébert, "Wage Cobwebs and Cobweb-Type
Phenomena: An Early French Formulation," *Western Economic Journal* (December 1973), pp.
394–403.)

Tâtonnement Walras called this rather complex process *tâtonnement*—a groping for equilibrium—and in contemporary analysis his concept has been of consummate usefulness in numerous models of microeconomic and macro-economic behavior. Microeconomic and general-equilibrium theorists such as Nobel Prize winners Sir John R. Hicks and Kenneth Arrow have devoted a great deal of time to such questions as: Is a competitive equilibrium possible, and if there is a displacement, will the system return to equilibrium?

The question of the existence and stability of the equilibrium the economy may be headed toward has been an issue of critical importance in the develop-ment of twentieth-century analysis. Whereas earlier writers (Cournot, for exam-ple) had only hinted at the importance of these topics, Walras and Marshall (par-ticularly the former) made stability an essential part of their analytical systems. From a modern perspective, it was a contribution of high order.

As an interesting historical footnote, both Walras and Marshall claimed pri-ority in the development of stability analysis. The issue of priority was raised in correspondence between Marshall and Jevons (Walras, *Elements,* p. 502, footnote 5). Marshall claimed to have developed the issue of stability in 1873, but as Professor William Jaffé noted, this "development" was little more than suggestive. Certainly, in his privately printed *Pure Theory of Foreign Trade* (1879), Marshall defined stable equilibrium in reference to reciprocal-demand curves (see the discussion of the Mill-Marshall theory of reciprocal demand in Chapter 8). But Walras had done so in print as early as 1874 and therefore clearly had priority in published form.

Far more important than this issue of priority (which is often a very difficult one to settle) is the fact that through the course of the discussion, neither Walras nor Marshall, but particularly the latter, seemed to have had any ap-preciation of the other's analysis. Simple jealously might be a good explana-tion for a debate on priority, but Marshall's failure to understand Walras cor-rectly is something else again. Nevertheless, it was in this aura of dissonance that the two giants of the neoclassical era appeared to perceive each other.

WALRASIAN GENERAL EQUILIBRIUM IN CONSUMPTION AND WALRAS'S LAW

The previous section presented a rather simplistic discussion of Walrasian market analysis. As noted in the introduction to the present chapter, the Walrasian general-equilibrium system is simple in concept but is of some com-plexity when formally expressed.[10] The reduced-form Walrasian equation (see equation [16-1]) for demand is relatively simple to master, for example, but the behavior that underlies it is considerably more complex. The purpose of the

---

[10] Readers unaccustomed to analyzing theories in algebraic terms are advised to skip the fol-lowing discussion. A short summary of general-equilibrium theory may be found in the concluding part of the present section, devoted to Pareto. Unfortunately, in the case of general equilibrium, geometry does not have obvious advantages (over algebra) in facilitating understanding.

following discussion is to analyze the individual behavior that is at the core of Walrasian general equilibrium in consumption. Though too lengthy to include here, a similar analysis of general equilibrium in production could be developed originating in the behavior of the profit-maximizing individual firm.

The basic concepts utilized by Walras in his construction of the general-equilibrium system were those used by Dupuit, Menger, Jevons, and others in the development of utility and demand theory. Whereas these pioneers dealt with utility and demand functions for single commodities, Walras systematically presented a model for the individual's maximization of utility, given all the commodities he or she consumes and a budget constraint. From these choices, the individual's demand and supply functions can be derived.

General Equilibrium in Mathematical Form

Walras's model can be described more fully and clearly with some simple algebraic expressions. The presentation by Walras in the *Elements* is unique and laborious. Lessons 5 through 10 of the *Elements* will reward the most tenacious reader with an understanding of the Walrasian system in the two-trader, two-commodity case. The reader is warned, however, that the graphics and the arithmetic of the "purchase" and "offer" curves developed there are undeniably tedious. In fairness to Walras, it should be noted that these labored developments of a general-equilibrium system are what one would expect of a pioneer. In addition, as Professor Jaffé has indicated, Walras's own knowledge of, and experience in, mathematics was not great (*International Encyclopedia of the Social Sciences*), and this, of course, makes his brilliant conceptual contribution to economic analysis even more astonishing.

Fortunately, Walras's notational system has been revised, and modernized revisions of Walrasian general equilibrium facilitate understanding. First, the utility and *rareté* functions (Walras's term for marginal utility) will be defined, and the concept of marginal rate of substitution will be developed. The individual's budget constraint, income, and endowment are then introduced, and an "optimum bundle" of goods and services for the individual (given his or her budget constraint) is defined. The marginal conditions for utility maximization are derived, and the demand and excess-demand functions are specified. Finally, Walras's law—which states simply that demand is just another way of looking at supply—is related to excess demand. This completes the Walrasian general-equilibrium system.

Utility and *Rareté* The economics of the post-Smithian era would probably be of little interest in a primitive society. In such a society each individual, for the most part, tends to his or her own survival needs and produces only for his or her immediate family. Though the individual must still decide how to allocate production time so as to maximize his or her well-being (or satisfactions), the problem is not nearly so complex as in a more advanced state of society, where specialization occurs in production and exchange. Specialization creates greater interdependence, which, as Adam Smith pointed out, has certain disadvantages. But specialization has one great and overriding advantage in that it leads to an increase in output. Since more goods are always preferred to fewer, an increase in satisfaction will accrue to societies that specialize.

One common assumption in economics concerning people, be they in primitive or in advanced societies, is that they are able to order or rank preferences between alternative bundles of goods and services. The level of the satisfactions that the individual receives from the alternative bundles is ordinarily called the individual's *utility*, but sometimes other words, such as "happiness" or "welfare," are used to denote the same concept. The whole set of tastes or preferences related to the various possible collections of goods and services is called a *utility function*.[11] A Walrasian statement of the individual's utility function may be expressed as

$$u = u(q_1, q_2, q_3 \ldots q_n) \tag{16-5}$$

where u denotes the level of total utility attained by the individual, $u(\ )$ is the functional notation for unknown relations existing between the goods and services consumed by the individual and his or her level of utility, and q_1, q_2, $q_3 \ldots q_n$ represents the quantities of goods and services that the individual consumes per unit of time; q_1 might be a haircut, q_2 might be four compact discs, q_3 might be eight slices of apple pie, and so on. Further, Walras assumed that any addition to the individual's consumption—such as a ninth slice of apple pie—would increase the level of his or her utility.

Walras used the term *rareté* to denote an individual's change in total utility as a result of consuming one more (or less) unit of any good. His intent was to "express the *rareté*, i.e., the intensity of the last want satisfied, as a decreasing function of the quantity consumed" (*Elements*, p. 43). *Rareté*, or marginal utility, is assumed to be always positive, so that with reference to equation (16-5), the *changes* in utility can be written $\Delta u / \Delta q_1 > 0$, $\Delta u / \Delta q_2 > 0$, and $\Delta u / \Delta q_n > 0$. This property of the utility function is called *nonsatiety of wants* in modern economic literature.

Another useful concept is that of a ratio of the marginal utilities of any two goods in the individuals's collection. This ratio is called the *marginal rate of substitution*, and it is simply the individual's internal valuation of any one good in terms of another that would keep his or her level of total utility or satisfaction the same. It can be expressed as

$$V_{ij} = \frac{mu_i}{mu_j} \tag{16-6}$$

which is read as the individual's valuation of any good i in terms of any good j. If, for example, the marginal utility of eggs per dozen to the individual is 10

---

[11] The reader will note that these ideas, albeit in much simpler form, were present in the work of several earlier writers, notably Dupuit and Jevons.

and the marginal utility of haircuts is 5, the marginal rate of substitution of eggs to haircuts is 10/5, or 2. This means simply that the individual can trade 2 haircuts for 1 dozen eggs without altering his or her level of total utility. The marginal rate of substitution declines, moreover, as units of good i (eggs in our example) are added to the individual's consumption relative to good j (haircuts). A moment's reflection tells us why: The marginal utility of eggs *declines* as more eggs are added to consumption relative to consumption of other goods.

Modern economics is, of course, concerned with maximizing behavior. That is, it assumes that an individual will maximize his or her well-being, given the environment the individual faces and the resources at his or her command. If resources are limited, the individual obviously cannot reach the ultimate in satisfaction. He or she is, as economists say, under a budget constraint. Allocating scarce resources so as to maximize utility is identified by the economist as rational behavior.[12]

Goods Endowment in a Mythical Kingdom   Since we are not interested here in considering the Walrasian general-equilibrium system in production, some simplification is required in order to get at Walras's theory of exchange and consumption. In effect, we must assume away all considerations of the production of goods, for to do otherwise would drastically complicate the model we seek to understand. Naturally, it is to be understood that the production half of Walras's model may be integrated with the exchange half—Walras, of course, accomplished the integration in the *Elements*.

In order to isolate a pure exchange economy for investigation, we must imagine an unreal society, say, the mythical island kingdom of Econ. Imagine, furthermore, that the people of Econ are ruled by a wizard who provides all their goods. (This provision takes the place of production; thus, it should be emphasized, the value theory discussed here is being illustrated in a zero-cost world.) The wizard does not provide goods in unlimited quantities, however; rather, he bestows on each citizen an equal endowment of each good every Monday. Assume further that all remaining (unconsumed) goods disappear into thin air the following Sunday night. Thus each individual in Econ is treated in identical fashion, receiving his or her weekly endowment much as the people of Israel received manna in the biblical story. These equal endowments from the wizard may be conveniently expressed as a collection of goods $q_1^e, q_2^e, \ldots, q_n^e$. Though each individual receives an equal amount of each good, the tastes or preferences of each citizen will not be the same. Thus the incentive for trade is present, and over time exchange rates or prices (that is, the

---

[12] It should be noted that many economists are not interested in what the individual's tastes *should* be. Whereas psychology and behavioral sciences study the *formation* of tastes, economics takes the tastes of the individual as given and calls "rational" that behavior which the individual exhibits in allocating his or her scare resources consistently with his or her tastes.

quantity of one good that must be exchanged in order to receive a unit of another good) will be established.

At this point it is convenient to introduce a base good, one in terms of which all other exchange rates may be expressed. Walras called this base good the *numéraire*. It is defined as "the commodity in terms of which the prices of all the others are expressed..." (*Elements,* p. 161). The *numéraire* is usually associated with a monetary unit, although it need not be. Nevertheless, suppose that gold is chosen as the *numéraire*. The value of all other goods (that is, p_1, $p_2,...,p_n$) could then be expressed in terms of gold, and the price of gold would always be unity, since its value is defined in terms of itself. Now the *value* of one of the equal, individual shares may be expressed in terms of the *numéraire*. If we let Y represent this value, then Y is simply the sum of the quantities of each good received by the individual multiplied by that good's price, or

$$Y = p_1 q_1^e + p_2 q_2^e + \ldots + p_n q_n^e = \sum_{i=1}^{n} p_i q_i^e \qquad (16\text{-}7)$$

Each individual will choose an optimum collection of goods, i.e., a utility-maximizing bundle of goods, given the price of each good and his or her budget constraint. Note that the individual is constrained by his or her income, which is the value of the weekly endowment. The individual's utility-maximizing collection may be denoted as $\hat{q}_1, \hat{q}_2,..., \hat{q}_n$, and the value of that collection is simply the sum of the prices of each good times the optimum quantity of it desired, or

$$E = p_1\hat{q}_1 + p_2\hat{q}_2 + \ldots + p_n\hat{q}_n = \sum_{i=1}^{n} p_i\hat{q}_i \qquad (16\text{-}8)$$

E represents the individual's expenditures, and each individual must necessarily limit them to the value of his or her weekly endowment. The budget constraint may therefore be expressed as $E = Y$, or as

$$\sum_{i=1}^{n} p_i q_i^e = \sum_{i=1}^{n} p_i\hat{q}_i \qquad (16\text{-}9)$$

Walras stressed again and again that the individual's demand for goods (E in our example) is but another way of looking at the supply of goods (Y). The act of demanding goods, in other words, presupposes that the individual is also supplying goods of equal value (though not of equal utility).

The Conditions of Utility Maximization   One of the marginal conditions for utility maximization should be well known from our discussions of Menger and Jevons (Chapters 13 and 14). This condition is that, given a budget constraint, the individual consumer will buy goods up to the point where the marginal utilities of all goods consumed per unit of the base good (usually money and thus, "per dollar") are equal. Symbolically, this may be expressed as

$$\frac{mu_1}{p_1} = \frac{mu_2}{p_2} = \cdots = \frac{mu_n}{p_n} \qquad (16\text{-}10)$$

An elaboration of this condition is required, however. Condition (16-10) implies that in order to maximize utility, an *individual's* valuation of each good in terms of the *numéraire* must also equal the *market* valuation of that good in terms of the *numéraire.* If *n̂* represents the *numéraire,* then this condition may be expressed as

$$\frac{mu_1}{mu_{\hat{n}}} = p_1, \frac{mu_2}{mu_{\hat{n}}} = p_2, \ldots, \frac{mu_n}{mu_{\hat{n}}} = p_n \qquad (16\text{-}11)$$

The reasoning behind this condition for utility maximization is explained by Walras for the two-commodity case:

> Given two commodities in a market, each holder attains maximum satisfaction of wants, or maximum effective utility, when the ratio of the intensities of the last wants satisfied [by each of these goods], or the ratio of their *raretés* is equal to the price. Until this equality has been reached, a party to the exchange will find it to his advantage to sell the commodity the *rareté* of which is smaller than its price multiplied by the *rareté* of the other commodity, and to buy the other commodity the *rareté* of which is greater than its price multiplied by the *rareté* of the first commodity (*Elements,* p. 125).

Walras's logic can be illustrated with respect to the relations expressed in equation (16-11). Suppose that, with respect to good 1, the condition does not hold. Specifically, assume that $[mu_1/mu_{\hat{n}}] < p_1$. What this means, assuming that the marginal utilities are constant, is that the individual could obtain p_1 units of the *numéraire* by giving up one unit of good 1. Given that $[mu_1/mu_{\hat{n}}] < p_1$, such a transaction would increase utility by $p_1 mu_{\hat{n}}$ and decrease utility by mu_1. On balance, the individual would experience a positive increase in utility. Ensuing trade, assuming negatively sloped marginal-utility functions, would raise mu_1 and reduce $mu_{\hat{n}}$, bringing the individual's valuation of the commodity in line with the market's valuation.

Walras summarized the general solution of the multicommodity problem after a rather tedious mathematical explanation of the systems of equations. He concluded as follows:

> Thus $m - 1$ prices of $m - 1$ of the m commodities are determined mathematically in terms of the mth commodity which serves as the *numéraire,* when the following three conditions are satisfied: first, that each and every party to the exchange obtain

the maximum satisfaction of his wants, the ratios of his *raretés* then being equal to the prices; second that each and every party give up quantities that stand in a definite ratio to the quantities received and vice versa, there being only one price in terms of the *numéraire* for each commodity, namely the price at which total effective demand equals total effective offer; and third that there be no occasion for arbitrage transactions, the equilibrium price of one of any two commodities in terms of the other being equal to the ratio of the prices of these two commodities in terms of any third commodity (*Elements*, p. 169).

The market guaranteed a solution to the problem through the mechanism of competition. In short, Walras believed that his scientific system had an empirical referent. He viewed himself as having described the solution that competitive forces would establish in the real world.

Walras's Law

An important aspect of Walrasian general equilibrium has come to be known as "Walras's law." The concept, along with the entire Walrasian system, has found much use in contemporary economic models, especially in macroeconomic models and in the analysis of monetary behavior.

Walras's law is related to the concept of excess demand, which we have already discussed in regard to Marshallian and Walrasian stability. The present discussion of excess demand relates the optimum holdings for each good to the prices of all goods and the endowments held by each individual. Specifically, this optimum holding for the individual will depend upon his or her utility function (see equation [16-5]) and upon his or her budget constraint (equation [16-9]). Thus the demand for any good—say, grapes—can be written as

$$\hat{q}_g = h^g(p_i, Y) \tag{16-12}$$

where $h^g(\ )$ is some unknown form that depends upon the individual's utility function.

The individual is a demander, supplier, or nontrader of grapes. The person who supplies at their going price p_g is said to have a negative excess demand or a positive excess supply of grapes. This excess demand for grapes is defined as

$$ED_g = (\hat{q}_g - q_g^e) \tag{16-13}$$

where ED_g is the excess demand for grapes, $\hat{q}_g$ is the desired quantity, and q_g^e is the amount of grapes presented him by the wizard. If the individual wishes to consume more grapes (q_g) than he or she is endowed with (q_g^e), the consumer is termed a "net demander." On the contrary, if $q_g^e > \hat{q}_g$, this consumer is a net supplier. Finally, if $q_g^e = q_g$, the individual is satisfied and does not trade. Since the functional expression for desired holdings of grapes is written $\hat{q}_g = h_g(p_i, Y)$, the excess-demand expression (16-13) may be reduced to

$$ED_g = H^g(p_i, q_g^e, Y) \tag{16-14}$$

where H^g ( ) is a new functional relation between grape demand and price and endowments. Thus we may summarize by saying that the demand for grapes, apple pie, or any other good is functionally related to the prices and endowments facing the individual.

With a bit more arithmetic we can achieve an understanding of Walras's law. Stated simply, it is the proposition that the excess demand for any good depends upon the *sum* of the excess demands for other goods. It can be expressed arithmetically as follows: If the value of the excess demand for the ith good is defined as $p_i ED_i$ and if we sum over all n goods that the individual consumes, expression (16-15) is obtained:

$$\sum_{i=1}^{n} p_i ED_i = \sum_{i=1}^{n} p_i(\hat{q}_i - q_i^e) \qquad (16\text{-}15)$$

The budget constraint (16-9) can be rewritten as

$$0 = \sum_{i=1}^{n} p_i \hat{q}_i - \sum_{i=1}^{n} p_i q_i^e = \sum_{i=1}^{n} p_i(\hat{q}_i - q_i^e) \qquad (16\text{-}16)$$

If the individual is forced to live within his or her budget constraint (within an income, or endowment), the sum of the values of his or her excess demand must necessarily be zero. To put it another way, the individual having excess demands for some goods equal to a given value must have excess supplies of other goods of precisely equivalent values. Equation (16-16) may thus be rewritten as follows:

$$\sum_{i=1}^{n-1} p_i (\hat{q}_i - q_i^e) = - p_n(\hat{q}_n - q_n^e) \qquad (16\text{-}17)$$

Equation (16-17) tells us, in other words, that the sum of the values of the excess demands for all goods *except one* must be equal to minus the value of the excess demand for the other good. Clearly, not *all* the individual's choices are independent (a fact implied by equation [16-17]), since once the individual chooses $n - 1$ goods, a budget constraint determines whether he or she is an excess demander or supplier of the final good. Equation (16-17) expresses Walras's law.

Fundamentally, Walras's law is a manner of expressing basic interrelations in individuals' economic behavior. It is a valuable shorthand tool that expresses the conclusion that, given individual tastes and an income constraint, the excess demands and supplies of all goods must sum to zero. The demands and supplies of goods in real terms, in other words, are not independent.

Interrelations that exist for individuals in their economic activity apply also to consumer behavior in the economic system as a whole. When a production side, including the behavior of profit-maximizing firms, is added, Walrasian general equilibrium describes the entire set of factor and product markets in the economy. Most importantly, Walrasian theory describes the necessary *interconnections* between input and output markets in a competitive, idealized economy. Walras's law in consumption (which we have discussed here) and in production (which has not been discussed in this chapter) is a shorthand expression for describing these interesting and crucial interconnections.

A brief example from contemporary monetary-macroeconomic theory might aid in understanding the usefulness of Walras's law. Professor Don Patinkin, in his book *Money, Interest and Prices,* has attempted an integration of Keynesian and classical monetary and macro theory. He does so by analyzing the economy's aggregate demand and supply sides. The demand side contains an analysis of equilibrium conditions in three markets: the consumption and investment goods market, the money market, and the bond market. Without going into the complexities of Patinkin's meticulous study, these three markets are assumed to be interrelated in the Walrasian sense. That is, price, interest rate, and income variables are connected such that equilibrium (zero excess demand) in any *two* of the markets presupposes, by Walras's law, equilibrium in the third.

At any time, in analogy to our discussion of general equilibrium in consumption (equation [16-17]), the sum of the excess demands (which may, of course, be negative) in two of the markets must equal *minus* the value of the excess demand in the third market. When two markets are characterized by zero excess demand, the third must be in equilibrium also. Thus the aggregate demand of any interrelated economy that contains three sectors may be analyzed using only two. Walras's law has therefore found special use in recent macro and monetary models.[13]

On any reasonable scale, Walras's theory of general equilibrium was a contribution of the highest order of importance for the development of twentieth-century economic analysis. Yet this was not the only service Walras performed for economics. After a brief detour to review the contributions of his able successor at Lausanne—Vilfredo Pareto—we shall turn to another of Walras's most important contributions, namely, his tireless efforts to help professionalize the modern discipline of economics.

PARETO, GENERAL EQUILIBRIUM, AND WELFARE ECONOMICS

Vilfredo Pareto (1848–1923) was an early adherent of Walrasian general equilibrium, and he utilized that framework to explore and establish several areas of economic analysis, including a brilliant contribution to methodology (see

---

[13] This statement is not meant to imply that modern *micro* theorists have not made good use of Walrasian general equilibrium. Nobel Prize winner Sir John R. Hicks, for example, used Walras's approach in his important reformulation of value theory.

Notes for Further Reading at the end of this chapter). In his *Cours d'économie politique* (1896–1897) and his *Manuel d'économie politique* (1906), Pareto explored the conditions in exchange and production that are the foundations of modern welfare economics. Unlike the English tradition (Marshall-Pigou) in welfare theory, which was cast in a partial-equilibrium setting, Pareto built upon Walrasian general equilibrium. Although Pareto did not derive all the conditions for a global welfare maximum, those relating to production and consumption bear his name.

Pareto Maximum in Consumption

Pareto utilized F. Y. Edgeworth's consumer "indifference curves" (*Mathematical Psychics*, 1881) to show that in the case of a fixed supply of goods, a welfare optimum in exchange would occur when no individual could benefit from trade without injuring someone else. A more specific formulation of Pareto's point might be given by identifying a marginal rate of substitution. For any individual the marginal rate of substitution between any two commodities—say, *x* and *y*—measures the number of units of *y* that must be sacrificed per unit of *x* so that the level of satisfaction remains the same. (The marginal rate of substitution is the slope of the indifference curve.)

A Pareto optimum in exchange requires that the marginal rate of substitution between any pair of consumer goods be the same for *any* two individuals (selected at random) who consume both goods. If this is not the case, then one or both parties could gain from exchange. Exchange is Pareto optimal, in other words, as long as at least one of the parties to the trade is made better off without leaving the other party worse off.[14] Once trade reaches a point where one party can benefit only at the expense of another, any further statements concerning exchange require additional specification. In fact, a whole area of modern welfare economics centers on the attempt to specify the conditions under which a value-free answer can be given when policy changes involve gainers and losers. It is perhaps too early to decide whether the quest for a value-free social welfare function is illusory or not, but it is certain that Pareto, at least implicitly, inaugurated the attempt. He did so, moreover, by applying ordinal utility analysis to Walrasian general equilibrium.

Paretian Factor Substitution

Analogous to the consumer's marginal rate of substitution, a *marginal rate of technical substitution* between any two inputs may be defined. The marginal rate of technical substitution measures the number of units of an input *i* that

---

[14] Traditionally, Paretian welfare theory is presented with the aid of an Edgeworth "box diagram," which is a useful graphical technique for illustrating the relations between two economic activities with fixed inputs. See C. E. Ferguson, *Microeconomic Theory,* 3rd ed. Homewood, Illinois: R.D. Irwin, 1972, pp. 467–473, for a lucid exposition of general equilibrium and welfare economics utilizing box diagrams. See also Chapter 22.

can be substituted for another input *j* in such a way as to maintain a constant level of output. Thus, as with an indifference curve, one might construct a curve (convex to the origin) depicting the manner in which one input may be substituted for another while output is held constant. In microeconomic theory, this curve is called an *isoquant,* and its slope is the marginal rate of technical substitution.

Although Pareto did not develop isoquants, he did state the conditions necessary for the optimum distribution of resources, given a *fixed supply* of inputs. The Pareto condition is that the marginal rate of technical substitution between any pair of inputs must be the same for all producers (chosen at random) who use both inputs. If this were not the case, reallocation of inputs could result in larger total output without a reduction in the output of any single commodity. An optimum further implies that each factor receives a wage equal to the value of its marginal product, a state of affairs that occurs under perfect competition (see Chapter 18 for a partial-equilibrium demonstration of this point). Analysis of this issue is a staple in undergraduate courses in microeconomic theory.

Welfare and Competition

There are many serious problems connected with Pareto's development of welfare theory, including the possibility of deriving a nonnormative social-welfare function. The assumption of nonaugmentable supplies of inputs and outputs is another severe limitation. In addition, the whole model is of *static* equilibrium, thus omitting the effects of uncertainty and a host of other factors. Beyond these problems, however, Pareto's welfare theory, which rests upon the maximizing behavior of individuals, adds a great deal of support to the assertion (made by Adam Smith) that a freely competitive system leads to an optimum of social welfare. Consumers, in an attempt to maximize satisfaction, are led to trade until their marginal rates of substitution are equal. Producers, in their attempt to maximize profits, are led to hire inputs up to the point where their marginal rates of technical substitution are equivalent. Pareto's demonstration, assuming that "externalities" do not exist (see Chapter 15), places the case for competition on a more objective basis. His emphasis upon the *effects* of maximizing behavior is in sharp contrast to the somewhat metaphysical premises of many other developers of competitive theory. Consequently, Pareto helped to hasten the acceptance of Walras's general-equilibrium analysis.

WALRAS'S CORRESPONDENCE AND ITS IMPACT
ON THE DISCIPLINE OF ECONOMICS

Léon Walras was a true believer in the system that he developed, and with the fervor of a religious zealot, he attempted to proselytize economists and policymakers all over the world to the general-equilibrium "faith." Between 1857 and 1909, he communicated with virtually every major economist in the world.

The definitive collection of Walras's extraordinary correspondence was published in 1965 under the editorship of Professor William Jaffé. With meticulous care and incredible scholarship, Jaffé selected, edited, and commented upon almost eighteen hundred of Walras's letters (from a still larger correspondence) dealing with economic analysis, with the profession of economics, and with the enormous array of topics that interested Walras. A search through the correspondence—which spans fifty years and five different languages—reveals the many sides of Walras: his petty debates over the priority of theoretical ideas; his general contempt for English economists (especially Mill and Marshall); his personal lobbying for a Nobel Peace Prize in recognition of his scientific discoveries and their alleged application to society and social problems; his evaluation of theoretical criticism of his system; and his polemics on mathematical economics as the mainspring of social reform.[15] Mainly, however, we find Walras marketing, advertising, and hawking the general-equilibrium system—here lobbying shamelessly with journal editors for summaries of his system to be printed, there on the offensive, attacking partial-equilibrium analysis.

As revealed in the *Correspondence,* Walras was willing to make significant sacrifices in the course of spreading his conception of economic science. He was concerned not only that the errors he perceived in others' writings be corrected but also that his own place be established in the profession. In a letter of April 11, 1893, to his student Vilfredo Pareto, Walras noted that it would give him

> ...great pleasure (if I am still there to enjoy it) to have others eventually recognize that only Gossen, Jevons, and I have conceived the degree of utility as the central element in valuation and that I, alone, have demonstrated the *proportionality* of the final degrees of utility to all exchanges, prices, or values to the state of general equilibrium and production. And as for Dupuit, Menger, Wieser, Böhm-Bawerk, Auspitz and Lieben, Marshall, Edgeworth, and *all the rest,* they have confused price and the final degree of utility through identification of the curve of utility and the demand curve (*Correspondence,* II, letter 1123).

Walras, moreover, was wont to mask his anglophobe sentiments. With the single exception of William Stanley Jevons, who with Walras's help added a large appendix on mathematical writings in economics to the 1879 edition of his *Theory of Political Economy* (see Chapter 14), Walras had very little good to say about traditional British political economy or economists. He never missed an opportunity to take a swipe at Ricardo, Edgeworth, or Marshall, the latter being regarded in the "English tradition." In a letter (May 25, 1877) to his friend Jevons, he even noted that J. S. Mill "is as poor a logician as he is a mediocre

---

[15] A favorite subject of Walras the socialist was land nationalization. The revenues derived therefrom, he argued, could be used to finance government expenditures.

economist''—in spite of the incredible pains, Walras added, that Mill took to avoid giving proofs.[16]

In more general terms, Walras's correspondence is a shimmering mirror of a most unusual man, his era, and the birth of the international cultivation of the science of economics. Although some of the issues taken up in the *Correspondence* seem trifling, they are nevertheless issues that helped shape the modern profession of economics. Walras's unflinching attempt to sell economics as a science was a seminal force in molding the character of the discipline in the twentieth century. The barriers of national interests and separate languages tended to fall away with the increasingly mathematical character of the science. More than any other single economist, Léon Walras established and ''sold'' an analytical method whose cultivation transcended national boundaries. How he did so—with incessant but often rewarding debates and arguments—is in itself fascinating, but is not really the main point. Walras was an economist whose analytical invention placed him among the giants of the field.

Walras in Retrospect

Walras's most original contribution to economics was his mathematical specification of a general-equilibrium system. Such a system stresses the vast and intricate web of interrelations in a modern economy. It may be contrasted with partial-equilibrium analysis, which ignores such interrelations in order to focus on specific firms or individuals. Before Walras, Cournot had pointed out that a complete and rigorous solution of the problems relative to specific parts of the economic system requires consideration of the entire system and its interconnections. Even before Cournot, Quesnay had presented a clear vision of the economy consisting of many interconnected parts. But Cournot thought the problem of general equilibrium was beyond the reach of mathematical analysis, and Quesnay never got as far as a mathematical specification of microeconomic relations. Walras's genius lay in his grasp of the problem anticipated by Quesnay and Cournot and in his demonstration that the problem was solvable, at least in principle.

It is generally held by most economists that Walras's contribution was one of form more than of substance. Clearly there is an architectonic quality to Walras's general-equilibrium system. The pattern of the system is precise, but Walras did not undertake the vast statistical research necessary to provide concrete solutions to each of the equations in the system. There are, in fact, tremendous problems in specifying the relevant equations in precise terms and in gathering data on such a large scale. The recognition of such problems is not meant to diminish the importance of Walras's contribution. Himself a mediocre mathematician, Walras nevertheless demonstrated the power of mathemat-

---

[16] Walras, in fairness, was only agreeing with Jevons's own assessment of the value of Mill's writings on logic (see *Correspondence*, letter 337). Jevons was ready to identify Richard Cantillon, and not Adam Smith, as the first great developer of liberal economic doctrine!

ics in solving complex theoretical problems. He made it possible, moreover, to see that equilibrium of the household and the markets for final goods was consistent with equilibrium of the firm and factor markets. The attempts of Jevons and the Austrians to find a simple causal relation between marginal utility, input prices, and goods prices seem naive and unsophisticated by comparison.

NOTES FOR FURTHER READING

Up until his death in 1980, William Jaffé was the leading authority on the life and writings of Léon Walras. In addition to his translation of Walras's *Elements*, Jaffé collected and edited the voluminous *Correspondence* (see References), a product that ranks as one of the great contributions to research in the history of economic thought. Virtually every major and minor figure of the neoclassical period is presented or discussed in the *Correspondence*. Jaffé's comments on the *Correspondence* and the writers who people it are invaluable and exhaustive. It is a must, not only for any serious researcher on Walras but also for almost any research on any facet of neoclassical economics. Some idea of the content of the *Correspondence* may be obtained from the following review articles: S. C. Kölm, "Léon Walras' Correspondence and Related Papers: The Birth of Mathematical Economics," *American Economic Review,* vol. 58 (December 1968), pp. 1330–1341; D. A. Walker, "Léon Walras in the Light of His Correspondence and Related Papers," *Journal of Political Economy,* vol. 78 (July/August 1970), pp. 685–701; and V. Tarascio, "Léon Walras: On the Occasion of the Publication of His Correspondence and Related Papers," *Southern Economic Journal,* vol. 34 (July 1967), pp. 133–145.

At the time of his death, Jaffé was engaged in writing a comprehensive biography of Walras, a project cut short by his demise. Jaffé's literary leavings were collected by his student Donald Walker and published posthumously; see William Jaffé, "The Antecedents and Early Life of Léon Walras," *History of Political Economy,* vol. 16 (Spring 1984), pp. 1–57, which devotes more attention to the influence of Auguste Walras on his more famous son. In a series of articles stretching over an academic lifetime, Jaffé has also explored many aspects of Walras's economics. See, for example, William Jaffé, "A. N. Isnard, Progenitor of the Walrasian General Equilibrium Model," *History of Political Economy,* vol. 1 (Spring 1969), pp. 19–43. Also by the same author, see "The Birth of Léon Walras's *Elements*," *History of Political Economy,* vol. 9 (Summer 1977), pp. 198–214; "Léon Walras's Role in the 'Marginal Revolution' of the 1870's," *History of Political Economy,* vol. 4 (Fall 1972), pp. 379–405; "The Walras-Poincaré Correspondence on the Cardinal Measurability of Utility," *Canadian Journal of Economics,* vol. 10 (May 1977), pp. 300–306; "The Normative Bias of the Walrasian Model: Walras versus Gossen," *Quarterly Journal of Economics,* vol. 91 (August 1977), pp. 371–388; and "Léon Walras: An Economic Adviser Manqué," *Economic Journal,* vol. 85 (December 1975), pp. 810–823.

For the last decade, Donald Walker has been carrying on where Jaffé left off. See, for example, D. A. Walker, "Is Walras' Theory of General Equilibrium a Normative Scheme?" *History of Political Economy,* vol. 16 (Fall 1984), pp. 445–469, in which Walker raises anew a question posed by Jaffé in 1977; same author, "Walras and His Critics on the Maximum Utility of New Capital Goods," *History of Political Economy,* vol. 16 (Winter 1984), pp. 529–554, in which Walker attributes to Walras an adumbration of the marginal conditions for a Pareto optimum in the market for capital goods; and same author, "Walras's Theory of the Entrepreneur," *De Economist,* vol. 134 (1986), pp. 1–24, in which Walker tries to rescue Walras from "the misunderstandings and decades of neglect" surrounding his treatment of the entrepreneur in economic theory. For even more Walker on Walras, see "Walras's Theories of *Tâtonnement,*" *Journal of Political Economy,* vol. 95 (August 1987), pp. 758–774; and "Edgeworth versus Walras on the Theory of *Tâtonnement,*" *Eastern Economic Journal,* vol. 13 (April/June 1987), pp. 155–165.

Outside of the Jaffé-Walker circle, see Milton Friedman, "Léon Walras and His Economic System," *American Economic Review,* vol. 45 (December 1955), pp. 900–909, for an evaluation of Walras's work on the occasion of the first English translation of the *Elements;* David Collard, "Léon Walras and the Cambridge Caricature," *Economic Journal,* vol. 83 (June 1973), pp. 465–476, for an assessment from within the Marshallian tradition; and R. J. Rotheim, "Equilibrium in Walras's and Marx's Theories of Capital Accumulation," *International Journal of Social Economics,* vol. 14 (1987), pp. 27–43, for the socialist perspective.

Walras's theory of money has not drawn as much attention as other aspects of his thought, but see S. G. F. Hall, "Money and the Walrasian Utility Function," *Oxford Economic Papers,* vol. 35 (July 1983), pp. 247–253; and R. Cirillo, "Leon Walras' Theory of Money," *American Journal of Economics & Sociology,* vol. 45 (April 1986), pp. 215–221.

A brief nontechnical discussion of Walras and Marshall on stability is provided by A. Leijonhufvud, "Notes on the Theory of Markets," *Intermountain Economic Review,* vol. 1 (Fall 1970), pp. 1–13. Milton Friedman has also proposed a resolution of the Walras-Marshall stability paradox in his *Price Theory: A Provisional Text,* rev. ed. (Chicago: Aldine, 1962), p. 93. Peter Newman's *The Theory of Exchange* (Englewood Cliffs, N.J.: Prentice-Hall, 1965), pp. 106–108, argues that the Marshall-Walras models are not comparable because the Marshallian stability conditions were designed for production theory, while the Walrasian ones were devised for a theory of exchange. Akira Takayama presents a nonmathematical summary of Newman's argument, enlarges on it, and remarks in *Mathematical Economics* (Hinsdale, Ill.: Dryden Press, 1974), pp. 295–301, that both "Marshall and Walras clearly recognized that there are these two types of adjustments and they both used them in the proper context."

A number of nontechnical expositions of Walrasian general equilibrium exist. J. R. Hicks's "Léon Walras," *Econometrica,* vol. 2 (October 1934), pp. 338–348, may still be read profitably. A graphical description of general equilibrium and Paretian welfare theory is contained in C. E. Ferguson, *Micro-*

economic Theory, 3d ed., chaps. 15 & 16 (Homewood, Ill.: Irwin, 1972). A more advanced and thorough discussion is presented in Don Patinkin, *Money, Interest and Prices* (see References). On Walras's capital theory as the basis for a theory of economic growth, see W. D. Montgomery, "An Interpretation of Walras's Theory of Capital as a Model of Economic Growth," *History of Political Economy,* vol. 3 (Fall 1971), pp. 278–297. Some comparative questions of method are discussed by A. N. Page, "Marshall's Graphs and Walras's Equations: A Textbook Anomaly," *Economic Inquiry,* vol. 18 (January 1980), pp. 138–143; and D. Pokorny, "Smith and Walras: Two Theories of Science," *Canadian Journal of Economics,* vol. 11 (August 1978), pp. 387–403.

Maurice Allais and Talcott Parsons give an overview of Pareto and his thought in "Vilfredo Pareto," *International Encyclopedia of the Social Sciences.* Pareto's *Manuel* (the French edition was published in 1906) has been translated; aspects of the translation have been disputed, however. See W. Jaffé, "Pareto Translated: A Review Article," *Journal of Economic Literature,* vol. 10 (December 1972), pp. 1190–1201; and the exchange between J. F. Schwier, Ann S. Schwier, Jaffé, and Vincent Tarascio in the *Journal of Economic Literature,* vol. 12 (March 1974), pp. 78–96. Vincent Tarascio has published widely on Pareto's scientific methodology and welfare theory. See, in particular, two works by Tarascio: *Pareto's Methodological Approach to Economics: A Study in the History of Some Scientific Aspects of Economic Thought* (Chapel Hill: The University of North Carolina Press, 1968) and "Paretian Welfare Theory: Some Neglected Aspects," *Journal of Political Economy,* vol. 77 (January–February 1969), pp. 1–20. Also by the same author, see "Vilfredo Pareto and Marginalism," *History of Political Economy,* vol. 4 (Fall 1972), pp. 406–425; "Pareto on Political Economy," *History of Political Economy,* vol. 6 (Winter 1974), pp. 361–380; and "Pareto: A View of the Present through the Past," *Journal of Political Economy,* vol. 84 (February 1976), pp. 109–122. For a condensed but useful overview of the development of welfare economics, see R. F. Hébert and R. B. Ekelund, "Welfare Economics," John Creedy and D. P. O'Brien (eds.), *Economic Analysis in Historical Perspective* (London: Butterworth & Co., 1984), pp. 46–83.

REFERENCES

Allen, William R. "Stable and Unstable Equilibrium in the Foreign Exchanges," *Kyklos,* vol. 7 (1954), pp. 395–408.

Jaffé, William. "Léon Walras," in *International Encyclopedia of the Social Sciences,* vol. 16. New York: Macmillan, 1968, pp. 447–552.

Pareto, Vilfredo. *Manual of Political Economy,* Ann S. Schwier (trans.) and Ann S. Schwier and Alfred Page (eds.). New York: A. M. Kelley, Publishers, 1971 [1906].

Patinkin, Don. *Money, Interest and Prices,* rev. ed. New York: Harper & Row, 1965.

Walras, Léon. *Elements of Pure Economics,* William Jaffé (trans.). Homewood, Ill.: Irwin, 1954 [1874].

——. *Correspondence of Léon Walras and Related Papers,* William Jaffé (ed.), 3 vols. Amsterdam: North-Holland Publishing Company, 1965.

PART FIVE

TWENTIETH-CENTURY
PARADIGMS

JOHN MAYNARD KEYNES   KARL MARX   ALFRED MARSHALL   WILLIAM STANLEY JEVONS   ADAM SMITH

17

THORSTEIN VEBLEN AND AMERICAN INSTITUTIONAL ECONOMICS

INTRODUCTION

Important criticism of economic orthodoxy was not indigenous to the nineteenth century, although as we saw in Chapters 10 and 11, the landscape of nineteenth-century thought was strewn with vociferous and sometimes shrill critics of classical and early neoclassical theoretical economics. Like theory, criticism possesses a tradition of its own—a tradition that is alive and well in contemporary assessments of capitalism and the capitalist process.

The present chapter features the "institutional economics" of Thorstein Veblen (1857–1929), a study constituting one of the most important twentieth-century installments of the ongoing critique of received theoretical economics. Veblen, who was and remains the progenitor of the only uniquely American school of economics, contributed a critical "Darwinian" view of the capitalist process, but a mood of large-scale dissatisfaction had already surrounded British neoclassical economics for forty years before Veblen penned his critical works. In very much the same spirit as their German counterparts, British historicists were touting a method of economic study that featured the search for broad laws of historical development, use of inductive empirical generalizations rather than deductive logic, and the general irrelevance of economic science as it was then constituted. Veblen was certainly sympathetic to some of these views, but he went far beyond the British historicists in terms of methodology and cohesiveness. Indeed, it is essentially Veblen's methodological contribution that makes his criticism of capitalism lasting and singularly important. The economics of Veblen and some of his followers (including John Kenneth Galbraith) is thus the primary feature of this chapter, but the stage must be set for Veblen's achievement with a brief discussion of the leading

449

British historicists' "case against economic method." While some of these writers surely had an impact upon Veblen's institutionalism, it will become obvious that he was, intellectually, very much his own man. Veblen's preconceptions were unique, but in his case, as we shall discover presently, they also produced creative understanding of social and economic relations to an astonishing degree. First, however, we must consider the possible origins of some of Veblen's preconceptions.

NINETEENTH-CENTURY BRITISH HISTORICISM

As late as the 1840s, intellectual conditions in England had decidedly solidified around Ricardian economics, a situation that strongly contrasted to the intellectual "anarchy" on the Continent (see Chapter 10). Eric Roll has noted that "The legacy of Ricardo was considered sacrosanct; and even as late as 1848 John Stuart Mill regarded himself in matters of theory as little more than a proponent of pure Ricardianism." J. R. McCulloch, James Mill, and Harriet Martineau (who penned moralistic fairy tales replete with "lessons" from classical economics) turned out to be quite effective popularizers of what they thought to be the Ricardian legend. The charisma surrounding Ricardian abstraction had grown to formidable proportions.

Ironically, however, a cohesive historicist revolt originated on British soil. The Reverend Richard Jones, sometimes regarded as the first institutionalist, published *An Essay on the Distribution of Wealth and on the Sources of Taxation* in 1831. In it he complained that the matrix of the Ricardian analysis was far too narrow to be of practical use. He felt that economic assumptions should be *historically determined* and empirically justifiable. In his words, the Ricardians "confined the observations on which they founded their reasonings to the small portion of the earth's surface by which they were immediately surrounded." But the voice of Richard Jones was drowned in a sea of Ricardian dogma. Methodological criticism of classical economics nevertheless resurfaced in England as the century wore on.

Bagehot, Spencer, and Darwin

The many-faceted editor of the conservative periodical *Economist* and author of *Lombard Street*, Walter Bagehot, espoused the heretical cause in an essay that appeared in the *Fortnightly Review* in 1876 (the *Fortnightly* became the unofficial mouthpiece of the historicists). Although Bagehot was an early follower of Ricardo, his writing is filled with concern for interrelating institutional structures with economic theory. Bagehot found economic theory guilty of the pretentious and fallacious claim of general applicability. This theory, he charged, was particularly useless in discussing economic development in countries outside Great Britain, since the institutional backdrop was seldom the same. Again the indictment was that the major assumptions of economic science were unverified and that the resultant theories were too abstract to be of practical value.

This growing intellectual despair at the alleged uselessness of classical postulates was due in large measure to philosophical ferment. Herbert Spencer, himself subeditor of the *Economist* from 1848 to 1853, was partly responsible for this agitation, although he in no way condoned it. Spencer's first love was biology, but his writings clearly spelled out the relation between biological and social evolution, even before Darwin. He sketched this relation as follows:

> A social organism is like an individual organism in these essential traits: that it grows; that while growing it becomes more complex; that while becoming more complex, its parts acquire increasing mutual dependence; that its life is immense in length compared with the lives of its component units... that in both cases there is increasing integration accompanied by increasing heterogeneity (*Autobiography*, II, pp. 55–56).

Along with other social sciences, economics was being interpreted in the light of this type of analysis. The fast-declining atomism of firms and their movement toward monopoly and oligopoly structures could be explained in terms of Spencer's concept of integration, while increasing economic interdependence manifested itself in the growing division of labor and burgeoning British trade.

In 1859 Darwin's *Origin of Species* dropped into the philosophical stew. To the orthodox economist, and of course to the extremely individualistic Spencer, Darwin's work merely reiterated what had been known all along about the "inevitable" forces of laissez faire. But the British historicists, eclectic in their appraisal of Spencer and Darwin, enlisted biological evolution in the service of their theories of institutional and social development. Bagehot even applied Darwinian principles of natural selection to the political struggles of nation-states. And, importantly, one of the strongest and most important foundations of Veblen's institutional economics—his theory of change—finds its origin in the Spencer-Darwin conceptions of "process" and "evolutionary and quasi-random change." But, Bagehot notwithstanding, the British historicists did not apply Spencerian-Darwinian evolutionist principles to economic institutions in any significant and cohesive manner. Rather, they looked to other "deterministic" theories of change in forming their concepts of economics.

Comte, Ingram, and Cliffe-Leslie

A most important determinist-philosophical influence, that of the French positivist philosopher Auguste Comte, was very much in vogue among certain British intellectuals at this time. Comte's direct influence was felt in England by the historicists, especially by the classical scholar and historical economist, John Kells Ingram.

Ingram, who had ubiquitous interests, accepted much more than his mentor's views on social and economic progress; indeed, he was the leading British expositor of Comtian thought, going to the extremes of writing sonnets on the "religion of humanity." The "social dynamics" of Comte, which impregnate Ingram's *History of Political Economy* (British historicism's only full-length critique of economic theory), are far from the modern economic meaning of the term and farther still from the Darwinian conception of evolution. The Comtian conception is one of a necessary and continuous movement of humanity toward a teleological and predictable end. In Comte's view, social dynamics, relating as it did to the development of society, derives its basic data from history and is therefore the science of history. Ingram eagerly applied these principles to what he conceived to be the proper method of economic inquiry. In his *History,* published in 1888, he maintained that:

> These general principles [Comte's] affect the economic no less than other branches of social speculation; and with respect to that department of inquiry, they lead to important results. They show that the idea of forming a true theory of the economic frame and working of society apart from its other sides is illusory (pp. 193–194).

The application of Comtian principles to the social sciences was not new in England. J. S. Mill attempted it in Book IV (on social reform) of his *Political Economy,* but Ingram, speaking for the historicists, declared that this "appears to us one of the least satisfactory portions of his work."

Other orthodox economists were much more critical of the Comtian infiltration. J. E. Cairnes, while acknowledging that political economy "has no panacea to offer for the cure of social evils" and that "practical application of scientific principles are...not the proper fruit, but the accidental consequence of scientific knowledge," nonetheless thought that the subordination of political economy to the more general field of sociology would be a barren endeavor, at least until cognate social sciences were brought up to a like stage of advancement. But even Cairnes was forced to lament that this "important field of economic research [empirical and historical] has as yet produced but scanty fruit" ("M. Comte and Political Economy," p. 602).

Critics aside, the historicists used the Comtian and other deterministic philosophy of change as a starting point for their assault on abstraction. British writings were often more vitriolic in their critique of classicism than those of the Germans. T. E. Cliffe-Leslie, for example, joining in the chorus of wages-fund criticisms of the period, categorically attacked wanton deduction. Leslie presented a case for "positive economics" regarding statistical verification of all laws and assumptions as crucial to social theory. The formal incorporation of empiricism with economic science is seen as having the great advantage of forcing the economist to use much neglected and ever-changing facts. The alternative was metaphysics. Unverified abstraction was attacked as alien to the very conception of a social science.

Some historicists simply felt that the existing body of theory was untenable. Cliffe-Leslie proposed a purge of all heuristic postulates from the science, hoping to clear the air for new "theory." Arnold Toynbee, uncle of the famous historian by the same name, not so unguarded in his appraisal of existing abstraction, proposed a symbiotic relation between history and theory and felt that "Ricardo becomes painfully interesting when we read the history of his time" (*Lectures on the Industrial Revolution*). Toynbee abandoned the attempt to discover a universal body of economic truths, however, feeling that economics is, of necessity, relativistic. Theories would be derived by placing political economy on a broader base, i.e., as a branch of sociology. Ingram underlined this point in an analogy comparing society to the human body and the economist to the physician:

> The physician who had studied only one organ and its function would be very untrustworthy even in the therapeutics of that organ. He who treats every disease as purely local, without regard to the general constitution, is a quack; and he who ignores the mutual action of the physique and the moral in disease, is not properly a physician, but a veterinary. These considerations are just as applicable, mutatis mutandis to the study of society, which is in so many respects kindred to biology ("The Present Position and Prospects of Political Economy," p. 50).

In the historicist paradigm, economics was conceived as a science, but its abstractions were not to be a priori, and deduction was assigned a minor role. Theory would be derived not only by induction but also by historical processes. Economists would find the material for their studies by instituting a comparison of the successive states of society in order to discover the laws of social affiliation—a process similar in principle to the comparison of organisms at different degrees of development. Society and social facts could not be studied apart from their history. History was therefore seen as the mainspring from which the science of economics would emerge.

The Impact of British Historicism

The work of the British historicists had noteworthy practical effects. Although the attempts to make economics a branch of sociology and to derive a body of theory via historical processes failed, the writings of Cliffe-Leslie, Ingram, Bagehot, and Toynbee had a positive influence on major British theorists of the day. W. Stanley Jevons (see Chapter 14), largely under the influence of Cliffe-Leslie, qualifiedly repudiated the laissez faire principle, judging the orientation of the historicists to be "indispensable"; but he also asserted that the deductive method was a necessary adjunct to economic science. Indeed, it was an element in the very process of induction. Jevons grew to believe that statistical verification was required to rescue economics from public hostility as well as from the more basic level of idle speculation. Although he was in accord with the general methodological prescriptions of Cliffe-Leslie and Ingram, and although he thought that their criticism could "hardly fail to overcome in the end the prestige of the false old doctrines," Jevons was suspicious of the attempt to supplant orthodox theory with the historical approach. To do so, he thought, would be to make of political economy a barren and occult science.

In 1890 the great neoclassical economist Alfred Marshall (see Chapter 15) lauded the work of the historicists, finding it "one of the great achievements of our age; and an important addition to our real wealth." Somewhat later he affirmed his alliance to the "new generation" of economists, those holding to a less didactic and modified orthodoxy. In many respects, Marshall's *Principles* reflects the growing concern of economists over the issue of social reform, and his "evolutionary" approach to economics may be said to be a direct result of his brush with historicism. John Neville Keynes, father of John Maynard and the foremost methodologist of the day, under the impetus of the British school found that the "study of economic history plays a distinct and characteristic part in the building up and perfecting of political economy," although Keynes, along with Jevons and Marshall, thought that the study of history and the "inductive" method should actually supplement economic theory. The truth is, of course, that neoclassical *theoretical* economics ultimately served as the training ground for economists in England, and economic history (with the emphasis on the noun) largely became as it has in the United States, a subfield of general economics.

THORSTEIN VEBLEN AND AMERICAN INSTITUTIONALISM

Conditions within the economics profession in late-nineteenth-century America were markedly different from those in Europe. Eclecticism had always been the hallmark of American economists. From Thomas Jefferson and Alexander Hamilton to Henry Carey and Henry George, English and continental ideas were filtered through the uniquely American experience and institutions. Pragmatism permeated both philosophy and economics well into the twentieth century. Classical and neoclassical *theoretical* analysis consequently never had the hold upon American economists that it did on English economists.[1] American economists, such as Henry Carey and Francis A. Walker, turned classical theoretical ideas on their heads in order to fit them, they believed, to the situation in the United States. In such a freewheeling intellectual environment, the ideas of historicists were able to take root. Richard T. Ely and E. R. A. Seligman, who were (along with the more orthodox Walker) the organizers of the American Economic Association in 1886, were sympathetic to the historicist cause (Ely was educated in Germany under the aegis of historicists). In many respects, these writers represented a left wing of the AEA and its professional economists. J. K. Ingram himself, in the preface to Ely's *Introduction to Political Economy,* suggested a growing acceptance of historicist views, declaring that "A more humane and genial spirit has taken the place of the old dryness and hardness which once repelled so many of the best minds from the study of economics" (Ely, *Introduction to Political Economy,* pp. 5–6). Into this very receptive milieu stepped a formidable American critic of received economic orthodoxy, Thorstein Veblen. Although influenced by myriad philosophical and intellectual forces (including those of the histori-

---

[1]American Nobel laureate Kenneth Arrow reports that, as late as his graduate student days a Columbia University (1940–1942), no required course in price theory was offered, thoug Veblenian economics was prominently displayed. Further, Arrow notes, "The corrosive skepti cism of Veblen towards 'received' theory had, belatedly and even posthumously, underminded th never-very-secure hold of neoclassical thought on the teaching of American economics' ("Thorstein Veblen as an Economic Theorist," p. 5).

cists), Veblen's ideas on economists may nevertheless be clearly stamped "Made in U.S.A."

Veblen: The Critic's Life and Preconceptions

Thorstein Bunde Veblen was born in Wisconsin of Norwegian ancestry (his first name means "son of Thor") and at the age of eight moved to a large farm in Minnesota. In 1874 he entered Carleton College, a religious training school, where he quickly demonstrated his brilliance along with a calculatingly critical attitude toward everything (including religion). Veblen also studied at Johns Hopkins University, where he was greatly influenced by J. B. Clark, and at Yale University, where he received his Ph.D. in philosophy in 1884. Unable to secure an academic position, he returned to his father's farm, where for seven years he was a voracious and eclectic reader of social science literature, including economics. In 1890 Veblen entered Cornell University as a graduate student, but he soon joined the faculty of the University of Chicago, where he became editor of the *Journal of Political Economy*.

During his twelve-year tenure at Chicago and afterward (he was dismissed in 1904 for sexual indiscretions with female undergraduates), Veblen became the most visible and highly regarded social and economic critic of his time. In numerous journal contributions and books, including the exceedingly popular *Theory of the Leisure Class* (1899), he assessed problems in then-existing social institutions and scathingly criticized classical and neoclassical economic analysis. Veblen's prestige as a thinker and academician (he was, by all accounts, an awful teacher) was not sufficient to overcome his flagrant and frequent violations of social mores and his biting attacks on businessmen supporting the university. He was asked to leave.

After leaving Chicago, he took positions at Stanford University, at the University of Missouri, and at the New School for Social Research, never rising above the rank of assistant professor. In 1927 he returned to California, where he died on August 3, 1929, a few months before the great stock market crash (which in a sense he had predicted and probably would have enjoyed a great deal). In the ultimate epitaph, his student Wesley C. Mitchell summed up Veblen's life:

> A heretic needs a high heart, though sustained by faith that he is everlastingly right and sure of his reward hereafter. The heretic who views his own ideas as but tomorrow's fashion in thought needs still firmer courage. Such courage Veblen had. All his uneasy life, he faced outer hostility and inner doubt with a quizzical smile. Uncertain what the future had in store, he did the day's work as best he might, getting a philosopher's pleasures from playing with ideas and exercising "his swift wit and his slow irony" upon his fellows. However matters went with him, and often they went ill, he made no intellectual compromises ("Thorstein Veblen," in *What Veblen Taught*, p. *xlix*).

While the facts of Veblen's life are relatively simple, Veblen's mind and "preconceptions" were not. Throughout his very productive life Veblen was uncannily able to view the real world and the world of ideas (circa turn-of-the-century America) from the "outside." He once attributed the intellectual and scientific predominance of European Jews to their *lack* of contemporary preconceptions and to their initial immersal in a culture stamped "B.C." Like them, and perhaps because of the essentially Nordic cultural background of his youth, Veblen was able to view society in much the manner of a pathologist approaching an autopsy. He was insatiably curious about what makes social and economic processes "tick" and especially about the mode and method of how societies—as the totality of cultural and technological institutions—change.

The formative forces of Veblen's own preconceptions were numerous. His views on human nature were shaped by behaviorism and, specifically, by theories of instincts and habits. His view of human nature, as we shall see, was in strong contrast to the rationalistic and utilitarian conceptions of the classical and neoclassical writers. The Spencer-Darwin view of social and biological evolutionary change had a primary impact upon Veblen's "world view," as did the instrumentalist philosophy of William James. Veblen also much distrusted mathematics and statistics as tools of science, sarcastically labeling those who resorted to such calculations as "animated slide-rules." (The term most frequently heard today is "computer jockeys.")

Veblen's thoughts on particular subjects are often hard to decipher. Scattered and piecemeal statements, often contradictory, are dispersed throughout his many publications. An appreciation of his "system" is not rendered easier by the fact that polemical speculation, personal prejudices, gratuitously normative statements, cynicism, and outright jokes pepper his writings. His brilliant control of the English language has sent more than a few of his readers running to the dictionary. At base, the study of Veblen is akin to a Ferris wheel ride. It matters not where one gets on, for the rider always returns to the same spot. The essentials of Veblen's theory were formed early and remained virtually unchanged throughout his life's work. Indeed, one might say that his later works were merely extensions and elaborations of a central thesis set forth earlier. We now turn to that thesis, beginning with Veblen's views on human nature and his ideas on the method of economics.

Human Nature and Economic Method

The classical writers, as we have seen in Part 2 of this book, placed people in the role of the rational calculators of pleasures and pains. The "invisible hand" or the so-called natural law kept people on course and in general promoted the greatest good for the greatest number in society. Veblen railed against this belief as superficial nonsense. Humans, in Veblen's view, are significantly more complex creatures led by particular instincts and characterized by instinctive behavior and habits.[2] People aren't "lightening fast calculators"

---

[2] Veblen's instinct-habit psychology and its interactions with human propensities of thought has been criticized as one of the less satisfactory parts of his work. We do not take these matters up in this chapter, but the interested reader may consult Notes for Further Reading at the end of the chapter.

of pleasures and pains but rather are *curious* beings who, *by nature,* hit upon new ways of doing things. In sum, people are creatively curious and are creatures of propensities and habits.

In an anthropological study of human culture, Veblen concluded that certain instincts, such as the "instinct of workmanship" (the title of one of his most interesting books) applied to all humans in all societies. Veblen found that the material circumstances surrounding humans composed the most significant factor in determining their propensities and preconceptions about the world. We may view the matter in the following sequence. The foundation of a world view, whether of an individual or of society (the accurate reflection of the mass of individuals), rests primarily upon the particular material (and thus technological) circumstances in which humans find themselves. These, in turn, give rise to relations between humans and property, humans and philosophy, humans and religion, humans and the legal-political system, and so on. A *world view* is thus premised upon the material conditions of any particular age. Institutions—ways of doing things, thinking about things, and distributing the rewards for work, etc.—arise to support a set of material circumstances. Most beings are indelibly stamped with a set of preconceptions unique to their particular time and place, and most particularly, these preconceptions rest upon a given technological system. Veblen's posited interactions between technological institutions, on the one hand, and ceremonial institutions, on the other, constitute the mainsprings of change in his system.

All this should sound somewhat familiar to readers of Marx (see Chapter 11). Marx's view of human nature and the impact of technology upon culture was in part analogous to Veblen's, but with an essential difference—Marx's view was pre-Darwinian, deterministic and teleological (purposive), leading to an ultimate transformation of society into the socialist state. Veblen's theory of cultural and institutional change follows the Darwinian theory of biological evolution in which "ends" are not exactly predictable. The application of evolutionary principles to human culture was, in Veblen's view, even more critical since human *biological* evolution and mental capacity had been essentially *fixed* for thousands of years, while cultural evolution has progressed at a much more rapid pace. The impress of evolution is almost exclusively cultural, in other words. Thus the principal underlying difference between Marx and Veblen is the theory of change each advanced. This is an essential difference between Veblen and practically *all other* economic writers as well, including the classical writers. In order to get a fuller appreciation of this important concept of economic and cultural change, we must examine the critical differences that Veblen drew between the "proper" method of economic study and the one adopted by practically everyone else.

"Matter of Fact" versus Animistic Preconceptions

In a long and brilliant critical essay entitled "The Preconceptions of Economic Science" (first published in the *Quarterly Journal of Economics* in 1899–1900),

Veblen attacked the philosophical foundations of economic orthodoxy. He argued that Adam Smith was, in part, possessed of a matter-of-fact, empirical preconception, though he was guilty of fostering an "animistic" view of the world in economic science. In an animistic preconception, the ultimate ground of reality is a design of God, a teleological natural outcome. Thus we find Smith (and other classical economists) discussing a *natural* or *equilibrium* price, which, when disturbed, would return through an assumed natural order (see Chapter 5). In Veblen's words:

> The animistic preconception enforces the apprehension of phenomena in terms generically identical with the terms of personality or individuality. As a certain modern group of psychologists would say, it imputes to objects and sequences an element of habit and attention similar in kind, though not necessarily in degree, to the like spiritual attitude present in the activities of a personal agent. The matter-of-fact preconception, on the other hand, enforces a handling of facts without imputation of personal force or attention, but with an imputation of mechanical continuity, substantially the preconception which has reached a formulation at the hands of scientists under the name of conservation of energy or persistence of quantity. Some appreciable resort to the latter method of knowledge is unavoidable at any cultural stage, for it is indispensable to all industrial efficiency. All technological processes and all mechanical contrivances rest, psychologically speaking, on this ground. This habit of thought is a selectively necessary consequence of industrial life, and, indeed, of all human experience in making use of the material means of life. It should therefore follow that, in a general way, the higher the culture, the greater the share of the mechanical preconception in shaping human thought and knowledge, since, in a general way, the stage of culture attained depends on the efficiency of industry ("The Preconceptions of Economic Science," p. 141).

According to Veblen, the utilitarianism of Bentham and Mill simply substituted hedonism (utility) for achievement of purpose as a ground for legitimacy. The result was that utilitarian philosophy made economics a science of wealth, in which the individual is inert, because human nature and institutions are given and values are therefore eliminated. Economics became (and remained, Veblen thought) a deterministic and categorical discipline that attributed all good things (good = normal = right) to a functionless and static, but beneficent, competitive system. The outcomes of all interferences with, or departures from, this competitive system, based upon an incessant quest for monetary gain, were predictable, and the effects of the removal of interferences were equally predictable.[3] One of Veblen's persistent themes was that the instincts and habits emerging from pecuniary hedonism characterized American society both on *the supply and on the demand sides*. Absentee ownership and conspicious consumption and leisure were the expected responses to a pervasive utilitarian preconception that created a "consumption economy." (This matter is investigated in greater detail below.)

---

[3] This type of competitive system was described by numerous neoclassical writers, including the Austrians and Alfred Marshall. But it must be remembered that in the case of Wieser, and particularly of Marshall, strong undercurrents of dissent from this method were in evidence.

From a methodological point of view Veblen's critique may be summarized as follows. First, he argued that the orthodox neoclassical view of the economic system, and the theoretical superstructure it supported, was sterile and essentially useless. But he did *not* argue, as is sometimes supposed, that neoclassical analysis was invalid, given its assumptions. One difficulty was its simplistic view of human nature—Bentham's concept of "pecuniary rationality"—rather than an instinct-habit conception, and another was its outmoded concept of change. Second, in a positive vein, Veblen based his own theory upon (1) an implicit hypothesis that historical events (social, economic, and political) are determined and best described by *group* characteristics formed by the sum of instinct-habitual human behavior, and (2) a Darwinian (evolutionary), not a deterministic, view of change as the appropriate tool for dealing with social and economic phenomena.

Veblen's assumption regarding group behavior is common to many dissident writers, including most of the radicals and socialists examined in Chapters 10 and 11. His Darwinian view of change, an insight of genuine originality, is based upon his belief in a *causal sequence* or process. Consider a movement from some situation A to some state B. Given some displacement from, say, competitive equilibrium at state A, the determinist would argue that when the factor causing the displacement was removed or permitted to impact upon the situation for a long period of time, equilibrium either would be restored or would change in some predictable way. That is, assuming that fundamental economic data (utility functions, costs, institutions, etc.) do not change from A to B, the *effects* of a single disturbing change may be analyzed. (See the Marshallian method of *ceteris paribus* discussed at length in Chapter 15.) In Veblen's concept of causal sequence, the mere cessation of interference with the system or the introduction of a single "permanent" change at state A will not leave the outcome the same as if no interference had taken place. Moreover, the effects of single changes at A will not be predictable. Because tastes, technology, and institutions are *constantly* changing, states A and B are not comparable in any meaningful way. Orthodox economic analysis, since it employs a deterministic method, requires that the underlying data of the system remain the same over the period of analysis. Veblen, on the other hand, described a system of constant and ineluctable change. To him, economics was most accurately described as a process, or as a "proliferation."

Veblen's Positive Analysis: The Interaction of Ceremony and Technology

Veblen featured these methodological concepts and his instinct-habit psychology in the core of a positive theory of economic change. While his analysis may be applied to specific institutions, as we shall see, the overall design of his theory incorporated a grand view of economywide institutional change. Figure 17-1 will be helpful in describing Veblen's concept of economic change.

Veblen developed an evolutionary "science" of economics based upon

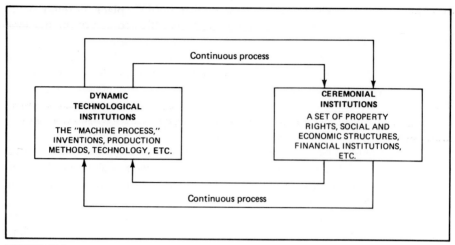

FIGURE 17-1
The intersection of technological and ceremonial institutions are based on unchangeable characteristics of human nature and the anthropological and historical processes.

ever-changing institutions. Roughly, he identified two groups of institutions, both shown in Figure 17-1: "technological" and "ceremonial." The existence and characteristics of these dichotomized sets of institutions rest upon so-called unchangeable characteristics of human nature and the anthropological and historical processes these characteristics have produced.

What prime factors have been central in shaping these institutions through time? Veblen thought that human instincts were a root of human institutions, and he specifically identified what he called the instincts of workmanship and humans' innate "idle curiosity" as the source of dynamic technological institutions. Crucial to this conception is the "machine process," or technology, which gives rise to a characteristic set of property rights, social and economic structures, certain habits of thought, and so on. The machine process is the *dynamic* force in society, whereas the companion set of ceremonial institutions tends to be the relatively static result of a given *state* of the machine process. Thus the social and economic institutions characteristic of a "long primitive stage" of society are inextricably bound to the nature (and growth) of technology over that period. Feudal social and economic institutions were as essentially characteristic of the technology extant over the Middle Ages as contemporary "ceremonial" institutions were characteristic of the more advanced production methods of the nineteenth and twentieth centuries.

Two aspects of the institutional process described in Figure 17-1 must be expanded. Specifically, (1) the relations between the two "types" of institutions are not quite as simple as described above, and (2) certain forms of social and economic behavior, as well as mental "preconceptions" associated with them, were associated with humans throughout their development but were *amplified* under a given "machine process." In the first place, ceremonial institutions, including property rights, not only were the product of the machine process of any given time but also impinged upon technology, thwarting or encouraging it as the case may be. This interrelation could last only over a "short" period of time (perhaps several hundred years), however, since in the long run a technology based upon the human ability to invent and upon human idle curiosity was *dynamic*. Stated differently, ceremonial institutions could constrain the machine process, but only temporarily. Technological institutions, in the *long run*, would shape social and economic relations.

A second point concerns the interrelations between instincts and preconceptions. Certain preconceptions or behaviorial characteristics may be common to humans *throughout* their entire development but may be emphasized by a particular state of technology. Thus, as we shall see, conspicuous consumption and leisure, while very much in evidence over a certain stage in development, rest upon certain *general* behaviorial characteristics of humans typical to them since the beginning of time. Humans are born with certain instincts and with a set of preconceptions about the way in which the world works. For example, emulation is a behaviorial characteristic of humans, and such activity is most in evidence in societies dominated by a pecuniary culture. Likewise, a pecuniary culture is the *product* of a technology that permits and even fosters the divorce between ownership and management, between proprietary accumulation and the actual productive process, between "business" and enterprise.

How did Veblen view this process at the beginning of the twentieth century? As we shall see below, the process he envisioned generated an indigenous business cycle within capitalist economies, but the institutional framework itself was always the product of past and present interactions of ceremonial and technological institutions. Ceremonial institutions surrounding private property, like economic science itself, were increasingly characterized by a love of money. Advancing technology permitted a separation of production from finance. "Making goods" became very different from "making money." In this well-known distinction Veblen noted that, after the industrial revolution, the functions of owner-producers and managers became increasingly separated. Businessmen and *captains of finance* attempted to subvert the progress of technology, reducing output and increasing pecuniary returns through monopoly contrivances. Making money, not goods, became the object of the game. According to Veblen, acquisition of money through subversion and "warlike traits" were characteristic of businessmen. (Veblen's infamous attacks on the role of businessmen in commerce were pitiless.) At the same time workers and engineers—those close to the machine process—were rejecting old technology and developing new (and presumably cheaper) means of production. The outcome of the dynamic process of technological change and the cyclical forces produced by it will be considered later in this chapter. An important aspect of the social process must be considered first—Veblen's famous teachings on conspicuous consumption.

Conspicuous Consumption: A Digression on Sociology and Economics

Veblen's most famous and subtle idea juxtaposed psychology, economics, and sociology.[4] In *The Theory of the Leisure Class* (subtitled "An Economic Study of Institutions") Veblen launched a very detailed study of the practice of consumption and of the formation of tastes.[5] Neoclassical economists had assigned *given* utility functions to individuals and assumed that each expenditure purchased a utility independent of the utility from any other expenditure, either by the same consumer or by any other. (In more formal jargon, utility functions, thus conceived, are said to be additive.) Veblen's conception of taste formation challenged this very simple view, arguing implicitly that a study of the formation of tastes and consumption patterns was an *essential* part of the economic process and that the neoclassical writers were off base in their simplistic assignment of a given utility function to each individual. In his well-known characterization of their view, Veblen argued:

> The hedonistic conception of man is that of a lightning calculator of pleasures and pains, who oscillates like a homogeneous globule of desire of happiness under the impulse of stimuli that shift him about the area, but leave him intact ("Why Economics Is Not an Evolutionary Science," p. 389).

As a practical matter, however, Veblen recognized the prime importance of higher consumption to the maintenance of aggregate demand in a pecuniary economy. Moreover, he viewed a complex theory of consumption as an inextricable part of the ceremonial institutions of capitalism. But his view was rooted in a theory of *pecuniary emulation* rather than in that of simple utility maximization.

In Veblen's conception, the instinct to emulate others was second in strength only to the instinct of self-preservation. In his lengthy anthropological study of the "emulatory instinct" (*Theory of the Leisure Class*, pp. 22–34), Veblen argued that, early in the history of humankind, property acquisition became the conventional basis for social esteem. Initially acquired through plunder, over a long transition in human development wealth acquired *passively* becomes "more honorable" than gains made through predatory efforts. In addition to the "honorifics" of passively acquired wealth, a person's status is determined by how well his or her holdings square with those of an immediate peer group and with the group immediately above the person. In the crux of his argument Veblen noted that:

> In any community where goods are held in severalty it is necessary, in order to his own peace of mind, that an individual should possess as large a portion of goods as

---

[4] The idea of "conspicuous consumption" did not originate with Veblen, having been discussed at some length during mercantile times by Bernard de Mandeville and later in the classical period by John Rae. Veblen brought the concept to its highest expression, however.

[5] Critics of academic economists have often accused them of enjoying "the leisure of the theory class."

others with whom he is accustomed to class himself; and it is extremely gratifying to possess something more than others. But as fast as a person makes new acquisitions, and becomes accustomed to the resulting new standard of wealth, the new standard forthwith ceases to afford appreciably greater satisfaction than the earlier standard did. The tendency in any case is constantly to make the present pecuniary standard the point of departure for a fresh increase of wealth; and this in turn gives rise to a new standard of sufficiency and a new pecuniary classification of one's self as compared with one's neighbours (*Theory of the Leisure Class,* p. 31).

Nonsatiety is as much a part of Veblen's theory of consumption as it is of the neoclassical one. "More is better than less" in both paradigms. But in Veblen's theory of pecuniary emulation, the human basic "instinct of workmanship" becomes compacted into a straining for pecuniary achievement, which itself takes on still another important aspect. In the striving for pecuniary achievement productive work becomes a mark of infirmity and leisure becomes evidence of pecuniary strength. Thus a *leisure class* emerges in all stages of culture, but its ultimate expression takes place in a "quasi-peaceable" stage of society (such as Veblen's turn-of-the-century America).[6] Leisure itself becomes a consumption good, and conspicuous consumption and conspicuous leisure are thus two sides of the same coin. Although there is an elite "leisure class," no class in society is exempt from such strivings.

The bulk of Veblen's book is composed of wide-ranging (and largely sociological) applications of this bold generalization. With profound insight he extended his theory to such matters as the consumption of "immaterial goods by leisure-class gentlemen—quasi-academic, quasi-scholarly pursuits, awards, and trophies" that stand in evidence of unproductive leisure. Gift giving, fashion, the leisure consumptions of middle-class wives, the place of athletics, manners, and higher learning are all ingeniously built into Veblen's conception.[7] The entire book should not be missed, but Veblen's economic conclusion is that conspicuous consumption is a waste of goods and conspicuous leisure is a waste of time. Just what Veblen would do about these matters is not clear, but the avoidance of productive work and the enjoyment of conspicuous waste were part and parcel of contemporary society as he saw it. They were institutions, explainable, but regrettable.

While Veblen's brilliant analysis of consumption cannot be said to have per-

---

[6] Veblen tells in his anthropological study of Polynesian chiefs who, "under the stress of good form, preferred to starve rather than carry their food to their mouths with their own hands," and of a certain French king who died through an excess of moral stamina in the observance of good form. Veblen relates that "In absence of the functionary whose office it was to shift his master's seat, the king sat uncomplaining before the fire and suffered his royal person to be toasted beyond recovery. But in so doing he saved his Most Christian Majesty from menial contamination" (*Theory of the Leisure Class,* pp. 42–43.)

[7] Among other Veblenian gems is his treatment of children as conspicuous waste, i.e., as a consumer good. Says Veblen: "The conspicuous consumption, and the consequent increased expense, required in the reputable maintenance of a child is very considerable and acts as a powerful deterent. It is probably the most effectual of the Malthusian prudential checks" (*Theory of the Leisure Class,* p. 113).

meated twentieth-century orthodox analysis, it has been incorporated by degrees into both macroeconomic and microeconomic discussion. A major attempt at reconciliation with neoclassical analysis has been made by Harvey Leibenstein, who studied interdependent utility functions and demand curves. In his 1950 article "Bandwagon, Snob, and Veblen Effects in the Theory of Consumers' Demand" Leibenstein identified a "Veblen good" as one whose utility derived not only from the direct use of the good but also from the price paid for it. Thus a conspicuous price is the price that a consumer *thinks* that other people think he or she paid for a commodity. It is this price that determines a good's "conspicuous consumption utility." Quantity demanded may then be regarded as a function of a good's money price, P, and its *expected* conspicuous price, P', as in Figure 17-2 (adapted from Leibenstein). Alternative demand curves for consumers may be derived by changing the money price on the assumption that some expected conspicuous price is constant. Thus, demand curve D_1 is derived by assuming that expected conspicuous price P_1 is constant, and varying the money price. In a perfect market with perfect information, equilibrium occurs when expected conspicuous price and actual real price are equal, i.e., where $P_1 = P'_1$, $P_2 = P'_2$, and so forth. If the expected conspicuous price increases, the demand curve shifts to the right for every money price. Alternative possible equilibriums may then be traced out as points *A, E, F* in Figure 17-2, yielding an *upward-sloping* Veblenian demand curve (not to be confused with the Giffen good of orthodox analysis).

A *Veblen effect* may be isolated, moreover, by supposing a decline in price from equilibrium at P_2 to P_1. In the absence of any changes in expected conspicuous price, quantity demanded would expand along demand curve D_2 from Q_0 to Q_2. But when expected conspicuous price falls to P'_1, output thereby declines by an amount Q_2Q_1. Thus the pure price effect is *positive*, Q_0Q_2, and the Veblen effect is *negative*, Q_2Q_1, producing a net negative effect on quantity of Q_0Q_1. Price reduction of a Veblen good *may* produce a reduction in quantity if the Veblen effect outweighs or overbalances the price effect. The point of this discussion is that although the consumption concepts propounded by Veblen are complex and subtle, at least one form of his idea may be utilized within the neoclassical framework of microeconomics.

Economic Change, Capitalism, and the Future

In a number of studies, including the *Theory of Business Enterprise* (1904) and a set of essays entitled *The Engineers and the Price System* (1921), Veblen enlarged upon his theory of institutional change under capitalism. In the process, he spelled out a theory of the business cycle and a prognosis for the capitalist system.

Veblen saw economic and social change as the result of the interaction of technological and ceremonial institutions. This interaction is made more concrete by identifying the two institutions with certain groups in the process of change. Specifically, Veblen identified absentee owners, "captains of indus-

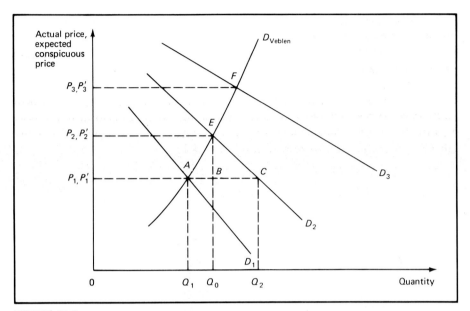

FIGURE 17-2
As the expected conspicuous price rises from P'_1 to P'_2 to P'_3, the demand curve shifts to the right, from D_1 to D_2 to D_3. Tracing out the alternative equilibriums, A, E, F yields an upward-sloping Veblenian demand curve.

try,'' corporate financiers, investment bankers, and businessmen as part of the ceremonial process, while technicians, engineers, and certain workers were part of the technological process. Originally, the functions of directly overseeing the "machine process" and the management of the firm were one. This melding of functions created the preconditions for maximum production, which was Veblen's goal. The two functions were divorced, however, as the pecuniary aspects of culture became predominant and as specialized knowledge grew apace. Veblen described this process:

> ...a new move in the organization of business enterprise has come in sight, whereby the discretionary control of industrial production is shifting still farther over to the side of finance and still farther out of touch with the requirements of maximum production. The new move is of a twofold character: (a) the financial captains of industry have been proving their industrial incompetence in a progressively convincing fashion, and (b) their own proper work of financial management has progressively taken on a character of standardized routine such as no longer calls for or admits any large measure of discretion or initiative. They have been losing touch with the management of industrial process...(*Engineers and the Price System,* p. 41).

At bottom, then, the businessman (financier, captain of industry, etc.) is interested in keeping aggregate profits as high as possible. In order to accomplish this objective, he or she may either restrict output in monopoly fashion and/or lower production costs. According to Veblen, businessmen had in the main followed the former practice because (among other reasons) it required less familiarity with the workings of the machine process.

Business interests thus have chosen to restrict output rather than to reduce the amount of income flow to the "vested interests" (stockholders, investment bankers, etc.). They are interested in "making money" rather than in "making goods," which should be the end of economic activity in Veblen's scheme of things. Due to the sole interest of making money, businessmen mismanage resources and even sabotage the technological-productive process to keep profits high.

Technicians, engineers, and workers "close to the machine process" are generally imbued with a different habit of mind. Their goal is to encourage and devise means and machines for maximizing real output. Though they work for the businessmen-corporate financiers, Veblen argued that they were becoming increasingly aware of the utter wastes of business enterprise. Veblen pointed to several developments affecting this state of affairs. But it was the industrial experts, not the businessmen, who finally began to criticize this businesslike mismanagement and neglect of the ways and means of industry:

> ...two things have been happening which have deranged the régime of the corporation financier: industrial experts, engineers, chemists, mineralogists, technicians of all kinds, have been drifting into more responsible positions in the industrial system and have been growing up and multiplying within the system, because the system will no longer work at all without them; and on the other hand, the large financial interests on whose support the corporation financiers have been leaning have gradually come to realize that corporation finance can best be managed as a comprehensive bureaucratic routine...(*Engineers and the Price System*, pp. 44–45).

Engineers and other industrial experts were thus to assume a role in reordering the system of production, a role that may be better integrated into Veblen's theory of the business cycle.

Veblen, like Marx (see Chapter 11), believed that business cycles were *endogenous* to capitalism and for many of the same reasons. While Veblen did not attempt to juxtapose business cycles with a labor theory of value, he explained recession and prolonged depressions in much the same way as Marx. There were two basic factors leading to recession, according to Veblen: (1) banker uncertainty after a period of expansion and new capitalization of industry and (2) technological displacement by new and more efficient inventions and processes. In the course of a business boom, businesses accumulate debt as business capitalization continues apace. The banker-lender becomes uncertain as to repayment and begins to "call in" loans (or not renew them). The underlying capital structure (possibly due to maturity structure) is unable to meet banker demands, and as more and more uncertainty develops, the entire system proves unsound and recession takes hold of the economy.

A second recession scenario involves the technological displacement of old firms by new firms. Business firms capitalize at some point in time, but new cost-lowering inventions are later adopted by new competing firms. Rates of return are thereby driven down on the older assets, causing lower-than-anticipated profits or, at the limit, bankruptcies. Investment is reduced, and the psychology of recession leads to a downturn of business activity.[8] Thus, depression results both from instabilities in the financial system and from technological displacement caused by new invention. After a depression phase, the cycle "bottoms out" as the overhead burden is "worked off." Financial expansion takes place along with increases in employment and new capital investment. Rising prices and overexpansion occur, once more precipitating a new cycle.

A number of aspects of the Veblenian cycle are of interest. In the first place, Veblen characterized the expansion phase of the cycle as one of overproduction and overcapitalization. Overproduction is the result of an explicit *underconsumption* argument in Veblen's conception of the cycle. Joining such underconsumptionists as Malthus before him and J. M. Keynes after him (see Chapter 19), Veblen believed that the business cycle was exacerbated by the saving and investment motives of financiers and owners of business enterprises. Though the instinct to emulate and to consume conspicuously was operative in all classes, Veblen apparently thought it insufficient to maintain aggregate demand. Underconsumption and the psychological effect of falling prices and redundant capital were the factors leading to prolonged recession.

A second interesting feature of the recession phase of the Veblenian cycle is the nature of the businessman's attempt to avert the crisis. Veblen believed that declining profit rates led to business concentration and to other forms of "sabotage." Consolidations of industry took place in order that reductions in total capitalization could be avoided. Thus, after progressive cycles, capitalist industry became more and more consolidated in exactly the same manner as premised in Marx's laws of "increasing concentration" and the "declining rate of profit" (see Chapter 11).

Still other forms of sabotage take place. In an argument that is clearly anticipatory of an important contemporary idea (see Chapter 24) Veblen charged that businessmen would attempt to "capture" the government's regulatory apparatus and use it for orderly and organized sabotage against the public. Veblen saw through the incestuous relation between government and business in the matter of external trade restrictions and tariffs:

> Where the national government is charged with the general care of the country's business interests, as is invariably the case among the civilized nations, it follows from the nature of the case that the nation's lawgivers and administration will have some share in administering that necessary modicum of sabotage that must always go into the day's work of carrying on industry by business methods and for business purposes. The government is in a position to penalize excessive or unwholesome traffic. So, it is always considered necessary, or at least expedient, by all sound mer-

---

[8] Contemporary writers have amplified Veblen's point and argued that initial investment problems caused by anticipated technological innovations lead to government regulation or to "administered controls" (see Notes for Further Reading).

cantilists, as by a tariff or by subsidies, to impose and maintain a certain balance or proportion among the several branches of industry and trade that go to make up the nation's industrial system (*Engineers and the Price System,* pp. 18–19).

In a brilliantly incisive passage Veblen turned his "capture theory" loose on internal regulation and restrictions:

> Of a similar character, in so far that in effect they are in the nature of sabotage— conscientious withdrawal of efficiency—are all manner of excise and revenue-stamp regulations; although they are not always designed for that purpose. Such would be, for instance, the partial or complete prohibition of alcoholic beverages, the regulation of the trade in tobacco, opium, and other deleterious narcotics, drugs, poisons, and high explosives. Of the same nature, in effect if not in intention, are such regulations as the oleomargarine law; as also the unnecessarily costly and vexatious routine of inspection imposed on the production of industrial (denatured) alcohol, which has inured to the benefit of certain business concerns that are interested in other fuels for use in internal-combustion engines; so also the singularly vexatious and elaborately imbecile specifications that limit and discourage the use of the parcel post, for the benefit of the express companies and other carriers which have vested interest in traffic of that kind (*Engineers and the Price System,* pp. 20–21).

Veblen thus saw, correctly, that the aim of much regulation was the protection of vested interests at the expense of the public interest.[9] That is, the formation of legalized cartels legitimized monopolies at the public expense.

The Future of Capitalism

These examples of sabotage constituted what Veblen called *a conscientious withdrawal of efficiency* by business. All such withdrawals attempt to subvert the productive process, i.e., to reduce output to the most profitable levels. This scarcity was, of course, accompanied by business cycles of increasing severity. In Veblen's scheme, the representatives of technological institutions could be expected to resist the imbecile activities of businessmen. But from where would the resistance come, and what sort of institutions would triumph?

In Marx's scheme, propertyless workers developed a class interest to challenge the propertied bourgeosie, but not in Veblen's. Organized labor, in Veblen's view, exercised its *own* conscientious withdrawal of efficiency in order to keep its returns above the "competitive level" earned by the "common man." The American Federation of Labor (AFL) was a frequent target.

---

[9] The government's perversions of the system did not end with the "real goods" sector. Veblen originated a common twentieth-century-radical complaint against the Federal Reserve System by charging that the "process of pooling and syndication that is remaking the world of credit and corporation finance has been greatly helped on in America by the establishment of the Federal Reserve System....That system...has very conveniently left the substantial control in the hands of those larger financial interests into whose hands the lines of control in credit and industrial business were already being gathered...." (*Engineers and the Price System,* pp. 50–51). How many times since 1921 has the Fed been accused of favoring big business interests at a high cost to workers and small owners and investors?

Veblen considered American labor organizations, and specifically the AFL, to be one of the vested interests always ready to do battle for its own privilege and profit (*Engineers and the Price System*, p. 88). The AFL leadership dominated the politics of the organization, but what of the rank-and-file workers? "The rank and file assuredly are not of the kept classes, nor do they visibly come in for a free income. Yet they stand on the defensive in maintaining a vested interest in the prerogatives and perquisites of their organization. They are apparently moved by a feeling that so long as the established arrangements are maintained they will come in for a little something over and above what goes to the common man" (*The Vested Interests and the Common Man*, p. 165).

Both business and *organized* labor were in cahoots to subvert the productive process, so how could change representing the ascendance of technological interests develop? For Veblen, engineers and industrial managers were the key. Though these types represented less than 1 percent of the population, Veblen believed they could alter the industrial order of finance capitalism. (Presumably, socialism of some form would result, but just what that order would be is unclear from Veblen's writings.) Engineers and other industrial-production personnel were trained largely at public expense, and they alone would be competent to run the system. Although the nature of the evolutionary (or possibly revolutionary) struggle is unclear, Veblen often hinted that nonaligned workers, the "common man" (and even the rank and file), were becoming more cognizant of the profitable abuse of technology perpetrated by business and organized labor. Some type of socialism was the likely result, but Veblen was short on definite predictions of the outcome of this process. Marx could predict within his system, but Veblen could not since he consistently maintained an evolutionist's outlook on the prospects of capitalism. Thus, the outcome of Veblen's profound study of institutional interactions was not clear, and in the end he could only speculate. His intriguing speculation was that capitalism, and specifically American capitalism, was at the turning point:

> In effect, the progressive advance of this industrial system towards an all-inclusive mechanical balance of interlocking processes appears to be approaching a critical pass, beyond which it will no longer be practicable to leave its control in the hands of businessmen working at cross purposes for private gain, or to entrust its continued administration to others than suitably trained technological experts, production engineers without a commercial interest. What these men may then do with it all is not so plain; the best they can do may not be good enough; but the negative proposition is becoming sufficiently plain, that this mechanical state of the industrial arts will not long tolerate the continued control of production by the vested interests under the current businesslike rule of incapacity by advisement (*Engineers and the Price System*, p. 58).

Veblen's Economics: A Brief Assessment

Veblen's prognostication that society was about to explode certainly appeared to come true in 1929. Although the causes of the onset and the severity of the great depression are in debate, there is no debate concerning the extent of the financial collapse and the human and material unemployment that followed in its wake. Was this the "critical pass" Veblen spoke of in referring to the probable collapse of the capitalist system? In order to answer the question, Veblen's analysis of the capitalist system must be viewed from both the theoretical and the practical side.

First, consider Veblen's theoretical scenario. The stock market crash of 1929 and the depression that followed did not bring on an "age of engineers" or an end to the price system of resource allocation and distribution. Veblen failed to perceive that self-interested behavior would have extended to *any* group of individuals in control of the productive process. Engineers and the "common man" were not "philosopher kings" any more than businessmen, financiers, and organized labor were. The ascendance of the engineers would simply have created new "vested interests" in money-making. Institutional changes occurred in American capitalism after the depression but they were not the result of the development of a new engineering power elite.

Further, in Veblen's analysis, engineers, or some central group, would emerge to *maximize production* without regard to prices in a type of socialist system. But, empirically, no communistic or socialistic state has survived in the twentieth century without some recourse to a price system. Prices (or shadow prices) have often been found to be necessary *payments* in socialist systems in order to obtain efficient allocations of resources. Profits, rents, and other factor payments may not be necessary receipts, however, and may be taxed away by socialistic central planners. Veblen and Marx were both naive in their understanding of markets. To date nothing has proved superior to prices as providers of economic information in the marketplace.

From a more practical point of view, Veblen underestimated the ability of the system to adjust. His profound hatred of businessmen led him to the erroneous belief that virtually all output markets were characterized by monopoly or oligopoly. Veblen never appreciated the fact that real competition constrains the attempted "withdrawal of efficiency" by businessmen in most instances. In addition, Veblen neglected the role of government and the legal system in addressing problems of social costs and externalities. For good or evil, the government instituted numerous interventions to alter income distribution in the post-1930s era, interventions that have sometimes acted as a political filter between "vested interests" and the "common man."

The economic critique of Thorstein Veblen cannot itself be criticized or dismissed as easily as his speculations concerning the future of capitalism. Veblen's critique of orthodox economic method and his theory of institutions must command the serious attention of economists. While parts of Veblen's theory of instincts and of propensity formation are of questionable merit, it is clear that he was (unlike Marx) attempting to build a theory of human behavior outside the utilitarian mold. Further, he was attempting the development of a theory of property rights and other concerns of contemporary economists, especially in the area of economic development.

Much of Veblen's writing is of a sociological and quasi-philosophical nature, but his ideas are especially relevant to economics. While the Veblenian paradigm has never substituted for the usefulness of neoclassical economic analysis (as perhaps Veblen thought it should), it is not necessary to choose one or the other. The long-run institutional studies of Veblen may be employed as a useful supplement to short-run price theoretical analysis. Surely there is room for discussion within the economics profession along the lines of Veblen's "grand vision." If for no other reason, Veblen may be read for the gainful reminder that economics is a *social* science, not a mere branch of mathematical inquiry.

SECOND- AND THIRD-GENERATION VEBLENIANS

The fields of Veblenian thought, unlike those of Adam Smith and Alfred Marshall, were not so easily cultivated. Although it may be said that Veblen had a *theory* of economic and social development, there was far less specificity and cohesiveness about his work than, say, the neoclassical paradigms of Alfred Marshall or Léon Walras. Moreover, whereas Marx was orderly in arranging his (often obscure) ideas, Veblen was not. A research program for future scholars is difficult to flesh out of his turgid, rambling prose. In addition, as noted in the introduction, Veblen wore different "hats," sometimes that of the economic scientist, sometimes that of the iconoclastic polemicist and social critic. Thus, some of the theoretically inclined followers of Veblen have imitated him by studying the role of specific institutions and processes, while studies of other Veblenians have taken a more practical bent. The ideas of four Veblenians (a much looser term than "Marshallians") are considered below in order to demonstrate the sheer diversity of what has been termed institutional economics. Three writers—J. R. Commons, W. C. Mitchell, and C. E. Ayres—are discussed briefly. The fourth Veblenian, J. K. Galbraith, is reserved for a somewhat more detailed treatment.

Commons, Mitchell, and Ayres

Although John Rogers Commons (1862–1945), Wesley Clair Mitchell (1874–1948), and Clarence E. Ayers (1892–1972) are all American institutionalists in name, one could hardly imagine a more disparate group of individuals.

Commons was born in Ohio, did graduate work at Johns Hopkins University, and was perhaps the foremost scholar at the University of Wisconsin between 1904 and 1932. Commons was less of a theoretician than an adamant champion of the social and economic reform achieved through codified regulations. Along with Wisconsin's liberal governor Robert M. LaFollette, Commons wrote and sponsored labor, antitrust, and public-utility regulations for the state. Commons's legislative proposals and Wisconsin's enactments became a model from which federal regulations of similar activities were later drawn. His numerous publications are a potpourri of criticism, demand for social reform, historical-empirical information, and classical, socialist, and marginalist ideas. He was not a pure institutionalist of the Veblenian stripe, choosing instead to focus on the operation of manmade institutions (such as regulatory or antitrust agencies) and how they are affected by private property, legislation, and court decisions.

In the *Legal Foundations of Capitalism* (1924) Commons emphasized law and the courts as the constraining elements in the economic system, an idea that is very much alive today in the economics of government regulation (see Notes for Further Reading at the end of the chapter). But in his multivolume (and practically incomprehensible) *Institutional Economics* (1934) Commons took the definition of institutionalism beyond Veblen's original vision. To Commons, markets and their effects could be judged good or bad through (admittedly normative) criteria of efficiency and justice. A just and efficient system therefore could be devised and effected through optimal legislative regulations and through the judiciary. As we have seen, Veblen was far more skeptical about government's ability to raise the general welfare through institutional change. Commons was unable to effect any fundamental reorientation of economics, but he did have a profound impact on a number of his students at Wisconsin.

Yet another institutionalist direction was taken by Wesley Clair Mitchell, student of Veblen's, professor at the University of Chicago from 1922 to 1940, and one of the two or three most famous American economists of his generation. Mitchell, who gave economics in general, and institutional economics in particular, a statistical foundation, established the National Bureau of Economic Research in 1920. (The NBER is alive and well today as a functioning research institution.) It is difficult to overestimate the importance of Mitchell's pioneering attempts to quantify simple economic concepts such as "money," "prices," and "income." Jevons's earlier pathbreaking analyses of index-number construction and statistical studies of price series (see Chapter 14) came to life under Mitchell's able supervision. In his magnum opus entitled *Business Cycles* (1913), Mitchell analyzed booms and depressions from the nineteenth century through the monetary panic of 1907, utilizing masterfully reconstructed data on bond prices and yields, wages, commodity prices, the money stock (a central variable in Mitchell's interpretation), and monetary velocity. His approach to economic analysis—theory interrelated with empirical explanation—had a profound impact on the direction taken by economic studies in twentieth-century America. Studies in GNP accounting, business-cycle analysis, growth, antitrust, and industrial organization henceforth could be accompanied by empirical referents. Thus, Mitchell established a program for the collection and use of empirical data that, together with subsequent mathematical and statistical analysis, has given much of modern economics its particular character.

But how did Mitchell's great contribution relate to his mentor's institutionalism, especially since Veblen vigorously opposed mathematical and statistical complements to economic theory as unproductive? Veblen sought to establish the cultural and psychological bases for certain types of institutions and for institutional change, whereas Mitchell's aim was to objectivize pecuniary institutions and business fluctuations. As such, Mitchell's work was an extension of Veblen's, but one that Veblen himself did not pursue or find extremely useful. Again, as in the case of Commons, "institutional economics" took a direction not particularly close to Veblen's own conception.

Closest of all institutionalists to Veblen's original theoretical conceptions was Clarence Edwin Ayres. Educated at Brown University and at the avant-garde University of Chicago, Ayres spent the lion's share of his career (1930 until his retirement in 1968) at the University of Texas. Indeed, owing to the influence of Ayres, the University of Texas became the locus of the institutionalist school in America over these years.

In a number of important publications, including *The Theory of Economic Progress* (1944) and *Toward a Reasonable Society: The Value of Industrial Civilization* (1961), Ayres returned to the theoretical concerns of Thorstein Veblen, but with some important differences. Like Veblen, Ayres was steeped in philosophy, but his particular orientation was to John Dewey's pragmatist-instrumentalist approach. In terms of economic policy, Ayres advocated pragmatic, liberal modifications of capitalism, akin to those of Commons. But he rejected socialism and fascism. Like Veblen and J. M. Keynes, Ayres was an underconsumptionist who supported modified economic planning and regulation as a palliative to what he judged to be the excesses of capitalism.

In terms of theory, however, Ayres was a technological determinist. Ayres held technology to be an *absolute value* toward which society should be gravitating. He spoke of a life process to which institutions either did or did not contribute. "Full production," which included maximization of human creativity, artistic pursuits, etc., in addition to material well-being, was the human maximand of Ayres's system.

Ayres contrasted institutional values with technological values, indicating that "contribution to the life process" could serve as a criterion for judging "true" and "false" institutional values.[10] In his view technology was an ultimate value since it alone was independent of cultural considerations. In effect, Ayres made institutional economics a study of technology and of technological change. Unlike Veblen, he did not totally repudiate the value of markets and the price system, but he did argue that prices and markets were less important than technology and institutions in determining the direction of "full production." Like Veblen, however, Ayres was unable to provide a consistent and cohesive framework within which to analyze the momentum and life history of economic societies. In spite of Ayres's very creative work there are numerous lacunae in the institutionalists' theoretical paradigm, gaps and contradictions that remain to be filled and resolved by others.

---

[10] During the 1960s one of the authors of this book attended a lecture by Ayres in which Coca Cola was attacked as representing a "false" value, i.e., one detracting from the "life process."

Thus, institutional economics took several divergent paths after Veblen. An inductive-statistical component was added by Mitchell, Commons translated institutional economics into a program for social (chiefly legislative) reform, and Ayres extended Veblen's conception into a theory of technological values. The concerns of modern institutionalists reflect all these diverse interests and many others. But, perhaps more than any other writer of institutionalist leanings, John Kenneth Galbraith has cornered the interest of social scientists and the reading public.

John Kenneth Galbraith: The Institutionalists' Popularizer

Galbraith is one of the best-known social critics on the contemporary American scene. He has donned hats as Harvard faculty member, economic adviser to the President, novelist, and U.S. ambassador to India, among others. He has also written numerous influential and heretical books on the social and economic system. In part, Galbraith's work is a modern repository of heterodox thought. His thought includes elements of many writers from that tradition, especially Veblen. Though Galbraith's intellectual scope has been broad, we might identify in this brief treatment at least two ideas as distinctly Galbraithian: (1) the process of *countervailing power* and (2) the identification of a *social imbalance* within the context of an affluent society.

As early as 1952, in his book *American Capitalism*, Galbraith was concerned with the traditional (orthodox *Marshallian*) explanation of "how things work" in the American economic system. In brilliant rhetoric he was already arguing that affluence ("unseemly opulence") was a mixed blessing. Most particularly, he charged that orthodox economic theory was unrealistic, since any acquaintance at all with the facts of the real world would negate the relevance of the competitive model—the stock-in-trade of Marshallian economics. In his criticism, however, Galbraith encased certain value judgments in a dynamic social theory that forms a springboard for his criticism of static, orthodox political economy. Thus he argued that income inequality "distorts the use of resources," since "it diverts them from the wants of the many to the esoteric desires of the few—if not from bread to cake at least from Chevrolets to Cadillacs. Unneccessary inequality in income—unnecessary in the sense that it does not reward differences in intelligence, application, or willingness to take risks—may also impair economic stability" (*American Capitalism*, pp. 104–105).

Countervailing Power Most importantly, Galbraith argued that the model of a smoothly operating competitive system, which assumed a built-in regulating force of many buyers and sellers in the market, was academic hokum. The members of orthodox tradition, or anyone else for that matter, failed to recognize the existence of the process of countervailing power.[11] Competition had

---

[11] Wieser, of course, had formulated this concept and explored some of its implications in his *Social Economics* (see Chapter 13).

broken down, according to Galbraith, creating concentration and monopoly power. Yet it only *appeared* as if all restraints had dissolved. Galbraith argued that:

> In fact, new restraints on private power did appear to replace competition. They were nurtured by the same process of concentration which impaired or destroyed competition. But they appeared not on the same side of the market but on the opposite side, not with competitors but with customers and suppliers. It will be convenient to have a name for this counterpart of competition and I shall call it countervailing power (*American Capitalism*, p. 111).

It is clear that Galbraith envisions countervailing power as a process in the *Veblenian* sense, since he argues that the orthodox theory of bilateral monopoly, which at first blush appears so similar to his thesis of countervailing power, is a mere "adventitious occurrence." On the other hand, countervailing power is a process that develops in response to the private economic power that emerges from the original breakdown of competition. Though there are exceptions to this theory, Galbraith advances the tool as an important explanation for many developments, including trade unionism, retail cooperatives, chain stores, and the like. His concept of market and product, needless to say, is of much broader meaning than that of traditional theory. It most closely resembles E. H. Chamberlin's concept of differentiated products in monopolistic competition (see Chapter 18).

The existence or nonexistence of countervailing power has great relevance for public policy. Specifically, Galbraith viewed the failure of countervailing power as a *raison d'être* for government intervention in a private economy. As he put it:

> Without the phenomenon itself being fully recognized, the provision of state assistance to the development of countervailing power has become a major function of government—perhaps the major domestic function of government. Much of the domestic legislation of the last twenty years, that of the New Deal episode in particular, only becomes fully comprehensible when it is viewed in this light (*American Capitalism*, p. 128).

He said further:

> The groups that sought the assistance of government in building countervailing power sought that power in order to use it against market authority to which they had previously been subordinate (*American Capitalism*, p. 136).

Galbraith also feels that antitrust policy should be modified to permit the implementation of those policies that encourage the development of countervailing power so that original monopoly power may be checked wherever possible. Moreover, Galbraith asserts that where government intervention has occurred, this has been the result of a breakdown in countervailing power, not competition.

There are, however, gaps of a serious nature in Galbraith's theory of countervailing power. If it is to be used as a tool of public policy, one must be able to determine original as opposed to generated countervailing power. In *American Capitalism*, Galbraith identified two categories of monopoly: (1) monopoly that emerges as a result of the breakdown of competition (original) and (2) monopoly that develops in response to existing market power (countervailing). He might well have added a third category, which arises because of industry demands for regulation—in the form of assistance, subsidies, and contracts, not to mention control over entry. (Veblen, as we have seen, anticipated this development.)

More generally, Galbraith's theory lacks a cogent explanation of how power emerges in the first place and how it affects market processes and the political system, all of which is an interesting and legitimate concern of the economist as social scientist. One wonders how countervailing power is supposed to affect prices and the distribution of income, a subject that should be of high interest in Galbraith's socialist state. When does the government step in to socialize or control areas of the economy (low-cost housing)? How long do we wait for market processes to develop in "defenseless" areas of the economy before the government steps in? Unfortunately, Galbraith's theory does not give us the answers to these queries. Nevertheless, his discussion may yet point the way to a neoinstitutionalist synthesis.

Social Imbalance   In *The Affluent Society* (1958), a book that has sold more copies than Adam Smith's *Wealth of Nations,* Galbraith seemed to object to American society because it is rich and because its values are misdirected. This time Galbraith took on the orthodoxy through the theory of consumer demand. He maintained (1) that the received theory, to its detriment, has disallowed "any notion of necessary versus unnecessary or important as against unimportant goods" (p. 147) and (2) that having neglected certain implications of diminishing marginal utility, economists have been unable to see that more of certain goods—through time—is not better than less. This, of course, is normative stuff. In criticism of positive economics, Galbraith remarked: "Any notion of necessary versus unnecessary or important as against unimportant goods was rigorously excluded from the subject....Nothing in economics so quickly marks an individual as incompetently trained as a disposition to remark on the legitimacy of the desire for more food and the frivolity of the desire for a more elaborate automobile" (*The Affluent Society,* p. 147). With scholarly impertinence, Galbraith asserted that consumer sovereignty is a myth and that in modern times the chain of cause and effect runs from production to consumption. In order to maintain an affluent society, one in which production and income are growing, new wants must be manufactured. Thus Galbraith focused on the crucial role of advertising in creating and manipulating wants for new consumer goods, which are provided at the expense of social goods. The social imbalance that results is considered unconscionable by Galbraith.

In the tradition of Henry George, another American maverick, Galbraith maintains that economic problems lead to social ills. "The more goods people procure, the more packages they discard and the more trash that must be carried away. If the appropriate sanitation services are not provided, the counterpart of increasing opulence will be deepening filth. The greater the wealth the thicker will be the dirt'' (*The Affluent Society,* p. 256). Rebellion of the young is similarly explained since ''schools do not compete with television and the movies,'' and ''the dubious heroes of the latter, not Miss Jones, become the idols of the young'' (p. 257).

Galbraith details a whole litany of social ills that result from a breakdown of the economic forces of competition and a value system that encourages wasteful private consumption at the expense of the provision of public goods. At the heart of this ''inappropriate'' value system is the fact that advertising and emulation work primarily on the creation of private wants. In fact, a large part of Galbraith's theory rests upon Veblen's concept of conspicuous consumption treated earlier in this chapter.

In order to redress social imbalance, Galbraith proposes increased government taxation at all levels and redirection (away from national defense, to be sure) of government expenditures. He is of the opinion (as he explains more fully in *The New Industrial State*) that ''In the absence of social intervention, private production will monopolize all resources'' (*The Affluent Society,* p. 310). Consequently, government must take a more active role to see that social balance is engendered and preserved in the process.

Some Comments on Galbraith's System   By intellect, at least, John Kenneth Galbraith is a lineal descendant of former American heterodox thinkers, especially Henry George and Thorstein Veblen. There is a commonality among these writers insofar as group behavior is the focal point of analysis. Also, like Veblen, Galbraith takes an institutional approach in his attempt to provide a theory of the unfolding process of modern capitalism.

But Galbraith's ideas—like those of his distinguished predecessors—lack specificity. There are many gaps, moreover, in his theory of the process of an evolutionary interpretation of capitalism. A case in point relates to the government's redress of social imbalance. According to Galbraith, ''affirmative action'' on the part of the government is required, but he does not spell out how social needs and their magnitudes are to be assessed. One wonders whether it is to be on the basis of conjecture, special pleading, or value judgments. Principles of modern public finance (which developed within the orthodoxy) such as benefit-cost analysis are admittedly imperfect, but they appear to be incomparably more useful as a guide to policy than those suggested by Galbraith and his camp.

Galbraith's neglect of the individual, and especially of the individual's intellectual independence and his preferences, leads him to argue that individuals cannot discern what is in their own best interests. The usefulness of the price system in allowing individuals to register their choices between economic and social alternatives (for example, to choose less costly gasoline and more pollution rather than more costly gasoline and less pollution) is similarly ignored or discounted. Galbraith and others have felt frustration at the distribution of income and the level of social-goods provision that free markets provide. This frustration has led them to champion the extension of government as a palliative.

There is no question that social goods must be provided. Modern economists who defend the neoclassical theory of markets are at least as interested as Galbraith in the problem of the provision of public goods. The debatable point, of course, is the method of provision and the theory and philosophy behind it.

CONCLUSION: THE INSTITUTIONALIST PARADIGM

The fate of a *pure* institutionalist paradigm remains somewhat uncertain. In the first place no one, not even a self-proclaimed institutionalist, pretends to identify a single, cohesive, and consistent body of thought. Should one identify the "system" of Veblen, or some combination of the writings of Veblen, Commons, Mitchell, and Ayres, as the foundation for a school of neoinstitutionalism? "Institutional economics" appears to be an open-ended inquiry.

Moreover, there is a strong and growing recognition within the traditional body of American economics that institutions, and specifically property-rights institutions, cannot be assumed "given" in studies where temporal matters are important. In other words, a property-rights literature is developing that highlights the interactions of legal institutions, economic behavior, and economic outcomes. Theories of economic growth and development, law and economics, comparative economic organization, and economic regulation have been major beneficiaries of these broader approaches. At a time when a large segment of American economists have retreated from policy matters and forced economic theory into tighter mathematical straitjackets, others have been expanding economic theory and policy in very interesting and fruitful ways (see, for example, Chapters 23 and 24). Institutional economics may yet have much to contribute to the latter development.

In short, institutional economics is an umbrella under which many interesting and productive ideas may be hiding. As a separate inquiry, the "school" has largely consisted of an organon for strident criticism of neoclassical economics. Progress may well require compromise with more traditional strains of American economic thought. Compromise and eclecticism, after all, have been distinctly American characteristics.

NOTES FOR FURTHER READING

Two excellent summaries of the historical movement are T. W. Hutchison, *A Review of Economic Doctrines, 1870–1929,* chaps. 8, 12 (Oxford: Clarendon Press, 1953), and Ben B. Seligman, *Main Currents in Modern Economics,* chap. 1 (New York: Free Press, 1962).

Social Darwinism was an important influence on the philosophical and social thought of the time. In this regard, see William Graham Sumner, *Social Darwinism: Selected Essays* (Englewood Cliffs, N.J.: Prentice-Hall, 1963) and the brilliant overview by Richard Hofstadter, *Social Darwinism in American Thought,* rev. ed. (Boston: Beacon Press, 1955).

On British historicism and its development, see R. B. Ekelund, "A British Rejection of Economic Orthodoxy," *Southwestern Social Science Quarterly,* vol. 47 (September 1966), pp. 172–180; and, especially, A. W. Coats, "The Historicist Reaction in English Political Economy, 1870–1890," *Economica,* vol. 21 (May 1954), pp. 143–153. John Neville Keynes's *Scope and Method of Political Economy* (New York: A. M. Kelley, Publishers, 1963 [1890]) is still one of the most penetrating contributions to economic methodology in the literature. With incredible skill and thoroughness Keynes sorted out the issues and the supposed conflicts between the orthodox methods of Mill and Cairnes and those defended by the German and British historicists. In the process, the elder Keynes produced a work of lasting significance.

An interesting and growing literature exists on specific members of the British historical school demonstrating their eclecticism vis-à-vis orthodox political economy and their great diversity of interests. Cliffe-Leslie's interest in Irish and English social reform and his role in the origins of the historical movement are the subject of G. M. Koot's "T. E. Cliffe-Leslie, Irish Social Reform and the Origins of the English School of Economics," *History of Political Economy,* vol. 7 (Fall 1975), pp. 312–316. A leading doctrinal opponent of orthodox laissez-faire principles regarding labor and union policy in the mid-Victorian period is considered in P. Adelman, "Frederic Harrison and the Positivist Attack on Orthodox Political Economy," *History of Political Economy,* vol. 3 (Spring 1971), pp. 170–189. The most extensive study of the methodological and philosophical underpinnings of the British historical movement is contained in Craig Bolton, *The British Historical School in Political Economy: Its Meaning and Significance* (unpublished Ph.D. dissertation, Texas A & M University, 1976). The Reverend Richard Jones's actual use of induction is the subject of W. L. Miller's "Richard Jones: A Case Study in Methodology," *History of Political Economy,* vol. 3 (Spring 1971), pp. 198–207. Miller's careful studies of the evolutionist and economist–social scientist Herbert Spencer may be consulted with profit. See, for example, his treatment of Spencer's conception of public policy in the "static" state of society: "Herbert Spencer's Theory of Welfare and Public Policy," *History of Political Economy,* vol. 4 (Spring 1972), pp. 207–231.

The joy and pleasure of reading Veblen in the original should not be missed by any student of economic and social thought. In addition to the works listed in the References to this chapter, all of Veblen's major works have been reprinted by A. M. Kelley and are generally accessible. The secondary literature on Veblen is vast and kaleidoscopic. The best biographical study of Veblen and his times remains Joseph Dorfman's *Thorstein Veblen and His America* (New York: A. M. Kelley, 1961 [1934]). Veblen's "economic" methodology is treated by A. W. Coats in "The Influence of Veblen's Methodology," *Journal of Political Economy,* vol. 62 (December 1954), pp. 529–537; and excellent overviews of Veblen's economic system and his economic critique of capitalism are contained in two essays: Thomas Sowell, "The Evolutionary Economics of Thorstein Veblen," *Oxford Economic Papers*, n.s., vol. 1 (July 1967), pp. 177–198; and, especially, Donald A. Walker, "Thorstein Veblen's Economic System," *Economic Inquiry*, vol. 15 (April 1977), pp. 213–237. A brief but incisive paper by Kenneth J. Arrow, "Thorstein Veblen as an Economic Theorist" (see References), is also recommended.

Veblen's concept of conspicuous consumption is echoed in some twentieth-century economic analysis, as Leibenstein's microeconomic formulation suggests. In a macroeconomic context, see James S. Duesenberry's *Income, Saving and the Theory of Consumer Behavior* (Cambridge, Mass.: Harvard University Press, 1949). A modern reaffirmation of the "given tastes" assumption of neoclassical microanalysis—one that Veblen challenged—is found in G. J. Stigler and G. S. Becker, *"De Gustibus Non Est Disputandum,"* *American Economic Review*, vol. 67 (March 1977), pp. 76–90.

Veblen's explication of the role and mechanism of habits and habit formation in institutional development and change has been the subject of recent discussion. That there is a genetic component or predisposition in habit formation is indisputable, and Veblen may have very well appreciated the fact. Beyond a possible appreciation for the role of evolution and genetics, however, Veblen focused upon the inexact forces of "expedience, adaptation and concessive adjustments" in his explanation of the role of habits in economic change. Richard W. Ault and Robert B. Ekelund, Jr., argue that a blending of Veblen's anthropological view of habits with a neoclassical cost-choice framework wherein habits are considered endogenous to the choice process produces a more cogent and satisfactory *analysis* of economic and institutional change than either alone: see "Habits in Economic Analysis: Veblen and the Neoclassicals," *History of Political Economy*, vol. 20 (Fall 1988), pp. 431–445. Ault and Ekelund also believe that Veblen's analysis suffered from his refusal to view economizing and habit formation in the manner of neoclassical economics (i.e., as largely endogenous to economic processes). The combination of Veblen's views on habits and habit formation and neoclassical cost-choice theory yields something very much like the new institutionalist analysis of economic history and change: see D. C. North and R. P. Thomas, *The Rise of the Western World* (London: Cambridge University Press, 1973). On these issues, also see Malcolm Rutherford, "Thorstein Veblen and the Processes of Institutional Change," *History of Political Economy*, vol. 16 (1984), pp. 331–348; and Alexander James Field, "On the Explanation of Rules Using Rational Choice Models," *Journal of Economic Issues*, vol. 13 (1979), pp. 49–72.

J. E. Biddle, "Twain, Veblen and the Connecticut Yankee," *History of Political Economy*, vol. 17 (Spring 1985), pp. 97–108, draws a tenuous link between Mark Twain and Thorstein Veblen, particularly the shared view that human actions are motivated more by custom and habit than by reason. On the other hand, divergence between Veblen and Commons on how to treat a specific form of business property is the subject of A. M. Endres, "Veblen and Commons on Goodwill: A Case of Theoretical Divergence," *History of Political Economy*, vol. 17 (Winter 1985), pp. 637–650.

Veblen's judgment that classical-neoclassical economics was pre-Darwinian and that his analysis provided a new evolutionary theory is disputed in an interesting paper by L. B. Jones, "The Institutionalists and *On the Origin of Species:* A Case of Mistaken Identity," *Southern Economic Journal,* vol. 52 (April 1986), pp. 1043–1055. On the basis of information recently come to light in Darwin's early diaries, Jones argues that it was Adam Smith's theories of competition and the division of labor that led Darwin to develop the theories of speciation and natural selection. The prior conventional wisdom held that Malthus was the source of Darwin's evolutionary concepts.

Veblen applied the concept of technological displacement and the reduction of capital values to business cycles, and Commons used the idea in a regulatory framework that has been buttressed recently with a modern (neoinstitutionalist) defense of the regulatory process by Victor Goldberg; see his "Regulation and Administered Contracts," *Bell Journal of Economics,* vol. 7 (Autumn 1976), pp. 425–448. The writings on capitalist dynamics of another great "evolutionist," Joseph A. Schumpeter, are contrasted with Veblen's in L. A. O'Donnell's "Rationalism, Capitalism and the Entrepreneur: The Views of Veblen and Schumpeter," *History of Political Economy,* vol. 5 (Spring 1973), pp. 199–214. An interesting paper contrasts the contemporary "radical critique of economics" (mainly of 1960s origin with Marxian overtones) with the theoretical structure of Veblenian economics, showing why Veblen has has so little influence on the radicals; see Joseph E. Pluta and Charles G. Leathers, "Veblen and Modern Radical Economics," *Journal of Economic Issues,* vol. 12 (March 1978), pp. 125–146. (The *Journal of Economic Issues* and the *American Journal of Economics and Sociology* regularly carry articles dealing with institutionalist topics.)

The renaissance of interest in Commons-type legal analysis is discussed in Victor Goldberg's "Commons, Clark, and the Emerging Post-Coasian Law and Economics," *The Journal of Economic Issues,* vol. 11 (December 1976), pp. 877–893. A real insight into the theoretical structure of Commons (and into his substantial ego) may be sifted from his autobiography, *Myself.* Mitchell was the "economist's economist" of his generation. That he was a superb historian of thought is reflected in his lecture notes, edited by Joseph Dorfman in the two-volume *Types of Economic Theory* (New York: A. M. Kelley, Publishers, 1967). Kelley has also reprinted a number of Mitchell's works, including *The Backward Art of Spending Money and Other Essays* [1937], which is a very fine Mitchell "sampler." One of Mitchell's specialties was monetary economics, and an interesting essay by Abraham Hirsch brings out the interrelations of Mitchell's unique views of theory, policy, and economic verification in this area; see "Mitchell's Work on the Causes of the Civil War Inflations in His Development as an Economist," *History of Political Economy,* vol. 2 (Spring 1970), pp. 118–132. Hirsch also examines Mitchell's ambivalence toward methodology and his use of mainstream economic theory in "The *A Posteriori* Method and the Creation of New Theory: W. C. Mitchell as a Case Study," *History of Political Economy,* vol. 8 (Summer 1976), pp. 152–206. Perhaps the best assessment of Mitchell as an economist and quantity theorist is the tribute of his admirer Milton Friedman; see "Wesley C. Mitchell as an Economic Theorist," *The Journal of Political Economy,* vol. 58 (December 1950), pp. 465–493. An institutionalist-labor theorist contemporary of Mitchell's at Chicago, Robert F. Hoxie, is discussed in P. J. McNulty's essay "Hoxie's Economics in Retrospect: The Making and Unmaking of a Veblenian," *History of Political Economy,* vol. 5 (Fall 1973), pp. 449–484. Hoxie and others fell under Veblen's ideas and were somewhat influential in forming FDR's economic policies over the depression years. FDR's "brain trust" was heavily influenced by institutionalist ideas.

C. E. Ayres's full and quietly rebellious life is aptly chronicled by W. L. Breit and W. P. Culbertson in "Clarence Edwin Ayres: An Intellectual's Portrait," *Science and Ceremony* (see References). In addition to the Coats essay, this volume contains essays on Ayres by a number of leading social and economic scholars, including Talcott Parsons, James M. Buchanan, Gordon Tullock, Joseph J. Spengler, and Alfred F. Chalk (the epistemology of Ayres is clearly revealed in Chalk's essay). While most of these papers do not concern Ayres's thought per se, they are very much in the spirit of the broad inquiries he sponsored. Three other papers on Ayres provide helpful background: W. B. Breit, "The Development of Clarence Ayres' Theoretical Institutionalism," *Social Science Quarterly,* vol. 54 (September 1973), pp. 244–257; D. A. Walker, "The Institutionalist Economic Theories of Clarence Ayres," *Economic Inquiry,* vol. 17 (October 1979), pp. 519–538; and, by the same author, "The Economic Policy Proposals of Clarence Ayres," *Southern Economic Journal,* vol. 44 (January 1978), pp. 616–628. In the latter paper Ayres is shown to have become a rather commonplace "liberal" with respect to policies designed to alter income distribution, although his "minimum income proposal" contained a negative income tax provision. The influence of John Dewey on Ayres is chronicled by Floyd McFarland, "Clarence Ayres and His Gospel of Technology," *History of Political Economy,* vol. 18 (Fall 1986), pp. 617–637.

Some works by Galbraith not cited in this chapter are *The Great Crash, 1929* (Boston: Houghton Mifflin, 1955); *A Theory of Price Control* (Cambridge, Mass.: Harvard University Press, 1952); *Economics and the Art of Controversy* (New Brunswick, N.J.: Rutgers University Press, 1955); *The Liberal Hour* (Boston: Houghton Mifflin, 1960); and *Economics and the Public Purpose* (Boston: Houghton Mifflin, 1973). For an interesting assessment of Galbraith's "system" see Scott Gordon's "The Close of the Galbraithian System," *Journal of Political Economy,* vol. 76 (July/August 1968), pp. 635–644; and Galbraith's reply, "Professor Gordon on 'The Close of the Galbraithian System,'" *Journal of Political Economy,* vol. 77 (July/August 1969), pp. 494–503. Veblen and Galbraith are compared and contrasted by C. G. Leathers and J. S. Evans, "Thorstein Veblen and the New Industrial State," *History of Political Economy,* vol. 5 (Fall 1973), pp. 420–437; while Harold Demsetz makes a provocative attempt to discover and test the empirical content of Galbraith's theory in "Where Is the New Industrial State?" *Economic Inquiry,* vol. 12 (March 1974), pp. 1–12. Finally, lucid overviews of

Galbraith and Veblen are contained in W. L. Breit and Roger Ransom, *The Academic Scribblers* (New York: Holt, 1982).

REFERENCES

Arrow, Kenneth. "Thorstein Veblen as an Economic Theorist," *American Economist,* vol. 19 (Spring 1975), pp. 5–9.

Bagehot, Walter. *Lombard Street: A Description of the Money Market.* Homewood, Ill: Irwin, 1962 [1873].

———. "The Postulates of English Political Economy," *Fortnightly Review,* vol. 19 (1876), pp. 215–242, 720–741.

Cairnes, J. E. "M. Comte and Political Economy," *Fortnightly Review,* vol. 7 (1870), pp. 579–602.

———. "Political Economy and Laissez-Faire," *Fortnightly Review,* vol. 10 (1871), pp. 80–97.

Coats, A. W. "Clarence Ayres' Place in the History of Economics: An Interim Assessment," in W. L. Breit and W. P. Culbertson (eds.) *Science and Ceremony: The Institutional Economics of C. E. Ayres.* Austin: University of Texas Press, 1976.

Ely, Richard T. *Introduction to Political Economy.* New York: Hunt and Eaton, 1891.

Galbraith, J. K. *American Capitalism: The Concept of Countervailing Power.* Boston: Houghton Mifflin, 1952.

———. *The Affluent Society.* Boston: Houghton Mifflin, 1958.

———. *The New Industrial State.* Boston: Houghton Mifflin, 1967.

Ingram, John K. *History of Political Economy.* London: A. & C. Black, 1915 [1888].

———. "The Present Position and Prospects of Political Economy," in R. L. Smythe (ed.), *Essays in Economic Method.* New York: McGraw-Hill, 1963 [1898].

Jones, Richard. *Literary Remains on Political Economy of the Late Rev. Richard Jones,* William Whewell (ed.), London: J. Murray, 1859.

Leibenstein, Harvey. "Bandwagon, Snob, and Veblen Effects in the Theory of Consumers' Demand," *The Quarterly Journal of Economics,* vol. 62 (May 1950), pp. 183–207.

Mitchell, W. C. (ed.). *What Veblen Taught: Selected Writings of Thorstein Veblen.* New York: A. M. Kelley, 1964.

Smythe, R. L. (ed.). *Essays in Economic Method.* New York: McGraw-Hill, 1963.

Spencer, Herbert. *Autobiography.* New York: Appleton, 1904.

Veblen, Thorstein. "Why Economics Is Not an Evolutionary Science," *Quarterly Journal of Economics,* vol. 12 (July 1898), pp. 373–426; vol. 14 (February 1900), pp. 240–269.

———. "The Preconceptions of Economic Science," *Quarterly Journal of Economics,* vol. 13 (January 1899), pp. 121–150, (July 1899), pp. 396–426; vol. 14 (February 1900), pp. 240–269.

———. *The Theory of the Leisure Class.* New York: Modern Library, 1934 [1899].

———. *The Vested Interests and the Common Man.* New York: Capricorn Books, 1969 [1919].

———. *The Engineers and the Price System.* New York: Viking, 1921.

CHAPTER 18

COMPETITION RECONSIDERED: CHAMBERLIN AND ROBINSON

INTRODUCTION: DEVELOPMENT OF IMPERFECT COMPETITION

Of the numerous directions taken in twentieth-century economics, perhaps the most important one related to microeconomics has been the search for models descriptive of actual markets. Alfred Marshall, as will be recalled from Chapter 15, devoted the lion's share of his attention to models of perfect competition on the one hand and pure monopoly on the other.

Perfect competition is a model containing the assumption that a large number of sellers produce a homogeneous product. Further, since the number of firms is indefinitely large, no one seller can affect the price and profits of other firms; i.e., the actions of one firm have no effect on the price and output decisions of other firms. Since complete freedom of entry and exit is assumed, neither long-run economic profits nor rents exist.

In contrast, the monopoly model, first accurately described by Cournot and Dupuit and expanded by Marshall and others, is characterized by a single firm with exclusive control over the output of the good in question. Economic profits are greater under this market structure than under any that includes more than one seller.

These two models, the essentials of which had been worked out fairly early in the nineteenth century, are polar extremes. Marshall, though he displayed some awareness of a middle ground between the two extremes, perpetuated the cultivation of these two diverse models of the firm, and economists through 1933, with a few important exceptions, did not bother to analyze price and output equilibriums of firms whose decisions had an effect on one another's policies. But in 1933 two important (and independently written) books appeared in America and England whose titles and central themes were addressed to this very problem: Edward H. Chamberlin's *Theory of Monopolistic Competition* and Joan Robinson's *Economics of Imperfect Competition*.

Interest in the problem of imperfect markets did not originate with Chamberlin and Robinson, of course, but it is clear that a number of factors explain the reception of their ideas in the early 1930s. At this point it is instructive to recount briefly some of these developments.

Duopoly Analysis

Augustin Cournot was probably the first writer to analyze an imperfect market. In Cournot's case of duopoly, it will be recalled from Chapter 12, there were two sellers whose profit-maximizing behavior depended upon each thinking the other's output would remain constant. Cournot did obtain a solution, but it was dependent upon this rather naive assumption.

Still other early models of duopoly were based on other assumptions. Chief among these were the models of Joseph Bertrand in 1883 and F.Y. Edgeworth in 1897. Bertrand, a French mathematician, argued that given the assumption that the prices of the rival seller are assumed constant (by each of the sellers), price and output will reach competitive levels. Edgeworth, on the other hand, placed output constraints on each of his duopolists, producing an indeterminate range over which prices and outputs of the two sellers will oscillate.

Clearly, the Cournot-Bertrand and Edgeworth results depended upon the special assumptions that each made concerning the behavior of the duopolists. Perhaps it was this tenuousness of result that led Alfred Marshall to avoid contributing to duopoly theory (though he was certainly aware of Cournot's solution). Nonetheless, Marshall unwittingly paved the way for the large reception given to imperfect competition in the 1930s. It will be recalled that in the *Principles,* Marshall discussed the possibility of the existence of industries characterized by increasing returns or decreasing costs. A debate ensued principally in the 1920s, involving several important disciples of Marshall, over whether competitive equilibrium was compatible with increasing returns.

Sraffa and Imperfect Competition

Marshall's great student, A. C. Pigou, participated, but Cambridge economist Piero Sraffa set out the issues clearly in 1926 in an article entitled "The Laws of Returns under Competitive Conditions." Sraffa had proved elsewhere that decreasing-cost conditions were indeed incompatible with long-run Marshallian competitive equilibrium. One or the other had to be given up. But in 1926 he noted an emptiness in the exclusive cultivation of the market models of competition and monopoly. Sraffa commented on market imperfections which defenders of the competitive model dismissed as "frictions." According to Sraffa, these obstacles are not frictions, "but are themselves active forces which produce permanent and even cumulative effects" upon market prices and outputs.

Establishing a basis for models of imperfect competition, Sraffa further argued that these obstacles to competition "are endowed with sufficient stability to enable them to be made the subject of analysis based on statistical assumptions" ("The Laws of Returns," p. 542).

Sraffa, moreover, suggested some obstacles that might affect monopoly strength or the elasticity of the demand curve faced by the imperfectly competitive seller: possession of unique natural resources, legal privileges, the control of a greater or lesser proportion of the total production, and the existence of rival commodities. Thus, out of a contradiction in Marshall's analysis of competition, Sraffa suggested a new approach to market theory. In 1933, Robinson explicitly credited Sraffa and the increasing-returns controversy as having led her to analyze imperfect markets. Sraffa's obstacles to pure competition, as we shall see, were an important aspect of Chamberlin's approach. Chamberlin's development of monopolistic competition was not directly influenced by Sraffa, however, but by Cambridge economist A. C. Pigou and by an imbroglio over the explanation of railway rates. The debate has come to be known as the "Taussig-Pigou controversy."

Taussig and Pigou on Railway Rates

The Taussig-Pigou controversy centered on the question of whether the observed pattern of multiple railway rates could best be explained by the Mill-Marshall theory of joint supply (see Chapter 8), which was Taussig's position, or by the presence of high rail common costs accompanied by the ability to price-discriminate between buyers (Pigou's position).

In 1891, scarcely one year after the publication of Marshall's *Principles,* F. W. Taussig of Harvard University put the joint-cost argument to use in attempting to fit the pattern of existing multiple railway rates into orthodox competitive theory. Taussig entered the debate over railway rates to combat the widely accepted (and erroneous, he thought) notion that the government should own the railroads, a notion arising from the belief that monopoly and discriminatory rates were inherent in, and exclusive to, any system of private control. But varying rates for rail service would persist, Taussig argued, even under government ownership, since the expenses were preponderantly joint.

The essentials of Taussig's supportive reasoning may be set out simply. First, Taussig noted (correctly) that railway expenses are largely independent of the traffic carried; i.e., railroads are characterized by high fixed costs that have no influence on rates. From this premise, Taussig concluded:

> We have here [on the railroads] commodities produced in part at least, at joint cost. For the explanation of the values of commodities produced under such conditions, the classic economists developed a theory which they applied chiefly to cases like wool and mutton, gas and coke, where practically the whole of the cost was incurred jointly for several commodities. But obviously it also applies, *pro tanto,* to cases where only part of the cost is joint. The conditions for its application exist in any industry in which there is a large plant, turning out, *not one homogeneous commod-*

ity, but several commodities, subject to demand from *different quarters with different degrees of intensity* ("A Contribution to the Theory of Railway Rates," p. 443, italics supplied).

Thus Taussig attempted to fit the railway case into the theory of competitive joint supply by asserting (1) that the unit of rail supply is not homogeneous but is, in a dimension relevant to pricing, heterogeneous, and (2) that somehow, different demand elasticities for rail service contribute to, or are the sole cause of, the heterogeneous nature of the output unit. He concluded, inevitably, that, excepting a small element of direct costs, demand price for the separate items (services) must allocate the *joint costs* of all outputs, just as it alone sets prices for wool and mutton. Different rates would persist for the transport of copper and coal under a regime of competition, and although such discriminations would be magnified with monopolistic market structures, they could not be eliminated with government ownership or regulation because monopoly is not the source of differential rates. These principles, Taussig concluded, explain pricing in many other industrial operations, but railways "present on an enormous scale a case of the production at joint cost of different commodities."

Pigou, in his *Wealth and Welfare,* published in 1912, presented a trenchant criticism of the widely accepted view that rates could be explained on the basis of joint cost, and he named Taussig as its sponsor. Devoting an entire chapter to the issue of rail rates, Pigou argued (1) that Taussig was in error in identifying rail costs as preponderantly joint and (2) that he was led to the error by regarding the transport service supplied as a heterogeneous unit of output. Pigou was convinced that monopoly coupled with the presence of the necessary conditions for price discrimination explained multiple rates. The large mass of rail *common* costs were allocated by differing demand elasticities for the homogeneous unit of output.

Although it is generally conceded that Pigou won the debate and that price discrimination is the essential explanation for rail rates, F. W. Taussig's reasoning concerning the nonhomogeneous product greatly affected E. H. Chamberlin and his development of imperfect competition. In a 1961 essay, Chamberlin attributed the origin of his theory to the controversy. He admitted that Pigou had the upper hand in the debate but that "a very slight element of monopoly" would have supported Taussig's position. This slight element of monopoly, that is, some ability to control price, was the *result* of the ability to differentiate products. Taussig had noted in the course of the debate that: "We speak of railways and the like industries as 'monopolies.' Yet they are far from being industries to which the strict theory of monopoly price can be applied." Railways, in other words, are subject to degrees of competition, from other railways and from other modes of transportation. From this literature on railway rates, then, Chamberlin derived one of the essentials of his theory—product differentiation—though he presented the idea in a far more general form.

E. H. CHAMBERLIN'S QUEST FOR A NEW THEORY OF VALUE

Product Differentiation

One of the most important elements of Chamberlin's new theory of monopolistic competition was that most firms involve themselves not only in price competition but in nonprice competition as well. Though a large number of firms might exist in a market (the competitive element in monopolistic competition), each was viewed by Chamberlin as having a unique product or advantage that gave it some control over price (the monopoly element in monopolistic competition). Each seller, because of this monopoly element, would be able to vary price.

What were these monopoly elements? Sraffa had already described some of them in a general way, as we have seen, but Chamberlin specifically noted such items as copyrights, trademarks, brand names, and economic space (i.e., where products might be identical but where buyers, because of the distances involved, would have locational allegiances). Chamberlin clearly expounded the dual nature of most markets:

> In this field of "products" differentiated by the circumstances surrounding their sale, we may say, as in the case of patents and trade-marks, that both monopolistic and competitive elements are present. The field is commonly regarded as competitive, yet it differs only in degree from others which would at once be classed as monopolistic. In retail trade, each "product" is rendered unique by the individuality of the establishment in which it is sold, including its location (as well as by trademarks, qualitative differences, etc.); this is its monopolistic aspect. Each is subject to the competition of other "products" sold under different circumstances and at other locations; this is its competitive aspect. Here, as elsewhere in the field of differentiated products, both monopoly and competition are always present (*The Theory of Monopolistic Competition*, p. 63).

Many examples of Chamberlin's theory come to mind. Take aspirin (for the moment, ignore the issue of whether all aspirin is the same). Numerous brands exist: Advil, Empirin, Bufferin, Cope, Bayer, and many, many others. Through advertising and packaging, each brand is established and differentiated, thus creating a market of buyers who demand a *specific* product. Depending upon the size and intensity of demand in any specific case, the seller can charge a monopolistic price that may differ from that of his or her competitors. Although a large number of substitutes compete for the consumer's aspirin dollar, price differentials can exist.

These differences can exist, of course, whether or not all aspirin is alike. Product differentiation, in other words, may convince the consumer that differences exist, even when they in fact do not. The aim of this activity is to increase buyer allegiance for, and the number of buyers of, the product. In this manner, profits are increased (in the short run, at least).

Product differentiation, as Chamberlin suggests in the quotation above, may be of yet another form—economic space. Location may differentiate the products of sellers, and it may indeed be the overriding consideration. Suppose, for example, that five drugstores exist in a large city and further assume that they are alike in service and range of offerings. Though the products—drugstores—appear to be alike in every respect, Chamberlin would point out that they are differentiated with respect to location. The degree of monopoly and the degree of freedom with which any store can price will depend upon the number and dispersion of drugstore demanders, as well as upon the location of competing sellers. Location is then part and parcel of product differentiation.

A multiplicity of other examples of differentiation could be cited. Automobiles are differentiated, but substitutability still exists. Furniture, toothpaste, suppliers of identical but locationally differentiated raw materials, fine china, the neighborhood grocer, clothing, etc., are all differentiated markets. Chamberlin's point was well made and may be summarized as follows: There exists practically no market that is not characterized by monopoly elements. These monopoly elements are manifested by some form of differentiation: product, location, or service, for example. This fact means that each seller has some control over price, however small. When much (little) substitutability exists, the demand for the product is more (less) elastic, giving the individual seller less (more) control over price. Whereas Marshall regarded price as the sole variable under analysis in value theory, Chamberlin regarded both price and the product itself as variables under the control of firms in markets characterized by elements of both competition and monopoly.

Advertising: The Method of Most Differentiation

A little reflection will reveal that competitive advertising is largely unnecessary under either pure competition or pure monopoly (a single seller with no substitutes). The purely competitive seller is assumed to produce a homogeneous product and to be able to sell all the firm's output at the given market price. There would be no need to advertise, and if it did so, the firm, by increasing its costs, would go out of business. Indeed, under most formulations, wants are given, and *perfect knowledge* is assumed to prevail. By definition, a pure monopolist, facing no competitors and no substitutes, would not need to advertise and would reduce profits by doing so.

Chamberlin recognized, however, that advertising is the modus operandi of monopolistic competition, and he lumped a number of items into what he called "selling costs." In his words, "Advertising of all varieties, salesmen's salaries and the expense of sales departments, margins granted to dealers (retail and wholesale) in order to increase their effort in favor of particular goods, window displays, demonstrations of new goods, etc., are all costs of this type" (*The Theory of Monopolistic Competition*, p. 117). The purpose of all these costs is clear, however: to alter the position and/or elasticity of the demand function facing the individual firm.

The individual entrepreneur's reasons for advertising are obvious: "to shift to the right the demand curve for the advertised product by spreading knowledge of its existence, by describing it, and by suggesting utilities it will provide the purchaser'' (*The Theory of Monopolistic Competition,* p. 119). In addition, Chamberlin claimed that advertising affects demands by manipulating wants. Some ads are simply not informative at all, in other words, but are competitive in attempting to rearrange wants.[1] Such advertising is well known to any television viewer who regularly groans at uninformative and often tasteless exhortations. The intent of such advertising is to shift the demand curve of the advertised good to the right, at the expense of goods that substitute in the product group. Such advertising allocates demand among competing sellers, but unless the consumer's saving is reduced, it does not increase aggregate demand. Advertising, in sum, plays a crucial role in establishing and maintaining product differentiation in the monopolistically competitive firm.

Chamberlin's Two Demand Curves

It is now time to consider the demand situation actually facing the monopolistically competitive firm. Chamberlin described the firm as actually facing two demand curves, although he behaved as if only one is relevant. A diagram might clarify his rather cryptic statement. Figure 18-1 depicts two demand functions, *DD* and *dd,* which intersect at point C. Both of these functions are negatively sloped since the firm is assumed to have some control over price. Suppose that the firm, which is assumed to be in a monopolistically competitive market, is charging price P_M and selling quantity Q_M. How does the firm (whose product faces a large number of competing substitute products) view the situation? Given that all firms in his product group produce substitutable goods, the seller believes that he could increase sales considerably by lowering his price P_M. *The seller also believes that a marked reduction in sales will result from raising his price above P_M,* however, since he believes that none of his competitors will follow. Thus, assuming that the seller believes that his action will go unnoticed by his rivals, the demand curve facing the firm would be *dd.*

A slight problem renders the individual seller's assumption unwarranted, however. If our representative seller can profit from a price reduction, so can any of his rivals, assuming, as Chamberlin did, that costs for all firms are identical. Thus it is reasonable to expect that all the monopolistic competitors would have an incentive to reduce prices. If all reduced prices vis-à-vis our representative seller's reduction, sales would expand to the firm only from the general price reduction and not at the expense of his rivals. *DD* depicts the demand curve, given that rival firms follow the price actions of any one firm.

Both curves *dd* and *DD* are drawn under the assumption that advertising expenditures are at a constant level for each firm. Should the firm under con-

---

[1] Social unrest in underdeveloped countries is often said to rest upon a ''demonstration effect.'' The advertisement of Cadillacs, appliances, and luxury goods in these countries is said to alter the individual's ''utility function'' or want pattern. Finding such goods unobtainable under the constraints of existing institutions, individuals take steps to alter these institutions.

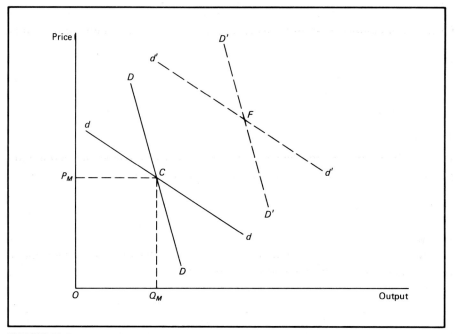

FIGURE 18-1
A monopolistically competitive firm can increase its sales along demand curve *dd* by reducing its price below P_M. However, if rival firms follow the price actions of any one firm, the demand curve will change to *DD*.

sideration increase its amount of competitive advertising, *given that other firms do not react similarly,* the demand functions facing the firm in Figure 18-1 would shift to the right, and profits could be increased. Advertising expenditures would be optimized for the firm when $1 of additional selling costs added exactly $1 to the firm's receipts.

Chamberlin's Tangency Solution: Long-Run Equilibrium

We are now in a position to discuss Chamberlin's famous "tangency solution" to the market model of monopolistic competition. Once his solution is described, its conclusions may then be contrasted to those of the perfectly competitive Marshallian model.

First it would be well to summarize the assumptions of the model. Chamberlin focused upon a single firm in an industry composed of many sellers producing and selling closely related and substitutable products.[2] Each

---

[2] It is perhaps worth repeating that products or product groups do not have to have similar physical characteristics. A new boat may be highly substitutable for a vacation in Hawaii. Although the two are obviously not physically similar, they could constitute a product group in Chamberlinian terms.

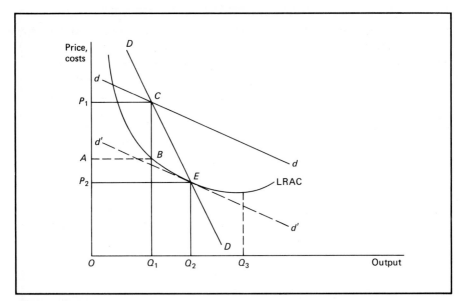

FIGURE 18-2
At price P_1, and output Q_1, each seller will make profits of $ABCP_1$. If a seller lowers the
price below P_1 and rival sellers follow suit, the *dd* function will slide down the *DD* function
until it (new schedule *d'd'*) intersects *DD* at point *E*.

seller has some control over price, and since he is in a large group of sellers, he
assumes that his price actions would not provoke any reaction from the competitive field. He would, in short, view his demand curve as *dd* or *d'd'* of Figure 18-1, and assuming that the degree of product differentiation had been determined, he would manipulate *prices* in order to increase profits. Chamberlin,
moreover, assumed the existence of a representative firm, not unlike
Marshall's, so that every firm's cost and demand were treated as identical.

A model reproducing demand curves, like those of Figure 18-1 (*dd*, *d'd'*,
and *DD*), as well as a long-run average cost *LRAC*, is represented in Figure
18-2 (which closely follows Chamberlin's Figure 14 in *The Theory of Monopolistic Competition*, p. 91).[3] Let the representative seller (of, say, 100 sellers)
find herself at the intersection of curves *dd* and *DD* (point *C*), charging price
P_1 and producing quantity Q_1. Each firm will produce the same price and
quantity, and each will earn profits of $ABCP_1$. Now consider the manner in
which any one of the firms views its situation. The seller believes, erroneously
it turns out, that she may increase her profits by lowering price; i.e., she believes that demand curve *dd* is relevant in that her rivals will not reduce prices
when she does. But each one does in fact reduce prices, and instead of expanding along curve *dd*, the firms expand along *DD*.

---

[3] See Ferguson, *Microeconomic Theory*, Chap. 10, for a discussion of the dynamics of this
equilibrium.

Each seller continues to believe that he or she could increase profits by lowering price, and each one does so. The $d'd'$ function continues sliding down the DD function until it (now dashed $d'd'$) intersects DD at point E. Here the firm's demand curve is tangent to the long-run average costs, and economic profits are eliminated. If the dashed $d'd'$ function fell *below* its position in Figure 18-2, losses would ensue and prices increase. In short, the tangency equilibrium is stable. Quantities greater than Q_2 would produce a loss to the firm since long-run average cost would be greater than average revenue or demand.[4] Chamberlin's equilibrium exists uniquely at the tangency of $d'd'$ with $LRAC$ and simultaneously at the intersection of $d'd'$ and DD.

Monopolistic Competition: A Waste of Resources?

A charge often leveled at monopolistic competition is that its economic effects are inefficient compared with those of perfect or pure competition. Specifically, it is alleged that excess capacity exists at a monopolistically competitive equilibrium such as point E in Figure 18-2. Let us look into the nature of this charge.

Figure 18-3 abstracts some of the functions of Figure 18-2, including the dd demand function and the long-run average-cost function. The $LRAC$ function, as the reader might recall from Chapter 15, is often called an "envelope" or "planning" curve. It is composed of a series of tangencies of points on the short-run average-cost curve. $SRAC_1$ and $SRAC_2$ are two such short-run curves, and for simplicity assume that between any two short-run U-shaped curves, another could be drawn for a slight alteration in scale of plant. The firm is producing an *optimum rate of output* when it utilizes the existing scale of plant (i.e., existing resources invested) to produce at the lowest average cost of production. Given a scale of plant characterized by $SRAC_1$, this optimum rate of output would be Q_m^1. Since, from the point of view of the firm, output Q_m is a profit-maximizing equilibrium state, from *society's* viewpoint the plant is being underutilized in that $Q_m Q_m^1$ is not being produced.

A second reason proffered for the inefficiency of monopolistic competition is that it does not produce a competitive rate of output, that is, one that achieves an optimum scale of plant from society's point of view. Firms' demand curves, it will be recalled, are horizontal or infinitely elastic, given perfect competition. Such a demand curve is represented in Figure 18-3 as the horizontal $P_c d_c$. The long-run output for the purely competitive firm would be Q_c, corresponding to both an optimum rate of output and an optimum scale of plant from society's point of view. Thus, it is alleged, waste exists for two reasons: (1) because the monopolistically competitive firm does not utilize its existing resources to produce a socially optimum rate of output and (2) because

---

[4] The total number of sellers was kept constant throughout the analysis. See Chamberlin's *Theory of Monopolistic Competition*, p. 92.

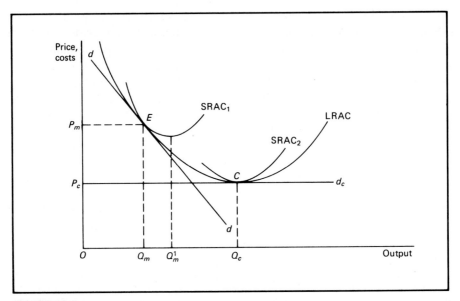

FIGURE 18-3
A monopolistically competitive firm will maximize profits at price P_m and output Q_m, but given the scale of plant represented by $SRAC_1$, the optimum rate of output from society's point of view will be Q_m^1. "Excess social capacity" is measured by Q_mQ_c, where Q_c is the competitive rate of output.

a socially optimum scale of plant is rendered impossible as a result of product differentiation, which creates a negatively sloped demand function. "Excess social capacity" is then measured as Q_mQ_c.

Chamberlin, however, did not agree with this conclusion. Product differentiation, he argued, introduces variety and expands the continuum of the consumer's choices. Certainly a comparison of social benefits under pure competition and monopolistic competition must take this crucial difference into account. Variety might be desirable, i.e., possess utility for its own sake, and such variety would not be possible given homogeneous output under perfect competition. The increased social welfare from variety that monopolistic competition represents may well be greater than the loss in terms of excess social capacity that the market model necessitates. The theorist can only speculate.[5]

Chamberlin: A Tentative Evaluation

Chamberlin's *Theory of Monopolistic Competition* was an important benchmark in the development of value and the theory of industrial organization. A

---

[5] The whole foundation of monopolistic competition has been questioned in a number of important recent contributions (see Notes for Further Reading at the end of the chapter). The substance of this modern argument is that what may appear to be excess capacity is simply a *competitive* market's working out of a means to reduce "waiting time," transactions costs, or time-associated costs.

great deal of interest developed in models of monopolistic competition in the 1930s, 1940s, and 1950s. Professors Fritz Machlup, Robert Triffen, William Fellner, Arthur Smithies, and many others have built upon Chamberlin's work. Practically every text in principles of economics and in intermediate microeconomic analysis devotes space to Chamberlin and his ideas.[6]

Chamberlin himself devoted his entire life to the selling of his theory. In article after article he amplified, corrected, expanded, and contrasted issues surrounding monopolistic competition, and many of these appeared as appendixes to successive editions of *The Theory of Monopolistic Competition* (it went through seven editions).

Although a number of theorists continue to work Chamberlinian "realism" into value theory, a large and ever-growing coterie has come to defend an expanded model of perfect competition as a more consistent and useful approach to microeconomic problems. Why? Not because the assumptions of perfect competition seem more realistic, but because a modified competitive analysis seems to yield very fruitful predictions concerning the behavior of price and quantity in individual markets. The outcome is uncertain, but it is clear that at the time, Chamberlin struck a responsive chord in economic analysis in emphasizing monopolistic elements in the competitive process. Interest in the market conditions of specific industries, which gave impetus to industry studies and to the field of industrial organization, owes much to E. H. Chamberlin's work. In addition, many of his ideas have raised questions that are still relevant to economic analysis. Chamberlin's major achievement, then, seems to have suggested and partially implemented interesting new paths of analysis rather than to have provided economics with a well-cultivated and finished alternative to the competitive model. Thus Chamberlin's contributions were noteworthy, substantial, and important for the future of economic theory.

ROBINSON AND IMPERFECT COMPETITION

Another economist's interest in imperfect competition blossomed almost simultaneously with Chamberlin's. Joan Robinson's early training in Marshallian economics, particularly as expanded and debated by A. C. Pigou and Piero Sraffa, led her to a comparative analysis of monopolistic and competitive markets that she called *The Economics of Imperfect Competition*.

Published in 1933 (completed in late 1932), Robinson's *Economics of Imperfect Competition* is an analytical tour de force. Robinson in the main eschewed Chamberlin's emphasis upon product differentiation and advertising as elements of monopolistic markets, but her book introduced and used a "set of tools" (a term of her invention) that has become valuable in the partial-equilibrium analysis of markets and market structures. Specifically, Robinson

---

[6] The reader is encouraged to read Chamberlin's *Theory of Monopolistic Competition* and to remember that the ideas presented here are only a sample. His assessments of the duopoly models of Cournot, Bertrand, Edgeworth, and Hotelling are particularly recommended.

reintroduced Cournot's untitled concept of marginal revenue into the theory of the firm, be it a competitive or a monopoly firm or one somewhere in between.

Fully cognizant of the fact that *degrees* of monopoly exist, Robinson chose the pure monopoly model as a proxy for all those intermediate structures that Chamberlin had begun to classify.[7] In this sense, Robinson's approach was both more traditional and more general than Chamberlin's. Within the confines of her method of analysis, however, she was able to make contributions of the first rank to the theory of the firm under all imperfectly competitive market structures. After a brief discussion of the reintroduction of the marginal-revenue concept, two of Robinson's major contributions will be considered: her analysis of monopoly and price discrimination and her discussion of the effects of monopolistic elements in the market for labor.

Marginal Analysis

As noted above, one of Robinson's great contributions was the revival of marginal analysis. Alfred Marshall and all the neoclassical economists had clearly understood marginalism, but practically all had framed their graphic analyses of firm profit maximization in terms of total cost and total revenue. The latter approach can be cumbersome and tedious, as can be verified by a cursory look at some of Marshall's expositions (see his analysis of monopoly and the "constant revenue schedules" to which he must resort in his *Principles,* p. 335).

Concave and Convex Functions   Robinson readopted Cournot's convention of graphically analyzing monopoly equilibrium in terms of marginal quantities.[8] As she noted, "The first tool required for the monopoly analysis of value is a pair of curves, marginal and average." Emphasizing the generality of the approach, she said further that, "The conceptions of average and marginal value can be applied to costs of production, utility, revenue, the productivity of factors of production, and so on" (*Economics of Imperfect Competition,* p. 26). Thus Robinson explored the general relations between average and marginal curves, indicating their applicability to various types of economic quantities. Some of these important relations are summarized in Figures 18-4*a* and 18-4*b*. In Figure 18-4*a* a concave (viewed from above) average function is drawn, and in Figure 18-4*b* a similar function, though convex, is depicted. One might visualize these as cost functions, but the general and simple rules drawn from them apply to all marginal and average behavior. Clearly, when a marginal quantity is less (greater) than an average quantity, the average must be declining (rising). When the marginal quantity equals the average, the average is either at a maximum or at a minimum.

---

[7] Chamberlin's classifications of market structures (polypoly, etc.) were expanded by Machlup and others. See References at the end of this chapter.

[8] Robinson freely acknowledged that others in the post-Marshallian era had, at least partly, utilized this approach.

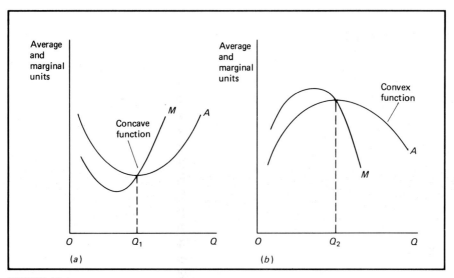

FIGURE 18-4
Portions of the concave function to the left of Q_1 in (a) and portions of the convex function to the right of Q_2 in (b) represent the nonlinear relation between average revenue and marginal revenue. Portions of the concave function to the right of Q_1 in (a) and portions of the convex function to the left of Q_2 in (b) represent the nonlinear relation between average cost and marginal cost.

Applied to costs, it is clear that when marginal costs are less than average costs, average costs must be declining (see Figure 18-4a) and that when marginal costs are greater than average costs, average costs are rising. Since monopoly demand curves are negatively sloped, the relations between the demand curve, which is of course the *average* revenue curve to the firm, and the marginal-revenue curve are described by portions M and A of Figure 18-4a for quantities less than quantity Q_1 and by portions M and A of Figure 18-4b for quantities greater than Q_2. Indeed, Robinson presented an exhaustive examination of the behavior of average revenue and marginal revenue and, moreover, utilized these relations in her important extension of the theory of price discrimination. Beyond her own specific applications of the tool kit, Robinson's presentation and systematic review of the mathematical behavior of economically intersecting functions were themselves a contribution of great merit. Perhaps more than any other theorist, Robinson was responsible for the propagation of contemporary methods in analyzing microeconomic aspects of firm behavior.

Pigou, Robinson, and the Theory of Price Discrimination

In Chapter 12, Dupuit's analysis of price discrimination was discussed at some length. It will be recalled that his contribution was concerned primarily with the welfare advantages of price discrimination over simple monopoly pricing.

It remained for A. C. Pigou and Joan Robinson to refine and develop foundations of discrimination in pure theory. Unfortunately, the Pigou-Robinson analysis of price discrimination is a rather complex and difficult subject in pure theory. Thus only a verbal overview is presented here.[9]

Price discrimination is an activity carried on by a firm with monopoly power because it is profitable. Essentially it involves the selling of *identical* units of a commodity to different individuals and groups of individuals at *different* prices. Perhaps it would be well to comment upon the formal conditions necessary for price discrimination at the outset.

Conditions Necessary for Price Discrimination   First, a degree of monopoly power is required. The firm, in short, need not be a single seller, but it must face a downward-sloping demand curve for its product. Any firm (including the whole range from monopolistically competitive to pure monopoly) that has any degree of control over the price of its product possesses one of the prerequisites for price discrimination.

Second, the firm must be able to discern (or artificially create) more than one market for its product. These markets must be separable—such as the markets for children's and adults' movie tickets—ordinarily by some identifiable characteristic (age in the case of movie tickets). Retrading between consumers in the several markets must be either too costly or impossible. In the case of movie tickets, for example, a market wherein exchange of children's for adults' tickets might take place must be prohibited. Such retrading might be effectively disallowed by the use of different-colored tickets and/or by an age check at the theater door.

A third prerequisite for price discrimination relates to the entrepreneur's profit motive. Simply stated, the *relative* profitability in the two or more markets must be different or different enough, measured at simple monopoly price. Specifically, the condition is that the elasticities of demand, or the ratios of simple monopoly price to marginal revenue, must be different in two (or more) markets facing the monopolist. This condition makes good economic sense. If a monopolist is selling some given quantity X and if he or she can separate and discern two markets, one of which will yield a higher addition to revenue for every unit sold, it will be profitable for the monopolist to transfer units of output from the market yielding lower revenues to that producing higher revenues. Such transfers of output units from one market (the low marginal revenue market) to the other (the high marginal revenue market) will have the effect of finally producing an equality of the marginal revenues in both markets.

These conditions for discrimination can be illustrated with the use of the simple model (which only appears complex) given in Figure 18-5. In Figure 18-5

---

[9] The reader interested in detailed analysis is directed to Robinson's *Economics of Imperfect Competition,* Chaps. 15 and 16, or to other sources listed in the References at the end of this chapter.

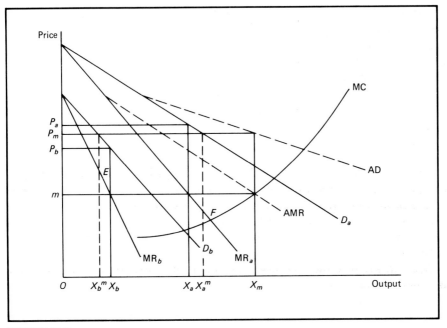

FIGURE 18-5
A single-price monopolist will produce output X_m and charge price P_m, selling output X_b^m and X_a^m in the two markets. A discriminating monopolist will equate the single-value marginal cost to the marginal revenue in each market, and produce output X_a for market A at price P_a, and output X_b for market B at price P_b.

the demand curves of two discernible markets, represented by D_a and D_b, are depicted. The aggregate demand and marginal revenue facing the monopolist are found by summing (horizontally) the demand and marginal revenue functions of the two separable markets. These two aggregate functions are represented by the dashed curves AD and AMR, respectively. These are the only curves relevant for a monopolist who charges only *one* price, and under this system he or she would produce output X_m, which corresponds to the equating of marginal cost (MC) with aggregate marginal revenue AMR. Price, read off AD at output X_m, would correspond to P_m. Total output X_m would be allocated in the two markets from the demand curves D_a and D_b. In other words, if price P_m is charged for the product, X_b^m will be sold in one of the markets (B), and output X_a^m will be sold in the other, yielding a total monopoly output X_m.

The Discriminating Monopolist Let us now evaluate the situation facing the monopolist. If the necessary conditions exist for price discrimination in the situation depicted in Figure 18-5—i.e., if the markets are separable, etc.—the monopolist can increase her or his profits by transferring sale units from market A to market B! Why? Because the addition to revenue from an addition to sales in B is *greater* than that in A. Figure 18-5 verifies this point. At simple monopoly price P_m the marginal revenue of sales in market B (A) corresponds to some value E (F). Thus the transfer of a unit of output from A to B would add more to the firm's revenue (E, approximately) than the firm would lose by doing so (F, approximately). Thus the profit-maximizing monopolist would find it in her or his interest to adjust sales and price in the two markets so that the revenues produced there were exactly the same. This equation of revenues is accomplished by equating MC and AMR as before but also by equating this single value MC to the marginal revenues in the *separate* markets. Graphically, in Figure 18-5, this single value of MC is shown as the line drawn to point m on the vertical axis from $MC = AMR$. Discriminating outputs and prices are determined by the intersection of this line with the MR's in the separate markets. Output OX_a for market A is produced and sold at price P_a, and output OX_b is sold at price P_b in market B. Note that output is *increased* in market B by the same amount as it is *decreased* in market A. Thus in the case described in Figure 18-5, total output remains unchanged, irrespective of whether the monopolist discriminates. Monopoly profits are clearly increased by price discrimination, however.

Output Effects: Robinson's Contribution With the model of Figure 18-5 firmly in hand we are in a position to comment upon Robinson's contribution to price discrimination. Pigou had clearly described this model as early as 1912 in his *Wealth and Welfare* (a revised version entitled *The Economics of Welfare* was published in 1920). In the case depicted in Figure 18-5, the simple monopolist via discrimination simply redistributes utility to her or himself from consumers of her or his product. This utility takes the form of increased profits at the expense of consumers' surplus. This is so because the total quantity sold remains the same before and after a two-price system is employed.[10] In other words, a simple redistribution of welfare takes place.

One of the most important arguments raised against monopoly in the economic literature (by Dupuit, Wieser, Marshall, and many others) has been that it restricts output and thus diminishes the economic welfare that would be produced if the good or service were sold under competitive conditions. The case considered in Figure 18-5 does not provide any objective social basis for choosing simple monopoly structures over discriminating monopoly structures, or vice versa. Output remains the same in either case, and one might argue that the redistribution that occurs with discrimination outrages a popular sense of equity; i.e., one might argue against discrimination and in favor of simple monopoly pricing.

Pigou, however, used only *linear* curves (like those in Figure 18-5) in concluding that output would remain unchanged with the introduction of price discrimination. In the course of refining Pigou's analysis of discrimination, Robinson brilliantly demonstrated that his conclusion was only a special case

---

[10] At this point the reader might profit from rereading those sections of Chap. 12 dealing with price discrimination.

and that discriminatory output could be greater or less than that sold under simple monopoly pricing.

Although Robinson's proof of this crucial point is fairly complex, the method and conclusions of her analysis can be stated simply. Basically, the question of whether output changes hinges upon the shape, or concavity, of the demand curves in the separate markets. Concavity, as has been depicted in Figure 18-4, relates to the change in the *slope* of the demand curves. Robinson's view may be stated succinctly: Output will be larger (smaller) under discrimination than under simple monopoly pricing if the demand curve in the more elastic market is relatively more concave (convex) than the demand curve in the less elastic market.[11] If the demand curves are linear, as in the case Pigou describes (Figure 18-5), Robinson demonstrated that the curves are of *equal* concavity and that output remains unchanged with the introduction of a multiple-price system.

At this point, one might justifiably wonder whether Robinson's theory is not of purely academic interest. Stated differently, does her difficult theoretical analysis of relative concavities in monopoly pricing have anything to do with the real world or not? The answer, as with many economic questions, depends on the empirical evidence respecting the shapes of demand curves in noncompetitive markets. Antidiscriminatory policies may be somewhat misguided from the point of view of social welfare if discrimination does in fact produce higher outputs than simple monopoly. Robinson drew one possibility from international trade:

> This is probably a common case where the more elastic market is an export market in which the exported goods are in competition with those produced locally. It will often happen that only a small amount can be exported at relatively high prices but that as the price of the exported goods approaches and falls below the price of the local rival goods the demand for them increases very rapidly—in short the demand curve is highly concave (*The Economics of Imperfect Competition*, p. 205).

As with "dumping" in international markets, discrimination on the part of transportation firms of all kinds and public utilities might well result in increases in output.

Many other examples of the possible importance of Robinson's analysis come to mind. The Robinson-Patman Act of 1936 (which expanded the Clayton Act of 1914) proscribed certain types of price discrimination, and, indeed, the antidiscriminatory statutes have become one of the most important parts of antitrust legislation.[12] Since antitrust legislation is designed to deal with monopoly market structures wherein discrimination or the expansion of discriminatory pricing is a possibility, the law would appear to thwart or im-

---

[11] The concavity of the demand curves in the two markets is to be evaluated at simple monopoly price.

[12] There is an irony in the fact that a legislative act, authored by one of the same surname and clearly antidiscriminatory in tone, followed Robinson's unique theoretical demonstrations by only three years.

pede the welfare gains of potential output increases. In short, the traditional presumption in antitrust enforcement must be reevaluated where the policy alternatives are between single-rate monopoly pricing and multiple discriminatory rates. These multiple-pricing systems, as Robinson demonstrated, might possess certain welfare advantages over simple monopoly pricing. Only careful empiricism can sort out the probable results in any particular case.

Labor Exploitation: Monopoly and Monopsony

Perhaps one of the most famous concepts to emerge in Robinson's discussion of a "world of monopolies" relates to the market for labor. In traditional (Marshallian) competitive theory it is assumed that workers will be paid a wage that is equivalent to the value of the marginal product they produce. A simple arithmetic illustration will make the point clear. If the addition of one worker adds 2 additional bushels of corn to a farmer's output, the marginal product of that worker is said to be 2 bushels.[13] If competition exists in the market for corn, the price of the product to the firm will not change with the addition of 2 bushels of output. Assuming that the price per bushel of corn is $1.50, the value of the marginal product of the worker is $3. If competition exists in the market for farm workers, *all* workers will receive a wage of $3. Definitionally, then, the value of the marginal product is equivalent to the product of the worker's physical marginal product (2 bushels) and the price of the final output ($1.50 per bushel). In equilibrium the worker receives a wage equivalent to this product. Symbolically, if $VMP_L = MP_L \times P_x$, this equilibrium is expressed as

$$W = VMP_L = MP_L \times P_x$$

The above expression is to be evaluated in the following manner. When competition exists in both input and output markets, the wages of all workers will equal the marginal product of the nth worker times the price of the final output (P_x). Economic theory tells us that the demand curve for the perfectly competitive firm is horizontal (infinitely elastic)—i.e., price equals marginal revenue—and the firm can sell additional units of output at the going market price. Thus price is assumed not to change when workers are added. Yet the VMP_L ultimately *declines* when units of input are added, and a moment's reflection on simple theory tells us why this is so. It is because labor's marginal product falls as a result of diminishing returns when more labor inputs are added to the firm's employ. These relations are summarized in Figure 18-6, where the demand curve for labor is equal to the value of the marginal product of labor. As labor inputs N are increased, the VMP *declines* because of a decline in the marginal productivity of labor (P_x, of course, remains constant under perfect

---

[13] The complexities of multiple inputs are neglected here.

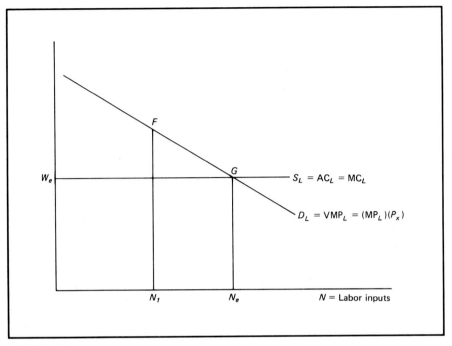

FIGURE 18-6
At wage rate W_e, the profit-maximizing firm will hire N_e units of labor because at lower levels of labor utilization, the value of labor's marginal product (for example, N_1F) is greater than the firm's cost of each labor unit (W_e).

competition in the product market). The supply function for labor is horizontal, indicating that the wage rate does not change with additional employment of labor and reflecting the assumption of perfect competition in the labor market. Given the wage rate W_e and the VMP schedule, the profit-maximizing employer will hire N_e units of labor. A look at Figure 18-6 will tell us why. If the firm (or farmer, in our simple example) hired only N_1 units of labor, the value of labor's marginal product would be an amount N_1F. In practical terms, N_1 units of labor would add more to the firm's receipt (an amount N_1F) than to the firm's costs (W_e per unit). The rational employer, then, will continue to hire inputs up to the point where the addition to the firm's receipts from hiring additional inputs is exactly equivalent to the addition to the firm's costs of doing so. This occurs at point G, where N_e units are hired at a wage of W_e for all units.

Imperfections on the Supply Side   Now that we have established the necessary backdrop, we may turn to Robinson's contribution, which, essentially, was to analyze the labor market when two of the competitive assumptions of the traditional analysis, described in Figure 18-6, were dropped. Specifically, Robinson identified labor market imperfections due to (1) monopoly conditions in the market for the firm's final output and/or (2) market imperfections in the hiring of labor. The former leads to monopoly exploitation of labor, and the latter to monopsony exploitation. These two cases may be treated together graphically, but the two concepts are discussed separately here.

How are the elements of competitive-input equilibrium altered when monopoly elements exist in the market for the firm's product? The answer clearly relates to the demand curve for labor (see Figure 18-6), or, what is the same thing, the value of the marginal-product curve. Recall that the demand for labor under competitive conditions (*VMP* in Figure 18-6) was determined by multiplying the marginal product of labor by the price of final output. Under conditions of perfect competition the firm is a "price taker"; that is, it faces a perfectly elastic horizontal demand for its product. Price, under such conditions, equals the marginal revenue to the firm. When each firm possesses a degree of monopoly, however slight, the price of the commodity does not equal the marginal revenue that the firm receives from selling additional units of product. The seller faces negatively sloped demand and marginal revenue in this case. Clearly, if a firm must reduce the price of its commodity to sell more units, it must reduce the price on *all* the units it sells (unless, of course, it can discriminate). Under such circumstances the *addition* to revenue (the marginal revenue) is not simply the price of the additional unit sold. Rather, it is *less* than the price of the unit since the loss from lowering the price on all previous units must be subtracted. Thus marginal revenue is lower than price under monopoly conditions.

The ramifications of this feature of monopoly for demand for labor should be clear. Since the firm calculates the addition to receipts from hiring additional inputs, the increase will be determined by the marginal product of the input and the marginal revenue of the output sold, rather than by the price obtainable therefrom. This means that, given monopoly in the output market, the firm's demand for labor will be the marginal revenue product of labor, found by multiplying the marginal revenue of final output by the marginal product of labor; that is, $MRP_L = MP_L \times MR_x$. Recall that $VMP_L = MP_L \times P_x$ and that since under monopoly $P_x > MR_x$, then $VMP_L > MRP_L$. In equilibrium workers are paid a wage equivalent to their marginal revenue product, not the value of their marginal product. Robinson identified this difference as monopoly exploitation of labor.

Although the issue of monopoly exploitation will be treated graphically in Figure 18-7, we must first turn to the second of the imperfections Robinson discussed, monopsony in the *hiring* of labor. Exploitation, Robinson maintained, also arises because "the supply of labor is imperfectly elastic to the unit of control." This imperfection in the supply of labor is not due to any differences in the quality of labor. Rather, laborers are explicitly assumed to be homogeneous in efficiency. Why, then, might a firm have to pay higher and higher wages in order to hire additional workers? Robinson offered the following reasons, among others: "because it was necessary to tempt labour away from better paid occupations, to overcome the cost of movement from more distant regions, or to overcome a preference for other occupations" (*The Economics of Imperfect Competition,* p. 292).

Translated into economic terms, monopsony means that the average cost to the firm of hiring labor (which is the wage rate) rises as additional units of labor are employed. As we learned in the section on marginal and average functions above, the marginal cost of hiring labor must *exceed* the average cost when the average is rising. In the case of labor inputs, this situation makes good sense. If additional workers can be acquired only at higher wage rates, the marginal cost of hiring more labor must be above the wage, since all workers must receive the higher wage. Thus the incremental cost, which is engendered by paying present workers the higher wage, must be added to the wage of the new worker.

If a firm is maximizing profits, it will always hire inputs up to the point where the addition to its costs is equivalent to the addition to its revenue. In the competitive case the equilibrium occurs when $W = VMP_L$, since the wage rate *is* the marginal cost of hiring inputs and the value of the marginal product *is* the addition to revenue resulting from the addition of a worker. Where monopoly exists in the output market and where monopsony exists in the input market, the condition is changed. The equilibrium quantity of inputs is now determined when the marginal cost of additional inputs (MC_i) equals the marginal revenue from employing them, the *marginal revenue product*. Thus a more general formulation of input equilibrium would be

$$MC_i = MRP_i = MR_x \times MP_i$$

Since, under competition, $MC_i = AC_i = W$ and $MR_x = P_x$, the above equation is also the correct expression for input equilibrium under competitive conditions.

Graphic Analysis   Robinson's theory of exploitation and imperfections in the labor market is summarized in Figure 18-7, which is very similar to her own illustration of the issue. In Figure 18-7, the *VMP* schedule is computed on the same basis as before, i.e., as in the competitive case. Since $P > MR$ when a degree of monopoly exists in the product market, MRP_L is less than the VMP_L curve. The revenue to the *firm* for hiring additional labor units is depicted by this function. In addition, given monopsony elements in the hiring of labor, the *AC* and *MC* of labor curves in Figure 18-7 do not coincide. The addition to the firm's cost from hiring additional labor inputs is obviously *MC*. Thus the profit-maximizing firm will hire N_e units of labor, the quantity that equates MRP_L and MC_L. Further, it will pay those inputs a wage W_e, read off the *AC* curve (the supply curve) of labor inputs to the firm.

An important argument raised by Robinson and directly related to the analysis of Figure 18-7 regards labor exploitation. Robinson did not define exploitation in Marxian terms. Rather, she defined it as "the payment to labor of less than its proper wage" (*The Economics of Imperfect Competition,* p. 281). By "proper wage" Robinson meant a wage equal to the value of labor's marginal

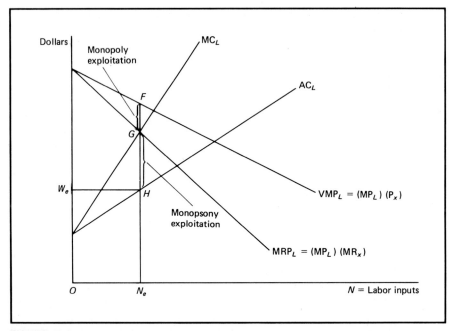

FIGURE 18-7
The amount of monopoly exploitation at labor utilization N_e is approximated by *FG*, and
the amount of monopsony exploitation is approximated by *GH*.

product, the one paid in competitive equilibrium. Market imperfections, both
in the demand for products and in the supply of labor, are the root cause of
exploitation. The exploitation, then, is of two types: that which exists under
monopoly and that which exists under monopsony. Both types are explained
in Figure 18-7. Monopoly exploitation exists, in the first instance, because
price and marginal revenue diverge under imperfect competition. The latter
situation causes MRP_L to be lower than VMP_L, and the amount of exploitation
at equilibrium employment N_e is approximated by *FG* in Figure 18-7. The second type of exploitation occurs because monopsony exists in the employment
of labor, which causes the *AC* of workers to the firm to be *less* than their *MC*.
The amount of exploitation due to monopsony is approximated by an amount
GH in Figure 18-7. Total exploitation in the amount *FH* takes place when N_e
inputs are hired at wage W_e. It is important to note that, according to
Robinson, pervasive market imperfections are the reason why labor is exploited (not paid the value of the marginal product). Exploitation is built into
the structure of the economy since monopoly is the rule rather than the
exception.[14] Indeed, this theme—"a world of monopolies"—pervades her

[14] Robinson also sponsored the argument, not discussed here, that a properly devised minimum wage imposed by the government might eliminate monopsony (but not monopoly) exploitation. The total number of workers employed may be lower with such a scheme, however (see *The*

book, and its application to the labor market makes her analysis of input returns distinctly original.

Imperfect Competition in Perspective

The present chapter has considered only a few of the unique features of Robinson's book, and at only a superficial level. Her discussions of rent and comparisons of monopoly and competitive output, for example, are important parts of received microanalysis. The publication of her book (and Chamberlin's) was unquestionably an important theoretical event.

Two issues of some moment in appreciating these contributions remain to be discussed, however. First, there are several crucial differences in the two models of imperfect competition discussed in the present chapter. Second, it is not at all clear that the so-called revolution in value theory, wrought by Chamberlin and Robinson, has won the day—theoretically, at least—judged from the vantage point of fifty or so years. We now turn to these issues.

As noted earlier in this chapter, E. H. Chamberlin spent a great deal of his productive life defending and simplifying his model. Moreover, he never tired of contrasting it to Robinson's. He noted, for instance, in a 1950 article:

> *Imperfect Competition* followed the tradition of competitive theory, not only in identifying a commodity (albeit elastically defined) with an industry, but in expressly assuming such a commodity to be homogeneous. Such a theory involves no break whatever with the competitive tradition. The very terminology of "imperfect competition" is heavy with implications that the objective is to move towards "perfection" ("Product Heterogeneity and Public Policy," p. 87).

Although Chamberlin's contrast was a bit overdrawn, there are important differences between the Chamberlin and Robinson approaches to imperfect competition. Clearly, Robinson did not try to develop a concept of product differentiation or "quality differences" in her analysis of monopoly, though she did allude at points in the book to heterogeneous products, patents, and all types of monopolistic restrictions that make firms unique. In many parts of her book Robinson's chosen level of analysis *was* the industry, but, as we have seen, the models of price discrimination were couched in terms of the firm. Further, she envisioned degrees of monopoly and, in so doing, underlined the great varieties of monopoly strength. In short, product differentiation with product as a variable does not play a starring role in her book, as it clearly does in Chamberlin's, but it may easily be worked into her conceptual framework.

Second, was Robinson's work simply a continuation of the Marshallian

---

Economics of Imperfect Competition, pp. 294–295, and the References at the end of this chapter). A large problem, of course, centers on Robinson's "scientific terminology." Just because she called $W = VMP_L$ the "proper" wage, for example, there is no economic justification for considering it to be the proper wage and all other wages to be "improper." It is simply her definition of proper wage, and it might be argued, cogently, that it would be improper for labor to receive anything other than its marginal revenue product when monopoly elements exist.

competitive tradition, as Chamberlin suggests? Stated differently, was Chamberlin's work the only original break with competitive value theory? Marshall and the Marshallians had, of course, studied monopoly as an extreme in value theory. But Robinson's insistence upon the pervasiveness of monopoly and degrees of monopoly power certainly departs from Marshall's general characterization of markets in the economy; i.e., it departs from the traditional one. Though she did not view monopolistic competition or anything approaching it as a norm or as a general theory of value (as Chamberlin did), it is clear that she accepted the inevitability of a continuing world of monopolies. Thus she recommended policies (minimum-wage legislation, etc.) that would soften their impact or partially increase welfare (allowance of price discrimination when output increased over simple monopoly). Such attitudes are hardly traditional, since monopoly, not competition, is the subject of analysis. All in all, it would perhaps be best to combine Chamberlin's and Robinson's approaches, calling the whole mélange "imperfect competition." Apart from a distinct difference in emphasis, and in levels of analysis, the two works do in fact have a single message: The competitive model is, in the main, inappropriate for describing observable pricing structures. In its stead, monopoly models are what economists should develop and expand.

As a final note, it is important to indicate that, notwithstanding the initial surge of interest in models of imperfect competition, lately the focus of many economists has turned back to the competitive model. It would, of course, be an overstatement to suggest that the nadir of such models is at hand, but it is the case that realism in model building often brings complexities that theory and empiricism cannot handle. Such is probably the case in some areas of imperfect competition. Indeterminacies in duopoly-oligopoly models of the type suggested by Chamberlin have repelled some theorists interested in firm behavior. The competitive model and its accoutrements, on the other hand, offer appealing and simple explanations of firm behavior. Many economists are attracted to such simple, though analytically satisfying, models. (In this arena Robinson—since her tool kit was more like Marshall's—has fared much better than Chamberlin.)[15] Still, Chamberlin's and Robinson's ideas are aired in contemporary books and courses on price theory. It is probably much too soon to judge the outcome of the value revolution. But whether it is viewed as a simple skirmish with the neoclassical tradition or as a full-fledged victory of analysis, the Chamberlin-Robinson reorientation continues to play a major role in twentieth-century economic thought.

NOTES FOR FURTHER READING

Today there exist a number of alternative theories of imperfect competition, depending on the premises established and the market to be analyzed. Fritz

---

[15] As for herself, Robinson has questioned the value of most of partial-equilibrium price theory, including her own! (see her "Imperfect Competition Revisited").

Machlup, *The Economics of Sellers Competition* (see References), and William Fellner, *Competition among the Few* (New York: A. M. Kelley, 1960), provide excellent treatments of monopolistic competition, imperfect competition, and oligopoly theory, along with many theoretical extensions. The question of efficiency and monopolistic competition is discussed in a number of papers by Harold Demsetz. See, for example, "The Nature of Equilibrium in Monopolistic Competition," *Journal of Political Economy,* vol. 67 (February 1959), pp. 21–30. Also see A. S. Devany, "An Analysis of Taxi Markets," *Journal of Political Economy,* vol. 83 (February 1975), pp. 83–94, for an extension of the theme of monopolistic competition in a particular market, that of taxicabs.

A neglected pioneer in the development of monopolistic competition theory is Heinrich von Stackelberg, a German economist. See his *Marktform und Gleichgewicht* (Vienna: Julius Springer, 1934), published just one year after the appearance of Chamberlin's and Robinson's works. Von Stackelberg developed a Cournot-type graphic technique to analyze the market results from various types of conjectural assumptions on the part of competitors. Concluding that instability and disequilibrium characterized many markets, von Stackelberg urged state intervention. His book is reviewed in Wassily Leontief's "Stackelberg on Monopolistic Competition," *Journal of Political Economy,* vol. 44 (August 1936), pp. 554–559; this article provides a mathematical treatment of von Stackelberg's theory. The best non-technical exposition of his alternative models may be found in Fellner, *Competition Among the Few*. Stackelberg geometry has been put to use in analyzing certain aspects of public-goods theory. See William L. Breit, "Public Goods Interaction in Stackelberg Geometry," *Western Economic Journal,* vol. 6 (March 1968), pp. 161–164. Von Stackelberg's *Theory of the Market Economy* has been translated by A. T. Peacock (London: William Hodge, 1952).

An even earlier pioneer in duopoly-oligopoly analysis must also be mentioned. In 1929 the American economist Harold Hotelling, in "Stability in Competition," *Economic Journal,* vol. 39 (March 1929), pp. 41–57, constructed a model wherein location of firms itself is a variable. He demonstrated the quasi-monopolistic power of each firm to set price on the basis of locational advantages (akin to product differentiation). Paul Sweezy utilized Chamberlin's two-demand curve analysis (see Figure 18-1) to discuss the alleged rigidity of oligopoly prices in his "Demand under Conditions of Oligopoly," *Journal of Political Economy,* vol. 47 (August 1939), pp. 68–73. One of the most exciting developments in twentieth-century economic theory can be applied to the analysis of duopoly-oligopoly behavior. John von Neumann and Oskar Morgenstern's *Theory of Games and Economic Behavior* (Princeton, N.J.: Princeton University Press, 1943) combined the considerable talents of a mathematician and an economist to produce a mathematical theory of business and social organization. The far-reaching implications of the book extend to decision strategies on the part of duopolist-oligopolist competitors.

The early history of the theory of price discrimination, so closely tied to product differentiation and imperfect competition, is analyzed by Robert B. Ekelund, Jr., "Price Discrimination and Product Differentiation in Economic Theory: An Early Analysis," *Quarterly Journal of Economics,* vol. 84 (May 1970), pp. 268–278. Along with Dupuit, Pigou, and Robinson, F. Y. Edgeworth also pioneered in the theory of price discrimination; see his "Contribution to the Theory of Railway Rates," *Economic Journal,* vol. 22 (June 1912), pp. 198–218.

Two recent articles by C. P. Blitch trace the influence of the neglected economist Allyn Young (Chamberlin's dissertation director) on the development of Chamberlin's theory of monopolistic competition. See Blitch, "Allyn A. Young: A Curious Case of Professional Neglect," *History of Political Economy,* vol. 15 (Spring 1983), pp. 1–24; and same author, "The Genesis of Chamberlinian Monopolistic Competition Theory: Addendum," *History of Political Economy,* vol. 17 (Fall 1985), pp. 395–400. A somewhat different view, which is highly speculative and does not fit the historical evidence, is offered by T. P. Reinwald, "The Genesis of Chamberlin's Monopolistic Competition Theory," *History of Political Economy,* vol. 9 (Winter 1977), pp. 522–534; and same author, "The Genesis of Chamberlinian Monopolistic Competition Theory: Addendum—A Comment," *History of Political Economy,* vol. 17 (Fall 1985), pp. 400–402. Two articles by A. S. Skinner delve more deeply into the origins of Chamberlin's analysis: "The Origins and Development of Monopolistic Competition," *Journal of Economic Studies,* vol. 10 (1983), pp. 52–67; and "Edward Chamberlin: The Theory of Monopolistic Competition: A Reorientation of the Theory of Value," *Journal of Economic Studies,* vol. 13 (1986), pp. 27–44. In the latter appraisal, Skinner explores Chamberlin's reaction to the Marshallian perspective.

Chamberlin's debt to Veblen (see Chapter 17) and the affinity of monopolistic competition to institutional economics are issues raised by R. D. Peterson in "Chamberlin's Monopolistic Competition: Neoclassical or Institutional?" *Journal of Economic Issues,* vol. 13 (September 1979), pp. 669–686.

REFERENCES

Chamberlin, Edward H. "Product Heterogeneity and Public Policy," *American Economic Review,* vol. 40 (May 1950), pp. 85–92.
———. *The Theory of Monopolistic Competition: A Re-orientation of the Theory of Value,* 8th ed. Cambridge, Mass.: Harvard University Press, 1962.
Ferguson, C. E. *Microeconomic Theory,* 3d ed. Homewood, Ill.: Irwin, 1972.
Machlup, Fritz. *The Economics of Sellers Competition.* Baltimore: Johns Hopkins, 1952.
Pigou, A. C. *Wealth and Welfare.* London: Macmillan, 1912.
Robinson, Joan. *The Economics of Imperfect Competition.* London: Macmillan, 1933.
———. "Imperfect Competition Revisited," *Economic Journal,* vol. 63 (September 1953), pp. 579–593.
Sraffa, Piero. "The Laws of Returns under Competitive Conditions," *Economic Journal,* vol. 36 (December 1926), pp. 535–550.
Taussig, Frank. "A Contribution to the Theory of Railway Rates," *Quarterly Journal of Economics,* vol. 5 (July 1981), pp. 438–465.

CHAPTER 19

JOHN MAYNARD KEYNES, THE GENERAL THEORY, AND THE DEVELOPMENT OF MACROECONOMICS

INTRODUCTION

One of the most startling developments in twentieth-century economic analysis has been the resurgence of the classical economists' interest in aggregate economics—that is, in both monetary and macroeconomic theory. While the quantity theory of money was the means for organizing economists' thoughts about the aggregate economy for well over 200 years, events both internal and external to the discipline led to the emergence of a different approach to the macroeconomy in the mid-1930s. This movement, encompassing both economic theory and economic policy, took on the name of its leader, the British economist John Maynard Keynes. For decades, especially in the 1950s and 1960s, Keynesian thought emphasizing fiscal policy dominated the economic policy of the United States and many other western nations. However, with the emergence of inflationary pressures in the 1970s and 1980s, the policy emphasis has once again shifted to money and to the reassertion of the underlying principles of the quantity theory. The *theoretical* shift to monetarism occurred even earlier. Both paradigms coexist in contemporary thought on aggregate economics. We cannot hope to air all of these views in detail here. We seek only to survey some major ideas in contemporary macroeconomics in this and the next chapter. Chapter 19 is devoted to Keynes and Keynesian theory, and Chapter 20 considers the twentieth-century development of quantity-theory/monetarist thought.

John Maynard Keynes was the most famous and perhaps the most influential economic theorist of the twentieth century. While many economists today would minimize the analytical importance of Keynes's contribution, probably none would deny that his impact inside and outside the profession has been as great as, say, Ricardo's, Mill's, or even that of Keynes's great teacher, Alfred Marshall. Modern fiscal policy—i.e., the use of government taxation and expenditure policy to affect prices, employment, and income—owes much to Keynes. His importance as a thinker is thus undeniable, and so we devote an entire chapter to an introduction to Keynesian theory and policy. But before tackling this job, the reader should become aware of certain features and limitations of our treatment of Keynes in the present chapter.

First, although Keynes's magnum opus, *The General Theory of Employment, Interest and Money,* is popularly thought to represent a great break with past ideas, it is more likely that Keynes's ideas on economic theory were changing over a fairly long period of time. The treatment of Keynesian theory in this chapter focuses solely upon the Keynesian economics that appeared in the *General Theory* and neglects the transitional aspects of his thought.

Second, this chapter develops a standard and popular version of what Keynes "really" said in the *General Theory.* This version is known as the "income-expenditure model," and it has been a staple of Keynesians almost since the *General Theory* was off the press. This translation of Keynes was chiefly the work of Nobel laureate (1972) John R. Hicks and Harvard economist Alvin H. Hansen. Both writers were early propagators of Keynesian ideas, and the graphs used to depict these ideas are often called (understandably) Hicks-Hansen diagrams. Our discussion derives much from the Hicks-Hansen approach to Keynes, but the student must be aware of the fact that several recent studies have provided alternative interpretations of Keynes's intent in writing and in the standard analysis of the *General Theory.*[1]

Third, the reader should also be warned that the Keynesian legend has a policy theme. The legend has it that Keynes was the first (at least with respect to the great depression of the 1930s) to advise governments to engage in discretionary spending and taxation (budget deficits) to cure depression and unemployment. But the policy legend has been open to question recently. It has even been convincingly demonstrated that typically Keynesian advice regarding compensatory spending was forth-coming in the *early* 1930s, but from economists at the University of Chicago and elsewhere who have, in the lore of economic thought, been pictured as extreme defenders of orthodox, neoclassical, and monetarist government policies (see J. Ronnie Davis, *The New Economics and the Old Economists*). Our discussion, owing to space constraints, perpetuates the (inaccurate) legend of a typically Keynesian policy, however.

Fourth, the reader may well wonder how Keynes's ideas could still be the subject of so much debate. One might think, in other words, that what Keynes

[1] For the most interesting of these alternative interpretations, the serious student should consult Axel Leijonhufvud's *On Keynesian Economics and the Economics of Keynes.* Specifically, Leijonhufvud argues that Keynes's chief concern was a presentation of a macroeconomic quantity adjustment model rather than an analysis of unemployment equilibrium per se. The latter has been the traditional interpretation of Keynes's interests.

really thought should be well settled by now. At least two important factors contribute to modern controversy over Keynes.

The first of these is the fact that Keynes's own statements of his ideas were often ambiguous. Moreover, he left many lines of analysis undeveloped or underdeveloped. A second and related point is that interpretations of Keynes's ideas by influential post-Keynesians have fixed opinions about what Keynes thought, although reinvestigations can be instituted at any time. In this latter sense, the fate of Keynes is not unlike that of Ricardo, whose ideas were and are the subject of debates (witness, for example, Stigler's discussion of Ricardo's value theory—see References at the end of Chapter 7). The reader should always bear in mind the simple fact that there may be vast differences between Ricardo and Ricardians, Saint-Simon and Saint-Simonians, and so on. Naturally, all this implies that a definitive assessment of Keynes and Keynesian economics or history of economic thought is not yet possible. Here we seek only to provide a simple introduction to basic Keynesian thought and policy. In order to orient ourselves, however, let us first consider Keynes's very interesting life.

J. M. KEYNES, DILETTANTE AND ECONOMIC THEORIST

John Maynard Keynes was born in 1883, ten years after Mill's death and seven years before Alfred Marshall was to publish his *Principles of Economics*. He died in 1946. If heredity has an important impact on mental achievement, John Maynard was certainly as fortunate as John Stuart Mill. His father, John Neville, and his mother, Florence Ada, were both intellectuals. Maynard's father was a famous logician and writer on economic methodology. John Neville Keynes's most important work was *The Scope and Method of Political Economy,* published in 1890 (see Chapter 17). From his father, John Maynard inherited a great intellectual curiosity and a lifelong love for the arts, especially the theater. His devotion to his father, who outlived him (J. N. Keynes died in 1949), was lasting.

Keynes was educated at Eton, with all that such an education implies. Keynes was alternatively immersed in classical literature, in logic, in mathematics, in dramatics (he once played Hamlet), and in the high jinks of school life. This frenetic intellectual activity was carried over into his life at King's College, Cambridge. Keynes described his pace in a letter (November 13, 1902) to his good friend B. W. Swithenbank:

> Immediately after hall I went to a Trinity Essay Society and heard a most brilliant satire on Christianity. From there I went to an informal philosophical debating society of interesting people where I stayed till nearly twelve; I then went to see Monty James where I stayed till one; from there I went on to another man with whom I talked till half past four. At half past seven I got up and read the Lesson in Chapel. I had four hours' work that morning, and rowed half a course in the afternoon. In the evening I went as a visitor to the Political Society to hear a paper on the Jesuits...(cited in Harrod, *The Life of John Maynard Keynes,* p. 68).

And so it was during his whole career, first as a student and then as an author, government official, and fellow at King's College.

Keynes was always surrounded by individuals of similar interests. Friendship was very important to him, and as a member of the famous Bloomsbury group (named for an area of London), he was in intimate and stimulating contact with leading British intellectuals. In addition to Keynes, the original Bloomsbury group included Leonard and Virginia Woolf, Duncan Grant, Clive and Vanessa (Virginia's sister) Bell, E. M. Forster, and, perhaps its most important member, Keynes's good friend Lytton Strachey. Anti-Victorian and bohemian, the Bloomsbury group considered all issues (philosophy, social convention, art, literature, and music) with the utter frankness and conceit born of a firm belief in their own intellectual superiority. Keynes clearly contributed to, and drew cultural sustenance from, the group, although his major interest and achievements were to depart significantly from those of the Bloomsbury set.

Economics had always interested Keynes. In 1905, Alfred Marshall wrote to J. N. Keynes of his pupil: "Your son is doing excellent work in Economics. I have told him that I should be greatly delighted if he should decide on the career of a professional economist. But of course I must not press him." Marshall probably did not find it necessary to press him much, for Keynes's interest grew steadily. He was a natural. And, what is more, he knew it.

Keynes's precociousness and wide range of activities carried over into his entire brilliant career, which by 1906 was leading him toward civil service as well as economics. In that year, Keynes passed the civil service examination and was assigned to a position in the Indian office. Soon becoming bored with his administrative duties, Keynes devoted a large part of his time to a study of probability theory, the fruits of which were his highly praised (by Bertrand Russell and others) *Treatise on Probability* (1921).

In 1911 Keynes became coeditor (with F. Y. Edgeworth) of the *Economic Journal,* the official organ of the Royal Economic Society. He held this formidable position until 1945. In 1913 he published a work on international finance related to the gold exchange standard, *Indian Currency and Finance.* Quickly becoming famous as a monetary expert, Keynes entered the treasury department in 1915 and remained there until the end of the war. He was assigned as a British treasury representative to the conference of Versailles. With grave forebodings concerning the terms of European recovery, he resigned from the treaty conference. In 1919 Keynes attacked the conditions of the treaty (and Lloyd George's policies) in *The Economic Consequences of the Peace,* which was an immense critical success, urging as it did moderation in the demands upon defeated Germany.[2]

---

[2] In other ways, Keynes had turned a handsome profit from his wartime experience. While Big Bertha was shelling Paris, Keynes was at an art auction representing London's National Gallery. (The auction was to improve France's exchange position.) On that occasion, he acquired a number

During the 1920s, Keynes taught at King's College. Although he was an enthusiastic and successful lecturer, he soon reduced his teaching load in order to engage in a multitude of other activities. They included amassing a fortune (about half a million pounds in 1937) by speculating in the foreign exchanges (Keynes wished to be independent of salaried employment); becoming chairman of the board of the *Nation,* a liberal weekly; and assuming the duties of bursar (financial analyst and manager) of King's College, for which he received, in the beginning, £100 per year.

In 1923, Keynes published his *Tract on Monetary Reform,* which was a polemic in favor of discretionary management of the internal money stock and against the gold standard as a capricious determinant of the internal economy. In 1925, Keynes married Lydia Lopokova, one of the great Diaghilev's prima ballerinas. With his marriage, the strange confluence of economics and Bloomsbury in Keynes's interests began to separate, and the former became and remained the major focus of his life.

The two-volume *Treatise on Money* appeared in late 1930. Keynes intended that the book should bring together his lifework in the field of money. However, it was only a "still" picture of his ideas at that time. Nevertheless, the *Treatise* anticipated and even developed some of the important ideas that were later to receive extended treatment in the *General Theory.* Specifically, the key roles of saving and investment in influencing the level of income—ideas that owe much to the influence of Keynes's friend and colleague Dennis H. Robertson—are first discussed in the *Treatise.*

Keynes's post-1930 productivity, even if we exclude the *General Theory,* was large. His persuasive and pedagogical skills are manifest in the *Essays in Persuasion* (1931) and, most especially, in the *Essays in Biography* (1933), both of which can still be read for enlightenment and enjoyment. In addition to his defenses of the *General Theory,* Keynes continued his lecturing, civil service, and duties to his college during the period.

In the late 1930s Keynes became increasingly concerned with the financial burdens imposed by the impending war with Germany. The problems of reordering wartime resource priorities and the excess demand thereby created are dealt with in *How to Pay for the War,* published in 1940. Between 1941 and 1946, Keynes negotiated wartime lend-lease financing, and in 1946 he was instrumental in arranging the Marshall loan to Britain. That same year Keynes was made a vice president of the World Bank, and he was a leading figure, along with Harry Dexter White, in the plans to restore the international monetary system (which were made in Bretton Woods, New Hampshire). This dizzying array of activities took its toll on a heart weakened by a previous attack, and in the summer of 1946, at the age of sixty-three, Keynes died. The world lost a mind that probably could have reached high flights of achievement in any one of a number of areas. But Keynes himself chose economics.

of fine pieces for the gallery, but he bought a Cézanne and an Ingres for himself. As Keynes's biographer Harrod reports, the shelling depressed prices.

THE GENERAL THEORY: MAJOR THEORETICAL IDEAS

As noted earlier, the actual writing of the *General Theory* took place in a milieu of depression. From the beginning of the 1930s, Keynes had been much concerned with the employment crisis, which had been deepening drastically in the United States and England. He voiced this concern in several communiqués to President Roosevelt, including a famous open letter to him in *The New York Times*. Keynes's advice was to make vigorous use of fiscal policy (government tax and expenditure policy) to supplement the market mechanism of the private sector, which, in Keynes's view, was failing to get at the employment problem. Roosevelt appeared to follow Keynes's advice, but only guardedly. Whatever other meaning the episode had, it clearly indicates that the environment of the early 1930s was much on Keynes's mind prior to the actual writing of the *General Theory*.

Pressures internal to the discipline of economics were also of large moment at the time of Keynes's writing. Marshallian microeconomics was going through some radical extensions, including those of E. H. Chamberlin and Joan Robinson (see Chapter 18). Keynes himself had raised questions concerning the adequacy of neoclassical monetary theory in his *Treatise on Money,* and several of his colleagues were focusing upon the importance of expenditures in aggregate output determination. Richard Kahn had developed a concept of an investment multiplier, and departures from standard theory were much discussed topics at Cambridge among Kahn, Robinson, R. G. Hawtrey, and R. F. Harrod, all of whom Keynes mentions in the preface to the *General Theory*. A general rethinking of neoclassical economic theory and, specifically, Marshall's economics must have contributed to Keynes's seminal work. Thus a confluence of internal and external pressures led him to offer an alternative to neoclassicism. Keynes firmly believed that he was making a significant departure, but he freely admitted that preparations for the trip were extremely tortuous. He spoke of a "long struggle of escape" from traditional methods of thought and expression, and he was at pains to emphasize these differences, to which we now turn.

Keynes's Reaction to the Classics

The classics, in Keynes's use of the term, included a whole retinue of classical and neoclassical writers, from Smith and Ricardo through Marshall and Pigou (Keynes thought Pigou's writings to be the repository of the whole tradition). Classical economics, moreover, in Keynes's frame of reference, was an *idealized* model not unlike the one considered in Chapter 7 of this book. It was this idealized model of classical macro theory to which Keynes addressed himself, though he freely acknowledged anticipators of his ideas.[3]

---

[3] Keynes's anticipators were, for the most part, dissenters from the classical tradition. A superb historian of thought, Keynes reviewed and evaluated these heretics in Chap. 23 of the *General Theory,* "Notes on Mercantilism." In this connection, see Chap. 3 of the present book.

Keynes's essential break with the classics was over the notion of Say's law, which, broadly and naively stated, holds that supply creates its own demand. A belief in Say's law (with all its accoutrements) was supposed to imply that unemployment, as a long-term proposition at least, was not possible. Moreover, it implies that the economy would be self-adjusting, that is, that disturbances from a full-employment–full-production equilibrium would be only temporary.

The classics had reasoned that the modern economy functioned much like a barter economy. Goods were exchanged for goods, and money represented simply a standard of value and a medium of exchange. In Pigou's words, money was a "veil." It hid the *real* workings of the economy. It was the grease of trade, not the wheel.[4]

An equivalent way of stating Say's law is to say that aggregate savings (that taken out of the expenditure stream) will always equal investment (that returned to the expenditure stream) at full employment. People generally prefer present consumption to future consumption, but given that savings is a function of the reward for savings, or a rate of interest, they can be induced to hold more assets in the form of savings if offered a positive rate of interest. Thus the classics reasoned that the amount of savings was positively related to the rate of interest.

Investment, on the other hand, was negatively related to the interest rate. Why? Because, among other reasons, the productivity of given investments declined with incremental increases in investment (technology being constant, of course). This declining marginal productivity of investment meant that lower rates of interest were required in order to increase the quantity of investment. All this is summarized in Figure 19-1, in which economywide saving and investment schedules are depicted against the rate of interest. At interest rate r_0, the classics reasoned, saving equaled investment, which meant that what is not consumed (saved) was invested (returned to the expenditure stream). A flexible interest rate mechanism guaranteed this result. Flexibility in this context means that if investment exceeds savings, say, at interest rate r_1, the rate of interest would be bid up to r_0 by investors. Conversely, if savings are greater than investment, savers will bid the interest rate down to r_0.

The classical model could handle an increase in investment (which might have resulted from inventions or innovations). The level of investment simply increased, and the amount of consumption *decreased*. With reference to Figure 19-1, the dashed line represents the new investment schedule. Society is induced to save more by a rising rate of interest. At the new equilibrium the rate of interest rises to r_0^*, and the *amount* of savings and investment increases to s_0^* and i_0^*, respectively. The real increase in savings ($s_0^* - s_0$) represents the *decrease* in consumption, but the decrease in consumption caused thereby is exactly matched by the increase in investment ($i_0^* - i_0$). *In equilib-*

---

[4] All this has been emphasized in Chap. 6 of this book, which dichotomizes the real from the monetary aspects of the macro economy.

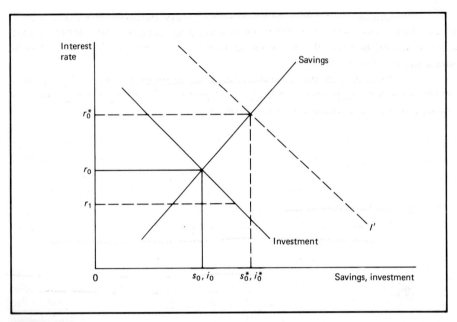

FIGURE 19-1
At interest rate r_0, saving equals investment. If investment increases from I to I', the new equilibrium rate of interest rises to r_0^* and the amount of saving and investment increases to s_0^* and i_0^*, respectively.

rium the economy would neither overproduce nor underproduce. Given free markets, general laissez faire, and rapid interest rate responses, Say's law was a sure thing. A ready demand for goods (consumption and investment) could always be depended on. The market would always clear at full employment.

Another classical proposition that amplifies and supports Say's law is that regarding the flexibility of wages and prices in the economy. If, for some reason, the economy was sluggish in adjusting to fundamental changes in savings and investment (say, as a result of a massive change in the desire to save), flexible prices and wages would guarantee a smooth short-term adjustment. With a dearth of aggregate demand, money, wages, and prices would fall such that full employment and full production would be resumed. Workers would always be willing to take lower money wages, and entrepreneurs would be willing to accept lower prices in order to sell their goods. Any disturbance that caused unemployment and output reductions was bound to be temporary since the competition in labor and product markets would always adjust the real variables of the system to equilibrium.

Keynes flatly and boldly took exception to these propositions. These exceptions will be analyzed in detail later in this chapter, but they may be summarized here briefly. First, Keynes denied Say's law. To Keynes, the equilibrium of savings and investment was not such a simple matter as it was to the classical economists. Savings and investment were determined by a complex host of factors in addition to the interest rate, and there was no guarantee that the two would necessarily be equal at a level of economic activity that produced full employment.

Second, rigidities in the economy such as monopolies and labor unions thwarted the fluid movement of wages and prices, which might bring about an adjustment of the economy to full employment. Laborers, he believed, were under "money illusion"; i.e., their behavior was related to the money wage (*W*) rather than to the real wage (*W/P*). They would *refuse* to take cuts in their money wages. And, along with the classical economists, Keynes believed that the level of employment was *inversely* related to the real wage rate and that this refusal of laborers to take money wage cuts was a direct denial of the classical wage-rate adjustment mechanism.

But Keynes pushed further, asking the question: What if workers were prepared to take cuts in their money wages? Such wage cuts meant lower real wages and increased employment (a movement down the demand curve for labor) if and only if prices remained constant. Keynes argued, however, that prices could not remain constant in the face of falling money wages since falling wage incomes mean declining demands for goods and lower prices for those goods. Lower prices meant, however, that real wages might not fall and that employment would probably not increase (unless the Keynes effect, which we shall consider later on, was operative). To sum up, adjustments of money wage rates were an ineffective way of getting at unemployment.

Unemployment, Keynes argued, could be efficiently attacked only by manipulating aggregate demand. Workers would be willing to accept increases in prices that resulted from an increase in demand, given stable money wage rates. Such increases would *lower* real wages, thereby stimulating employment. Keynes turned the classical proposition around: Employment does not rise by lowering real wages, but real wages fall because of increased employment resulting from an increase in aggregate demand. A more complete explanation of this important point will be given later in this chapter, but in order to understand Keynes's critique of classical employment theory, we must first look at some distinctly Keynesian inventions that laid the groundwork for his system. First we look at a concept to which we have already alluded, that of aggregate consumption and investment demand.

Aggregate Demand

In approaching the concept of aggregate demand, Keynes turned away from the quantity of total output suggested in the quantity theory of money and set out to look at the determinants and characteristics of the component parts of the total demand for goods. Chief of these was the total consumption of private goods and services, that is, a *consumption function.*

A consumption function relates the consumption of all private goods and services to the aggregate level of income. It is conveniently expressed as

$C = f(Y)$, to be read as consumption (C) is a function of aggregate income (Y). Consumption, as Keynes well knew, is related to a host of other factors—price expectations, the utility of saving for future consumption versus present consumption, income expectations, institutions, mores, and so on. But Keynes wished to hold these variables in abeyance in order to look at consumption and income (aggregate factor returns and profit). Thus, with regard to income *receipt*, income may be consumed or saved, and thus aggregate saving is also regarded as a function of income. These functions, as Keynesian economics has come to be understood, have specific forms, as depicted in Figure 19-2.

Several fundamental points must be made concerning this figure. The first relates to the underlying assumptions made about the nature of the consumption function. As drawn in Figure 19-2, the *average propensity to consume* is assumed to decline as income declines. The *marginal propensity to consume,* or the ratio of a change in consumption to an incremental change in income ($\Delta c/\Delta y$ read off the consumption function in Figure 19-2), remains constant. Similarly, Keynes defined average and marginal propensities to save with the former *increasing* with income and the latter constant. Any alteration in the propensity to consume would create alterations (shifts or rotations) in the consumption and savings functions. Any of the aforementioned nonincome determinants of consumption (tastes, price, and income expectations) would have this effect.

FIGURE 19-2
The intersection of aggregate demand and aggregate supply schedules (point *A*) determines an equilibrium level of income, Y_0. If income exceeds Y_0, then aggregate supply will exceed aggregate demand.

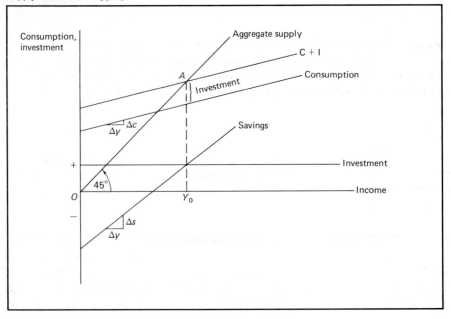

Keynes defined an aggregate supply function as the aggregate supply price of output from employment of N men [and in functional form, $Z = \phi(N)$]. Along this function depicted as a 45° line in Figure 19-2, the demand for goods at given prices exactly equals the supply of goods.[5] A part of the total aggregate demand for goods comprised investment demands (plant, equipment, etc.), and Keynes believed that a large mass of these expenditures (at least in the short run) may be regarded as autonomous or independent of the level of income. The assumption might be perfectly reasonable given that large businesses make long-term investment commitments that take place in the short term irrespective of income conditions. Such an autonomous investment schedule is also depicted in both the positive and the negative part of Figure 19-2, being added (vertically) to consumption in the upper part and set against the savings function in the lower part. Total aggregate demand equals consumption expenditures and investment expenditures. Now all the elements for an explanation of income determination are present.

The consumption and investment schedules depicted in Figure 19-2 determine an equilibrium level of income Y_0. At the intersection of the aggregate supply and aggregate demand schedules (point A), the aggregate sale proceeds of Y_0 level of output precisely equal the aggregate cost (factor payments) of producing output Y_0. If the level of income were greater than Y_0, aggregate supply would exceed aggregate demand. In other words, the aggregate cost of producing that higher level of output would exceed the receipts obtainable from consumption and investment expenditures at that level. This is so because consumption would not increase sufficiently to absorb the increased supply. Barring price changes (which are ignored in this simple model), unsold inventories would pile up, and entrepreneurs would cut back production to Y_0. For the opposite and analogous reason, output would increase to Y_0 should it temporarily fall from Y_0. The output level is thus considered stable.

Keynes's major point in all this is that an output level, such as Y_0, generated by consumption and investment, though stable, is not necessarily a full-employment level of national output. There could be, Keynes concluded, an equilibrium level of income in an economy at less than full employment.

The Role of Investment

In the admittedly simplistic model summarized in Figure 19-2, two sources of private expenditures were introduced, consumption and investment. Of the two, Keynes viewed investment expenditures as by far the more volatile. Investment demands are determined by a host of factors besides the interest rate, including expected future returns. Indeed, a well-known Keynesian concept, the *marginal efficiency of capital* (actually investment), relates the cost

---

[5] There is small doubt that Keynes's terminology here is confusing. Aggregate supply is at present usually thought of as a function setting output produced against alternative price *levels* of output.

of investment capital to the expected returns over the life of investment projects. Keynes viewed expectations, dependent upon capricious psychological factors, as having direct, important effects on investment and hence on income.

Beyond psychological effects on investment, however, lay a more fundamental problem for income determination; i.e., that investment expenditures (like all other types) have multiple effects upon income. A change in investment expenditures, for example, did not result in a change in income by the amount of the spending change but, rather, by some multiple.

The investment multiplier can be illustrated with a diagram, Figure 19-3, similar to the one developed previously. The initial consumption and investment expenditure level $C + I$ determined an equilibrium level of income Y^0. This level is stable in the sense described in the previous section. Now, suppose that one of the determinants of investment changes—say, expectations—and that investment increases from I to I' (ΔI). The effect on total expenditures is depicted in Figure 19-3 as a shift upward in the aggregate demand function by ΔI. Income, in equilibrium, increases from Y^0 to Y^1 (ΔY). The point is, of course, that the change in income (ΔY) will be greater than the initial change in investment (ΔI).

FIGURE 19-3
If investment increases from I to I', the aggregate demand function will shift upward by ΔI. Income will also increase from Y^0 to Y^1.

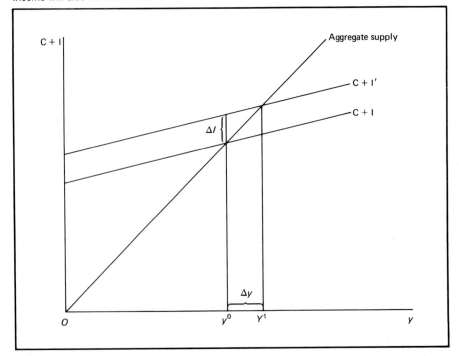

The multiplier effect, moreover, is theoretically predictable because it depends upon the numerical value of the marginal propensity to consume. The dependence is easily explained. The initial injection of investment (ΔI) is received as income by factor-share recipients. That means that income is increased by ΔI. These recipients have marginal propensities to consume and save that, of course, add up to 1. Imagine that the marginal propensity to consume is 75 percent, in which case 75 percent of the initial new receipt of income is spent. At this point income is generated in the amount $\Delta I + 3/4(\Delta I)$. But the process continues. The $3/4(\Delta I)$ spent by the initial recipients is received as income by other factors. When the process approaches the limit, the change in income ΔY is equal to $1/(1 - MPC)$, or, in our example, $1/(1 - 3/4) = 4$, *times* the initial investment increase. If the initial investment injection was $10 billion, the ultimate change in income would be $40 billion. The value of the multiplier is obviously 4; or k, the multiplier, equals $\Delta Y/\Delta I$.

Thus, the capriciousness of private investment, coupled with its multiplier effects upon income, meant that prediction of aggregate income was complex and difficult. But even if income levels and changes could be predicted with a high degree of accuracy, such levels would only *by accident* be full-employment levels. To see why Keynes believed this to be so, we must turn to a discussion of his theory of unemployment equilibrium and relate it to the present discussion of aggregate demand. Though difficult (and sometimes ambiguous), it is an essential part of Keynesian analysis.

Unemployment Equilibrium

The classical writers believed that the demand for labor was equivalent to the marginal productivity of labor and that labor supply was an increasing function of the real wage. This classical view of labor functions is reproduced in Figure 19-4a. Equilibrium real wage $(W/P)_0$ produces full employment of labor inputs N_0. Should the equilibrium real wage be displaced, say, to $(W/P)_1$, unemployment would occur in the amount AB. Workers would competitively bid the money wage down and reestablish full employment at N_0.

Keynes, as we have already seen, disagreed. He argued that laborers could be involuntarily unemployed. Theoretically, he joined the classical economists in their conception of the labor demand curve or the marginal product of labor. But laborers, in the Keynesian view, did not supply labor with respect to the real wage, but rather with respect to the money wage. Workers were under money illusion, moreover, and would not take cuts in their prevailing money wage. These points are illustrated in Figure 19-4b, where money wage W_0 is a floor. In Figure 19-4b, the employment level N^* represents full employment of labor, and the labor demand functions D_N and D'_N are now the value of the marginal product of labor (because the demand is set against the money wage instead of against the real wage).

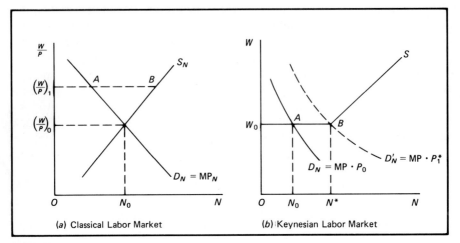

FIGURE 19-4
The classical labor market automatically adjusts itself to full employment whereas the
Keynesian labor market does not automatically adjust.

The question is whether there could be any involuntary unemployment in
the economic system. The classical economists recognized that at an equilibrium real wage, such as $(W/P)_0$ in Figure 19-4a, voluntary and frictional unemployment could exist. Unemployment could be voluntary in the sense that certain amounts of labor would voluntarily exempt themselves from the labor force at wage $(W/P)_0$.

Keynes, on the contrary, viewed the matter differently. In Figure 19-4b, labor would supply quantity N^* at money wage W_0, but demand might be such that only a lesser quantity N_0 would be demanded at real wage $(W/P)_0$. The result would be what Keynes called *involuntary* unemployment. Labor was involuntarily unemployed in the amount *AB,* and yet an equilibrium in the labor market existed in the sense that no automatic tendency for employment to change from N_0 could be expected. No unique full-employment level of output could be presupposed, therefore. Economywide equilibrium could be achieved at any utilization of labor. Laborers, in the first place, would not take money wage cuts, thereby reducing the real wage rate for increased employment. In the second place, even if they did, prices would likely fall in the same proportion, causing the labor demand function to shift to the left and leaving the unemployment level the same.

Thus a situation like that described in Figures 19-5a and 19-5b might be observed. Outputs Y^0 and Y^* are functions of inputs. An equilibrium occurs at input and output levels N^0 and Y^0, but at these levels involuntary unemployment exists in the amount *AB*. Aggregate demand would have to increase by *MN* in order to bring the economy to full employment. Keynes believed that private investment would not be likely to bring this about, and he suggested compensatory government expenditures and taxation (fiscal policy) in order to

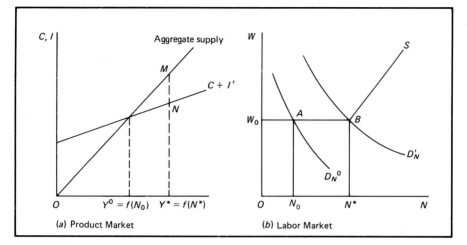

FIGURE 19-5
At equilibrium levels N^0 and Y^0, involuntary unemployment exists in the amount AB.
Aggregate demand would have to increase by MN to bring the economy to full employment.

relieve unemployment and underproduction. These aspects of Keynesian policy will be discussed later, but we must first turn to another Keynesian theory, the liquidity-preference function, or, equivalently, the speculative demand for money. An understanding of the Keynesian position goes far toward explaining his views on the role of monetary policy (and fiscal policy) in controlling the level of economic activity.

Liquidity Preference and the Role of Money in the Keynesian System

The neoclassical economists adhered to a well-known theory about money, the so-called quantity theory of money. Keynes himself had adhered to the Cambridge version early in his academic life. The quantity theory, as we shall see in Chapter 20, emphasized the holding of money for transactions purposes. Specifically, the transactions holdings of cash were viewed as positively related to income and (in the typical treatment) as a constant proportion of income. In fact, the V in the quantity-theory identity can be regarded as the *reciprocal* of the transactions demand for money. An increase in transactions demand for money, or an increase in the average amount of cash balances individuals hold as a percentage of income, meant that velocity, or the turnover of the average dollar facilitating national income, was reduced.

The factors changing velocity (institutions, etc.) were not thought of as being constant, but as being relatively stable and predictable. A moment's reflection indicates what this meant for theory and policy. If V is constant or predictable, M is controllable, and P is (relatively) stable up to full employment,

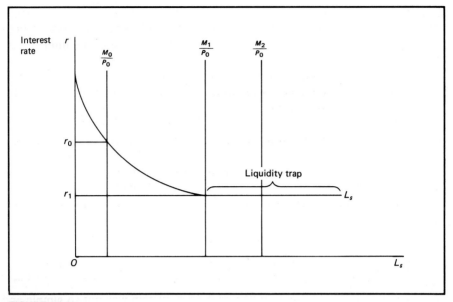

FIGURE 19-6
Increasing the nominal money stock from M_0 to M_1 will reduce the interest rate from r_0 to r_1, but increasing the money stock further, to M_2, will not have any effect on the interest rate.

then M can be adjusted to produce changes in income (Y) when there are un-employed resources in the economy.[6]

Keynes did not disagree that people hold money for transactions purposes or that the transactions demand was related to income. He argued, however, that individuals hold money for at least one other important reason—to spec-ulate in the bond market. In other words, while the classical economists con-sidered that individuals hold money for transactions and even for precaution-ary (saving for a rainy day) motives, Keynes argued that they would hold money in order to speculate in the bond market. This so-called liquidity-preference function is depicted in Figure 19-6.

The function L_s shows society's demand for money for speculative pur-poses. The alternative between holding bonds and holding money is presented to society. Keynes theorized that at high interest rates (which meant low bond prices, since there is an inverse relation), individuals would prefer to hold bonds. Tritely, bonds are a "good deal" at high rates of interest. As the inter-est rate falls, however, bond prices rise, and buying bonds becomes less and less attractive. The yield on the bond becomes lower and lower. But now *sell-*

---

[6] At all other times, of course, the classical economists viewed money as having a stabilizing role and as oiling the wheels of trade. Current proposals by Milton Friedman and others, related to a rule of a constant growth rate in the money stock, reflect this traditional concern; see Chap. 20 for details.

ing bonds becomes more and more attractive because of the rise in bond prices (capital gains). Thus, individuals will choose to hold more and more of their assets in the form of money (and less in the form of bonds) as the interest rate falls. Such a function, L_s, is traced out in Figure 19-6.

The liquidity-preference function of Figure 19-6 has one typically Keynesian feature, the liquidity trap, although Keynes's followers emphasized the "trap" far more than Keynes himself. Keynes had argued in the *General Theory* that the interest rate might fall so low (price of bonds so high) as to make all believe that bonds were a bad investment. All, in short, would want to hold the *more liquid asset,* money. Such a situation is described by the horizontal (infinitely elastic) portion of Figure 19-6, and it is called the liquidity trap. It shows that at some *positive* rate of interest, society regards bond holding as unsafe and would hold money balances instead for speculative purposes.[7]

What has all this to do with monetary policy and its effectiveness? Keynes argued that although the rate of interest was determined by a combination of real and monetary factors in the economic system, the existence of the speculative demand for money meant that the mechanism by which money influenced income and employment in the economic system was not so simple and predictable as the classical economists believed. Specifically, one of the major impacts of money upon spending, income, and employment was through its effect upon interest rates. Lower interest rates ordinarily meant, *ceteris paribus,* higher levels of investment and consumption (since lower interest rates made present consumption more attractive relative to future consumption, i.e., saving). Typically, monetary policy might lower the interest rate and thereby increase spending to a full-employment level.

This situation is described in Figure 19-6. The real money stock (M/P) is increased by increasing the nominal money stock (M). The increase from M_0 to M_1, assuming that prices remain constant, reduces the interest rate from r_0 to r_1. Assuming a reaction of consumers and investors to the lowered rate, aggregate demand will be increased, and income and employment will rise. The hoped-for result does not occur if unemployment exists at interest rate r_1, for when the real money supply available for speculative purposes increases from M_1/P_0 to M_2/P_0, the rate of interest *does not change.* Society will hold all the new assets in the form of money balances. Since the interest rate does not fall, investment and consumption—for this reason at least—will be unaffected. Given the liquidity trap situation, Keynes concluded that monetary policy (working through the interest rate at least) is helpless in the face of depression and unemployment.

---

[7] Sir Dennis Robertson once provided an amusing description of the liquidity trap: "The rate of interest is what it is because it is expected to become other than it is; if it is not expected to become other than it is, there is nothing left to tell us why it is what it is" (*Essays in Money and Interest,* p. 174).

Prices and Price Changes

Did the liquidity trap exist? Keynes, and particularly the "Keynesians," believed that the monetary and psychological conditions surrounding the depression did seem to support the existence of such a trap. (Subsequent empirical evidence does not add support to the existence of a trap.) For this reason and a complex of other reasons, he supported a strong fiscal policy, as opposed to sole reliance upon monetary policy for economic stabilization. As theoretical matters, however, some of Keynes's ideas respecting prices and stabilization need to be considered.

Keynes regarded prices, as we have already seen in this chapter, as fairly inflexible downward. Monopoly and other collusive practices could prevent the price level from falling even in the face of declining aggregate demand in the economy. But what if prices were flexible downward? As a theoretical proposition, Keynes did believe that falling prices and a set of additional circumstances could improve the situation. In fact, it is often called the *Keynes effect*. Given that the nominal money stock remains constant, a reduction in prices would increase the real stock of money. As is easily seen from Figure 19-6, the interest rate would fall with a constant M and a reduced P. Given the twin circumstances that the economy is not in the liquidity trap and that investors and consumers are in fact responsive to lower interest rates, aggregate demand, income, and employment would increase. Otherwise, falling prices would have no effect.

What of the practical effects of falling prices? Keynes appeared to believe that a declining price level that could have some effect on the economy would have other, opposite, and deleterious effects. To wit, there is the effect that falling prices have upon fixed business indebtedness, not to mention the effects upon expectations. As we have seen, Keynes believed that aggregate investment is conditioned largely by price and profit expectations. A rapid decline in the price level may, practically, reduce the level of investment even in the face of declining interest rates. Bankruptcies and adverse business conditions would almost certainly follow falling prices. In sum, Keynes believed that economic catastrophe could not be averted by a flexible and falling price level.

Keynes and Economic Policy

As the whole tenor of our discussion reveals, Keynes did not regard the economic mechanisms of the private sector as fail-safe against prolonged unemployment. An equilibrium could exist at less than full employment. The existence of downwardly flexible wages and prices, though unlikely to exist in the economy, would not guarantee full employment. Because of other limitations, namely, special forms of the speculative demand for money and the investment function, monetary policy was not predictably useful. How, then, might the unemployment gap in aggregate demand (see *MN* in Figure 19-5a) be bridged?

As has been suggested already, Keynes argued on the basis of his theoretical developments that the government should use its powers to tax and spend in order to influence the business cycle. Government spending is a direct injection of public investment in the income stream. Government spending could be financed by taxation (which would reduce consumption, but by less than the amount of the tax), by the sale of bonds to the Federal Reserve, or by some other means. The income- and employment-generative effects of all these alternatives must be assessed, and action might then be taken to achieve economic stability.

Keynes did not believe that single injections, or "pump priming," would be enough. What was required was a full-scale and planned program of discretionary fiscal policy as well as a strengthening of built-in stabilizers (such as progressive taxation). The government must stand ready, in short, to provide the conditions for full employment. Keynes's basic message is clear.

Eventually, all these ideas became part of a new economic orthodoxy. Even the most academically untrained legislator in Washington is at least aware of Keynesian policy prescriptions, if not of the theoretical underpinnings. Keynes's ideas, especially in the 1940s, 1950s, and 1960s, permeated most institutions of higher learning in the United States and elsewhere. Indeed, they were commonplace thanks to their relatively early introduction into one of the most successful contemporary textbooks since Alfred Marshall's *Principles:* Paul Samuelson's *Economics* (1st ed., 1948).

All this should not imply that Keynesian economic analysis has not been tinkered with, refined, remolded, criticized, and/or maligned. As we shall detail in Chapter 20, monetarism has emerged, especially in the 1970s and early 1980s, as a substantive and significant challenge to the Keynesian view of the world. Just as Marshall's *Principles* was the subject of heated discussion after its publication in 1890, so Keynes's *General Theory* has suffered (or enjoyed) a similar fate. Before turning to a tentative assessment of Keynes and, in Chapter 20, to the monetarist challenge of his ideas, we shall consider briefly the Pigou-Patinkin assessment of Keynesian theory in terms of the Keynesian model.

Neoclassicism Reviewed in Keynesian Terms

Thomas Kuhn, in his seminal work entitled *The Structure of Scientific Revolutions* (see Notes for Further Reading at the end of Chapter 1), notes that the introduction of new paradigms of thought, such as the Keynesian model, comes about when old paradigms are no longer capable of providing good answers to the questions posed to them. But old paradigms may be firmly entrenched, and their defenders may rise to protect them and perhaps to show that a paradigm that is considered new may really be just a subset of an old one (thereby, of course, renewing and rejuvenating it). It appears that, to a certain extent, Kuhn's theory of the nature of ideational progress fits the case of J. M. Keynes.

Keynes, it might be recalled, used A. C. Pigou's *Theory of Unemployment* as his straw man in attacking the classical model. But one of Pigou's ideas, widely known as the "Pigou effect" and later as the "real-balance effect," returned to haunt Keynesian theory. Keynes had argued that prices and wages were not flexible downward because of the agglomeration of monopoly power on both the input and the output sides of the market. But he argued further that price and wage declines would likely not increase income and employment because declining wages would lead to declining prices (since declining wage income means reduced demand for final output), which would mean that the real wage would not be reduced appreciably. The Keynes effect, discussed above, was a theoretical possibility, but its impact was limited by the inelasticity of the investment function and by the liquidity trap, discounting all the practical difficulties with falling prices.

Pigou, however, had identified another effect of falling prices. To wit, when prices fall, individuals' real balances rise—that is, the real value of their money holdings (*M/P*) increases—thereby creating a wealth effect on consumption. In short, consumption will increase with increases in real balances. A simple example makes this clear: A beach bum with $1 to his name can become a millionaire (in real terms) if the price level falls low enough.

The theoretical conclusion is inescapable. With falling prices the Keynes effect might be rendered impotent by the liquidity trap and an inelastic investment function, but the Pigou effect would not. *Given that the price level would fall,* aggregate demand would rise to a full-employment level.

As a theoretical proposition, then, the Pigou effect saves neoclassical theory. This conclusion was elegantly and thoroughly analyzed in an important book, Don Patinkin's *Money, Interest and Prices,* which first appeared in 1956 but was initially submitted as a doctoral dissertation at the University of Chicago in 1947. Patinkin utilized an expanded Pigou effect, a Walrasian general-equilibrium model containing three markets (money, commodities, and bonds), and a Keynesian expenditure approach (in the commodity market) to demonstrate the theoretical consistency of neoclassical macroeconomics.

Much of Patinkin's analysis is very complex, although his conclusions are clear—namely, that given the classical assumptions of full employment and price flexibility (and, of course, the absence of money illusion), the conclusions of the quantity theory of money hold; that Keynes's analysis of the speculative motive for holding money was a genuine contribution but that its introduction (unless money illusion is introduced) does *not* upset the conclusions of neoclassical theory; and, finally, that because of the stickiness of prices and wages in an actual economic system, Keynesian policy prescriptions have merit. Patinkin also showed balance in his refurbishments of classical theory by criticizing gaps and inconsistencies therein.

Though Patinkin's contribution was promptly dubbed "Much Ado about Pigou," its importance lies in its thoroughness and in its clear exposition of the assumptions by which Keynes obtained his results. It also demonstrated how the speculative demand for money along with the expenditure approach to national income, as well as other Keynesian ideas, could be worked under the umbrella of neoclassicism, thereby exposing the alleged weakness of naive neoclassical economics.

CONCLUSION: KEYNES AND THE HISTORY OF THOUGHT

Whether the Keynesian paradigm (in modern dress) ever emerges as a preferred model, as the last section indicated, is problematical. So much depends upon empirical estimates of the elasticities of the theoretical functions in question—estimates that are difficult and sometimes impossible to obtain. Price declines of the type required by the Pigou effect for full employment are not within our experience, and even if feasible, they may present the same practical difficulties required for the Keynes effect. Thus the Keynesian model itself rests in limbo, but there are strong indications that the rejuvenated neoclassical model is beginning to win the day theoretically.

It is no secret that in matters of policy, Keynesian ideas on compensatory finance became the reigning economic orthodoxy. Orthodox Keynesians viewed the Employment Act of 1946 as a victory, but Keynesian ideas continued to permeate the highest policy echelons of government, especially during Democratic administrations. Presidential economic advisers were schooled in the tradition of Keynes. As a by-product, mountains of data on unemployment, income, and expenditures have been built up for use by the policymakers.

Where, then, shall we place Keynes in the history of economic thought? As noted in the introduction, only a very tentative assessment is possible at such close distance, but several facts do stand out. At the very least Keynes is, and probably will continue to be, an important figure in the history of economic thought. That he stirred the waters of economic policy and analysis is unquestionable. Apart from the charismatic quality of Keynesian ideas, out of which a veritable modern legend has developed, Keynes was an interesting economist. Between the ridiculous excesses of certain Keynesians and the apologetics of certain neoclassicists (who refuse to find anything of value in Keynes), there is at least a minimum legacy. It is the legacy of an interest in, an orientation toward, and a restatement of macroeconomic theory and consequent policy concerns inside and outside the professional discipline of economics. The tremendous resurgence of interest in monetarism (and in other macroeconomic concepts) might not have been possible without the counterpoint of Keynesian thought and policy. Keynes did not live to see the massive influence of his ideas, but politicians, economists, citizen-taxpayers, and historians of economic thought have. In season and out, Keynes has stirred the waters of economic ideas.

NOTES FOR FURTHER READING

Although a large and detailed literature exists on Keynes and his ideas, only a small sample can be mentioned here. A useful source on traditional Keynesian economics and on post-Keynesian developments in cycle, growth, investment, and inflation theory is Gardner Ackley's *Macroeconomic Theory* (New York: Macmillan, 1961). For an abbreviated summary of aggregate analysis before the *General Theory* see James L. Cochrane's *Macroeconomics before Keynes* (Glenview, Ill.: Scott, Foresman, 1970). Utilizing a model of behavior appropriate to each, Cochrane analyzes physiocratic, classical, Marxian, and neo-classical macroeconomics. As should be expected, there were anticipators of Keynesian ideas. The British economist Richard Kahn anticipated Keynes's multiplier analysis, and it now seems clear that a number of Swedish authors, including Erik Lundberg and John Åkerman, were toying with ideas very similar to those of Keynes, especially in the field of monetary theory. O. Steiger, "Bertil Ohlin and the Origins of the Keynesian Revolution," *History of Political Economy*, vol. 8 (Autumn 1976), pp. 341–366, up-plays the independence of the Stockholm school's writings, which proceeded, according to Steiger, within a neo-Wicksellian framework (see Chapter 20 on Wicksell). The origins of a stock-in-trade of (what has been thought to be) Keynesian fiscal theory—the balanced budget multiplier—is explored in two early papers by William A. Salant and Jørgen Gelting, with commentaries by Walter S. Salant, Bent Hansen, and Paul Samuelson: see "Origins of the Balanced-Budget Multiplier, I-IV," *History of Political Economy*, vol. 7 (Spring 1975), pp. 3–55. In the area of fiscal policy, Keynes was "scooped" by Chicago economists of the early thirties (see J. Ronnie Davis, *The New Economics and the Old Economists*). In this regard, also see B. L. Jones, "Lauchlin Currie and the Causes of the 1937 Recession," *History of Political Economy*, vol. 12 (Fall 1980), pp. 303–315. John M. Robertson, an underconsumptionist and pre-Keynesian philosopher, stated the paradox of thrift as early as 1892; see R. T. Nash and W. P. Gramm, "A Neglected Statement of the Paradox of Thrift," *History of Political Economy*, vol. 1 (Fall 1969), pp. 395–400. Of special interest in appreciating Keynes's differences with classical writers is John R. Hicks, "Mr. Keynes and the Classics: A Suggested Interpretation," *Econometrica*, vol. 5 (April 1937), pp. 147–159. In a similar vein, see B. T. McCallum, "On the Observational Inequivalence of Classical and Keynesian Models," *Journal of Political Economy*, vol. 87 (April 1979), pp. 395–402.

Important post-Keynesian developments in the area of economic dynamics include P. A. Samuelson, "Interactions between the Multiplier Analysis and the Principle of Acceleration," *Review of Economics and Statistics*, vol. 21 (May 1939), pp. 75–78; and J. R. Hicks, *A Contribution to the Theory of the Trade Cycle* (London: Oxford, 1950). Also see M. Fisher, "Professor Hicks and the Keynesians," *Economica*, vol. 43 (August 1976), pp. 305–414. Keynes's emphasis on consumption as the major component of total spending initiated a number of alternative formulations of consumption. See, for example, J. S. Duesenberry, *Income, Saving, and the Theory of Consumer Behavior* (Cambridge, Mass.: Harvard University Press, 1949); and Milton Friedman, *A Theory of the Consumption Function* (Princeton, N.J.:Princeton University Press, 1957).

Assessments of Keynesian economics abound. On the genesis and subsequent evolution of Keynes's ideas, see D. E. Moggridge, "From the *Treatise* to the *General Theory:* An Exercise in Chronology," *History of Political Economy*, vol. 5 (Spring 1973), pp. 72–88; D. Patinkin, "John Maynard Keynes: From the Tract to the *General Theory*," *Economic Journal*, vol. 85 (June 1975), pp. 249–271; H. Johnson, "Keynes' *General Theory:* A Revolution or War of Independence?" *Canadian Journal of Economics*, vol. 9 (November 1976), pp. 580–594; and E. G. Davis, "The Correspondence between R. G. Hawtrey and J. M. Keynes on the *Treatise:* The Genesis of Output Adjustment Models," *Canadian Journal of Economics*, vol. 13 (November 1980), pp. 716–724.

On Keynes's life and ideas, see Roy Harrod's *Life of John Maynard Keynes* (see References) and J. A. Schumpeter's "Keynes, the Economist," in *The New Economics: Keynes' Influence on Theory and Public Policy* (New York: A. M. Kelley, Publishers, 1965). This volume also contains useful essays on specific aspects of Keynesian theory by Seymour Harris, Abba Lerner, Paul Samuelson, Wassily Leontief, and others. Numerous assessments of Keynesian economics appeared in the 1960s. Three are mentioned here: Harry G. Johnson, "The *General Theory* after Twenty-Five Years," *American Economic Review*, vol. 51 (May 1961), pp. 1–17; Robert Lekachman (ed.), *Keynes' General Theory: Reports of Three Decades* (New York: St. Martin's, 1964); and, in a much more critical vein, David McCord Wright, *The Keynesian System* (New York: Fordham University Press, 1961). On the relevance of Keynes for today, see J. Tobin, "How Dead Is Keynes?" *Economic Inquiry*, vol. 15 (October 1977), pp. 459–468.

Some recent elaborations and/or clarifications of Keynes's work include: J. A. Trevithick, "Keynes, Inflation and Money Illusion," *Economic Journal*, vol. 85 (March 1975), pp. 101–113; C. Casarosa, "The Microfoundations of Keynes' Aggregate Supply and Expected Demand Analysis," *Economic Journal*, vol. 91 (March 1981), pp. 188–194; R. T. Froyen, "The Aggregative Structure of Keynes' General Theory," *Quarterly Journal of Economics*, vol. 90 (August 1976), pp. 369–388; and W. M. Corden, "Keynes and the Others: Wage and Price Rigidities in Macroeconomic Models," *Oxford Economic Papers*, vol. 30 (July 1978), pp. 159–180.

Don Patinkin, "A Study of Keynes' Theory of Effective Demand," *Economic Inquiry*, vol. 17 (April 1979), pp. 155–176, touched off a mini-debate on the proper interpretation of Keynes's demand theory. B. Littleboy and G. Mehta, "Patinkin on Keynes's Theory of Effective Demand," *History of Political Economy*, vol. 19 (Summer 1987), pp. 311–328, contend that the theory of effective demand is more completely developed by Keynes in his *Treatise on Money* than Patinkin gives him credit for. Patinkin's rejoinder is contained in *History of Political Economy*, vol. 19 (Winter 1987), pp. 647–658.

Much of Keynesian macroeconomics deals with the theory of investment. The effect of Keynes's notion of uncertainty on calculations of expected yields on investments is discussed by Mark Stohs, "Uncertainty in Keynes' *General*

Theory," History of Political Economy, vol. 12 (Fall 1980), pp. 372–382. Stohs claims that Keynes rejected the idea of numerical measures of prospective yields but believed some kind of nonnumerical calculation is possible. This interpretation has been questioned by C. A. Garner, "Uncertainty in Keynes' *General Theory:* A Comment," *History of Political Economy,* vol. 15 (Spring 1983), pp. 83–86, followed by Stohs's rejoinder, in which he argues for a modified Cartesian approach to economics. S. F. LeRoy, "Keynes' Theory of Investment," *History of Political Economy,* vol. 15 (Fall 1983), pp. 397–421, tries to elucidate what Keynes "really meant" by his theory of investment. Among other things, LeRoy claims that Keynes had in mind a temporary, general-equilibrium, two-sector model with nonshiftable capital, and that this is at variance with practically all previous interpretations of Keynes's investment theory. Also at issue is the entrepreneur's motivation in initiating new investments. Harold Dickson, "How Did Keynes Conceive of Entrepreneur's Motivation? Note on Patinkin's Hypothesis," *History of Political Economy,* vol. 15 (Summer 1983), pp. 229–248, raises an objection to Patinkin's interpretation that Keynes's entrepreneur based his decision to expand output on the fact that aggregate receipts exceed aggregate variable costs. See Patinkin, "New Materials on the Development of Keynes' Monetary Thought," *History of Political Economy,* vol. 12 (Spring 1980), pp. 1–28. Dickson maintains that said decisions are based, instead, on whether or not the expansion of output is *expected* to increase profits. On a related issue, P. G. McGregor, "Keynes on Ex-Ante Saving and the Rate of Interest," *History of Political Economy,* vol. 20 (Spring 1988), pp. 107–118, defends Keynes's post-*General Theory* view of interest rates against charges of confusion and inconsistency.

Although Keynes was not very sympathetic to Marx, several writers have emphasized the affinities between the two. See P. Kenway, "Marx, Keynes and the Possibility of Crises," *Cambridge Journal of Economics,* vol. 4 (March 1980), pp. 23–36; Dudley Dillard, "Keynes and Marx: A Centennial Appraisal," *Journal of Post-Keynesian Economics,* vol. 6 (Spring 1984), pp. 421–432; and Claudio Sardoni, "Marx and Keynes on Effective Demand and Unemployment," *History of Political Economy,* vol. 18 (Fall 1986), pp. 419–441.

Michael Hudson, "German Economists and the Depression of 1929–1933," *History of Political Economy,* vol. 17 (Spring 1985), pp. 35–50, shows how German economists, particularly Wilhelm Lautebach (the "German Keynes"), employed Keynesian public policy during the depression. The contrasting approaches to macroeconomic theory between Keynes and Hayek is the subject of R. W. Garrison, "Intertemporal Coordination and the Invisible Hand: An Austrian Perspective on the Keynesian Vision," *History of Political Economy,* vol. 17 (Summer 1985), pp. 309–321. The chief difference, Garrison argues, is that Keynes ignored the problem of intertemporal coordination. Garrison has been challenged by J. Snippe, "Intertemporal Coordination and the Economics of Keynes: Comment on Garrison," *History of Political Economy,* vol. 19 (Summer 1987), pp. 329–333, but see Garrison's rejoinder in the same issue for the final word.

The Keynesian model depicted in Figure 19-3 of this chapter has become the staple of beginning textbooks, and yet it is considered by some to be analytically weak and unsophisticated. D. R. Fusfeld, "Keynes and the Keynesian Cross: A Note," *History of Political Economy,* vol. 17 (Fall 1985), pp. 385–390, defends the Keynesian cross diagram against its supposed shortcomings, and claims that Keynes himself explicated the strengths of the model, although he never documented them in his writings.

Disputes on the real nature of Keynes's system continue among post-Keynesians as well as among historians of economic thought. On the spread of the Keynesian system and particularly the role of John R. Hicks in popularizing the Keynesian model, see Farhad Mahloudji, "Hicks and the Keynesian Revolution," *History of Political Economy,* vol. 17 (Summer 1985), pp. 287–308. Leijonhufvud's interpretation of the Keynesian system (see References) remains the most provocative, but the entire *Journal of Post-Keynesian Economics* is devoted to grappling with interpretative issues of this sort. Those who would allow Keynes to speak for himself should consult his own summary of the *General Theory,* "The General Theory of Employment," *Quarterly Journal of Economics,* vol. 51 (September 1937), pp. 209–223.

It is certain that Keynes was a brilliant biographer and historian of thought as well as a first-rate theorist. See his *Essays in Biography,* rev. ed. (New York: Norton Library, 1951); and Donald A. Walker, "Keynes as a Historian of Economic Thought: The Biographical Essays on Neoclassical Economists," *History of Political Economy,* vol. 17 (Summer 1985), pp. 159–186. On what Keynes himself was really like, the record still makes interesting and somewhat titillating reading. See Michael Holroyd, *Lytton Strachey: A Critical Biography,* 2 vols. (New York: Holt, 1968), which contains a considerable amount of information on Keynes; E. S. Johnson and H. G. Johnson, *The Shadow of Keynes: Understanding Keynes, Cambridge, and Keynesian Economics* (Chicago: University of Chicago Press, 1978); C. H. Hession, *John Maynard Keynes: A Personal Biography of the Man Who Revolutionized Capitalism and the Way We Live* (New York: Macmillan, 1984); and R. J. A. Skidelsky, *John Maynard Keynes* (New York: Viking, 1986).

REFERENCES

Davis, J. Ronnie. *The New Economics and the Old Economists.* Ames: The Iowa State University Press, 1971.

Hansen, Alvin H. *A Guide to Keynes.* New York: McGraw-Hill, 1953.

Harrod, R. F. *The Life of John Maynard Keynes.* New York: Harcourt, Brace, 1951.

Keynes, John Maynard. *The General Theory of Employment, Interest and Money.* London: Macmillan, 1936.

Leijonhufvud, Axel. *On Keynesian Economics and the Economics of Keynes.* New York: Oxford University Press, 1968.

Patinkin, Don. *Money, Interest and Prices,* 2d ed. New York: Harper & Row, 1965.

Pigou, A. C. *The Theory of Unemployment.* London: Macmillan 1933.

Robertson, Dennis. *Essays in Money and Interest.* London: Fontana Library, 1966.

CHAPTER 20

CONTEMPORARY MACROECONOMICS: THE QUANTITY THEORY, MONETARISM, AND RATIONAL EXPECTATIONS

INTRODUCTION

Despite a few notable exceptions discussed in Chapter 6, money in the aggregate sense was not of prime importance to classical writers. There were important debates about money, such as the bullionist and currency school arguments, but the prime concern was for the institutions affecting the supply of money. The determinants of the wealth of a nation were identified as *real* factors related to thrift and productivity. The determinants of the general price level was the stock of money, of course, but this magnitude had nothing to do with real wealth or *relative* prices. Most industrial nations, moreover, supported gold or specie standards that were viewed as "self-regulating." Inflations could and did occur, but they were attributed to wars and other disasters (during which the gold standard was very often abandoned) or to the money-printing tendencies of improvident governments or politicians. In classical theory, then, value theory (determined by real forces) was dichotomized from monetary theory.

Neoclassical writers in the early twentieth century, particularly Irving Fisher, Knut Wicksell, and A. C. Pigou, began to put aggretate monetary theory on a par with value theory. The transmission mechanism from money to prices, the determinants of the velocity of circulation and of the demand for money, and the general role of interest rates in the process of monetary expansions and contractions were all matters of concern to these writers. All the elements of a rather sophisticated version of the quantity theory were on hand well before Keynes penned the *General Theory*. But ideas and events coalesced in the 1930s to produce a macroeconomics that (Keynesians believed) could deal with problems of massive unemployment, depression, and general economic malaise. In this Keynesian scenario, money mattered very little or not at all.

The lack of faith in monetary policy as a central stabilizing device in the macro economy persisted well through the 1960s. It has been the case, however, that Keynesian suggestions about deficit spending were easily followed during periods of recession, whereas surpluses or balanced budgets during periods of inflation have been extrèmely rare and most unpopular within the political establishment. The very Keynesian principles that made the economy deflation- or depression-proof, in other words, may have made it inflation-prone. Events of the 1960s, especially the (largely) deficit-financed Vietnam war, led to large rates of increase in the money stock. Such increases in the money stock led to serious and persistent problems with inflation. Predictably, these events of the past few decades have led to a confrontation with Keynesian economics and to a real and practical resurgence of interest in "monetarism," which is but a refinement of the neoclassical quantity theory. (In theoretical terms, monetarism in the form of the quantity theory was never absent from the economic intellectual scene.) The purpose of this chapter is to chronicle twentieth-century developments leading up to and including the contemporary form of monetarism and rational expectations.

THE NEOCLASSICAL ORIGINS OF MONETARISM

Despite a noticeable lack of unanimity in early formulations of the quantity theory, they all established a more or less direct relation between money and prices. With a few notable exceptions, such as Locke and Thornton, no writer assigned an explicit role to the interest rate as an important determinant of economic activity. On the other hand, the quantity theory was not purely mechanical, since increases in the quantity of money were seen by Cantillon, Thornton, Ricardo, and Mill as affecting the demand for commodities and, through greater demand, as raising prices. But classical monetary theory did not appreciate the adjustment process in the transition to a new equilibrium, nor did it analyze the stability conditions of new equilibriums following monetary disturbances. Classical writers often discussed the forces that would preserve (or destroy) that new equilibrium. A large part of this void was initially filled by the neoclassical writers Irving Fisher and Knut Wicksell.

Irving Fisher and the Equation of Exchange

In 1911, Yale University professor Irving Fisher (1867–1947) took the lead from John Stuart Mill and derived a mathematical framework for expounding the conclusion of the quantity theory. Fisher wrote: $MV + M'V' = PT$, where M is the stock of currency in circulation; V is currency's annual velocity of circulation, or the rate at which currency changes hands; M' is the volume of demand deposits held by banks; V' is annual demand-deposit velocity of circulation; P is the aggregate price level; and T is an index of the physical vol-

ume of transactions. Since our modern definition of money includes bank demand deposits, the above equation can be rewritten more simply as $MV = PT$,
hereafter referred to as Fisher's equation of exchange.

Fisher's mathematical expression finds its verbal antecedent in Mill, who
wrote:

> If we assume the quantity of goods on sale, and the number of times those goods are
> resold, to be fixed quantities, the value of money will depend upon its quantity; to-
> gether with the average number of times that each piece changes hands in the
> process.... Consequently, the amount of goods and transactions being the same, the
> value of money is inversely as its quantity multiplied by what is called the rapidity of
> circulation [velocity]. And the quantity of money in circulation is equal to the money
> value of all the goods sold, divided by the number which expresses the rapidity of
> circulation (*Principles of Political Economy,* p. 494).

Fisher realized that his equation of exchange was an accounting identity,
therefore a truism. But that does not render it useless from the standpoint of
economic theory. In fact, Fisher used it to assert once again the proportionality between increases in M and increases in P. The equation of exchange, with
certain assumptions, subsequently became a mathematical expression of the
quantity theory. Fisher's assumptions were that velocity (V) and the volume of
trade (T) were independent of the money supply and that the price level was a
passive rather than an active variable. Hence he could and did affirm the strict
proportionality between M and P as a long-run phenomenon. His specification
of the determinants of V and T was incredibly complete. In essence, V and T
were assumed determined by *real* factors (habit and custom, technology and
institutional arrangements), so that changes in the stock of money did not
cause changes in any of the real determinants of V and T.

A Missing Link: The Real-Balance Effect   More important than his mathematical rendition of the strict quantity theory was Fisher's identification of the
connection between an increase in the quantity of money and the ensuing increase in prices. The missing link (which ensures the stability of monetary
equilibrium) is the real-balance effect. It can be explained this way. An increase in individual money holdings disturbs the optimum relation between the
individual's cash balances and expenditures. In Walrasian terms, more money
at the existing price level creates an excess supply of money balances in individual hands. Thus individuals seek to reduce their excess money balances by
increasing expenditures. Furthermore, if output remains unchanged (as Fisher
assumed), the increased money demand will push prices up until they have
risen in the same proportion as the increase in money. In this way a new equilibrium is reached and maintained because individual money balances are returned to their optimum level.

This idea was absent from earlier formulations of the quantity theory, although having discovered it, Fisher did not exploit the real-balance effect
fully. He never showed, for example, how excess money balances could be
used to purchase securities, thereby pushing security prices up and the interest

rate down. In other words, Fisher never demonstrated how an increase in money could cause increased output *indirectly* through lower interest rates (although Wicksell went far in filling this gap, as we shall see). Instead, Fisher turned to the interrelation between inflation, interest rates, expectations, and the holdings of real-cash balances.

Inflation and the "Fisher Effect"   In seminal works such as *The Purchasing Power of Money* and *The Theory of Interest*, Fisher explored the ramifications of actual and expected inflation and its interactions with nominal interest rates and the demand for real balances. First consider the demand for real-money balances, which may be expressed as follows:

$$m_d = f(y, i)$$

where m_d, the demand for real balances, is a function of y, real income, and i, the nominal rate of interest. Money demand is the reciprocal of velocity. This functional form of money demand was understood by Fisher, but it was not elaborated upon until the writings of A. C. Pigou and Milton Friedman, two writers considered later in this chapter. However, Fisher did discover the important process through which the *nominal* interest rate, which is the *opportunity cost of holding money*, is determined.

In a flash of practical wisdom Fisher saw that the *nominal* interest rate was the product of two factors: (1) the *real* rate of interest, which reflects the basic underlying forces of borrowing and lending (the classicals' thrift and productivity) in the economy, and (2) the *expected* inflation rate at some point of time. In some sort of "global equilibrium"—i.e., with constant rates of inflation—the actual rate equals the expected rate. In general, with some simplifications, Fisher's concept may be expressed as follows:

$$i = r + P^*$$

where i is the nominal rate, r is the real rate, and P^* is the *expected* rate of inflation. Naturally, when the expected rate equals the actual rate of inflation, the nominal interest rate is equal to the real rate.

The logic of Fisher's equation is quite clear. The nominal rate is formed by lenders as the sum of the real rate plus whatever inflation is expected to be over the course of the lending period. If the expected rate of inflation is 5 percent per year and the real rate is 4 percent, lenders would be generally unwilling to lend funds at less than 9 percent. If, ex post, the rate of inflation turns out to be 10 percent, the borrower has obtained funds at a *negative* real rate of interest and lenders will adjust in succeeding periods. Thus, inflationary expectations affect nominal interest rates. The implications of the "Fisher effect" will be considered in more detail below, but it is important to note that Fisher discovered a mechanism whereby inflation may be self-perpetuating. Higher rates of monetary expansion may thus lead, initially, to lower nominal interest rates (through an increase in the supply of loanable funds), but eventually higher *prices* lead, through inflationary expectations, to increases in the nominal rate and higher inflation. This principle, a stock-in-trade of modern monetarists, was one of Fisher's major discoveries. We will return to these matters later in the present chapter, but at this point we pause to consider Wicksell's contributions to the monetarist paradigm.

Knut Wicksell and Modern Monetary Theory

The task of extending the Walrasian framework to monetary theory fell to the Swedish economist Knut Wicksell (1851–1926), who opposed quasi-mechanistic formulations such as Fisher's. Two items of minor surgery performed by Wicksell on the quantity theory brought it into the realm of modern monetary theory. First, Wicksell took a hint from Thomas Tooke (1779–1858), an early critic of the quantity theory, and asserted that prices are determined by income (i.e., that money works through income to determine the aggregate price level). Second, Wicksell used the two-rate analysis of Thornton to underline the role played by the interest rate in monetary theory.[1]

In his restatement of the quantity theory, Wicksell made an important step toward integrating monetary theory with value theory. He constructed an aggregate-demand–aggregate-supply framework for investigating changes in prices, as demonstrated in the following passage:

> Every rise or fall in the price of a particular commodity presupposes a disturbance of the equilibrium between the supply of and demand for that commodity, whether the disturbance has actually taken place or is merely prospective. What is true in this respect of each commodity separately must doubtless be true of all commodities collectively. A general rise in prices is therefore only conceivable on the supposition that the general demand has for some reason become, or is expected to become, greater than the supply.... Any theory of money worthy of the name must be able to show how and why the monetary or pecuniary demand for goods exceeds or falls short of the supply of goods in given conditions (*Lectures on Political Economy*, II, pp. 159–160).

What is noteworthy in this passage is the way in which Wicksell made the transition from the partial-equilibrium approach of Marshall (i.e., supply equals demand for a single product) to the aggregate-supply–aggregate-demand framework later employed by Keynes. Moreover, Wicksell accepted the challenge that he set down in the last sentence quoted above: he did show how monetary demand exceeds or falls short of aggregate supply through the effects of changes in money on cash balances.

---

[1] A leading student of Wicksell, Professor Carl Uhr, has concluded that Wicksell was probably never exposed to Thornton's writings directly but that he had studied the currency debate between Tooke and Ricardo at length and was most likely exposed to Thornton's ideas through Ricardo (*The Economic Doctrines of Knut Wicksell*, p. 200). On Thornton's analysis, see Chap. 6 of this book.

Real Balances The passage that most vividly describes Wicksell's understanding of the real-balance effect appears below. The reader is cautioned that the analysis is worked through for a *decrease* in the stock of money:

> Let us suppose that for some reason or other...the stock of money is diminished while prices remain temporarily unchanged. The cash balances will gradually appear to be *too small in relation to the new level of prices....*(It is true that in this case I can rely on a higher level of receipts in the future. But meanwhile I run the risk of being unable to meet my obligations punctually, and at best I may easily be forced by shortage of ready money to forego some purchase that would otherwise have been profitable.) I therefore seek to enlarge my balance. This can only be done— neglecting for the present the possibility of borrowing, etc.—through a *reduction* in my *demand* for goods and services, or through an *increase* in the *supply* of my own commodity...or through both together. The same is true for all other owners and consumers of commodities. But in fact nobody will succeed in realizing the object at which each is aiming—to increase his cash balance; for the sum of individual cash balances is limited by the amount of the available stock of money, or rather is identical with it. On the other hand, the universal reduction in demand and increase in supply of commodities will necessarily bring about a continuous fall in all prices. This can only cease when prices have fallen to the level at which the cash balances are regarded as *adequate* (*Interest and Prices*, pp. 39–40).

In this way, Wicksell demonstrated the real-balance effect as the equilibrating mechanism that ensures stability in the wake of monetary disturbances. He thereby filled in what Don Patinkin called the "missing chapter" in neoclassical monetary theory.[2]

By emphasizing the relation between savings and investment in his aggregate-supply–aggregate-demand analysis, Wicksell also rescued the interest rate (as a monetary variable) from the oblivion into which it had sunk after Thornton. Wicksell did not accept the interest rate as a purely monetary phenomenon, but he used the two-rate thesis to synthesize nonmonetary theories of the rate of interest. Moreover, he made the divergence between the natural rate and the actual rate the main element of his dynamic analysis.

The Cumulative Process Neoclassical monetary theorists have been criticized for complacently accepting the comparative-static, mechanical conclusion (that is, $2M = 2P$) of the Hume-Mill-Fisher quantity theory. Although a number of neoclassical monetary theorists seemed to have grasped the real-balance effect, "they frequently failed," in Professor Patinkin's words, "to provide a systematic dynamic analysis of the way in which the monetary increase generated real-balance effects in the commodity markets which propelled the economy from its original equilibrium position to its new one" (*Money, Interest and Prices*, p. 167). Wicksell was the exception. His dynamic analysis, which focused on the interest rate as the point of departure, constitutes what he called the "cumulative process."

---

[2] See Patinkin's *Money, Interest and Prices*.

What is important to note beforehand in Wicksell's dynamic process is that short-run discrepancies between aggregate supply and demand are revealed by shifts between the normal and actual rates of interest. Thus he makes the interrelation between money and product markets explicit. The cumulative process is illustrated in the following passage:

> If the banks lend their money at materially lower rates than the normal rate as above defined [e.g., in Thornton—see Figure 6-1], then in the first place saving will be discouraged and for that reason there will be an increased demand for goods and services for present consumption. In the second place, the profit opportunities of entrepreneurs will thus be increased and the demand for goods and services, as well as for raw materials already in the market for future production, will evidently increase to the same extent as it had previously been held in check by the higher rate of interest. Owing to the increased income thus accruing to the workers, landowners, and the owners of raw materials, etc., the prices of consumption goods will begin to rise.... What is still more important is that the rise in prices, whether small or great at first, can never cease so long as the cause which gave rise to it continues to operate; in other words, so long as the loan rate remains below the normal rate (*Lectures,* II, pp. 195–196).

Wicksell also hinted at the role played by expectations in aggregate analysis when he pointed out that the effects of the cumulative process may be irreversible. He maintained that entrepreneurs who had been able to pay higher wages and raw material prices when the loan rate was below the natural rate will, "*even if* [the] *bank rate reverts to the normal natural rate,* on an average be able to offer the same high price, because they have reason to expect the same increased prices for their own products in the future" (*Lectures,* II, p. 196). Thus if banks maintain artificially low interest rates, they merely tempt entrepreneurs to bid up the prices of labor and raw materials, and thus the prices of final goods.

Despite his innovations, however, Wicksell's monetary analysis did not depart radically from that of the classical economists. He set out, in fact, to defend the quantity theory against its critics, and this he did for the long-run variant of that theory. Yet he elaborated a process of adjustment better than anyone had done before. He also gave a prominent role to the interest rate and to aggregate demand in explaining aggregate adjustments to changes in money. (This last aspect of Wicksell's researches is also characteristic of Keynesian analysis, as we have seen.) In assessing contemporary monetary theory, however, which incorporates Wicksell's contribution, we must also look to a tradition begun at Cambridge University near the turn of the century.

The Cambridge Equation

We learned in Chapter 15 that Marshall founded a Cambridge tradition in partial-equilibrium analysis near the end of the nineteenth century. This tradition extended to monetary theory as well, although Marshall's tortuous delay in publishing his ideas robbed his monetary theory of most of its novelty by the time it appeared in print. Nevertheless, a leading characteristic of the Cambridge tradition was the desire voiced by Marshall himself to integrate monetary theory and value theory. As Keynes wrote in his biography of Marshall: "He always taught that the value of money is a function of its supply on the one hand and the demand for it, on the other, as measured by 'the average stock of command over commodities which each person cares to keep in ready form'" (*Memorials of Alfred Marshall,* ed. A. C. Pigou, p. 29).

Ironically, the Cambridge economists never fully succeeded in the integration of monetary and value theories; they were surpassed in this respect by Wicksell. But Marshall's supply-and-demand framework did lead to the famous Cambridge equation, and in so doing, it provided for the first time a focus on the demand for money as well as its supply. In this respect Marshall's monetary economics is the spiritual father of the Keynesian theory of liquidity preference (see Chapter 19) as well as the more modern formulation of the demand for money as a part of the general theory of asset choice.

Marshall asserted that the demand for money (i.e., the desired quantity of cash balances) could be expressed at any time as a fraction of income, which led to the familiar Cambridge equation, summarized here as $M = KPT$. M is the stock of money, which Marshall assumed to be an exogenous variable; K is the fraction of income that the community seeks to hold in the form of cash balances and demand deposits; P is the general price level; and T is total output. Thus the right-hand side of the above equation is an expression of the quantity of money supplied. Analytically, K in the cash-balance equation is the reciprocal of V in Fisher's equation of exchange. Thus both Fisher and Marshall accepted the quantity theory as a fundamental truth, and both concentrated on the medium-of-exchange function of money while neglecting the interest rate.

This omission led to some serious shortcomings in neoclassical monetary analysis, the chief of which was the neglect of the interdependence between the product and money markets. Wicksell avoided this pitfall, as we have seen, but the too exclusive emphasis by the Cambridge group[3] on the demand for money possibly prevented their systematic analysis of the way in which changes in real balances are transmitted into the commodity market. This is curious because the cash-balance effect is inherent in the Cambridge equation. It can be rearranged, in other words, to express an excess supply of money $(E_s = M - KPT)$ or an excess demand for money $(E_d = KPT - M)$, either one of which is capable of generating a real-balance effect.

Professor Patinkin also finds it curious that the Cambridge group did not apply the test of stability conditions to the monetary sector of the economy, since they never failed to do so in examining the product markets. This discrepancy is especially obtrusive in the case of Walras, as Patinkin noted in his critique of neoclassical monetary theory:

---

[3] Along with Marshall, this group included his students A. C. Pigou and D. H. Robertson.

> Walras was a man who never tired of establishing the stability of his system by elaborating on the corrective forces of excess supply that would be called into play should the price lie above its equilibrium value, and the forces of excess demand that would be called into play should it lie below. He did it when he explained how the market determines the equilibrium prices of commodities; he did it again when he explained how the market determines the equilibrium prices of productive services; and he did it a third time when he explained how the market determines the equilibrium prices of capital goods. But he did not do it when he attempted to explain how the market determines the equilibrium "price" of paper money. And Walras is the rule, not the exception (*Money, Interest and Prices,* p. 168).

This omission and the general neglect of the interest rate in the cash-balance equation tended to preserve the separation of monetary theory and value theory well into the twentieth century. However, some advances were made by other predecessors of Keynes in explaining the dynamic relation between money, income, and the business cycle.

MODERN MONETARISM: THEORY AND POLICY

It is now time to return to the main theme of this chapter and to demonstrate how some of the basic elements of the modern monetarist position are straightforward extensions of earlier works on the quantity theory. As pointed out previously, the popularity of monetarism as a policy prescription was preceded by continuous contributions (even during the heyday of Keynesianism) to the development of the quantity theory. No writer, perhaps, has brought forth the monetarist case in more forceful and elegant terms than Nobel laureate Milton Friedman, whose ideas have shaped a generation of "monetarists."

Friedman's Theory of the Demand for Money

In 1956 (during the utter dominance of Keynes's ideas within the academic community) Chicago economist Milton Friedman published a set of essays enlarging upon (and "testing") the quantity theory of money (*Studies in the Quantity Theory of Money*). In his essay entitled "The Quantity Theory of Money: A Restatement" (contained in *Studies*) Friedman set out a new version of the demand for money. In functional form Friedman's equation was

$$m_d = \alpha \, (Y_p, \, w, \, i, \, P^*, \, P, \, u)$$

where the demand for money is seen to be a function (α) of permanent income (Y_p), the proportion of human to nonhuman wealth (w), the *nominal* interest rate (i), *expected* changes in the rate of change in the price level (P^*), the actual price level (P), and the preference function for money vis-à-vis other goods (u). Friedman offers this specification as a *theory* of money demand, and it is set up in testable form.

   An elaboration of all of the independent variables in Friedman's equation would take us too far afield here. (The interested reader is invited to read the original essay.) But several points about the equation are of principal importance.

Friedman's restatement is essentially a theory of a demand for money, not a theory of prices (as was the older version of the quantity theory). In this respect, his approach to monetary theory is similar to Keynes's. There is an important difference, however. What is unique in Friedman's restatement of the quantity theory is that he begins with a basic premise from capital theory: that "income" is the yield on capital. This means that the concept of income Friedman uses in his construction of the quantity theory is not that used by Keynes in his income-expenditure model. Friedman calls his income measure "permanent income," which is to say that he treats income as a discounted, present-value stream of payments derived from an existing stock of wealth, including human wealth. The latter consists of "qualitative" improvements such as education and training. Keynes neglected wealth almost entirely, which was appropriate for the type of short-run analysis he was trying to develop.[4] But when the emphasis shifts to the long run, permanent income is a more appropriate variable.

Friedman does not argue that the demand for cash balances or its reciprocal, velocity, is constant, as implied in earlier naive formulations. Rather he argues that money demand is a stable and predictable function of the independent variables. This implies that money is still the crucial variable in predicting prices and, as we shall see, short-term fluctuations in output and employment. In other words, if velocity is predictable, changes in the rate of monetary expansion will explain changes in the rate of inflation (or deflation) as well as short-term alterations in output and employment.[5]

Friedman's money-demand equation will be recognized as an elaboration of the money-demand function we looked at earlier in this chapter. It can be simplified to include only income (current, not permanent) and nominal interest rates (y and i). While this simplification does not do justice to Friedman's elegant conception, it will make our elementary explanation of "monetarism" easier. For example, when the Fisher effect and Friedman's conception of money demand are combined, a very lucid explanation of inflation emerges.

The Monetarist Explanation of Inflation: A Simple Treatment

Recall that Fisher argued that the nominal interest rate was equal to the sum of the real interest rate and the *expected* inflation rate. This immediately raises

---

[4] Keynes's matter-of-fact justification for short-run analysis was that "in the long run, we are all dead." Modern monetarists would undoubtedly retort that the reason we are dead in the long run is that Keynesian policies have killed us with inflation and excessive government.

[5] Although Friedman's statistical evidence is the subject of much controversy, his role as a leading monetary theorist is undisputable. On this point, at least, other leading monetary theorists agree. Harry Johnson has written that "Friedman's application to monetary theory of the basic principle...that income is the yield on capital, and capital the present value of income—is probably the most important development in monetary theory since Keynes' *General Theory*" ("Monetary Theory and Policy," p. 350).

questions about how expectations are formed. One popular theory about expectations is the so-called *adaptive expectations* theory, which simply states that price expectations are formed on the basis of past experience with inflation, with more recent past price experience weighing more heavily than that of the distant past. Uncertainty about future prices dominates expectations. Laborers, for example, contract for future wages and businesses set future prices on the basis of some (uncertain) expectations about future prices. The adaptive expectations theory says that these expectations will be formed principally by the most recent past experience.

Remember that the *nominal* interest rate is partly a function of price expectations and that the demand for cash balances is in turn a function of the nominal interest rate. Higher nominal rates mean higher opportunity costs for holding money, which means a *reduced* demand for cash balances (and vice versa).

A simplified explanation for inflation may thus be given utilizing the concepts of adaptive expectations, the Fisher effect, and Friedman's (modified) money-demand function. Assume (1) that there is a constant rate of money expansion by the central bank; (2) that expected inflation rates and actual inflation rates are equal (and equivalent to the rate of monetary expansion); (3) that the nominal interest rate is equal to the real rate plus the rate of inflation (or monetary expansion), which is constant; (4) that actual and desired holdings of cash balances are equal; and (5) that real income is growing at a constant rate. Given these conditions, assume a once-and-for-all increase in the rate of monetary expansion.

The initial results of the increase in monetary expansion are to increase actual cash balances of individuals and firms above their desired levels and to *initially* depress the nominal rate of interest (because loanable funds have increased, temporarily reducing the real rate of interest—the "Wicksell effect" if you will). The excess of cash balances leads to increased spending on commodities, securities, and all other assets. Actual prices begin to rise (as do nominal wages somewhat) due to the increased nominal spending. Expectations, *after a time*, "adapt" to the price increases, causing the nominal interest rate, which fell initially, to rise. The process does not end until: (1) the new rate of inflation is equal to the new and higher rate of monetary expansion; (2) the nominal interest rate has increased by an amount equal to the difference between the old and the new inflation rate; (3) actual cash balances are again equal to desired cash balances; and (4) the *real* rate of interest is restored to its former level. Notice that the *level* of cash balances held will be *lower* than that before the new rate of money growth because of a higher nominal interest rate, which means a higher cost of holding money.

What are the implications of the process for economic policy? Some are obvious. How often have we heard that "tight money and high interest rates are the causes of inflation"? Many business people and politicians adhere to this naive view. The monetarist version of events tells us that exactly the opposite is the case. While monetary expansion *initially* lowers the nominal interest rate, inflation and the Fisher effect take over and eventually cause nominal interest rates to rise. The only way that interest rates could be depressed over long periods is to enact higher and higher rates of monetary expansion, a very dangerous policy in the view of monetarists.

Friedman has argued that, always and everywhere, inflation is a *monetary phenomenon,* and he has convincingly demonstrated this proposition for the United States in a massive empirical study (conducted with Anna Schwartz) entitled *A Monetary History of the United States, 1867–1960.* As in the earlier and more naive versions of the quantity theory, inflation can be explained by increased velocity (reduced money-demand growth), reduced income growth, or an increased rate of monetary expansion. In the contemporary monetarist's view, there are limits to the growth of velocity—people can economize just so much on cash balances. Further, the growth in income and employment is, in the longer run, determined by real and other factors (see the following section). The remaining culprit is *monetary expansion.* Ultimately the monetarist interpretation of inflation, as we shall see in a later section, is that it is produced by erratic discretionary changes in money growth rates.

Inflation and Unemployment: The Monetarist Reaction

Monetarism has been extended to the problems of employment and income growth and to their relation to inflation. In 1958, in a famous paper establishing an "effect" that bears his name, British economist A. W. Phillips discussed a relation between the rate of unemployment and inflation ("The Relation between Unemployment and the Rate of Change of Money Wage Rates in the United Kingdom, 1861–1957").[6] The "Phillips curve" described an inverse relation between the unemployment rate and the inflation rate such that higher and higher inflation rates were required to reduce the unemployment rate by a given percentage. If correct, this would present the ultimate policymaker's dilemma. Problems of definition arose. The definition of unemployment itself—taken as including both frictional and structural factors—is open to question. Does the economist accept the Labor Department's definition, the Council of Economic Advisers' conception, or what?

Macroeconomic events such as "stagflation" led to strong doubts about the Phillips relation. Friedman once again rose to the occasion and offered an elegant alternative conception of both unemployment and the short-run Phillips curve. In his 1968 presidential address to the American Economic Association ("The Role of Monetary Policy") Friedman argued that the *long-run* Phillips relation was vertical at some *natural* rate of unemployment. That is, in the long run, any particular rate of monetary expansion and inflation has little or nothing to do with the *natural* unemployment rate. The question of what constitutes the natural rate of unemployment has been set forth by Friedman in the following terms:

---

[6] Actually, as the title of this essay suggests, Phillips used money wage rates rather than the inflation rate in his relation. Further, it is apparent that Irving Fisher invented the Phillips conception; see Fisher's essay "A Statistical Relation between Unemployment and Price Changes" (1926).

It refers...to that rate of employment which is consistent with the *existing real conditions* in the labor market. It can be lowered by removing obstacles in the labor market, by reducing friction. It can be raised by introducing additional obstacles. The purpose of the concept is to separate the monetary from the nonmonetary aspects of the employment situation—precisely the same purpose that Wicksell had in using the word *natural* in connection with the rate of interest (*Price Theory,* p. 228).

In Friedman's conception, then, the natural rate of unemployment is determined by all *real* conditions affecting the supply and demand for labor. These factors would include all institutional arrangements, such as the degree of unionization, minimum-wage laws, the proportion of women in the work force, the status of worker education, and so on.

In the short run, however, the actual unemployment rate may diverge from the natural rate. It may be higher or lower than the natural rate. To see intuitively how this is possible we need merely return to our analysis of money and inflation in the previous section, changing only the assumption stated there that output and employment remain constant over the adjustment to a new rate of monetary expansion.

The key to understanding the short-run-inflation–unemployment relation is to note that after an increase in the rate of money expansion, business people's and workers' perceptions or expectations diverge from actual price experience. Specifically, as individuals begin to rid themselves of excess cash balances, the prices of goods and services rise. Individual entrepreneurs perceive an increase in demand (and price) for their own products (not an increase in the general price level) and produce more, simultaneously hiring more labor at a lower actual real wage. Why will laborers be willing to supply more labor? (Nominal wages may *rise* somewhat, but inflation tends to drive down real wages, indicating a *reduced* quantity of labor input!) The answer is that laborers' perceptions of prices lag behind—workers are, in Keynesian terms, under *money illusion.* In other words, increased *nominal* wages fool laborers into thinking that real wages have increased, and therefore they supply more labor. Consequently, unemployment falls below the natural rate until laborers (and businesses) catch on and readjust. There is, therefore, a short-run inverse relation between unemployment and inflation, but in the long run the Phillips relation is vertical at the natural rate of unemployment. Monetarists thus argue that in the long run employment and, consequently, output growth are determined by *real factors* affecting input markets. Altering money-supply growth rates only temporarily affects output and employment. Nevertheless, money-supply changes have long-term effects on the rate at which prices change.

Economic Policy from a Monetarist Perspective

The monetarist theoretical scenario also has a strong policy message. The existence of an "expectations component" in the argument means that lags of various kinds exist within the implementation of monetary policy. There are both *inside* and *outside* lags in the monetary policy of a central bank. Inside lags exist because of administrative delays and delays in the recognition of adverse macroeconomic developments in output, employment, and prices. While these may be of shorter actual duration than in the case of fiscal policy (which goes through a political process), the "outside" lag is very significant. Milton Friedman first called attention to the outside lag, which is simply the length of time it takes before actual changes in monetary expansion or contraction are felt on the "target" variables of inflation, output, and employment.

In the monetarist view, as we have seen, expectations adjustment is a time-consuming process. While a number of studies present conflicting evidence on the matter, there is likely a six- to nine-month lag between monetary alterations and changes in total spending. Output changes are ordinarily thought to be the first target affected, the full effects of monetary expansion on the rate of inflation taking as long as a year and a half. Comparatively little is known, however, about the formation of expectations and other factors affecting the length of lags. Thus, it is clear that a good deal of uncertainty surrounds the conduct and effectiveness of monetary policy.

The Federal Reserve Board, moreover, has targeted the money variables in attempting to control macroeconomic activity. The Fed's attempt to target interest rates (such as the federal funds rate)—i.e., to keep it within a certain range—has led to very costly mistakes. When interest rates climb due to market factors such as excessive government borrowing, the Federal Reserve often reacts with a monetary expansion that temporarily lowers the interest rate but lays the groundwork for new upward pressures on interest rates in the future (preceded, of course, by higher inflation rates). This problem has led many monetarists, including and most especially Friedman, to espouse the targeting of bank reserves and monetary aggregates rather than interest rates. To some extent, the Federal Reserve has altered operating procedures somewhat to target money aggregates, but the outcome of these piecemeal changes has been far from clear. At base, monetarists view monetary policy from a "rules-versus-discretion" perspective. They strongly question whether discretionary policy—given the state of existing or future knowledge of macroeconomic processes—can ever create stability. Let us consider this important matter in more detail.

Rules versus Authority   The United States, of course, operates under an independent monetary authority. The members of the Federal Reserve Board are chosen by the president of the United States—with the advice and consent of the Senate—but once chosen, they operate independently of the body politic. Friedman sees in this arrangement a threat to individual liberty, since it is money more than anything else that affects the price level and employment.

We might expect Friedman to be led to such a view on the basis of philosophical persuasion alone, but his argument against an independent monetary authority receives added force from investigation of historical monetary data. For example, in his lengthy study with Anna Schwartz, *Monetary History of the United States* (1963), Friedman revealed that during the great depression the Federal Reserve Board allowed the money stock of the United States to fall by one-third, which he contends caused the depression to last much longer than it would have in the presence of a "proper" monetary response.

A deeper acquaintance with monetary facts in this and other countries led Friedman to assert that severe depressions have always been accompanied by sharp reductions in the money stock and that sharp reductions in the money stock have always been accompanied by depressions. On the other end of the spectrum, Friedman feels that severe inflations have always been accompanied by sharp increases in the money stock and vice versa. With respect to the great depression, Friedman concludes:

> The Great Depression in the United States, far from being a sign of the inherent instability of the private enterprise system, is a testament to how much harm can be done by mistakes on the part of a few men when they wield vast power over the monetary system of a country (*Capitalism and Freedom*, p. 50).

Friedman therefore advocates an alternative that has long been in the University of Chicago tradition: that automatic rules replace independent monetary authority. In Friedman's view the past performance of the Federal Reserve Board has not been unlike that of a nervous teenager learning to drive. When pressing on the accelerator (i.e., increasing the money stock), our nervous tyro frequently gives the car too much gas; when stepping on the brakes (reducing the money stock), he or she pushes too hard. In a phrase, monetary overacceleration and overbraking are predictable. Rather than proceeding smoothly on a path of economic growth, the economy is subject to fits and starts—inflation and/or depression results, harming individuals in the process.

To counteract this tendency, Friedman proposes that the Federal Reserve Board be directed by law to increase the money stock month by month at an annual rate of between 3 and 5 percent. A rate of increase in this range is consistent, in Friedman's view, with attainable economic growth in the United States and relative price stability. Moreover, it would eliminate the destabilizing effects of, say, a 12 percent increase in the money supply one month and a 3 percent increase the next.

Among academicians, the rules-versus-authority question is most controversial. Friedman's result of stable economic growth under the monetary rule depends crucially on the stability of velocity. While his statistical evidence supports this assumption, his critics dispute that evidence, or they challenge Friedman's statistical procedures. Some critics contend that while velocity may be stable in the long run, it is not stable in the short run. They therefore argue that discretionary monetary policy is required to head off short-run, destabilizing changes in velocity. As is true of so many other issues championed by Friedman, the debate on this matter rages still. But those who share Friedman's views could hardly have a more effective spokesman for the monetarist position in contemporary macroeconomic theory.[7]

---

[7] So razor-sharp is Friedman's intellect and so skillful an adversary in debate, that he has been compared to the philosopher Nietzsche, of whom H. L. Mencken said, "when he took to the floor

Supply Siders and Monetarists—The Bottom Line As we have seen in the present and previous chapters, a great debate is ongoing over the fundamentals of macroeconomics. Specifically, the Keynesians and post-Keynesians support discretionary manipulation of fiscal or budget policy as the principal tool for macroeconomic stabilization with discretionary monetary policy used as an auxiliary control. These discretionary enactments are sometimes referred to as "demand management policies." In the Keynesian view, then, the economy is in constant need of manipulation and tinkering. (The success of these policies obviously presupposes a strong governmental apparatus.) Monetarists view the problem from the other way around. The economy is basically stable and self-regulating, and government's role (especially that of the Federal Reserve) is to provide a predictable and stable environment within which unfettered economic processes can work most efficiently so as to maximize economic well-being. Thus minimum government, balanced budgets, deregulation of business and industry, and a monetary growth rule are all part of the monetarist policy "package." However, both monetarists and post-Keynesians have emphasized the "demand side" of the economy in their policy prescriptions.

A new view of the macroeconomy emerged over the 1970s and the 1980s. These writers, known as *supply siders,* have been concerned with lagging growth rates in labor productivity and output in the United States and other advanced economies. This has caused a general reinvestigation of factors affecting incentives to save, invest, and acquire capital. Most importantly, factors affecting technology and the labor market came under the purview of supply siders. Part of the inflation of the 1970s, for example, has been blamed on reduced growth in labor productivity. (In monetarist terms, a reduced growth in Y would, *ceteris paribus,* create greater increases in inflation.)

What, then, do the supply siders propose? They advance tax and spending cuts and a balanced budget as a major fiscal tonic. The net result, it is hoped, will be the creation of greater incentives to save and invest. The deregulation of industry, including reduced business "standards" regulation, an emphasis on private labor-training programs, and reduced social welfare subsidies that create disincentives to work and save are also part of most of the supply siders' policy prescriptions.

RATIONAL EXPECTATIONS: THE NEW CLASSICAL ECONOMICS

Another contemporary (and in its details, very complex) theory of the economy's functioning is called the *rational expectations hypothesis.* Although much of this work is extremely technical, the basic outlines of the idea are simple and build on classical ideas (hence the "new classical economics") and upon the monetarist concepts of Milton Friedman and others.

The basic idea of rational expectations theory is straightforward and appeal-

to argue it was a time to send for ambulances" (in Breit and Ransom, *The Academic Scribblers,* p. 259).

ing: Market participants do not ignore or "throw away" information and predictions about the future course of the economy and about economic activity. Rather, they rationally anticipate the effects of governmental policies and react in the present in accordance with the formed expectations. The rational expectationists believe that consumers of goods, services, and financial instruments and the producers of these items will react to fiscal, monetary, and other policies of government by (at least ultimately) learning the effects of these policies and actions. Consumer and producer *reactions* based on the rational expectations of the effects of these policies will either partly or totally *counteract* the intended effects of the government's discretionary fiscal and monetary policies.

For example, market participants will learn through experience that increases in the rate of monetary expansion by the Federal Reserve Board will generally be followed by a higher inflation rate, which is then followed by higher nominal interest rates. Actions taken in the present upon this information will, in part or in whole, thwart the intended policy goals of the Federal Reserve. If the Federal Reserve Board increases the money supply in order to increase employment (a Keynesian prescription to alleviate recession), but workers and firms perfectly anticipate the resulting price increases, then workers will demand nominal wage increases. (A fall in *real* wages is required to obtain an increase in employment.) Firms anticipating the price increase and the increase in revenues will be willing to give workers the nominal wage increase. In this event, however, real wages remain the same and the intended policy of the Federal Reserve is soon neutralized. Discretionary policymakers are pitted against market participants. Ultimately—after learning takes place and expectations are adjusted accordingly—the policymakers have little or no effect on the economy. Policymakers may try to "surprise" market participants, but on average, they cannot do so forever. In order to have any effect on the economy, policy would have to be conducted in a "random" manner.

The rational expectations theory is clearly an extension of the monetarist hypothesis examined earlier in this chapter. It is a view that stems from classical and neoclassical microanalytic foundations of behavior in the product and labor markets. The "old classical view" of such writers as Adam Smith, John Stuart Mill, and, in this century, A. C. Pigou emphasized the rationality of market participants, but it was a rationality based upon an assumption of perfect information. There was not, of course, an explicit modeling of individual markets in classical economics, but the ideas of those writers were riddled with a belief that individual market participants could not be manipulated by government and its policymakers. Adam Smith made this principle of classical economics clear even before he wrote the *Wealth of Nations*. In the *Theory of Moral Sentiments* Smith wrote the broad outline of the rational expectations hypothesis:

> [The economic planner] seems to imagine that he can arrange the different members of society with as much ease as the hand arranges the different pieces upon a chessboard; he does not consider that the different pieces upon the chessboard have no

other principle of motion besides that which the hand impresses upon them; but that, in the great chessboard of human society, every single piece has a principle of motion of its own, altogether different from that which the legislator might choose to impress upon it (*Theory of Moral Sentiments,* p. 325).

A great deal of interest has been generated by the rational expectations hypothesis in the potential for modern policymakers to affect players in "the great chessboard of human [economic] society." No definitive answers yet exist. Much of the contemporary research has been devoted to the matter of whether or not and under what conditions discretionary policy will be neutral or "quasi-neutral." Sophisticated econometric testing (using actual data in mathematical-statistical tests of hypotheses) has left open the answer to the critical question, Can discretionary policy work? Some of the evidence does not support the conclusions of the rational expectationists. Until consistent answers are provided by such testing, the policy effects as well as the theoretical foundations of rational expectations theory will remain in limbo. The idea, whatever its ultimate fate, is at the cusp of contemporary debates in macroeconomic and monetary theories.

CONCLUSION

The French have a saying that "the more things change, the more they remain the same." This maxim appears especially appropriate to an evaluation of modern macroeconomic and monetary theory. Supply-side economics and the fundamentals of modern rational expectations theory (the idea without the technical accoutrements) were the stock-in-trade of Adam Smith and many of the other important classical economists! Underlying their conception of the wealth of a nation were the factors of labor productivity and capital formation. They coupled this with a belief in as little government "policymaking" as possible. These principles are very close to the philosophical and theoretical conceptions of modern supply siders, monetarists, and rational expectationists. As such, contemporary macroeconomics and monetary theory appear to be returning to the timeless concerns of any economy. However, it has returned far richer. We now know, thanks in large measure to the Keynesian interlude and to the refurbishment of neoclassical ideas by Milton Friedman and the rational expectationists, a great deal more about the workings of the aggregate economy. As such, modern macroeconomics—conceived of as including monetary economics—is a major and ongoing study of the contemporary economist.

NOTES FOR FURTHER READING

An excellent survey of monetary theory that in some respects parallels the one presented in this chapter is contained in J. Ascheim and C. Y. Hsieh, *Macroeconomics: Income and Monetary Theory* (Columbus, Ohio: Merrill, 1969). For a broader sweep, see Charles Rist, *History of Money and Credit Theory from John Law to the Present Day,* J. Degras (trans.) (New York: Macmillan, 1940).

Space does not permit our doing justice to the many talents of Irving Fisher, certainly a prime candidate for "greatest American economist." A glimpse at the personal side of Irving Fisher is provided in J. P. Miller, "Irving Fisher of Yale," in William Fellner et al., *Ten Economic Studies in the Tradition of Irving Fisher* (New York: Wiley, 1967). The same volume also contains an instructive and perceptive assessment of Fisher's theoretical work written by P. A. Samuelson. Fisher's role as policymaker and presidential adviser is detailed in W. R. Allen, "Irving Fisher, F.D.R., and the Great Depression" *History of Political Economy,* vol. 9 (Winter 1977), pp. 560–587. Fisher's very important foundation for the theory of risk and uncertainty is developed in J. H. Crockett, Jr., "Irving Fisher on the Financial Economics of Uncertainty," *History of Political Economy,* vol. 12 (Spring 1980), pp. 65–82.

Possibly the best single source of information on Wicksell and his ideas is Uhr's *Economic Doctrines of Knut Wicksell* (see References). See also Ragnar Frisch, *Knut Wicksell: A Cornerstone in Modern Economic Theory* (Oslo, 1951); D. Patinkin, "Wicksell's Cumulative Process in Theory and Practice," *Banca Nazionale del Lavaro Review,* vol. 21 (June 1968), pp. 120–131; same author, "Wicksell's 'Cumulative Process,'" *Economic Journal,* vol. 62 (December 1952), pp. 835–847; E. J. Nell, "Wicksell's Theory of Circulation," *Journal of Political Economy,* vol. 75 (August 1967), pp. 386–394; and Jacob Marschak, "Wicksell's Two Interest Rates," *Social Research,* vol. 8 (November 1941), pp. 469–478.

Alfred Marshall's monetary theories are best described in his *Money, Credit, and Commerce* (New York: A. M. Kelley, Publishers, 1960 [1923]). Perhaps the best spokesman for the Cambridge group was Marshall's student Pigou. See A. C. Pigou: "The Value of Money," *Quarterly Journal of Economics,* vol. 32 (November 1917), pp. 38–65; "The Monetary Theory of the Trade Cycle," *Economic Journal,* vol. 39 (June 1929), pp. 183–194; and "Marginal Utility and Elasticities of Demand," *Quarterly Journal of Economics,* vol. 50 (May 1936), p. 532.

Don Patinkin's *Money, Interest, and Prices* (see References) is valuable on two counts: (1) it is a monumental effort to fully integrate monetary theory and value theory, and (2) the supplementary notes at the end of the book provide useful information on the historical antecedents of neoclassical monetary theory. While the text is heavy going for undergraduates and possibly even graduates, the notes might be read with much profit.

The literature on modern monetarism and its satellite ideas is vast and growing. A superb introduction accessible to the general reader is J. Huston McCulloch's *Money and Inflation: A Monetarist Approach* (New York: Academic, 1975). A more extensive treatment of the monetarist approach to money and inflation may be found in L. Auernheimer and R. B. Ekelund, Jr., *The Essentials of Money and Banking* (New York: Wiley, 1982). The relation between modern monetarism and classical economics generally, and David Hume in particular, is interestingly handled in Thomas Mayer, "David Hume and Monetarism," *Quarterly Journal of Economics,* vol. 95 (August 1980), pp. 89–101.

History from a monetarist view is beautifully exposed in the Friedman-Schwartz volume (see References). The great depression, analyzed from this vantage, has stirred up a good deal of controversy. See Milton Friedman and Anna J. Schwartz, *The Great Contraction* (Princeton, N.J.: Princeton University Press, 1966); then read Peter Temin's *Did Monetary Factors Cause the Great Depression?* (New York: Norton, 1976).

Rational expectations theory is explained in a clear, nontechnical fashion by Rodney Maddock and Michael Carter, "A Child's Guide to Rational Expectations," *Journal of Economic Literature,* vol. 20 (March 1982), pp. 39–51. Although complex in its advance formulations, the theory of rational expectations developed rapidly over the 1970s: see T. Sargent, "Rational Expectations, the Real Rate of Interest, and the Natural Rate of Unemployment," *Brookings Papers in Economics Activity 2* (1973), pp. 429–472; T. Sargent and N. Wallace, "Rational Expectations and the Theory of Economic Policy," *Journal of Monetary Economics,* vol. 2 (April 1976), pp. 169–184; and R. E. Lucas, "An Equilibrium Model of the Business Cycle," *Journal of Political Economy,* vol. 83 (December 1975), pp. 1113–1144. Michael C. Lovell, "Tests of the Rational Expectations Hypothesis," *American Economic Review,* vol. 76 (March 1986), pp. 110–124, has attempted to test the conclusions of the theory and found them lacking in empirical support.

Readers interested in learning more about lags and "targets" in monetary (and fiscal) policy would do well to consult L. C. Anderson and J. L. Jordan, "Monetary and Fiscal Actions: A Test of Their Relative Importance in Economic Stabilization," *Federal Reserve Bank of St. Louis Review,* vol. 50 (November 1968), pp. 11–24; see also B. M. Friedman, "Even the St. Louis Model Now Believes in Fiscal Policy," *Journal of Money, Credit and Banking,* vol. 9 (May 1977), pp. 365–367; and J. E. Tanner, "Are the Lags in the Effects of Monetary Policy Variable?" *Journal of Monetary Economics,* vol. 5 (January 1979), pp. 105–121.

For a general introduction to the aspects of supply-side economics see L. R. Klein, "The Supply Side," *American Economic Review,* vol. 68 (March 1978), pp. 1–7. The "Laffer curve"—showing the relation between tax *rates* and government revenues—has been an integral part of modern supply-side economics. Economist Arthur Laffer argues that lowering tax rates would create additional incentives to work and invest, increased incomes, and increased revenues for government; see A. B. Laffer and R. D. Ranson, "A Formal Model of the Economy," *Journal of Business,* vol. 44 (July 1971), pp. 247–270; and the simplified treatment in J. Wanniski's "Taxes, Revenues, and the 'Laffer Curve,'" *The Public Interest,* vol. 50 (Winter 1978), pp. 3–16. For a "fiscalist" criticism of Laffer logic see W. Heller, "The Kemp-Roth-Laffer Free Lunch," *The Wall Street Journal* (July 12, 1978), p. 20. Whether the Laffer relation exists or not is debatable, but no one denies the onset of a productivity problem in the U.S. economy of the 1970s. An excellent overview of the problem is provided in J. A. Tatom, "The Productivity Problem," *Federal Reserve Bank of St. Louis Review,* vol. 61 (September 1979), pp. 3–16. Also, for contrasting approaches to the productivity problem, see Paul Samuelson and Milton Friedman, "Productivity: Two Experts Cross Swords," *Newsweek* (September 8, 1980), pp. 68–69.

The reemergence of the quantity theory in the 1950s and 1960s, along with the monetarist school that it spawned, is the subject of a spate of papers, all contained in *History of Political Economy*. Three separate papers concerning the effect of statistical and theoretical developments on the early quantity theory may be profitably read as a unit. T. M. Humphrey treats the statistical tests of the theory in the first three decades of this century, stressing that the major contribution of such tests was empirical rather than theoretical in nature. See "Empirical Tests of the Quantity Theory of Money in the United States, 1900–1930," *History of Political Economy,* vol. 5 (Fall 1973), pp. 285–316. Anticipatory and actual contributions to theoretical monetarism are the subjects of two papers about C. F. Bickerdike and Clark Warburton. On Bickerdike's anticipatory developments related to the role of money in business fluctuations see V. J. Tarascio, "Bickerdike's Monetary Growth Theory," *History of Political Economy,* vol. 12 (Summer 1980), pp. 161–173. Before the seminal writings of Friedman, Clark Warburton was the staunchest defender of monetarism. Although very much out of the mainstream of Keynesian times, Warburton deserves a good deal of credit for kindling the fires of monetarism when it was most unpopular to do so; see T. F. Cargill's "Clark Warburton and the Development of Monetarism since the Great Depression," *History of Political Economy,* vol. 11 (Fall 1979), pp. 425–449. Finally, important parallels between indexation as a hedge against inflation and the development of monetarism are the topic of R. Brenner's "The Concept of Indexation and Monetary Theory," *History of Political Economy,* vol. 11 (Fall 1979), pp. 395–405.

REFERENCES

Breit, William, and Roger Ransom, *The Academic Scribblers,* rev. ed. New York: Holt, 1982.

Fisher, Irving. "A Statistical Relation between Unemployment and Price Changes," *International Labor Review* (June 1926). Reprinted as "I Discovered the Phillip's Curve," *Journal of Political Economy,* vol. 81 (March/April 1973), pp. 496–502.

———. *The Purchasing Power of Money.* New York: A. M. Kelley, Publishers, 1963 [1911].

———. *The Theory of Interest.* New York: Macmillan, 1930.

Friedman, Milton. *Studies in the Quantity Theory of Money.* Chicago: The University of Chicago Press, 1956.

———. *A Program for Monetary Stability.* New York: Fordham University Press, 1960.

———. *Capitalism and Freedom.* Chicago: The University of Chicago Press, 1962.

———. "The Role of Monetary Policy," *American Economic Review,* vol. 58 (March 1968), pp. 1–17.

———. *Price Theory.* Chicago: Aldine, 1976.

————, and Anna Schwartz. *A Monetary History of the United States, 1867–1960.* Princeton, N.J.: Princeton University Press, 1963.

Hansen, Alvin. *Monetary Theory and Fiscal Policy.* New York: McGraw-Hill, 1949.

Johnson, H. G. "Monetary Theory and Policy," *American Economic Review,* vol. 52 (June 1962), pp. 335–384.

Mill, J. S. *Principles of Political Economy,* W. J. Ashley (ed.). New York: A. M. Kelley, Publishers, 1965 [1848].

Patinkin, Don. *Money, Interest and Prices,* 2d ed. New York: Harper & Row, 1965.

Phillips, A. W. "The Relation between Unemployment and the Rate of Change of Money Wage Rates in the United Kingdom, 1861–1957," *Economica,* vol. 25 (November 1958), pp. 283–299.

Pigou, A. C. (ed.) *Memorials of Alfred Marshall.* London: Macmillan, 1925.

Smith, Adam. *The Theory of Moral Sentiments.* Indianapolis: Liberty Classics, 1976 [1759].

Uhr, Carl G. *Economic Doctrines of Knut Wicksell.* Berkeley: University of California Press, 1962.

Wicksell, Knut. *Lectures on Political Economy,* 2 vols., L. Robbins (ed.). London: Routledge & Kegan Paul, 1935.

————. *Interest and Prices,* R. F. Kahn (trans.). London: Macmillan, 1936.

CHAPTER 21

AUSTRIAN ECONOMICS

INTRODUCTION

Chapter 13 reviewed the contributions of the "older" Austrian school within the context of a "marginal revolution" in value theory that occurred in the closing decades of the nineteenth century. The common tendency among historians of economic thought has been to lump Menger, Jevons, and Walras together as independent discoverers of the same approach to value. This tendency served to obscure the essential differences in the original intent and design of their theoretical constructions and in the influence their major works exerted, each in its own way, on the subsequent development of economic thought.

One important difference, of course, is that Walras, alone of the three, was the architect of the general-equilibrium system. Joseph Schumpeter singled out this accomplishment as the really important one of the period, and concluded that, "in itself, the principle of marginal utility is not so important after all as Jevons, the Austrians, and Walras himself believed" (*History,* p. 918). There is some question, however, whether the Austrians ever considered the marginal-utility principle alone to be as important as Schumpeter seems to think they did. Recent research, in particular, has shown the marginal-utility principle to be *incidental* to Menger's economic analysis, not an integral part of it. Menger nowhere concerned himself with the relative maxima or minima of functions, which many take to be the essence of marginalism. The focus of his economic analysis, instead, was on the study of institutions and the conditions of disequilibrium.

This last concern constitutes a sharp cleavage between the Austrian brand of "neoclassical" economics and the French (Cournot-Walras) or English

(Jevons-Marshall) variants of neoclassical theory. Overlooking for the moment the fact that Walras rode the high road of general-equilibrium theory while Marshall took the low road of partial-equilibrium analysis, both showed a theoretical concern for the determination of prices under a hypothetical regime of perfectly free competition. By contrast, it is important to note that Menger did not try to explain prices nor did he assume that competition could be "perfect." He forged no analytical link between "the importance of satisfactions" (i.e., marginal utility) and market prices. In fact, he regarded market prices as superficial and incidental manifestations of much deeper forces at work in the exchange of goods and services. He believed that economics should investigate these deeper forces and essential causes rather than concern itself with mathematical formalism.

Menger's view of human beings and their nature inevitably colored his approach to economic analysis. In the words of William Jaffé, an authority on the period:

> Man, as Menger saw him, far from being a "lighting calculator" [Veblen's derogatory phrase], is a bumbling, erring, ill-informed creature, plagued with uncertainty, forever hovering between alluring hopes and haunting fears, and congenitally incapable of making finely calibrated decisions in pursuit of satisfactions. With his attention [thus] unswervingly fixed on reality, Menger could not, and did not, abstract from the difficulties traders face in any attempt to obtain all the information required for anything like a pinpoint equilibrium determination of market prices to emerge, nor did his approach permit him to abstract from the uncertainties that veil the future, even the near future in the conscious anticipation of which most present transactions take place. Neither did he exclude the existence of noncompeting groups, or the omni-presence of monopolistic or monopoloid traders in the market ("Menger, Jevons and Walras De-Homogenized," pp. 520–521).

The institutional component is also of paramount importance in the Austrian paradigm, albeit in a different way from that conceived by Veblen. The fundamental goal of Menger's economics was to make social phenomena intelligible in terms of individual goals and plans. Economic and social institutions affect human action by influencing the interaction of individual plans. In Menger's framework an institution is any coordinated pattern of individual interaction. A market or a legal system is an institution, but so is money and so are prices. How does it come about that so many people of diverse backgrounds come to agree on a certain pattern of interaction? How is it possible that so many individual exchanges take place under mutually advantageous conditions without central direction? The Austrian tradition is not a ready-made set of answers to these and other major theoretical questions. It is instead a way of conceiving "the economic problem." It is a research program with a peculiar *gestalt*. The key concepts in this particular approach concern the role and influence of subjectivity, time, uncertainty, disequilibrium, process, knowledge, and coordination.

THE GESTALT OF AUSTRIAN ECONOMICS

Although it was Menger who first gave meaning to the phrase "Austrian economics," his influence went far beyond the national boundaries of his native land. The "Vienna circle" nurtured second-generation Austrians, most notably Ludwig von Mises (1881–1973) and Joseph Schumpeter (1883–1950), both of whom emigrated to America. Mises in turn taught a third generation that includes Friedrich Hayek (b. 1889), Oskar Morgenstern (1902–1977), Fritz Machlup (1902–1983), Paul Rosenstein-Rodan (1902–1985), and Gottfried Haberler (b. 1901). In London, Hayek's influence touched G. L. S. Shackle and Ludwig Lachmann, the latter also a holder of a Vienna doctorate. On American soil, Mises' influence extended to Israel Kirzner and Murray Rothbard, who attended his seminars at New York University. In this way, successive generations of "Austrians" were spawned long after the geographic connotation of the word ceased to have any substantive meaning.

Modern expositors of the Austrian approach underscore five major points of emphasis that distinguish, in their view, Austrian economics from mainstream neoclassical analysis. The five distinguishing features are: (1) radical subjectivism, (2) methodological individualism, (3) purposiveness in human action, (4) casual-geneticism, and (5) methodological essentialism. Each of these requires some elaboration.

Radical subjectivism is a wide net that snares a number of particular Austrian themes. Basic to the Austrian approach is the conviction that all underlying permanent relations of economic theory are consequences of human choice. Austrians therefore emphasize the roles of knowledge and error in individual decision making. What is important is that people *differ* with respect to their knowledge, interpretations, expectations, and alertness, so that subjectivism has a much broader meaning than merely tastes. All decisions are by their very nature subjective. Certain information cannot be reasonably expected to be held by anyone other than the individual making a decision, e.g., the intensity and form of his or her preferences and expectations. Since decision making is the province of the entrepreneur, entrepreneurship is consequently given a wide berth in Austrian economics.

The most unique and radical aspect of the Austrian approach, however, lies in its emphasis on the primacy of utility and the denial of costs as a coterminous element (with utility) in the determination of value. This last point constitutes the sharpest break with the English variant (Marshall and Jevons) of neoclassical value theory. Essentially, Austrians argue that economic costs are themselves subjective, based as they are on calculations of utility *forgone* whenever a choice is made. In other words, Austrians associate costs with a decision, a neutral act, not with an event or a thing. This means that costs are subordinate to, but inextricably joined with, utility. Costs are subjective because they are perceived by the chooser. The price paid for an item therefore represents the utility of it to the purchaser alone, not necessarily its utility to anyone else. This line of thought runs against the strict Marshallian tradition that associates costs with events and therefore regards costs as in some sense objective.

Methodological individualism asserts that the most appropriate way to study economic phenomena is at the level of the individual. If economics is a science of choice, then one must look to the chooser to understand economic relations. But aren't some choices collective in the sense that they are made by a body of people (e.g., a committee) rather than by a single individual? There are two things to consider in response to this question. One is that any collective decision-making body is composed of persons whose individual decisions make up the collective judgment. The other concerns the nature of aggregates and what kind of information they convey. Austrians argue that aggregates only matter where individual considerations don't matter; yet for Austrians, individual decisions *always* matter. In the final analysis the choice between individual or aggregate is at least partly a normative issue, and Austrians are quite explicit about their methodological preference in this regard.

There is an element of teleology in the Austrian approach expressed in their emphasis on *purposive* human action. However, it is a kind of teleology that does not take goals as absolute. Goals may change over time, and they obviously vary from one individual to the next. The basic proposition Austrians assert in this connection is that individual choice is not the consequence of some mere gravitational pull toward utility. Rather, individuals act with a purpose, even if that purpose is frequently frustrated by error or imperfect knowledge. In this regard, Austrians are decidedly anti-Benthamite, for Bentham saw people as being passively pushed about by pleasure and pain. Austrians regard all choices as forward-looking; consequently expectations are very important economic variables. These expectations, along with the purpose behind each person's actions, shape individual plans and the decisions consequent to the carrying out of each plan.

To say that Austrian economics is causal-genetic is to say that it emphasizes essences rather than functional relationships. Functionalism stresses the working out of conditions that must be met in order for some end to be fulfilled (e.g., the enumeration of characteristics that constitute the competitive model). Austrians claim to be more interested in the nature and essence of things and less interested in their form. There is an Aristotelian strain that runs through the Austrian approach; for example, attempts to mathematize economic relations are considered fruitless because mathematics is functional and form-oriented and therefore incapable of contributing any real understanding of basic economic relations.

Finally, Austrian economics claims to be *nonscientistic*. "Scientism" is a word coined by Hayek to refer to the (illegitimate, in his view) application of the principles of natural science to the study of humans. Hayek finds this attempt decidedly *unscientific* because it involves the mechanical and uncritical application of habits of thought to fields different from those in which they have been formed. According to Hayek, "the scientistic as distinguished from the scientific view is not an unprejudiced but a very prejudiced approach which, before it has considered its subject, claims to know what is the most appropriate way of investigating it" (*The Counter-Revolution of Science*, p. 24). For Hayek, the chief culprits in promoting the slavish imitation of the method and language of science by the social sciences were Saint-Simon and Comte (see Chapter 10). As a consequence of this Hayekian view, the claims of Austrian economics are fairly modest. Austrians seek to understand human society and to make it more intelligible, without concern for making predictions.

It is beyond the limited scope of this chapter to deal with all aspects of Austrian economics. We offer a brief treatment of several Austrian themes: money, credit, the trade cycle, and the nature of competition.

LUDWIG VON MISES: THE THEORY OF MONEY AND CREDIT

The classical economists treated money as neutral in its economic effects (see Chapter 6), and the Walrasian neoclassical economists, past and present, do not recognize the uniqueness of money. In general-equilibrium models money is merely a *numéraire*—it has no properties distinguishing it from the many nonmoney goods in the model. Austrian monetary theory rejects both these propositions. It considers money to be unique because of its intertemporal exchangability, and it concentrates on the relative price effects of changes in the money supply. The theory begins with a theory of the evolution of money and concludes with an analysis of the effects of changes in money on the fundamental economic decisions of individuals.

Although Carl Menger (see Chapter 13) fashioned a theory of the evolution of money that stressed the unintended consequences of individual (self-interested) behavior, he did not succeed in solving the question of what determines the value of money. Thus, monetary theory remained separated from value theory until the two were integrated by Ludwig von Mises, one of Böhm-Bawerk's students at the University of Vienna. Mises achieved the integration of monetary and value theory by founding both on the same principle, the marginal utility of subjective individual wants.

Subjective Use Value versus Objective Exchange Value

Mises recognized that the marginal utility of money comes from two separate sources. On the one hand, money has value derived from the value of the goods it can buy. On the other hand, money has a subjective use value of its own because it can be held for future exchange. What we call the value of money in common parlance springs from the ability of money to be exchanged for other things. Mises called this characteristic of money its objective exchange value in order to distinguish it from money's subjective use value. Today we call it the purchasing power of money.

How then do we measure the purchasing power of money? Conventional theory advanced the concept of a unitary (aggregate) price level, whereby the purchasing power of money (the reciprocal of the price level) is the outcome of the total volume of transactions in society divided by the velocity of circulation. In terms of the familiar equation of exchange (see Chapter 20) where $MV = PT$, the price level P would be derived as follows: $P = MV/T$, and its reciprocal (the purchasing power of money), $1/P = T/MV$. Mises recognized the grain of truth in the quantity theory, namely "the idea that a connection exists between variations in the value of money on the one hand and the supply of it on the other hand," but "beyond this proposition," he argued, "the Quantity Theory can provide us with nothing. Above all, it fails to explain the mechanism of variations in the value of money" (*Money and Credit,* p. 130).

True to the Austrian tradition, Mises rejected the macroeconomic approach to monetary theory in favor of the individualistic approach. All valuation is done by individuals; therefore the key to understanding the value of money must be in the mind of the individual. The purchasing power of a dollar is the vast *array of goods* that can be purchased with that dollar. This array is heterogeneous and specific. At any point of time a dollar might buy three packs of chewing gum, one pair of socks, two floppy computer disks, two sodas, one pack of cigarettes, one-tenth of a haircut, and so forth and so on. The purchasing power of money therefore cannot be summarized in some unitary price-level figure. At all times a homogeneous good must be defined in terms of its usefulness to the consumer rather than by its technological properties. Likewise, price must be related to the specific usefulness of a good, and not to its technological properties. An apartment with the same technological properties in Manhattan and in Peoria will not have the same price because they are not equally useful to the purchaser. The apartment in New York has a more desirable location with more extensive consumption possibilities and hence will be more highly priced on the market. Mises emphasized locational (and temporal) aspects in explaining differences in the value of technologically similar goods, and this in turn complements the Austrian notion that the purchasing power of money is equal to an array of goods.

In applying the theory of marginal utility to the price of money, Mises confronted a thorny analytical problem. When an individual ranks coffee or shoes or vacations on a value scale, he or she values those goods for their direct use in consumption, and each valuation is independent of and prior to its price on the market. However, people hold money not because it can be used directly in consumption but because it can eventually be exchanged for goods that will be used directly. In other words, money is not useful in itself. It is useful because it has a prior exchange value—a preexisting purchasing power. The demand for money therefore not only is *not* independent of its existing market price but derives precisely from its preexisting price in terms of other goods and services. And therein lies the problem. If the demand for money, and hence its utility, depends on its preexisting price or purchasing power, how can that price be explained by the demand? Mises' critics accused him of falling into a circular trap.

Mises avoided the trap by means of a regression theorem. The demand for money on any given day, say day D, is equal to its purchasing power on the previous day, $D - 1$. The demand for money on the previous day, $D - 1$, in turn was equal to the purchasing power of money on $D - 2$, and so on. In other words, the demand for money always has a historical (i.e., temporal) component. But is this not an infinite regression backward in time? No, Mises answered, we must push the analysis backward only to that point when the commodity used as money was not used as a medium of indirect exchange but was demanded instead solely for its own direct consumption use. Suppose we go back in time to the point when gold was introduced as money. Let us assume that before this day, all trade took place by barter. On the last day of barter, gold had value only for its direct consumption use, but on the first day of its use as money, it took on an additional use as a medium of exchange. In other words, on the first day of its use as a medium of exchange, gold had two dimensions of utility: first, a direct consumption use; and second, a monetary use which had a historical component in its utility.

Evaluating this regression theorem, Murray Rothbard, a student of Mises, pointed out the continuity between Mises and Menger, who emphasized the evolutionary and institutional elements of money:

> Not only does the Mises regression theorem fully explain the current demand for money and integrate the theory of money with the theory of marginal utility, but it also shows that money must have originated in this fashion—on the market—with individuals on the market gradually beginning to use some previously valuable commodity as a medium of exchange. No money could have originated either by a social compact to consider some previously valueless thing as a 'money' or by sudden governmental fiat. For in those cases, the money commodity could not have a previous purchasing power, which could be taken into account in the individual's demand for money. In this way, Mises demonstrated that Carl Menger's historical insight into the way in which money arose on the market was not simply a historical summary but a theoretical necessity ("The Austrian Theory of Money," p. 169).

The Effect of Changes in Money on Relative Prices

Utilizing an insight first attributed to Richard Cantillon (see Chapter 4), Mises focused his monetary analysis on the effects of changes in the stock of money on economic activity. Once again, he rejected the macroeconomic approach in favor of methodological individualism. In response to the quantity theory advanced by John Locke, Cantillon had argued that the result of an increase in the stock of money will not be uniform across the economy, but rather will cause prices to rise at uneven rates in different sectors, thereby changing *relative* prices in the process. Mises combined the marginal-utility theory of money with this "Cantillon effect" to elucidate the impact of changes in the supply of money.

In modern societies, when governments or central banks increase the supply of money, they do not do so in a way that affects everyone equally. Instead, new money is created by the government or by banks to be spent on specific goods and services. The demand for these specific goods rises, thereby raising their prices first. (The elements of this in a Misesian economy should now be clear: as money holdings increase, the marginal utility of money declines so that certain goods are revalued ahead of money on subjective preference scales, pushing the prices of these goods upward.) Gradually the new money ripples through the economy, raising demand and prices as it goes. Income and wealth are thereby redistributed to those who receive the new money early in the process, at the expense of those who receive the new money later, or those who live on fixed incomes and receive none of the new money.

Recognizing these relative price effects and the ensuing wealth redistribution they entail, Mises took a very strong stand against inflationary expansion of the money supply. Indeed, he argued that because the exchange services of money are not increased by a higher stock of money, inflation will always be a zero-sum game, benefiting some at the expense of others.

> The services money renders are conditioned by the height of its purchasing power. Nobody wants to have in his cash holding a definite number of pieces of money or a definite weight of money; he wants to keep a cash holding of a definite amount of purchasing power. As the operation of the market tends to determine the final state of money's purchasing power at a height at which the supply of and the demand for money coincide, there can never be an excess or a deficiency of money. Each individual and all individuals together always enjoy fully the advantages which they can derive from indirect exchange and the use of money, no matter whether the total quantity of money is great or small. Changes in money's purchasing power generate changes in the disposition of wealth among the various members of society. From the point of view of people eager to be enriched by such changes, the supply of money may be called insufficient or excessive, and the appetite for such gains may result in policies designed to bring about cash-induced alterations in purchasing power. However, the services which money renders can be neither improved nor impaired by changing the supply of money.... The quantity of money available in the whole economy is always sufficient to secure for everybody all that money does and can do (*Human Action*, p. 418).

It is clear from the above passage that Mises' economic analysis made him wary of the potential abuse present in every concentration of economic power. Monetary expansion is a method by which the government, its controlled banking system, and favored political groups are able to partially expropriate the wealth of other groups in society. Having witnessed firsthand the German hyperinflation after World War I, Mises remained skeptical of any government's willingness to show monetary restraint over long periods of time. It is for this reason, and not because he attributed any mystical qualities to gold, that Mises championed a gold standard as the best form of money.

F. A. HAYEK AND THE MONETARY OVERINVESTMENT THEORY OF BUSINESS CYCLES

Mises' theory of money and credit led to an Austrian theory of business cycles based upon changes in the supply of money, a theory elaborated most completely by one of Mises' students, Nobel laureate Friedrich A. Hayek. Like Mises, Hayek broke with the quantity theory tradition because it ignored the effect of money on relative prices. He continued the integration of monetary theory and value theory that Mises had begun by exploring the effect of changes in the supply of money on the *composition* of output, rather than upon the quantity of output or the aggregate price level.

Hayek's business-cycle theory is a blend of the Austrian theories of money, capital, and prices. In a nutshell, his explanation of the cycle runs like this. A monetary disturbance (e.g., an increase in the money stock) brings about a reduction of interest rates below an equilibrium level, which stimulates investment in capital, thereby reallocating resources away from the production of consumption goods toward production of intermediate (capital) goods. As a consequence, prices of capital goods rise and prices of consumption goods fall. This change in relative prices changes the *structure of production*. (Hayek viewed the entire process of production as a multistage activity through which raw materials pass until they finally emerge as end products. Therefore, a change in the number of stages or a reallocation of resources among the different stages constitutes a change in the structure of production.) Such a change in the structure of production, because of the longer time component of capital, leads to overinvestment in "longer" or more "roundabout" methods of production and thereby upsets the coordination of plans between consumers and producers and between savers and investors.

Although Hayek's chief technical contribution to economic theory was his monetary theory, his important conception of equilibrium as the coordination of economic activities became the unifying theme in all of his writings. Coordination is achieved when the plans of all economic decision makers mesh. How does this come about? Decision makers look for signals. The appropriate signals are relative prices. Hayek argued that if relative prices change due to the "natural" forces of technology, tastes, time preference, etc., the ensuing adjustments will reestablish a coordinated plan. But purely *monetary* disturbances evoke perverse signals by artificially raising rates of return on certain types of economic activity. These rates of return can only be sustained as long as additional monetary stimulus is forthcoming, so eventually every boom will be followed by a bust.

Hayek centered his business cycle theory on the market signals utilized by savers and investors to make their decisions. He emphasized that although these decisions are independently arrived at, they are interdependent in terms of their implications for equilibrium. Cycles occur when a general inconsistency of plans comes about. In the case of a monetary stimulus, firms tend to switch to more capital-intensive methods at the expense of consumption-goods production, despite the fact than no additional planned savings has taken place. According to Hayek:

> [T]his sacrifice is not voluntary, and is not made by those who will reap the benefit from the new investments. It is made by the consumers in general who, because of

the increased competition from the entrepreneurs who have received the additional money, are forced to forego part of what they used to consume. It comes about not because they want to consume less, but because they get less goods for their money income. There can be no doubt that, if their money receipts should rise again, they would immediately attempt to expand consumption to the usual proportion (*Prices and Production*, p. 57).

Hayek completed his research on monetary theory and business-cycle theory in the 1930s, at a time when Keynesian macroeconomics was on the ascendancy. Eventually his monetary theory was eclipsed by the so-called Keynesian revolution. In more recent times, Hayek has turned his attention to other important analytical issues, especially, the role of information in economic activity. This latter contribution has shown a greater survival value than Hayek's earlier one, and Hayek has been timely in anticipating a revival and reformulation of contemporary theories of competition. Several aspects of the new theory of competition are discussed in Chapter 23, particularly the ideas of knowledge, information, and transactions cost. While present space and organizational structure impede a complete discussion of Hayek's contribution to this literature, his pioneer efforts have had a major influence on the development of contemporary economic thought.

JOSEPH SCHUMPETER: COMPETITION, DYNAMICS, AND GROWTH

Joseph Schumpeter was a third-generation Austrian economist who rose to prominence as finance minister of the Austrian government. A student of Böhm-Bawerk's at the University of Vienna, he later emigrated to the United States in order to avoid Hitler's onslaught. Although steeped in the Austrian tradition, Schumpeter reopened a classic line of economic inquiry—the subject of economic development. In 1911, he published his *Theory of Economic Development,* a book that won critical acclaim but made little impact on English-speaking economists until it was translated into English in 1934. His second major work, *Business Cycles,* followed in 1939.

Schumpeter blended ideas from Marx, Walras, and the German historian and sociologist, Max Weber, with insights from his Austrian forebearers, Menger, Wieser, and his teacher, Böhm-Bawerk. Like Marx, for whom he professed great admiration, Schumpeter was no mere imitator—he borrowed ideas from his intellectual heroes but melded them into something uniquely his own. He shared Marx's view that economic processes are organic and that change comes from *within* the economic system, not merely from without. He admired the blend of sociology and economics that comprised the theories of both Marx and Weber. From Walras he borrowed the notion of the entrepreneur, but in place of the passive figure of Walras's general-equilibrium system, Schumpeter substituted an active agent of economic progress. Reflecting the Austrian economists' interest in disequilibrium processes, Schumpeter made the entrepreneur the chief agent who causes *disequilibrium* (i.e., change) in a competitive economy.

To Schumpeter, development is a dynamic process, a disturbing of the economic status quo. He looked upon economic progress not as a mere adjunct to the central body of orthodox economic theory, but as the basis for reinterpreting a vital process that had been crowded out of mainstream economic analysis by the static, general-equilibrium approach. The entrepreneur is a key figure for Schumpeter because, quite simply, he is the *persona causa* of economic development.

Entrepreneurs and Innovation

Like Menger and the second-generation Austrians, Schumpeter described competition as a process involving mainly the dynamic innovations of the entrepreneur. Schumpeter used the concept of equilibrium as Weber had used the stationary state—as a theoretical construct, a point of departure. He coined a phrase to describe this equilibrium state: "the circular flow of economic life." Its chief characteristic is that economic life proceeds routinely on the basis of past experience; there are no forces evident for any change of the status quo. Schumpeter outlined the nature of production and distribution in the circular flow in the following terms:

> [I]n every period only products which were produced in the previous period are consumed, and ... only products which will be consumed in the following period are produced. Therefore workers and landlords always exchange their productive services for present consumption goods only, whether the former are employed directly or only indirectly in the production of consumption goods. There is no necessity for them to exchange their services of labor and land for future goods or for promises of future consumption goods or to apply for any "advances" of present consumption goods. It is simply a matter of exchange, and not of credit transactions. The element of time plays no part. All products are only products and nothing more. For the individual firm it is a matter of complete indifference whether it produces means of production or consumption goods. In both cases the product is paid for immediately and at its full value (*Economic Development*, pp. 42–43).

In this hypothetical system, the production function is invariant, although factor substitution is possible within the limits of known technological horizons. The only real activity that must be performed in this state is "that of combining the two original factors of production, and this function is performed in every period mechanically as it were, of its own accord, without requiring a personal element distinguishable from [mere] superintendence...." (*Economic Development*, p. 45). In this artificial situation, the entrepreneur is a nonentity. There is nothing for him or her to do because equilibrium is automatic and permanent. But such a state of being does not apply to the dynamic world in which we live.

Schumpeter wrote in *Capitalism, Socialism, and Democracy* (p. 84) that the really relevant problem is not how capitalism administers existing structures, but how it creates and destroys them. He called this process "creative destruction," and maintained that it is the essence of economic development. In other words, development is a *disturbance* of the circular flow. It occurs in industrial and commercial life, not in consumption. It is a process defined by the carrying out of new combinations in production. It is accomplished by the entrepreneur.

Schumpeter reduced his theory to three elemental and corresponding pairs of opposites: (1) the circular flow (i.e., tendency toward equilibrium) on the one hand versus a change in economic routine or data on the other, (2) statics versus dynamics, and (3) entrepreneurship versus management. The first pair consists of two real processes; the second, two theoretical apparatuses; the third, two distinct types of conduct. The theory maintained that the essential function of the entrepreneur is distinct from that of capitalist, landowner, laborer, inventor. According to Schumpeter, the entrepreneur may be any and all of these things, but if he or she is, it is by coincidence rather than by nature of function. Nor is the entrepreneurial function, in principle, connected with the possession of wealth, even though "the accidental fact of the possession of wealth constitutes a practical advantage" (*Economic Development,* p. 101). Moreover, entrepreneurs do not form a social class, in the technical sense, although they come to be esteemed for their ability in a capitalist society.

Schumpeter admitted that the entrepreneur's basic function is almost always mingled with other functions. "Pure" entrepreneurship is difficult to isolate from other economic activity. But "management" does not describe the truly distinctive role of the entrepreneur. "The function of superintendence in itself, constitutes no essential economic distinction," Schumpeter wrote (*Economic Development,* p. 20). The function of making decisions is another matter, however. In Schumpeter's theory, the dynamic entrepreneur is the person who innovates, who makes "new combinations" in production.

Schumpeter described innovation in several ways. He first spelled out the kinds of new combinations that underlie economic development. They encompass the following: (1) creation of a new good or new quality of good, (2) creation of a new method of production, (3) the opening of a new market, (4) the capture of a new source of supply, and (5) a new organization of industry (e.g., creation or destruction of a monopoly). Over time, of course, the force of these new combinations dissipates, as the "new" becomes part of the "old" in the circular flow of economic activity. But this does not change the essence of the entrepreneurial function. According to Schumpeter, people act as entrepreneurs only when they actually carry out new combinations, and lose the character of entrepreneurs as soon as they have built up their business, after which they settle down to running it as other people run their businesses.

Later, and in a more technical sense, Schumpeter defined innovation by means of the production function. The production function, he said, "describes the way in which quantity of product varies if quantities of factors vary. If, instead of quantities of factors, we vary the form of the function, we have an innovation" (*Business Cycles,* p. 62). Mere cost-reducing adaptations of knowledge lead only to new supply schedules of existing goods, however, so this kind of innovation must involve a new commodity, or one of higher quality. Schumpeter recognized that the knowledge behind the innovation need not be new. On the contrary, it may be existing knowledge that has not been utilized before. According to Schumpeter:

> [T]here never has been anytime when the store of scientific knowledge has yielded all it could in the way of industrial improvement, and, on the other hand, it is not the knowledge that matters, but the successful solution of the task *sui generis* of putting an untried method into practice—there may be, and often is, no scientific novelty involved at all, and even if it be involved, this does not make any difference to the nature of the process ("The Instability of Capitalism," p. 378).

In Schumpeter's theory, successful innovation requires an act of will, not of intellect. It depends, therefore, on leadership, not intelligence, and it should not be confused with invention. Schumpeter was explicit on this last point:

> To carry any improvement into effect is a task entirely different from the inventing of it, and a task, moreover, requiring entirely different kinds of aptitudes. Although entrepreneurs of course *may* be inventors just as they may be capitalists, they are inventors not by nature of their function but by coincidence and vice versa. Besides, the innovations which it is the function of entrepreneurs to carry out need not necessarily be any inventions at all (*Economic Development*, pp. 88–89).

Business Cycles

Schumpeter's emphasis on the entrepreneur as the active agent for change in a competitive economy provides a bridge between the microeconomics of the firm and the macroeconomics of government policy. Within a Schumpeterian framework, the transmission mechanism through which tax and spending policies affect economic behavior is the ultimate impact that such policies have on individual incentives. Once again, the entrepreneur is the focal point. Citing the experience of the U.S. economy in the 1920s, Schumpeter raised the issue of whether taxes significantly affect the profit motive and economic progress. The United States inaugurated a federal income tax in 1913, so the issue was a timely one in the 1920s. Schumpeter evaluated the effects of a progressive income tax on the entrepreneurial function:

> Any tax on net earnings will tend to shift the balance of choice between "to do or not to do" a given thing. If a prospective net gain of a million is just sufficient to over-balance risks and other disutilities, then that prospective million minus a tax will not be so, and this is as true of a single transaction as it is of series of transactions and of the expansion of an old or the foundation of a new firm. Business management and enterprise...will for its maintenance depend, at least in the long run, on the actual delivery, in case of success, of the prizes which that scheme of life holds out, and, therefore, taxes beyond a percentage that greatly varies as to time and place must blunt the profit motive (*Business Cycles*, pp. 291–292).

True to his Austrian training, Schumpeter always kept an eye on the competitive process, that maelstrom of economic activity that is composed of in-

dividual decisions based on reigning economic incentives. Schumpeter retained the Austrian perspective on macroeconomics, namely that it concerns
aggregates, which in turn represent collective outcomes of individual decisions. The causation runs from the individual to the collective, however, as
Menger taught, never the other way around. There may be numerous institutional forces promoting or discouraging economic growth, but a key one, in
Schumpeter's judgment, lies in a "do no harm" fiscal policy that includes low
and/or declining rates of taxation. In the vernacular of the Reagan administration, Schumpeter was an early "supply sider."

Schumpeter's influence on the theory of economic development has been
enormous, even among those economists who reject the theory outright. And
among economists, especially those lacking historical perspective, the term
"entrepreneur" has become virtually synonomous with the name of
Schumpeter. As theories of economic change go, Schumpeter's analysis occupies the middle ground between Marshall and Max Weber. Marshall's theory
adapted incrementally to shifts in preference and production functions, the result being a continuous improvement in moral qualities, tastes, and economic
techniques. Its shortcoming was that it did not explain business cycles, a deficiency that Marshall's student Keynes set about to remedy. Marshall's approach also implied a theory of unilinear progress, which Schumpeter's theory
denies. Weber's theory developed its own set of moral imperatives and used
them to explain rapid social and economic transitions that punctuate long periods of historical continuity. Schumpeter postulated the *continuous* occurrence of innovations and waves of adaptation simply because entrepreneurs
are always present and are a force for change.

Ultimately, the appeal of Schumpeter's theory of economic development
derives from its simplicity and its power, characteristics evident in the
Schumpeterian phrase: "The carrying out of new combinations we call 'enterprise'; the individual whose function it is to carry them out we call 'entrepreneurs'" (*Economic Development,* p. 74). Yet despite the importance of
Schumpeter's contribution to economic development, his dynamic approach
and his holistic vision of economic activity have failed to dominate economic
analysis. Conventional economics still works mainly by intellectual specialization and division of labor.

COMPETITION AND THE MARKET PROCESS

As a result of the combined influence of many economic theorists, but especially Cournot and Walras, "competition" took on a meaning in the nineteenth
century quite apart from the practical but ambiguous sense it was given in classical economics. Early use of the term meant simply rivalrous behavior (e.g.,
in Adam Smith); in other words, two or more parties seeking the same prize,
which usually meant economic profits. The subtle but lasting influence of
Cournot and Walras was to change this notion from what may basically be described as a *process* to what may be described as a *situation*. Emphasis turned

away from the institutional setting and the personalities involved and toward the *conditions* that must be fulfilled in order to yield an equilibrium result. Thus the notion of "perfect competition" emerged, a notion that encapsulated the following conditions: (1) perfect knowledge of every relevant utility function of both buyers and sellers and of all relevant prices, (2) an infinitely large number of buyers and sellers, (3) complete and open entry and exit of all firms, (4) constant expectations, and (5) homogeneous products. When these conditions are operative, the "competitive equilibrium" results—that is, a uniform price for each good, a "normal" level of profits for each producer, utility maximization for each consumer, and no further tendency for things to change. The assumptions of competition are, therefore, nothing else but the conditions necessary to make equilibrium "determinate."

The "competitive model" so briefly sketched here has performed yeoman service in the evolution of economic theory because it has made it possible to give an exact account of the course of economic events solely with the aid of scientific generalizations. In any analytical study, forces whose operations are known must be separated from those that exhibit no uniform principles. The only satisfactory way of recognizing and accounting for the influence of the latter in the real world is to assume them away and observe what happens in their absence. This method of omission and comparison also offers the best hope that we can gradually extend the range of phenomena over which we can make generalizations. But it should be obvious that this technique requires constant awareness of its limitations as well as its strengths.

It has never been easy to convince people that the way to discover reality is through unreality—yet that is what the neoclassical competitive model requires. Modern Austrians offer an alternative that purports to be more realistic because it attempts to incorporate aspects of the human personality excluded from the neoclassical, "mechanistic" model. In particular the Austrian approach seeks to deal explicitly with individuals': (1) knowledge about their own tastes and the opportunities available, (2) interpretations of current events and others' actions, (3) expectations about future events and behavior, and (4) alertness to new opportunities previously unrecognized. In the Austrian view the key insight into competition is that different people know different things. The market is a process whereby scattered and often contradictory bits of information are assimilated and transmitted to individual market participants; in Hayek's phrase, the competitive market process is a *discovery procedure*. Competition—not in the technical sense of "perfect competition," but in the older sense of rivalry—is the engine that drives the market process down the road to *coordination of individual plans* (the Austrian conception of equilibrium).

Hayek has never tired of pointing out that if all that needed to be known was *already* known, then every market decision would correctly anticipate every other decision and the market would automatically have attained full equilibrium. The market is necessary precisely because it is an institutional device for mobilizing existing knowledge and making it available to market participants who are not omniscient. Taking the argument one step further, Austrians argue that the competitive market process is needed not only to mobilize existing knowledge but also to generate awareness of new opportunities. The discoverers of these new opportunities are the entrepreneurs, who take on a far more crucial role in the Austrian paradigm than was previously assigned to them by classical or neoclassical economics. Indeed, in the Austrian framework, the competitive process is by its very nature an entrepreneurial process.

The standard neoclassical theory employs the concept of "economizing," or maximizing utility subject to given tastes and prices, which is inadequate to explain the search for *new* opportunities, whether they consist of new products or variations on existing ones. Likewise, the terms "prices" and "profits" have a more restricted definition in standard use. Conventional theory assumes that the firm confronts known and given cost and revenue possibilities. Profit maximization does not entail discovery of a profit opportunity; it merely requires calculative action to explain already existing and recognized opportunities. In the Austrian view, this takes too much for granted. The Austrian approach views prices as (disequilibrium) exchange ratios representing the incomplete discoveries and current errors made up to the moment by profit-seeking entrepreneurs. Thus market prices offer opportunities for pure profit, and it is up to the alert entrepreneurs to sniff out these opportunities and act on them.

This view of profit, significantly, has nothing to do with monopoly power. It is merely the reward for noticing some lack of coordination in the market. As such, it is a necessary incentive for the discovery of new knowledge, not, as in the standard theory, a minimal payment to a disembodied economic agent to stand pat.

ADVERTISING AND DEMAND DISCOVERY

In light of the attempts by Chamberlin and Robinson to replace or supplement the notion of perfect competition (see Chapter 18), the Austrian approach takes on additional interest. Among contemporary Austrian economists, Israel Kirzner, for one, views the Chamberlin-Robinson reformulation as misguided:

> The new theories failed to perceive that the characteristic features of the real world are simply the manifestations of entrepreneurial competition, a process in which would-be buyers and sellers gropingly seek to discover each other's supply and demand curves. The new theories merely fashioned new equilibrium configurations—based, as was the theory of perfect competition—on *given* and known demand and supply curves—differing from the earlier theory only in the *shapes* assigned to these curves. In the course of attempting to account for such market phenomena as quality differentiation, advertising, markets in which few producers were to be found, the new theories were led to conclusions which grossly misinterpret the significance of these phenomena (*Competition and Entrepreneurship*, p. 29).

The basis for Kirzner's claim is that the theory of monopolistic competition rules out the discovery process. There is no awareness of the need for manufacturers and consumers to experiment in order to find those products and variations that are most wanted. Like the theory it was supposed to supplement, it assumed the market demand to be given beforehand. A second weakness noted by other writers besides Austrians is that the theory offers no explanation of how product differentiation can persist in equilibrium, that is, why rival firms cannot duplicate those product variations that prove successful.

In particular, Austrian economics has provided fresh insights into advertising, which proved to be something of an embarrassment to traditional economic theory. If consumers always have perfect information about the products available, there is no rational explanation for the persistence of advertising. Indeed, it would seem wasteful. To Chamberlin and others, advertising was one way of conveying information to consumers about a product they knew existed. But mere persuasion was another matter. Most economists objected to persuasive advertising as unabashed hucksterism. Austrian thinking departs substantially from the conventional view. Consumers do not always know what products are available, and even if they do, they are not usually informed about their properties. Consequently, the seller has a role in capturing the consumer's attention. It matters not whether advertising is purely informational, purely persuasive, or some combination of the two. What matters is that the products are noticed, for then and only then can consumers act entrepreneurially—that is, exercise their decision-making ability.

In a similar fashion, the Austrian notion of monopoly stands apart from the orthodox view. Standard theory traditionally assumes that a monopolist's demand curve is known and that his or her ability to raise price and increase profits depends on the shape of that curve. It is not always explained how monopolists came to know the demand curve, why they are single producers, and why the threat of competition from other firms does not prevent them from acting as they do. These questions are confronted in the Austrian approach, in which the presence of monopoly in no way obviates the need for market discovery. Whether or not a firm is a monopolist, it must discover what its customers want and what they are willing to pay for it. Therefore, monopolists are subject to the same competitive market process as other firms. Moreover, monopolists must compete with producers of new and better products even if they do not face competition from producers of the *same* product. Hence it is misleading to characterize monopoly as "the absence of competition." Rather, monopoly implies barriers to entry. Kirzner has noted:

> The existence of rivalrous competition requires *not* large numbers of buyers and sellers but simply *freedom of entry*. Competition places pressure on market participants to discover where and how better opportunities, as yet unnoticed, might be offered to the market. The competitive market process occurs because equilibrium has not yet been attained. This process is thwarted whenever non-market barriers are imposed blocking entry to potential competitors ("The Perils of Regulation," p. 9).

One way to gain an appreciation for the operation of the market process is by reviewing the socialist calculation debate that took place over an extended period of time between Mises and Hayek on the one hand and Oskar Lange and H. D. Dickinson on the other. Mises and Hayek illuminated the enormous difficulties confronting socialist planners trying to emulate the market's result without an actual market in operation. Lange and Dickinson, joined later by Abba Lerner and others, maintained that efficient allocation is achievable under socialism so long as socialist managers follow well-prescribed rules in decision making.

THE SOCIALIST CALCULATION DEBATE

Mises fired the opening salvo in the socialist calculation debate in 1922 by questioning whether socialism was possible at all—whether modern industrialized society could continue to exist if organized along socialist lines. Mises attacked the basic premise of socialist theorists that the economy could be planned and directed efficiently after a socialist state had abolished money, markets, and the price system. He argued that money prices determined in a market context were necessary for rational economic calculation. The price system allows resources to freely flow to their most highly valued uses, indeed, directs resources to their highest valued use. For example, it is technically feasible to construct subway rails out of platinum rather than steel, but to use platinum would be inefficient in the face of less expensive substitutes. Only the price system, representing the competing bids of all potential users of platinum, guarantees that such judgments are made. Without the price system, Mises argued, resources could not be allocated efficiently and the economy would function at a primitive level.

Socialist economists took Mises' challenge seriously, with some of the most prominent socialist writers, particularly Oskar Lange and Abba Lerner, acknowledging that Mises had uncovered an important weakness in the socialist theory. Lange even half-seriously proposed that in the future socialist commonwealth a statue be erected to Mises so that no one would forget that prices and markets are essential under socialism too. But of course, the socialists launched a counterattack. Partially retreating from the theory of pure socialism, Lange claimed that socialism would work if socialist planning were substituted for the market mechanism. In other words, the state would set prices for goods and factors of production instead of the market. Managers of state-owned firms would then produce until the marginal cost of their output equaled the "shadow" price of the good. Resources needed to produce finished goods would be requisitioned in accordance with this rule, and the state would stand ready to adjust prices in response to any shortages or surpluses that might result.

As clever as this response appears on the surface, Mises and Hayek now responded with an even more devastating critique. The problem with the state "imitating" the market, they argued, is that the ex ante prices established by government functionaries could never convey accurate information regarding the true opportunity costs associated with resource use. The enormous amount of detailed, specific information required for state-determined prices to match market prices, if it *could* be made available to government bureaucrats, would only be forthcoming at huge transactions cost. In addition, for socialism to approximate market performance, individual incentives would have to be structured to ensure that people within the system would use information and resources efficiently. This could only happen if property were privately owned, a circumstance that clashed directly with socialism.

At its most fundamental level, the socialist calculation debate was a contest over theoretical models. Socialist economic theory is based on Walrasian general-equilibrium models within which the central planning board substitutes for the Walrasian auctioneer. Lange proposed that a central planning board administer resource prices and allow consumer goods to be priced in free markets in order to provide accurate information for factor evaluation. Factor prices would then respond to market eventualities, and the whole process would, by trial and error, simulate the Walrasian *tâtonnement* process. For their part, Mises and Hayek rejected the Walrasian model as unrealistic and inappropriate. In either its pure form or its socialist guise it could not capture enough important features of the real world to make it applicable. In particular, Hayek argued that the information required by the socialist calculation theory was not *given,* but is the subject of continuous discovery. The Austrian criticism was essentially the same as that leveled at the neoclassical model, namely that the proponents of socialism did not understand the *nonparametric* function of prices. Somewhere along the way in the evolution of economic theory, neoclassical economists had forgotten or ignored Cantillon's original vision of the market as an arena in which market participants (i.e., entrepreneurs) nudge prices in the direction of equilibrium by exploiting profit opportunities offered by disequilibrium prices. This vision has been more consistently grasped and maintained by Austrian economists than by any other group. Consequently, they attributed the socialists' myopia to a perception of the market's operation primarily in terms of perfect competition.

As usual, Hayek gave the most forceful counterargument to the socialist position. In a nutshell, he argued as follows. The information that individuals use to guide their economic activity is vast, detailed, fragmented, and often idiosyncratic. It is not neatly captured in objective demand and supply functions that are at the ready command of the central planners. The major reason Hayek gave was that such information is the subject of *continuous discovery* through entrepreneurial action and counteraction. Neoclassical economics stresses only one kind of knowledge—the "engineering knowledge" of technical input-output relations. Austrian economics also spotlights the specific knowledge of "time and place," which leads to the perception of profit opportunities in advance of the crowd, and the kind of knowledge that enables an individual to conceptualize new methods and new products that may bring large rewards. Market prices in this framework are not parameters. They are the unique and timely results of numerous transactions by individuals possessed of these various bits and forms of knowledge. In turn these prices serve as the signals by which decentralized knowledge is collected and coordinated into a systematic whole. In the words of Karen Vaughn, "To try to summarize all this information into a set of simultaneous equations would be quixotic at best" ("Economic Calculation under Socialism," p. 546).

The problem that Mises and Hayek were attacking at base was the effects of different specifications of property rights on individual economic decision making. This is a wide-ranging issue that does not confine itself to the dichotomy between socialism and capitalism. It also pervades the issue of economic regulation, which is a major theme of Chapter 24.

Almost seven decades after the socialist calculation debate began, we may well ask how relevant was the debate in retrospect. Among existing socialist economies, only Yugoslavia resembles the "market socialist" proposals of Lange and Lerner. Several of the socialist countries, particularly Hungary and Poland, but including also the largest, China and the Soviet Union, have introduced reforms enlarging the role of the private sector, even though large segments of these economies remain directed from the center. Before we conclude, however, that the "workability" of nonmarket socialist economies belies the Austrian critique of socialism, we must take into account two established facts about centrally planned economies. First, their economic performance is poor by comparison with capitalist market economies, in some cases, disastrously so. Second, the private sector in socialist economies, usually existing in the form of illegal underground economies, is typically large and important. These facts offer at least a partial vindication of the Austrian critique of socialism.

CONCLUSION

The tradition of economic inquiry begun by Menger continues in the writings of many contemporary economists who profess to be "Austrians." In this chapter, we have seen that the Austrian tradition is wide-ranging, starting with the theory of subjective wants but building on that primal insight in a methodologically consistent fashion to elucidate such broader topics as money, credit, banking, business cycles, economic development, and the very nature of competition. The distinguishing feature of Austrian macroeconomics is its overriding concern for the microeconomic foundations of macroeconomics principles. While this same concern has been expressed with renewed fervor by many conventional economists in the wake of the perceived failures of Keynesian macroeconomics, many "Austrian" ideas have been ignored by mainstream economic theory. For example, if contemporary monetary economics seems far removed from the concerns of Mises and Hayek, the reason is that it treats all increases in the quantity of money as being essentially alike and disregards the question of the "transmission mechanism" by which the new money makes its impact felt on the macroeconomy, by assuming that relative prices are left unchanged in the wake of the monetary change.

In the final analysis, the monetarists and the Austrians are closer together than the monetarists and the Keynesians. What the monetarists and the Austrians share is the belief that changes in the quantity of money are the primary cause of aggregate instability. The Austrians, however, have been more sensitive to the ubiquitous effects of changes in relative prices caused by monetary changes. Understanding these differences helps to sort out the various policy proposals that are likely to emanate from each camp. In the face of the Keynesian challenge that "money does not matter," the monetarists have counterattacked that "money does matter." In essence, Mises' monetary theory takes the phrase one step further. In the Austrian view, "money matters all the time!"

NOTES FOR FURTHER READING

Two good introductions to the Austrian *gestalt* are L. H. White's monograph, *The Methodology of the Austrian School* (New York: The Center for Libertarian Studies, 1977); and A. H. Shand, *Subjectivist Economics: The New Austrian School* (Exeter: Short Run Press, 1980). See also E. G. Dolan (ed.), *The Foundations of Modern Austrian Economics* (Kansas City: Sheed & Ward, 1976); S. C. Littlechild, *The Fallacy of the Mixed Economy* (London: Institute for Economic Affairs, 1978); L. S. Moss (ed.), *The Economics of Ludwig von Mises* (Kansas City: Sheed, 1976); G. P. O'Driscoll, *Economics as a Coordination Problem: The Contributions of Friedrich A. Hayek* (Kansas City: Sheed, 1977); W. D. Reekie, *Industry, Prices and Markets* (New York: Wiley, 1979); M. J. Rizzo (ed.), *Time, Uncertainty and Disequilibrium: Exploration of Austrian Themes* (Lexington, Mass.: Heath, 1979); L. M. Spadaro, *New Directions in Austrian Economics* (Kansas City: Sheed, 1978); and K. I. Vaughn, "Does It Matter That Costs Are Subjective?" *Southern Economics Journal,* vol. 46 (January 1980), pp. 702–715.

For particularly cogent views from notable "insiders," see Ludwig von Mises, *The Historical Setting of the Austrian School* (New Rochelle, N.Y.: Arlington House, 1969); L. M. Lachmann, "The Importance in the History of Ideas of the Austrian School of Economics," J. H. McCulloch (trans.), *Zeitschrift für Nationalökonomie,* vol. 26 (1966), pp. 152–167; and F. A. Hayek, "Economic Thought: The Austrian School," *International Encyclopedia of the Social Sciences,* vol. 4 (1968), pp. 458–462. Earlene Craver, "The Emigration of the Austrian Economists," *History of Political Economy,* vol. 18 (Spring 1986), pp. 1–32, recounts the early academic careers of the third-generation Austrians, especially Mises, Hayek, and Schumpeter.

We will not attempt to give an exhaustive bibliography of Hayek's writings here (but see the work by O'Driscoll). A significant number of Hayek's early and later writings on Austrian topics have been collected and published in three works: *Prices and Production* (London: Routledge, 1935); *Individualism and Economic Order* (Chicago: The University of Chicago Press, 1948); and *New Studies in Philosophy, Politics, and the History of Ideas* (Chicago: The University of Chicago Press, 1978). Mises' magnum opus is *Human Action: A*

Treatise on Economics (New Haven, Conn.: Yale University Press, 1949), a much neglected book that still repays careful reading. Mises' opening salvo in the socialist calculation debate has been translated and reprinted in Hayek (ed.), *Collectivist Economic Planning* (London: Routledge, 1935). See also L. Mises, *Socialism: An Economic and Sociological Analysis*, J. Kahane (trans.) (New Haven: Yale University Press, 1951). Additional appreciations of the problems involved in socialist planning can be found in G. W. Nutter, "Markets without Property: A Grand Illusion," in N. A. Beadles and L. A. Drewry, Jr. (eds.), *Money, the Market and the State: Essays in Honor of James Muir Waller* (Athens: University of Georgia Press, 1968); and in D. T. Armentano, "Resource Allocation Problems under Socialism," in W. P. Snavely (ed.), *Theory of Economic Systems: Capitalism, Socialism, Corporatism* (Columbus, Ohio: Merrill, 1969).

The socialist side of the debate was put forth most energetically by Oskar Lange and F. M. Taylor, *On the Economic Theory of Socialism*, B. E. Lippincott (ed.) (New York: McGraw-Hill, 1964); H. D. Dickinson, *Economics of Socialism* (London: Oxford University Press, 1939); and A. P. Lerner, *The Economics of Control* (New York: Macmillan, 1944). Karen I. Vaughn (see References) provides a worthy summary of the debate as well as a bibliography in her 1980 article. Peter Murrell, "Did the Theory of Market Socialism Answer the Challenge of Ludwig Von Mises? A Reinterpretation of the Socialist Controversy," *History of Political Economy*, vol. 15 (Spring 1983), pp. 92–105, contends that the socialist answer given to Mises was not definitive and that modern economics now has the tools to confront the issues raised by Mises long ago.

The Misesian tradition has been carried on in America by Rothbard and Kirzner. See particularly M. N. Rothbard, *Man, Economy and State: A Treatise on Economic Principles* (New York: Van Nostrand, 1962); I. M. Kirzner, *Competition and Entrepreneurship* (Chicago: The University of Chicago Press, 1973); same author, *Perception, Opportunity and Profit* (Chicago: The University of Chicago Press, 1979); and same author, *Discovery and the Capitalist Process* (Chicago: The University of Chicago Press, 1985). For a recent treatment of advertising (a favorite Austrian theme) that poses a "process" view of competition in contrast to the conventional view, see R. B. Ekelund, Jr., and D. S. Saurman, *Advertising and the Market Process* (San Francisco: Pacific Research Institute for Public Policy, 1988). Ludwig Lachmann reflects an Austrian influence absorbed from Hayek. See his *Capital, Expectations and the Market Process* (Kansas City: Sheed, 1977); and "From Mises to Shackle: An Essay on Austrian Economics and the Kaleidic Society," *Journal of Economic Literature*, vol. 14 (March 1976), pp. 54–61.

Some works that are not strictly Austrian but bear closely on the nature of subjectivism, especially in regard to costs, include A. A. Alchian, *Economic Forces at Work* (Indianapolis: Liberty Press, 1977), particularly pp. 273–334; J. M. Buchanan, *Cost and Choice* (Chicago: Markham, 1969); and Buchanan and G. F. Thirlby (eds.), *L. S. E. Essays on Costs* (New York: New York University Press, 1981). For an Austrian perspective on some of the topics not treated in this chapter, see L. M. Lachmann, *Capital and Its Structure* (Kansas City: Sheed, 1977); F. A. Hayek, *Monetary Theory and the Trade Cycle* (New York: A. M. Kelley, 1975); R. W. Garrison, *Austrian Macroeconomics: A Diagrammatic Exposition* (Menlo Park, Calif.: Institute for Humane Studies, 1978); J. R. Hicks, *Capital and Time: A Neo-Austrian Theory* (Oxford: Clarendon Press, 1973); and M. N. Rothbard, *America's Great Depression* (Kansas City: Sheed, 1975).

G. L. S. Shackle has written at length on the problem of time and uncertainty, notably in *Uncertainty in Economics* (London: Cambridge University Press, 1955) and in *Epistemics and Economics* (London: Cambridge University Press, 1972). T. W. Hutchinson and Brian Loasby (a student of Shackle's) have sounded related themes, the former in *Knowledge and Ignorance in Economics* (Chicago: The University of Chicago Press, 1977) and the latter in *Choice, Complexity and Ignorance* (London: Cambridge University Press, 1976).

Historical development of the mainstream notion of competition of which the Austrians are so critical is the subject of several papers. See G. J. Stigler, "Perfect Competition, Historically Contemplated," in Stigler (ed.), *Essays in the History of Economics* (Chicago: The University of Chicago Press, 1965); P. J. McNulty, "Economic Theory and the Meaning of Competition," *Quarterly Journal of Economics,* vol. 82 (November 1968), pp. 639–656; and K. G. Dennis, *'Competition' in the History of Economic Thought* (New York: Arno Press, 1977). On the importance and significance of property rights in economic theory, see A. A. Alchian, "Some Economics of Property Rights," in Alchian (ed.), *Economic Forces at Work* (Indianapolis: Liberty Press, 1977); and E. G. Furubotn and S. Pejovich (eds.), *The Economics of Property Rights* (Cambridge, Mass.: Ballinger, 1974).

The entrepreneur, who assumes such a central role in the neo-Austrian paradigm, emerges chameleon-like from a study of past economic thought. Different writers have conceived the concept and role of this prime economic actor in many different ways, so much so that in contemporary economics the term is often used indiscriminately, or at best, ambiguously. A recent attempt to review the historical record and to distill meaning and direction for the notion of entrepreneurship is contained in R. F. Hébert and A. N. Link, *The Entrepreneur: Mainstream Views and Radical Critiques,* 2d ed. (New York: Praeger, 1988).

REFERENCES

Hayek, F. A. *Prices and Production,* 2d ed. London: Routledge & Kegan Paul, 1935.
———. *The Counter-revolution of Science: Studies on the Abuse of Reason.* Indianapolis: Liberty Press, 1979.
Jaffé, William. "Menger, Jevons and Walras De-homogenized," *Economic Inquiry,* vol. 14 (December 1976), pp. 511–524.

Kirzner, I. M. *Competition and Entrepreneurship*. Chicago: The University of Chicago Press, 1973.

———. "The Perils of Regulation: A Market Process Approach." Miami: Law and Economics Center Occasional Paper, 1978.

Mises, Ludwig von. *The Theory of Money and Credit,* H. E. Batson (trans.). New York: The Foundation for Economic Education, 1971 [1912].

———. *Human Action: A Treatise on Economics*. New Haven: Yale University Press, 1949.

Rothbard, M. N. "The Austrian Theory of Money," in E. G. Dolan, (ed.), *The Foundations of Modern Austrian Economics*. Kansas City: Sheed & Ward, 1976.

Schumpeter, J. A. "The Instability of Capitalism," *Economic Journal,* vol. 38 (1928), pp. 361–386.

———. *The Theory of Economic Development,* 2d ed., R. Opie (trans.). Cambridge: Harvard University Press, 1934.

———. *Business Cycles*. New York: McGraw-Hill, 1939.

———. *Capitalism, Socialism, and Democracy,* 3d ed. New York: Harper & Row, 1950.

———. *History of Economic Analysis,* E. B. Schumpeter (ed.). New York: Oxford University Press, 1954.

Vaughn, K. I. "Economic Calculation under Socialism: The Austrian Contribution," *Economic Inquiry,* vol. 18 (October 1980), pp. 535–554.

THE DEVELOPMENT OF MATHEMATICAL AND EMPIRICAL ECONOMICS

INTRODUCTION

A highly visible feature of modern economics is the suffusion of mathematical and empirical tools into the core of practically every economist's research. The quest to formalize economic theory and to gauge its validity, at least tentatively, has been an ongoing concern in economics throughout the twentieth century and, most particularly, in the post-World War II period. While all major journals in the field carry papers with mathematical and empirical content, there are no fewer than five periodicals exclusively devoted to mathematical and econometric technique, which publish no fewer than 6,000 pages per year on the subject.[1] Few graduate or undergraduate programs in economics offer a degree without requiring some evidence of proficiency in mathematics or statistics. (Advanced students would be unable to read most economic research without it.) Some economists appear to eagerly await new mathematical and statistical techniques so that they may begin to use them in conjunction with or to elaborate new economic theories or new tests of economic theories.

This headlong rush to mathematical economics has been greeted with mixed enthusiasm. To be sure, not all in the economics profession have welcomed

---

[1] In a recent survey article, Nobel laureate Gerard Debreu (see References) cites the following journals as playing a major role in the spread of the mathematical technique in economics: *Econometrica* (founded in 1933), the *Review of Economic Studies* (1933), the *International Economic Review* (1960), the *Journal of Economic Theory* (1969), and the *Journal of Mathematical Economics* (1974). The *Journal of Econometrics* (1973) might also be added to this list. Debreu's survey of the evolution of mathematical economics informed certain aspects of this chapter and is highly recommended to readers seeking an overview of modern developments in the field.

these developments or welcomed them uncritically. Some believe that the costs of further developments along mathematical/empirical lines heavily outweigh the possible or probable benefits. Defenders argue that economics can never be truly "scientific" without a continuous pursuit and cultivation of technique. Although a definitive resolution of these issues is illusive, certain important questions must be addressed by the historian of economics. What, for example, are the origins of these important methodological developments? How and to what end are mathematics and statistics applied in economics and in economic theory? What are the gains and losses from such applications? What is the current state and what is the probable future of mathematics and testing techniques in the profession and in economic inquiry? The purpose of this chapter is to provide tentative assessments of these critical and ongoing issues and to develop an understanding of some elementary applications of mathematical and empirical tools to economic theory. Since methods of testing economic theory paralleled or followed the acceptance and development of mathematical and statistical techniques, attention is devoted first to mathematical methods and their long history in economics.

ORIGINS AND DEVELOPMENT OF THE MATHEMATICAL METHOD

From the beginnings of economic analysis, economists have sought methods to explain and display their ideas. Some ideas, such as those related to economic institutions and history, and some eras, such as that which includes the earliest stirrings of economic theory, produced an economic analysis encased in purely literary style. But numerical calculations accompanied economic theory in some writings from the beginning.[2] These primitive calculations were natural developments, since economics deals not only with "tendencies" but also with the numerical calculation of phenomena. Indeed, the kind of deductive reasoning employed or implied by Adam Smith, David Ricardo, and other pioneers of the science invited and encouraged researchers to employ mathematics.

Augustin Cournot on the Mathematical Method

Cournot, as we learned in Chapter 12, was the real founder of mathematical economics. One could hardly improve on Cournot's understanding of the *role* and advantages of using mathematics in economics. The employment of mathematics, in Cournot's embryonic understanding, was not different from the use

---

[2] For example, Aristotle's views on exchange were informed by mathematical concepts, e.g., mean, proportion, etc. In the seventeenth century, Sir William Petty developed "Political Arithmetick" to describe a primitive national income accounting system (see Chap. 4). A few decades later, Charles Davenant, building on earlier work by Gregory King, estimated a demand curve (see John Creedy, "On the King-Davenant 'Law' of Demand," cited in the References, and the discussion later in the present chapter).

of words or graphical representations of economic theory. Ricardo, claimed Cournot, had only disguised his algebra under "numerical calculations of tedious length" (*Mathematical Principles,* p. 4). But Cournot knew full well that numerical calculations were not the only or even the major benefits of the use of mathematics. He wrote:

> I have said that most authors who have devoted themselves to political economy seem also to have had a wrong idea of the nature of the applications of mathematical analysis to the theory of wealth. They imagined that the use of symbols and formulas could only lead to numerical calculations, and as it was clearly perceived that the subject was not suited to such a numerical determination of values by means of a theory alone, the conclusion was drawn that the mathematical apparatus, if not liable to lead to erroneous results, was at least idle and pedantic. But those skilled in mathematical analysis know that its object is not simply to calculate numbers, but that it is also employed to find the relations between magnitudes which cannot be expressed in numbers and between *functions* whose law is not capable of algebraic expression (*Mathematical Principles,* pp. 2–3).

Although good data were hard to come by in Cournot's day (as in our own), he nevertheless foresaw a role for mathematics to facilitate economic intuition about how nonquantitative values (e.g., price and quantity) were related to each other and to other magnitudes. Mathematical symbols, in Cournot's own words, are able to "facilitate the exposition of problems, to render it [sic] more concise, to open the way to more extended developments, and to avoid the digressions of vague argumentation" (*Mathematical Principles,* p. 4). Since the functions developed by Cournot were in finite commodity and price spaces, Euclidian geometry (i.e., graphs) could be used (and was used by Cournot) to provide renderings of economic theory that are equivalent to mathematical treatment.[3]

Common Mathematical Tools Used in Economics

In principle, then, literary, graphical, and mathematical expressions of economic theory do not differ in any fundamental respect. But there are costs and benefits to the use of each means of expression. By way of analogy, consider the use of computers and software. The use of software is basically a means by which we process information; i.e., it gets us from input to output. An ordinary typewriter allows us to put words and thoughts (the input) on paper, which can be read (the output). Computer software programs (e.g., word processors) permit us to do the same thing. Each software package, whether for word processing or data processing, permits us to transfer inputs to output, and each software package does it differently. Of course, it takes time to learn

---

[3] We do not wish to imply that isolated, well-formed technical developments of portions of economic theory did not exist before Cournot. Indeed the evidence is overwhelmingly to the contrary; see, for example, the treatment by Theocharis, *Early Developments in Mathematical Economics* (see References).

any given software package, but once learned, the tool may be used again and again for any task that may be adapted to it.

One of the tasks of the economic theorist is to reason deductively from postulates (assumptions about economic behavior) to conclusions about the way the world works. Just as words and thoughts may be processed by typewriter or by computer software, there are more and less efficient ways to get from postulates to conclusions in expressing economic theory. Each kind of software has advantages and disadvantages, just as each mode of economic expression has pluses and minuses.

A purely verbal argument is readily intelligible to the largest audience, but as Cournot recognized, literary exposition has some definite limitations. Literary exposition can lead to digressions and vague arguments. Where elaborate reasoning is required, graphical and mathematical expositions offer more precision. Graphs of economic relations and theories provide a very useful picture and help the economist grasp and extend complex relations. Graphs have taken and still take economists far as a mode of expressing economic ideas. But graphs also have limits. When problems extend beyond two dimensions (i.e., a demand relation involving changes in prices, quantities, *and* income), graphs become cumbersome. Moreover, graphs are limited to three dimensions, so they are inappropriate to problems involving more than three dimensions. Mathematics was used by neoclassical writers such as Jevons (Chapter 14) to explicate simple theories of consumer behavior, but as economists began to tackle larger problems (e.g., Walrasian general equilibrium; see Chapter 16), new modes of expression ("software") became necessary, and mathematics became an essential tool of the economic theorist. The benefits that mathematics brings to economics are at least threefold: (1) mathematics makes assumptions and premises explicit, thereby eliminating "hidden" biases of theory; (2) it makes the presentation of economic theory more concise and more precise; and (3) it allows the economist to deal more easily with more than two-dimensional economic problems.

Mathematical theorems of many kinds, some of them exceedingly complex, have become part and parcel of the economist's "software." We cannot identify all of the major mathematical theorems employed by economics in this chapter, but we will identify some major, elementary tools here, and we will introduce others (at least intuitively) later in this chapter.

Calculus Beyond simple arithmetic, the most useful mathematical tool of the economist is differential calculus. As we have seen, early econo-engineers such as Dupuit, Ellet, and Lardner (see Chapter 12) and economists such as Jevons, Marshall, and Walras utilized forms of calculus. Purely *qualitative* economic models deal with direction. Thus, a hypothesis that states that an increase in demand (supply remaining constant) increases both equilibrium price and quantity makes a qualitative statement about the direction of price and quantity. But the issue of how much price and quantity will change in response to a change in demand is a *quantitative* question (the answer to which includes the qualitative). Differential calculus, which essentially deals with *rates of change,* is thus the natural tool for the economist to employ in constructing and discussing economic theories.

Economists are not so much interested in total quantities as they are in marginal quantities. In the theory of the firm, for example, the business person is interested in the *marginal* cost and the *marginal* revenue of this or that action or policy change. Differential calculus is uniquely suited to provide such answers. Take, for instance, the standard theory of consumer behavior. The consumer, with a given set of preferences for all goods and services, faces a certain set of prices and is constrained by his or her income. The mathematical procedure which describes the consumer's solution to the problem of utility maximization in these circumstances is called *constrained optimization,* which is a straightforward application of differential calculus. Another example is given by Cournot's theory of profit maximization. Cournot specified the solution as requiring the rates of change of the firm's revenue (i.e., *marginal* revenue) and costs (i.e., *marginal* costs) to be equal. Marginal revenue and marginal cost are determined by taking the first derivative of the total-revenue and total-cost functions, respectively, thus providing another illustration of the straightforward application of the differential calculus.

Other branches of calculus, such as *integral* calculus, also find ready application to economic problems, especially in the fields of industrial organization and public finance. The decision whether to provide a new bridge or public park should be informed by, among other things, a calculation and comparison of the economic costs and benefits. A common means of calculating benefits is the computation of consumers' surplus (see Chapters 12 and 15), i.e., the maximum prices consumers would be willing to pay for the good or service rather than go without it. The mathematical measure of this aggregate "benefit" is the integral (i.e., summing up) of the benefits of all individuals under the demand curve for the good in question. Once the demand curve is estimated and the costs of the project are calculated, integral calculus provides the economist with a ready-made tool for making an actual calculation and comparison.

Linear Systems and Algebra   Algebra, whether simple or complex, provides the economist with a wealth of tools or "software" by which to express economic theory. This is especially so when the economist is faced with the task of estimating general-equilibrium (Walrasian) relations and interrelations. A branch of algebra called *matrix algebra* has proved especially useful in dealing with large numbers of equations and variables which summarize or approximate those in a real-world economy.

The combination of linear and matrix algebra provides economists with an estimation procedure that depicts production or consumption (or other) relations as being linear, or as being reducible to, or approximated by, linear relations. The advantage of the procedure is that huge systems of equations can be calculated rapidly by computer to uncover complicated relations in an economic system. A possible disadvantage to using linear relations is that, even as approximations, they may not capture accurately the features of production or consumption relations.

THE CHILDREN OF COURNOT: SOME APPLICATIONS
OF MATHEMATICS TO ECONOMIC IDEAS

Calculus and algebra are two general mathematical tools that have proved useful to the economist. There are many other kinds of mathematical "software" of varied complexity that economists have adapted for use with economic theory. Calculus, however, has been the tool of choice from the beginning, because the concept of "small changes" lies at the heart of many economic problems. The early intellectual descendants of Cournot applied calculus to economic problems in ingenious ways. Francis Y. Edgeworth, a neoclassical contemporary of Jevons and Marshall, was perhaps the premier Anglo-Saxon economist of his era in adapting mathematics to the social sciences. Although his presentation of ideas is somewhat obscure (a fact that accounts in part for the neglect by his contemporaries), Edgeworth applied calculus and other mathematical tools to economic topics such as monopoly, price discrimination, index numbers, and taxation (see Notes for Further Reading). Edgeworth also exerted a major influence on the direction of economic method by his long editorship of the *Economic Journal,* England's foremost economic periodical. Furthermore, his invention of the "core" theory of an exchange economy, as we will see below, has had an enormous impact upon contemporary mathematical economists.

Alfred Marshall, although an enthusiastic and capable mathematician, largely eschewed the application of formal mathematics in his academic writings. Marshall's aim was to portray economics as a tool of social change to the business person and to the intelligent layperson (see Chapter 15). He wished his ideas to be accessible to the widest possible audience, and saw mathematics as a device that would thwart this goal. Yet while Marshall was reluctant to employ mathematics, his students and successors have taken his (and Léon Walras's) ideas to new heights of mathematical sophistication. Important advances of this sort were accomplished by two contemporary Nobel prize winners, Sir John R. Hicks (b. 1904) and Paul A. Samuelson (b. 1915). In 1934, Hicks and R. G. D. Allen (1906–1983) undertook a complete revision of Marshallian value theory in terms of calculus. Hicks later expanded this "new" neoclassical microeconomics in 1939 (*Value and Capital*) to include dynamic and monetary considerations. His rigorous mathematical presentation of key components of economic theory eventually became a standard for modern practice.

Paul Samuelson, an American economist who won the Nobel Prize in Economic Science in 1970, has also been an important force for mathematical rigor in economic theory. In his *Foundations of Economic Analysis* published in 1947 (a work stemming from his Harvard doctoral dissertation of six years earlier), Samuelson transformed the style of economic analysis from predominantly verbal-graphical exposition to systematic and thorough mathematical treatment. In the *Foundations* and in many other works, Samuelson applied mathematics to general economic theory and to specific elements of that theory, including the theory of consumer behavior, growth and capital theory, welfare economics, and international trade theory. The detailed nature of these pioneer contributions is too intricate and far afield of the task at hand, but a general discussion of several useful techniques is in order.

Linear Relations

Linear algebra and its elaborations, as suggested above, provide an important mathematical tool that finds ready application in economic theory. Numerous early attempts to apply algebra, often in conjunction with calculus, highlight the development of economic theory in the nineteenth century. It might be recalled that Friedrich von Wieser in his book *Natural Value* (1884) introduced a "system" of input-to-value equations in order to determine the productive contribution of each input (see Chapter 13). These are simple, linear equations (for various industry inputs and values) that yield a simultaneous algebraic solution. Elaborations on this theme abound in twentieth-century economics.

Linear Programming One of the most important applications of linear techniques has come through the development of *linear programming* by mathematicians John von Neumann and George Dantzig in the late 1940s and by economists Robert Dorfman, Paul Samuelson, and Robert Solow in 1958. (See Notes for Further Reading.) While linear programming (and certain nonlinear varieties) has been brought to increasingly useful and elaborate stages of development, the fundamental idea is basically uncomplicated. It models optimizing behavior as the choice of processes or activities under some set of *linear* constraints. Dantzig's first applications were to logistical planning and to the optimal deployment of military forces, but the tool has proved to have an enormous range of applications in economics and business, especially in choosing least-cost production techniques or inputs to produce some desired level of output.

The idea applies to many other areas as well. Consider an important problem in the theory of the firm: profit maximization. Suppose that a firm owns a small fabricating plant that produces semifinished athletic equipment of two types, e.g., tennis rackets and barbell sets.[4] Let X_1 = tennis rackets and X_2 = barbell sets. Suppose that the production of semifinished tennis rackets and barbell sets requires the use of three machines, A, B, and C, all of which can be employed 8 hours per day—i.e., 8 hours is the "production period." Suppose, further, that the firm owns 6 A-type machines, 4 B-type machines,

---

[4] The example provided here is adapted from Charles Maurice and Charles Smithson, *Managerial Economics*, Chap. 7 (see References).

and 10 C-type machines. One might think of machine A as a "cutting" machine, B as a lathe, and C as a "finishing" machine. The object of the firm is, presumably, to maximize profits, which we here characterize as "gross" profits—profit net of all other input costs, such as labor and raw materials. The *objective* of the firm is to obtain the greatest profits by selecting profit-maximizing production amounts of tennis rackets and barbell sets. In linear programming language these are the *choice variables*. But this selection of X_1 and X_2 can only be made under certain constraints. Since machines are only worked 8 hours per day, the following total machine-hours are available given the number of machines the firm owns:

Type A—cutting machines	48 hours
Type B—lathes	32 hours
Type C—finishing machines	80 hours

To make matters somewhat more complicated for the firm's decision maker, each output—tennis rackets and barbell sets—requires different numbers of machine-hours. Suppose that the following are the physical requirements for tennis rackets (X_1) and for barbell sets (X_2):

Cutting machine
X_1 requires 12 hours
X_2 requires 6 hours

Lathe
X_1 requires 4 hours
X_2 requires 8 hours

Finishing
X_1 requires 16 hours
X_2 requires 16 hours

The firm's decision maker now has his or her *inequality constraints* for each type of machine. On the basis of the above information, these constraints may be written notationally in the following way:

Cutting	$12X_1 + 6X_2 \leq 48$
Lathe	$4X_1 + 8X_2 \leq 32$
Finishing	$16X_1 + 16X_2 \leq 80$

These inequality constraints may be visually depicted in Figure 22-1, where barbell sets are shown on the vertical axis and tennis rackets on the horizontal axis. For example, the cutting machine constraint is a straight line which shows all of the possible alternatives between producing barbell sets and tennis rackets, *but only on the cutting machine*. If all cutting machine time were devoted to tennis rackets, a maximum of four rackets could be produced. If only barbell sets were produced, the maximum output would be 8 (48 divided by 6 as given in the inequality constraint above). Constraints given by the

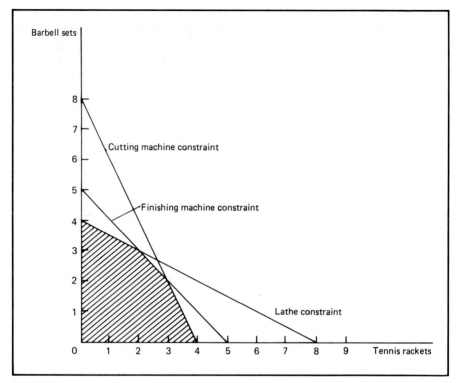

FIGURE 22-1
The inequality constraints for cutting, lathe, and finishing machines are straight lines showing all of the possible alternatives between producing barbell sets and tennis rackets but only for *each* machine. The feasible region of production is shown by the hatched area of the figure.

physical capacities of the other two machines are likewise shown in Figure 22-1. Clearly the firm is going to be limited by what economists call a *feasible region* of production. Although the ability of the firm to produce more than four tennis rackets per period is not constrained by lathes or finishing machines, it is limited by the number of cutting machine-hours it controls. Thus the feasible region of production is indicated by the crosshatched area of Figure 22-1. Each point in that region is a feasible solution to the problem the firm faces of selecting that quantity of X_1 and X_2 that maximizes profits.

What precise solution will the firm choose? The choice will depend upon the prices it can get for tennis rackets and barbell sets along with the relative profitability of those two items. In general the firm is said to maximize profits subject to physical constraints and availability of machines. If, for example, market prices are fixed to the firm so that it realizes a profit of $24 per semifinished racket and $16 per semifinished barbell set, profits will be maximized subject to the above constraints when

$$\pi = 24X_1 + 16X_2$$

From this expression for profits, a whole set of parallel *isoprofit* curves (actually straight lines) may be added to Figure 22-1 in order to produce an equilibrium solution to the firm's problem. These isoprofit curves are of the form

$$X_2 = \frac{\pi}{16} - \frac{3X_1}{2}$$

The graphic depiction of these isoprofit lines is shown in Figure 22-2 as a parallel series of lines with a slope of $-\frac{3}{2}$. The maximum profit attainable by the firm is shown at the optimal solution where isoprofit curve II touches the "outermost" point on the feasible region of production. Note that isoprofit curve I is in the feasible region, but more profit could be earned by producing different

FIGURE 22-2
Maximum profit attainable by the firm is given where the isoprofit curve II just touches the outermost point on the feasible region of production.

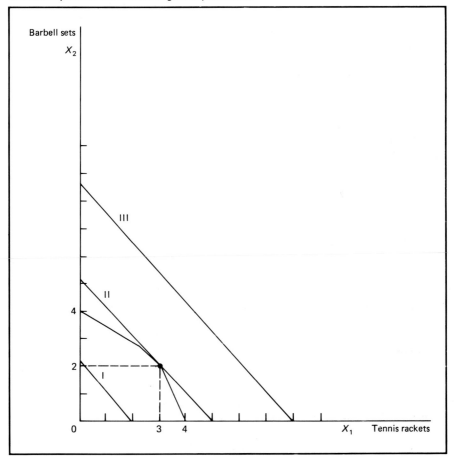

quantities of X_1 and X_2. For example, higher profits might be earned from isoprofit curve III, but that is unattainable by the firm given the production-machine constraint it faces. As in all linear programming problems, the optimal solution will be at a point called the *extreme point:* the intersection of two constraints, or an intersection of axes.[5] In this simple case, the optimal production will be the output combination of three tennis rackets (X_1) and two barbell sets (X_2), as shown in Figure 22-2. Profits will be maximized at $104 per production period (3 times $24 plus 2 times $16).

While this simple example illustrates some fundamental principles of linear programming, it does not reveal the multitude of problems that can be understood and solved by linear programming methods. Linear programming is useful in *any* case where constrained choice is involved. It has been used repeatedly in problems of cost minimization for given output levels, in the selection of production techniques in industry and agriculture, and in the minimization of transport costs, but it is applicable also to problems involving consumer behavior. How, for example, should you allocate your given work (or leisure) time in order to maximize your income (or satisfaction)? Linear programming models can provide answers to this question and a wide range of others.

Leontief's Input-Output Analysis   Linear programming is actually an offshoot of a broader mathematical technique called input-output analysis, which was invented by the 1973 Nobel laureate Wassily Leontief (b. 1906), a Russian-born American economist. Input-output analysis is a mathematical technique that emphasizes the general interdependence of inputs and outputs of whole economies, regions, or, indeed, even the entire world. Leontief, who joined the Harvard faculty in 1932, published the first input-output tables for the U.S. economy during World War II. His early tables described the American experience between 1919 and 1929 (see References).

Input-output analysis contains both inductive and deductive components. It draws inductively upon actual data and actual interdependencies of all of the various sectors of the economy. These interdependencies, however, are analyzed within mathematical models which facilitate computations and analyses of the effects of exogenous changes such as changes in the composition of final demand or input supplies—the deductive component of input-output investigations. Input-output analysis may also be contrasted with the highly aggregative Keynesian theory (Chapter 18), insofar as actual tables are usually based on disaggregated economic data.

As an introduction to this important branch of mathematical analysis, consider an elementary input-output table with only three sectors in a simple economy. Actual input-output tables may contain hundreds of sectors and subsectors describing real-world economies. Ours is kept simple for illustration, and is contained in Table 22-1. This simple economy contains three in-

---

[5] A nonnegativity condition is attached to linear programming problems of this sort.

TABLE 22-1
AN INPUT-OUTPUT TABLE*

Sector	Food and raw materials	Manufacturing	Household	Total
Food and raw materials	200	100	400	1,000 bu. corn
Manufacturing	100	150	25	300 tons plastics
Household	250	200	—	450 work-years

*The production requirements of the various sectors of an economy are summarized in rows and columns.

terrelated sectors: a food-and-raw-materials sector, a manufacturing sector, and a household sector. Like all input-output tables, Table 22-1 is composed of rows and columns arranged in the form of an input-output *matrix*. (A 3 × 3 matrix contains three rows and three columns; a 75 × 75 matrix contains seventy-five rows and an equal number of columns.) Each row and its corresponding column represent one particular sector of the economy, e.g., automobiles, toasters, avocados, and so on. In the simple case described in Table 22-1, the food-and-raw-materials sector has produced 1,000 bushels of corn which are delivered in the various amounts shown to the sectors listed in the column headings. Two hundred bushels have been retained in the food-and-raw-materials sector (for replenishment of seed), 100 bushels have been delivered to the manufacturing sector, and 400 bushels have been delivered to the household (final demand) sector. Other sectors, not shown in the table, receive the balance, so the row does not add up to the total produced. Entries may also be zero for some column sectors since some sectors may deliver nothing to other sectors of the economy. Like the agricultural sector, the manufacturing sector delivers output to other sectors. The manufacturing sector is represented in Table 22-1 by a producer of plastics, and we see that manufacturing delivers 100 tons of plastic to the agricultural sector, supplies 25 tons to the household sector, and retains 150 tons for its own use.

Each column may be interpreted as displaying the requirements for production in the sector represented. Consider the food-and-raw-materials column in Table 22-1. It tells us that the production of 1 bushel of corn requires ⅕ (200/1,000), or 0.20, of a bushel of corn; ⅒ (100/1000), or 0.10, ton of plastics; and ¼ (250/1,000), or 0.25, man-year of labor. The production of 1 ton of plastics (reading down column 2) requires ⅓ (100/300), or 0.33, bushel of corn; ½ (150/300), or 0.50, of a ton of plastics; and ⅔ (200/300), or 0.66, man-year of labor.

While this example may seem artificial, its purpose is to show how the *technical coefficients of production* are built up and arranged in mathematical form. Once the technical coefficients (a fancy term for the production requirements for any good or service) are known, and once final actual output is known, equations relating inputs to outputs may be developed. These equations, which can be manipulated through the use of matrix algebra, then provide critical information on *intersectoral* changes in input and production requirements that would emerge, say, if the final demand for corn or plastics were to change. The general interdependence of any economic system means that a change in demand in one sector will and must affect many other sectors in the economy. In any real-world economy these interdependent intersectoral changes will have an enormous impact upon resource utilization in certain sectors, including employment in specific sectors.

Input-output analysis is a useful tool for estimating changes in intersectoral production requirements that emerge from changes in final demands. One early use of Leontief's model, for example, was to predict the extent of steel shortages during World War II. The impact on total production due to technological change in one sector may be estimated by means of the device. Input-output analysis is thus both a descriptive tool that permits the modeling of an economy from actual data and an analytical tool that permits the estimation of intersectoral shortages or surpluses under the assumption of a specific change in final demand or technology. While the technique itself is politically neutral, it obviously lends itself readily to problems of socialist planning and economic development. Nevertheless, Marxist economists have not uncritically accepted the technique. The Soviet Union, for example, has used computer-driven techniques to determine target outputs and so-called shadow prices with mixed success. The reasons for their limited successes are, of course, a matter of intense debate, as you will recall from the socialist calculation controversy described in Chapter 21.

Summary: Linear Relations   The use of linear mathematical systems, as exemplified by linear programming and input-output analysis, has been supported in critical ways by the invention and development of the computer. Greater capacity and increased speed of calculations have permitted the development of highly sophisticated econometric forecasting models of the economy (such as the St. Louis Federal Reserve model or the MIT models). Input-output matrices may now be manipulated and analyzed with hundreds of sectors, thanks to advanced computer technology. In addition, the concepts of linear programming and input-output theory have helped bridge the vast gap between the highly aggregative kind of Keynesian macroeconomic theory so popular in the precomputer age and the microeconomic principles of general-equilibrium theory.[6]

Total accuracy in predictions has, of course, been illusive. The quality of the "output" (predictions of GNP, employment, inflation, sectoral input re-

---

[6] There are, of course, differences between types of linear systems. Input-output analysis describes actual input-output situations using historical data. It then attempts to predict input requirements given demand alterations or economywide effects of specific input shortages. Linear programming, on the other hand, is most often a means of determining, a priori, one optimal strategy out of an array of optimal strategies given some predetermined goal, or "objective function." At this point, a look back at our discussion of Walras and general equilibrium in Chapter 16 provides an appreciation of the usefulness of mathematical and computer manipulation in linking his ideas to economywide calculations.

quirements, etc.) of even the most sophisticated computers is dependent upon the quality of the "input"—data derived from varied and sometimes dubious sources. Furthermore, it must be remembered that economics remains a *social* science which depends on human (and therefore not strictly predictable) behavior. Actual production and consumption relations, moreover, may not be strictly reducible to linear functions. In other words, economies or diseconomies may exist in production and consumption patterns in the real world. But these problems do not vitiate the usefulness of contemporary applications of the mathematical tools of algebra to economic questions. In most cases, some estimations are better than none at all, and estimates can usually be improved over time by better economic theory and intuition aided by better methods of calculation. Properly used, linear algebra is a powerful tool that can enlighten and enliven contemporary economic research.

Game Theory

One of the most interesting and robust tools of modern economic analysis is the technique called game theory. Game theory was applied initially to such topics as politics and military strategy, but many of its applications are of great help to economics. Although the idea was anticipated by Cournot (see Chapter 12), the formal origins of game theory are ascribed to John von Neumann, a mathematician, and Oskar Morgenstern, an economist, who set forth the formal theory in *The Theory of Games and Economic Behavior,* published in 1944.

Von Neumann and Morgenstern pointed out that Cournot's duopolists played a kind of "game" in that each had some independent *conjecture* about the other's output decision. One duopolist conjectured or believed that the other would hold output constant in the face of profit-maximizing adjustments in his or her own output. Given Cournot's assumptions, neither of the duopolists learned that this conjecture was unrealistic, so the outcome of the rivalry is that each seller shares the market equally and together produce a level of output in equilibrium equal to two-thirds the level of output that would be produced under conditions of competition output. (Actually, Cournot generalized the solution so that total output in his model always equals $n/(n + 1)$ times competitive output, where n is the number of sellers.)

Game theory employs the concept of behavioral conjectures, but it is less naive than Cournot's "game" because it considers the payoffs associated with alternative conjectures. Consider the following problem, which is attributed to the mathematician A. W. Tucker. Suppose that two kidnappers are caught in the act but that the FBI only has hard evidence to convict them for a lesser offense. In an attempt to improve their evidence, the FBI sequesters the prisoners separately and tries to get confessions from them in the following manner. Each kidnapper is separately informed that (1) if one confesses, the one that confesses goes free and the other gets the death penalty; (2) if neither confesses, both will receive the light penalty that accompanies the lesser crime;

(3) if both confess, both will receive a severe penalty but one less than death. Given the payoffs and the uncertainty, the expected solution is that both kidnappers confess to kidnapping.

This problem, which has come to be known as the "prisoner's dilemma," finds a direct analogy in many kinds of economic behavior. Consider one behavior that is observed from time to time by auto manufacturers—increasing the warranty period paid for by the manufacturer of new cars. Warranties are a method of making new cars more attractive to buyers, and they are often viewed as a type of oligopoly behavior. More extensive warranties, however, are costly to institute since they increase production costs and tend to reduce profits. Yet we often observe new and more inclusive warranties being offered by automakers on new cars. Such warranties are in the manufacturers' self-interest, and game theory helps explain why.

Figure 22-3 is a matrix that presents a hypothetical situation in which two auto manufacturers, Toyota and General Motors, are trying to maximize profits. Profits are shown as the dollar amounts in each grid. Toyota and General Motors could maximize joint profits in grid A where neither manufacturer provides extended warranties. Industry profits total $120 million dollars (GM earns $55 million; Toyota earns $65 million). Total profits are $100 million in grids B and C and $90 million in grid D. Acting independently, however, both General Motors and Toyota could make higher profits.

General Motors would maximize profits in grid B ($70 million) where it provides new warranty protection and its competitor does not. Consider the company's options. Regardless of Toyota's behavior, GM's profits are higher when it offers extended warranties. If GM offers a warranty and Toyota does not, its profit is $70 million. If it offers a warranty and Toyota does likewise, GM's profit drops to $40 million. However, if GM elects *not* to offer the warranty and Toyota does, GM's profit falls to $30 million. Toyota's management, assessing the possibilities, will reach the same conclusion, namely that it will always be better off by offering the warranty. Independent decisions to maximize profits by each firm will lead to the introduction of warranties. This means that the sum of profits between the two firms will be lower ($90 million) than it would have been if each firm did not offer warranties ($120 million). In other words, they are "prisoners" of a game.

While such behavior may benefit auto consumers at the expense of General Motors' and Toyota's stockholders, the problem for stockholders could be avoided if the manufacturers were allowed to communicate and to reach grid A in Figure 22-3. Communication in this case, as in the case of the prisoner's dilemma, would produce a different solution, but such collusion is usually prohibited by antitrust laws.

In the simple case illustrated in Figure 22-3, the game between General Motors and Toyota has a stable outcome, an equilibrium solution. In this simple case the participants minimize their opponents' maximum—what von Neumann and Morgenstern call a *minimax solution*. More complex games—those with more players and multiple strategies—may not result in stable equi-

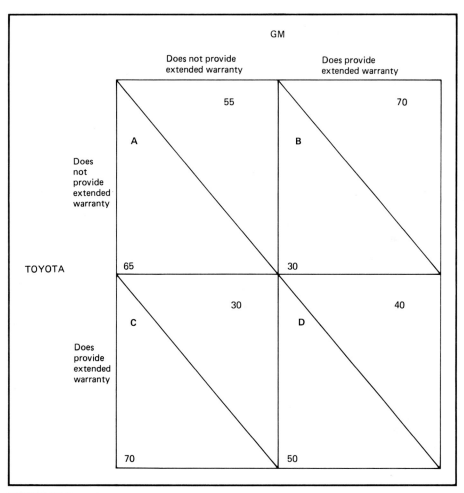

FIGURE 22-3
Automakers are depicted in a "game" to maximize profits. While they will earn lower total profits ($90 million) from doing so, game theory predicts that individual decisions on the part of both firms to maximize their profits will lead to the introduction of warranties.

libria. In treating the issue of stability of equilibrium, von Neumann and Morgenstern introduced a valuable concept: the principle of *convexity*. Convexity, which is a condition of stable equilibrium in game theory, allows two-dimensional graphical relations to be transformed into Euclidian *n*-space, which has promoted the analysis of economic behavior under less stringent and restrictive assumptions. One area in which this technique has provided an important breakthrough is in specifying the so-called core of an economic system, a concept invented by the neoclassical economist Francis Y. Edgeworth (1845–1926). In the context in which Edgeworth used the term, the "core" refers to the mathematical conditions of exchange in any exchange-based economy.

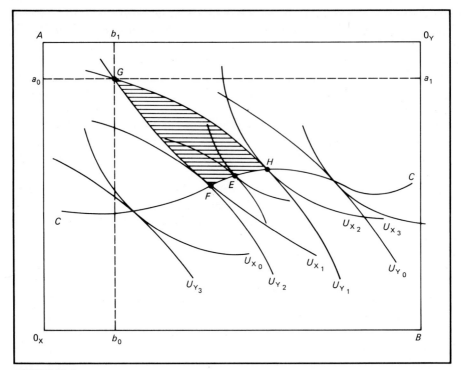

FIGURE 22-4
The box diagram displays the utility-maximizing possibilities of two traders, X and Y. Once the contracting parties reach the contract curve (*CC*), any improvement in the utility level of one of the parties must mean a reduction in that of the other party.

Contracting and the Core

The theory of utility invented by such writers as Jules Dupuit and W. S. Jevons (Chapters 12 and 14) provided the foundation for theoretical concepts that explain a central feature of an exchange economy: contracting. The theory of contracting that lies at the core of the economy is not a mathematical tool itself, but it has become a subject to which the most sophisticated tools of modern economics have been applied.

Edgeworth, who was a contemporary of Alfred Marshall (see Chapter 15), employed utilitarian ethics and (mathematical) utility theory to develop the notion of contracting. Figure 22-4, the Edgeworth box diagram, is a simplified description of Edgeworth's chief idea, although he was not the sole inventor of the "box" representation so often attributed to him.[7] At the heart of

---

[7] Claims of priority regarding the representation of core contracting in a "box" (as in Figure 22-4) have been disputed. Some argue for the priority of Arthur L. Bowley (1869–1957), who built on the work of Edgeworth and constructed a "Bowley box diagram." Others insist on joint priority by labeling the concept an "Edgeworth-Bowley box diagram." Still others credit the Italian

Edgeworth's contribution is the notion of an individual preference function, or "indifference curve." Underlying the preference function are the individual's calculations regarding the number and kind of trades that will maximize his or her utility.

Under perfectly competitive conditions any individual is free to recontract with anyone else in markets that contain large numbers of individuals. Edgeworth argued that "any individual is free to *contract* (simultaneously) with an indefinite number; e.g., any X (and similarly Y) may deal with any number of Y's" (*Mathematical Psychics,* p. 18). Recontracting does not require the consent of third parties, moreover, so that any individual is free to contract with another individual independently of a third party.

These and other fundamental principles translate into the important concept of the core of an exchange economy. In Figure 22-4 the preference functions, or indifference curves, of two contracting individuals, X and Y, are shown as $U_{X_0}, U_{X_1}, \ldots, U_{Xn}$ and $U_{Y_0}, U_{Y_1}, \ldots, U_{Yn}$ respectively. The origin for individual X is in the southwest corner of the box, while that of individual Y is "flipped over" and located in the northeast corner. Individuals X and Y are valuing alternative quantities of two goods or bundles of goods A and B. Along any *given* preference function, i.e., U_{X_0} or U_{Y_0}, each individual is indifferent between alternative quantities of A and B. The utility level along any indifference curve is constant—i.e., more A may substitute for less B, or vice versa. These curves are convex to the respective origins O_X and O_Y because of diminishing marginal rates of substitution. (A diminishing marginal rate of substitution implies that the amount of good A a consumer is willing to give up in order to acquire more good B decreases as he or she accumulates more B, and vice versa.) Indifference curves with higher-numbered subscripts indicate that the utility level of individuals X and Y would increase as they hold higher amounts of one or both of goods A and B. If quantities of commodities are infinitely divisible, as Edgeworth assumed, an indifference curve or preference function can be drawn between any two indifference curves.

In Figure 22-4 the total available quantities of A and B are given (and constitute the exact dimensions of the box) so that more A (B) for X means less $A(B)$ for Y, and vice versa. The goods or bundles of goods are distributed randomly so that production considerations are eliminated from the simple exchange economy described in Figure 22-4. As a next stage of the analysis, assume that individuals X and Y each receive an endowment of A and B, placing them at point G in Figure 22-4. Individual X holds quantity a_0 of good A and b_0 of B, while Y holds a_1 of A and b_1 of commodity B. At point G, individual X is

---

economist Vilfredo Pareto (1848–1923) with priority. We consider the debate largely academic since Edgeworth is the unchallenged inventor of the theory of contracting and its relation to the core. While not patterned as a "box," moreover, Edgeworth's own diagram (Figure 1, page 28, of *Mathematical Psychics*), and its related discussion, conveys the same information as that represented in Figure 22-4.

at a satisfaction level designated by preference function U_{X_1}, and Y is at satisfaction level U_{Y_1}. Note that at point G the indifference curves intersect.

The critical question addressed by Edgeworth is whether X and/or Y can reach higher levels of satisfaction (than that enjoyed at point G) through voluntary contracting. The model tells us that all contracts to trade A for B within the space GFH will improve the utility or satisfaction of either or both X and Y. A trade of B for A between X and Y which moves both individuals from point G to point F clearly improves Y's satisfaction without diminishing X's. Y moves to preference function U_{Y_2}, which is an increase in his or her utility; while X remains at utility level U_{X_1}, with no change in his or her satisfaction. A move from point G to point H would, contrariwise, improve X's satisfaction *without diminishing* Y's. Naturally, trades from G within these boundaries (the crosshatched area) will benefit both traders. Trades within these boundaries are said to be within the *core* of the economy.

The curve labeled CC in Figure 22-4 is called the *contract curve;* it connects all the points of tangency between preference functions X and Y. Once the contracting parties reach curve CC, any improvement in the utility level of one of the parties must mean a diminution in that of the other party. Edgeworth describes this line as one "along which the pleasure-forces of the contractors are mutually antagonistic" (*Mathematical Psychics*, p. 29). In terms of Figure 22-4, movements from point G to, say, point E will improve the lot of both traders, but once point E is attained, further trades will improve the utility of one party only at the expense of the other.[8]

Edgeworth recognized that the theory of core exchanges was central to economic theory. He also knew that contracting at the core did not necessarily lead to a *unique* competitive equilibrium in exchange (*Mathematical Psychics*, pp. 47–48). Rather, different initial positions and different constraints produce different solutions. When trading complications such as imperfect information between traders or the presence of third-party bargainers are introduced, solutions can become indeterminate. Some of the most complex and elaborate tools of mathematics have been applied to these issues. Tools such as game theory, set theory, and measure theory, which call into play fixed-point theorems and other forms of advanced mathematics, have all been used to analyze technical questions raised by Edgeworth's theory of the core. Indeed, several Nobel prizes, those of Kenneth J. Arrow in 1972 and Gerard Debreu in 1983, have been awarded for contributions related to this issue.

As mathematical tools, old and new, have influenced the direction of technical economic theory in the modern period, so have mathematics and statistics established a new area in contemporary economic inquiry. The aim of the

---

[8] The definition of market exchange as "Pareto optimal," i.e., a trade that improves one party's utility without reducing another party's utility, was clearly established by Edgeworth before Vilfredo Pareto investigated this central proposition of welfare economics. Pareto, a member of the "Lausanne school" founded by Léon Walras, did, however, translate Edgeworth's ideas into a general-equilibrium context.

inquiry is nothing less than to make economics "scientific," in the same way that the physical sciences are so regarded. This has induced more and more economists to emulate the successful techniques of the physical sciences. In other words, more and more emphasis has been placed on "testing" the validity of economic hypotheses.

EMPIRICAL ECONOMICS: THE TESTING OFECONOMIC THEORY

The modern field of empirical economics, or *econometrics,* broadly speaking, is the application of mathematical and statistical methods to economic data in order to verify and improve economic theory. Its object is both to explain and to predict economic behavior within the context of theory. Within the limits of statistical inference, econometrics attempts to test economic theory using historical data, and to forecast economic events utilizing a combination of economic theory and economic data.

Descriptive Statistics and Economic Theory: Origins

The attempt to enliven economic theory with real-world facts is centuries old. An interesting early example involves the efforts of the political arithmeticians of the late seventeenth and early eighteenth centuries to come to grips with quantitative data concerning gross national product, the balance of trade, consumer demand, and a variety of other subjects. One of the earliest and best-known illustrations of empirical economics comes from the researches on consumer demand of Gregory King and Charles Davenant. King established the empirical foundations of the inverse relationship between price and quantity purchased. This "law," which was refined considerably by Charles Davenant, appeared in Davenant's mercantilist treatise of 1699, *An Essay upon the Probable Methods of Making a People Gainers in the Balance of Trade.* Davenant's version of the demand law, which we now refer to as the "King-Davenant law of demand," is as follows:

> We take it, that a defect in the harvest may raise the price of corn in the following proportions:

Defect		Above the common rate
1 tenth		3 tenths
2 tenths	Raises	8 tenths
3 tenths	the price	1.6 tenths
4 tenths		2.8 tenths
5 tenths		4.5 tenths

> So that when corn rises to treble the common rate, it may be presumed that we want above ⅓ of the common produce; and if we should want ⁵⁄₁₀, or half the common produce, the price would rise to near five times the common rate (*Political and Commercial Works,* pp. 224–225).

King's actual statement of the demand relation was considerably less sophisticated, but it is clear that both writers drew upon observations of actual price and quantity behavior. Although this early attempt at estimating a statistical demand curve was naive and quite obviously simplistic, it nevertheless demonstrates the desire to establish economic theory on firm empirical foundations.

During the nineteenth century the field of descriptive statistics made great strides. Besides applications of statistical theory to such problems as population and public health, the technological revolution in transportation provided a backdrop for statistical investigations of a purely economic type. Early railway engineers from Europe and America attempted to identify cost data in order to assess the costs and benefits of particular railroads and proposed rail systems. The American engineer Charles Ellet (1810–1862), educated in Paris at the École des Ponts et Chaussées (the French School of Civil Engineering), is especially noteworthy in this regard. In contributions published between 1840 and 1844 (see Notes for Further Reading), Ellet attempted to determine a "predictive" total cost function for a "typical" American railroad. He did this by building up the constants in an equation for rail costs involving various components of rail expenses.

William Stanley Jevons (see Chapter 14) also advanced the subject of descriptive statistics in his famous essays of the 1860s on commercial fluctuations and on price series. Jevons improved the notion of index numbers and the nature of sampling techniques. But as S. M. Stigler has remarked, "Jevons' lack of use and development of probability-based statistical methods in his empirical work was typical of even the best efforts before the 1880s" ("Francis Ysidro Edgeworth, Statistician," p. 288). It was left for three other pioneers, Francis Galton, Karl Pearson, and Edgeworth, to develop the essential foundations of modern statistics. These writers developed the probabilistic basis for the more advanced statistical techniques of regression and related analyses, which form the foundation of modern statistics and econometrics.[9]

Regression analysis is an econometric tool commonly used by economists to gauge a relationship between a dependent variable and an independent variable, or set of independent variables. If one wished, for example, to study the effect of advertising expenditures upon the levels of concentration in some industry or set of industries, one might set up the following relationship:

$$C_i = B_0 + B_1 A_i + e_i \qquad (i = 1, \ldots, n)$$

where C_i is a measure of industrial concentration in some (ith) industry, B_0 is a constant, A_i is a measure of advertising intensity in the ith industry, and e_i is a catchall (error) term designed to capture discrepancies in the posited rela-

[9] Stephen M. Stigler, *The History of Statistics: The Measurement of Uncertainty before 1900* (Cambridge, Mass.: Harvard University Press, 1986), provides a complete chronicle of the formative period in statistics.

tionship. In this equation, C is the dependent variable (also called the regressand), and advertising intensity is the independent variable (also called the regressor). The B values, such as B_1, which measures the *strength* of the marginal effect of advertising intensity on concentration in this simple example, are estimated from data. (While B values may be estimated in a number of ways, the most common estimation procedure is called the method of least squares.)

Simple regression means that the regression equation contains only one independent variable, as shown in the above expression. In effect, our equation seeks to determine the impact of a one-unit change in advertising intensity upon industry concentration which, of course, could be positive or negative. The impact is measured by a *regression coefficient* (B), which is a number that contains two pieces of information. In addition to indicating whether the proposed relationship is positive or negative, it indicates how the dependent variable would change when the independent variable changes by one unit. This number, it must always be remembered, is only an *estimate* of the theorized cause-and-effect relation. In other words, the researcher employing this technique can never be entirely certain that the coefficient reflects the true relationship. He or she can be confident only that the estimate is correct within certain (probabilistic) intervals (i.e., a 5 percent confidence interval means that the technique will yield the correct answer 95 percent of the time.)

Other subtle issues often raise more complex statistical questions. Consider the simple relationship between concentration and advertising once again. If our theory is that advertising intensity causes concentration, can we be sure that a positive and significant B_1 coefficient is conclusive evidence of that result? Might it not be the case that industries that are more profitable can afford to advertise more, or that more profitable industries are more concentrated? Insofar as other variables may affect industrial concentration besides the one posited in a simple regression, econometricians most often test such theories with *multiple regression* techniques. Multiple regression includes more than one explanatory (independent) variable and is usually of the following general form:

$$Y_i = B_0 + B_1 X_{1_i} + B_2 X_{2_i} + \cdots + B_k X_{k_i} + e_i \qquad \text{where } i = 1,\ldots,n$$

This equation describes n observations and the relation between some dependent variable, Y, and k independent variables. Contemporary theoretical econometrics is concerned chiefly with the development of more powerful tools so that complex equations such as these can be better fit to the data. As indicated above, however, regression techniques are incapable of providing conclusive proof of selected hypotheses. We can never be 100 percent sure that an estimator captures true relationships. Nevertheless, econometrics can develop statistical techniques that add confidence to estimates.

The quest for improved technique has been a vital part of the development of econometrics. Early in the present century, certain key economists distinguished themselves in this respect. In Britain, G. U. Yule (1813–1886) pioneered economic and social science applications of statistics, whereas in the United States, Henry L. Moore (1869–1958) championed empirical methods in his studies of business cycles and agricultural production (see Notes for Further Reading). Moore was particularly influential in fostering a zeal for econometric studies among a number of important students, particularly Henry Schulz (1893–1938), whose *Theory and Measurement of Demand* (1938) became an early classic.

Econometrica and Modern Econometrics

While the empirical nature of economic theory was the subject of much attention in the late nineteenth and early twentieth centuries, the formal beginnings of econometric research as a distinctive (and somewhat separate) field of economics may be traced to 1933. In that year an international coterie of scholars founded the Econometric Society and inaugurated the journal *Econometrica,* which is dedicated to the pursuit of empirical economics. A distinguished international group of economists made up the society's charter membership. Harold Hotelling (1895–1973), a prominent American economist and statistician, and Ragnar Frisch (1895–1973), a Norwegian economist who won the Nobel Prize in Economic Science in 1969, were among the founders. The society and its journal have supported research for more than half a century on the theory and method of testing economic ideas. On occasion, inadequate methods have been attacked (e.g., Frisch presented devastating early critiques of measurement errors). At the same time, new and superior testing tools have been generated (e.g., the development of probabilistic rationalizations of regression analysis and the use of probabilities to develop maximum-likelihood estimation methods). These developments continue to the present day, not only in the first of the econometric journals, but also in a number of later journals which have appeared in the wake of *Econometrica*'s success.

CONCLUSION: DIRECTIONS AND DANGERS OF FORMALIZATION AND TESTING OF ECONOMIC THEORY

No abbreviated survey of mathematical and empirical techniques could possibly do justice to the full range of their use in modern economics. Virtually no area of modern microeconomic or macroeconomic theory has remained untouched by mathematical methods. Mathematical and econometric tools have permeated the microeconomic subfields of labor, public finance, and antitrust and government regulation, to name a few. Macroeconomic model building and forecasting of national income and employment would be inconceivable without such tools. Courses in mathematics and econometrics form the basis of most graduate curricula at major and minor universities around the world. Few could read and fully understand research in most general economic journals without command of these tools.

Historians of economic thought are in a unique position to address critical questions related to these ongoing developments. A meaningful evaluation must rest on the costs and benefits, the advantages and deficiencies, of this development as it relates to some conception of *progress* in economics. The chief argument for continued formalization (i.e., mathematization) of economics is that the discipline cannot become truly scientific until it attains the rigor and completeness of science—in other words, until its fundamental propositions have been tested and proved. Theory without verification (or potential verification) is of limited usefulness. Facts without theory forged in the logic of mathematics are meaningless. Mainstream economists argue, therefore, that increased respect for economics as a separate, scientific discipline will only come from the steady application of rigorous mathematical and statistical tools.

Some critics have strong reservations concerning this view. They argue that the nature of social science, of which economics is a part, makes exact formulation and verification impossible. Some of the central problems of contemporary econometrics relate to inexact or incomplete formalizations of economic theory and to various insufficiencies in data samples and in the random errors inherent to the measurement of variables. Modern econometric techniques are, generally speaking, most appropriate when data samples are large; yet in many instances, large-sample data do not exist. Thus, the quantities and *qualities* of economic data are often insufficient to the task. In contrast to conditions in the physical and natural sciences, the collection of most economic data is not predetermined or predesigned to fit tests of economic theory. Indeed, most economic data are collected by government agencies for far less specific purposes, often for purely political reasons. While inadequate theory and poor data are not sufficient reasons in themselves to reject quantitative methods, some critics argue that the design costs and the collection costs necessary to secure high-quality data are prohibitive.

Numerous critics, especially neo-Austrian and institutional economists, argue that the attempt to make economics a science through mathematical formalization and empirical verification is illusory. In the opinion of these critics, the fruits of decades-long intellectual investment in mathematical and statistical techniques have been small, if not negative. According to this argument, these futile attempts at rendering economics scientific has engendered widespread distrust of the economic pronouncements of policymakers and an almost total breakdown in communication between economists and other social scientists. Even worse, mathematics and calculation in the hands of those equipped with tools but no ideas can lead economists away from the basic truths about markets and market functioning. The march to socialism, so the argument goes, is likely to be led by "calculators" who have no practical understanding of how real-world markets function. In this view, mathematics inevitably diverts attention away from the basic truths of the economic process developed by Adam Smith.

There is, moreover, a persistent danger that antiseptic and highly technical analysis tends to be self-perpetuating. Those who have made heavy human-capital investments in mathematical and econometric techniques have a strong incentive to perpetuate the "mystique of the cognoscenti" despite the general failure of these lines of inquiry to achieve much progress. Moreover, the formalization of economics can too often lead to the erection of entry barriers in academics, whereby graduate curriculum requirements, university hiring standards, journal editorial policies, and professional recognition all hinge on the mastery and application of mathematical and empirical techniques. Some observers believe that the cultivation of technique for technique's sake has fostered an environment wherein intellectual fads readily come and go. The "shelf life" of such fads is often notoriously short. As soon as today's new technique fails to live up to the unrealistic expectations placed upon it, it falls out of favor, only to grease the skids for a new fad to replace it. Economists who indulge in the latest fad run the risk of becoming obsolete. Worse yet, the ongoing process tends to drive a wedge between those who regard economics as a powerful, though somewhat imprecise, behavioral science and those who regard the discipline as a branch of applied mathematics. According to some skeptics, the very survival of economics will ultimately require a formal split between the "economists" and the "mathematicians."

There is some recent evidence of a slowdown in the production of formal mathematical articles that find their way into the economic literature (Debreu, "Mathematical Economics," Figure 1, p. 401).[10] Furthermore, there is a growing awareness of the dangers of technical pursuits as substitutes for the study of economics. Some skepticism is undoubtedly healthy, and yet the complete or substantial abandonment of mathematical formalization would be a bigger mistake than its uncritical acceptance. Economists, of all people, must avoid this pitfall because they, more than other scientists, deal with quantities *at the margin*. An appreciation of the limits to mathematics and econometric technique fosters an understanding of their correct and useful place in economic science. So long as these limits are understood, the value of mathematics and econometrics in formulating and testing economic *ideas* is very great. No science is perfect, and perfect truth, as Protagoras told us long ago, is always elusive, whether it is sought in physics, astronomy, microbiology, or economics. Mathematical and statistical tools, properly used, can reduce ambiguity and raise or lower confidence in new *and* old economic ideas. The problem facing today's economists is to capture the benefits of mathematical formalization without making economics moribund or irrelevant—the ultimate potential cost.

NOTES FOR FURTHER READING

Introduction to the vast literature of economics containing formalized mathematics and econometrics must begin with the learning of the essentials of these

---

[10] Indeed Debreu warns of the "seductiveness" of mathematical tools whereby researchers "may be tempted to forget economic content and to shun economic problems that are not readily amenable to mathematization" (p. 403).

areas. Although several basic texts contain excellent treatments of mathematical economics, the following two are especially noteworthy and useful to the upper-division or first-year graduate student: Alpha Chiang, *Fundamental Methods of Mathematical Economics* (New York: McGraw-Hill, 1967), and Akira Takayama, *Mathematical Economics* (Cambridge: Cambridge University Press, 1985). Those interested in basic calculus applied to consumer demand should master the mathematical appendix to Hicks's *Value and Capital* (see References). Similarly, those seeking an introduction to econometrics should, along with mastery of a basic statistics course, find the following work very useful: G. S. Maddala, *Introduction to Econometrics* (New York: Macmillan, 1988), and Domodar Gujarati, *Basic Econometrics,* 2d ed. (New York: McGraw-Hill, 1988). For a historical approach to the subject that makes use of previously unknown manuscript material, see R. J. Epstein, *A History of Econometrics* (Amsterdam: North-Holland, 1987).

Early works in mathematical economics and statistics (the handmaiden of modern econometric techniques) tended to be isolated contributions until the late nineteenth and early twentieth centuries. The most cited example of an early empirical statement of demand is the King-Davenant law of demand, but both the priorities of the two writers and the quality of their statements have been debated. Two papers, one published and one unpublished, deal with these issues: John Creedy, "On the King-Davenant 'Law' of Demand" (unpublished manuscript; see References), and A. M. Endres, "The King-Davenant 'Law' in Classical Economics," *History of Political Economy,* vol. 19 (Winter 1987), pp. 621–638. See also A. M. Endres, "The Functions of Numerical Data in the Writings of Graunt, Petty, and Davenant," *History of Political Economy,* vol. 17 (Summer 1985), pp. 245–264.

The splendid work of Cournot is graced not only by his contributions to mathematical economics, but also by a treatise on probabilities. Theocharis (see References) provides good coverage of mathematical economics in its infancy. Those interested in early attempts by engineers to measure cost functions should consult the papers of Charles Ellet, "Cost of Transportation on Railways," in *Journal of the Franklin Institute of the State of Pennsylvania* (September, December 1842; November 1943). Also see R. B. Ekelund, Jr., "Economic Empiricism in the Writing of Early Railway Engineers," *Explorations in Economic History,* vol. 9 (Winter 1971), pp. 179–196.

W. S. Jevons, *Investigations in Currency and Finance,* H. S. Foxwell (ed.) (London: Macmillan, 1909), provides a starting point for the "middle" period of mathematico-statistical writings in economics. But pride of place should go to Edgeworth. In addition to his *Mathematical Psychics,* Edgeworth produced an enormous literature, largely published in the *Economic Journal,* devoted to the application of mathematical tools to index numbers, theories of taxation, the theory of monopoly and price discrimination, and theories of economic welfare. Many, but not all, of these are contained in Edgeworth's *Papers Relating to Political Economy,* 3 vols. (London: Macmillan, 1925). The birth of modern statistics in the writings of Galton, Pearson, and Edgeworth is detailed by S. M. Stigler, *The History of Statistics: The Measurement of Uncertainty before 1900* (Cambridge, Mass.: Harvard University Press, 1986). Stigler takes his readers on a journey strewn with multiple attempts to obtain improved measurement in fields as diverse as astronomy, psychology, heredity, and the social sciences. The book reads like a well-crafted mystery story, in which Stigler demonstrates how the development of modern tools of correlation and regression analysis, which required sound analyses of probability and measurements of uncertainty, were remarkably slow in flowering. The key figures in the drama, as Stigler shows, were Francis Galton, Karl Pearson, and, most importantly, F. Y. Edgeworth.

Henry L. Moore, the American pioneer in statistics and econometrics, made several important contributions, e.g., "The Statistical Complement of Pure Economics," *Quarterly Journal of Economics,* vol. 23 (November 1908), pp. 1–33; *Generating Economic Cycles* (New York: Macmillan, 1923); and *Synthetic Economics* (New York: Macmillan, 1929). See George J. Stigler, "Henry L. Moore and Statistical Economics," in *Essays in the History of Economics* (Chicago: University of Chicago Press, 1965), for more details on Moore's place in the history of mathematical economics.

The foundations for the mathematics of linear programming were established by the great mathematician John von Neumann in the 1920s and 1930s and brought to fruition by George B. Danzig in his work entitled *Programming in a Linear Structure* (Washington, D.C.: U.S.A.F., 1948). For an analysis of linear programming applied to economic analysis, see R. Dorfman, P. A. Samuelson, and R. M. Solow, *Linear Programming and Economic Analysis* (New York: McGraw-Hill, 1958).

Prior to his book-length contribution to input-output analysis mentioned in this chapter, Wassily Leontief published the elements of his famous idea in an article entitled "Quantitative Input-Output Relations in the Economic System of the United States," *Review of Economics and Statistics,* vol. 18 (August 1936), pp. 105–25. This complicated topic was made more accessible by William H. Miernyk, *The Elements of Input-Output Analysis* (New York: Random House, 1965). Miernyk not only clearly develops the analytical principle involved, but also shows how to apply it in regional, interregional, and international contexts, concluding his discussion with a lucid review of the mathematics required by the technique (e.g., matrices and determinants). Chiousshuang Yan, *Introduction to Input-Output Economics* (New York: Holt, Rinehart and Winston, 1969), is another useful source on the subject.

Besides the classic work by von Neumann and Morgenstern, Martin Shubik, in *Game Theory in the Social Sciences, Concepts and Solutions* (Cambridge, Mass.: MIT Press, 1982) and *A Game Theoretic Approach to Political Economy* (Cambridge, Mass.: MIT Press, 1984), outlines the many applications of game theory, actual and potential.

Edgeworth's theory of the core, and its importance in modern economic theory, is set forth in lucid fashion by Peter Newman in *The New Palgrave* (see References), and on a more technical plane, in *The Theory of Exchange* (Englewood Cliffs, N.J.: Prentice-Hall, 1965). See also John Creedy,

Edgeworth and the Development of Neoclassical Economics (Oxford: Basil Blackwell, 1986).

Students who wish to learn more about a particular mathematical technique or about the application of mathematics to a particular area of economic theory might profitably consult *The New Palgrave: A Dictionary of Economics* (see References). In general, the entries provide readable, nontechnical introductions to particular subject areas written by specialists (and sometimes by the pioneers themselves). Another excellent basic source on such matters is William Baumol, *Economic Theory and Operations Analysis,* 4th ed. (Englewood Cliffs, N.J.: Prentice-Hall, 1977). Baumol's chapter-length treatments of such subjects as game theory and linear programming, not to mention his succinct statements of the mathematical concepts used in developing them, are masterpieces of clarity and brevity. Those in search of shorthand definitions of terms and concepts used in mathematical economics should consult W. A. Skrapek, B. M. Korkie, and T. E. Daniel, *Mathematical Dictionary for Economics and Business Administration* (Boston: Allyn and Bacon, 1976).

REFERENCES

Cournot, Augustin. *Researches into the Mathematical Principles of the Theory of Wealth,* N. T. Bacon (trans.). New York: A. M. Kelley, 1960 [1838].

Creedy, John. "On the King-Davenant 'Law' of Demand," unpublished manuscript. University of Durham, 1985.

Davenant, Charles. *The Political and Commercial Works of That Celebrated Writer Charles D'Avenant, Relating to the Trade and Revenue of England,* collected and revised by Sir Charles Whitworth in five volumes, vol. II. London: Farnborough Gregg, 1967.

Debreu, Gerard. "Mathematical Economics," in *The New Palgrave: A Dictionary of Economics,* John Eatwell, Murray Milgate, and Peter Newman (eds.), vol. 3, pp. 399–404. London: Macmillan, 1987.

Edgeworth, F. Y. *Mathematical Psychics: An Essay on the Application of Mathematics to the Moral Sciences.* London: Kegan Paul, 1881.

Hicks, J. R. *Value and Capital.* Oxford: Oxford University Press, 1939.

———, and R. G. D. Allen. "A Reconsideration of the Theory of Value," *Economica,* vol. 1 (February, May 1934), pp. 52–76, 196–219.

Leontief, Wassily. *The Structure of the American Economy: 1919–1929.* Oxford: Oxford University Press, 1941.

———. "Input-Output Analysis," in *The New Palgrave: A Dictionary of Economics,* John Eatwell, Murray Milgate, and Peter Newman (eds.), vol. 2. London: Macmillan, 1987, pp. 860–864.

Maurice, S. C., and C. W. Smithson. *Managerial Economics.* Homewood, Ill.: Irwin, 1981.

Newman, Peter. "Francis Ysidro Edgeworth," in *The New Palgrave: A Dictionary of Economics,* John Eatwell, Murray Milgate, and Peter Newman (eds.), vol. 2. London: Macmillan, 1987, pp. 84–98.

Pesaran, M. Hashem. "Econometrics," in *The New Palgrave: A Dictionary of Eco-*

nomics, John Eatwell, Murray Milgate, and Peter Newman (eds.), vol. 2. London: Macmillan, 1987, pp. 8–22.

Samuelson, P. A. *Foundations of Economic Analysis.* Cambridge, Mass.: Harvard University Press, 1947.

Schultz, Henry. *The Theory and Measurement of Demand.* Chicago: University of Chicago Press, 1938.

Stigler, Stephen M. "Francis Ysidro Edgeworth, Statistician," *Journal of the Royal Statistical Society,* ser. A, vol. 141 (1978), pp. 287–322.

Theocharis, Reghinos D. *Early Developments in Mathematical Economics,* 2d ed. Philadelphia: Porcupine Press, 1983.

von Neumann, John, and Oskar Morgenstern. *Theory of Games and Economic Behavior.* Princeton, N.J.: Princeton University Press, 1944.

MODERN
MICROECONOMICS:
A RICH AND
MOVABLE FEAST

INTRODUCTION

Static microeconomics in the traditions of Marshall and Walras have enjoyed and still enjoy great prestige in modern economic theory. These traditions emphasize microeconomic and macroeconomic behavior within an equilibrium framework. In recent decades, economists have ventured beyond the standard neoclassical theory of competition into such "new" realms as the nature of market disequilibrium, the development of modern public-choice theory, and the reevaluation of the theories of regulation and industrial organization.

Microeconomic theory in particular has brimmed over with new insights and applications. Although contemporary microeconomics is firmly rooted in static Marshallian principles, it has added new analytical twists. Much of this modern development can be ascribed to what might be termed a "Chicago" school of thought, led over the past three decades mainly by economists George Stigler (b. 1911) and Gary Becker (b. 1930). Marshall, it might be recalled, made many important simplifying assumptions respecting markets. Specifically, he abstracted from quality differences in products, costly consumer information, the costs of time forgone in consuming and producing goods, and the locations of sellers and buyers. The new twists of contemporary microeconomic theory consist of (1) providing a formal analysis of how market outcomes change when we relax these and other simplifying Marshallian assumptions about consumers and firms and (2) applying these new tools to interesting and novel questions that were previously thought to be beyond the purview of the economist (e.g., crime, drug use, family relations, and so on).

This chapter reviews a small sample of these new developments in economic theory. These new developments serve as examples of how past ideas

611

continually shape present and future ideas. Novel tools are emerging to address modern problems, but such tools are usually refinements of earlier principles discovered in the classical and neoclassical periods. For example, the new theory of household production pioneered by Gary Becker rests on the principles of utility maximization established by Jevons, Menger, and Walras. Further extensions of earlier theories of costs and benefits have resulted in an economic theory of marriage, child rearing, and crime. Like other scientists, economists build the present and the future on the contributions of the past.

CONSUMPTION TECHNOLOGY: MODERN VIEWS

Traditional neoclassical microeconomics imposes a distinct cleavage between producers and consumers, whereas contemporary microeconomics treats the cleavage as an oversimplification of the process by which goods are purchased and consumed.

The Household as a Factory

Following Gary Becker, many modern economists regard the household as analogous to a small factory that "combines capital goods, raw materials and labour to clean, feed, procreate and otherwise produce useful commodities" (Becker, "A Theory of the Allocation of Time," p. 496). The individual neoclassical consumer becomes part of both household production and consumption in this broader approach. Most importantly, contemporary analysis recognizes that the production and consumption of goods (children are sometimes regarded as consumer goods in Becker's model) *take time*. Time is an opportunity cost that must be calculated along with the market prices of any good or activity in making economic decisions. Earlier economists (e.g., Senior, Böhm-Bawerk, Marshall) also understood the nature of time as both a resource and a constraint, but their concepts were sometimes vague and never fully integrated into mainstream economic theory.

Figure 23-1 gives a schematic view of the combination of market goods and time necessary to produce ultimate goods or services ("commodities"). Just as it takes inputs of human resources, capital, and time to bring children to adulthood, the production and consumption of any ultimate good or service may be viewed as combining inputs to consume an output. If we identify an *ultimate* good consumed by an individual, such as "healthful behavior," we see that the production of such a good requires the combination of numerous "market goods" (those purchased directly by consumers in the marketplace) and time inputs. Athletic equipment, health foods of all sorts, medical services, and time spent in doing exercises and in consuming goods are all *inputs* in a process that yields the ultimate good. The individual or the household transforms these inputs into outputs through a production function.

Ultimate consumption is therefore a function of both market goods and time inputs. Since it takes time to see a play, read a book, or consume a meal, the

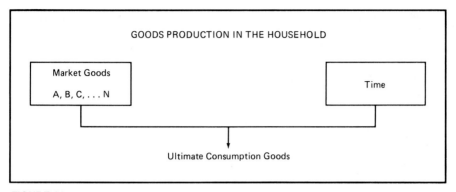

FIGURE 23-1
The household as a miniature factory combines market goods and time to produce ultimate consumption goods.

full price of these activities must include the opportunity cost of using time to engage in these consumption activities. The measurement of this opportunity cost can be approximated by the market wage of the individual under consideration. Assume, for example, that an individual who can make $10 an hour in market work is choosing between a restaurant meal which takes an hour and a "fast-food" meal which takes 15 minutes. Assume further that the money cost of both meals is $6. While both meals require the same money outlay, the full price of consumption differs substantially. The full price of the fast-food meal is $8.50 ($6 plus $2.50 in forgone income) versus $16 for the restaurant meal ($6 plus $10 in forgone income). The determining factor in the individual's final decision will be the amount of utility each meal produces per (full-cost) dollar of expenditure.

This approach also has the benefit of highlighting the full costs of household production. The value of household production—producing and raising children, performing household chores and maintenance activities, etc.—may also be expressed in terms of opportunity costs. Also, when the cost of time is placed on an equal footing with the cost of market goods, new insights into the traditional choice between work and leisure (now a choice between market work, leisure, and household production) and new views of the consumption patterns of households in terms of both quantity and quality are made possible.

The implications of the new consumer theory are expressed in the following examples. As earnings from market work rise (with equal reductions in other income), the opportunity cost of in-home productions rises, and we expect to see more goods and less time used in household production. In general, the development and widespread use of time-reducing appliances may be explained partly by this phenomenon. Greater use of child-care services, outside contracting for household services, and the emergence of condominiums and other low-maintenance housing (and lawn care) arrangements are all related to wage and earnings increases over time.

Another implication of this new theory of consumer behavior involves *patterns* of consumption. As family incomes rise, goods-intensive commodities and activities tend to be substituted for time-intensive ones. There is, in effect, a bias against time-intensive production and consumption within the household produced by economic growth. The development of time-saving devices and products is, in some measure, a reflection of the increased opportunity cost of time-intensive consumptions. The decline of time-intensive "gourmet" cooking and the substitution of high- (and increasing) quality frozen foods and take-out meals, all suitable for time-saving microwave cooking, are a manifestation of the effect that Becker emphasizes.

Many modern inventions are successful because they permit substitutions which allow people to economize by reallocating time-intensive consumptions. The growth of airline travel, portable computers, videotape recorders, and "talking" books (on cassettes) provide everyday examples. In other words, not only do households combine market goods and time inputs as raw materials (e.g., a piano, printed music, and piano lessons) to produce ultimate goods (e.g., music appreciation), but the *proportions* in which they are combined change over time as market wage rates and incomes change.[1]

Household Production

More complex contemporary theories of consumer behavior permit many new evaluations of hitherto unexplained behavior by individuals and by households. For many years, household production by individuals, male or female, such as housekeeping and child care, was routinely and implicitly left out of economic analysis. The usual choice examined was the simple and straightforward one between market work and leisure. When an individual was not engaged in a market job, he or she was enjoying leisure, analytically speaking. The problem with such an unrealistic scenario is that it assigns no value to household work.

In 1977 Reuben Gronau (b. 1937) provided a choice-theoretic framework for analyzing decisions between leisure, market (out-of-home) work, and home production.[2] Gronau questioned the implicit assumption of the traditional work-leisure tradeoff, namely that the productivity of market work is always greater than the productivity of home work, or equivalently, that the market wage always exceeds the implicit return to housework. Figure 23-2 depicts the issues that Gronau examined. In this diagram, time is measured on the horizontal axis and the quantity of all goods (i.e., tangible and intangible output,

---

[1] The assumption of taste stability is examined within the framework of a household production function by George Stigler and Gary Becker in their paper *"De Gustibus Non Est Disputandum"* (see References). In addition, Stigler and Becker give form to their concept by investigating the implications of taste stability for "addictions," custom and tradition, advertising, fashions, and fads.

[2] "Leisure, Home Production, and Work—The Theory of the Allocation of Time Revisited," *Journal of Political Economy.*

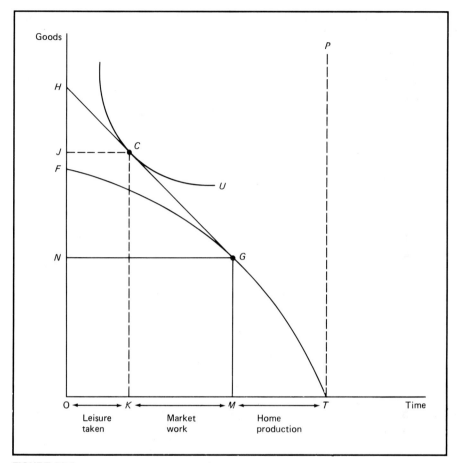

FIGURE 23-2
When goods produced in the home are given economic value, the home producer will
ordinarily allocate effort among three activities: home production, market work, and leisure.

leisure, etc.) is measured on the vertical axis. The function FT describes how
individuals may transform resources from the production of goods to the production of leisure and/or household services. The distance from O to T is the
total time available. Time spent in leisure activities is measured in a rightward
direction from the origin O, whereas time spent in home production plus market work is measured in a leftward direction from point T. The difference between the total available time and the sum of the time spent on leisure and
home production is the amount of market-work time engaged in. In this model,
child care and housecleaning are equivalent to BMWs, haircuts, or stereo TVs.

In Figure 23-2 the slope of the home-production transformation curve FGT
measures the marginal productivity of time spent in home production versus
leisure. Neglecting for a moment the other aspects of the diagram, consider the

vertical line *PT*. As traditional theory had it, the tradeoff facing the individual between leisure and home production is always such that only leisure is chosen. Therefore, the slope of *PT* is everywhere greater than the slope of the transformation curve *FGT*. In traditional theory, then, the individual never devotes time to home production, because such time is not given value in the individual's choice set. Consequently, the return to market work always dominates the return to home production. By contrast, the contemporary approach to this problem allows time *TM* devoted to home production to produce *ON* "goods" in terms of housekeeping, child care, and so on.

Insofar as additional time devoted to home production will yield diminishing marginal productivity, the curve *FGT* is concave to the origin at *O*. (The marginal product of each additional hour devoted to home production declines.) Whether an individual will engage in market work depends upon the marginal return to market work versus home production. When, at some point, the marginal return to market work (expressed as a wage rate) exceeds that of home production, the individual undertakes some market work. In terms of Figure 23-2, this occurs when the individual faces the wage rate represented by line *HG*. Given the tradeoff between leisure and *all* work (market and home production) represented by the preference function *U* in Figure 23-2, the individual chooses *OK* in leisure time and *KT* in *total* work time, *KM* of which is devoted to market work and *MT* devoted to home production.

Insofar as Gronau's model stresses the fact that time imposes a costly constraint on human behavior, it marks a new departure from traditional neoclassical analysis. However, its conclusions rest on several simplifying assumptions. For example, it implicitly assumes that individuals are able to choose freely the number of hours devoted to market work. We all know that, in the short run at least, this may not be true. The fixed-period, eight-hour workday is standard operating procedure in most western countries and in most types of jobs. Nevertheless, the very existence of this rigidity implies that other market adjustments are likely. Thus we find twenty-four-hour grocery stores and other similar accommodations that allow workers to make partial adjustments to the time and productivity constraints that they face. Such marketing innovations allow workers to have more flexibility in making decisions and thereby achieve higher levels of utility in scheduling combinations of leisure, home production, and market activity.

Information and Search

The modern theory of consumption technology has let another genie out the bottle. In a Marshallian world, consumers are assumed to be immediately aware, at zero cost, of any price differences in a given market for a given product. By buying low and selling high, they will drive market price to a single value. One price for a product will prevail when a perfectly competitive market is in equilibrium.

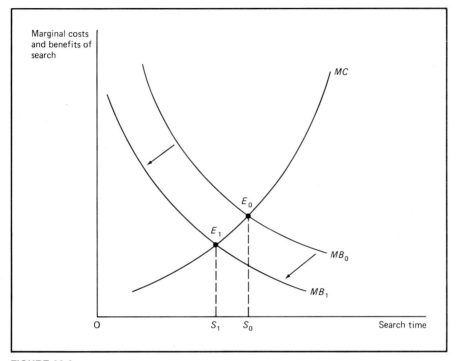

FIGURE 23-3
Advertising in its role as information reduces optimal search time spent acquiring goods and servicing.

In 1961 George J. Stigler (b. 1911) enlarged and developed the argument that information is an economic good which is costly to produce and obtain.[3] For example, when gas stations put up signs with prices on them, an act of producing information, they must pay for the construction of the signs, including raw materials and labor. Furthermore, consumers must spend valuable time (and other resources) looking for the prices that are posted. Since information concerning prices is costly to produce and obtain in most markets, transaction prices will be "dispersed" (more than one price) for the same commodity *even when the market is in equilibrium.*

A Simple Information Model   Figure 23-3 provides a framework for understanding the economics of information. The marginal cost to the consumer of searching for a lower price for some particular good or service is represented by *MC* in Figure 23-3. Since additional search is typically more and more costly, *MC* rises over time. If you are in the market for a used car, for example, the marginal cost of search can be thought of as the costs of visiting and

---

[3] "The Economics of Information," *Journal of Political Economy.*

negotiating with one or more used-car dealers. The level of the MC curve will naturally vary across goods. It will be low, for example, when shopping for clothes by mail-order catalog, but it will be high when searching for a new home.

The marginal benefit curve (MB_0) depicts the marginal benefit to the consumer of searching for a lower price. As the consumer checks the prices of more and more sellers, the prospect of finding a lower price from the next seller declines, and so MB_0 declines as search time increases. The marginal benefits of additional search will also vary across markets. For example, it ordinarily pays the consumer to search longer for a lower price when the good in question is a high-ticket item (e.g., consumer durables, such as houses, refrigerators, and automobiles), but it will usually not pay to search widely for a lower price of toothpicks or chewing gum. Generally, the larger the share of the consumer's budget represented by any one expenditure, the greater the benefit of longer search, i.e., the further to the northeast the MB_0 curve will locate in Figure 23-3.

The consumer will search until the marginal cost (MC_0) of search equals the marginal benefit (MB_0) of search. This coincides with the point of optimal or efficient search, shown by point E_0 in Figure 23-3. At levels of marginal cost and benefit to the left of point E_0 (ignore point E_1 and curve MB_1 for the moment), the extra benefits of more search exceed the extra costs. To the right of point E_0, the marginal costs of search exceed the marginal benefits. Point E_0 represents the correct or equilibrium amount of search for a given consumer for some particular good or service. Consumers employ such optimal search procedures in their shopping behavior, not so much in the rigid fashion of the diagram, but in an intuitive, instinctive manner. Since point E will not be the same for all consumers for all products or services, the fact that information about prices is costly to produce and to obtain means that in most markets there will be a dispersion of final transaction prices and not a single price for a product at all locations.[4] Again, as stressed in earlier examples, this line of reasoning recognizes time as part of the *full cost* of consuming goods and services.

A New Role for Advertising Neoclassical writers such as Marshall (see Chapter 15), and even post-Marshallians such as Chamberlin (see Chapter 18), when not overtly critical of advertising in a market economy, at least deemphasized or ignored advertising. Static, competitive models that assume perfect information regard advertising as wasteful and/or unnecessary. In contrast, the new economics of search provides a rational explanation for the ex-

---

[4] Common sense and personal experience support the idea of search costs. The following experiment may be conducted in any community. Collect the prices for a single product of a particular quality such as a specific brand and size of aspirin or toothpaste at six or seven different stores. An array of prices will likely be observed across locations, which is a result consistent with Stigler's thesis. Real-cost differences to consumers may therefore provide a plausible explanation for different *money* prices of a particular good or service.

istence of advertising. In the new microeconomics advertising is a low-cost means of producing information. We have seen that gathering information is costly in terms of time forgone and that time has an implicit value. In the simplest of terms, advertising saves the consumer time in his or her effort to acquire information about prices or qualities of products.

Consider an example whereby the marginal cost of an additional hour of search is rising along curve MC_0 in Figure 23-3. An additional search of one hour requires that the individual give up utility in the form of time forgone. The curve MB_0 represents the marginal benefit to search (i.e., information gained), assuming that the consumer knows nothing about existing prices. Optimal search time is therefore S_0 for this consumer.

Suppose, alternatively, that the consumer originally had knowledge of some (but not all) prices charged by some sellers and that the information was obtained through newspaper advertising. With such information already in his or her possession, the consumer cannot expect to find price differentials as large through search as in the former instance in which no price information was had firsthand. Therefore, the additional benefit to any given amount of search (in terms of finding price reductions) is less in the case where the consumer starts with some price information. Marginal benefits to search in the second case may be depicted as MB_1, reflecting the fact that for any given amount of search time, additional benefits to search are less if consumers have some information ahead of time. The existence of advertising reduces the amount of time consumers spend in searching for lower prices. If consumers spend less time searching for lower prices, they necessarily have more time left to devote to other, more desirable activities such as earning income from market work, producing goods at home, or enjoying leisure.

There are, in effect, two sacrifices involved in consuming most goods: (1) the money price of the good and (2) the value of time forgone in search and other transactions costs. Together these elements constitute the full price of any good or service. In the informed modern view, advertising economizes on search time and therefore lowers the full price of goods and services.[5]

Demand Theory Innovations

Marshallian demand theory assumes that consumers purchase goods and services that are desired directly for their utility. As we have seen, this approach has been modified by more recent developments. Thus, the household is viewed now as purchasing combinations of market goods *and* time to produce more ultimate and desirable commodities. A separate, but related, new devel-

---

[5] In his important contribution to this topic, Phillip Nelson (see References) distinguishes between "search" goods (those whose characteristics are readily determined before purchase) and "experience" goods (those whose characteristics are primarily determined after purchase). The theory of consumer search for low prices and advertising as information is also used by Nelson to explain quality discovery by consumers.

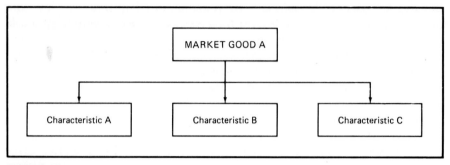

FIGURE 23-4
Modern demand theory emphasizes that individuals do not demand market goods per se, but
the characteristics and attributes provided by market goods.

opment in modern demand theory emphasizes the attributes of goods and services rather than the good or service itself. This new perspective holds that
consumers do not demand market goods for the direct utility provided by the
good or service itself, but for the utility derived from certain combinations of
utility-producing *characteristics*. This feature of demand is represented graphically in Figure 23-4, where a single market good (*A*) produces multiple characteristics or joint dimensions (*X, Y,...*, *N* characteristics).

The demand for characteristics is well known to most consumers. Most
goods are capable of satisfying utility on the basis of several different dimensions. For example, individuals purchase automobiles for reasons other than
mere transportation—prestige, status, and other psychological motives usually
are involved also. A Porsche produces these characteristics in different proportions than a small economy car, which, in turn, produces characteristics in
different proportions than a large Cadillac or Lincoln sedan. The point, commonly attributed to Kelvin Lancaster (b. 1924),[6] is that consumers actually demand jointly produced characteristics rather than products or services themselves.

This new approach has some clear advantages over the traditional Marshallian analysis of demand. For example, it provides a basis for examining goods
that are obviously related but that cannot be compared easily (or at all) in standard theory. Motorcycles, bicycles, subways, buses, taxis, railroads, airlines,
and walking shoes all provide one or more of the characteristics of automobiles, and yet standard theory provides no meaningful way to compare them.

Lancaster's approach to consumer behavior, along with Becker's innovations discussed earlier, serves to remind economists that the purchase of market goods is merely an intermediate step to the satisfaction of some more ultimate demand. The demand for market goods is therefore a derived demand—
the demand for an automobile or a subway token is *derived* from a demand for

---

[6] "A New Approach to Consumer Theory," *Journal of Political Economy*.

certain utility-creating attributes (e.g., transportation and other things) provided by the good or service. It must be remembered that quality itself is one of those attributes. This enlarged focus on goods as bundles of characteristics, where the characteristics are numerous and variable, sheds light on the sometimes sudden emergence (and rapid disappearance) of market goods in the consumption bundles of individuals or households.

Summary: Consumption Technology

New developments relating to consumer behavior, including nuances of the kind discussed here, dot the landscape of modern literature in microeconomics. As with most new economic ideas, these, too, have been cast in the formal dress of mathematical models, and the result of the process has been to expose the limitations of the new developments as well as their relevance to real-world situations. On balance, however, the modern theory of consumer behavior has widened the boundaries of microeconomic theory.

NEW THEORIES OF THE FIRM

Broadly speaking, the economic function of a firm is to combine economic resources in order to produce goods and services demanded by consumers. Standard theory tells us that firms that succeed in meeting these demands efficiently survive and prosper while those that do not make losses and fail. In traditional economic theory, cost curves based on resource productivity are combined with demand and other revenue curves to make models of competitive or monopolistic (including monopolistically competitive) firms. (Figures 20-2 and 20-3 of Chapter 20 are examples of such models.) This sort of analysis *describes* firms and their mechanical activities, but it does not answer some deeper questions. Why, for example, do firms exist at all?

All advanced economies are based upon the division of labor. In a market economy the division of labor is vented in an incredible array of activities based upon the different skills and talents of individuals. But what mechanism or mechanisms ensure that such consumables as food, clothing, and airline travel are produced when and where they are wanted? The answer is found in the concept of economic coordination. In order to explain why firms exist, market coordination must be distinguished from firm coordination. Market coordination exists when the price system *directly* provides signals (through supply and demand) that guide production and consumption. Firm coordination exists when the division of labor is carried on and directed by managers. Market coordination is by nature decentralized, whereas firm coordination is by nature centralized. Firm coordination is therefore not unlike central planning in a socialist economy. Within the firm, resources are not bought and sold but are transferred through managerial command.

In the language of economics, a firm is a voluntary institution characterized by free contract. Employees agree voluntarily to follow the dictates of managers, but these "commands" are but a figure of speech. Successful managers must mimic the price system by transferring and allocating resources in an efficient manner, given the prices of equivalent resources "outside" the firm.

But if market and firm coordination are so similar, why are firms necessary at all? Why do some automobile manufacturers purchase tires for their cars rather than make their own? Why do some firms purchase advertising and travel services from outside agencies (i.e., other firms) rather than produce them within the firm. Why is market coordination used for some resource inputs and firm coordination used for others? Contemporary microeconomics seeks to provide satisfactory answers to such questions.

Why Firms? The Coasian Perspective

Why are firms necessary? In a classic paper entitled "The Nature of the Firm," published in 1937, Ronald Coase (b. 1910) proposed a simple and elegant answer to the question. Coase argued that firms emerge and exist as a least-cost means of economic coordination. There are, in short, costs to using market coordination. The hiring of inputs (e.g., temporary labor) typically involves transaction costs, search costs, and negotiation costs. If contracts are used, they must be negotiated as well as policed. The other side of the coin is that market coordination provides certain benefits. The firm is only obligated for a short term (a day's worth of labor) and is able to hire resources more flexibly. When firms hire "Kelly Girls" or other temporary secretarial services, they are using market coordination rather than firm coordination.

At some point, however, market coordination may give way to firm coordination. Entrepreneurs begin to use firm coordination when a comparison of the costs and benefits between alternative forms of coordination indicates positive benefits to coordination *within* rather than without. It may pay to organize secretarial tasks *within* the firm by hiring a secretary on a regular, longer-term basis rather than hire temporary help. A firm therefore emerges as a conglomeration of resources that are gathered together under the centralized (quasi-socialistic) direction of a manager because it is cheaper than organizing and directing resources through overt (outside) market mechanisms.

The next compelling question is, When do firms stop growing in size? Coase argued that firms face a limit to growth in the form of rising marginal costs of organization and direction. When the net benefits derived from internal organization and direction fall below the net benefits of organizing tasks through market contracts, the firm stops growing and again resorts to market coordination. Economic reality rarely presents us with an either-or situation, however. Many firms use *both* forms of resource coordination simultaneously. Market coordination may be more efficient for some specialized tasks, e.g., a "temp" secretary to type rarely needed legal documents, whereas frequent and repetitive tasks may be accomplished at lower cost by a full-time secretary with a wide array of office skills. As a practical matter, therefore, each task within the firm may be examined from the standpoint of whether the net benefits derived from inside coordination exceed those from outside coordination.

Team Production and Shirking in the Firm

Coase's innovative theory of the firm has spawned a number of theoretical extensions. One of the more promising off-shoots of the theory has been the "team production" view of how activities are organized within firms. Most of the activities of firms, including the production of goods and services, involve team effort, and a team, like a chain, is only as strong as its weakest link. How, then, can the firm prevent its team members from shirking or engaging in unproductive behavior? One answer has been given by Armen Alchian and Harold Demsetz,[7] who maintain that the manager acts as a team monitor to ensure efficiency in those instances where several individuals or groups of individuals must work together to accomplish a task.

Specialization, as Adam Smith recognized long ago, leads to increased productivity. But without someone policing their behavior, all individuals have an incentive to shirk. Yet at the same time workers have an incentive to be monitored, since their returns are, to a large degree, adversely affected by the shirking behavior of other members of the team. These circumstances explain the emergence of the manager as the person given the responsibility to discipline those who shirk and to reward superior performance.

In the absence of team production, individual producers are disciplined by market competition, i.e., the actions of rivals. The worker can shirk, but he or she bears the full costs of such behavior by receiving lower earnings. In such circumstances, an internal monitor is not necessary. Firms that employ monitors obviously face increased costs over those that do not, so it is only when the benefits of increased productivity to team production outweigh the costs of monitoring that team production replaces individual production. In the evolutionary scheme of things, when teams can produce goods and services at a lower cost than individuals can, firms emerge and survive. The Alchian-Demsetz view therefore regards a firm as the logical consequence of positive net benefits that derive from team production even in the face of the higher costs of monitoring team performance.

The manager-as-monitor view of team production raises some rather obvious questions. Who, for instance, will monitor the manager? Does not the manager also have an incentive to shirk? The answers to these questions are to be found in the institutional composition of the firm, specifically in the pattern of incentives, both positive and negative, given to managers. On the one hand, managers are disciplined by the market. If they perform poorly, monitor-managers will be fired and competing managers will be installed by owners or stockholders. On the other hand, managers can be rewarded as residual claim-

---

[7] "Production, Information Costs and Economic Organization," *American Economic Review.*

ants who share in the profits or rewards of team production. Managers thus have both positive and negative incentives to be efficient monitors of team production.

OTHER APPLICATIONS AND EXTENSIONS

Interest in the economics of information as a central part of the new microeconomics has raised a number of provocative issues related to the qualities of products. The central question concerns the determination of product quality and the kind of information buyers and sellers have before the purchase of products. If sellers possess information concerning product qualities that buyers do not, sellers may have incentives to sell substandard products or services. This rather obvious observation has generated various approaches to the issue of quality.

Asymmetric Information: The "Lemons" Problem

In the labor-market variant of the information problem, different employees may have different productivity potentials which are unknown to employers. In order to improve information, therefore, employers may develop screening techniques for sorting prospective employees. Good screening techniques should "signal" which workers have the highest productivity potential. There are certain worker attributes that tend to be highly correlated (i.e., provide strong "signals") with productivity, such as educational attainment or innate math and language skills. As economic theory would predict, employers will tend to utilize screening techniques that emphasize characteristics which can be measured reliably at low cost. From the standpoint of the potential employee, it should be noted that individuals have more control over certain desirable attributes than others, e.g., education versus physical appearance, race, or sex.

Ever since Hayek (see Chapter 21) pioneered the notion of markets as processors of information, it has generally been recognized that price itself is a "signal." But how reliable a signal is it? Information can be asymmetric. The possibility and the implications of asymmetric information in economic markets have been analyzed by George Akerlof in a study of the automobile market.[8] In this market, it is difficult for the buyer to get complete information before the purchase. A new car may be dependable and trouble-free, or it may be in constant need of repair. The customer usually does not know, nor can he or she know, if a car is a lemon or not until after the purchase.

Consider an instructive example from the used-car market. Used-car buyers demand cars, among other things, on the basis of the used car's price and on the probability that it is a lemon. If the initial price of used cars does not clear the market—suppose that price is "too high" and quantity supplied exceeds

---

[8] "The Market for 'Lemons': Quality Uncertainty and the Market Mechanism," *Quarterly Journal of Economics.*

quantity demanded—it is not clear whether a reduction of price will improve matters. Why not? The quantity demanded may not increase as traditional demand theory tells us. In fact the entire demand curve for used cars may shift leftward due to the customer's perception that the car offered for sale at the lower price is more likely a lemon. The excess supply of used cars may not be reduced at all, and, in the limit, the market for used cars may disappear completely. A more likely outcome is that used cars will sell at a "discount" below their normally depreciated value. But discounting may discourage owners of "good"-quality used cars from selling, thereby reducing the number of potentially welfare-enhancing trades that take place between buyers and sellers.

Factors which mitigate these "lemon" effects tend to emerge in such markets over time. Seller reputation is one means of reducing the lemons problem. Auto dealers with good reputations for honoring promises through warranties or guarantees gain an advantage in selling used cars over fly-by-night firms. Institutions, in short, develop in order to compensate for (but possibly not offset) information problems in markets where the lemons problem exists.

Economics and Sociology

Economic analysis has also intruded on matters that used to be considered within the purview of sociology. Once again, Gary Becker (*The Economic Approach to Human Behavior*) has been a pioneer in formulating economic theories of social interactions and family organization. While sociologists and psychologists typically view the family as a complex set of interpersonal activities and relations, Becker sees it as a form of economic organization. In the language of the economist, marriage is a two-party, incompletely defined contract carrying explicit and implicit obligations. Prenuptial dating may be viewed as an investment in information about prospective mates. Being "in love" implies interdependent utility functions: most successful marriages are made by people whose preferences and values are closely related, in addition to their sense of mutual caring.

The economic theory of the family also maintains that a "head of household" who cares for the welfare of family members directs and allocates household resources in Pareto-optimal fashion. In what Becker calls the "Rotten Kid Theorem," all family members have incentives to act so that the household head's utility function is maximized. This arrangement, e.g., allocation of resources by the head of household in Pareto-optimal fashion, allows every family member to be better off than he or she would be in isolation. The household head's single utility function is said to capture the utility of the entire household, so that decisions by the head of household normally take into consideration the collective utility of the family. In turn, the family, according to Becker, will behave in accordance with the household head's utility function. It is within this context that decisions regarding the transformation of leisure into household work or market work, as analyzed above, are made. In this interpretation, the sociological-psychological category of "role playing" within the family unit becomes an expression of specialization that follows rational economic principles of cost and choice. Although this approach is controversial, Becker's insights give meaning to a number of social phenomena that sociologists have been at pains to understand and explain. For example, consider marriage rates and birthrates.

When marriage is viewed as an incompletely defined contract that is entered into according to the perceived costs and benefits of the participants, it is possible to bring those costs and benefits explicitly into the decision nexus. On the cost side, marriage means that each partner sacrifices some independence and makes many compromises regarding personal habits, friendships, and the direction of expenditures. On the benefit side, marriage provides companionship and reciprocal caring and love, and it facilitates the production and rearing of children. In addition to these benefits, however, marriage provides an opportunity to enjoy the economic gains from specialization and division of labor. Traditionally, division of labor has placed the male marriage partner as the primary earner of market income through outside-the-home market work. Until recent decades, in developed economies, the female partner has more or less specialized in household production and in child rearing. Although this pattern is changing in developed nations, the important point is that so long as skills vary widely between spouses, the gains to husband and wife from specialization and trade are potentially large and positive.

The "women's revolution" of the past three or four decades has changed this configuration for a significant number of individuals. Laws and practices have greatly lessened discrimination against women in the workplace. Women have, in increasing numbers, become engineers, lawyers, and physicians. In many areas of the marketplace, opportunities for educational attainment and other investments in human capital have been expanded for women. The result is that skill levels of men and women are drawing closer together. With more and more similar skills, the economic gains from specialization and trade between men and women within the organizational framework of marriage are clearly lowered. On economic grounds alone (neglecting all other factors), economic theory predicts that a reduction of the gains to marriage will lead to a decline in marriage rates and an increase in divorce rates—precisely the experience in recent times of many developed nations.

As more women have entered the (market) work force and as family incomes have risen, we have observed another phenomenon with economic implications: a decline in the birthrate. Population growth requires a sustained demand for children on the part of parents. Long ago the classical economists argued that income increases would encourage an increase in the production of children, which, in Ricardo's scenario, would eventually lead to the stationary state. Becker's analysis goes beyond the simple Malthusian framework of population growth by adding an important additional consideration: it is not only the level of income that explains population growth, but also the relative "price" of children.

The full cost of raising children depends not only on the direct expenditures entailed but also on the *opportunity* costs incurred by parents. These opportunity costs increase as family income increases, particularly as the mother's opportunity costs increase. Consequently, there is a bias against child production that accompanies economic growth. In most underdeveloped countries, especially those surviving on subsistence agriculture, children represent direct labor inputs, and are considered valuable to their parents as a source of labor. Low wages in such countries keep the opportunity costs of having children at a low level. By contrast, the "price" of additional children is high in developed countries because children have less value to their parents as direct labor inputs and because parents' opportunity costs are high. Instead of raising an additional child, parents may decide to improve their living standards and that of their existing children by spending more on education, housing, or a wide array of other goods. In part, then, rational economic decision making and a novel application of the law of demand explain low birthrates in developed nations and high birthrates in underdeveloped countries.

Despite these recent forays by contemporary microeconomics into areas traditionally considered outside the province of economics, no economist, including Becker, argues that economics is the sole or even the central factor in explaining sociological phenomena. Rather, contemporary microeconomics offers additional insights into certain aspects of human behavior which complement and/or supplement explanations proposed by other social scientists.

CONCLUSION

Contemporary microeconomics teems with many provocative issues and interesting applications. To borrow Hemingway's aphorism about Paris, today's microeconomics is a movable and ever-changing feast. We have tried to give the flavor of several new developments in this chapter. Even a small taste of the feast conveys the clear and correct impression that economic theory has made and is making giant leaps in the direction of "realism." Economists are learning to recognize and to account for all kinds of actual market circumstances that were held in abeyance when markets were being analyzed by Alfred Marshall. This is not, of course, to criticize the genuine pioneers of microeconomic theory such as Marshall, Jevons, or Robinson. Rather, it is evidence that the operation of markets is a more complex process than the earlier conceptual apparatus was able to handle. In reality, the modern directions of microeconomic theory are testimony to the ongoing nature of earlier contributions and to the vibrance of economics.

NOTES FOR FURTHER READING

No short narrative of contemporary trends in microeconomic analysis (or any other subject) could possibly do justice to the ideas themselves. As always, there is no substitute for the original sources. One source stands out in bringing the largest number of original papers on the "new" microeconomics together under one cover: see William Breit, Harold M. Hochman, and Edward Saueracker (eds.), *Readings in Microeconomics* (St. Louis: Times Mirror/

Mosby College Publishing, 1986). For another excellent compendium of original essays on the "new microeconomics" and its broad applicability, see Richard B. McKenzie and Gordon Tullock, *The New World of Economics: Explorations into the Human Experience,* 3d ed. (Homewood, Ill.: Irwin, 1981). The authors take up such matters as marriage, child production, law, crime, presidential elections, and college and university education, examining each issue as a straightforward application of basic microeconomic principles. Most of Gary Becker's works treating familial and interpersonal relations are reprinted in his *Economic Approach to Human Behavior* (see References). Also see Becker, "A Theory of Marriage," *Journal of Political Economy,* part I, vol. 81 (July/August 1973), pp. 813–46; and part II, vol. 82, suppl. (March/April 1974), pp. s11–s26.

Those interested in the historical background on the economics of crime should first review the ideas of Bentham and Chadwick discussed in Chapter 9, and the references cited there to the early literature. Gary Becker, "Crime and Punishment: An Economic Approach," *Journal of Political Economy,* vol. 76 (March/April 1968), pp. 169–217; and Gordon Tullock, "The Welfare Costs of Tariffs, Monopolies, and Theft," *Western Economic Journal,* vol. 5 (June 1967), pp. 224–232, present the modern "pioneer" view of the subject. The question of whether punishment is a deterrent to crime is answered in the affirmative in most economic studies of the issue; see, for example, Isaac Ehrlich, "Participation in Illegitimate Activities: A Theoretical and Empirical Investigation," *Journal of Political Economy,* vol. 81 (May/June 1973), pp. 521–565; and Gordon Tullock, "Does Punishment Deter Crime?" *The Public Interest,* vol. 36 (Summer 1974), pp. 103–111.

Many other important innovations in resource allocation and the theory of the firm and firm operations bear careful study. In our view one of the most interesting extensions of time costs and resource allocation involves the problem of welfare dissipation under differing schemes of distribution and retrade. A central contribution which clearly reveals the implicit costs of queuing is that of Yoram Barzel, entitled "A Theory of Rationing by Waiting," *Journal of Law & Economics,* vol. 17 (April 1974), pp. 73–95. Another basic study which raises and evaluates the question of whether firms minimize costs as assumed in orthodox theory is by Harvey Leibenstein, "Allocative Efficiency vs. 'X-Efficiency,'" *American Economic Review,* vol. 56 (June 1966), pp. 392–415. Problems relating property rights and contracting to firm size and organization have been developed in a number of contributions by Oliver E. Williamson: see, for example, "Hierarchical Control and Optimum Firm Size," *Journal of Political Economy,* vol. 56 (April 1967), pp. 123–138, and his book *Markets and Hierarchies* (New York: The Free Press, 1975). The modern approach to the theory of the firm is evaluated and expanded in an unpublished doctoral dissertation by Donald J. Boudreaux, *Contracting, Organization, and Monetary Instability: Studies in the Theory of the Firm* (Auburn, Ala.: Auburn University, 1986). A contemporary brief for the generally positive contribution of advertising to efficient market functioning and information provision is given in Robert B. Ekelund, Jr., and David S. Saurman, *Adver-*

tising and the Market Process: A Modern Economic View (San Francisco: Pacific Research Institute for Public Policy, 1988).

Experimental economics with both animal (primarily rats and pigeons) and human subjects has mushroomed over the past decade and a half. A classic study using human subjects was undertaken by Vernon Smith, "An Experimental Study of Competitive Market Behavior," *Journal of Political Economy,* vol. 70 (April 1962), pp. 111–137. A research team of economists and psychologists have designed experiments to test the "rationality" of animal (nonhuman) subjects with respect to demand, labor supply, and other well-known theoretical microeconomic relations. For a sample of this important work see Raymond C. Battalio, John H. Kagel, H. Rachlin, and L. Green, "Commodity Choice Behavior with Pigeons as Subjects," *Journal of Political Economy,* vol. 84 (February 1981), pp. 116–151; and same authors, "Demand Curves for Animal Consumers," *The Quarterly Journal of Economics,* vol. 96 (February 1981), pp. 1–14.

Finally, the revolution in microeconomic theory has created a revolution in the applied areas of economic theory. One important example is the "new" industrial organization where broadened views of the competitive process and the concepts of full price and full costs are reorienting traditional thought on economic policy toward "monopoly." See, among many contributions to this developing field, William J. Baumol, "Contestable Markets: An Uprising in the Theory of Industry Structure," *American Economic Review,* vol. 72 (March 1982), pp. 1–15.

REFERENCES

Akerlof, George A. "The Market for 'Lemons': Quality Uncertainty and the Market Mechanism," *Quarterly Journal of Economics,* vol. 84 (August 1970), pp. 488–500.

Alchian, Armen A., and Harold Demsetz. "Production, Information Costs, and Economic Organization," *American Economic Review,* vol. 62 (December 1972), pp. 777–795.

Becker, Gary S. "A Theory of the Allocation of Time," *The Economic Journal,* vol. 75 (September 1965), pp. 493–517.

———. *The Economic Approach to Human Behavior.* Chicago: University of Chicago Press, 1976.

Coase, Ronald H. "The Nature of the Firm," *Economica,* vol. 4 (November 1937), pp. 386–405.

Gronau, Reuben. "Leisure, Home Production, and Work—The Theory of the Allocation of Time Revisited," *Journal of Political Economy,* vol. 85 (December 1977), pp. 1099–1123.

Lancaster, Kelvin J. "A New Approach to Consumer Theory," *Journal of Political Economy,* vol. 74 (April 1966), pp. 132–157.

Nelson, Phillip. "Advertising as Information," *Journal of Political Economy,* vol. 82 (1974), pp. 729–754.

Stigler, George J. "The Economics of Information," *Journal of Political Economy,* vol. 69 (June 1961), pp. 213–225.

———, and Gary S. Becker. "De Gustibus Non Est Disputandum," *American Economic Review,* vol. 67 (March 1977), pp. 76–90.

THE NEW POLITICAL ECONOMY: PUBLIC CHOICE AND REGULATION

INTRODUCTION

The great classical writers, such as Adam Smith and Jeremy Bentham, considered economics to be a social science in the broadest possible sense. Political economy, with the adjective given as much weight as the noun, was an inquiry into analysis, institutions, policy, and policy formation. As economics progressed through the nineteenth and twentieth centuries, however, the scope of its inquiry gradually narrowed. Indeed, we have now come to the point that in some graduate institutions in the United States and abroad, economics is seen more as a branch of applied mathematics than as a social science. In the quest to formalize the subject, political and institutional concerns, in spite of Veblen's influence, have often been relegated to second-class status within economics curricula.

But there have always been economists who have maintained an interest in the interface between "politics" (political behavior and institutions) and the motives of self-interested economic actors. In the broader view of these economists, there is no such thing as strictly "economic behavior." Politicians are not regarded as selfless lawgivers, exogenous to the economic happenings in society. They are seen, rather, as self-interested competitors maximizing returns (power, position, votes, etc.) under certain constraints (reelection, for instance). The important point is that in seeking to optimize their own interests, politicians impact upon the entire economic system, for example, through fiscal policy or through the supply of industrial regulation. The germ of these notions—especially that of endogenous politicians—has always been present in economic literature, but in the past twenty or thirty years a veritable revolution has taken place. In this modern development, economics has been reborn as a political and social science.

The purpose of this chapter is to show how the self-interested economic motives postulated by classical and neoclassical economists are being applied and extended to an analysis of the modern world. Two major contemporary themes—public choice and the economic approach to regulation—are treated. Even a cursory investigation of these two important and developing areas reveals a fundamental continuity in economic analysis stretching from Adam Smith to the present. In addition, such active concerns on the part of prominent modern writers are evidence that, despite the recent surge of mathematical formalism in the discipline, economics is not down at the heels as a *social* science.

PUBLIC CHOICE: CONTEMPORARY POLITICAL ECONOMY

Modern public choice is a study of the political mechanisms or institutions through which taxes and expenditures are determined; that is, it is a study of the demand for and the supply of *public* goods. Further, public choice is the use of the simple analytics of competition to make positive statements concerning institutions and events in the public sector. Although the economics of the *private* sector has been well developed over the last two centuries, until recently an analysis of how social goods are supplied and demanded took a back seat to the central concerns of most economists.

Some classical and neoclassical writers, such as Alfred Marshall and A. C. Pigou, always paid attention to public finance. However, the Marshallian-Pigovian approach to public finance, antedated as we have seen by the French engineers, focused on "problem solving" in the provision of *specific* public goods. Moreover, its concern was almost exclusively on the tax side of the fiscal equation. The welfare and efficiency effects of various types of taxes were stock-in-trade for neoclassical (Marshall-Pigou) analysis; but it never occurred to writers in this somewhat insular Anglo-Saxon tradition that fiscal decisions were the result of choice on the part of both demanders and suppliers acting through a process of political filtration.

Modern research has demonstrated conclusively that intellectual efforts to place fiscal theory on more broad-based interdependencies were emerging in Italian and Scandinavian writings. James M. Buchanan, Nobel laureate and founder-pioneer of modern public-choice theory, investigated the classical, Italian tradition in public finance (1880–1940) and contrasted it to the Anglo-Saxon (Marshallian-Pigovian) development.[1] Buchanan noted:

> As early as the 1880s, Mazzola, Pantaleoni, Sax, and De Viti De Marco made rudimentary efforts to analyze the public economy within an exchange framework. Sax and Mazzola discussed the demand side of public goods by identifying collective as distinct from private wants. Pantaleoni extended the marginal calculus to apply to

---

[1] Buchanan chronicles this tradition in his essay "La scienza delle finanze: The Italian Tradition in Public Finance" (see References).

the legislator who makes choices for both sides of the budget. De Viti De Marco explicitly constructed a model in which the consumers and the suppliers-producers of public goods make up the same community of persons ("Public Finance and Public Choice," p. 384).[2]

In addition, the Swedish economists Knut Wicksell (1851–1926) and Erik Lindahl (1891–1960) were hard at work developing a holistic approach to the public sector, one that included a public budget determined within a political process rather than as the endogenous dictates of Platonic philosopher-kings. Contemporary movements among public-choice theorists to establish the entire fiscal sector of the economy within a general-equilibrium theory owe much to the efforts of these continental economists.

As a matter of doctrinal development, we must agree with Buchanan's assessment that the real surprise is not the emergence of continental contributions to public-sector equilibrium—these could be expected as somewhat straightforward extensions of the emergent neoclassical (marginalist) theory of *private* markets in the 1870s (see Chapters 13 through 16). Rather, the riddle for the historian of thought is to explain "the long-continued failure of English-language economists to make comparative extensions of their basic framework or to acknowledge an interest in the continental efforts" ("Public Finance and Public Choice," p. 384). The bridge between these early continental contributions and the emergence of modern public-choice theory is a long one that has, in the main, spanned the Atlantic and reached American economists. Contemporary public-choice theory is essentially an ongoing American achievement, originating in the late 1930s and the 1940s.[3] The content of this achievement is both extensive and detailed. Voting theory, for example, is an integral and complex part of public choice. Space constraints in a book such as this prohibit a detailed account of the entire field. We therefore confine our discussion to some simple concepts and areas of concern in public-choice theory so that we might provide the reader with an overview of this developing paradigm in contemporary economics.

Public-Goods Demand and the Median-Voter Model

The theory of public-goods demand is an integral aspect of contemporary public-choice theory. Further, it is a good example of how economic analysis

---

[2] Buchanan's essay "Public Finance and Public Choice" (see References) provides a fine introduction to contemporary public choice and its history, as does Randall G. Holcombe's "Concepts of Public Sector Equilibrium" (see References). With permission, the spirit of our discussion, as well as some details, follows these two papers closely.

[3] The early, seminal American contributions were those of Musgrave ("The Voluntary Exchange Theory of Public Economy," 1938), Bowen ("The Interpretation of Voting in the Allocation of Resources," 1943), and Buchanan ("The Pure Theory of Government Finance: A Suggested Approach, 1949), all cited in the References at the end of this chapter. This ongoing tradition in contemporary American economics is exemplified in the Center for the Study of Public Choice, founded by Professor Buchanan, and in *Public Choice,* a journal devoted to the subject and edited by Professor Gordon Tullock.

developed to handle one problem can often be applied to new problems. In this case the theory of public-goods demand is analogous in most respects to the Mill-Marshall joint-supply theory developed to analyze simultaneous production of such items as beef and hides, mutton and wool, and so on (see Chapter 8 for this discussion). Originally articulated by Howard Bowen in 1943, the necessary conditions for allocative efficiency in the provision of a public good were developed by Paul Samuelson in 1954 in a classic paper "The Pure Theory of Public Expenditures." A public good in this context may be distinguished from a private good in that, in the public-good case, an individual's consumption of the public good does not reduce all other individuals' *simultaneous* consumption. In the private-good case, if X_T is the total consumption of shoes, then $X_T = x_1 + x_2 + \ldots + x_n$, where $x_1 + x_2$, etc., is the sum of all individuals' consumption of shoes. In the public-goods case, X_p may be total consumption of, say, national defense, and $X_p = x_1 = x_2 = \ldots = x_n$, where all individuals consume the *same* amount of defense. In the latter case, one individual's consumption of defense does not detract from another's, and all consume the *same quantity* of defense.

Here, units of measurement are important. A "unit" of a good is defined as the minimum quantity of that good required to provide more than one consumer simultaneously with that particular bundle of services that serves to distinguish the good in question from all other goods. Accordingly, a dozen pencils would not be considered a unit of a public good even though twelve individuals could consume this good simultaneously. The reason is that one pencil is capable of providing the unique bundle of services (writing, erasing, etc.) usually associated with the term "pencil." A unit of pencils would be a private good because its services are provided to only a single individual.

A Polaris submarine, on the other hand, can be viewed as a unit of a public good because it provides "safety from nuclear attack" simultaneously to more than one individual. While the provision of "safety from nuclear attack" as a private good might be possible (individual concrete underground silos, for example), the cost per individual presumably is less when the service is provided as a public good.

Some other characteristics of public goods are important though they are not unique to public goods. For instance, in the public-good case described by Samuelson, the *marginal* cost of supplying additional users would be negligible—sometimes zero—and the exclusion of nonpaying consumers would be impossible. Some goods in the private sector approximate the above cost conditions (a bus trip for a particular journey, perhaps). Moreover, it may always be possible to exclude consumers. Even in the case of national defense it would theoretically be possible to remove nonpayers to (nonprotected) islands in the Pacific Ocean although such exclusion would be costly. The conceptual difficulties of defining a *pure* public good are many, therefore, but these matters need not detain us here. Let us assume that joint-consumption, zero marginal cost, and nonexcludability conditions apply and turn to the Bowen-Samuelson equilibrium of Figure 24-1. (Note that the details of this case are

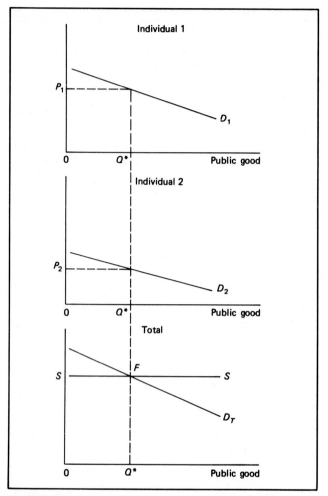

FIGURE 24-1
The total demand for the public good is the vertical sum of
individual demands D_1 and D_2, with each demander consuming Q^*
quantity of the good.

analogous to Mill's model of joint supply for jointly produced private goods
[such as steers] depicted graphically in Figure 8-1.)

The two upper quadrants of Figure 24-1 depict the demands for a public
good (education, Polaris submarines, etc.) on the part of a closed community
of two individuals. These demands are summed vertically in order to get the
total demand for the public good shown (with a constant-cost supply curve) in
the lowest quadrant of Figure 24-1. Vertical summation of individual demand
curves is called for in the public-goods case since consumption between individuals is noncompeting. Individual A's consumption of nuclear submarines

does not compete with individual B's. Consumption is simultaneous and "complementary." Most importantly, note that the equilibrium described in the public-goods case with simultaneity of consumption requires (in exact contrast to the private-goods example) that the *same* quantity of the good be consumed by *each* consumer (quantity Q^* in Figure 24-1). Different prices are required in equilibrium to get different individuals with different demands to hold Q^* of the commodity. The equilibrium prices would not be equal except in the unlikely event that the two individuals' demands are identical.

Samuelson's description of the demand for public goods is perfectly abstract and general, but in fitting the principle to real-world applications several difficulties emerge. When the good in question is not *purely* public in Samuelson's sense, the optimal size of the consuming group will not be known, and the question that begs answering is: What quantity should be produced (i.e., what Q^*)? In his 1943 paper, Howard Bowen reviewed this last issue and answered: "It is, of course, no more difficult to obtain information on the cost of producing social goods than to get data on individual goods; but to estimate marginal rates of substitution [public-goods demands] presents serious problems, since it requires the measurement of the preferences for goods which, by their very nature, cannot be subjected to individual consumer choice" ("The Interpretation of Voting in the Allocation of Resources," pp. 32–33).

Some sort of proxy for public-goods demands is needed, in other words, and Bowen suggested that, under certain conditions, voting (in a democratic setting) is the closest substitute for consumer choice.[4] This so-called *median-voter model* (actually a whole set of models) became the major tool of public-choice theorists in the 1960s and 1970s owing in large part to the pioneering efforts of Duncan Black and Kenneth Arrow. While this literature is central to modern public-choice theory, it is fairly technical and would take us too far afield.[5] Nevertheless, the Bowen model and its variants (along with possible complications and problems) may be presented in simple terms.

Any individual's demand for public goods will be determined by two things: (1) the satisfaction he or she expects to receive from various amounts of it, and (2) the cost to the *individual* of alternative amounts of the public good. In order to look at even a basic model of voting behavior, we must invoke simplifying assumptions. First, assume that all members of a community actually vote and thereby correctly reveal their individual preferences for the social good. Sec-

---

[4] Bowen was not the first economist, and certainly not the last, to deal with this general problem. Harold Hotelling broached the issue of the median voter in 1929 (see References).

[5] The interested reader should consult two works central to the argument, Duncan Black's *The Theory of Committees and Elections* (1958) and Kenneth Arrow's *Social Choice and Individual Values* (1951) (see References and Notes for Further Reading). These works faced the question of the efficiency and workability of majority rule through the median voter in registering individual preferences for social goods. The fascinating intellectual history of the efficiency of voting rules is presented in Black's book. The contributions of the Rev. C. L. Dodgson, better known to history as Lewis Carroll, are particularly interesting (see Black's *Theory*, pp. 189–213).

ond, suppose that the total and average cost of the good to the community is known and that it is divided equally among all citizens. Finally, assume with Bowen "that the several curves of individual marginal substitution [i.e., the individual demand curves] are distributed according to the normal law of error" ("The Interpretation of Voting," p. 34). This simply means that there are a large number of demand curves and that, for any quantity of the public good provided, there will be demands clustered symmetrically about a mode. Such a community may be illustrated easily in terms of Figure 24-2, which shows the clustering of demands about the demand of the median voter. The pro rata tax share (AC/N) is the same for each voter-consumer. Now consider a provision of some quantity of the public good Q_1 in Figure 24-2. Clearly for the *same* quantity of the good, different demanders would be willing to pay different tax shares. Thus, for Q_1, those who value the good highly would be willing to pay D_7, those placing little value on the public good would only be willing to pay D_1, and so on. The median voter, however, values Q_1 at some rate D_4, which is *higher* than the pro rata tax share to all taxpayers who receive the public good AC/N (MC/N). Thus in, say, a town-meeting process employing majority rule, any Q proposed above Q_1 will win approval; any Q proposed above Q^*, such as Q_2, will fail to carry. In this process, the quantity preferred by the median voter, Q^*, will always defeat any other motion.

The median-voter process, under certain circumstances, can yield similar

FIGURE 24-2
At quantity Q_1 of a public good, the median voter values Q at some rate D_4 which is higher than the pro rata tax share. Thus, with majority rule, any Q proposed above Q_1 will win approval and any Q proposed above Q^* will fail to carry.

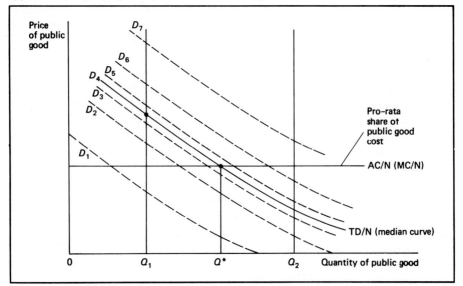

results in other variants of the model, such as voting for marginal increases of a public good in a referendum process or through elected representatives. In the latter case, if the people are consulted on *particular* policies and if representatives identify with specific issues, the results of the process can approximate those of Figure 24-2. Many factors affect voting. Public officials working through certain institutions may upset the results of Bowen equilibrium by manipulating the agenda or simply by representing and voting on a large variety of issues. Thus, majority-rule election processes do not ensure that voter preferences for public goods will be optimized. It does seem to be a practical system for approximating preferences, however.

Lindahl Tax Prices and Wicksellian Public Finance

Distribution of the tax share, as noted above, is a crucial feature in the provision of public goods, since any individual will demand a good both on the basis of its (marginal) value and on the basis of its cost. The "marginal cost" is simply the share of taxes that the citizen-consumer pays for his or her portion of the output. A major problem in public choice, then, is to devise a means for providing an optimal quantity of any public good such that, for the *single* quantity produced, some distribution of the tax burden may be found that equates the marginal valuation of the good to the marginal tax share for each citizen-consumer. Two early writers on public choice, Erik Lindahl and Knut Wicksell, were interested in different aspects of this question and originated different paths of analysis in modern public-choice theory.

Lindahl Equilibrium In his 1919 contribution entitled "Just Taxation—A Positive Solution" (a part of his book *Die Gerechtigkeit der Besteuerung*), Lindahl treats the problem of tax-share determination as one of bilateral exchange in an "isolated" community with two categories of taxpayers, one "well-to-do" and the other "relatively poor." The problem of the distribution of the tax shares is then considered to be one settled by free argument, or "a kind of economic exchange." (Lindahl of course recognized that this process was filtered through protagonists in a political process and that resultant tax-share distributions assigned would be influenced by their relative power, but he assumed initially that such political "blocs" did not influence the model under free exchange.)

Lindahl's solution is straightforward. In a "solution in which both parties have equally safeguarded the economic rights to which they are entitled under the existing property order," the price of the collective good "tends to correspond to marginal utility for each interested party" ("Just Taxation," pp. 172–173). This means that tax price will equal the affected voter's (or group of voters') marginal valuation of the public good.

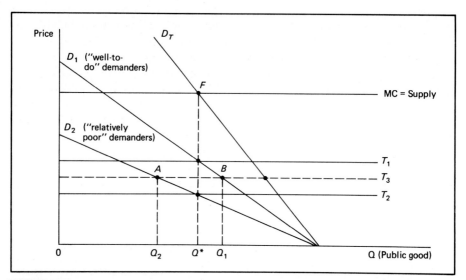

FIGURE 24-3
Lindahl equilibrium is achieved when well-to-do demanders are charged a marginal tax rate T_1 for Q^* and relatively poor consumers are charged a lower tax rate T_2. At a tax rate of T_3 the poor will prefer Q_2, a less-than-optimal quantity, and the rich will prefer Q_1, a more-than-optimal quantity.

Consider the modern adaptation of Lindahl equilibrium in Figure 24-3 (Figure 24-3 is constructed in the same manner as Figure 24-1, except that the two demand curves and their summation are contained in one graph in Figure 24-3.)[6] In Figure 24-3, D_T is the *vertically* summed demand curve for the public goods, with D_1 and D_2 being the separate demand curves of the two groups. Lindahl equilibrium would occur, through voluntary exchange, when for quantity Q^*, well-to-do demanders are charged a marginal tax rate T_1 and the relatively poor consumers are charged a lower tax rate T_2. Under this tax system, each group is paying a marginal cost (T_1 and T_2, respectively) equal to its marginal valuation of the public good. Efficiency is achieved in the Bowen-Samuelson sense because a single quantity of the good is produced, Q^*, which corresponds to the equation of total demand D_T and marginal cost of production (at point F in Figure 24-3).

The establishment of Lindahl prices is *not* necessary in order to obtain efficiency in the production of public goods in the Bowen-Samuelson sense. All that is required for efficiency is that total output of the good be established at point F (producing Q^*) in Figure 24-3. In order to understand this fact, consider the imposition of some "average" tax rate T—one that would be imposed on both groups of demanders and that would cover the costs of producing Q^*.

---

[6] Figure 24-3 is adapted with modifications from R. G. Holcombe's "Concepts of Public Sector Equilibrium," p. 82.

It is easy to see that the well-to-do demanders would prefer this system and would, if possible, foist it on the poor through a political process (Lindahl considered this case). Note, however, that at tax rate T_3 the poor would prefer Q_2, a less-than-optimal quantity of the public good. If the poor were politically powerful, they might force society to take a less-than-optimal quantity of the good.[7] In general, however, a system of Lindahl-tax prices would produce Bowen-Samuelson efficiency—everyone would agree on how much of the public good should be produced. While a Lindahl system is not the only one capable of producing this result, it is also the case that a Lindahl model features *unanimous* agreement of the taxed parties in voluntary exchange given differential tax rates. Probably this feature of Lindahl's work is very strong because his conception of public finance was deeply influenced by his mentor, Knut Wicksell.

Wicksell and Wicksellian Extensions Swedish economist and reformer Knut Wicksell was probably the most important early progenitor of contemporary public choice. In his long essay of 1896, "A New Principle of Just Taxation," Wicksell attacked the orthodox approaches to public finance and simultaneously laid the groundwork for both normative and positive public choice. In a concern for how decisions in the public sector are reached, Wicksell emphasized the dual nature of the fiscal side of the economy. In his view, normative comments concerning the welfare effects of alternative tax systems were of no value unless the expenditure side of the fisc (benefits to taxpayers) was simultaneously considered. "Most importantly," as Professor Buchanan has pointed out, "Wicksell admonished economists for their failure to recognize the elementary fact that collective or public-sector decisions emerge from a political process rather than from the mind of some benevolent despot" ("Public Finance and Public Choice," p. 385).

As the title of his famous paper suggests, Wicksell was most concerned that a fiscal system conform to justice and efficiency. In his view justice and efficiency demanded *unanimity* among all parties that participate in public-sector decisions. Wicksell was clear on this matter:

> When it comes to benefits which are so hard to express numerically, each person can ultimately speak only for himself. It is a matter of comparatively little importance if perchance some individual secures a somewhat greater gain than another so long as everyone gains and no-one can feel exploited from this very elementary point of view. But if justice requires no more, it certainly requires no less. In the

---

[7] In a most ingenious extension based upon the above problem, Charles M. Tiebout noted in 1956 that people may "vote with their feet" in choosing local communities ("A Pure Theory of Local Expenditures"). In other words, local communities may be thought of as offering a continuum of public-service quantities. In terms of Figure 24-3, given that both groups of demanders face tax rate T_3, the poor would move to a local community offering quantity Q_2 and the well-to-do would seek out one offering Q_1 of public goods. Tiebout's idea certainly offers a testable hypothesis, but there are of course many reasons why citizen-consumers are attracted to local communities.

final analysis, unanimity and fully voluntary consent in the making of decisions provide the only certain and palpable guarantee against injustice in tax distribution. The whole discussion on tax justice remains suspended in mid-air so long as these conditions are not satisfied at least approximately ("A New Principle," p. 90).

State activity in Wicksell's view must thus be of general usefulness, and more, the sacrifice must be weighed against the expected utility of the project. Whether individuals favor a project or not depends on a number of variables, e.g., one's position in the income distribution, relative tastes for private versus public consumption, and subjective evaluation of the public project. The tax-price distribution of the costs will determine whether the project would be approved or not. Some distributions of costs would win majority approval and others would not. In a slap against "authoritarian" tax allocations, Wicksell argued that alternative financing and spending proposals should be submitted to the public for vote. Wicksell then argued that it would be possible, theoretically, to find a distribution of the costs that would produce *unanimity*. Any other results would provide, in Wicksell's words, "the sole possible proof that the state activity under consideration would not provide the community with utility corresponding to the necessary sacrifice and should hence be rejected on rational grounds" ("A New Principle," p. 90).

Although no other principle would be "just" in Wicksell's positive notion, he did recognize that unanimity, though ideal, was not to be expected in any practical circumstance. Society is then faced with a set of voting-rule options, none efficient in Wicksell's ideal sense. This apparent impasse set the stage for a notable development in the modern literature on public choice. In *The Calculus of Consent*, published in 1962, James Buchanan and Gordon Tullock analyzed less-than-Wicksellian-optimal rules within a framework of methodological individualism. Within this positive (value-free) framework, Buchanan and Tullock modeled the calculus of a utility-maximizing, rational individual as he or she faces the choice of constitutional design. In their model, a "construction" is simply a set of rules decided upon in advance that determines the manner in which future action will be conducted.[8]

The institutions of collective choice making in the Buchanan-Tullock conception are themselves variables. Buchanan and Tullock argue that:

> The constitutional choice of a rule is taken independently of any single specific decision or set of decisions and is quite rationally based on a long-term view embodying many separate time sequences and many separate collective acts disposing of economic resources. "Optimality" in the sense of choosing the single "best" rule is something wholly distinct from "optimality" in the allocation of resources within a given time span (*Calculus of Consent*, p. 95.).

---

[8] Further: "Collective action is viewed as the action of individuals when they choose to accomplish purposes collectively rather than individually, and the government is seen as nothing more than the set of processes, the machine, which allows such collective action to take place" (Buchanan and Tullock, *Calculus of Consent*, p. 13).

Optimality, or the determination of the "best" decision rule (one of which could be majority rule), takes place in the presence of individuals' uncertainty concerning their future preferences about a series of individual collective acts or proposals to be voted upon. Given such uncertainty about the nature of future preferences, individuals may vote on criteria *unrelated to their respective position in income distribution*. Optimality in the more "dynamic" Buchanan-Tullock framework does not mean the same thing as in the time-constrained decision-making model of Wicksell. Strict unanimity is required for optimality ("justice") in Wicksell's conception, whereas the choices facing the Wicksellian community are later in time than the constitutional choices analyzed by Buchanan and Tullock. At this earlier point a voting rule that is nonoptimal from a Wicksellian perspective can be optimal in the presence of future preference uncertainty. Buchanan and Tullock thus provide a theory of constitutions and a design of political institutions that augments the unanimity rule as the sole criterion for efficiency in the narrow Wicksellian sense. Their analysis, especially when combined with the norm of "individualism," has had a large impact on contemporary research on political behavior and institutions.

Bureaucracy, the Supply Side, and Empirical Public Choice

Demand analysis—that is, the interconnections between voting and the demand for public goods—has taken center stage in the contemporary public-choice literature. The primary focus on this issue implies that goods and services demanded in the public sector are *automatically* supplied. Public-goods supply, however, takes place through government bureaucracies, and the incentive mechanisms of "bureaus" have, with very few exceptions, not been the subject of much inquiry in public choice. Two exceptions have been the work of the Austrian economist Ludwig von Mises (*Bureaucracy,* 1944) and the more recent study by Gordon Tullock, *The Politics of Bureaucracy* (1965). These books, especially the latter, originated the attempt to model the process of bureaucratic output and most particularly the motivations through which "public-sector supply" takes place.

How do bureaucrats behave? What are their motivations? Is there a discernible quantity that they optimize in their public-good-supplying operations? The works mentioned above, especially through Tullock's intellectual influence, resulted in a singularly interesting recent contribution in this area. In 1971, William A. Niskanen, Jr., published his *Bureaucracy and Representative Government,* which, in the author's words, "focuses on the relations between a bureau and its environment, particularly the environment of representative government, and develops the consequences of these relations for the bureau's budget and output" (*Bureaucracy and Representative Government,* p. 9).

Niskanen views the bureaucrat as an "endogenous" maximizer in the system, not unlike the entrepreneurial suppliers of private goods in the economic system. But one crucial difference stands out. While private entrepreneurs can maximize profits, government bureaucrats cannot, at least not legally. Though illegal side payments are not unknown in the political arena, it is far more reasonable to point to such variables as income, prestige, the size of the bureau, the bureau's budget, job promises after retirement, and so on as candidates for the bureaucratic maximand. Niskanen assumes that bureaucrats are budget maximizers, and he models government bureaus as individual budget-maximizing units. Budget maximization enables the individual bureaucrat to increase his or her salary, have an easier (or more "pleasant") working environment, or both.

Bureaus, in this scenario, are "nonprofit organizations which are financed...by a periodic appropriation or grant" (*Bureaucracy and Representative Government,* p. 15). In essence, a *total* budget is transformed into a level of *total* output, since marginal adjustments are not feasible within the bureaucratic context. One of the (many) implications of the model is that in their attempt to maximize budget size (and thus the size of the bureau), suppliers will "eat up" the consumers' surplus that results from public-goods supply. The sheer growth of bureaucracy is also an obvious implication of this theory. There have been difficulties, moreover, in integrating the theories of public-goods demand and Niskanen's notion of supply into a "general-equilibrium model." Niskanen's model has stimulated a good deal of research into the "supply problem," however, and it has become an ongoing research concern in the economics of public choice.

Positive public choice has yielded a large number of testable implications and extensions. Economists, especially since 1970, have been hard at work expanding and empirically estimating some of these propositions. A very large literature, some of which might be called "empirical public choice" has grown up in the field.[9] The list of contributions delving into these matters is long and pertains to such issues as (1) what the economics of campaign contributions are and how they affect political competition, (2) how self-interest leads to length of political terms in office and to the rules of succession, (3) how the independent judiciary affects cartel behavior, (4) how entry barriers into politics are determined by economic variables, (5) how and why coalitions are formed within legislatures, and (6) why state and federal legislatures contain more lawyers as representatives than any other occupation. A whole branch of literature has developed on the "political business cycle," that is, how self-interested politicians acting under reelection constraints can *cause* swings in inflation, income, and employment. Some of these interesting contributions are discussed below, while others are referenced in the Notes for Further Reading at the end of this chapter.

The Median-Voter Model Consider the median-voter model described earlier in this chapter. It has been shown that, assuming competition among po-

---

[9] See "Public Choice: A Survey," by Dennis C. Mueller, for an annotated discussion of contributions up to 1975 or so (see References at the end of this chapter).

litical parties, the party that most appeals to the interest of the median voter will be elected. It is not likely that the strongest supporters of a political party will be most rewarded by favors from the party. In order to get elected, the party must sacrifice some of the benefits to its strongest supporters and reallocate them in a taxing-spending-program offer to the median voter. Holcombe has shown that when tax shares can be offered as part of a political platform, "democracy has a natural bias in favor of electing the political party that has the highest demand for public sector output" ("Public Choice and Public Spending," p. 382). He has also studied the empirical relevance of the Bowen median-voter model (see Figure 24-1). Utilizing data from Michigan millage referenda on educational expenditures in 275 elections in 1973, Holcombe provided empirical support for the assertion that the median-voter model is consistent with local governmental referenda on educational expenditures ("An Empirical Test of the Median Voter Model," pp. 272–273).

The Economics of Political Representation Empirical models in public choice have extended to testing very practical questions. For instance, do methods of paying legislators (say, set in the state constitution or by state legislators themselves) determine "outside earnings?" A recent study by Robert McCormick and Robert Tollison suggests that in higher-paying states, with legislators setting their own salaries, individuals find it less in their own interest to seek outside payments or bribes ("Legislatures as Unions," p. 77). In another interesting empirical study, entitled "Legislators as Taxicabs: On the Value of a Seat in the U.S. House of Representatives," Mark Crain, Thomas Deaton, and Robert Tollison investigated the question of why the size of the U.S. House of Representatives has remained constant at 435 (with the minor exception of a temporary expansion after Alaska and Hawaii were admitted to the Union). The only two constitutional requirements respecting size are (1) that there be *no more* than one representative per 30,000 population and (2) that there be at least one representative from each state. The House, given these restrictions, could have supported 5,977 members in 1977. Why, then, were there only 435? The answer, according to Crain, Deaton, and Tollison, is that legislators, like the situation where taxicabs are controlled, are able to restrict their own numbers. The result is that economic rents are earned by the existing units of supply—at least partially by the legislators themselves. Thus, some "economic" answers to "political" questions are provided by the axioms of self-interest, the ability of U.S. representatives to control the number of their own members, and the theory of rent seeking (see the following section).

The richness of the emerging literature on public choice is suggested in the brief discussion above. But beyond that, the public-choice paradigm has been a fertile source of advances in the theory of economic regulation. Indeed, an endogenous political process is central to most contemporary theories of economic regulation.

THE NEW POLITICAL ECONOMY OF REGULATION

Deregulation of some industries became stylish among both Democratic and Republican politicians in the 1970s, a fact that represents a distinct and dramatic shift in emphasis from the philosophy of "New Deal liberalism" in the United States. Historically, regulation of some industries, especially those regarded as "utilities," or natural monopolies, has been considered in the "public interest." After the establishment in 1887 of the first large federal regulatory agency (the Interstate Commerce Commission), economists spent great quantities of paper and ink trying to devise better pricing tools to be implemented in the regulatory process.[10] A vast literature developed on such subjects as marginal-cost pricing, price discrimination, and peak-load pricing, all ostensibly to be of some use in implementing public policy in the regulated areas of the economy. The whole regulatory process was seen as stemming directly from market failure and from the consequent necessity of government actions in the interests of the public. While imperfections in the regulatory process were acknowledged, most economists lined up behind the view that regulation was required due to the presence of "natural monopoly" and, further, that the process could be perfected by successive approximations in control.

Unfolding intellectual events of the 1960s changed all of this within the economics profession and, ultimately, among politicians and the public as well. We have already discussed one of these developments—the emergence of the public-choice paradigm with its emphasis upon politicians as endogenous actors in economic processes. It simply remained to apply these principles to the regulatory process through a theory of rent or profit creation by politicians and regulators ("the government"). The stage was set by two important papers appearing in 1962. George Stigler and Claire Friedland broke the ice with an essay questioning the effects of regulation on such variables as rate levels, the degree of price discrimination, and the rate of return ("What Can Regulators Regulate? The Case of Electricity"). Their surprising conclusion, based on statistics before and after electrical-utility regulation, was that regulation was almost totally ineffective at controlling the quantities it was designed to control. They noted:

> The theory of price regulation must, in fact, be based upon the tacit assumption that in its absence a monopoly has exorbitant power. If it were true that pure monopoly profits in the absence of regulation would be 10 or 20 percent above the competitive rate of return, so prices would be on the order of 40 to 80 percent above long run marginal cost, there might indeed be some possibility of effective regulation. The electrical utilities do not provide such a possibility ("What Can Regulators Regulate?" p. 12).

---

[10] An early "Chicago school" economist, Henry Simons, went so far as to suggest that failures in the regulatory process demanded government *ownership* of some industries (*A Positive Program for Laissez Faire*). However, this position is distinct from the modern Chicago view (deregulation plus competitive franchise bidding for rights to supply in some cases), and it is even more distant from the views of a majority of economists up to the 1990s.

A second contribution was no less influential in questioning long-held beliefs about regulation. Harvey Averch and Leland L. Johnson developed a theory about the firm's actions when facing a regulated rate of return constraint ("Behavior of the Firm under Regulatory Constraint," 1962). They concluded that, under certain conditions, regulated firms would overinvest in fixed capital, at least from society's point of view. Although optimal (i.e., profit maximizing) from the regulated firm's position, too much capital (relative to labor inputs) could force up the costs of utility services to society. The empirical relevance of this Averch-Johnson effect is still being debated by economists and econometricians, but their allegations, along with those of Stigler and Friedland and other writers, helped agitate a general rethinking of the whole regulatory process. This reassessment was, moreover, strongly influenced by the economics of politics and rent seeking.

Rents, Politics, and Regulation

Before turning to forms of the contemporary theory of regulation, let us review what "rent seeking" means.[11] A basic model is presented in Figure 24-4.

For simplicity, assume linear demand and marginal-revenue curves plus a constant average and marginal-cost function. Under competitive conditions a quantity Q_c would be produced and sold at price P_c. A monopoly, or a legalized cartel such as that provided under a regulatory system, could have the effect of causing a reduction of output to Q_m, and a rise in price to P_m. It is important to be clear about the nature of the losses. Triangle AFG corresponds to a deadweight loss due to monopoly—one that was first noticed by the French engineer Jules Dupuit (see Chapter 12). Such a loss is always present whenever price exceeds marginal cost (excise taxes and monopoly prices are analogous in this regard).

But what of area $P_c P_m AF$? Many economists have claimed these "rents" represent only a redistribution from consumers to the monopolist. In the context of regulatory processes, however, they may be viewed by any given competitor as the value of gaining the franchise.[12] In other words if a single award is given, *each* individual competitor will have an incentive to spend an amount $P_c P_m AF$, less an infinitesimal amount, for the exclusive monopoly-granting franchise. Likewise, a cartel, assuming that shares among firms can be cheaply and efficiently devised, would be willing to bid a similar amount for protection from competition. The disposition and dissipation of these rents could be in lobbying or legal fees. With these principles in mind, let us return to the political and economic interconnections in the regulatory process.

A clear imperfection exists in the above argument. Legally, of course, pol-

---

[11] A "rent-seeking" interpretation of the mercantile age was presented in Chap. 3, although a specific model, such as Figure 24-4, was not developed.

[12] These "rent-seeking" arguments originated in the writings of Gordon Tullock (1967, 1975) and Richard Posner (1975); see References.

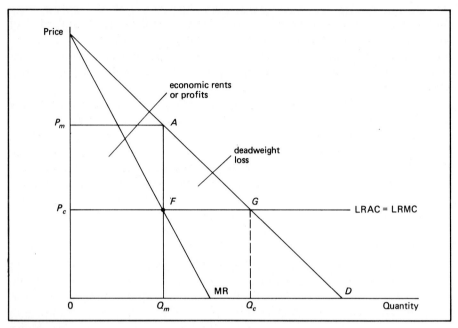

FIGURE 24-4
In the regulatory process, individual competitors will be willing to spend $P_c P_m AF$ less an infinitesimal amount for the exclusive monopoly rights.

iticians and regulators cannot take bribes, although, as stated earlier, *sub rosa* and illegal side payments have on occasion been unseemly features of government at all levels. Payments from business interests may take other forms, of course, and these motives are the key to the modern theory of regulation. Regulation, like any other good, such as shoes or beer, is demanded and supplied with underlying motives of self-interest. In a provocative paper published in 1971 ("The Theory of Economic Regulation") George Stigler fleshed out a "capture" theory of regulation based upon self-interested motives of demanders and suppliers. This view, it must be emphasized, is only superficially similar to the Marxian notion that "capital" uses the state and the political apparatus to capture benefits. In the modern theory capital or "business" does not always win. Groups of any kind, e.g., labor, farmers, or consumers, may institute or take over the regulatory system at different times. In Stigler's view regulation benefits politically effective groups. Let us consider his view in more detail.

The Capture Theory Who benefits from and who is burdened by regulation? Regulated firms may benefit from the process by direct subsidies of money, entry control, price fixing, or control over substitutes or complements. Regulation is almost never an unmixed blessing. Regulated industries (railways, electrical utilities, etc.) or occupations (barbers, funeral directors, local contractors, etc.) must submit to certain rules, regulations, "standards" of conduct, or other interferences. These are costly and reduce the net return to the regulated firm, but as long as the *net* benefit is positive and lobbying costs are not prohibitive, those who stand to gain from the regulatory process will demand it.

Why will politician-regulators supply regulation? Stated another way, how do businesses go about demanding regulation in a system where outright bribes are illegal? Politically effective coalitions (e.g., nurses, carpenters, "the Moral Majority," etc.) do so with votes and other resources such as monetary support or "campaign contributions." A more basic question is, how do regulations get passed that hurt many people (consumers) a little but benefit a few people (industry) a lot? Certain characteristics of a democratic political process make this possible. Stigler noted that (1) political decisions must be made simultaneously, unlike market decisions, and that (2) a democratic process (through representatives) must involve all parties simultaneously—those very interested in a decision, those somewhat interested, and those uninterested ("Theory of Economic Regulation," pp. 10–11). In these circumstances, the larger damage to majorities (the "deadweight loss" analyzed above) may not find expression against the smaller gains of minorities. Information acquisition is a good with costs and benefits. An individual has no incentive to acquire costly information on issues of no concern to him or her, but the individual votes on these issues anyway, ordinarily through a full-time representative affiliated with a political party. As Stigler argues:

> The representative and his party are rewarded for their discovery and fulfillment of the political desires of their constituency by success in election and the perquisites of office. If the representative could confidently await reelection whenever he voted against an economic policy that injured the society, he would assuredly do so. Unfortunately virtue does not always command so high a price. If the representative denies ten large industries their special subsidies of money or governmental power, they will dedicate themselves to the election of a more complaisant successor: the stakes are that important. This does not mean that the representative and his party must find a coalition of voter interests more durable than the anti-industry side of every industry policy proposal. A representative cannot win or keep office with the support of the sum of those who are opposed to: oil import quotas, farm subsidies, airport subsidies, hospital subsidies, unnecessary navy shipyards, an inequitable public housing program, and rural electrification subsidies ("Theory of Economic Regulation," p. 11).

Politics and the voting process are thus a *gross* filter of individual preferences. Regulations of all kinds are simply the result of interactions of self-interested demanders, i.e., effective coalitions of individuals who stand to gain from regulation and political suppliers who must endure periodic reelection constraints.

Does this mean that the "public interest" comes in last in this process? In the modern approach to regulation, the term "public interest" itself takes on a different meaning. The public interest is not some abstract legalism; rather, it is merely a *summation* of *individuals'* interests on some issue. If transactions costs among consumers were zero, they would most certainly buy out monopolies such as that depicted in Figure 24-4. In other words, for a sum $P_c P_m AF$, consumers could buy out the monopolist and gain triangle AFG, the deadweight loss. But in an imperfect world where coalition costs are positive and where the state is permitted to coerce (in a democratic setting), monopolies created by regulation can reduce the welfare of consumers.

It is important to recognize that regulation does not always support the special interests of industrial market groups. Consumer or environmental groups may also form effective coalitions to impact upon the political process. Preferences of nonmarket groups may be registered, and different groups may capture the process at different points in time.[13] Identification of the specific configurations of costs and benefits facing demanders and politician-suppliers of regulations is an ongoing task engaging contemporary economists in this field. One of the central problems is to develop a sound single theory of political decision making within bureaucracies. The important point is that the outlines have been developed of a positive economic theory of the regulatory process assuming self-interested, endogenous politicians.

Other Modern Approaches to Regulation   The economic and political approaches to regulation outlined above suggest that *any* effective coalition might obtain regulation through the political process. This view assumes, for example, that regulation may be obtained by some industry irrespective of whether the firms' long-run costs are declining over large blocks of output. The presence or absence of natural monopoly conditions, in other words, is not the foundation of an explanation for government regulations. Altering constraints faced by suppliers and demanders of regulation is the only way to get a diminution of the activity. But what if natural monopoly conditions (declining marginal costs, great capital fixity) are present? Does that mean that agency regulation of the type discussed in early sections of this chapter is inevitable?

The so-called Chicago theory of regulation has dealt with this question. In a view derivative of Sir Edwin Chadwick's nineteenth-century assessment of similar problems (see Chapter 9), Harold Demsetz in 1968 questioned the necessity of regulating (in traditional fashion) industries having scale economies in production ("Why Regulate Utilities?").[14] Demsetz proposed that formal

---

[13] The central paper here was written in 1976 by Sam Peltzman. Peltzman's "Toward a More General Theory of Regulation" is a powerful generalization of Stigler's earlier theory that coalitions of producers, consumers, and politicians compete for economic rents. In this view regulation redistributes wealth or "rents" from some consumers to coalitions of consumers and/or producers or politicians.

[14] Actually, the modern rediscovery of the "Chadwick principle" was made three years earlier by Gordon Tullock, who applied it to political party competition. See Tullock's "Entry Barriers in Politics."

regulation of utilities would be rendered unnecessary where governments could allow "rivalrous competitors" to bid for the exclusive right to supply the good or service over some indefinite "contract" period. In such a system, as Demsetz shows, the existence of natural monopoly does not imply monopoly price and output, given (1) an elastic supply of potential bidders and (2) prohibitive collusion costs on the part of potential suppliers.

Under certain restrictive conditions a "competitive" price and output could be achieved under Demsetz's plan (see Figure 9-1 and the related discussion). Critics of this idea have strongly questioned the plan as a *substitute* for traditional forms of regulation, and they cite problems of market uncertainty, information and policing costs, investment criteria, and so on as making the plan practically unworkable. Government ownership of certain basic property rights would also attach to the scheme. All of this might be somewhat irrelevant, however, since it is probable that Demsetz never intended his conception to serve as a "Chicago theory of regulation." There is not much empirical support for the existence of natural monopoly in utilities and other regulated industries, and the "Chicago position" on the matter—if there is a unified position—is that *deregulation* and the return of competition to most regulated activities would improve consumer welfare.

A final contemporary view of the regulatory process offers a possible avenue through which regulation may be supported. Victor Goldberg's view ("Regulation and Administered Contracts") is that regulation is very much akin to private or public long-term contracts to serve and be served. Further, he argues that the vast complications associated with long-term contracts may provide a rationale for regulation. Goldberg's analysis is principally concerned with natural monopolies, though his considerations are important for the regulation of other industries as well.

There is a similarity between the regulatory process and long-term relational contracts giving producers a right to serve and consumers a right to be served. Owing to uncertainty and other problems, both parties to the contract limit future options in order to achieve optimality *over time* (all other theories considered in this chapter are static and carry no intertemporal implications). Contracts, or regulation, in Goldberg's view, provide procedural mechanisms for adjudicating future contingencies. Increasing the producers' right to serve makes the contract more attractive to producers while simultaneously making the contract *less* attractive to consumers. The opposite is true of the consumers' interest in the right to be served. In Goldberg's words:

> [C]onsumers want to maintain freedom to terminate the agreement so that they can take advantage of lower prices and/or superior technologies as they appear. The only variable under the agent's control is the level of production of the right to serve.
>
> The optimal protection will be that at which the expected marginal benefits to the consumers of increased durability and decreased producer risk (lower prices) are

just offset by the expected marginal costs of decreased flexibility ("Regulation and Administered Contracts," p. 433).

Thus Goldberg's justification for regulation is that long-term contracts are difficult to define and enforce because it is costly to delimit, ex ante, their many provisions. The regulatory body is an ongoing monitoring agent that continually defines the relation between consumers and producers over time in much the same way that common-law courts continually interpret rights and obligations of citizens vis-à-vis other citizens and the state. (Goldberg is not optimistic about the efficiency of private contracting under public laws of contract.) Goldberg has not proved a case *for* regulation. No market failure is cited. But he has demonstrated an intriguing possibility. With risk-averse consumers and capital fixity, some regulation may be appropriate when viewed over a period of time. These views are, of course, in strong contrast to those developed earlier.

Schumpeter's Perspective on Market Processes

Arguments about the intertemporal optimality of regulation and its related problems of risk and uncertainty in long-term contracting can be found in economic literature much earlier than the contemporary writings of Goldberg and others. Earlier in this century, Joseph Schumpeter (see Chapter 21) characterized the market function as an intertemporal competitive process which implies certain things about the role of government regulation. According to Schumpeter, risk is an unavoidable and natural element of market activity. Schumpeter discussed the critical nature of risk and uncertainty and the problems they pose for entrepreneurs in a capitalist society.

> Practically any investment entails...certain safeguarding activities such as insuring or hedging. Long-range investing under rapidly changing conditions, especially under...the impact of new commodities and technologies, is like shooting at a target that is not only indistinct but moving—and moving jerkily at that. Hence it becomes necessary to resort to such protecting devices as patents or temporary secrecy of processes or, in some cases, long-period contracts secured in advance. But these protecting devices which most economists accept as normal elements of rational management are only special cases of a larger class....
>
> If for instance a war risk is insurable, nobody objects to a firm's collecting the cost of this insurance from the buyers of its products. But that risk is no less an element in long-run costs, if there are no facilities for insuring against it, in which case a price strategy aiming at the same end will seem to involve unnecessary restrictions and to be productive of excess profits. Similarly, if a patent cannot be secured or would not, if secured, effectively protect, other means may have to be used in order to justify the investment. Among them are a price policy that will make it possible to write off more quickly than would otherwise be rational, or additional investment in order to provide excess capacity to be used only for aggression or defense. Again, if long-period contracts cannot be entered into in advance, other means may have to be devised in order to tie prospective customers to the investing firm (*Capitalism, Socialism, and Democracy*, p. 88).

The point that Schumpeter stresses in this passage is that elements of competition that may appear to be anti-competitive from a purely static perspective (patents, etc.) may be elements of progress in a more dynamic competitive setting. Expressing a few reservations about the adverse effects of cartels, Schumpeter characterized a number of static "monopolistic" practices as "natural" tools of dynamic (long-run) competition. But he was also alert to the possibilities of utilizing regulatory procedures to subvert the welfare effects of the marketplace. Since government is the only permanent source of monopoly privilege, its regulatory actions should be scrutinized intensively:

> The power to exploit at pleasure a given pattern of demand...can under the conditions of intact capitalism hardly persist for a period long enough to matter for the analysis of total output, unless buttressed by public authority.... Even railroads and power and light concerns had first to create the demand for their services and, when they had done so, to defend their market against competition (*Capitalism, Socialism, and Democracy*, p. 99).

Schumpeter's perspective on market processes provides a forceful case for a clear delineation between "static" competition and "dynamic" competition. Nongovernmental restrictions on competition, when viewed in a static sense, are usually considered suboptimal, when in fact they may help regulate the introduction of new technology that improves economic welfare. Government regulation, on the other hand, is the major source of long-term economic rents associated with output reductions and welfare losses.

Ultimately, the debate over natural market processes versus regulation is a debate over economic efficiency. Schumpeter and other economists have argued that precontracting may be a natural response to the uncertainty and risk involved in intertemporal sales policies. Market contracting to avoid risk may take the form of warranties, guarantees, futures contracts, etc. Other economists are more inclined to reduce risk and uncertainty through government regulation. Does the market provide a necessary bridge between present and future supplies at a lower cost to society than government measures aimed at the same objective? This is an issue that remains hotly debated. Only a well-executed, case-by-case, empirical study seems capable of providing convincing support for one view or the other. In the absence of such complete documentation, Schumpeter's insights, combined with the modern theory of regulation, remind us that the mere existence of regulation and of intertemporal problems of production and consumption does not constitute proof that the market has failed to work properly.

CONCLUSION

The purpose of the present chapter has not been to attempt to settle contemporary theoretical disputes in the theory of public choice or regulation. Rather, it has been to demonstrate that new and ongoing inquiries in political economy have utilized and are utilizing the simple models of competition and self-interest sponsored so long ago by Adam Smith. The twist here—and the essential lesson within our discussion—is that self-interest as a basic economic motive does not differ in form whether one is buying an ice cream cone or running a campaign for city treasurer. These motives—in form if not in kind— pervade the activities of *all* humans. Public-choice theory and application, linking both taxation and expenditures and including the theory of regulation, is a valuable means of transforming economic analysis into other realms of human action. In doing so it is stretching the reaches of the discipline toward the original conception of Adam Smith, a conception of economics as part of a broader social and political inquiry.

NOTES FOR FURTHER READING

In addition to the classic writings of Lindahl and Wicksell mentioned in the References to this chapter, Musgrave and Peacock's important volume contains a number of translated international classics in public finance. For much insight into the development of public finance see the essays of Maffeo Pantaleoni, Ugo Mazzola, F. Y. Edgeworth, Enrico Barone, and Friedrich von Wieser. A part of the French (Marshall-style) tradition is developed by R. B. Ekelund, Jr., and Robert F. Hébert, "French Engineers, Welfare Economics, and Public Finance in the Nineteenth Century," *History of Political Economy,* vol. 10 (Winter 1978), pp. 636–668.

Contemporary literature on public goods is plentiful. A central question concerns the "competitive provision" of public goods, that is, whether such goods can be supplied competitively and whether such equilibriums are "stable." See J. M. Buchanan, *The Demand and Supply of Public Goods* (Chicago: Rand McNally, 1968); J. G. Head, "Public Goods and Public Policy," *Public Finance,* vol. 17, no. 2 (1962), pp. 197–219; and Harold Demsetz, "The Private Production of Public Goods," *Journal of Law & Economics,* vol. 8 (October 1970), pp. 293–306. In addition to the literature on voting cited in the text, two early papers may be consulted: Duncan Black, "On the Rationale of Group Decision Making," *Journal of Political Economy,* vol. 56 (February 1978), pp. 23–24; and Kenneth Arrow, "A Difficulty in the Concept of Social Welfare," *Journal of Political Economy,* vol. 58 (August 1950), pp. 328–346. Also see T. Nicholas Tideman and Gordon Tullock, "A New and Superior Process for Making Social Choices," *Journal of Political Economy,* vol. 84 (December 1976), pp. 1145–1160.

The "constitutional rules" taken up by Buchanan and Tullock in their extension of Wicksell's optimal tax rules are considered in a somewhat different context in John Rawls, *A Theory of Justice* (Cambridge, Mass.: Harvard University Press, 1971). Buchanan's reaction to Rawls, in addition to a very sizable contribution to the question, is contained in his *Freedom in Constitutional Contract: Perspectives of a Political Economist* (College Station: Texas A & M University Press, 1977).

In addition to Niskanen's major work on bureaucracy, see his "The Peculiar Economics of Bureaucracy," *American Economic Review,* vol 58 (May

1968), pp. 293–305. Emendations and extensions of Niskanen's work may be found regularly in the journal *Public Choice;* see also Bruce L. Benson, "Why Are Congressional Committees Dominated by 'High-Demand' Legislators?— A Comment on Niskanen's View of Bureaucrats and Politicians," *Southern Economic Journal,* vol. 48 (July 1981), pp. 68–77.

The literature on "empirical public choice" is wonderfully diverse and varied. On the economics of internal organization of legislatures, see W. Mark Crain and Robert D. Tollison, "Campaign Expenditures and Political Competition," *Journal of Law & Economics,* vol. 19 (April 1976), pp. 177–188; Arleen Leibowitz and Robert D. Tollison, "A Theory of Legislative Organization: Making the Most of Your Majority," *Quarterly Journal of Economics,* vol. 95 (March 1980), pp. 261–267; and W. Mark Crain, "On the Structure and Stability of Political Markets," *Journal of Political Economy,* vol. 85 (August 1977), pp. 829–842. An article by Randall G. Holcombe and Asghar Zardkoohi uses a regression model to show that grants are determined by political rather than economic variables; see "The Determinants of Federal Grants," *Southern Economic Journal,* vol. 47 (October 1981), pp. 393–399. An excellent contribution to interest-group theory is provided by Robert E. McCormick and Robert D. Tollison, *Politicians, Legislation, and the Economy: An Inquiry into the Interest-Group Theory of Government* (Leiden: Martinus Nijhoff, 1981).

An important aspect of the empirical public-choice literature has been the modeling of a political business cycle wherein inflation, employment, and disposable income are manipulated by politicians in attempts to win elections. One of the most interesting and comprehensive studies of the electoral cycle is that of Edward R. Tufte, *Political Control of the Economy* (Princeton, N.J.: Princeton University Press, 1978). Also see the following works of Bruno S. Frey and Friedrich Schneider: "On the Modeling of Politico-Economic Interdependence," *European Journal of Political Research,* vol. 3 (December 1975), pp. 339–360; and "An Empirical Study of Politico-Economic Model of the United Kingdom," *Economic Journal,* vol. 88 (June 1978), pp. 243–253. Frey and Schneider use ex ante measures of actual popularity rather than ex post electoral success as the "independent variable" in their studies. A model meshing political manipulations and the monetarist conception of the so-called inflation-unemployment tradeoff (called the "Phillips curve") is developed in Richard E. Wagner's "Economic Manipulation for Political Profit: Macroeconomic Consequences and Constitutional Limitations," *Kyklos,* vol. 30 (1977), pp. 395–410. An empirical study of why deficits are demanded as well as supplied may be found in W. Mark Crain and Robert B. Ekelund, Jr., "Deficits and Democracy," *Southern Economic Journal,* vol. 44 (April 1978), pp. 813–828.

An excellent summary of the "early" regulation literature and of the institutional structure of broad areas of regulation in the United States through the 1960s is in Alfred E. Kahn's two-volume study, *The Economics of Regulation: Economic Principles* (vol. I) and *Institutional Issues* (vol. II) (New York: Wiley, 1971). A good survey of post-1962 regulatory theories—those discussed in the present chapter—is contained in the introductory chapters of Bruce M. Owen and Ronald Braeutigam's *The Regulatory Game: Strategic Use of the Administrative Process* (Cambridge: Ballinger Publishing Co., 1978).

The general topic of rent seeking and its role in regulation and income distribution is covered in *Toward a Theory of the Rent-Seeking Society,* James Buchanan, Robert Tollison, and Gordon Tullock (see References). Empirical papers (those presenting statistical evidence) on rent seeking and regulation have appeared regularly in most academic journals over the 1970s and 1980s, especially in journals such as the *Journal of Law & Economics,* the *Journal of Legal Studies,* and the *Rand Journal of Economics.* A very small sample of these papers includes: Don Bellante and James Long, "The Political Economy of the Rent-Seeking Society: The Case of Public Employees and Their Unions," *Journal of Labor Research,* vol. 2 (Spring 1981), pp. 1–14; Paul W. McAvoy, "The Regulation Induced Shortage of Natural Gas," *Journal of Law & Economics,* vol. 14 (April 1971), pp. 167–199; Stanley Besen, "The Economics of the Cable Television 'Consensus,'" *Journal of Law & Economics,* vol. 17 (April 1974), pp. 39–52; and Raymond Urban and Richard Mencke, "Federal Regulation of Whiskey Labeling: From the Repeal of Prohibition to the Present," *Journal of Law & Economics,* vol. 15 (October 1972), pp. 411–426.

Over the 1970s and 1980s, a veritable revolution in the study of industry structure has been under way, called *contestable markets* theory. The basic argument is simple: when potential competitive rivalry is costless or inexpensive, i.e., when entry and exit possibilities exist in a market, and price and output configurations are "sustainable," the market may be characterized as perfectly contestable. The theory of contestable markets may be used to show that the principal conclusion of the traditional competitive model—that price equates to marginal and average cost—may occur when numbers of competitors are as small as two (or even one). In this theory the degree of concentration cannot reveal anything about competitiveness. Under certain conditions even a "natural" monopoly can behave as a competitive firm and industry. The degree of contestability (and not the number of firms) is the benchmark for understanding the competitiveness of markets. See William J. Baumol, John C. Panzar, and Robert D. Willig, *Contestable Markets and the Theory of Industry Structure* (New York: Harcourt Brace Jovanovich, 1982).

REFERENCES

Arrow, Kenneth. *Social Choice and Individual Values.* New York: Wiley, 1951.

Averch, Harvey, and Leland L. Johnson. "Behavior of the Firm under Regulatory Constraint," *American Economic Review,* vol. 52 (December 1962), pp. 1052–1069.

Black, Duncan. *The Theory of Committees and Elections.* London: Cambridge University Press, 1958.

Bowen, Howard R. "The Interpretation of Voting in the Allocation of Resources," *Quarterly Journal of Economics,* vol. 58 (November 1943), pp. 27–48.

Buchanan, J. M. "The Pure Theory of Government Finance: A Suggested Approach," *Journal of Political Economy,* vol. 57 (December 1949), pp. 496–505.

————. "La scienza delle finanze: The Italian Tradition in Public Finance," in *Fiscal Theory and Political Economy*. Chapel Hill, N.C.: University of North Carolina Press, 1960.

————. "Public Finance and Public Choice," *National Tax Journal,* vol. 28 (December 1975), pp. 383–394.

————, and Gordon Tullock. *The Calculus of Consent.* Ann Arbor: The University of Michigan Press, 1962.

Crain, W. Mark, Thomas H. Deaton, and Robert D. Tollison. "Legislators as Taxi-cabs: On the Value of a Seat in the U.S. House of Representatives," *Economic Inquiry,* vol. 15 (April 1977), pp. 298–302.

Demsetz, Harold. "Why Regulate Utilities?" *Journal of Law & Economics,* vol. 11 (April 1968), pp. 55–65.

Downs, Anthony. *An Economic Theory of Democracy.* New York: Harper & Row, 1957.

Goldberg, Victor. "Regulation and Administered Contracts," *The Bell Journal of Economics,* vol. 7 (Autumn 1976), pp. 426–448.

Holcombe, Randall G. "Public Choice and Public Spending," *National Tax Journal,* vol. 31 (December 1978), pp. 373–383.

————. "An Empirical Test of the Median Voter Model," *Economic Inquiry,* vol. 18 (April 1980), pp. 260–275.

————. "Concepts of Public Sector Equilibrium," *National Tax Journal,* vol. 33 (March 1980), pp. 77–88.

Hotelling, Harold, "Stability in Competition," *Economic Journal,* vol. 39 (March 1929), pp. 41–57.

Lindahl, Erik. "Just Taxation—A Positive Solution," in Richard Musgrave and A. T. Peacock (eds.), *Classics in the Theory of Public Finance.* New York: St. Martin's, 1958 [1919].

McCormick, Robert E., and Robert D. Tollison, "Legislatures as Unions," *Journal of Political Economy,* vol. 86 (February 1978), pp. 63–78.

Mises, Ludwig. *Bureaucracy.* New Haven, Conn.: Yale University Press, 1944.

Mueller, Dennis C. "Public Choice: A Survey," *Journal of Economic Literature,* vol. 14 (June 1976), pp. 395–433.

Musgrave, Richard A. "The Voluntary Exchange Theory of Public Economy," *Quarterly Journal of Economics,* vol. 53 (February 1938), pp. 213–237.

Niskanen, William A. *Bureaucracy and Representative Government.* Chicago: Aldine-Atherton Press, 1971.

Peltzman, Sam. "Toward a More General Theory of Regulation," *The Journal of Law & Economics,* vol. 9 (August 1976), pp. 211–240.

Posner, Richard A. "The Social Costs of Monopoly and Regulation," *Journal of Political Economy,* vol. 83 (August 1975), pp. 807–827.

Samuelson, Paul A. "The Pure Theory of Public Expenditures," *Review of Economics and Statistics,* vol. 36 (November 1954), pp. 387–389.

Schumpeter, J. A. *Capitalism, Socialism, and Democracy.* New York: Harper & Row, 1942.

Simons, Henry. *A Positive Program for Laissez Faire,* in Harry D. Gideonse (ed.), Public Policy Pamphlet no. 15. Chicago: The University of Chicago Press, 1934.

Stigler, George J. "The Theory of Economic Regulation," *The Bell Journal of Economics and Management Science,* vol. 2 (Spring 1971), pp. 3–21.

————, and Claire Friedland. "What Can Regulators Regulate? The Case of Electricity," *Journal of Law & Economics,* vol. 5 (October 1962), pp. 1–16.

Tiebout, C.M. "A Pure Theory of Local Expenditures," *Journal of Political Economy,* vol. 64 (October 1956), pp. 416–424.

Tullock, Gordon. "Entry Barriers in Politics," *American Economic Review,* vol. 55 (May 1965), pp. 458–466.

———. *The Politics of Bureaucracy.* Washington: Public Affairs Press, 1965.

———. "The Welfare Costs of Tariffs, Monopolies, and Theft," *Western Economic Journal,* vol. 5 (June 1967), pp. 224–232; also published in James M. Buchanan, Robert D. Tollison, and Gordon Tullock, *Toward a Theory of the Rent-Seeking Society.* College Station: Texas A & M University Press, 1981.

———. "The Transitional Gains Gap," *The Bell Journal of Economics,* vol. 6 (Autumn 1975), pp. 671–678.

Wicksell, Knut. "A New Principle of Just Taxation," James M. Buchanan (trans.), in Richard Musgrave and A. T. Peacock (eds.), *Classics in the Theory of Public Finance.* New York: St. Martin's, 1958.

ACKNOWLEDGMENTS

We are indebted to the following publishers for permission to quote from works published by them:

Aldine Press, Chicago: Milton Friedman, *Price Theory,* copyright 1976.

Arno Press, New York: K. G. Dennis. *'Competition' in the History of Economic Thought,* copyright 1977.

Beacon Press, Boston: *Primitive, Archaic and Modern Economies: Essays in Honor of Karl Polanyi,* G. Dalton (ed.), copyright 1968.

Bell Journal of Economics, New York: George Stigler, "The Theory of Economic Regulation," copyright © 1971, American Telephone and Telegraph Company; Victor Goldberg, "Regulation and Administered Contracts," copyright © 1976.

Cambridge University Press, London: *Works and Correspondence of David Ricardo,* P. Sraffa (ed.), copyright 1951–1955.

The Duke University Press, Durham, N.C.: R. B. Ekelund, Jr., and C. L. Fry, "Cournot's Demand Theory: A Reassessment," *History of Political Economy,* copyright © 1971; R. B. Ekelund, Jr., and E. O. Price III, "Sir Edwin Chadwick on Competition and the Social Control of Industry: Railroads," *History of Political Economy,* copyright © 1979.

Economic Inquiry (Journal of the Western Economic Association), Los Angeles: R. B. Ekelund, Jr., and R. Tollison, "Economic Regulation in Mercantile England: Hecksher Revisited," copyright 1980; R. F. Hébert, "Edwin Chadwick and the Economics of Crime," copyright 1977; William Jaffé, "Menger, Jevons and Walras De-Homogenized," copyright 1976.

The Free Press, New York: Carl Menger, *Principles of Economics,* James Dingwall and Bert F. Hoselitz (trans.), copyright 1950.

Harcourt, Brace and Company, Inc., New York: R. F. Harrod, *The Life of John Maynard Keynes,* copyright 1951.

Harper and Row Publishers, Inc., New York: Don Patinkin, *Money, Interest and Prices,* copyright © 1965.

Harvard University Press, Cambridge, Mass.: E. H. Chamberlin, *The Theory of Monopolistic Competition,* copyright © 1962; R. B. Ekelund, Jr., "Price Discrimination and Product Differentiation in Economic Theory: An Early Analysis," *Quarterly Journal of Economics,* copyright © 1970.

Houghton Mifflin Company, Boston: John K. Galbraith, *The Affluent Society,* copyright © 1958; *American Capitalism: The Concept of Countervailing Power,* copyright © 1952.

International Publishers Company, Inc., New York: Karl Marx, *Precapitalist Economic Formations,* J. Cohen (trans.) and E. J. Hobsbawm (ed.), copyright © 1965; Karl Marx, *Economic and Philosophic Manuscripts of 1844,* Martin Milligan (trans.) and D. J. Struik (ed.), copyright © 1964.

Richard D. Irwin Company, Inc., Homewood, Ill.: Léon Walras, *Elements of Pure Economics,* William Jaffé (trans.), copyright 1954.

Journal of Economic Issues, East Lansing, Mich.: R. B. Ekelund, Jr., and Emilie S. Olsen, "Comte, Mill and Cairnes: The Positivist-Empiricist Interlude in Late Classical Economics," copyright © 1973.

Augustus M. Kelley, Publishers, New York: Knut Wicksell, *Lectures on Political Economy,* copyright 1935; Edgar Furniss, *The Position of the Laborer in a System of Nationalism,* copyright 1957.

Longman Group, Ltd., Edinburgh: Alexander Gray, "Adam Smith," *Scottish Journal of Political Economy,* copyright 1976.

Macmillan London and Basingstoke: Alfred Marshall, *Principles of Economics,* copyright 1920; Joan Robinson, *The Economics of Imperfect Competition,* copyright © 1933.

Macmillan London and Basingstoke and the International Economic Society: Jules Dupuit, *Annales des Ponts et Chaussées,* in the *International Economic Papers,* copyright 1952 and 1962.

Macmillan Publishing Co., Inc.: W. E. Baumol, *Economic Dynamics,* 3d ed., copyright © 1970; William Jaffé, "Léon Walras," *International Encyclopedia of Social Sciences,* vol. 16, copyright © 1968; Alfred Marshall, *Principles of Economics,* copyright 1948.

McGraw-Hill Book Company, New York: Alvin Hansen, *Monetary Theory and Fiscal Policy,* copyright 1949.

Monthly Review Press, New York: A. L. Morton, *The Life and Times of Robert Owen,* copyright © 1963.

National Tax Association—Tax Institute of America, Columbus, Ohio: James M. Buchanan, "Public Finance and Public Choice," *National Tax Journal,* copyright 1975; R. G. Holcombe, "Concepts of Public Sector Equilibrium," copyright 1978.

North-Holland Publishing Company, Amsterdam: Léon Walras, *Correspondence of Léon Walras and Related Papers,* W. Jaffé (ed.), vol. II, copyright © 1965.

Review of Social Economy, Chicago: R. B. Ekelund, Jr., "Power and Utility: The Normative Economics of Friedrich von Wieser," copyright © 1970.

Princeton University Press, Princeton, N.J.: Alan Ritter, *The Political Thought of Pierre-Joseph Proudhon,* copyright © 1969.

Routledge & Kegan Paul, Ltd., London: Knut Wicksell, *Lectures on Political Economy,* copyright 1935; Knut Wicksell, *Interest and Prices,* copyright 1936.

Routledge & Kegan Paul, Ltd., London: Knut Wicksell, *Lectures on Political Economy,* copyright 1935; Knut Wicksell, *Interest and Prices,* copyright 1936.

Royal Statistical Society, London: J. M. Keynes, "William Stanley Jevons, 1835–1882," copyright 1936.

Schocken Books, Inc., New York: Eduard Bernstein, *Evolutionary Socialism: A Criticism and Affirmation,* E. C. Harvey (trans.), copyright © 1965.

Southern Economic Journal, Chapel Hill, N.C.: R. B. Ekelund, Jr., and W. P. Gramm, "Early French Contributions to Marshallian Demand Theory," copyright © 1970; R. B. Ekelund, Jr., "A Note on Jules Dupuit and Neo-Classical Monopoly Theory," copyright © 1969.

Southwestern Social Science Quarterly, Austin Tex.: R. B. Ekelund, Jr., "A British Rejection of Economic Orthodoxy," copyright 1966.

Texas A & M University Press, College Station, Tex.: R. B. Ekelund, Jr., and R. D. Tollison, *Mercantilism as a Rent-Seeking Society: Economic Regulation in Historical Perspective,* copyright © 1981.

The University of Chicago Press, Chicago: R. B. Ekelund, Jr., "Jules Dupuit and the Early Theory of Marginal Cost Pricing," *Journal of Political Economy,* copyright © 1968; Milton Friedman, *Capitalism and Freedom,* copyright © 1963; Israel M. Kirzner, *Competition and Entrepreneurship,* copyright © 1973; George Stigler and Claire Friedland, "What Can Regulators Regulate? The Case of Electricity," *Journal of Law & Economics,* copyright © 1962.

University of Miami Law and Economics Center, Miami, Fla.: Israel M. Kirzner, "The Perils of Regulation," copyright 1978.

University of Michigan Press, Ann Arbor, Mich.: James M. Buchanan and Gordon Tullock, *The Calculus of Consent,* copyright 1962.

NAME INDEX

SUBJECT INDEX